Uncle John's 24-KARAT GOLD BATHROOM READER®

By the Bathroom Readers' Institute

Bathroom Readers' Press
Ashland, Oregon

OUR "REGULAR" READERS RAVE!

"Your books are the greatest written word since Homer's *Iliad* and *Odyssey*. Uncle John and all his staff at the BRI must be the smartest rubber duckies in the pool."

—**Steven**

"I've been a fan of your series for years, and I have two shelves devoted to them. I'm now equipped with an arsenal of fun facts for any occasion."

—**Alex**

"I have been an avid reader of *Uncle John's Bathroom Readers* for years. Everyone knows what to buy me for presents. Just wanted to let you folks know that you keep me mesmerized (and seated) for long periods of time!"

—**Mitch**

"I LOVE your books! It is so nice to be able to impress my family and friends with an arsenal of wacky, fun facts!"

—**Shayla**

"My whole family loves your books. We wait anxiously for each new one to come out. The most recent one we are reading has definitely brought conversation out of the bathroom and to the dinner table!"

—**Trena**

"I have about 30 of your books, and I want the whole collection! Do you know how much fun it is to start a conversation with a weird little tidbit from Uncle John?"

—**Rose**

UNCLE JOHN'S 24-KARAT GOLD
BATHROOM READER®

"When Life Was 'Simpler'" is reprinted from Secrets of the Great Old-Timey Cooks by Barbara Swell, © 2001. Used by permission of Native Ground Music, Asheville, North Carolina (nativeground.com)

For information, write:
The Bathroom Readers' Institute, P.O. Box 1117,
Ashland, OR 97520
www.bathroomreader.com • 888-488-4642

Cover design by Michael Brunsfeld, San Rafael, CA
(Brunsfeldo@comcast.net)
BRI "technician" on the back cover: Larry Kelp

ISBN-13: 978-1-60710-320-2 / ISBN-10: 1-60710-320-6

Library of Congress Cataloging-in-Publication Data
Uncle John's 24-karat bathroom reader.
    p. cm.
Includes indexes.
ISBN 978-1-60710-320-2 (pbk.)
1. American wit and humor. 2. Curiosities and wonders.
I. Bathroom Readers' Institute (Ashland, Or.)
 PN6165.U46 2011
 081.02'07—dc23

2011020177

Printed in the United States of America
First Printing
1 2 3 4 5 6 7 8 15 14 13 12 11

Hiya, Sophie! Hiya, Jesse!

THANK YOU!

The Bathroom Readers' Institute sincerely thanks the people whose advice and assistance made this book possible.

Gordon Javna

John Dollison

Jay Newman

Brian Boone

Thom Little

Kim Griswell

Amy Miller

Michael Brunsfeld

Angela Kern

Jack Mingo

Megan Todd

Stephanie Fretwell

Eddie Deezen

Brandon Hartley

Eleanor Pierce

Jill Bellrose

William Dooling

Michael Kerr

Michael Conover

Ed Krenzolok

Claudia Bauer

Claire Breen

JoAnn Padgett

Melinda Allman

Monica Maestas

Annie Lam

Ginger Winters

Jennifer Frederick

Maggie Javna

Nate & Dena

Wayne Erbsen

Barbara Swell

Tom "Deli Style" Mustard

Sydney Stanley

David Calder

Erin Corbin

Julie Pigeon

Joseph Pisco

Media Masters

Publishers Group West

Bloomsbury Books

Raincoast Books

Porter the Wonder Dog (R.I.P.)

Thomas Crapper

CONTENTS

Because the BRI understands your reading needs, we've divided the contents by length as well as subject.

Short—a quick read
Medium—2 to 3 pages
Long—for those extended visits, when something a little more involved is required
* Extended—for those leg-numbing experiences

INTRODUCTION

WELCOME TO OUR GOLDEN 24th
After one score and four years of bringing *Bathroom Readers* to our growing legion of throne-sitters, we're rolling along stronger than ever! And in a way, we feel like we're just getting started. In fact, one of our favorite articles in this new edition, *Uncle John's 24-Karat Bathroom Reader*, chronicles people who have been in the same job for more than *70 years*! How do they do it? Simple—they love showing up to work every day.

And so do we.

We never know what golden nugget of information is out there, just waiting to be mined. Like the fact that the Soviet Union's 1957 launch of *Sputnik I* into space was part of a much bigger plan enacted by the world's leading scientists (page 255), or that for all his genius, automobile pioneer Henry Ford was actually a *horrible* businessman (page 486). That's just fascinating! Yeah, we could definitely stand another 50 years or so of sharing this stuff.

And here's the best part: All *you* have to do is start reading. Here's a bit of what awaits you...

• **Origins:** The Tupperware Lady that time forgot, the history of the humble umbrella, and the inventor of the toilet tank flap

• **Helpful hints:** How to run a clock on potato power, how to measure distances with your thumb, and why you should never say "fanny pack" in Australia

• **Pop science:** What is nano-gold, and could it be a cure for cancer? All about metal, a bra that may help you breathe, the used space suit that became an orbiting ham radio, and the notorious nuclear accidents now known as the "Curse of the Demon Core"

• **Odd happenings:** The guy who got inflated by his semi-truck's pressure hose, the lady who cracked an egg on a TSA agent's head, and the tale of the Swedish shotgun-guitar

• **Bizarre eats:** Caffeinated marshmallows, hair remover in breakfast sandwiches, and a cocktail made from rattlesnake blood

- **Critters and beasties:** Scary spiders, horse-racing lingo, how fishes got their names, and an octopus with an attitude problem

- **Strange places:** Travel beneath Paris and Atlanta. *Don't* travel to two forbidden Islands—one in the Bay of Bengal, and the other in the middle of the Pacific. (But you can read all about them.)

- **That's entertainment:** Bill Murray's tall tales; how MacGyver always escaped; all about *The Price Is Right*; and the story of what *really* happened to Michael Jackson, Elizabeth Taylor, and Marlon Brando after the 9/11 terror attacks

- **Games people play:** Football…Canadian style, legendary sports goofs, action figure facts, a killer video game, Parcheesi, and the athletic shoes that tore apart a family *and* a town

- **Forgotten history:** Jack Daniels's untimely end, what Nikola Tesla said to Mark Twain, and why Americans don't speak French

- **Wordplay:** Funny license plates (like "GOTTA P"), plus a cacophony of caca words, and why **Comic Sans** is the world's most reviled font

Before you dive in, we'd like to take a moment once again to thank our dedicated team of writers, researchers, editors, designers, and everyone else who helped make this book glitter. Give yourselves a gold star! And a big welcome to Kim, the latest writer to be "institutionalized" at the BRI! Bet you didn't think it would be *this* crazy, Kim. (Insert maniacal laugh here.)

So, just like the element gold is ever malleable but always full of luster, we plan on shining and increasing in bathroom-reading value for decades to come. Happy reading. And as always…

Go with the Flow!

—Uncle John, Felix the Dog, and the BRI Staff

YOU'RE MY INSPIRATION

*It's always interesting to find out where the architects of
our culture get their ideas. Some of these may surprise you.*

THE GRINCH. Dr. Seuss's 1957 book *How the Grinch Stole Christmas* was illustrated in black and white, but in 1966, when the book was made into a TV special—in color—animator Chuck Jones decided to make the Grinch green. Why? Jones had always loved the "ugly" shade of a green car he'd rented once, but never knew what character to give it to...until the Grinch.

TWITTER. Jack Dorsey got the idea for a micro-blogging website, in part, from listening to "the way cab drivers and dispatchers succinctly convey locations by radio." He designed Twitter to do the same thing: to convey important information quickly.

SUE SYLVESTER. The mean high-school cheerleading coach on Fox's Glee is based on *American Idol*'s Simon Cowell. Said actress Jane Lynch: "Simon and Sue say the things people wish they could in their jobs or at their school, but can't."

NELSON MANDELA. The South African political leader was born in 1918 as Rolihlahla Mandela. His grade-school teacher couldn't pronounce his first name, so she called him "Nelson," after British naval hero Lord Horatio Nelson. The name stuck.

ANCHORMAN. In 2002 Will Ferrell was watching a documentary about pioneering TV journalist Jessica Savitch, who became the first female newscaster at a Philadelphia station in the early 1970s. When a former coworker described how chauvinistically he and his male colleagues had treated her, Ferrell got the idea to tell Savitch's story, but from the men's point of view.

SHERIFF WOODY. The *Toy Story* character was named after one of director John Lasseter's heroes, Woody Strode—the first African American to play in the NFL (LA Rams, 1946), and later an actor in dozens of movies, including *The Man Who Shot Liberty Valence* (1962) and *Spartacus* (1960).

IT WASN'T MY FAULT!

Real—and really odd—excuses filed on car insurance claim forms.

"I pulled away from the side of the road, glanced at my mother-in-law, and headed over the embankment."

"I thought my window was down but I found it was up when I put my head through it."

"The other car collided with mine without giving me warning of its intention."

"To avoid hitting the bumper of the car in front I struck a pedestrian."

"I was sure the old fellow would never make it to the other side of the road when I struck him."

"Going to work at 7:00 this morning I drove out of my driveway straight into a bus. The bus was 5 minutes early."

"My car was legally parked as it backed into another vehicle."

"I told the police that I was not injured, but on removing my hat I found that I had a fractured skull."

"I didn't think the speed limit applied after midnight."

"Windshield broken. Cause unknown. Probably voodoo."

"I had been learning to drive with power steering. I turned the wheel to what I thought was enough and found myself in a different direction going the opposite way."

"I started to slow down, but the traffic was more stationary than I thought."

"I bumped into a lamppost which was obscured by human beings."

"I knew the dog was possessive about the car, but I would not have asked her to drive it if I thought there was any risk."

"First car stopped suddenly, second car hit first car, and a haggis ran into the rear of second car."

"No one was to blame for the accident but it would never have happened if the other driver had been alert."

Since the 1770s, there has been a global flu pandemic about once every 20 years.

JOLT-ERNATIVES

The U.S. seems to run on caffeine—90 percent of adults consume it every day. But the demand for an energy boost is so strong that it can now be found in all sorts of unusual products, far beyond coffee and energy drinks.

Marshmallows. Remember the Stay Puft Marshmallow Man who wreaks havoc on New York City at the end of *Ghostbusters*? Stay Puft Marshmallows were fictional… until ThinkGeek licensed the name and image to sell mail-order marshmallows. A box of 24 costs $20, but it's worth it—each piece contains as much caffeine as half a cup of coffee.

Beef Jerky. Guarana, a caffeine-rich South American fruit that's been used for centuries, is now a common ingredient in energy drinks like Red Bull and Rockstar. It can also be used as an ingredient in marinade. That's how Perky Jerky can be beef jerky that's infused with caffeine. (Also available: Turkey Perky Jerky.)

Popcorn. Ordinary caramel corn will probably give you energy—it's loaded with sugar and carbohydrates, after all. Biofuel Caffeinated Popcorn, however, has a caffeine-laced caramel coating. One bag provides as much stimulation as three cups of coffee.

Bloody Marys. The Bloody Mary is an alcoholic drink—many consider it a "hair of the dog" cure for a hangover. Hot-D Wake Up Juice caffeinated Bloody Mary mix contains tomato juice, hot sauce, and all the other usual ingredients along with a cup of coffee's worth of caffeine to really help you recover from the night before.

Breath spray. Available in mint or cinnamon, Primer Energy Breath delivers 33 mg of caffeine in one spray into the mouth. That's as much as half a cup of coffee, but it doesn't have to pass through the stomach, so it's absorbed into the bloodstream immediately.

Water. Drinking coffee is the most common source of caffeine, but what if you hate the taste? Believe it or not, there's Water Joe—caffeinated water. The caffeine is flavorless, and one bottle has as much stimulant as a cup of coffee. (Ironically, caffeine dehydrates you, so after you have Water Joe, you'll probably want to drink some *decaf* water.)

Number of footballs made exclusively for use in the Super Bowl every year: 72.

OBSCURE-O-NYMS

Caution: Reading the definitions of these obscure words may lead to sophomania.

Castrophenia: The belief that one's thoughts are being stolen by enemies.

Eugonic: Rapid and luxuriant growth, such as bacteria bred in labs (and teenagers).

Rhytiscopia: A neurotic pre-occupation with wrinkles.

Nyctalopia: An inability to see at night.

Gyrovagues: Medieval Christian monks who wandered from monastery to monastery, or traveling salesmen and others who go door to door.

Tegestologist: A collector of beer coasters.

Limophoitos: Insanity caused by lack of food.

Ventoseness: A tendency to fart.

Necromimesis: A morbid state in which the sufferer believes himself to be dead.

Cumberworld: One so idle as to be a burden on his friends.

Ozostomia: Evil-smelling breath.

Maulifuff: A woman who makes a fuss about everything but does little or nothing.

Frugivore: An animal that eats fruit, such as the orang-utan, whose diet is 65% fruit.

Collywobbles: Intestinal cramps, such as colic, or a feeling of apprehension.

Quodlibetarian: One who argues about anything.

Chiliarch: In ancient Greece, the commander of 1,000 men (*chilioi*, a thousand; *archos*, leader).

Booboisie: Coined in the 1920s by social critic H. L. Mencken to describe the gullible masses. A parody of the French word *bourgeoisie*.

Orchiectomy: From the Greek word *orkhis* (testicles), the surgical removal of one, or both.

Flyspecked: Marked with tiny stains from the excrement of flies.

Sophomania: A delusional state in which the sufferer believes he or she is of exceptional intelligence.

Largest national forest in the US: the Tongass, in Alaska. It's larger than West Virginia.

OOPS!

*Everyone loves tales of outrageous blunders, so go
ahead and feel superior for a few moments.*

DIVERSIFICATION OF FUNDS

None of the news reports explained exactly *how* Mr. Lin managed to drop the bag full of money into an industrial shredder, but all agreed that it was an accident. In December 2010, the distraught Taiwanese factory owner called his local government office in a panic, explaining that his 200,000 Taiwan dollars (about $6,000 U.S.) had been reduced to a pile of shreds. Luckily for Mr. Lin, the Taiwanese government has a policy of repairing damaged money for free. They put their best forensics worker, Liu Hui-fen, also known as the "jigsaw expert," on the job. Working around the clock for a week, she was able to piece together every single bill to at least 75 percent of its former shape, which qualifies it as legal tender. Then Mr. Lin traded in the tattered currency for brand-new bills…which he vowed to keep safely away from his industrial shredder.

DAMN THE TORPY…D'OH!

How much does Eric Torpy admire NBA legend Larry Bird? So much that when Torpy was sentenced to 30 years in prison for armed robbery and attempted murder in 2005, he said to the judge, "Why not make it 33?" (That was Bird's jersey number.) Equally bizarre: The judge granted Torpy's request. However, after serving the first few years of his sentence, Torpy wasn't happy with the situation anymore. "Now I wish that I had 30 years instead of 33," he said in 2011. "I've wisened up." Adding insult to injury, the story made the rounds in the press and Torpy was made fun of on *The Tonight Show*…which means that Larry Bird himself has most likely heard about it. "He must think I'm an idiot," said Torpy, who will be eligible for parole in 2033.

THE SAD HATTER

For Halloween 2010 a young British man named Shawn Merter decided that he would complete his costume by wearing a sequinned top hat at an angle on his head. But instead of attaching the hat to his head with a string, Merter decided to glue it on. He tried fabric glue. That didn't work, so he used Super Glue. Good news: The hat stayed on. Bad news: It wouldn't come off. After unsuccessfully trying soap and warm water, Merter went to the emergency room. "Super Glue is actually quite strong," the ER doctor told him. "If I rip the hat off, it will tear your scalp and could lead to an infection." So a nurse cut it off with scissors. "I cut off the top of the hat, leaving only the brim," she told reporters, "so he won't look like that much of an idiot." (The brim finally did come off, but only after Merter soaked his head in warm water for 12 hours.)

SALT IN HIS WOUNDS

In the panic that followed the March 2011 Japanese tsunami and nuclear catastrophe, people all over the world began buying iodine tablets—or anything containing iodine, such as iodized salt—in the belief that it would protect them from radiation. Seeing that salt prices were rising, a Chinese entrepreneur named Guo purchased 4.5 tons of iodized salt, and had it trucked to his home. Not long after he had filled up nearly every room in his house with bags (and bags) of salt, news reports reassured the public that iodine was unnecessary in this type of disaster. Almost immediately, the price of salt dropped to pre-disaster levels. Guo couldn't return the salt because he didn't have the proper documentation. He also couldn't sell it, because he had no license to do so. At last report, Guo's house was still filled with salt.

A FABULOUS MISTAKE

A 2011 English-language booklet issued by the German tourism board to promote a music-awareness campaign in Düsseldorf city schools was marred by a typo that no one caught until two-thirds of the 90,000 booklets had been printed. The cause of the typo was a spelling error in the original German version of the booklet: The phrase *der Schulen*, meaning "of the schools," was misspelled as *der Schwulen*, which is a disparaging way of saying "of the homosexuals." The English text should have read "School's Day of Action," but read "Gay's Day of Action" instead. Result: Officials had to print 65,000 stickers with the correct word and then place each one over the typo by hand.

Unlike most big cats, which go for the throat, jaguars kill their prey by biting through the skull.

SIMPSONS STORES

Over 20+ seasons, The Simpsons *has shown hundreds of these blink-and-you-miss-'em sight gags: funny business names. Here are a few favorites.*

Something Wicker
This Way Comes

Donner's Party Supplies

Ah, Fudge
(chocolate factory)

Eastside Ruff-Form School
(dog obedience school)

Tokyo Roe's Sushi Bar

The Three Seasons Motel

All Creatures Great and
Cheap (pet store)

Miscellaneous, Etc.

Wee Monsieur
(kids clothing store)

Restoration Software

Dr. Zitofsky's
Dermatology Clinic

King Toot's Music Store

Louvre: American Style
(museum)

Kentucky Fried Panda

General Chang's
Taco Italiano

I Can't Believe
It's a Law Firm!

Red Rash Inn

Rubber Baby Buggy Bumpers

Hillside Wrangler Steakhouse

Goody New Shoes

The Frying Dutchman
(seafood restaurant)

Texas Cheesecake Depository

Much Ado About Muffins

International House of
Answering Machines

Taj Mah-All-You-Can-Eat

The Sole Provider
(shoe store)

Pudding on the Ritz

The Brushes Are Coming,
The Brushes Are Coming

T.G.I. Fried Eggs

Call Me Delish-Mael
(candy store)

The Buzzing Sign Diner

You can eat 'em, but only once: More than 2,000 plant species contain cyanide.

BASEBALL BIZARRE

Assorted weirdness from around the baseball diamond.

• Cleveland Indians pitcher Bob Feller and Minnesota Twins outfielder Denard Span have something odd in common: Both hit their mothers in the stands with a foul ball. Feller hit his mom in 1939 (he broke her collarbone); Span hit his during a spring training game in 2010. Both moms made full recoveries.

• On September 30, 1934, Charley O'Leary of the St. Louis Browns became the oldest big leaguer to get a hit and score a run. He was 51.

• In Japan, catchers learn to crouch by having spiked boards placed under their behinds.

• From 1936 to '46, Hall-of-Famer Joe "Flash" Gordon played exactly 1,000 games for the Yankees. In that time, he had exactly 1,000 hits.

• Breaking Babe Ruth's home-run record will never be 4-gotten: It happened in the 4th inning of the 4th game of '74, when the Braves' Hank Aaron, #44, hit a homer off the Dodgers' Al Dowling, #44.

• In the 1960s, Kansas City A's owner Charlie Finley installed a mechanical rabbit that popped up out of the ground behind home plate to deliver new baseballs to the umpire. Finley wanted the rest of the owners to install rabbits too, but none did.

• What minor leaguer—who never played in the majors— made a $4 million salary? Michael Jordan. In 1994 he played for a Chicago White Sox farm team. Jerry Reinsdorf, who owned the Sox and the Chicago Bulls, honored Jordan's basketball contract even as Jordan fizzled out as a baseball player.

• In 1989 the Reds' temperamental outfielder Paul O'Neill dropped a fly ball. He angrily kicked the ball. It went directly to the cutoff man and stopped a runner from scoring.

• In 1957 the Phillies' Richie Ashburn fouled a ball that hit a fan named Alice Roth. As she was being taken away on a stretcher, Ashburn fouled off another…and hit her again.

Hot running water: The Nile River has frozen only twice in recorded history.

THE GOLD WATCH AWARDS

Uncle John has been at the BRI for 24 golden years. If he keeps it up for another 30, maybe he'll qualify to be in an article like this one.

AWARD WINNER: Mike Ryterski, of St. Louis, Missouri
POSITION: Master grease maker
YEARS ON THE JOB: 71

STORY: Mike Ryterski was a 20-year-old Illinois farmboy when he went to Schaeffer Manufacturing, a St. Louis company specializing in industrial lubricants, and asked for a job. That was 1940, and as of 2011 he's still working there. The 91-year-old is down to three days a week, but he's still the "master grease maker" (one of only a few left in the world today, according to the company), overseeing the company's production of new grease products. Ryterski, who personally hired nearly every person who works at the plant today—including the person who is now his own boss—said in 2010 that he'd be on the job "as long as my health permits." (Sounds like it could be a long time.)

AWARD WINNER: Jack Ingram, of Manchester, England
POSITION: Columnist
YEARS ON THE JOB: 71
STORY: In December 29, 1933, 14-year-old Jack Ingram wrote his first newspaper column for the *Heywood Advertiser*, a local paper in northwest England. Titled "Scouts and Scouting," it was about Ingram's local Boy Scouts troop. The column, which ran under the byline "White Eagle," Ingram's scout nickname, appeared every week (with a break when Ingram served during World War II)—for the next 71 years. Ingram retired the column in 2004, at the age of 85—and was recognized by *Guinness World Records* as the longest-serving newspaper columnist in history. (Ingram died in November 2004.)

AWARD WINNER: Mary Whitehead, of Watkinsville, Georgia
POSITION: Church pianist

Tallest Miss America contestant: 6'2" Jeanne Robertson, Miss N. Carolina, 1963. (She lost.)

YEARS ON THE JOB: 75

STORY: Mary Whitehead started playing piano at the Winterville United Methodist Church in 1936 at the age of 15. She liked it so much that she came back every week for the next 75 years. When she finally decided to call it quits in February 2011, the congregation organized a "Mary Whitehead Day," just so she could play for them one more time. "I think it's awful nice of them to put on a special day for me," she said. "But I'm 91 years old. It's not so easy for me to get around as it used to be."

AWARD WINNER: Mavis Blakey, of Durban, South Africa
POSITION: Secretary of Durban's Central Gymnastics Club
YEARS ON THE JOB: 73

STORY: Blakely began studying gymnastics in Durban in 1926 at the age of 13. Ten years later, in 1936, she became secretary of the local gymnastics club. She was still organizing fundraising drives, helping set up competitions, and even coaching kids—all part of her duties as secretary—seven decades later. "Marvelous Mavis," as she was known, remained the club's secretary for nearly 73 years, until shortly before her death in 2009 at the age of 96.

AWARD WINNER: John Netherland Heiskell
POSITION: Editor-in-Chief, the *Arkansas Gazette*
YEARS ON THE JOB: 70

STORY: Heiskell graduated from the University of Knoxville in 1893, and for the next nine years worked as a reporter for various newspapers in Tennessee and Kentucky. Then in 1902 his family bought the *Arkansas Gazette*, a paper based in Little Rock, and Heiskell—29 at the time—was appointed editor-in-chief, a position he retained...for a very long time. Among the stories covered during his tenure: the first successful sustained flight of an airplane (by the Wright Brothers), the sinking of the *Titanic*, World War I, the Great Depression, World War II, the Korean War, desegregation, the Vietnam War, and the Apollo moon landing. Heiskell never retired: Although he stopped actually going to the office when he was 99, he remained the paper's editor-in-chief until December 1972...and only stopped then because he died. He was 100 years old.

Okapi, a species of antelope, are the only mammals whose females are taller than the males.

FAMOUS FOR 15 MINUTES

It's our latest installment based on Andy Warhol's observation, "In the future, everyone will be famous for 15 minutes." Here's how some people have used their allotted quarter hour.

THE STAR: Samuel Joseph Wurzelbacher, 35, a plumber from Holland, Ohio

THE HEADLINE: *Plumber Makes Waves in Presidential Race*

WHAT HAPPENED: On October 12, 2008, Wurzelbacher was playing catch with his son in his front yard when Senator Barack Obama's campaign bus rolled through the neighborhood. While cameras rolled, the bald, brawny plumber asked Obama, "I'm getting ready to buy a company that makes $250,000 to $280,000 a year. Your new tax plan's going to tax me more, isn't it?" Obama explained the nuances of his proposed tax plan, and how it wouldn't affect 90 percent of small businesses. But the media repeatedly ran a comment that Obama made at the end of his answer: "I think when you spread the wealth around, it's good for everybody." Three days later during the presidential debate, Obama's Republican rival, Senator John McCain, equated the statement with socialism, and mentioned "Joe the Plumber" 20 times, at one point referring to him as "my old buddy."

AFTERMATH: Many pundits on the left accused Wurzelbacher of being a plant for the right (he wasn't); many on the right tried to turn him into a folk hero. McCain's camp asked him to appear at rallies, and an Ohio Young Republicans chapter tried to recruit him to run for Congress. But when the press went digging into Wurzelbacher's personal life, they discovered that he didn't have a valid Ohio plumbing license, that he owed back taxes, and that he really didn't plan to buy the company he worked for. (And he goes by Sam, not Joe.) For his part, Wurzelbacher didn't have many nice things to say about *either* candidate. Obama, he said, doesn't hold true to American values, and he thought McCain tried to use him for his political gain, calling him "the lesser of two evils." After the election, Wurzelbacher wrote a book about his experiences and became a public speaker, appearing at several Tea Party political rallies. (And he still hasn't ruled out a run for office.)

Highest legal drinking age in the world: 21, in the United States.

THE STAR: Steven Slater, 38, a flight attendant from New York

THE HEADLINE: *JetBlue Gets the Blues after Attendant Grabs a Beer and Says, "Take This Job and Shove It!"*

WHAT HAPPENED: On August 9, 2010, Slater had a rough flight from Pittsburgh to New York. According to him, he got in a squabble with a passenger whose carry-on was too big and had to be checked. Allegedly, she hit Slater in the head with her bag—so hard that he started bleeding. At the end of the flight, just as the plane finished taxiing to the gate at JFK Airport, the woman demanded her bag "now!" Slater told her it would be in the baggage claim area. She started yelling, and then she slapped him. Slater snapped. With the intercom microphone in his hand, he announced to the cabin, "To those of you who have shown dignity and respect these last 20 years, thanks for a great ride." Then he told the lady and the rest of the passengers to go f*** themselves. He put down the mic, grabbed two bottles of Blue Moon beer from the galley, opened the emergency slide, and deplaned onto the tarmac. He then walked through two secure areas, got into his car, and drove home.

AFTERMATH: Slater's dramatic exit landed him in jail for reckless endangerment. His standing as a "working-class folk hero" was knocked down a peg when passengers didn't corroborate his version of events. Slater was fined $10,000 and ordered to get treatment for substance abuse. He made the rounds on the talk show circuit and was even offered a part on a reality show, which he turned down. One of the strangest parodies came in a Republican National Committee attack ad against Democrats in which they are shown "sliding off the emergency chute" to escape from President Obama's bad policies. Not laughing was JetBlue CEO David Barger. He was slammed by the press, who blamed the high tension on his baggage fee policy. Barger called Slater a "coward" and admonished the press for treating the slide deployment as a joke. "Slides can be as dangerous as a gun," he said, also noting that Slater's stunt cost the airline $25,000 in delays (and a replacement slide). At last report, Slater, still unemployed, was writing a book about his years as a flight attendant called *Cabin Pressure.*

THE STAR: Michael Brown, 49, head of the U.S. Federal Emergency Management Agency (FEMA) from 2003 to '05

When the Prince of Wales visited the White House in 1860, he brought...

THE HEADLINE: *Dubious Endorsement from Dubya Leaves FEMA Head Treading Water*

WHAT HAPPENED: "Brownie, you're doing a heck of a job." That's what President Bush said to Brown on September 2, 2005, four days after Hurricane Katrina caused major devastation along the Gulf Coast. Because the federal government was facing criticism for its slow response to the catastrophe, Brown became an example of the cronyism in the Bush administration. The administration was accused of appointing friends and business associates to positions for which they were unqualified. Case in point: Before being hired to run the nation's disaster response team, Brown was chairman of the International Arabian Horse Association, a post he resigned in 2001 amid allegations of corruption. Even more damning for Brown: His e-mails to staffers were leaked to the press. On the day Katrina made landfall, Brown wrote, "Can I quit now? Can I go home?" In another e-mail (sent while there were still corpses floating in New Orleans), he complained about the tacky suit he had to wear. "Call the fashion police!" Dozens of other petty e-mails were sent, all while his office took four days to respond to an urgent request for medical supplies.

AFTERMATH: Brown resigned from his FEMA post on September 12, stating that all the attention was hindering his agency from doing their job. He accused the press of making him a scapegoat for the administration's botched response, and added that most of the blame lay on the shoulders of local Louisiana officials. His biggest mistake, he claimed, was "underestimating" their incompetence. Brown made news again in 2007 when he was hired by Cold Creek Solutions, a company that specializes in data storage for big businesses, as their "Disaster and Contingency Planning Consultant." Said the company's CEO, "With Michael's experience and his unique view into what possibly could go wrong when looking at a plan, we can truly help clients be prepared for the unexpected." Brown is currently hosting a radio talk show in Colorado.

*　　　*　　　*

"He who angers you conquers you."

—**Elizabeth Kenny**

STAND-UP FOLKS

Comedian quips to pass the time.

"My husband thinks I'm crazy, but I'm not the one who married me."
—**Wendy Liebman**

"'Employee of the Month' is a good example of how somebody can be both a winner and a loser at the same time."
—**Demetri Martin**

"I wonder if deaf people have a sign for 'Talk to the hand.'"
—**Zach Galifianakis**

"My brothers would never let me play with them, so to get back at them I put Vaseline on the Twister mat. Left arm, BROKEN!"
—**Brian Regan**

"I realized I was dyslexic when I went to a toga party dressed as a goat."
—**Marcus Brigstocke**

"There's a metal train that's a mile long, and a lightning bolt strikes the back. How long until it reaches and kills the driver, provided that he's a good conductor?"
—**Bo Burnham**

"I was decorating, so I got out my step-ladder. I don't get along with my real ladder."
—**Peter Kay**

"I've never really thought of myself as depressed so much as I am paralyzed with hope."
—**Maria Bamford**

"Before birds get sucked into jet engines, do they ever think, 'Is that Rod Stewart in first class?'"
—**Eddie Izzard**

"I enjoy using the comedy technique of self-deprecation, but I'm not very good at it."
—**Arnold Brown**

"A lady with a clipboard stopped me in the street the other day. She said, 'Can you spare a few minutes for cancer research?' I said, 'All right, but we're not going to get much done.'"
—**Jimmy Carr**

"I was on the toilet for so long, I finally said to myself, 'I'm getting too old for this s***.'"
—**Doug Benson**

Cold-weather tip: Wearing a hat will help keep your feet warm.

FABULOUS FLOPS

*Some innovative products, like the Ford Model T and the
Sony Walkman, change the world forever. Others fail
miserably and give us something to laugh at.*

Product: OK Soda, introduced by Coca-Cola in 1993
What it Was: The cola giant's attempt to market a drink to
the teens and twenty-somethings known as "Generation X"
Details: If looks were all that mattered, OK Soda probably would
have done OK. Coca-Cola hired indie comic-book artists like
Daniel Clowse (*Ghost World*) to illustrate the cans. Clowse's cans
featured vacant-eyed slackers staring into space; others had similarly edgy images. "OK" was chosen as the brand name because it's
the most recognized word across all of the world's languages. (Second most recognizable: "Coca-Cola.")

Flop: What made OK *not* OK, aside from the fact that Generation
Xers resisted being pandered to, was the taste. Because the target
consumers drank everything from Starbucks to Snapple to Mountain Dew, product developers at Coke decided to mix multiple
flavors to create what it called a "unique fruity soda." Generation
Xers who tasted the reddish-brown stuff in test markets had other
names for it: "carbonated tree sap" was one description; "a mix of
all this crappy stuff" was another. The soda reminded tasters of
"suicides," a term for the do-it-yourself drinks that result when
kids mix all the flavors of a soft-drink dispenser together. OK Cola
lasted just over a year on store shelves before Coca-Cola canned it
for good.

Product: Thirsty Dog!
What It Was: A soft drink for dogs, introduced by the Original
Pet Drink Company in 1994
Details: Thirsty Dog! was a carbonated, "crispy beef" flavored soda
sweetened with fructose and glucose. Original Pet pitched Thirsty
Dog! as a superior alternative to tap water, even advocating elimi-
nating water from dog diets entirely in favor of Thirsty Dog!

Company president Marc Duke predicted pet sodas would be a
$500 million market by 2004.

A single teaspoon of seawater contains about 5 million living creatures.

Flop: He was off by $500 million. At 200 calories per bottle, the sugary soda made one of the most common pet health problems—obesity—even worse. And when pet owners tallied up the cost of replacing free tap water with Thirsty Dog! at $1.79 a liter, drinking out of the toilet didn't seem so bad after all. (Thirsty Cat!, the company's fish-flavored carbonated soda for cats, also bombed.)

Product: Persil Power

What it Was: A laundry detergent created by Unilever and introduced to the European market in 1994

Details: Persil Power contained a new active ingredient that regular Persil didn't—a patented manganese "accelerator" that cleaned clothes more quickly, and in cooler water, than regular detergent, which Unilever claimed would save consumers energy and money.

Flop: Consumers actually *lost* money, and lots of it, when Persil Power dissolved clothes into tattered rags in as few as a dozen washes. Unilever's rival, Proctor & Gamble, discovered the problem before Unilever did. P&G went public with the information out of fear that consumers who switched detergents would blame P&G products for damage caused by Persil Power. But Unilever ignored the warning, convinced that P&G was trying to kill a perfectly good product to avoid having to compete against it. By the time Unilever finally admitted the error eight months later and pulled the defective detergent from store shelves, Persil Power had dissolved more than $200 million of the company's money, along with all those ruined clothes.

*　　*　　*

THREE UNDERWATER RECORDS

• Most attendees at an underwater wedding: 261, at the nuptials of Italians Francesca Colombi and Giampiero Giannoccaro at Morcone Beach, Elba Island, Italy, on June 12, 2010.

• Longest time juggling three objects underwater on a single breath: 1 minute, 20 seconds, set by Merlin Cadogan in London, England, in November 2010.

• Most people playing checkers underwater: 52, at Valtu Sportshouse in Kaerepere, Estonia, on January 16, 2011.

CRAIGSLIST ODDITIES

A lot of newspapers are closing down in part due to revenue lost to Craigslist—more and more people are using the free online classified site to post their "room for rent," "for sale," and "help wanted" ads. It also tends to attract a lot of kooks. Here are some real Craigslist ads we found.

ROOMS FOR RENT

• "I have a bedroom available for a male or female roommate. The apartment is spacious and well lit. I work as a researcher and I'm also pursuing a Master's Degree. One more thing. On our bathroom door is a checklist. I like to keep a record of my bowel movements and I expect you to do the same."

• "I recently acquired a decommissioned Chinese nuclear submarine and am renting it out. The 'crew member' price is a low $120 per month and includes a bunk in the sleeping quarters, access to the mess hall, and a shared bathroom. Utilities included. We have enough uranium to power us through the 2060s."

FREE STUFF

• "Toilet: could be fixed up. A little dirty, and it leaked and overflowed last time it was used. My son stuffed an action figure down it, so if anyone picks this up and fixes it, can you drop the action figure back off at my house?"

• "One right New Balance shoe (never been worn). I broke my right foot and only used the left shoe, so now I have this new right shoe. Great gift for a one-footed person, or if you know anyone with a broken left foot."

• "Giving away absolutely free of charge, with no lien, mortgage, or other encumbrance of any sort, the undisputed world-record holder in the 'loudest vacuum cleaner on the face of the Earth' category! Act now to take advantage of this truly unique opportunity!"

• "Left-handed vintage air guitar for free. All that's needed is new strings and a good dusting."

FOR SALE

• "Fart Jar for sale: My hot girlfriend's fart in a mason jar. Need cash to pay the rent."

• "I have some banana slugs. I will lease them out for $1 per day. You just come and catch them, and keep sliding dollar bills under my front door. I am trying to save up for a flat screen TV."

• "I found four cockroaches in a box of Triscuits a few months back. I hate to have to get rid of them but I'm moving to a smaller place and won't really have the room for them anymore. Re-homing fee of $15 each or $50 for all four."

• "I have more than 1,300 pope hat replicas that I really need to get rid of. They are a little too small for most adult heads and are also irritating to the skin, so you would need to have long hair or wear a smaller hat underneath (just like the real pope). Dogs do not like to wear these pope hats, but maybe a large cat would wear one."

HELP WANTED

• "Looking for an assistant to help in texting duties—replies, deleting texts, alerting of new texts, reading texts, filtering texts. I get 40–50 texts an hour. I can't handle my workload plus texting responsibilities. My phone gets too full and needs to be deleted every couple of hours. This is a full-time position and you must be wherever I am, because my phone is always with me."

• "We have a complete business plan that aims to yield investors 1,000% returns within only a five-year period. We have all the pieces in place; the only missing piece is YOU! We are looking for a very motivated scientist who has experience in teleportation research and/or technology. Send a resume and any other information that may set you apart from other teleportation scientists."

• "I need someone to hide Easter eggs in my apartment when I am not there. They are small and filled with candy."

*   *   *

Life is half spent before one knows what life is.
—**French proverb**

Orthorexia is an unhealthy obsession with eating healthy foods.

BOUNCING BABIES

Call it luck, call it divine intervention, or just chalk it up to the fact that infants and toddlers are a lot tougher than meets the eye. Here are some incredible stories of survival.

BABY GOES ROUND AND ROUND

Three-month-old Ayden Robinson of Dunn, North Carolina, was unaware of the threat of the impending tornado, but his babysitter, Jonathan Robinson (also his cousin), was terrified. They were inside a mobile home, a notoriously unsafe place to be caught in a twister. But it was bearing down on them, and even though Robinson was holding onto Ayden as tight as he could, it wasn't tight enough. "The wind just took him straight out of my arms," said Robinson. After the storm passed, the trailer was in tatters. Robinson looked for Ayden but couldn't find him. Then he heard the faint sound of crying. He followed the sound and found the baby, unharmed, lying on a pile of debris, almost as if he were carefully placed there. "He's not supposed to be here now," said his mother, "but he is!"

BABY NEEDS A NEW CRIB

"All of a sudden, the house just shook," said Kenneth Enright, after a Toyota 4-Runner crashed into his Richmond, Kentucky, home in 2011. The truck had plowed into his 10-month-old daughter's bedroom while she was taking a nap. "We ran in, and we didn't see Aylinia," said Enright. "All I saw was the vehicle actually *on top* of her crib!" Enright shimmied under the truck but still couldn't see or hear any sign of his baby. But then, "She let out a cry, and there she was. She had her hands up, like, 'Get me out of here!'" The driver of the SUV, who'd simply lost control, was "extremely apologetic." Given that Aylinia was fine, the Enrights weren't too concerned about the gaping hole in the side of their house.

BABY BOUNCES

A couple in Paris went for a walk one day in 2010 and left their two children—a three-year-old girl and an eighteen-month-old boy—alone in their 7th-floor apartment. (The parents were later charged with reckless endangerment.) Both kids climbed through an open window onto the balcony. People on the ground yelled at them to go inside, and the girl did, but the boy climbed through the railing…and fell from 80 feet up. Thankfully, Dr. Philippe Bensignor was positioned just right. The boy bounced off a restaurant awning and landed softly in the doctor's arms. "He didn't have a scratch," said Bensignor. Making this truly lucky was that on just about any other day, the awning over the seating area would have been retracted, but because it was a bank holiday, the restaurant was closed and the awning was there.

BABY GOES FOR A SWIM

When three-year-old Demetrius Jones's grandmother awoke from her nap, the boy was missing. So was his battery-operated ride-on-top Chevy Silverado toy truck. After a frantic search, there seemed to be only one place the boy and the truck could have gone—into the Peace River next to the British Columbia campground where the family was staying. Family, neighbors, and Royal Canadian Mounted Police immediately started to hunt for Demetrius. "After three hours, we spotted what looked like some rocks or an eagle," neighbor Don Loewen recalled. "The 'rocks' were the black tires of the overturned toy sticking out of the water. And what we thought was an eagle was the little boy's blond head." And he was alive. When they plucked Demetrius from the water, *eight miles* downriver, "He wasn't even fazed," said Loewen, "although he seemed pretty excited to be dealing with the police."

BABY TAKES THE TRAIN

In 2009 just one day after Australian safety officials issued public service announcements warning parents at train stations to keep a close watch on their children, a mother at a Melbourne train station took her eye off her 15-month-old son's baby carriage. Suddenly, a gust of wind blew the carriage forward; it rolled over the ledge, flipped over, and landed upside down on the tracks. The mother lunged for the child, but it was too late—the train came along a split second later, forcing her back. The train ran over the carriage and dragged it 30 feet before rolling to a stop. No one wanted to look underneath, but someone had to. To everyone's amazement, the little boy was there, alive and okay. His only injury: a slight bump on the head.

BABY MAKES WAVES

Two Japanese parents had their worst fears realized when the
March 2011 tsunami swept through their home and ripped their
four-month-old daughter out of her mother's arms. Mom and Dad
survived but were told there was little hope for their baby girl.
Two agonizing days passed with no word. Then, on the third day, a
military search-and-rescue worker heard what sounded like a crying baby. He thought his ears were playing tricks on him; all they
had found so far were corpses. But when he heard more cries, he
yelled for his team. They began digging furiously, lifting away hundreds of pounds of rock, glass, and debris until they finally found
the baby, still in her pink woolen bear suit—and there was hardly
a scratch on her. No one knows how the girl didn't drown or get
crushed to death. Rescue workers called her a "tiny miracle."

*　　*　　*

FANCY BATHS

• **Milk Bath.** Roman scholar Pliny the Elder's *Natural History*
(A.D. 77) notes that emperor Nero's wife, Poppaea, traveled with
a herd of lactating female donkeys so that she could bathe in their
milk (with oils, lavender, and honey added in). Cleopatra was said
to bathe regularly in milk, too. As it turns out, the ancients were
on to something: The lactic acid in donkey milk contains *alpha
hydroxy*, a known exfoliant that is believed to improve the skin's
appearance. Milk baths aren't used much anymore, but hundreds
of modern beauty and bath products contain alpha hydroxy acids.

• **Bubble Bath.** Products that made baths burst with soapy bubbles appeared on the market not long after soap flakes were
invented by the Lever Brothers in 1899. In the 1950s, ads suggested that a bubble bath could soak bathers clean—with no
scrubbing needed—so their popularity for children took off. Sold
as either dry flakes or liquid, bubble bath isn't much different from
liquid soap, except for whatever scents are added in. All-time
bestselling bubble bath: Mr. Bubble, sold in bright pink bottles
since 1961.

FLUBBED HEADLINES

Whether silly, naughty, obvious, or just plain bizarre, they're all real.

Chick Accuses Some
of Her Male Colleagues
of Sexism

Westinghouse Gives
Robot Rights to Firm

How to Combat That
Feeling of Helplessness
With Illegal Drugs

World's Largest Stove
Destroyed by Fire

Deaf College Opens
Doors to Hearing

Young Marines Make
Tasty Christmas Treats

**Students cook & serve
grandparents**

Butts arrested in
Boob murder case

Parents keep kids home
to protest school closure

**Hispanics ace
Spanish tests**

Self Help Network asks
businesses for assistance

Most doctors agree
that breathing regularly
is good for you

Academics to dissect Bob
Dylan at NY conference

EXPERTS: FEWER BLOWS
TO HEAD WOULD
REDUCE BRAIN DAMAGE

Tiger Woods plays with
own balls, Nike says

Threat disrupts plan
to meet about threats

Mayor Parris to homeless:
Go home

**Police seeking man
handcuffed to chair**

Doobie tickets on sale
for Joint show

DENVER: A CITY
FULL OF BRIANIACS?

Dead man found
in graveyard

Rangers' Hamilton to get
shot for sore knee

NASA's original calculations predicted a 5% chance for a successful moon landing.

I SPY...AT
THE MOVIES

You probably remember the kids' game "I Spy, With My Little Eye..."
Filmmakers have been playing it for years. Here are some in-jokes
and gags you can look for the next time you see these movies.

THE HANGOVER (2009)

I Spy...a character from *Rain Man*

Where to Find Her: When the main characters approach a craps table, one of the women sitting there is played by Lucinda Jenney. She was reprising her role as the prostitute who tried to pick up Dustin Hoffman's autistic character, Raymond Babbit, in 1988's *Rain Man*. She was even wearing the same blue dress.

MAMMA MIA! (2008)

I Spy...two members of ABBA

Where to Find Them: The Swedish pop stars have cameos in the hit movie musical based on their music. Benny Andersson shows up as a piano-playing fisherman during "Dancing Queen"; Björn Ulvaeus appears at the end dressed as a Greek god.

ON GOLDEN POND (1981)

I Spy... Spencer Tracy's hat

Where to Find It: On Henry Fonda's head. The fishing cap that he wore in the film (his last) was a gift from co-star Katharine Hepburn. It was the first time the two legends had worked together. Spencer Tracy, who'd died in 1967, was Hepburn's longtime lover. On the first day of filming *On Golden Pond*, Hepburn told Fonda that she wanted him to have "Spencer's lucky hat."

TRUE GRIT (2010)

I Spy...the Boston Red Sox logo

Where to Find It: On Matt Damon's head. He tries to work in a nod to his favorite team in all his movies. But how could he do

---

It takes 5 liters of water to produce 1 liter of bottled water.

that in a Western set 20 years before the Sox formed? In the two buckles on his cowboy hat—they form the familiar Red Sox "B."

ROCKY BALBOA (2006)

I Spy... Sylvester Stallone

Where to Find Him: Ringside. Background footage from real boxing matches was used for the climactic fight scene. Stallone—who wrote, directed, and starred in the film—had attended one of those fights. If you look closely you can spot him watching his fictional alter-ego battle it out in the ring.

PLANES, TRAINS AND AUTOMOBILES (1987)

I Spy...the airplane from *Airplane!*

Where to Find It: In the exterior shot of the passenger jet where Steve Martin and John Candy meet. In a nod to the classic comedy film, director John Hughes used the same footage from the 1980 disaster spoof.

1408 (2007)

I Spy...a famous axe

Where to Find It: In a fireman's hands. In Stephen King's story about a malevolent hotel room, a firefighter uses an axe to break down a door. It's the same axe used in 1980's *The Shining* (another King story about an evil hotel), with which Jack Nicholson tried to kill his family after yelling, "Heeere's Johnny!" (Both films were made at London's Elstree Studios, where the axe lived in a prop closet.)

APOCALYPTO (2006)

I Spy... Waldo

Where to Find Him: In a pile of corpses. Remember the *Where's Waldo* picture-book series in which Waldo's tiny image is hidden among hundreds of other people? For some reason, in *Apocalypto*, a bloody epic about the final days of the Mayan civilization, director Mel Gibson inserted a single frame of a real man dressed like Waldo—blue jeans, red-and-white striped shirt, and red cap. (He appeared only in the theatrical release; Gibson took him out of the DVD version.)

T-ant-T? Some species of ants explode when attacked.

FORGOTTEN FOUNDERS

*Lots of cities are named after people, but sometimes
who those people were gets lost to history.*

BURBANK, CALIFORNIA

Home to many TV networks and TV studios (most
famously the "beautiful downtown Burbank" where Johnny
Carson made *The Tonight Show*), the former Spanish ranch land
was incorporated in 1887. The town began as 4,600 acres purchased by David Burbank, a dentist from New Hampshire.

LARAMIE, WYOMING

Wyoming conjures up images of plains and cowboys, but the
state's third-largest city was named after a French-Canadian fur
trapper. Jacques La Ramée settled there in 1815. In 1821 he
went on a trapping expedition and disappeared. He's believed
to have been killed by the Arapaho, but evidence was never
found. Nevertheless, he was such an economic influence that
the village he lived in and the nearby Laramie River were
named after him.

RENO, NEVADA

Jessie Reno was a war hero in both the Mexican-American
War and the Civil War, where he served as a general in the
Union army, and died at the Battle of South Mountain in 1862.
Reno was from Virginia, but he was such a popular military
figure that a number of emerging towns were named after him,
including Reno, Pennsylvania; El Reno, Oklahoma; and Reno,
Nevada.

SEDONA, ARIZONA

In the American West, towns were often "put on the map" when
they got mail service. Postal employees settled in unnamed, unin-
corporated towns and helped organize governments in addition to
mail service. That's what happened in the early 20th century with
Sedona, Arizona, named after Sedona Schnebly, wife of the town's
first postmaster.

Most commonly reported UFO shapes: hat-shaped, oval-shaped, and cigar-shaped.

YONKERS, NEW YORK

One of the town's first settlers in the 17th century was Adriaen van der Donck, a landowner who in his native Netherlands was a *jonkheer* ("yonk-ear"), the Dutch equivalent of "esquire" or "lord." In the New World, "Jonkeer" became his nickname. Yonkers is a corruption of that, and the New York City suburb was named after him.

PROVO, UTAH

Like many cities in Utah, Provo began as a Mormon settlement. They called it Fort Utah when they arrived in 1849, but a year later the town was officially incorporated and renamed Provo, after French-Canadian trapper and trader Etienne Provost, who'd helped settle the area in 1825.

MODESTO, CALIFORNIA

William Chapman Ralston founded the Bank of California and helped finance much of the settlement of Northern California in the late 1800s. He was so influential that a local government council decided to name a town after him. But at the naming ceremony for "Ralston, California," Ralston declined the offer. One of the Spanish-speaking workers there reportedly said that Ralston was "muy modesto," or very modest, to turn down the name. So Modesto it was.

ORLANDO, FLORIDA

Fort Gatlin was built near what is now Orlando in order to protect white settlers from the resident Seminole Indians. Skirmishes between the natives and the Europeans resulted, culminating in several conflicts known as the Seminole Wars, the first occurring in 1817. There, it's said, a soldier named Orlando Reeves was struck down in battle, and the city is named after him. Historians now believe that story was invented to explain the mysterious carving of the name "Orlando" into a tree as a grave marker. Or maybe it was named after Orlando Rees, a sugar mill owner who had lived nearby. A third origin story: It's named after Orlando, the lead character in William Shakespeare's play *As You Like It*. It makes sense—in the play Orlando was in love with Rosalind, and one of the city's main streets is Rosalind Avenue.

POLI-TALKS

When walking the halls of power, remember:
Walls (and reporters) have ears.

"No sane person is the country likes a war in Vietnam, and neither does President Johnson."
—**Hubert Humphrey**

"Sure, there are dishonest men in local government. But there are dishonest men in national government too."
—**Richard Nixon**

"Since a politician never believes what he says, he is surprised when others believe him."
—**Charles De Gaulle**

"If I were a Democrat, I suspect I'd feel a heck of a lot more comfortable in Boston than, say, America."
—**Rep. Dick Armey**

"What does an actor know about politics?"
—**Ronald Reagan,**
former actor, to SAG
president Ed Asner

"*Machismo gracias.*"
—**Al Gore, thanking**
Hispanic students at a school

"We see nothing but increasingly brighter clouds every month."
—**Gerald Ford**

"I don't understand it. Jack will spend any amount of money to buy votes but he balks at investing a thousand dollars in a beautiful painting."
—**Jacqueline Kennedy**

"Political skill is the ability to foretell what is going to happen tomorrow, and to have the ability afterward to explain why it didn't happen."
—**Winston Churchill**

"I tried to walk a fine line between acting lawfully and testifying falsely, but I now recognize that I did not fully accomplish that goal."
—**Bill Clinton**

"This is a great day for France."
—**Richard Nixon, at French**
president de Gaulle's funeral

"I've been subject to quite a lot of illegal leaking."
—**Hillary Clinton**

The Iron Pillar of Delhi, made of 98% pure wrought iron, hasn't rusted in 1,600 years.

AFTER THE FUNERAL

We all hope to rest in peace after we die, and most of us will. But an unlucky few of us…well, read on and see for yourself.

O LIVER CROMWELL (1599–1658)
Claim to Fame: Puritan, Member of Parliament, and leader of the forces that won the English Civil War in the 1640s, Cromwell presided over the trial and execution of King Charles I in 1649, then ruled England until his death in 1658.

After the Funeral: You can't kill a king without making enemies. By 1660 Charles I's son, Charles II, was back on the throne, and the royalists were ready for revenge. On January 30, 1661, Cromwell's body was removed from its burial vault in Westminster Abbey, hanged in a posthumous "execution," and decapitated. The body was then dumped in a pit; the head was impaled on a 20-foot spike and displayed for more than 20 years above Westminster Hall, the same building in which Charles I was tried and condemned to death. In 1685 the spike came down during a storm, and the weather-beaten head passed from one private collector to another for nearly three centuries. In 1960 the last owner arranged for it to be buried in a secret location at Sidney Sussex College in Cambridge, England, where it remains to this day.

What happened to the rest of Cromwell's body? It's either still in the pit where it was dumped in 1661, or was retrieved by Cromwell's daughter Mary and interred in a family crypt. No one knows for sure except, perhaps, the family: For more than 300 years, Cromwell's descendants have refused all requests to open the crypt to find out if the headless body is in there.

SIMON DE MONTFORT (1208–65)
Claim to Fame: An English nobleman who in A.D. 1264 led a rebellion against his brother-in-law, King Henry III, and then called the first *elected* parliament in English history. Because of this he's known as "the father of the (British) House of Commons." Unlike Oliver Cromwell, de Montfort did not execute the

---

Human tears have three layers: an oily layer, a liquid layer, and a mucus layer.

King or his son, Prince Edward, after capturing them in the battle of Lewes in 1264. He lived to regret it the following year, when Edward escaped from imprisonment, raised an army, and slew de Montfort and his son Henry (named after the King) in the battle of Evesham on August 4, 1265.

After the Funeral: The dead body of Montfort was decapitated, emasculated (that's the polite way of putting it), and otherwise cut into pieces, with the noblemen who defeated him taking the choicest parts home as souvenirs. (The first Baron Wigmore, Roger de Mortimer, got the head; he gave it to his wife, Baroness Maud, as a gift.) Afterward the parts that nobody wanted were buried beneath the altar of nearby Evesham Abbey, which soon became a popular pilgrimage site. When King Henry learned of this, he ordered de Montfort removed from the abbey and buried under a tree, the precise location of which has long been forgotten. Even the abbey is gone; it was destroyed during the reign of King Henry VIII (1491–1547). Today all that remains is a memorial stone where the altar once stood.

BENNY HILL (1924–92)

Claim to Fame: Bawdy British comedian and host of *The Benny Hill Show,* which aired from 1951 to 1989 in 140 countries around the world.

After the Funeral: Despite having a fortune estimated at $15 million, Hill was famously frugal. He lived simply, residing in a rented flat within walking distance of the TV studio where he taped his show. He never married and never even owned a car. So when he was found dead of a heart attack in his flat in April 1992, people couldn't help but wonder whatever happened to all that money.

Hill kept his millions in the bank, and when he died it all passed to his closest relatives. But that didn't stop rumors from spreading that Hill was buried with a large amount of gold jewelry, and one night in October 1992, thieves tried to dig up his body, apparently to steal the rumored jewelry. The thieves managed to dig all the way down to Hill's coffin, but were unable to get it open before daybreak, when they had to flee. A passerby discovered the desecrated grave soon after sunup, and within hours cemetery workers filled in the hole and covered the grave with a half-ton slab of concrete. Hill has rested undisturbed ever since.

BEFORE YOU GO

Overcome with wanderlust? Enjoy these random facts about travel.

• World's two busiest international airports: Atlanta, with 36 million passengers per year, and Beijing, with 31 million.

• Country most visited by vacationers: France, with 77 million visitors annually.

• Since 2007, the U.S. has issued e-passports. They're like regular passports but with a computer chip that enables face recognition, fingerprints, and iris scans at international borders. (Can you get yours without the chip? No.)

• Most common travel injury: a stubbed or broken toe incurred from walking barefoot in a poorly lit hotel room.

• Weird hotel: the eight-room Salt Palace in Bolivia, which sits atop a 12,500-foot high salt flat. The building, tables, chairs, and beds are all carved out of salt. Guests are warned not to lick the walls. (But they are encouraged to sample the barbecued llama meat.)

• Average weight gain on a week-long cruise: 8 pounds.

• Before flying, avoid onions, cauliflower, cabbage, baked beans, and other foods that cause bloating. At cruising altitude the air in your digestive tract expands by up to 30 percent, which may cause you (and your neighbors) distress.

• World's most visited tourist attraction: Times Square in New York, with 35 million out-of-towners each year.

• Travel tip: If stranded on a desert island and desperate for water, eat animal eyes (including fish eyes). They're a good source of pure water.

• A survey by a New York City hotel found that 70 percent of room lockouts and 65 percent of guests found wandering the halls in some state of undress were women. They also used twice as many towels as male guests.

• If you're traveling to Spain, consider visiting the town of San Pablo de Los Montes, which holds an annual Skirt-lifting Festival in January. For one day only, men can lift women's skirts without getting arrested (or clobbered).

FELINE FACTS

I tawt I taw a page of kitty facts. I did! I did taw a page of kitty facts!

• The only cats that hold their tails upright when they walk: domestic cats. All other cat species—lions, tigers, etc.—dangle their tails or hold them parallel to the ground.

• World's loudest domestic cat: Smokey, a 12-year-old tabby from Northampton, England. In 2011 Smokey's purr was recorded at 67.7 decibels—about the same volume as an electric shaver.

• Unlike dogs, most cat breeds are roughly the same size and body shape. Reason? They were all developed for the same job: catching rodents.

• In ancient Egypt, it was customary to mourn the death of a household cat by shaving your eyebrows.

• On average, outdoor cats "go" twice as often as indoor cats: They poop twice a day, and pee four times.

• When grooming, most cats clean their mouths and faces first, then the front legs and midsection. They usually clean their hindquarters and tail last. (Wouldn't you?)

• A cat rubs up against other cats to mingle its smell and reinforce its membership in the "pack." The lower a cat is in the pecking order, the more it rubs against other cats.

• Cats have scent glands in the pads of their paws that release a marking scent when they knead a blanket, a pillow...or you.

• The word "tabby" comes from the Arabic *al-Attabiyya*, a section of Baghdad where striped silk fabric was manufactured in the 16th century.

• Active ingredient in many allergy shots: pet dander (dead skin that clings to fur). Where do pharmaceutical companies get the dander? From pet groomers, who sell "leftover" fur for as much as $110 per pound.

• In 2004 a Pennsylvania cat named Colby Nolan was awarded an MBA from Trinity Southern University, an online college. It was part of a sting operation—Colby's owner, an attorney, enrolled him to expose the "university" as an Internet scam.

In 2004 the FDA approved maggots for use as "medical devices."

THE TUPPERWARE STORY

Today the word Tupperware is a generic term for any plastic food container with a sealable lid. That's thanks to two people: Earl Tupper, inventor of the product that bears his name, and Brownie Wise, who has been all but erased from the company's history.

BLACK GOLD

In the fall of 1945, a plastics manufacturer named Earl Tupper tried to place an order for plastic resin, one of the key ingredients in plastic, with the Bakelite Corporation. But the material was in short supply, and Bakelite couldn't fill his order. When Tupper asked if they had anything else for him to work with, the company gave him a black, oily lump of polyethylene slag, a rubbery by-product of the petroleum refining process that collected at the bottom of oil barrels. Bakelite, makers of an early plastic by the same name, couldn't find a use for the waste product, and neither could the chemical giant DuPont. Both companies had plenty of the stuff lying around. They told Tupper he could have as much as he wanted.

Tupper spent months experimenting with different blends of polyethylene—"Poly-T," as he called it—and molding them at different pressures and temperatures. He eventually came up with a process for forming it into brightly colored cups, bowls, and other household items. A year later he patented the idea that he's most famous for: the "Tupperware seal," which provided a spill-proof, airtight seal between Tupperware containers and their lids. (He borrowed the idea from paint-can lids.) Tupper called his first sealable container the "Wonderbowl."

UNDER COVER

Today plastic containers with airtight lids are so common that it's easy to forget just how revolutionary Tupperware was when it was introduced in the late 1940s. In those days, if you wanted to preserve food in the refrigerator, you could cover a dish with wax paper or foil. (Plastic wrap was still a few years away.) If you wanted something that you didn't have to throw away after a few uses, you could cover the dish with a shower cap or a damp cloth. Glass

A woman is more likely to be struck by lightning than to give birth to identical triplets.

containers were available, but they weren't cheap. They weren't airtight, either, and if you dropped them, they shattered into tiny, razor-sharp pieces—not a good thing during the post-war Baby Boom, when lots of households had small children underfoot. None of these options were very satisfactory. It was difficult to keep food fresh for more than a day or two, or to keep everything in the fridge from smelling like everything else in the fridge.

BLACK SHEEP

And yet for all the advantages that Tupperware had to offer, it just sat on store shelves, even when Tupper promoted the launch with national advertising. Consumers just weren't interested.

Part of the problem with Tupperware was that a lot of consumers couldn't figure out how to work the lids. Some people even returned their Tupperware, complaining that the lids didn't fit. But the real problem with Tupperware was that it was made of plastic. In those very early days of the plastics revolution, the stuff had a bad reputation: Many early plastics were oily; some were flammable. (They were smelly, too. One of the main ingredients in Bakelite was formaldehyde—the main ingredient in embalming fluid.) Some plastics were brittle and prone to chipping and cracking; others peeled, disintegrated, or "melted" and became deformed in hot water.

Tupperware didn't have any of these problems—it was odorless, non-toxic, lightweight. It was sturdy yet flexible and kept its shape in hot water. And if you dropped it, it bounced without spilling its contents. But consumers didn't know all that, and they were so turned off by earlier plastics that they didn't bother to find out.

SILVER LINING

As Earl Tupper pored over the dismal sales figures, he noticed that Tupperware was popular with two types of customers: 1) mental hospitals, which preferred Tupperware cups and dishes to aluminum because they didn't dent or make noise when patients threw them on the floor; and 2) independent salespeople who sold goods distributed by Stanley Home Products, one of the companies that pioneered the "party plan" sales method.

Stanley salespeople hawked their wares by recruiting a housewife to host a party for her friends and acquaintances. At the party, the salesperson demonstrated Stanley products—mops, brushes, cleaning products, etc.—in the hopes of selling some to the guests. Quite a few companies still sell goods using the home party system, and if you've ever been invited to such a party, you probably know that they aren't always the most pleasant of experiences. A lot of people attend only out of guilt or a sense of obligation to the host and buy just enough merchandise to avoid embarrassment. The same was true in the late 1940s: People could buy cleaning products anywhere, which made it kind of irritating to have to sit through a Stanley demonstration just because a friend had invited them. Even the Stanley salespeople knew it, and that was why growing numbers of them were adding Tupperware to their Stanley offerings.

LIFE OF THE PARTY

Tupperware was no mop or bottle of dish soap. It was something new, a big improvement over the products that had come before it. Once the salesperson explained its advantages and demonstrated how the lids worked—they had to be "burped" to expel excess air and form a proper seal—people were eager to buy it. They bought a lot of it, too: Tupperware sold so well at home parties that many Stanley salespeople were abandoning the company entirely and selling nothing but Tupperware.

One of the most successful of the ex-Stanley salespeople was a woman named Brownie Wise. By the early 1950s, she was ordering more than $150,000 worth of Tupperware a year for the sizable home party sales force she'd built up, this at a time when Earl Tupper couldn't sell Tupperware in department stores no matter how hard he tried. In April 1951, he hired Wise and made her a vice president of a brand-new division called Tupperware Home Parties, headquartered in Kissimmee, Florida. (Tupper remained in Leominster, Massachusetts, overseeing the company's manufacturing and product design.) Brownie's new job was to build the company's sales force, just as she'd been so successful building her own.

Tupper also pulled Tupperware from department stores. From then on, if you wanted to buy Tupperware (or *any* plastic container with an airtight lid, since Tupper controlled the patent), you had to buy it from a "Tupperware lady."

For Part II of the story, turn to page 232.

Black, green, and oolong teas all come from the same plant.

JUDGES GONE WILD

It's kind of a given that judges should have good judgment. And most of them do. But as for these folks, well...judge for yourself.

Judge: William F. Singletary, who was elected to the Philadelphia Traffic Court in 2008

Background: While running for the judgeship, Singletary was caught on video promising favorable treatment to campaign contributors at a "Blessing of the Bikes" motorcycle club gathering in a Philadelphia park. "If you all can give me $20—you're going to need me in traffic court, am I right about that?...Now you all want me to get there. You're going to need my hook-up, right?" he told the assembled crowd over the PA system. The footage soon found its way to YouTube. (Singletary is also a church deacon and blessed the bikes.)

What Happened: Singletary was charged with four counts of misconduct and found guilty of all four, enough to cost him his judgeship. But the state Court of Judicial Discipline let him off with just a reprimand and probation.

Legal Footnote: Singletary was perhaps the only traffic court judge in the country who was legally barred from driving: In 2007 his license was suspended after he racked up more than $11,000 in unpaid traffic tickets and fines for reckless driving, driving without a license, driving without insurance, and other charges. His license was reinstated in 2011.

Judge: C. Hunter King of the Orleans Parish Civil District Court in New Orleans

Background: Louisiana public officials are prohibited from using on-the-clock government employees as campaign workers. But that didn't stop King from suspending court for a week in October 2001 and ordering court employees to spend the week selling tickets to his $250-a-plate campaign fundraiser. When questioned under oath, Judge King denied everything...until he learned that his court reporter had recorded him threatening to fire any worker

---

During the 20th century, more than a third of San Francisco Bay was deliberately filled in.

who didn't sell at least 20 tickets. (King fired the court reporter when she didn't sell her tickets.)

What Happened: Judge King pled guilty to conspiracy to commit public payroll fraud and received a six-month suspended prison sentence. He was also thrown off the bench and disbarred.

Judge: Elizabeth Halverson, a Clark County, Nevada, District Court judge

Background: Halverson may have set some kind of unprofessional-conduct land-speed record after taking the bench in January 2007. In her first four months on the job, the state's Judicial Discipline Commission received more than a dozen complaints about her behavior. They alleged that Halverson abused court staff with racial and religious slurs, sexually harassed a bailiff and made him feel like a "houseboy" by assigning him menial personal chores, endangered courthouse security by hiring unqualified personnel as bodyguards and admitting them into secure areas of the courthouse, hired a computer technician to hack into courthouse e-mail accounts, made false statements to the media about three other judges she believed were conspiring against her, fell asleep on the bench during two criminal trials (and one civil trial), and ordered a clerk to swear in her husband so that she could question him under oath about whether he'd completed his chores at home. "Do you want to worship me from near or afar?" she reportedly asked one court employee.

What Happened: Halverson was suspended from the bench six months into her judgeship and charged with 14 counts of judicial misconduct. In 2008 she was removed from the bench for life. But by then she'd already lost her reelection campaign.

Judge: Timothy Blakely, a family court judge in Minnesota's First Judicial District Court

Background: For a number of years Judge Blakely was in the habit of referring people who came before his court to a St. Paul attorney named Christine Stroemer for divorce mediation. There's nothing particularly unusual about that, except that Stroemer had handled Blakely's own divorce, and she knocked more than $60,000 off of his $108,000 legal bill after receiving the referrals.

Blakely got caught when his ex-wife tipped off the state Board on Judicial Standards.

What Happened: The Board recommended that Blakely be removed from the bench, but the state Supreme Court let him off with a censure and a six-month suspension without pay in 2009. That made Dakota County prosecutor Larry Clark so angry that he ran against—and defeated—Blakely in 2010, winning 57 percent of the vote. (Blakely says that he didn't realize at the time that his conduct had created the "appearance" of a conflict of interest.)

Judge: Carlos Garza, a New Mexico magistrate judge

Background: After recusing himself from a 2006 drunk-driving case involving a woman he was dating, Garza told a court clerk to clear the woman's license of the charge before she met the legal requirements for having it cleared. In another incident with the same woman, Garza tried to intimidate a deputy marshal who pulled the woman over for speeding. Garza, a passenger in the car, reportedly told the deputy, "I'll take care of these tickets. Do you know who I am?" Garza got himself in even deeper trouble when he failed to comply with a Judicial Standards Commission order that he submit to a drug test. He eventually did take the test...and was found to have 14 times the legal limit for passive exposure to cocaine in his system. The commission also accused him of cutting the hair on his head and body to prevent samples being taken for the drug test. (Garza claims that's not why he cut his hair.)

What Happened: Garza ran for reelection unopposed in November 2006 and won; the next day the state Supreme Court barred him from the bench for life and ordered him to pay $16,000 to reimburse the Judicial Standards Commission for the cost of its investigation.

Update: Garza made headlines again in April 2008 when he was arrested for failure to appear in what had once been his own court, where he was scheduled to go on trial for driving with a suspended license, failure to display registered license plates, and speeding.

YOU'RE NEVER TOO OLD...

Because age is just a number.

At age 76: Min Bahadur Sherchan successfully climbed Mount Everest in 2008. He's the oldest person ever to do it.

At age 83: Thomas Edison applied for his 1,093rd—and final—patent (1931). The invention: a holder for items being electroplated.

At age 84: Eamon de Valera won a second term as Ireland's president (1966), making him the oldest democratically elected head of state in history.

At age 86: Doc Paskowitz, subject of the 2007 film *Surfwise,* still surfed every day.

At age 86: Katherine Pelton swam the 200m butterfly in 3:01:14, beating the 85- to 89-year-old *men's* record by more than 20 seconds (1992).

At age 87: Mary Baker Eddy founded *The Christian Science Monitor* newspaper (1908).

At age 87: Bob Hope entertained the troops, traveling with a USO show that went to Saudi Arabia in 1990 during Operation Desert Storm.

At age 88: Michelangelo drew the architectural plans for Rome's Santa Maria degli Angeli church (1563).

At age 89: Betty White won the 2010 Screen Actors Guild award for comedy actress (*Hot in Cleveland*)...a year *after* winning SAG's Lifetime Achievement Award.

At age 90: Painter Marc Chagall became the first living artist to be exhibited at Paris's Louvre museum (1977).

At age 92: Dr. Paul Spangler of San Luis Obispo, California, ran his 14th marathon.

At age 93: P.G. Wodehouse wrote his 96th book in 1975, the same year he was knighted.

At age 95: A retired union organizer named Bernard Herzberg earned a Master of Arts in Refugee Studies at the University of East London (2005).

At age 102: Alice Pollock published her memoir *Portrait of My Victorian Youth* (1971). It was her first book.

In 1978 Colorado outlawed using an apostrophe in Pike's Peak. Now it's "Pikes Peak."

Q&A:
ASK THE EXPERTS

*Everyone's got a question they'd like answered—basic stuff
like, "Why is the sky blue?" Here are a few questions,
with answers from the world's top trivia experts.*

OVER PRESSURE

Q: *Why do our ears "pop" at high altitudes?*

A: "As you go upward, the air gets thinner and lighter. If you have some heavier air from a lower level trapped inside your ears you may be able to feel the difference. As you go higher, the heavy air inside your ears presses outward on the eardrums harder than the light air pushes inward. If the heavier air escapes suddenly so that the pressure becomes equal all at once, you hear a tiny 'pop.' This is more apt to happen coming down than going up. Swallowing helps to keep the pressure on the inside of the ears even with the pressure on the outside." (From *Questions Children Ask*, by Edith and Ernest Bonhivert)

1 IF BY LAND, 0.868976 IF BY SEA

Q: *Why are a statute (land) mile and a nautical mile different lengths?*

A: "In 1593 Queen Elizabeth I established the statute mile as 5,280 feet (1,069 meters). It's based on walking distance, and originated with the Romans, who designated 1,000 paces as a land mile. The nautical mile isn't based on human locomotion, but on the circumference of the Earth. There was wide disagreement on the precise measurement, but by 1954 the United States adopted the International Nautical Mile of 1,852 meters (6,076 feet). So 1 nautical mile equals 1.1508 statute miles; and 1 statue mile equals 0.868976 nautical miles." (From *The Handy Science Answer Book*, by the Science/Technology Dept. of the Carnegie Library Assoc.)

BOUNCING AROUND THE ROOM

Q: *Where does the force come from when you are thrown across a room after touching a live electrical connection?*

A: "It's not the electricity itself that throws you. The force comes

---

Technically, the "high seas" are waters 12 or more nautical miles beyond a nation's territory.

from your own muscles. When a large electrical current runs through your body, your muscles are stimulated to contract powerfully—much harder than they can be made to contract voluntarily. The electric current typically flows into one arm, through the abdomen, and out of one or both legs, which can cause most of the muscles in the body to contract at once. The results are unpredictable, but given the strength of the leg and back muscles, the shock can send the victim flying across the room." (From *The Last Word: Questions & Answers*, edited by Mick O'Hare)

GENDER BENDER

Q: *Why do men have lower voices than women?*
A: "In the human voice box, known as the *larynx* and located in the throat, there are strings called vocal cords. These strings give sound to the voice when vibrated by wind from the lungs. The deeper voices of men are due to the longer and thicker cords in the voice box. In boys, vocal cords keep growing until about age 13, when they become fully grown. A boy's voice makes a sudden change when he reaches maturity because the greatest amount of growth takes place at that time. That's when his voice 'breaks.'" (From *How a Fly Walks Upside Down*, by Martin M. Goldwyn)

PALIN COMPARISON

Q: *Can you really see Russia from Alaska?*
A: "Yes, but only the boring parts. Russia and Alaska are divided by the Bering Strait, which is about 55 miles at its narrowest. In the middle of the Bering Strait are two small islands: Big Diomede, in Russian territory, and Little Diomede, which is part of the United States. At their closest, these islands are a little less than two and a half miles apart, which means that, on a clear day, you can definitely see one from the other. If you stand on high ground on the tip of St. Lawrence Island—a larger Alaskan island—you can see the Russian mainland, about 37 miles away. It's not as if Alaskans can see into the heart of the Kremlin, though. The region you'd see is Chukotka, a desolate expanse of about 285,000 square miles with a population of about 55,000. That's an area roughly the size of Texas with a population the size of Pine Bluff, Arkansas." (From *Slate* magazine, "Can You Really See Russia From Alaska?" by Nina Shen Rastogi)

THE WAY WE WEREN'T

Ah, this reminds Uncle John of a page he wrote a long time ago...

"Nostalgia is like a grammar lesson: You find the present tense, but the past perfect."
—**Owens Lee Pomeroy**

"Nothing is more responsible for the good old days than a bad memory."
—**Franklin P. Adams**

"The world is full of people whose notion of a satisfactory future is, in fact, a return to the idealized past."
—**Robertson Davies**

"It's never safe to be nostalgic about something until you're absolutely certain there's no chance of its coming back."
—**Bill Vaughn**

"There is no greater sorrow than to recall a happy time when miserable."
—**Dante Alighieri**

"When people talk about the good old days, I say to people, 'It's not the days that are old, it's you that's old.' I hate the good old days. What is important is that today is good."
—**Karl Lagerfeld**

"People have this obsession. They want you to be like you were in 1969, because otherwise their youth goes with you. It's very selfish...but it's understandable."
—**Mick Jagger**

"What is recalled by faded flowers, save that they did not last?"
—**Letitia Elizabeth Landon**

"Youth is like having a big plate of candy. Sentimentalists think they want to be in the pure, simple state they were in before they ate the candy. They don't. They just want the fun of eating it all over again."
—**F. Scott Fitzgerald**

"The best time is always yesterday."
—**Tatyana Tolstaya**

"Nostalgia is a file that removes the rough edges from the good old days."
—**Doug Larson**

"How sad and bad and mad it was—but then, how it was sweet."
—**Robert Browning**

A dirty spark plug can reduce your car's fuel efficiency by as much as 30%.

THE ECONOMY IN BRIEF(S)

When economists want to get a sense of how the economy is doing, they look at things like the prime lending rate, the unemployment rate, and the Dow Jones Average. It turns out that's not all they look at.

DOWN UNDER

Alan Greenspan was the chairman of the Federal Reserve from 1987 to 2006. He was one of the most influential economists of his day, and his grasp of how the American economy works was profound. He was also famous for keeping an eye on an economic indicator that, on the surface at least, didn't seem to have much to do with the economy at all: sales of men's underwear.

What interested Greenspan about men's underwear was that the sales figures rarely changed. For most men, underwear isn't something they treat themselves to when they feel like splurging; it's a purely utilitarian item. They buy it to replace underwear that has worn out. And since underwear wears out at a pretty steady rate, sales of new underwear are pretty steady too.

Greenspan noticed, however, that on occasion underwear sales did dip. When that happened, he interpreted it to mean that significant numbers of men were financially stressed enough that they had stopped replacing their worn-out shorts.

FIRST THINGS FIRST

How many people see you in your underwear? When funds are limited, most men will put off buying underwear—clothes that people *don't* see—before they stop buying shirts and pants that people *do* see, if for no other reason than to keep up appearances. If they have kids, men will put off buying their own underwear before they'll stop buying things for their children. For this reason, men's underwear sales tend to *lead* many other economic indicators—they register signs of economic distress months before sales of other items begin to slow. That's why Greenspan liked to keep an eye on it: If the economy was losing steam, he'd see it in men's underwear first.

Amount of fat in the McDonald's Big Macs America eats every year: 35 million lbs.

THIS, THAT, AND THE OTHER THING

Over the years, economists have developed theories based on a lot of other items besides men's underwear. For example:

• **Boxcars.** This is something that Uncle John can see right outside his window. A lot of freight is shipped by rail in the United States, and when the freight isn't moving, the unused boxcars are parked on railroad spur lines (including the one across the street from the Bathroom Readers' Institute) until the economy picks up and they're needed again.

• **Movie Tickets.** As expensive as a trip to the multiplex is nowadays, it's still a lot cheaper than a weekend at the beach. People who can't afford to take a vacation often compensate by going to the movies instead, causing ticket sales to rise in a recession.

• **Donuts.** People who can't afford a full breakfast in a restaurant will often trade down to a donut and coffee. Hot dog sales do well in hard times for the same reason: In the 1930s, they were known as "Depression sandwiches."

• **Laxatives.** When people are under stress and living on donuts and hot dogs…well, you figure it out.

• **Lipstick.** Studies show that women who don't have the money for a new dress or new shoes will spend $15 or $20 on lipstick instead. Belts, scarves, bracelets, and other fashion accessories that dress up old outfits also do well, as do home permanents and dye kits that offer a cheap alternative to hair salons.

• **Alligators.** Most gators that end up as boots, handbags, and other designer goods are raised on farms. Sales of these items tend to crash during a recession (they're too expensive *and* too flashy in hard times), and the alligator population on these farms explodes.

• **Lightbulbs.** When Jack Welch took the helm at General Electric in 1981, the company made more than just lightbulbs, but he still swore by sales of bulbs as an indicator of where the economy was heading. "When people are affluent, they go to the store and buy what's called 'pantry inventory,'" he told an interviewer in 2001. "They'll buy a pack of six or a pack of eight, and they'll wait for the lights to go out. When times are tough, a light burns out, they'll go buy one to replace the one went out. There are probably a thousand better indicators, but that one's never been wrong."

Banker slang for people who pay off their credit cards in full each month: "deadbeats."

BEN THERE, DONE THAT

Where has this awesome quote page Ben all our lives?

"A learned blockhead is a greater blockhead than an ignorant one."
—**Benjamin Franklin, statesman**

"We have to try to score more points than they do."
—**Ben Roethlisberger, QB, on how to win a Super Bowl**

"We don't point a pistol at our own forehead. That is not the way to conduct negotiations."
—**Benjamin Netanyahu, Israeli prime minister**

"Do unto others, then run."
—**Benny Hill, comedian**

"God help me if I ever do another movie with an explosion in it. You'll know I've lost all my money."
—**Ben Affleck, actor**

"A fool may talk, but a wise man speaks."
—**Ben Jonson, English poet**

"If you do nothing long enough, something's bound to happen."
—**H. Jon Benjamin, comedian**

"I'm not Jack Nicholson. I'm not Brando. But I do mumble."
—**Benicio Del Toro, actor**

"When a man recalls the good old days, he's really thinking of his bad young days."
—**Ben Stein, writer and actor**

"Who is more foolish: the fool, or the fool who follows him?"
—**Ben Kenobi, Jedi Master**

"The magician and the politician have much in common: They both have to draw our attention away from what they are really doing."
—**Ben Okri, Nigerian poet**

"The disappointment of manhood succeeds the delusion of youth."
—**Benjamin Disraeli, British prime minister**

"Relax? How can you play golf and relax? You have to grip the club, don't you?"
—**Ben Hogan, golf legend**

"Bonnnnnnng!"
—**Big Ben, clock**

Florida pharmacist Benjamin Green invented suntan lotion in 1944.

THERE'S A RECORD FOR THAT?

Anybody can run fast or eat a bunch of hot dogs, but it takes true commitment to be the world-record prune-eater.

• **BROOM-BALANCING.** Leo Bircher (Switzerland) holds the record for balancing a broom—on his nose—for a record time of two hours, one minute.

• **CHRISTMAS TREE-BALANCING.** David Downes (England) balanced a seven-foot-tall tree on his chin for 56.82 seconds.

• **TYPING.** In October 1987, Jens Seiler (Germany) typed 626 keystrokes, about 100 words, in a minute. More impressively, he typed the words backward.

• **BALLOON-STUFFING.** Ralf Schuler (Germany) holds two records: 1) the most people stuffed inside a latex balloon—23, and 2) the fastest time to stuff someone (himself) into a latex balloon—37.1 seconds.

• **PRUNE-EATING.** In 1984 Alan Newbold (USA) ate 150 dried plums in 31 seconds. (And then, presumably, a few hours later, Newbold set *another* record.)

• **WAITING.** Jeff Tweiten and John Goth (USA) queued up to see *Star Wars: Episode II—Attack of the Clones* outside a Seattle movie theater on January 1, 2002…and stayed there until the film opened four and a half months later, on May 16.

• **BEAN-EATING.** Kerry White (England) holds the world record for eating baked beans, consuming 12,547 beans (in sauce) in a 24-hour period. Barry Kirk (England) sat in a cold bath of baked beans for 100 hours in September 1986.

• **GUM-WRAPPER CHAIN.** Gary Duschl (USA) has been purchasing gum and collecting wrappers since 1965, and in 2004 he claimed the record for the world's longest gum-wrapper chain. He's still adding to it, and as of March 2011, it consisted of 1,581,159 gum wrappers and measured 66,835 feet—more than 12 miles.

- **EAR-WIGGLING.** Not many people can wiggle their ears at all. Jitendra Kumar (India) wiggled his 147 times in one minute.

- **EXTREME HULA-HOOPING.** In 2000 Roman Schedler (Austria) hula-hooped for 71 seconds straight. That may not seem very long, but he did it with a 53-pound tractor tire.

- **DRUMMING.** Tim Waterston (USA) is one the world's fastest drummers. In January 2002, he set a speed record, playing 1,407 beats in one minute…with his feet.

- **NAILING.** In October 1999, Chu-Tang-Cuong (Vietnam) drove 116 nails into a wooden board in just 11 minutes. The twist: He did it with his bare hand. (Ouch!)

- **PROPOSING.** In 1976 Keith Redman (USA) asked his girlfriend Beverly to marry him. She said no, the first of 8,801 rejections, a world record. (Happy ending: In 1999 Beverly finally said "Yes" after receiving Redman's proposals at a rate of more than one per day for 23 years.)

- **COTTAGE CHEESE-EATING.** In 1984 Peter Altman (England) shoveled down three pounds of cottage cheese in four minutes. Three years later, Altman set the 30-second record, consuming half a pound of it on a British talk show.

- **COCKROACH-EATING.** Ken Edwards (England) ate 36 in a minute in 2001. A more extreme record holder is Travis Fessler (USA), who held 11 live cockroaches (each at least 2.5 inches long) for 10 seconds…in his mouth.

- **BARF-BAG COLLECTION.** Niek Vermeulen (Netherlands) possesses the world's largest collection of airsickness bags He's a frequent flyer, and as of March 2008, owned 5,468 distinct bags from more than 1,065 different airlines, along with 10,000 duplicates. (Note: They are all unused.)

CANADA'S CAPTAIN UNDERPANTS

*You've heard of clothing drives; here's the story of
an underwear drive that involved a whole lot of
underwear…and a whole lot of driving.*

MAN ON A MISSION

Brent King is a mechanical engineer in Calgary, the largest city in the province of Alberta. Like many big cities, Calgary has a homelessness problem, and in the fall of 2008 King was curious to see how the city's social service agencies were tackling the issue. He was particularly impressed by the work an organization called the Mustard Seed was doing to help the homeless find jobs and housing and re-enter society. After visiting their facility, he asked if there was a problem he could help them solve. "They showed me their wish list, and on the top of it was men's underwear," he told the Montreal *Gazette*.

The people at Mustard Seed explained that while it's common for people to give used clothing to homeless shelters and thrift shops, used underwear isn't really the kind of thing that gets donated. And not many people think of donating new underwear, so homeless shelters rarely have enough.

ONE STRING ATTACHED

King formed a charity called Got Ginch ("ginch" is a slang term for men's briefs) and funded it with thousands of dollars of his own money, plus thousands more raised from friends. Rather than buy underwear at retail prices, he asked a business associate in China to help him work directly with a textile mill overseas to save money. The associate, a native of Vancouver, B.C., agreed…on one condition. "He said, 'I'll do it only if you do Vancouver next.'" That was fine with King, but why stop there? He decided to fill an RV full of underwear and spend his summer vacation driving 3,600 miles across Canada from Vancouver to Halifax, Nova Scotia, distributing underwear to homeless shelters in 10 different cities as he went. He hit the road in June 2009,

---

…rides in which they wore only underwear. Their slogan: "Insurance Is Stripping Us."

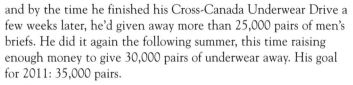

and by the time he finished his Cross-Canada Underwear Drive a few weeks later, he'd given away more than 25,000 pairs of men's briefs. He did it again the following summer, this time raising enough money to give 30,000 pairs of underwear away. His goal for 2011: 35,000 pairs.

The cross-country tours have helped raise awareness of the issue, and many Canadian homeless shelters have reported increased underwear donations. King hopes to distribute even more in future Underwear Drives…and after years of prodding about why he doesn't distribute underwear for *women*, he says he's working on that too. "I acknowledge that the need exists and that it is at least as important as the need for men's underwear," he writes in his blog, "but I maintain that two guys traveling cross country with a truck load of women's underwear is a little creepy. We are working to find a couple of like-minded ladies to take up the challenge."

OTHER CANADIAN UNDERWEAR CRUSADERS

• **The Underwear Affair.** The Underwear Affair is a charity race held by a number of Canadian charities to raise awareness for cancers that occur below the waist—including prostate, ovarian, testicular, bladder, and colorectal cancers—which make up 40 percent of all cancers. Weeks ahead of the race, volunteers promote the event by wearing skivvies over their clothing. On race day, participants run the 10k race or walk the 5k walk in their underwear or in underwear-themed costumes. "There's absolutely no shame in bringing a little awareness to down there-ness," says the website for the B.C. Cancer Foundation.

• **Mark McIntyre, a.k.a. GuyAtHome.com.** Who says you've gotta run a race in order to raise money for a good cause? In October 2010, McIntyre, a two-year survivor of testicular cancer (the most common cancer in males aged 15 to 29), fired up some webcams in a rented Toronto loft and spent 25 days lounging around in his underpants. That's it. For every "like" he received on Facebook during those 25 days, underwear maker Stanfield's agreed to donate $1 to the Canadian Cancer Society. "Since they're an underwear company, they're about as close to testicles as any company is," McIntyre says. He scored 50,000 "likes" and raised $50,000 for the charity.

IRONIC, ISN'T IT?

There's nothing like a good dose of irony to put the problems of day-to-day life into proper perspective.

LOW-GRADE IRONY

In 2011 the U.S. National Council on Teacher Quality announced that it would begin using letter grades to evaluate teaching instructors. The teachers objected to the plan, claiming letter grades are too simplistic to accurately measure anyone's achievements.

A FISTFUL OF IRONY

• In January 2007, Pakistan's *Daily Times* reported on violence at Dawood Engineering College in Karachi. "What started as an exchange of words," said the *Times*, "snowballed into a fistfight. At issue was a poster urging students not to fight on campus. The fight was over who would put up the poster."

• Inside the Erie County (New York) Correctional Facility, James Conlin and Lawrence Mule began arguing over a bag of potato chips. Before long, fists were flying...until a man standing nearby stepped in to break up the fight. What's ironic about that? Conlin and Mule are veteran prison guards; the man who broke up the fight was an inmate. (Both guards were suspended.)

HIS ©UNNING PLAN FAILED

A Taiwanese artist named Wu was awarded 50,000 Taiwan dollars ($1,600 in the U.S.) for submitting the winning entry in a contest to create a poster that discouraged people from violating copyright laws. He was ordered to return the prize money after it was discovered that he'd copied the design of another artist.

SEEKING CLOSURE

Warren and Maureen Nyerges paid $165,000 in cash for a home in Naples, Florida, in 2011. A few months later, Bank of America wrongly filed a foreclosure claim against them. The Nyergeses took the bank to court and won. The judge ordered the bank to pay their court costs (about $2,500), but the bank refused...until

Gramatically speaking, the first 8 lines of "The Star-Spangled Banner" are two sentences.

the Nyerges showed up at a Naples Bank of America branch with a court-approved "foreclosure of assets" notice and a moving-company crew. The workers began to seize furniture from the lobby. Less than an hour later, the bank paid up.

YIELD TO ONCOMING IRONY
A 200-foot-long fence was erected on an overpass of I-70 in St. Louis, Missouri, to prevent people from throwing things onto the highway, which could injure people and damage vehicles. In 2010 a motorist driving on the overpass lost control of his car and ran into the fence, sending the entire thing hurtling onto the highway. Several people were injured and several vehicles were damaged.

DEATH AND IRONY
• Elizabeth Taylor outlived Mel Gussow by six years. Mel who? He was *The New York Times* writer who penned Taylor's obituary.

• Michael Anderson Godwin was sentenced to death in the early 1980s for murder. After six years and numerous appeals, the South Carolina death-row inmate got his sentence reduced to life in prison. Not long after, Godwin was sitting on the metal toilet in his cell, watching TV. He was wearing nothing except a pair of headphones, which started to crackle. Trying to fix them, Godwin bit into the wire. He was electrocuted and died.

DETROIT ROCK-COCAINE CITY
In 2011 tourism officials in Detroit launched a new ad campaign in an attempt to counter the city's reputation as a place of rampant violence and drug use. After posters were put up all over the city, bloggers pointed out that the font designers had selected for the "Believe in Detroit" logo is called "Crackhouse."

THESE ARE THEIR STORIES...DUN DUN!
In 2011 Paterson, New Jersey, police received a tip regarding the whereabouts of a man who'd robbed a family at gunpoint. Informed that the man might be carrying one of the family's cell phones—which has a very distinctive ring tone—an officer dialed the number as he approached the suspect. Sure enough, the theme music to TV's *Law & Order* started playing. The man was arrested.

About 50% of people who are allergic to latex are also allergic to bananas.

NAME THAT TUNA

*The origins of the names of some common fish, and a few
that you may not have heard of before at all.*

BASS: Bass are *ray-finned* fish, meaning they have sharp,
boney spikes in their fins, as opposed to the *lobe-finned* fish,
which have loose, fleshy fins. Fishermen have known this
for eons, and that's how the fish got their name. "Bass" comes
from the ancient Germanic word *bærs*, which meant "sharp."

GUPPY: In 1866 an English clergyman and naturalist discovered a species of tiny fish on the Caribbean island of Trinidad
and sent samples to the British Museum in London. His name:
Robert John Lechmere Guppy. Later that year, the fish was given
the scientific name *Girardinus guppii* in his honor, and by the
1920s it was commonly known as the "guppy." Only problem:
The fish had been previously identified in America (in 1859)
and had already been given the name *Poecilia reticulata*. It's still
known by that name to biologists…but it's "guppy" to the rest
of us.

LAMPREY: The name for this family of jawless fish (often
referred to as "lamprey eels," even though they're not eels) comes
from the Old French *lampreie*, which etymologists believe was a
combination of the Latin *lambere* ("to lick") and *petra* ("rock"),
making it the "lick-rock" fish—a reference to lampreys' round,
sucker-like mouths, with which they attach themselves to rocks
(when they're not using them to suck the blood from other fish).

TUNA. The ancient Greeks ate a lot of this mackerel variety.
One of the most common fish in the Mediterranean, tuna was a
standard protein in Greek cooking. It was typically cooked with
vegetables and olive oil and served as an appetizer at banquets.
The Greeks called the large but speedy creature *thynnos*, from
thynein, which means "darter." By the 16th century, tynnos had
been anglicized into *tunny*, and by the 19th century, English-
speakers called it "tuna."

MARLIN: You probably know the marlin as a large ocean fish

The sketch that Jack drew of Rose in *Titanic* was actually drawn by director James Cameron.

with a very long and pointy snout. It got its name because that snout appeared to resemble a *marlinspike*, a large needle used by sailors to separate strands of rope. (The earliest recorded use of the word *marlin* in reference to the fish was in 1917.)

SALMON: Salmon are famous for their migrations from the ocean to rivers and streams, during which they leap their way up steep grades and waterfalls to make it to their spawning grounds. The name found its way into English back in the early 1200s via the Latin word *salmo*, which is believed to come from the Latin verb *silire*—meaning "to leap."

ORANGE ROUGHY: They're called "orange roughies" because they're orange…and they have very rough scales. But they used to be known as "slimeheads" because their heads are permeated with mucous glands. They became a very popular restaurant fish in the late 1970s (thanks to improved deep-sea trawling technology), and the name was changed to "orange roughy" because "slime-head" sounded about as appetizing as "poo eel" or "booger trout." Slimeheads, which can live for more than 140 years, have been so heavily fished since then that they are now severely threatened.

SHARK: Sharks were called "dog-fish" in several European languages since the days of the ancient Greeks. In the 1500s the Spanish started calling them *tiburons*, after their name in the Caribbean Arawak Indian language, and *tiburon* actually became the fish's English name for a while. Then, in 1569, a huge shark caught by the English slave trader John Hawkins was advertised for viewing in London. The ad read:

> "Ther is no proper name for it that I knowe but that sertayne men of Captayne Haukinses, doth call it a Sharke."

Nobody knows where the "men of Captayne Haukinses" got the name "sharke." But the big fish have been called that ever since.

MUSKIE: This long, narrow-bodied fish is found in North American freshwater systems from the Great Lakes to Hudson Bay. The Ojibwe people, who have inhabited the region since long before the arrival of Europeans, thought they looked like another local fish—the pike—and called them *maashkinoozhe*, which experts believe meant "ugly pike." In the early 1700s French trappers in

---

Doublespeak: Hummingbirds have split tongues. Hairs between the two halves draw in nectar.

the area took that name and twisted it into the French *masque allongé*, meaning "long mask," for the fish's long head, which the English adapted into *muskellenge* in the 1780s.

SARCASTIC FRINGEHEAD: These bizarre-looking, huge-mouthed, ferociously territorial fish make their homes in abandoned seashells along the west coast of North America. It's called "sarcastic" because of its temperamental nature, and "fringehead" because of the eyebrow-like appendages over its eyes. (Never heard of a sarcastic fringehead? Neither had we, but we liked the name so much that we just had to include it in this list.)

MANTA RAY: Rays are a flat, seemingly winged species of fish, closely related to sharks. They've been called "rays" in English since the 1300s, a derivation of their Latin name, *raia*—though why exactly they were called that is lost to history. (Etymologists say it is unrelated to the root words for "ray" as in "ray of light," "radius," or any other similar words.) *Manta* rays are the largest of all ray species. The Romans called them *mantellum*, the word for "cloak," after the manta ray's broad and flat body. That became "manta" in Spanish, and that came to English in around 1760.

SOLE: This is a name used for many types of ocean-going *flatfish*—fish with wide, flat bodies, like flounder. The name came to English in the 1300s and traces its way back to the Latin *solea*, which originally meant "sandal." (*Solea* is also the root of the *sole* of your shoe or foot.)

* * *

WHAT ARE...PANTS?

Just prior to the "Ultimate Tournament of Champions" game in 2005, *Jeopardy!* host Alex Trebek was informed that the three finalists were nervous, so they all decided to play the game without wearing any pants, just to ease the tension. They requested that out of solidarity, Trebek do the same. So he walked out onto the stage in his boxer shorts, only to discover that the contestants—Brad Rutter, Ken Jennings, and Jerome Vered—*were* wearing pants...and big smiles. Trebek turned around, walked back to his dressing room, and put on his pants.

In the 20th century, more than 3 million people died in earthquakes.

BATHROOM NEWS

*Here are a few fascinating bits of bathroom news
that we've flushed out from around the world.*

I WANT TO HOLD YOUR HAND(LE)

In the early 1970s, John Lennon had an antique china toilet replaced at Tittenhurst Park, the English country home where he lived from 1969 to 1972. When the plumber, whose name was John Hancock, asked Lennon what he wanted to do with the old toilet, the ex-Beatle reportedly told him to "use it as a plant pot." Hancock held on to John's john for the rest of his life (no word on whether he ever used it as a flower pot), and when Hancock died in 2010, his heirs put it up for auction during Liverpool's annual Beatles Week festivities. It sold for $14,740, about 10 times what auction organizers expected. "It's the most unusual item we've ever had," said auction spokesperson Anne-Marie Trace.

CRAPPER IN THE RYE

At about the same time John Lennon's old commode went under the gavel, a North Carolina collectibles dealer named Rick Kohl acquired a toilet once owned by J.D. Salinger, author of the 1951 novel *The Catcher in the Rye*, and put it up for auction on eBay. Asking price: $1 million. But unlike Lennon, Salinger was reclusive, and although he is believed to have continued writing until shortly before his death in January 2010, he published nothing after 1965, seeing even the publication of his own work as a violation of his privacy. When they learned of the listing, Salinger's family members found it hard to imagine that he would want to see his toilet sold at public auction. They sued to block the sale, and won. Kohl surrendered the throne and was reimbursed the $2,000 he paid for it.

IRON CHEF

In March 2009, a housing unit of Washington State's Clallam Bay Corrections Center was evacuated when a guard noticed smoke pouring out of a sewer vent pipe. One hundred and thirty inmates had to evacuate their cells and wait in the dining hall until guards finally tracked down the source of the smoke: a fire in a stainless-steel toilet, set by an inmate who was trying to heat up a snack sausage he bought in the commissary.

FACE TIME

In 2010 a Florida man named Pat McCourt ran for election to the Bonita Springs Fire Rescue District board. Shortly after he proposed cutting the fire department's budget, his campaign started getting some undesirable publicity: Urinal cakes bearing his photograph appeared in the men's room urinals of several local bars and restaurants. The proprietors of the establishments hadn't given permission for their urinals to be used in that way, and when customers complained ("Whose face am I peeing on?" was a common query), the offending cakes were removed. But it didn't matter. "As soon as we take them out they're being replaced," Gary Maurer, manager of the Landsdowne Street Pub, told reporters. Local firefighters denied any involvement: "Nope. It's not the firefighters, the union, or the fire department," said a spokesperson for Firefighters Union Local 3444. (McCourt lost the race.)

STRANDED

In November 2010, a 69-year-old woman living in a second-floor apartment in the Paris suburb of Epinay-sous-Senart got stuck in her bathroom when the lock on the door broke. There was no window in the bathroom for her to call for help, so she banged on the pipes instead, making a racket that could be heard throughout the building. No one investigated the sounds. The woman spent three weeks in her bathroom before worried neighbors, still ignoring the incessant banging, noticed she was missing and called the police. They broke into the apartment and found the woman, still locked in her bathroom, still banging away. For three weeks she had lived on tap water and toothpaste. So why did none of the other tenants investigate the noise? They assumed it was caused by someone doing repairs and were actually circulating a petition to get it stopped when the woman was finally rescued. (She made a full recovery.)

THE MANY FACES OF SANTA CLAUS

You probably think of Santa as a jolly guy in a red suit who hangs out with elves and reindeer. But that's only the American view. Saint Nick, it turns out, is a man of the world, and other countries have their own wildly varying versions.

KYRGYZSTAN

In this former Soviet republic, Santa is known as Ayaz Ata ("Snow Father") and he delivers presents on New Year's Eve, not Christmas Eve. Schools host "Christmas Tree Parties" in the week leading up to December 31 to help prepare for Ayaz's arrival. The celebration is part Christmas and part Halloween, as children dress in costumes. Ayaz doesn't have reindeer and elves—he walks with a staff and is assisted by his adopted daughter, Aksha Kar. According to legend, Aksha was once made out of snow, but she began to melt in the spring after Ayaz and his wife adopted her. Then she underwent a magical Pinocchio-like transformation and now serves as his helper.

ITALY

In Italy, Santa goes by Babbo Natale ("Father Christmas"), but he typically leaves the gift giving to a witch named La Befana. Italian children place their shoes by the front door of their homes in the hope that she'll stop by and place gifts in them on the night before Epiphany, a holiday that celebrates the 12th day of Christmas (January 5), the day the Three Wise Men arrived in Bethlehem. The legend says that as the Three Wise Men made their way to Bethlehem to greet the baby Jesus, they asked La Befana for directions and invited her to come along…but she declined because she was preoccupied with household chores. Later that night, she spotted a "great, white light" on the horizon, immediately regretted her decision to stay home, and flew off on her broomstick to join them. (She *is* a witch, after all.) But she got lost, so now she spends every Epiphany Eve searching for Baby Jesus, scattering gifts for kids along the way.

In the Dominican Republic, members of the armed forces and police are not allowed to vote.

JAPAN

Fewer than 1 percent of Japan's residents are Christian, so Christmas isn't considered a major holiday there, but many people enjoy it as a secular annual tradition. Children receive presents under their pillows from a Santa dubbed Santakukoru, who has taken on the characteristics of Hotei-osho, a mythological Buddhist monk who, according to legend, was once known for carrying gifts around in a large red bag. And it's become commonplace for couples (and families) to dine at Kentucky Fried Chicken on Christmas Day. The tradition started in the 1980s when Americans living in Japan couldn't find restaurants that served turkey dinners, so they got the next best thing: KFC. Result: Tables for Christmas meals at Japanese KFCs have to be booked months in advance.

TURKEY

Santa goes by Noel Baba ("Father Christmas") in Turkey, and his story is similar to the Turkish tales about St. Nicholas, who was born in the town of Patara around A.D. 270. The story goes that Nicholas inherited a large fortune from his father and decided to give it away to the poor, especially needy children. One night, Nicholas encountered a nobleman and three daughters, who had all fallen on hard times. Because their father couldn't provide dowries, the girls had no shot at marriage. One night Nicholas intervened and tossed a sack of gold coins through their window for the first daughter. He returned the following night and tossed in another sack for the second daughter. On the third night, the window was closed. Undaunted, Nicholas climbed onto the roof and dropped more gold down the chimney. The next morning, the daughters found the coins in the stockings they had hung to dry over the fireplace. (Sound familiar?) Now, every Christmas Eve, Noel Baba flies around Turkey delivering more presents via chimneys.

AUSTRIA

St. Nicholas is the Christmas icon here, and he isn't nearly as forgiving or jolly as the American Santa. Instead of Rudolph, he travels with Krampus, a hairy, demon-like monster with horns and sharp teeth. During the holiday season, children are encouraged to behave themselves: If they do, they get presents. If they don't, Krampus will beat them with his rusty chains. And what happens

There are more known reptile species in Australia than in all other countries combined.

if the creature finds children still awake on Christmas Eve when Nicholas shows up to deliver gifts? He will toss them into a sack and cart them away. Every December 5, the Austrian town of Schladming hosts an annual "Krampus Karnaval," which features volunteers who dress up as Krampus and march through the streets in a parade, threatening children along the route with tree branches and plastic chains.

THE NETHERLANDS

The tales surrounding the Dutch version of Santa may be the strangest of all. Here he goes by Sinterklaas, and he's taller, thinner, and more regal than the American version. He delivers presents on December 5 as part of a holiday called *Sinterklaasavond* ("Santa Claus Evening") or *Pakjesavond* ("Presents Evening"). But before that, on a Saturday in November, Sinkterklaas's "arrival pageant" is staged and televised across the country. Mounted atop a white horse, an actor dressed as Sinterklaas rides through a randomly selected Dutch city before he makes his deliveries. (Sinterklaas lives not at the North Pole, but in the distant, exotic land of…Madrid.) Accompanying him on his journey (via steamboat, not sleigh) is a group of African servants called the *Zwarte Pieten*, or "Black Peters." During the televised event, white Dutch actors wear black makeup and bright red lipstick to portray the Black Peters. They march alongside Sinterklaas, performing pratfalls while handing out candy to good children. Bad children are threatened with brooms, and according to Dutch legend, *really* bad kids are carted in sacks back to Spain to make the toys that Sinterklaas delivers to the good children. To keep up with the "politically correct" times, many Dutch parents now tell their children that the Pieten aren't really black— they're just covered in soot from sliding up and down so many chimneys. In 2006 the Dutch Program Foundation went even farther and attempted to replace Sinterklaas's helpers with rainbow-colored Pieten. It proved so unpopular that they reverted back to the traditional, all-black Pieten for the 2007 celebration.

*   *   *

"The one thing women don't want to find in their stockings on Christmas morning is their husband."
—**Joan Rivers**

Keiko the killer whale, star of *Free Willy*, was once shipped from Mexico to Oregon via UPS.

CELEBRITY CHECK-OUTS

We've all checked into hotel rooms that left us cold: bad room service, grungy sinks, bedspreads that haven't been washed—since the '80s. But at least we made it out alive. These famous folks didn't.

Celebrity: Irish writer and poet Oscar Wilde (1854–1900)
Where he died: Room 16, Hôtel d'Alsace, Paris
Story: At the height of his fame, Wilde was arrested for what *he* called "Uranian love." Victorian England had a less literary view of homosexuality: Wilde was convicted of "gross indecency" and sentenced to two years of hard labor. The years in prison destroyed his health and reputation, and forced him into bankruptcy, but he never lost his fabled wit. At age 46, as he lay dying of cerebral meningitis in his Paris hotel room, he raised a glass of champagne and gave his final toast: "I'm dying," he said, "as I have lived, beyond my means." It was true: Wilde left behind a very large—and unpaid—hotel bill.

Celebrity: Scientist and inventor Nikola Tesla (1856–1943)
Where he died: Room 3327, Hotel New Yorker, New York City
Story: This pioneering inventor contributed as much to the development of electricity as Thomas Edison did. In 1934 Tesla, who became increasingly eccentric late in life, claimed to have perfected a particle-beam ray that could bring down enemy planes from 250 miles away or drop a million men dead in their tracks. His ideas were so far-fetched that the first Superman cartoon, in 1941, featured a mad scientist, based on Tesla, terrorizing New York City with his death ray. But was he mad? When Tesla died in the hotel suite he'd occupied for 10 years, the U.S. Alien Property Custodian office—the only agency authorized to seize "enemy assets" without a court order—hauled away truckloads of paper, furniture, and artifacts, and sealed them away. What became of his effects is unknown, but the FBI reportedly feared there might be a working death ray among them. (There wasn't.)

Celebrity: Singer-songwriter Janis Joplin (1943–70)
Where she died: Room 105, Landmark Hotel, Los Angeles

"Flap-dragon": a 16th-century game of trying to eat hot raisins from a bowl of burning brandy.

Story: Joplin once said, "People like their blues singers miserable. They like their blues singers to die." On the evening of October 3, after a long day in the recording studio, Joplin shot up her final fix of heroin, went down to the hotel lobby for change, bought some cigarettes, and returned to her room. She was found dead the next day, wedged against a bedside table with a cigarette in her hand. Joplin had been finishing up the final songs for *Pearl*. The album was to include the song "Buried Alive in the Blues," but it remained an instrumental. Joplin died before recording the vocal track.

Celebrity: Playwright Eugene O'Neill (1888–1953)
Where he died: Suite 401, Shelton Hotel, Boston
Story: Because his father was a successful touring actor, O'Neill was born in a hotel and spent part of his childhood living in hotel rooms. He hated his early years and blamed his father's touring for his mother's morphine addiction. If nothing else, these hardships served him well as a playwright. O'Neill went on to garner Nobel and Pulitzer prizes for such works as *Strange Interlude* (1928) and *Long Day's Journey Into Night* (1941). But tragedy was never far away—he contracted a progressive nervous disorder that left him unable to write. He spent his final days in a hotel room overlooking the Charles River, grim, frustrated, and waiting for death. Among his final words: "I knew it. I knew it. Born in a hotel room—and g**damn it—died in a hotel room."

Celebrity: Bass guitarist John Entwistle (1944–2002)
Where he died: Room 658, Hard Rock Hotel, Las Vegas
Story: When the Who made it big, band members were finally able to quit their crappy day jobs and embrace the rock-star life. For Entwistle, that meant spending money—far more than he made. By 2002 the 57-year-old bassist owed a string of debts, including back taxes. "That 2002 tour was the last I ever intended to do with the band," said guitarist Pete Townshend. "My mission was to make enough money for John so that he could get out of debt." The night before the tour began, Entwistle snorted some cocaine and went to bed with a groupie. The next morning he was dead of a cocaine-induced heart attack. Entwistle's estate—including his beloved guitar collection—had to be auctioned off to pay the tax man. As for the crappy day job Entwistle quit back in 1963: He worked for the Inland Revenue Service, England's I.R.S.

ALTERED STATES

Think it's hard to remember the names of all 50 states? If lawmakers had had their way, there could have been even more.

CUBA

When the U.S. won the Spanish-American War in 1898, Spain ceded control of Puerto Rico, Guam, the Philippines, and Cuba. The first three were considered to be in the developing-colony stage, so they became U.S. territories. Cuba was far more established and was granted independence (although the United States reserved the right to intervene in Cuban affairs at any time). Things were fine until 1906, when opponents of Cuban president Tomas Estrada Palma accused him of voter fraud in his successful re-election. The protests that erupted created an instability that made the U.S. government nervous, and a small congressional delegation proposed annexing Cuba and making it a state—the easiest way to quell any uprisings. Ultimately, the cultural differences between the two nations were seen as too great, or, as Rep. John Sharp Williams of Mississippi said, "We have enough people of the Negro race."

GREENLAND

In 1945 Secretary of State James Byrnes offered Denmark $100 million for the gigantic, ice-covered Arctic island. Why? For its strategic location. This was at the very beginning of the Cold War, and Greenland was situated much closer to the Soviet Union's major cities than any current U.S. land, making it an ideal place for a missile-defense system. The Danish government did not entertain the offer.

FRANKLIN

When the United States established its Constitution in 1787, the 13 former colonies became the new nation's first states. There could have been 14. In 1785 a group of citizens in an isolated, sparsely populated mountainous region of western North Carolina proposed creating their own state, predicated on one idea: that doctors and lawyers were too highbrow, not representative of the

---

On average, Americans in 2001 bought seven times more fireworks than they did in 1976.

common man, and thus unfit to serve in the legislature. Despite that weird premise for independence, 7 out of 13 states voted yes. Franklin was denied statehood, but by only two votes. Nevertheless, Franklin's leading proponents acted like they *had* been granted statehood and proceeded to form a basic government: electing lawmakers (no doctors or lawyers), establishing a court system, and assembling a small militia. All that local power wasn't enough to prevent attacks from local Indian tribes, who saw Franklin residents as easy targets. Because they'd behaved like a rogue state, North Carolina and the federal government left them to their own devices and offered no protection. In 1796 "Franklin" was absorbed into Tennessee.

JACINTO

When the independent republic of Texas was annexed by the U.S. in 1845, it retained a right to split into as many as five separate states whenever and for whatever reason the state government saw fit. The Texas legislature entertained the idea in 1850, when the state's congressional delegation introduced a bill to divide the state in two, right along the Brazos River. The western portion would still be called Texas, while the eastern part was to be named Jacinto, commemorating the 1836 Battle of San Jacinto, which was decisive in Texas gaining its independence from Mexico (and lasted only 18 minutes). The bill never got enough support to make it to a vote, but the idea of partitioning Texas wouldn't go away—it resurfaced six more times over the 120 years.

GREAT BRITAIN

In the peacetime years that followed World War II, Senator Richard Russell Jr. of Georgia made a bizarre proposal to the news media: The United States should annex England, Scotland, Ireland, and Wales—at the time, the whole of Great Britain—as four new states. Why? The British were ravaged by the war, and the U.S. needed some strategically located sites in Europe. Russell reasoned that the U.S. getting military bases and the U.K. receiving an influx of American revenue would be good for both countries. The British government quickly dismissed the idea, noting that Russell's home state of Georgia still owed England money it had borrowed during the Civil War.

Bugsy Siegel named his Las Vegas casino the Flamingo for his leggy girlfriend, Virginia Hill.

THE BRIGHT SIDE OF THE MOON

*Unless you're an astronomy buff (or a werewolf), you don't keep track
of full moons and you've probably never heard of a "waning gibbous."
But you might still wonder why sometimes you can see the
whole moon, and other times you can't see any of it.*

WHEN THE MOON HITS YOUR EYE

It takes about a month—technically 29.5305882 days—
for the moon to go through one *synodic period*, the cycle
in which we see it go through its phases of full, half, crescent, and
"new," or invisible, and then back to full again. But the moon
really doesn't go anywhere—it's always orbiting Earth, and always
has the same side facing Earth, due to the powerful gravitational
pull the planet has on its satellite. The lunar phases we see are
created by the changing angles and positions of Earth, sun, and
moon in relation to each other. Moonlight is really just reflected
sunlight, so when the moon looks different, it's only because part
of it isn't visible from Earth—that part is shrouded in the moon's
own shadow. (But even that dark part isn't really invisible; you
can often see it, dimly, through a telescope or good pair of binoculars.) Here's a scientific look at where these celestial bodies have
to be positioned to make the moon look the way it does on any
given night.

NEW MOON (DAY 1): In most cultures, the beginning of the
moon's cycle is marked by the new moon. You can tell it's a new
moon if you can't find the moon anywhere in the sky, day or night.
That's because a new moon is virtually invisible—it hangs between
Earth and the sun, with all three more or less in alignment, so the
moon's far side is illuminated and the dark side faces us. (On the
rare occasions when all three are in *exact* alignment, the moon
hangs directly between Earth and sun, causing a solar eclipse.)

WAXING CRESCENT (DAY 5): In this "fingernail" phase, the
moon appears as a small sliver, with the long curve toward the

---

Largest gold coin ever minted: The Canadian $1 million Maple Leaf (diameter: about 20 in.).

right-hand side. "Waxing" means growing, so this means the moon is emerging from shadow and the lighted part will become larger—less shrouded in darkness—in the coming nights.

FIRST QUARTER (DAY 8): The name says "quarter," but really half of the moon is now visible, with the curve on the right, resembling a big letter "D." The moon is at a 90-degree angle in relation to Earth and the sun, leaving exactly half of the moon illuminated and the other half of it in shadow.

WAXING GIBBOUS (DAY 11): Again, the moon is waxing (growing), so the lighted part is getting bigger. The word *gibbous*, derived from Latin, means "more than half." In this case, it means that the moon is about three-quarters illuminated, with only a small portion on its left side still stuck in the shadows.

FULL MOON (DAY 15): Just as with a new moon, all three bodies are in near-alignment, but this time the moon is on the opposite side of Earth from where it was during the new moon. So the entire sunlight-illuminated part of the moon now faces Earth. The shadowed portion of the moon is on the far side, hidden from view. As with the new moon, on rare occasions the three bodies align perfectly, causing an eclipse—in the this case, a lunar eclipse, when Earth's shadow crosses the moon.

WANING GIBBOUS (DAY 21): After a full moon, the moon appears to "shrink" or recede into the shadows. *Waning* means the opposite of waxing, so in this phase, the moon is once again three-quarters visible and illuminated, but now its right side is the portion that is obscured.

THIRD QUARTER (DAY 23): This phase is similar to the first quarter: Half of the moon is visible, and half is obscured. But since the moon is now completing its cycle, the sides are reversed: The left side is illuminated; the right side is obscured.

WANING CRESCENT (DAY 26): Another crescent moon, in which there's a small sliver of moon in the sky, but now the curve is on the left.

And then it's the new moon again.

VIRAL VIDEOS

You probably already know that pop superstar Justin Bieber's career was launched when his mother posted some home movies on YouTube. Here's a look at some other folks who found fame—or infamy—when their videos went viral.

Internet Star: Dave Carroll, a Canadian country singer
Better Known As: The "United Breaks Guitars" guy
The Story: In March 2008, Carroll and his band were seated aboard a United Airlines plane at Chicago's O'Hare Airport when they and other passengers saw the airline's baggage handlers throwing the band's instrument cases around on the tarmac. When Carroll retrieved his $3,500 Taylor guitar at the end of the flight, the neck had been broken off. United refused to replace the guitar or pay for repairs, even after Carroll pursued the matter for nine months. Rather than accept defeat, he decided to make a music video about the experience and post it on YouTube.
What Happened: Carroll uploaded the video, "United Breaks Guitars," onto YouTube on July 6, 2009. By the end of the day it had received 150,000 hits. That got United's attention, but Carroll wasn't interested anymore. When the airline offered to buy him a new guitar, he told them to give the money to charity instead. As of March 2011, "United Breaks Guitars" had been seen more than 10 million times, making it the most successful song of Carroll's career. (Believe it or not, he still flies United.) The airline uses the video as a training tool.

Internet Star: Ardi Rizal, 2, the son of Indonesian street vendors
Better Known As: "The Smoking Baby"
The Story: Indonesia is well known as being a nation of smokers—one in three Indonesians smokes 12 or more cigarettes a day—and many of the smokers are children. But Ardi Rizal got an earlier start than most: When he was about 18 months old, his father let him smoke a cigarette. The toddler took to the habit quickly, and his parents were happy to let him smoke because it kept him occupied while they worked long hours in their street stall. By the spring of 2010, two-year-old Ardi was smoking two packs of cigarettes a day. That was when a reporter filmed the toddler puffing

---

More than 25% of Arizona is designated as Native American lands, the most of any state.

away like a pro. The video found its way onto the Internet; by the summer of 2010, millions of people had seen it.

What Happened: By then Ardi was hooked on smokes, and his parents could not get him to quit. "He's totally addicted," his mother told reporters. "If he doesn't get cigarettes, he gets angry and bangs his head against the wall." Luckily for Ardi, the story embarrassed the Indonesian government, and they arranged for him to be treated in a clinic in the capital city of Jakarta. They even promised to buy the Rizals a car if their boy kicked the habit. After a month of "play therapy," in which Ardi was distracted with toys and lots of attention from therapists and playmates, he quit smoking. (No word on whether his parents got their car.)

Internet Star: Jack Rebney, an on-air pitchman and producer of industrial videos in the 1980s

Better Known As: "The Winnebago Man" and "The Angriest Man in the World"

The Story: In the summer of 1989, Rebney filmed a sales training video for Winnebago Industries, the motor-home company. It was a difficult shoot in hot, humid weather, and Rebney was foul-mouthed and irate as he flubbed one take after another. The camera crew was so annoyed with his antics that they assembled a videotape of his outbursts and used it to get him fired. That was the last Rebney knew of the tape for nearly 20 years.

What Happened: Today anyone with Internet access can view a video clip or recommend it to friends with a couple of keystrokes, but the Winnebago Man phenomenon predates YouTube by more than a decade. Rebney's obscene rants were so compelling that people made bootleg copies of the VHS tape and circulated them *by hand* for more than 15 years before YouTube came along in 2005 and Rebney became one of the site's earliest stars. Since then his outtakes have been seen by more than 20 million people.

Update: Rebney's fans have long wondered what happened to him, as he seemed to have disappeared from the face of the Earth. A documentary filmmaker named Ben Steinbauer finally tracked him down with the help of a private detective. Rebney, now in his 80s, lives a hermitic existence on top of a mountain in Northern California. The search for Rebney is the subject of the 2009 documentary *Winnebago Man*.

Internet Star: Ghyslain Raza, 15, a Canadian high-school junior
Better Known As: "The Star Wars Kid"
The Story: In November 2002, Raza made a video of himself in his school's video lab swinging a golf-ball retriever like a *Star Wars* lightsaber. Some classmates found the tape and e-mailed it to their friends; it bounced around a small circle of kids until April 2003, when someone posted it on the Internet. Since then it has been viewed more than a billion times, making it perhaps the most-watched video of all time.
What Happened: Raza was humiliated by his sudden fame. He couldn't step into the hallway at school without his classmates chanting "*Star Wars* kid! *Star Wars* kid!" and had to drop out of school. He was treated for depression, and his parents sued three of his classmates for $250,000 in damages. The term "cyberbullying" was coined with him specifically in mind.
Update: Raza eventually overcame his humiliation, and his parents' lawsuit even helped him settle on a career: At last report he was studying law at McGill University in Montreal.

Internet Star: Casey Heynes, an Australian high-school student
Better Known as: "Casey the Punisher"
The Story: In March 2011, a kid named Ritchard Gale picked a fight with Casey at school while a third kid filmed the fight. In the video, Ritchard is clearly the aggressor as he punches Casey in the face. Casey fends off several blows then suddenly grabs Ritchard, lifts him over his shoulder, and slams him to the ground. Casey then walks off in triumph as Ritchard, injured, staggers away.
What Happened: The video was posted online a few hours after the fight. It must have struck a chord with people's own memories of childhood bullying, because by the end of the week it had spread worldwide. Casey, a loner who says he's been bullied at school for years, suddenly had millions of admirers, including more than 230,000 on Facebook alone.
Update: Casey and Ritchard were both suspended from school for four days. At last report Casey was transferring to another school; Ritchard blames Casey for provoking him and refuses to admit responsibility for starting the fight. (The families of both kids received $40,000 apiece for letting them be interviewed on TV.)

BILL MURRAY STORIES

Bill Murray has played funny and bizarre characters in Stripes, Caddyshack, *and* Ghostbusters. *His weirdest role: real-life Bill Murray.*

NO ONE WILL EVER BELIEVE YOU...

A "Bill Murray story" is a type of personal urban legend. It begins as a plausible description of an ordinary event on an ordinary day or night, but then veers into the surreal when Murray shows up and does something outrageous or absurd. It ends with him saying something to the effect of, "No one will ever believe you." And then he disappears. Here are some classic Bill Murray stories that have been circulating via word of mouth and the Internet for years.

• "My freshman year of college, I was hanging out in my dorm room with some friends playing Xbox when I hear this deep-pitched meowing coming from outside my window. I look outside, and there's *Bill Murray*, clinging to a branch about 10 feet up in the air, meowing at a kitten stuck in the tree. Then he looked at me and said, 'No one will ever believe you.' Then he climbed down the tree and ran off."

• "So I was visiting my friend out in Santa Monica. She works the reception desk at this upscale hotel and she's always telling me stories about which celebrity is there that week. Anyway, she was on break and we were having dinner together in the bar when *Bill Murray* walks up, leans over, and picks a piece of potato off my plate with his bare fingers and just pops it in his mouth. I just sort of stare at him and he's looking me right in the eye and smiling as he chews and swallows. And you know what the best part is? He finally says, 'No one will ever believe you.' And he walks away."

...NOR SHOULD THEY

While Murray is an eccentric person, the truth is that these stories, which have been making the rounds for over a decade, probably never happened. Or maybe one or two of them did. But that's the nature of tall-tale-telling: The stories are so absurd, they couldn't possibly be true, but they *might* be true.

Or maybe they used to be not true...but now they are. In this age of the camera phone and instant Internet distribution, Bill Murray has now been spotted *and recorded* doing crazy things. Whether the following sightings are Murray trying to make an urban legend come true, or he's just a weird guy doing funny things, is known only to Murray himself.

• MURRAY TENDS BAR WITH THE WU-TANG CLAN

During the 2010 SXSW festival in Austin, Texas, Murray showed up at the crowded Shangri-La bar with RZA and GZA of the legendary rap group the Wu-Tang Clan. Murray pushed his way behind the bar and began taking orders. But no matter what starstuck patrons ordered, Murray poured them shots of tequila. Then he ran off.

• MURRAY READS POETRY TO BUILDERS

In 2009, while construction workers were busy putting the finishing touches on the Poets House Library and Literary Center in lower Manhattan, Murray stopped by to read the workers some poetry. After a straight-faced recital of former poet laureate Billy Collins's "Another Reason Why I Don't Keep a Gun in the House," Murray told his confused audience (a small crowd had gathered), "They get worse, so if you want to lie down, get sick, or take a sick day, do it now." He then read poems by Lorine Niedecker and Emily Dickinson, among others. When he finished, he told the crew, "You have about three minutes left on this break, so smoke 'em if you've got 'em." Then he ran off.

• MURRAY WASHES DISHES AT A HOUSE PARTY

In the 2003 film *Lost in Translation*, Murray played a Hollywood actor who forms an unlikely friendship with a younger woman in a foreign city (Tokyo). In a case of life imitating art, while in Scotland in 2006 for a celebrity golf tournament, the 56-year-old actor met a pretty 22-year-old Norwegian university student named Lykke Stavnef in a pub. Stavnef invited Murray to attend a local house party with her. Murray surprised her by accepting. The incident was witnessed by dozens of partygoers and reported in the U.K.'s *Sunday Times*. The party got crowded as word spread that he was there, and he became concerned that there weren't enough clean glasses for all the guests, so he began hand washing the stack of dishes that had piled up in the sink. Then he ran off.

Road hogs: Before crash-test dummies, pig cadavers were used to simulate accident victims.

POINTS TO PONDER

Profound thoughts from some of the world's most respected thinkers.

"Nothing will ever be attempted if all possible objections must be first overcome."
—**Samuel Johnson**

"To love and win is the best thing; to love and lose the next best."
—**William Makepeace Thackeray**

"Nothing in life is to be feared. It is only to be understood."
—**Marie Curie**

"Could a greater miracle take place than for us to look through each other's eye for an instant?"
—**Henry David Thoreau**

"The greatest happiness of life is the conviction that we are loved, loved for ourselves, or rather loved in spite of ourselves."
—**Victor Hugo**

"Everyone has a talent. What is rare is the courage to follow the talent to the dark places where it leads."
—**Erica Jong**

"You don't get to choose how you're going to die or when. You can only decide on how you are going to live now."
—**Joan Baez**

"Our prime purpose in this life is to help others. And if you can't help them, at least don't hurt them."
—**The Dalai Lama**

"The possible's slow fuse is lit by the imagination."
—**Emily Dickinson**

"It is not true that love makes all things easy; it makes us choose what is difficult."
—**George Eliot**

"Hope awakens courage. He who can implant courage in the human soul is the best physician."
—**Karl Von Knebel**

"To finish the moment, to find the journey's end in every step of the road, to live the greatest number of good hours, is wisdom."
—**Ralph Waldo Emerson**

Florida's official state gem, the moonstone, is not native to Florida.

MISSED IT BY ONE LETTER

*It's a good thing that we at the BRI never make any
typos, or it would be really embarrassing to call
out these folks for getting one little letter rong.*

• **MICHIGAN ELECTION OFFICIALS** missed it by one letter
in 2006, when they printed 180,000 mail-in ballots that used the
word "pubic" where "public" should have been. By the time the
error was caught (by an election clerk *after* a professional proof-
reader missed it), 10,000 ballots had already been mailed out. The
remaining 170,000 ballots were reprinted at taxpayers' expense.
Total cost: $40,000.

• **PEDRO URZUA LIZANA** missed it by one letter when he
chiseled a new design for Chile's 50-peso coin in 2008. In his rush
to finish on time, he accidentally left off the bottom stroke of the
"L" in "CHILE." Result: 1.5 million coins—all in circulation—are
inscribed with "REPUBLIC DE CHIIE." Lizana was fired.

• **DAVID BECKHAM** missed it by one letter when he gave the
Hindi translation of his wife's name to a tattoo artist. It was supposed to be "Victoria," but instead it said "Vihctoria," which is
what ended up (in huge letters) on the soccer star's right forearm.

• **ERIC SCHMIDT** missed it by one letter on his business
card when he called himself "Chariman of the Executive Committee." (If you missed it, read that first word again.) If only
there were some Internet search engine that he could have used
to find a good spell-checking program. (Schmidt was the CEO
of Google.)

• **THE GEORGIA DEPARTMENT OF LABOR** missed it by
one letter when a clerk sent a business license application to a car-
pet-cleaning company called Rug Suckers. But the package wasn't
addressed to "Rug Suckers"—it was…something *very* naughty. The

Lewis & Clark left with 34 people, and came back with 33. (One died of a ruptured appendix.)

company's owner, Pepper Powell, called the Labor Department to complain, only to be told by the clerk, "I understood you to say that the company's name was Rug *uckers. I asked you twice and you replied, 'Yes, it was.'" Powell told the clerk that he would never dream of giving his company such a foul name. "What would be the point?" Georgia Labor officials agreed. They issued an apology and reprimanded the worker.

- **STRATFORD HALL**, a personalized holiday card company, missed it by one letter on the cover of its 2007 catalog: "Reliability: always upholding the highest standards for every detal."

- **THE VICTORIA, B.C., PARKS & REC DEPARTMENT** missed it by one letter when it unveiled a statue of Emily Carr (1871–1945), an influential post-impressionist landscape painter and a hometown hero. Apparently nobody proofread the plaque that accompanies the $400,000 statue, which is cast with this inscription: "Dedicated to honour Victoria's best know citizen."

- **KTXL-FOX40 SACRAMENTO** missed it by one letter in 2011 when it ran a graphic during a breaking news story that read "Obama Bin Laden Dead."

- *THE TORRANCE PRESS*, a newspaper in Southern California, missed it by one letter on a two-page advertisement: "Sleeping on a Sealy Is Like Sleeping on a Clod." Sealy terminated their contract. (That was the ad department's *second* chance with its potentially lucrative new client. A day earlier, the *Torrance Press* ran an ad that read, "Sleeping on a Sealy Is Like Slipping on a Cloud.")

- **E.S. GAFFNEY** missed it by one letter while working at the U.S. Department of Energy. She submitted a proposal to an official whose last name is Prono, but Microsoft Word's auto-correct feature changed it to "Porno." Gaffney's proposal was rejected.

- *THE MOSCOW-PULLMAN DAILY NEWS* in Idaho missed it by one letter when it printed a recipe for a "Bowel Full of Brownies." (Does that make it a "typoo"?)

RANDOM BITS ON BEATLES HITS

Trivia you don't know about the songs you definitely do know.

"**Penny Lane**": The song described real locations in Liverpool. Or at least they *were* real—the street called Penny Lane is no longer there, although the barber, banker, and "shelter in the middle of the roundabout" still stand. The barber and banker are still a barber and banker; the shelter is now a coffee shop.

"**Eleanor Rigby**": A statue of the song's subject sits on a bench on Stanley Street in Liverpool. It was sculpted by Tommy Steele, a 1950s British rock star, who gave it to the city in 1982. Unlike the song's Eleanor Rigby, each year several thousand people "come near" the statue, which is dedicated to "all the lonely people."

"**Dear Prudence**": John Lennon met Prudence Farrow—actress Mia Farrow's sister—on a spiritual retreat with the Maharishi in India. She seemed very depressed when she arrived there, so Lennon wrote this song in an attempt to cheer her up. (She later said that she was neither sad nor despondent, just very deeply into meditation.)

"**Yellow Submarine**": Paul McCartney intended it to be a children's song, and wrote a spoken introduction to go along with it, but the idea of the intro was abandoned—no recording of it exists.

"**Because**": The chord progression is Beethoven's "Moonlight Sonata" played backward. Lennon got the idea after hearing Yoko Ono play the original piece on the piano. The unique vocal is the result of Lennon, McCartney, and Harrison singing in unison, then overdubbing the parts twice to create nine-part harmony.

"**Got to Get You Into My Life**": In his autobiography, *Many Years From Now*, McCartney admitted who the song was about: nobody. It was actually about his need to smoke marijuana.

Granger, Iowa, has two water towers, labeled HOT and COLD.

"When I'm 64": Paul McCartney wrote this song when he was 15, then recorded it a decade later with the Beatles. It was about his hope that he would have someone to love him in his old age. In 2002 McCartney married former model Heather Mills. They split up in 2006...one month before McCartney's 64th birthday.

"Twist and Shout": The Beatles' first concert ever held in a stadium was their show at Shea Stadium in August 1965. The first song they played: "Twist and Shout." The Beatles' version came from a 1962 recording by the Isley Brothers, but the Isleys didn't originate it: a Philadelphia R&B group called the Top Notes did.

"Something": John Lennon and Paul McCartney controlled the Beatles' output—George Harrison wrote lots of songs with the group, but this was his only composition with the Beatles that was ever released as a single. It went to #1.

"I Want to Hold Your Hand": The crowds of screaming girls during live performances were so loud that neither they nor the band could really hear the lyrics. So, when performing this song, Lennon would sing "I want to hold your gland," meaning a breast.

"Strawberry Fields Forever": When John Lennon was a boy in Liverpool, he liked to play in a garden called Strawberry Field on the grounds of a Salvation Army house. His Aunt Mimi didn't want him playing there, though, because he was technically trespassing. She often warned him, "It's nothing to get hung about."

"I Saw Her Standing There": Rights-holders wouldn't allow Beatles songs to be used on *American Idol* until the series' sixth season, but now a "Beatles week" is an annual feature. The first Fab Four song, performed on the 2007 finale, was "I Saw Her Standing There," sung as a duet by Jordin Sparks and Blake Lewis.

"I Am the Walrus": Some of the lyrics to this psychedelic song seem to be nonsensical—who is "the eggman," for instance? Eric Burdon of the Animals claims that it's him. Burdon says that Lennon nicknamed him "Eggman" after he told Lennon about an intimate encounter he'd once had that involved an egg.

SYMBOL ORIGINS

They're on flags, packages, street signs,
trash cans, and even bathroom doors.
Where did they come from?

Meaning: Biohazard

Story: In 1966 Dow Chemical engineer Charles Baldwin was developing medical-hazard containers for the National Institutes of Health's cancer division. Scientists at all of the different medical facilities he visited dealt with dozens of biological hazards, such as used needles, viruses, and blood, urine, and stool samples. There was no one universal way of telling at a glance which substances were especially dangerous (or "biohazardous"). With the help of the Dow package-design team, Baldwin developed several "warning" symbols—all bold, universal, and easy to recognize. Market research meetings were held, and participants were presented with the different designs. But the one most remembered was a "blaze orange" circular symbol with sharp points. Today it's one of the world's most recognizable symbols. Even people who don't know what "biohazard" means quickly grasp that it's saying "beware."

Meaning: Islam

Story: Non-Muslims strongly associate the "star and crescent" with Islam. But Islam doesn't officially recognize it, and it didn't even start out as a Muslim symbol. Around 342 B.C. Philip of Macedon (Alexander the Great's father) was laying siege to Perinthus, a city in Byzantium. According to legend, after months of direct attacks, the Macedonians had decided to tunnel under the city walls when a meteor suddenly ripped through the sky. The omen terrified them, and they retreated. The meteor and the crescent moon—the symbol of the Byzantines' protector god, Hecate the Torch Bearer—became the symbols of the city of Byzantium (now Istanbul). The Ottoman Turks, who conquered the city in the 14th century, put the symbol on their flags. After the Turks adopted Islam, the symbol came to be associated with the religion as well.

Longest English word with alternating consonants and vowels: Honorificabilitudinitatibus.

Meaning: Life

Story: The *ankh* is an ancient Egyptian symbol that was adopted by other ancient cultures too. There are many theories on how this shape came to be associated with the idea of "life": a mirror used for self-contemplation, a phallic symbol, or a double-bladed axe representing life and death, for example. A recent theory by bio-Egyptologists Andrew Gordon and Calvin Schwabe suggests that the ankh is a representation of a bull's thoracic vertebra, which, when viewed in cross-section, does look like an ankh. The bone sits between the bull's shoulders, just above the forelimbs, which Egyptians believed held the animal's vital life-force.

Meaning: Male and female

Story: The conventional explanation is that the "male" symbol represents the shield and spear of the ancient Roman god Mars, a symbol of masculinity, and the "female" symbol is the mirror held by Venus, an icon of femininity. But taxonomist William Stearn says those symbols are actually corruptions of the ancient Greek letters used to spell out the names of those Roman gods. The Greek name for Mars was Thouros, which starts with the letter *theta*, or Θ. Venus was called Phosphoros, which starts with the letter *phi*, or Φ. Stearn claims that over time Greek writers shortened the words Thorous and Phosphoros into just theta and phi, which evolved into the symbols we're familiar with today.

Meaning: Poison

Story: The Pittsburgh Poison Control Center created this symbol in 1971 to coincide with the introduction of their 24-hour accidental-poisoning hotline. It was designed to replace the common skull-and-crossbones symbol on poisonous materials because children equated that one with pirates, adventure, and fun, instead of danger. Among the symbols tested, children responded most negatively to a neon green, grimacing face with a protruding tongue that looks like it just swallowed something horrible. One child called it "yucky," leading to the name Mr. Yuk. Regional poison control centers around the United States distribute over 40 million black-and-green 'Mr. Yuk' stickers every year.

Rough start: There were 12 honeymooning couples aboard the *Titanic*.

COOKIE CRUMBS

Trivia bits about cookies (or bisoketto, *if you're Japanese).*

• "Cookie" comes from the Dutch word *koekje*, meaning "small cake." They're called *biscuits* in England, *galletas* in Spain, and *keks* in Germany.

• Cookies probably originated in 7th-century Persia, the first culture to cultivate sugar.

• Best-selling cookie in the United States: Oreos for three out of four quarters of the year...but in the first quarter, Girl Scout Cookies are #1. (For each $4 box of cookies a Scout troop sells, they receive about 50 cents.)

• Fig Newtons were created in the 1890s as a digestion aid. Medical "wisdom" held that many health problems were caused by poor digestion, and that fruit and bland bread could help.

• In Uruguay, Chips Ahoy! are called Pepitos!

• Flop Fig Newton flavors from the 1980s: grape, cherry, blueberry, and apple.

• The "creme filling" in Oreos is primarily high fructose corn syrup and vegetable oil.

• In the late 1800s, American cookbook writers considered cookies a lowly cousin of the more important cake, and generally included only a few cookie recipes, with odd names such as kinkawoodles, graham jakes, tangle breeches, and jolly boys. The only one that's lasted: snickerdoodle.

• Product placement? According to the cartoon "Mickey's Surprise Party" (1939), Mickey Mouse's favorite cookie is the Fig Newton.

• Today you can buy Baskin-Robbins ice cream and Starbucks coffee in grocery stores. The first "restaurant-branded" item on supermarket shelves: Famous Amos, which expanded from chain stores to packaged cookies in 1980.

• June 23 is National Pecan Sandies Day.

• Shortbread cookies are believed to have originated in Scotland. That's how Lorna Doone shortbreads got their name—she's the Scottish heroine of an 1869 novel by British author R.D. Blackmore.

Landlocked Liechtenstein and Uzbekistan are both surrounded by other landlocked countries.

TWEET BEAT

Police work isn't what it appears to be on TV. To prove it, in 2010 the Manchester (U.K.) police posted to Twitter every call they received over a 24-hour period, no matter how ridiculous it was. Here's a sampling.

"Man shouts 'you're gorgeous' to woman."

"Piece of wood on road."

"Concern for the welfare of a relative living in Tunisia."

"Man says he's locked out of house. Wants police to break in for him."

"Confused man reporting his TV not working."

"Reports of four-foot doll or robot on Princess Parkway. Officers investigated but nothing there."

"Caller wants advice on where 16-year-old daughter can stay while the caller is on holiday."

"Woman reports her horse refuses to come back over bridge."

"Youths playing football outside house."

"Dead cat found."

"Rat in the house. Caller thinks her cat may be responsible."

"Report of man holding baby over bridge. Police immediately attended but it was man carrying dog that doesn't like bridges."

"A drunk woman asking for police officers to call her back."

"Loose cows."

"Report of people trying to break into property. When police arrived it was surveyors."

"Builders have turned up to complete work two months late."

"Mother calls regarding 14-year-old son being aggressive, throwing clothes on floor."

"Caller receiving anonymous phone calls."

"Man appears asleep at bus stop."

"Caller says her two missing cats have come back home. This is a regular caller."

"Suspicious smell."

A Cinnabon study found that the scent of cinnamon causes mall shoppers to be more polite.

CITY OF FRIGHT

If you think the streets of Paris are enchanting,
wait till you discover what lurks below.

THEY DUG PARIS

Most visitors to Paris have no idea that beneath the City of Light is a dark labyrinth of branching tunnels and abandoned quarries. Paris sits atop massive limestone and gypsum formations that have been quarried for more than 1,000 years. The Romans chiseled the fine-grained limestone into bathhouses and sculptures. The French used it to build thousands of buildings, everything from Notre Dame cathedral and the Louvre Museum to Paris Police Headquarters. As for the gypsum, ever heard of plaster of Paris? That's where it comes from.

When the mining started, the quarries were outside of town, but over the centuries the city spread and so did the quarries. Eventually Paris ended up with a 1,900-acre underground maze that starts about 15 feet below the streets and ends 120 feet underground. Parisians call the multi-level maze *gruyère* (Swiss cheese), and that's exactly what a cross-section of the ground beneath their feet looks like.

THAT SINKING FEELING

When an entire city ends up on holey ground, things get shaky. Residents got their first glimpse of how unstable their city had become in 1774, when one of the tunnels collapsed, gulping down houses and people along *Rue d'Enfer* ("Hell Street"). Parisians panicked, so Louis XVI created the Inspection Generale des Carrieres (quarry inspectors) and appointed architect Charles-Axel Guillaumot as its first chief. He instructed Guillaumot to do three things: 1) find all the empty spaces under Paris, 2) make a map of them, and 3) reinforce any spaces below public streets or below buildings belonging to the king. Personally inspecting the sinkholes to a depth of more than 75 feet, Guillaumot was horrified by what he found and told Louis the truth: "The temples, palaces, houses, and public streets of several parts of Paris and its surrounding areas are about to sink into giant pits."

Coneheads: A giraffe's horns are called *ossicones*.

MOLD LANG SYNE

That wasn't the only problem in Paris. Thanks to war, famine, and plague, the city's cemeteries were full to overflowing. One frosty February morning in 1780, a homeowner started down into his cellar but was immediately driven back upstairs by a terrible stench. Egged on by his neighbors (and wearing a vinegar-soaked handkerchief over his nose), he crept back down and found 20 decaying bodies, covered in graveyard mold, bursting through the wall. The graveyards had finally gone beyond their limits.

But where others saw a problem, King Louis saw an opportunity. He closed the cemeteries and had the bones dug up and stacked into the quarries. Six million skeletons—mounds and stacks of skulls and tibias, femurs and spines—turned the chambers into catacombs, an underground boneyard that became known as "The Empire of the Dead."

CATS IN A MAZE

As Paris grew, the *gruyère* got even more full of holes. Churches dug crypts. City engineers built aqueducts, sewers, water mains, and tunnels for Métro lines. They dug conduits for telephone and electrical lines, bunkers for shelter during World War II, and garages for underground parking. And at the very bottom: the ancient quarries, their ceilings braced by nothing but limestone pillars and stacked stones.

Of the 180 miles of tunnels maintained by the Inspection Generale des Carrieres (IGC), only one mile—the catacombs—is open to the public. That doesn't stop the *cataphiles*. After dark, these hardcore cavers scurry down drains and through ventilation shafts. They chisel open manhole covers and sneak through entrances in hospital basements, the cellars of bars, church crypts, and subway tunnels. Why? "At the surface there are too many rules," says one cataphile. "Here we do what we want."

While preparing an article for *National Geographic*, reporter Neil Shea got an inside look at what cataphiles do underground. Some carry scuba tanks for exploring and mapping abandoned wells. Some create art, such as a four-foot-high limestone castle complete with drawbridge, moat, towers, and even a little LEGO soldier guarding the gate. Others host events: An author and an illustrator staged a book signing for their graphic novel *Le Diable*

Vert (*The Green Devil*). A group of people held a banquet, their candelabra casting shadows across the stone table as they dipped into cheese fondue and listened to chamber music. With cataphiles scurrying through the *gruyère* like mice, the city decided to hire another kind of cat to hunt them down.

ON THE PURR-ROWL

"We believe deeply that the catacombs belong to us, and that no one has the right to take them away," says a longtime cataphile nicknamed Morthicia. The *cataflics* disagree. These special cops patrol the maze, chase offenders from their underground lairs, and hand out fines. That's business as usual...unless they stumble upon something unexpected.

In 2004, during a training exercise 50 feet below the surface, officers moved a tarp marked "Building site. No access." That triggered a tape recording of dogs barking. "To frighten people off," said an officer. Beyond the barking they found 3,000 square feet of subterranean galleries. In one gallery there was theater seating for 20 (carved into the rock), a full-size movie screen, and projection equipment, along with all kinds of films, from 1950s film noir classics to contemporary thrillers. In another room, they found tables and chairs, and a well-stocked bar. Three days later, they returned with an electrician to trace the wires being used to pirate power and phone service. But the galleries had been stripped; not a wire remained to offer a clue to the culprits. All that was left was a note in the middle of the floor: "Do not try to find us."

CHEESY PARISEE

A group calling itself "The Perforating Mexicans" later claimed responsibility for the theater. "There are a dozen more where that one came from," said Patrick Saletta, a photographer who documents the urban underground. "You guys have no idea what's down there." Perhaps not, but here's something they *do* know: Inspector Guillaumot's 18th-century warning is still valid. In 1961 the maze swallowed an entire southside neighborhood. Small collapses happen every year, yet Parisians seem unconcerned. They have the IGC—still vigilant more than 200 years after its founding—to keep the City of Lights from falling into the *gruyère*.

Reel money: About 1.5 billion movie tickets are sold in the U.S. every year.

BLOW IT LIKE BUCKNER

*The 1986 Boston Red Sox were one out away from winning the World Series
...until a ball rolled through first baseman Bill Buckner's legs. The NY Mets
won the game, forcing a decisive game 7, which they also won. Buckner
became a sports pariah, but he's not the only athlete ever to screw up.*

NICE GOING, SPIKE

In one of his first NFL games in 2008, Philadelphia Eagles
wide receiver DeSean Jackson caught a long pass from
quarterback Donovan McNabb. Running it in for his first pro
touchdown, Jackson spiked the ball and started celebrating. Then
the other team, the Dallas Cowboys, called foul: A videotape
review showed that Jackson had thrown the ball down on the one-
yard line, *before* he crossed into the end zone. Result: The touchdown was taken away. Amazingly, Jackson had lost a touchdown
the same way in a high-school football game six years earlier.

NO TIME FOR YOU
In the 1993 men's college basketball national title game, Michigan
trailed North Carolina by just two points, 73–71, with less than
30 seconds to go. After North Carolina missed a free throw,
Michigan's Chris Webber got the rebound and hustled the ball
down to the other end of the court. With 20 seconds left, Webber
called a time-out to reset the play. Except that Michigan didn't
have any time-outs left. For the mistake, Webber was issued a
technical foul, which gave North Carolina a couple more free
throws, securing them the win.

A VERY BIG OOPS
Colombia was one of the pre-tournament favorites to win soccer's
1994 World Cup. But in the opening rounds, the team surprisingly
lost to the United States 2–1, with the second goal for the U.S.
coming when star Colombian defender Andres Escobar accidentally
scored a goal on his own net. Colombia was eliminated from the
tournament. (Sad ending: When the 27-year-old athlete returned
home to Medellin, Colombia, he was murdered, reportedly by
someone related to angry members of a gambling syndicate.)

LETTDOWN

Just minutes into the 1993 Super Bowl, the Buffalo Bills fumbled the ball on their own 45-yard line, where it was recovered by Dallas Cowboys lineman Leon Lett. He then did what few linemen ever do: He ran it all the way to the other end for a touchdown. As he was about to cross the goal line, he slowed down to celebrate the moment, raising the ball in triumph...and it was knocked out of his hands by Bills receiver Don Beebe. Lett had no idea Beebe was on his tail. Instead of Dallas getting a touchdown, the Bills got the ball (although the Cowboys won the game anyway).

ERROR PRONE

Tommy John pitched for more than 20 years and won 200 games, but he's best known for two things: 1) for being one of the first to undergo arm-strengthening elbow surgery ("Tommy John surgery," as it's now known) and 2) for making three errors in a single play. John was on the mound for the Yankees in 1988 when Milwaukee's Jeffrey Leonard hit an easy ground ball to him. John bobbled it (error #1), and Leonard made it to first base. John threw the ball to first base anyway, but the throw was wild and wound up in right field (error #2). The right fielder then threw it back to the catcher in an attempt to tag a runner at home plate. John intercepted it and threw it to the catcher himself—again, his throw was wild (error #3, which tied the Major League record).

FRIEND OR FOE?

The 1982 men's college basketball championship game was a fight to the finish, with 15 lead changes and neither Georgetown nor North Carolina ever ahead by more than three points. Georgetown was leading 62–61 with under a minute left to play, when North Carolina freshman Michael Jordan hit a jump shot to make the score 63–62. Georgetown's Fred Brown quickly rebounded the ball and ran to the other end, where he confidently passed it to an open player, James Worthy. Only problem: Worthy played for *North Carolina*. Georgetown quickly fouled Worthy to stop the clock. He missed both foul shots, but it didn't matter—there wasn't enough time left for Georgetown to score, so North Carolina won the game.

Hula hoops were once banned in Japan for causing "obscene movements."

EDITED FOR AIRLINES

Plane crashes, gruesome stabbings, what's beneath Mel Gibson's kilt…if you're hurtling through the sky at 30,000 feet, there are some things you might not want to see in a movie. Airlines rely on movie editors for special cuts, but some of what they sliced out of these Hollywood blockbusters may surprise you.

Movie: *The Queen* (2006)
Edit: Delta Airlines passengers thought something was wrong with the movie soundtrack. It kept "bleeping." It turned out that a newly hired editor had been told to bleep out all "profanities" and "blasphemies." The editor's overzealous response: He cut every incidence of the word "God" from the film, including a scene that left a character saying to Queen Elizabeth (Helen Mirren), "*Bleeep* bless you, ma'am."

Movie: *Hellboy* (2004)
Edit: A scene in which a hideous-looking man rises from a pool of blood was deemed too gory for captive airline audiences, so editors tinted the color of the blood. They made it blue. So instead of rising from a pool of blood, the hideous man appeared to be stepping out of a puddle of what looks like blue cake batter.

Movie: *Little Black Book* (2004)
Edit: One character in this romantic comedy is a gynecologist named Dr. Rachel Keyes (Rashida Jones) and, like many MDs in search of fame and fortune, she's written a book. The title of the book, *Keyes to Your Vagina*, was deemed too titillating for airline viewing, so when Dr. Keyes holds up the book, audiences see an altered title: *Keyes to Your Fertility*.

Movie: *Casino Royale* (2006)
Edit: In the theatrical version of this James Bond film, Virgin Airlines chairman Sir Richard Branson has a cameo role as a passenger going through security at a Miami airport. But in the British Airways version, Sir Richard ended up on the cutting-room floor. According to a spokesman for British Airways, they

---

Largest cyclone on record: Typhoon Tip (1979). Diameter: half the size of the continental US.

had a very good reason for editing out their biggest competitor: "We want to ensure movies contain no material that might upset our customers."

Movie: *Last Holiday* (2005)
Edit: During an airplane scene in this comedy, when the passenger sitting in front of Georgia Byrd (Queen Latifah) reclines his seat-back, it hits her knees. The two passengers argue, and Byrd goes into a tirade about the greedy airline putting the seats so close together in the economy-class section. In the Qantas version of the film, the entire seat argument is deleted, including the part where everyone in economy class cheers Byrd's tirade.

Movie: *Up in the Air* (2009)
Edit: In this romantic comedy, corporate downsizing expert Ryan Bingham (George Clooney) has trainee Natalie Keener (Anna Kendrick) in tow while going through airport security. His advice for getting through quickly: "Never get behind old people. Their bodies are littered with hidden metal and they never seem to appreciate how little time they have left. Bingo, Asians. They pack light, travel efficiently, and they have a thing for slip-on shoes." And then Natalie says, "That's racist." In the United Airlines version instead of "Bingo, Asians," a Clooney-esque voice says, "Business people." To which Natalie replies, "That's racist."

Movie: *Speed* (1994)
Edit: The plot is all about keeping a bus moving at 50 mph or greater so that the bomb planted on it doesn't blow up. In the film's climactic scene, the bus plows into a cargo plane. Result: The bus and plane both explode in a gigantic fireball. The cargo plane was being towed across a runway—it wasn't flying, taxiing, taking off, or landing when the bus hit. Still, any frames showing the plane were cut from the airline version; all viewers saw was the fireball. As the movie's producer Mark Gordon said, "The audience was just left figuring, geez, I guess the bus must have crashed into…something."

Fire escapes, laser printers, and bulletproof vests were all invented by women.

CALCULATOR WORDS

When calculators became cheap in the 1970s, millions of kids discovered that they could spell out words using numbers that look like letters and flipping the screen upside down. Can you guess these? (Answers on page 536.)

1. What bacon does when it hits a hot pan: 372215

2. If you make an omelet, you'll end up with a lot of these: 577345663

3. Central American nation: 321738

4. Where caged creatures live: 0.02

5. Turtle hut: 77345

6. A traditional Inuit home: 0.0761

7. Norwegian city: 0.750

8. He has no home but the rails: 0.804

9. Similar to a clarinet, but with two reeds instead of one: 3080

10. Cowboys wear it instead of a tie: 0.708

11. The capital of Idaho: 35108

12. Emmy Award-winning TV show: 3376

13. Search me: 376006

14. If the tide doesn't flow, it...: 5883

15. Immigrant island: 51773

16. A paid male "companion": 0.70616

17. They're alive, with the sound of music: 57714

18. Black gold! Texas tea! 710

19. What black gold (or Texas tea) does when it emerges from the ground: 53200

20. Building block: 0.637

21. Where your boss might tell you to go: 7734

22. Letter-cube board game: 376608

23. Some people collect stamps, others go birdwatching: 5318804

24. Russian ballet company: 1045708

25. Uncle John's handwriting: 378163771

Caterpillars have mouths; butterflies don't. (They have a *proboscis* instead.)

STUNG!

In police lingo, a "sting" is a covert operation in which deception is used to catch a person committing a crime. Sometimes they're scary, sometimes they're ingenious, and sometimes they're just plain dumb. Here are a few examples.

THE RUSE: In 2001 two representatives from a London-based defense contractor met with government officials in India. They wanted to sell night-vision cameras, binoculars, and similar items to the Indian military, they said.

THE HOOK: Without having to show a single sample of their products, over the next few months the men secured several large contracts…in exchange for bribes.

GOTCHA! Later in 2001, the Indian political magazine *Tehelka* broke a blockbuster story: They had video of Indian government and army officials taking cash payments from a bogus British defense contractor. The "contractors" were actually journalists with the magazine. In all, 34 members of the Indian military and government were videotaped accepting bribes. They included colonels and generals and also Bangaru Laxman, the president of the Indian People's Party—the ruling party in the country at the time. Most of the people who took payoffs were forced to resign, but even though they were seen *on videotape* accepting bribes, not a single one went to prison. A few were finally arrested in 2006, but their cases are still unresolved.

THE RUSE: In November 2007, hundreds of people around Fargo, North Dakota, received letters containing invitations to a party. The invitations were printed on purple stationery, had images of spider webs and skulls on them, and were from an outfit called "PDL Productions."

THE HOOK: They weren't your average party invitations. They were for a party at a Fargo nightclub…with British rock legend Ozzy Osbourne. Osbourne was performing at the Fargodome later that night, so the invitees were also promised backstage passes to the show.

GOTCHA! Forty-four invitees showed up at the club…and were

---

arrested on the spot. It was all part of a sting set up by Fargo Sheriff Paul D. Laney (that's what "PDL" stood for), who had the specially made invitations sent to hundreds of people who had outstanding-arrest warrants. When Osbourne heard about the stunt, he was not amused. "This sheriff should be ashamed of himself for using my celebrity to arrest these criminals," he said in a statement. Laney said he "meant no disrespect toward Mr. Osbourne" and added that several of his deputies had gone to his show after the busts.

THE RUSE: In February 2011, a friend of Jennifer Green, 28, of Washington, D.C., told her he knew about a house that had drugs and cash in it, and that the owners of the house were out of town.

THE HOOK: If Green sat lookout for him, the man said, he'd burglarize the house and split the loot with her. Green agreed, so the two drove to the house, and she waited in the car while the man broke into the home with a crowbar. He came back with $1,050 in cash and what looked like crack cocaine in a Ziploc bag. Green took $600 and said she didn't want any drugs.

GOTCHA! Little did the man know that Jennifer Green was a cop! Oh, wait—yes, he did. The Internal Affairs Department of the D.C. police department had sent the man (a confidential informant) to see if Green, whom they suspected of criminal activity, would go along with the burglary plot, which she did. She was arrested, eventually pleaded guilty to second-degree burglary, and was sentenced to seven months in prison and two years' probation.

THE RUSE: In November 2006, two men knocked on the door of a home in Weymouth, Dorset, England. The people inside didn't let them in because 1) they didn't know the two men; 2) the men appeared to be very drunk; and 3) the men were dressed in Batman and Robin costumes. The two eventually went away.

THE HOOK: A short time later, a group of policemen showed up at the same house. The people inside willingly let the officers in, telling them about the masked and drunk visitors.

GOTCHA! When the officers entered the house, one of the people inside ran out the back door, and…POW!…was nabbed by the Dynamic Duo. Officers Tony Smith and Mike Holman had set up the bizarre costumed sting operation in an attempt to get the man who'd just run out the back door. (He was wanted on drug charges.) "The Batman costume was quite comfortable and not too restricting," said Smith afterwards.

THE RUSE: In 2009 some "consumers" in Maryland ordered milk from an Amish Farm in Pennsylvania over the Internet.

THE HOOK: The owner of the Amish farm, Daniel Allgyer, delivered the milk to the people in Maryland.

GOTCHA! Busted, Amish milk farmer! Those guys in Maryland weren't milk drinkers—they were FDA agents, and they'd been investigating Allgyer's farm for more than a year. Why? Because he was selling raw, unpasteurized, milk, which the FDA says "should not be consumed under any circumstances," as it can contain dangerous bacteria—and he was transporting it across state lines, which made it "illegal interstate commerce." Result: In April 2010, U.S. marshals and FDA inspectors staged a surprise early-morning raid on Allgyer's farm, during which they took pictures and notes. The next day, Allgyer got a letter from the FDA telling him to stop selling raw milk. He didn't. The FDA filed suit against him. That suit is still in court.

THE RUSE: In 1978 two wealthy Arab sheiks started inviting U.S. government officials to meetings. The purpose of the meetings: The sheiks had a ton of money, and they wanted help making "investments" in the United States.

THE HOOK: Several of the government officials happily took the sheiks' money and "invested" it into their own pockets, in exchange for helping the sheiks secure purchases of casinos, mining companies, and other American businesses.

GOTCHA! The sheiks weren't sheiks—they were undercover FBI agents. It was all part of the agency's "Abscam" operation (from "*Abdul*," the name of the fictitious company the "sheiks" owned, and "scam"). And the government officials? They included eight members of Congress. Five members of the House of Representatives went to federal prison, as did Senator Harrison Williams of New Jersey, who was videotaped promising the "sheiks" he'd secure them contracts to open a titanium mine in exchange for shares in the company. Williams remains one of only two U.S. senators in history who went to prison for crimes committed while in office.

THE AMAZING ZEER POT

In parts of the world without electricity, the cooling properties of the simple zeer pot help fight hunger by preventing food from spoiling in hot weather. Now, thanks to the BRI's Technology Department, you can build one, too.

WHAT YOU NEED

- **Two clay flowerpots—a large one and a small one.** The small pot must be able to fit inside the large pot. The large pot must be unglazed; the small pot can be glazed or unglazed.
- **Sand.** You need enough to fill the space between the small pot and the large pot when one is placed inside the other.
- **Water.** You need enough to saturate the sand between the pots.
- **A towel,** large enough to cover the top of the pots.
- **A stand** for the large pot, so that air can circulate underneath.

WHAT TO DO

- Plug the drain holes in the pots, if they have them, so that the large pot can hold water in, and the small pot can keep water out.
- Put the large pot on the stand and fill it with enough sand so that the tops of the pots are level with each other.
- Fill the space between the two pots with the sand, all the way to the top. Then pour the water into the sand until it's saturated.
- Put some food or drinks in the small pot, then soak the towel in water and use it to cover the pots.
- Replenish the water as it evaporates.

HOW IT WORKS

The zeer pot, also known as a pot-in-pot refrigerator, cools food through evaporation, in much the same way you cool off by sweating. The water in the sand is absorbed by the porous larger pot, then evaporates into the surrounding air. As the water molecules evaporate, they absorb heat, causing the smaller pot and any food it contains to cool significantly. On a 100°F day, food inside a zeer pot can be kept as cool as 49°F, enabling it to remain fresh for as long as a month instead of spoiling in a day or two.

Manatees (sea cows) and elephants are related.

WHAT IT'S ALL ABOUT

Who invented the Hokey Pokey? It depends on who
you ask, or where and when you lived.

DO "THE HOKEY COKEY"
In 1942 Irish songwriter and publisher Jimmy Kennedy, best known for "The Teddy Bear's Picnic," created a dance, and an instructional song to go along with it, called "The Hokey Cokey." Written to entertain Canadian troops stationed in London, the lyrics told dancers to "put your left leg in / your left leg out / in out / in out / shake it all about / Do the Hokey-Cokey and you turn around / That's what it's all about." Sound familiar? It should, but that's actually not the song familiar to us today.

DO "THE HOKEY POKEY"

Composer Al Tabor was also entertaining Canadian troops in wartime London, and in 1942 *he* wrote a participation dance song called "The Hokey Pokey"—he said the name came from the London ice cream vendors of his youth, called "hokey pokey men." The accompanying dance was very similar to Kennedy's. Tabor accused Kennedy of reneging on an agreement to publish his song and writing his own "Hokey Cokey" instead. An out-of-court settlement was reached, and Kennedy won all rights to "The Hokey Pokey" (or Cokey). But it still isn't the song we know today.

DO "THE HOKEY-POKEY DANCE"

In 1946, totally unaware of the British "Hokey Pokey" and "Hokey Cokey," two Scranton, Pennsylvania, musicians, Robert Degen and Joe Brier, recorded "The Hokey-Pokey Dance" to entertain summer vacationers at Poconos Mountains resorts. Theirs went like this: "Put your right hand in / Put your right hand out / Put your right hand in / and you wiggle all about / Everything is okey dokey / when you do the Hokey Pokey / That is what the dance is all about." The song was a regional favorite at dances and resorts for the rest of the 1940s. But even *that* isn't the song we know today.

Vanilla is mildly addictive.

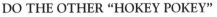

DO THE OTHER "HOKEY POKEY"

In 1949 bandleader Larry LaPrise, also without any knowledge of the other "Hokey Pokeys," came up with a dance and an instructional song called "The Hokey Pokey." He also wrote his to entertain wealthy vacationers, but this time in the remote ski resort town of Sun Valley, Idaho. Sample lyrics: "You put your left foot in / you put your left foot out / you put your left foot in / and you shake it all about / you do the Hokey Pokey and you turn yourself around / that's what it's all about." The song was a hit at the resorts, so LaPrise recorded it. It flopped, but Degan and Brier found out about it and sued LaPrise for ripping off their "The Hokey-Pokey Dance." Despite the fact that his version came out after theirs, LaPrise won the rights to anything to do with "The Hokey Pokey." In 1953 Ray Anthony's Orchestra recorded it—a double-A-side single with "The Bunny Hop"—and it went to #13 on the pop chart. And that's the version we know today.

SO *THAT'S* WHAT IT'S ALL ABOUT?

So that settles who wrote the popular incarnation of "The Hokey Pokey." But traces of the Hokey Pokey—an easy dance with a song telling you how to do it—appear in folk dances going back hundreds of years in North American and Europe. Pop culture historians believe that the reason so many different writers came up with what was essentially the same song was because it's part of our shared cultural heritage, including:

• **The Hinkum-Booby.** In 1857 the religious sect known as the Shakers had their own novelty song and dance popular in their New Hampshire community. The lyrics go something like this: "I put my right hand in, I put my right hand out; in, out, shake it all about." The ditty and corresponding gestures were then repeated, and went on to include the left hand, left and right feet, and the head…just like the modern-day Hokey Pokey.

• **Hincumbooby.** Of course, the Shakers' "Hinkum-Booby" is reminiscent of the Puritans' earlier "Hincumbooby" song and dance, which goes a little something like this: "Hincumbooby, round about, right hands in and left hands out." That dance dates to Massachusetts in the mid-1600s.

• **The Hincum Looby.** This one dates back even farther—to Tudor England in the 1500s. And *that's* what it's all about.

SMELLS FUNNY

And you thought candles were just for power outages.

• **Hot dog.** Sniff Candles offers a line of scented candles for dogs, including "Fart and Away," "Day in the Hamptons," and "Splendor in the Grass." Price: $28 each. They don't just give off smells that dogs like—they're aromatherapy candles. "These candles meet the most common needs of dog wellness and are pleasant and non-intrusive to humans," says the company's website. "By using each candle—the perfect blend of essential oils to offer emotional balance and energy—your dog will experience an overall improved sense of well-being."

• **Harold and Kumar stay home.** White Castle, the fast-food chain best known for its onion-flavored mini-burgers called "sliders," began selling a scented candle in 2010. It comes in a cardboard sleeve that looks like a White Castle burger package, and emits the aroma of steamed burgers and grilled onions. (The first 10,000 sold out in 48 hours; proceeds benefited Autism Speaks.)

• **Reading lights.** Paddywax sells a line called the Library Collection, a series of candles inspired by famous authors. According to Paddywax, a writer's "signature fragrance can enhance a book's literary stylings." The Edgar Allan Poe candle smells like absinthe and sandalwood; Walt Whitman's smells like (leaves of) grass; and the Charles Dickens candle combines juniper and clove to evoke Victorian London and burns for up to 60 hours—or about the length of a Bob Cratchit work week.

• **Urine for a treat.** Hotwicks specializes in novelty scented candles in nontraditional smells, including hot cocoa, pizza, coffee, and a "Hippie Candle" that smells like marijuana. But the weirdest is probably "urinal cake." According to Hotwicks, it was "modeled after a urinal cake our founder once relieved himself on at the Bellagio Hotel in Las Vegas."

• **Other real nonsense scents you can buy:** Beer, campfire, bacon, birthday cake, sawdust, leather jacket, dirt, lawnmower, nachos, pigskin, pancakes, and "patriot."

Oldest woman to pose nude in *Playboy*: actress Terry Moore (August 1984 issue, at age 55).

YOU'VE GOT A FRIEND

We once heard friendship defined as being close enough to someone to eat out of their fridge without asking. Here are some more thoughts on the subject.

"The bird a nest, the spider a web, man friendship."
—**William Blake**

"It is important to our friends to believe that we are unreservedly frank with them, and important to friendship that we are not."
—**Mignon McLaughlin**

"The only way to have a friend is to be one."
—**Ralph Waldo Emerson**

"A loyal friend laughs at your jokes when they're not so good, and sympathizes with your problems when they're not so bad."
—**Arnold H. Glasgow**

"A friend knows you and loves you just the same."
—**Elbert Hubbard**

"A true friend stabs you in the front."
—**Oscar Wilde**

"Each friend represents a world in us, a world possibly not born until they arrive."
—**Anaïs Nin**

"When a friend is in trouble, don't ask if there is anything you can do. Think up something appropriate and do it."
—**Edward W. Howe**

"A friend to all is a friend to none."
—**Aristotle**

"I value the friend who for me finds time on his calendar, but I cherish the friend who for me does not consult his calendar."
—**Robert Brault**

"You can always tell a real friend: When you've made a fool of yourself he doesn't feel you've done a permanent job."
—**Laurence J. Peter**

"The friend who holds your hand and says the wrong thing is made of dearer stuff than the one who stays away."
—**Barbara Kingsolver**

"Don't walk behind me; I may not lead. Don't walk in front of me; I may not follow. Just walk beside me and be my friend."
—**Albert Camus**

Heads up! People (or animals) with the condition *polycephaly* have two (or more) heads.

CHANCES THAT...

The odds that you'll read this list of odd statistics: 100%.

You'll survive for another year: 99.8 percent

You'll get married: 64 percent

Your car will be recalled for something: 60 percent

You'll be audited by the IRS: 57 percent

You'll have to wear glasses: 52 percent

Your drinking water is contaminated: 20 percent

A recovering alcoholic staying sober for good: 9 percent

A bill introduced into Congress will pass: 8 percent

You'll have a supernatural encounter: 5.9 percent

Your kid's a genius: 4 percent

You'll marry someone of another race: 2 percent

A pregnancy will result in twins: 2 percent

You'll be injured in a car accident: 1.33 percent

An asteroid will crash into the Earth and destroy all life sometime in the next 100 years: 0.02 percent

You'll date a supermodel: 0.1 percent

You'll win an Academy Award: 0.0083 percent

Your kid will earn a doctorate: 0.008 percent

You'll appear on *The Tonight Show*: 0.0002 percent

You'll be killed by terrorists in a foreign country: 0.000015 percent

Your kid will become a pro football player: 0.0001 percent

You'll spot a UFO tonight: 0.00003 percent

You'll win the big lottery: 0.000019 percent

You'll achieve sainthood: 0.000005 percent

You'll die from your pajamas catching on fire: 0.000003 percent

"Touching wires causes instant death. $200 fine." —sign seen in Newcastle, England.

FIRST, OR LAST, IN DEATH

For a few unfortunate souls, earning a place in the record books is the very last thing they ever do.

JANET PARKER (1938–78)

Claim to Fame: Last person on Earth to die from smallpox

Details: Parker, who worked in the anatomy department of England's University of Birmingham Medical School, one floor up from the smallpox lab, hadn't been vaccinated against the disease since 1966. But because she didn't work in that lab, she was not required to have a booster shot. Sometime on July 24 or 25, some live smallpox virus was accidentally sucked into the building's ventilation system, then blown into the room where Parker was making phone calls. Initially misdiagnosed with the flu and then chicken pox, by the time she was correctly diagnosed, she'd come in contact with a number of people, some of whom had to be quarantined. Only one of them, Parker's own mother, contracted the disease. She survived, but Parker died on September 11, 1978.

JEFF DAILY (1961–81) / PETER BURKOWSKI (1964–82)

Claims to Fame: First confirmed video-game fatality

Details: A 19-year-old named Jeff Daily *may* have been the first person killed by a video game. He is said to have dropped dead in January 1981, immediately after racking up a high score on the arcade game *Berzerk*. But the details are sketchy, and it's not clear that the video game was to blame. It's not even clear that Daily ever really existed; the story may be an urban legend.

Peter Burkowski, who died on April 3, 1982, after playing the same game for just 15 minutes, is a different story. He *did* exist. The 18-year-old spent his last quarter hour (and his last quarter) playing *Berzerk* at Friar Tuck's Game Room in Calumet City, Illinois. As he stepped away from the machine to play a different game, he collapsed and died. The coroner found that Burkowski had an undiagnosed heart condition. Apparently the stress of playing *Berzerk* was more than his weakened heart could handle.

In the 20th century, more people died of smallpox than in all wars of that century combined.

ROBERT WILLIAMS (1954–79)

Claim to Fame: First person ever killed by a robot

Details: Williams was an employee at a Ford Motor Company casting plant in Flat Rock, Michigan. On January 25, 1979, one of the one-ton "transfer robots" began to malfunction. Instead of removing parts from shelves that were stacked five stories high, the robot undercounted the number of parts on some of the shelves and then stopped retrieving parts from shelves it thought were empty. Williams climbed up onto a shelf to get the parts himself, but no one shut down the system. The robot's giant arm swung around and hit Williams in the head, killing him instantly.

RON HUBER (1945–2004)

Claim to Fame: First person to die in a Segway accident

Details: Huber, a vintage race car restorer who lived in Scottsdale, Arizona, was in Las Vegas for a go-kart race when he hopped on one of the two-wheeled, self-balancing electric vehicles and took it for a spin. He was only traveling about 5 mph when he fell off the Segway, struck his head on the pavement, and died.

Note: The second Segway fatality was James Heselden, the *owner* of the Segway company. In 2010 he was riding his Segway around his estate in Yorkshire, England, when he backed it off a footpath to make way for a neighbor walking his dog. Heselden lost control of the Segway and plunged off a 40-foot cliff into the river below.

WILLIE FRANCIS (1929–47)

Claim to Fame: First inmate to go to the electric chair *twice*

Details: Francis, an African American living in St. Martinville, Louisiana, was only 16 when he was convicted by an all-white jury of murdering the town pharmacist, who was also white. The first attempt to electrocute him failed; the guard and inmate responsible for wiring up "Gruesome Gertie," the state's electric chair, were drunk and botched the job. Francis' lawyers went to court to block the second execution attempt, arguing that it was unconstitutional to execute Francis for the same crime twice, not to mention cruel and unusual punishment. They fought the case all the way to the U.S. Supreme Court, which ruled against Francis. On May 9, 1947, Francis was strapped into Gruesome Gertie a second time and electrocuted again. This time it worked.

Twelve American presidents owned slaves, 8 while serving as president.

FAMILY FEUD: ADIDAS VS. PUMA

*Here's the strange story of a family-owned business
so dysfunctional that business schools teach it
as a lesson in how not to run a company.*

FOOT SOLDIER

Not long after the end of World War I in 1918, an 18-year-old German soldier named Adolf Dassler returned to his hometown of Herzogenaurach, in northern Bavaria. Shoemaking was the biggest industry in the area, so it was no surprise when he decided to become a cobbler.

Dassler started small, working in an empty laundry shed behind his parents' house. There he constructed his first shoes—work shoes—out of leather scraps salvaged from wartime army helmets and other gear. His interest soon turned to athletic footwear. An inveterate tinkerer, he made his first sports shoes for his friends. But as his designs improved, his reputation spread beyond Herzogenaurach, and he soon had more work than he could manage by himself. In 1923 his boisterous older brother Rudolf joined the business. "Rudi" handled sales while "Adi" made the shoes. In 1924 they formalized their partnership by founding the Dassler Brothers Shoe Company. Two years after that, they moved their growing business into a factory on the other side of town.

PARTY POOPERS

When Hitler seized power in 1933, Adi and Rudolf joined the Nazi Party. They certainly benefited from Hitler's use of sports as a propaganda tool, but they weren't the most dedicated of party members, something that became clear during the 1936 Summer Olympics, held in Berlin. Hitler intended the Olympics to serve as a showcase for the Nazi doctrine of Aryan racial superiority, but all the Dasslers cared about was getting Jesse Owens, the famous *African*-American track-and-field star, to wear Dassler Brothers shoes in the games. He did, and won four gold medals. Owens's victories gave the company its first international exposure. Soon athletes from all over Europe began making their way to tiny Herzogenaurach whenever they passed through Germany, to get a pair of Dassler Brothers shoes.

CAIN AND ADI

The brothers really had very little in common: Adi loved nothing more than to sit at his workbench and tinker with his shoes. Rudi, on the other hand, was a people person, but also short-tempered and loudmouthed. Their personalities complemented each other during the early years of the business. But as Germany moved closer to war in the late 1930s, their relationship became strained, made worse by the fact that they, their wives, their children, their parents, and their other siblings all lived together under the same roof in a villa in Herzogenaurach.

In December 1940, Adi was called up for military service, but he managed to get an exemption after just three months in uniform, perhaps with help from Rudi, who may have pulled strings from Herzogenaurach. If so, that probably made Rudi all the more bitter when *he* was called up for military service in 1943 and couldn't get out of it. He was convinced that Adi and his wife, Käthe, had schemed to get him sent to the front so that Adi could have the business to himself. Rudi retaliated by trying to get the factory shut down so that Adi would also be sent to the front, but he failed.

OH, BROTHER

In early 1945 Rudi deserted his post in Poland, fleeing just ahead of the advancing Russian army. He returned to Herzogenaurach, where a doctor friend declared him unfit for military service due to a frozen foot, but he was soon arrested by the Gestapo for desertion. He blamed that on Adi, too. There may actually have been some truth to Rudi's belief that Adi was out to get him, because not long after Rudi was released by the Gestapo, he was arrested by the Allies, this time on suspicion of working *for* the Gestapo. According to the report filed by the American investigating officer, both Adi and Käthe told investigators that Rudi had worked for the Gestapo. Result: Rudi spent a year in a POW camp. How did Adi spend the year? Rebuilding Dassler Brothers by selling athletic shoes to American GIs eager to buy the same kind of shoes that Jesse Owens had worn.

PAYBACK

Rudi retaliated in the summer of 1946, when Adi was hauled before the local denazification committee. Had Adi been classified as a *Belasteter*, or "profiteer," he could have lost control of Dassler Brothers—in which case Rudi might have been appointed to run the company—or he could have been stripped of ownership entirely.

Rudi appeared before the committee and did his best to paint Adi in a bad light, in the hope of assuming sole control of Dassler Brothers. And then he rejoined his wife and children under the same roof as Adi and his family. But not in the villa: That had been seized by the American occupation forces, who would be living in it until further notice. For the time being, Rudi and his family, and Adi and his family, and their widowed mother, and their other siblings, would all squat together in makeshift accommodations in a Dassler Brothers shoe factory. All the while, the brothers battled each other in public for control of the company.

SPLITSVILLE

Adi beat the rap in November 1946, when the denazification committee classified him as a *Mitläufer*, a "follower," or a Nazi who had not actively contributed to the party or profited from his association with it. He would not be barred from running Dassler Brothers.

But by that time neither of the brothers believed they could work together, so they decided to split the company in two. Rudi took the first step, moving his family and his mother (who sided with him) to new lodgings on the other side of the Aurach river, which runs through Herzogenaurach. He and Adi spent the next year and a half dividing the Dassler Brothers assets between themselves. Adi named his new company after himself, combining the first three letters of his first and last names to get *Adidas*. Rudi took two letters from his first and last names to get "Ruda." Then he decided that Ruda sounded pudgy and un-athletic, so he changed his company's name to the more powerful-sounding *Puma*.

Neither brother may have realized it at the time, but the Dassler family feud was just getting started.

For Part II of the story, turn to page 352.

They gave us the bird: Chickens were first domesticated in Vietnam about 10,000 years ago.

ODD SCHOLARSHIPS

*The bad news: College is more expensive than ever. The good news:
There are a lot of scholarships—and some really weird
scholarships—to help soften the financial blow.*

Grant: The David Letterman Scholarship
Scholarship amount: $10,000
Details: Students majoring or minoring in telecommunications at Ball State University in Indiana (Letterman's home state) are eligible for this scholarship. They must prepare a creative project: written, filmed, or audiotaped. The winner is selected solely on creativity. Grades don't matter at all, a stipulation Letterman made himself because he never got good grades.

Grant: FBI Common Knowledge Challenge
Scholarship amount: $1,000
Details: Any current college student can register to take this annual FBI-trivia quiz about the agency's history and procedures. Students are then sent the quiz along with a list of links to FBI websites that they can "investigate" to find the answers. The four students who score the highest each year get a scholarship.

Grant: Patrick Kerr Skateboard Scholarship
Scholarship amount: $5,000
Details: This award is given out by the family of Patrick Kerr, a 15-year-old boy who died in 2002 while he was skateboarding and ran into a truck. To qualify, entrants have to write essays telling how "skateboarding has been a positive influence" in their lives, along with demonstrating how they promoted skateboarding in their community. The winner gets $5,000; runners-up get $1,000 each, provided by Mountain Dew and the Tony Hawk Foundation.

Grant: Bernard Steur Scholarship
Scholarship amount: $1,000
Details: Most scholarship applications require a written essay or a list of relevant work or volunteer experience. This scholarship

---

First U.S. product sold wrapped in cellophane: Whitman's Candies.

for Philadelphia University textile engineering students calls for applicants to submit an article of clothing they've designed and knitted themselves, made entirely out of wool. Strangely, the grant's namesake, Steuer, had few ties to the textile industry— he was a painter.

Grant: Van Valkenburg Memorial Scholarship
Scholarship amount: $1,000
Details: Members of the Van Valkenburg family first came to the New World in 1644 and lived in New Amsterdam, present-day New York. In the 1970s, their descendants established a foundation that awards a scholarship to a student who has contributed positively to the Van Valkenburg family legacy (they have to write an essay proving it). Entrants must have the last name Van Valkenburg or a variation of it—Van Valkanburg, for example.
Other name-related scholarships: Texas A&M University has a scholarship for people named Scarpinato, and Loyola University in Chicago offers a full ride to a Catholic student named Zolp.

Grant: The Klingon Language Institute Scholarship
Scholarship amount: $500
Details: First of all, yes, there's an organization devoted to the appreciation and propagation of the made-up language from the *Star Trek* TV shows and movies (founded in 1992, or stardate 45493.9). And second, it will subsidize the education of a student who studies languages or linguistics. More good news: It can be *any* language program. (Although enrolling in a college that has a Klingon program—if you can find one—probably wouldn't hurt.)

Grant: Duck Brand Duct Tape Stuck on Prom Scholarship
Scholarship amount: $10,000 per couple
Details: Duck is a major manufacturer of duct tape—that incredibly sticky, durable, colored tape with a variety of uses, including, it would seem, making clothes. The high-school couple who makes the most creative his-and-hers formal dance ensembles out of Duck's duct tape (other materials can be incorporated into the garments) wins big. Entries are judged on workmanship, creativity, use of color, and how much Duck Tape you use.

UNCLE JOHN'S PAGE OF LISTS

Some random bits from the BRI's bottomless trivia files.

7 NATIONS THAT DRINK THE MOST ALCOHOL (PER CAPITA)
1. Moldova
2. Czech Republic
3. Hungary
4. Russia
5. Ukraine
6. Estonia
7. Andorra

8 THINGS YOU CAN'T SELL ON eBAY
1. Batteries
2. Catalytic converters
3. Guns
4. Food
5. Cable TV descramblers
6. Lock picks
7. Postage meters
8. Used airbags

4 ODD PIG BREEDS
1. Mulefoot
2. British Lop
3. Saddleback
5. Tokyo-X

4 DEFUNCT BOY SCOUT MERIT BADGES
1. Taxidermy
2. Invention
3. Blacksmithing
4. Beekeeping

THE 10 PLAGUES OF EGYPT
1. Blood (the waters of the Nile turned into blood)
2. Frogs
3. Lice
4. Flies
5. Diseased livestock
6. Boils
7. Hail (mixed with fire)
8. Locusts
9. Darkness
10. Death of the firstborn (of all Egyptians *and* their livestock)

3 NICKNAMES FOR THE DEVIL
1. Old Scratch
2. Hornie
3. Father of Lies

5 MOST COMMON TRANSPLANT SURGERIES
1. Cornea
2. Muscle graft
3. Kidney
4. Liver
5. Skin graft

8 ASIAN FLAVORS OF DORITOS
1. Coconut Curry
2. Tuna and Mayo
3. Fried Chicken
4. Winter Crab Pizza
5. Winter Cheese
6. Rock Taco
7. Olive
8. Corn Soup

SNOOPY'S 7 SIBLINGS
1. Andy
2. Belle
3. Marbles
4. Molly
5. Olaf
6. Rover
7. Spike

World's largest mall: the South China Mall, with space for 1,500 stores. (It's 99% vacant.)

DO TRY THIS AT HOME

We were saving this article about home science experiments for our next Bathroom Reader for Kids Only, *but then we thought, why should the kids have all the fun?*

POTATO-POWERED CLOCK

What You Need: 2 fresh, raw potatoes; 2 shiny pennies; 2 galvanized nails; 3 short pieces of insulated wire with small alligator clips at each end; 1 battery-operated LED clock (with battery removed); and 1 black Magic Marker. You should be able to get almost all of these items at any hardware store.

What to Do: Use the Magic Marker to mark the potatoes "1" and "2." Push the pennies edgewise into each potato, leaving some of each penny exposed. Stick the nails partway into each potato. Using the first wire, attach one alligator clip to the penny in potato #1 and the other to the positive (+) terminal in the clock. Using the second wire, connect one clip to the nail in potato #2 and the other to the negative (–) terminal in the clock. Take the third wire and clip one end to the nail in potato #1, and the other end to the penny in potato #2.

Result: Take a look at your clock. It's running…on potato power.

Explanation: What you're witnessing is an *electrochemical reaction*, or a chemical reaction that produces electricity. In this case, the zinc coating on the galvanized nails and the copper in the pennies are reacting with chemicals in the potato, resulting in the movement of electrons—that's electricity!—through the potato, the wires, and the clock. Bonus: You don't need potatoes. You can use lemons, apples, or bananas.

EGG IN A BOTTLE

Warning: Kids, this experiment uses fire—so don't do it in a barn full of hay. Or at a gas station. Or, more importantly, without a responsible adult present. (And don't be sneaky: It has to be an *awake* adult.)

What You Need: 1 hard-boiled egg; 1 glass bottle that's dry on the inside and has a fairly wide opening (like a fruit juice or iced tea bottle), but not wide enough to let the hard-boiled egg fall into it; a little vegetable oil; a small piece of paper (3 inches square); and a match or lighter.

What to Do: Rub a little bit of oil around the inside of the lip of the bottle. Fold the piece of paper into a strip that can be easily dropped into the bottle's opening. Ignite one end of the strip of paper and drop it into the bottle. Set the egg on the opening of the bottle while the paper is still burning.

Result: You'll be amazed…as the egg starts to wiggle…then squish…and squeeze through the opening, falling into the bottle.

Explanation: What you're seeing is a demonstration of how temperature affects air pressure. Before you drop the burning paper into the bottle, the temperature in the bottle and in the surrounding air are the same—so the pressure is the same, too. But when you drop the burning paper in, the heat from the fire causes the air in the bottle to expand—or increase in pressure. (That's why the egg wiggles: air was escaping.) After the fire.goes out (because the egg blocked oxygen from getting in), the air in the bottle cools down and contracts—or decreases in pressure. The air outside the bottle is now more highly pressurized than the air inside. High pressure naturally flows toward low pressure, so the air outside the bottle is drawn into it, and squishes the egg into the bottle in doing so. Once the egg is out of the way, the air pressure in and out of the bottle are equal again.

CABBAGE-JUICE pH TESTER

Warning: If you're not allowed to use the stove by yourself, find someone to supervise.

What You Need: Stove; pot; a head of red cabbage; white vinegar; baking soda; pencil and paper; and assorted things from around the house

What to Do: Chop up the cabbage and boil it in a medium-sized pot for 20 minutes. Pour the liquid into a measuring cup and let it cool. Use a spoon and put a little bit of the purple-blue cabbage juice on a white surface, or in a white cup, or just a glass if that's all you have handy. Now add a tiny bit of vinegar to it. Now start over, and add some baking soda to the cabbage juice instead.

The human body glows in the dark, but the light emitted is too dim for our eyes to see it.

Results: When you add vinegar to the cabbage juice, it turns bright red. When you add baking soda, it turns green.

Explanation: The reactions that you are witnessing are the result of the substances' *pH level*, or how *acidic* or how *basic* (or *alkaline*) they are. PH is measured from 0 to 14: Water is neutral, with a pH of 7. Anything less than 7 is an acid; the lower the number, the more *acidic* the substance is. Anything above 7 is a base; the higher the number, the more *basic* it is. (For "The ABCs of pH," go to page 496.) Acids cause the cabbage juice to change toward purple, pink, and red; bases make it change toward blue, green, and yellow. And you can now determine, pretty accurately, the pH level of anything you can dissolve in water, using the chart below, with the approximate pH level on the top, and color on the bottom.

Go ahead, test some other things: beer, yogurt, maple syrup, shampoo—whatever you like. Any colors you get, just try to place them where you think they belong on the chart.

0	2	4	6	8	10	12	14
red	light pink	dark pink	purple	blue	aqua	green	yellow

You now have a simple, homemade pH-level testing system, useful for a variety of purposes. Extremely acidic or alkaline foods, for example, will be very sour or bitter, respectively. And, more importantly, the water in your hot tub should have a pH level of between 7.2 and 7.8.

Extra: Cut some white paper into strips (coffee filters work well), soak them in cabbage juice for a few hours, take them out, and let them dry. You now have pH-level testing strips that work just as well as the ones you can buy in the store—and they'll last for months.

*   *   *

A GROANER

Did you hear about the hurricane
that lost its force? It was disgusted.

Bears don't raid beehives for honey—they're after the larvae. (But they'll eat the honey, too.)

SECRET INGREDIENTS

Great ice cream! You can really taste the beaver butt!

I ngredient: Sunscreen
Found in: Salad dressings
Explanation: Burger King's Fat Free Ranch Dressing and Wendy's Low Fat Honey Mustard Dressing both contain *titanium dioxide*. It has several commercial uses: In salad dressings it's used to create an appetizing, creamy-white color; in beauty products, it's used as a sunblock.

Ingredient: Pepper juice
Found in: Healthcare products
Explanation: *Oleoresin capsicum* is the active ingredient in pepper spray—when you spray the stuff in a bad guy's eyes, oleoresin capsicum is what makes his eyes burn, swell, and redden. That same ingredient is present in personal products that create a warming sensation to let you know they're working, like pain and itch creams.

Ingredient: Sheep oil
Found in: Multivitamin tablets
Explanation: If you take a multivitamin supplement that contains Vitamin D3—and most commercially available adult vitamins do—you're also consuming a byproduct of wool. The vitamin contains a chemical called *cholecalciferol*, a derivative of lanolin, a waxy oil that is extracted from sheep's wool.

Ingredient: Insect attractant
Found in: McDonald's cilantro-lime and orange glaze dressings
Explanation: These salad dressings and sandwich glazes contain *propylene glycol alginate*. It's considered safe for human consumption in small doses…but it's illegal to use in cat food, because the FDA doesn't think it's safe for cats. Propylene glycol is also used as an agent in bug traps because it both attracts and traps beetles.

Banana split: In a traditional Hawaiian burial, the body is wrapped in banana leaves.

Ingredient: Nuts

Found in: Artificial fire logs

Explanation: If you have a peanut allergy, you might want to stay away from light-and-burn artificial fireplace logs. The composite quick-burn material contains peanut shells and skins, which burn and become airborne in the smoke, and then can be inhaled.

Ingredient: Beaver secretions

Found in: Ice cream

Explanation: The male North American beaver marks its territory by urinating on things. Along with the urine, it secretes a liquid called *castoreum,* which gives off a sweet scent. Castoreum also enhances the intensity of vanilla flavor, which is why this extract, made in the beaver's anal glands, is used to flavor vanilla ice cream. (It's not listed in the ingredients—it's one of the "natural flavors.") Trappers harvest the scent glands and sell them to additive companies.

Ingredient: Animal fat

Found in: Those ubiquitous thin plastic shopping bags

Explanation: Plastic grocery bags are manufactured with an innate *slipping agent* to reduce friction, allowing the bags to be grabbed easily and opened without sticking to each other or themselves. What makes the best slipping agent? Animal fat.

Ingredient: Hair remover

Found in: McGriddle sandwiches

Explanation: Both the maple syrup-flavored "griddle cakes" and the egg patty of this breakfast sandwich contain *sodium acid pyrophosphate.* Generally regarded as safe by the FDA, it's used to maintain color and moisture in protein-heavy products (like eggs) and acts as a cheap alternative to yeast in manufactured baked goods: Coupled with baking soda, it makes bread rise. Elsewhere, sodium acid pyrophosphate aids the removal of hair, dandruff, and feathers in hog and poultry processing. It's also an effective stain remover, particularly when applied to leather goods.

LOU GEHRIG, RECONSIDERED

Even people who know nothing about baseball know that baseball legend Lou Gehrig died from "Lou Gehrig's Disease." Or did he?

THAT SINKING FEELING

In June 1939, New York Yankees first baseman Lou Gehrig checked into the Mayo Clinic in Rochester, Minnesota, for a series of tests that he hoped would tell him why playing baseball had suddenly become so difficult. After 14 seasons with the Yankees and a record 2,130 consecutive games played, Gehrig was having difficulty running, fielding balls, even holding the bat. When he began to have trouble even tying his shoes, he knew that whatever was wrong with him, it was serious.

The rest of the story is well known: Doctors diagnosed Gehrig with *amyotrophic lateral sclerosis*, or ALS, an incurable motor neuron disease that destroys the nerves that control muscles, causing paralysis and eventual death. The cause is unknown. Gehrig retired from baseball and lived with the disease for two years before passing away in 1941. Before Gehrig's illness, few people had heard of amyotrophic lateral sclerosis, and even afterward the name was difficult to remember, so it was probably inevitable that ALS would become known as "Lou Gehrig's Disease."

A NEW THEORY

The story didn't change much over the next 70 years. Then in August 2010, researchers with the Boston University School of Medicine and the Department of Veterans Affairs published a study that, while it didn't address Gehrig's case directly, called into question whether he ever really had ALS at all.

The researchers studied brain and spinal-cord samples from 12 deceased professional athletes who'd suffered a deterioration of brain function late in life. Three had been diagnosed with ALS; the other nine had suffered from *chronic traumatic encephalopathy*, or CTE, a condition believed to be caused by repeated concussions or other head trauma. Symptoms of CTE include depression,

---

Lou Gehrig's nickname during the 1920s: "Biscuit Pants."

impaired memory, and emotional instability. It often progresses to a full-blown dementia similar to Alzheimer's disease.

SIMILAR, BUT NOT THE SAME

People who suffer from CTE have abnormal deposits of a protein called *tau* in their brains. The researchers looked for, and found, abnormal tau deposits in all 12 athletes.

What was unusual about this finding was that ALS sufferers typically *do not* have tau deposits in their brains. When the researchers looked further, they found that the three athletes diagnosed with ALS also had the abnormal tau deposits in their spinal cords. Again, this is not something usually found in ALS patients.

The researchers also found that 10 of the 12 athletes had abnormal deposits of a second protein (called *TDP-43*) in their brains. Of these 10, only 3, the athletes diagnosed with ALS, also had deposits of TDP-43 in their spinal cords.

People who suffer from ALS can have abnormal deposits of TDP-43, but they typically are not as extensive as those found in the 12 athletes in this study. And ALS patients don't have abnormal deposits of tau. This led the authors to conclude that they had discovered a new disease, one with symptoms similar to ALS but with a different cause: abnormal tau and TDP-43 deposits in the brain and spinal cord, the result of repeated head trauma over many years. The researchers named the new disease *chronic traumatic encephalomyopathy*, or CTEM.

THE IRON HORSE

Gehrig may very well have suffered from CTEM, not ALS. During his 14 years with the Yankees, he sustained at least five serious concussions, the worst in 1934 when he was hit in the head by a fastball and knocked out cold for five minutes. He famously never missed a game during his years with the Yankees, and he routinely played through his injuries, which may have made matters worse. We can't test to see if Gehrig really did die from CTEM, because his remains were cremated. But the possibility is certainly intriguing. "Here he is, the face of his disease," lead researcher Dr. Ann McKee told the *N.Y. Times*, "and as a result of his athletic experience he may have had a completely different disease."

Stoners: Men are four times more likely than women to get kidney stones.

COME ON DOWN!

The Price Is Right has been around longer than Uncle John has. Here are some random facts about America's longest-running game show.

BACKGROUND
The Price is Right debuted on American television in 1956 on NBC, in both prime-time and daytime versions. Both were hosted by former radio announcer Bill Cullen, and they were huge hits—in the top 10 from 1959 to 1961, making it the most popular game show on TV. In 1963 the show moved to ABC, then was canceled after two years. CBS revived the show for its daytime schedule in 1972, bringing in former *Truth or Consequences* host Bob Barker and retitling it *The New Price is Right*. And it was a hit again. The "New" was dropped after a couple of years, and today it's one of only two network-produced game shows on the air.

• Prizes on the early version were often outlandish, like a chauffeured Rolls Royce, a Ferris wheel, or an island. A 1994 episode of *The Simpsons* in which Bart wins a contest and refuses the cash prize in favor of the "gag" prize—an elephant—is based on a *Price Is Right* incident in 1956 where a contestant demanded the real elephant he'd won instead of its $4,000 cash value. Producers finally acquiesced and flew one in from Kenya.

• Four men have sat in the announcer's chair of the current version. First was Johnny Olsen (1972–85), who was also the announcer for *Jeopardy!*, *The Match Game*, *Play Your Hunch*, and many other game shows. Rod Roddy and his sparkly suits replaced Olsen in 1985 and encouraged contestants to "Come on down!" until his death in 2003. Rich Fields followed, turning things over to *Junkyard Wars* host George Gray in 2011. Only two men have hosted the current incarnation of the show: Bob Barker, from 1972 to 2007, when he retired at age 83, and the current host, comedian Drew Carey.

• To honor Barker's 5,000th episode in 1998, the show's soundstage, Stage 33 at CBS Television City, was renamed Bob Barker Studio.

• As of the 7,000th episode, taped in November 2009, $250 million in prizes had been given out to nearly 62,000 contestants. The phrase "a new car!" had been shouted over 15,000 times; 7,000 contestants had actually managed to win one.

• In addition to other versions that have aired in syndication and during prime time in the United States, international editions have appeared on every continent except Antarctica. The show has also been licensed for slot machines, board games, scratch-off lottery tickets, and numerous video games.

• The most controversial of "Barker's Beauties," the models who introduced products on the show, was Dian Parkinson. She posed nude in *Playboy* twice in the early 1990s, and while CBS frowned on the pictorials, they couldn't fire her because they couldn't cross the powerful Barker…who was having an affair with Parkinson at the time. Parkinson's 18-year stint on the show came to end in 1994 when she filed a sexual-harassment lawsuit against Barker. She later dropped the charges, claiming the case was having a negative impact on her health.

• Debuting in 1976, "Cliff Hangers" is one of *The Price Is Right*'s oldest and most popular games. Contestants attempt to guess the prices of various products in order to prevent a miniature mountain climber dressed in lederhosen from falling off a cliff. The climber has no official name, but in 1977, guest host Dennis James (one of only four episodes Barker missed) called the climber "Fritz," unaware that Barker's Beauty Janice Pennington's husband, Fritz Stammberger, had recently disappeared in a mountain-climbing accident. After the game's tiny climber fell victim to a contestant's lousy guesses, James yelled, "There goes Fritz!" Pennington fled backstage, where she cried through the rest of the taping. Stammberger was never seen again; he was declared legally dead in 1984.

• During a Showcase (the show's final round) in 2007, a contestant named José bid $250,000 on a selection of prizes clearly worth a fraction of that amount (the show never gives out anything that valuable). Barker persuaded José to lower his bid, and he did…to $60,000, which ended up still being roughly $40,000 too high.

• Contestant who holds the record for netting the most cash and prizes on the show: Vickyann Sadowski. In 2006 she walked away with $147,517 in winnings—including…a new car!

HARDWARE STORE ORIGINS

Why get started on that home-improvement project when you can procrastinate and read these?

CHAIN-LINK FENCING

Chain link is made of long strands of wire bent into a zigzag pattern and woven together like cloth. It was invented in 1844 by Charles Barnard, one of the owners of "Barnard, Bishop and Barnard," in Norwich, England. The company originally produced cloth, and Barnard developed a machine fashioned after a textile weaver to make the fencing. (He used steel wire—still the most common material for chain-link fencing.) It was first made in the United States in 1891 by the Anchor Fence Company of Daly City, California. Chain-link fencing is relatively inexpensive and easy to install, as well as very strong. You can tell by looking around any town, virtually anywhere in the entire world today, to see that it became one of the most popular types of fencing—if not *the* most popular—in history.

LAMINATE FLOORING

In 1979 Perstorp, a Swedish company that had been making laminated surfaces for counters and tabletops since the 1950s, released Perstorp Golv GL80, a type of relatively cheap but attractive laminate flooring. It was a breakthrough, because the flooring, which came in pieces that could be fitted together easily, could be installed by nonprofessionals. It started a do-it-yourself flooring craze in Sweden, and in the late 1980s did the same for the rest of Europe. In 1989 Perstorp Golv (*golv* is Swedish for "floor") was shortened to "Pergo." A few years later, Pergo flooring was released in the United States and then worldwide. Today laminate flooring is one of the most popular styles of flooring in the world, and Pergo is still the most popular brand—so much so that in America all laminate flooring, even if it's not made by Perstorp, is referred to as "pergo."

Nothing to cry about: Your eyes produce about a teaspoon of tears every hour.

EMERY BOARDS

People have been using materials like pumice stone to smooth their fingernails since at least the 1500s, but the modern emery board—a piece of cardboard with abrasive powder affixed to it—was patented by J. Parker Pray on June 3, 1883. (Emery is a kind of rock that, because of its extreme hardness, makes an excellent abrasive when crushed into powder. Its primary source: the Greek island of Naxos.) Pray, who ran the "Dr. J. Parker Pray Co. Manicure & Chiropodist Parlour" on East 23rd Street in New York City, was one of America's first manicurists.

ROTATING CASTERS

In the early 1870s, David A. Fisher Jr. noticed that workers in his Washington, D.C., furniture factory had a hard time safely moving large pieces of furniture around the shop. "Casters," wheels fixed to the bottom of furniture, had been around since the 1700s, but they were simply fixed wheels, meaning you could only roll in one direction. Result: Large pieces of furniture still had to be lifted to maneuver them through a crowded room. Inspired by his workers' complaints, Fisher developed a free-turning wheel that could rotate in all directions, so furniture could easily be moved around obstacles. He received a patent for the idea on March 14, 1876, and casters quickly made their way out of furniture shops and onto furniture in homes. ("Caster" derives from *cast*, an old term for "turn.")

TOILET TANK FLAPS

This, as you might guess, is our favorite. Joseph Bramah was a cabinet maker in London, England, in the 18th century. Always a tinkerer, in 1778 he decided that English "water closets" needed to be improved. The valve that controlled the water level in the tank was prone to freezing, so Bramah designed a simple hinged leather flap that sealed the hole in the bottom of the tank and could be easily pulled open with a chain when the water was needed for flushing. He patented the device in 1778 and began selling toilets equipped with his patented flaps out of his shop. They were a huge success. (Some of Bramah's originals can still be found in working order in the U.K. today.) And the "flap"—now made of plastic—remains a standard part of toilets around the world today.

ROAD TRIP!

The idea of Elizabeth Taylor, Michael Jackson, and Marlon Brando fleeing New York in a rental car after 9/11 and driving cross-country sounds absurd, but it was widely reported as fact after Taylor died in 2011. Unfortunately, when things sound too weird to be true ...they usually are. Here's the story (and the real story).

LAST TANGO IN NEW YORK

On September 7 and September 10, 2001, Michael Jackson played Madison Square Garden as part of a "30 Years in Show Business" celebration. He brought two of his close friends along to see the shows: screen legends Marlon Brando, who gave a speech praising Jackson's efforts to help the world's children at the first concert, and Elizabeth Taylor, who introduced Jackson at the second concert.

A day after the 9/11 attacks on the World Trade Center, Jackson reportedly received a call from a well-connected friend in Saudi Arabia telling him that that was just the beginning—New York would continue to be bombarded by terrorist assaults. Jackson believed his friend and sprang into action. Yelling down the hall of his hotel (he'd rented out the entire floor), he ordered everybody out, including his entire entourage and Brando.

Jackson then released his staff to find safety on their own. He and Brando, meanwhile, purportedly called Taylor, who was staying in a different hotel, and met up with her. That's when things got weird. For some reason, the trio believed that it wasn't America that was under attack—they thought that because they were internationally famous American icons, *they* were the targets.

KENTUCKY-FRIED 8

They hatched a plan to flee. They couldn't fly—all planes were grounded in the days after 9/11, and not even these three could get permission for a private jet—so they decided to escape New York in a rental car. The plan: drive directly to Jackson's home in Southern California. Three days later, they'd traveled 535 miles, as far as Ohio, and by that time, planes were flying again, so the road trip was called off. The lasting legacy, according to

---

It takes 6 months to produce an episode of *The Simpsons*. An episode of *South Park*: 5 days.

friends of Taylor: She and Jackson grew closer on the trip, bonding over their common irritation with Brando's insistence on stopping at nearly every KFC and Burger King they passed on the highway.

ON SECOND THOUGHT

After Elizabeth Taylor died in 2011, this road trip story was relayed by hundreds of magazines and blogs after first being shared by *Vanity Fair*. It sounded extremely far-fetched, but it seemed like it could have been true. After all, weird things can occur in the wake of a tragedy. But the fact of the matter is that the road trip didn't happen. Why? *Vanity Fair*'s sources for the story are highly suspect. While Taylor's loyal personal assistant of 25 years, Tim Mendelson, shared the story with *Vanity Fair*, it was first told in the 2004 edition of J. Randy Taraborrelli's book *Michael Jackson— The Magic and the Madness*. Taraborrelli was a close friend of Jackson's...as well as his personal, authorized biographer. He was charged with spreading stories, whether true or not, that made his client look good.

A HOLE-Y STORY

There are several other factors that cast doubt on the likelihood of the adventure. For one, Jackson, Taylor, and Brando weren't all that close. Brando didn't introduce Jackson at the Madison Square Garden for free; he was paid $1 million to do it. As for Taylor, she and Jackson *had* been friends for years, but they'd had a rift in the late 1990s, reportedly over Taylor's discomfort with Jackson's "sleep-overs" with children. Still, Jackson wanted her at the shows, so he gave her what she asked for: a $660,000 diamond necklace.

It also would have been difficult for Taylor to be in Ohio in the days after 9/11 because she was repeatedly spotted in New York City during the post-9/11 recovery effort. Several media reports and photographs count Taylor among the celebrities who reported to Ground Zero to help out and talk with first responders. As for Jackson, he was accounted for, too: He and his children stayed with friends for two weeks in Franklin Lakes, New Jersey. Then he chartered a flight home.

Tough, but dumb: South African giant bullfrogs occasionally attack lions.

STRANGE CELEBRITY LAWSUITS

Step 1: Get famous. Step 2: Get a lawyer.

THE PLAINTIFF: Richelle Olson, a charity organizer from Palmdale, California

THE DEFENDANT: Sacha Baron Cohen, star of the movies *Borat* and *Brüno*

THE LAWSUIT: In 2007 Cohen was filming *Brüno*, a mockumentary in which the British comic plays a gay Austrian fashion reporter and puts himself into real situations and interacts with real—and unwitting—people. Olson had never heard of Cohen or his alter-ego Brüno. She knew only that a celebrity was scheduled to call the numbers at a bingo game for the elderly she was organizing. Cohen, the celebrity bingo caller, arrived provocatively dressed as Brüno and "used profanity and sexual innuendo." Aghast, Olson tried to take away his microphone. Cohen, claimed Olson, fought her, and in the scuffle she fell on the floor and hit her head. Cohen's camera crew then attacked her "to intentionally create a dramatic emotional response," from which she suffered two "brain bleeds" and lost the ability to walk. She sought $25,000. After the defense showed video of the incident that proved neither Cohen nor his crew ever touched Olson, she changed her story to say that she had been "emotionally attacked," which is actually what caused her to fall and hit her head.

THE VERDICT: Judges don't like it when litigants change their story. Olson not only lost the case, she was ordered to pay Cohen's court costs, $17,000. The bingo scene was cut from the final film.

THE PLAINTIFF: 1980s New Wave band Devo

THE DEFENDANT: McDonald's restaurants

THE LAWSUIT: Who knew Devo's red "Energy Dome" hats were copyrighted? McDonald's apparently didn't...until the band tried to sue the company in 2008. Reason for the suit: Devo was upset about a Happy Meal toy that promoted Fox's *American Idol*. The toys included Disco Dave, Country Clay, Rockin' Riley, Soul-

---

Over 60% of all home computers are infected with malicious software, or "malware."

ful Selma, and the subject of this lawsuit, New Wave Nigel, who wears a Devo-style red hat that looks like a futuristic flower pot. According to Devo member Jerry Casale, "They didn't ask us for permission. Plus, we don't like McDonald's or *American Idol,* so we're doubly offended." He added that it's "ironic" that a giant corporation would use a hat that was designed to "mock industrial and consumer culture."

THE VERDICT: The suit was dropped…by Devo. In a 2009 interview, Casale said he wasn't allowed to talk about the case, but then added, "McDonald's was so frightening with the legal process that I realized how true power works: What they say goes."

THE PLAINTIFF: Lindsay Lohan, actress and former child star
THE DEFENDANT: E-Trade Financial Corp.
THE LAWSUIT: E-Trade's popular ad campaign features babies who talk like adults about how easy it is to trade stocks online. In its 2010 Super Bowl commercial, seen by 100 million people, a male baby is arguing with a female baby over another female baby named Lindsay, who is called a "milkaholic." The ad aired at a time when Lohan's struggles with substance abuse were well-covered in the tabloids. Lohan accused E-Trade of capitalizing on her "infamy" without her permission. Her lawyer said, "These babies weren't just cute babies but were actually portraying Lohan and her friends." An E-Trade official called the suit "without merit," adding that there are "a lot of people named Lindsay."

THE VERDICT: Despite what the company said, it was pretty obvious to all concerned that E-Trade was in fact referencing Lohan. The case was settled out of court, and although it wasn't reported how much Lohan received from E-Trade, her publicist said she was "very happy" with the amount.

*　　*　　*

4 REAL SCHOOL NAMES
Butts Road Primary School
Goodenough College
Universidad de Moron
Pansy Kidd Middle School

BATHROOM FINDS

If you're reading this in the bathroom right now, look carefully around the room. There may be something very valuable within reach, and we're not just talking about this fabulous book in your hands....

Found in the bathroom: A Chinese brush pot
what it was doing there: Holding toothbrushes
Story: Gordon Murray was a pretty savvy antiques collector. He'd started buying antiques as a boy in Aberdeen, Scotland, in the 1950s, and even owned his own shop. Still, even he slipped up now and again. For example, he ran across a small unremarkable Chinese brush pot, used by scribes to hold their writing implements. Not knowing what else to do with it, he put it in the bathroom and used it as a *tooth*brush holder, where it did service for years. In 2010 Murray decided to put some of his curio collection up for auction, and tossed his Chinese pot into the mix, figuring it was good for maybe a few hundred dollars. He was way off. Buyers kept bidding the price up...and up...and up. How much did Murray's antique toothbrush holder ultimately bring? £30,000 ($49,000).

Found in the bathroom: A diamond
What it was doing there: Hiding
Story: In 2007 guards at Theo Branch Jail in Orange, California, removed a drain screen in the prisoners' shower and found a 2-karat diamond. They weren't surprised: A prisoner told them they'd find it there. And the prisoner, Bret Langford, knew what he was talking about: He was in prison on suspicion of stealing it.

The story begins two years earlier. Langford matched the description of a guy who, according to the owner of a mall jewelry store, strolled into his store and grabbed the $25,000 diamond, then dashed out. When police searched Langford's car, they discovered the diamond's certificate of authenticity stuffed inside the gas tank flap. They assumed they'd find the diamond, too—maybe in the gas tank—but the search revealed nothing. It turned out that when the cops pulled him over, Langford had swallowed the diamond, and after he was taken to jail, he regurgitated it. During the following 10 months, he'd played a cat-and-mouth game,

---

Scientists have discovered how to make diamonds out of tequila.

keeping the diamond tucked in the layers of his prison wristband and swallowing it whenever he knew he was going to be searched. One day, however, as Langford was preparing for a shower, guards staged a surprise inspection, allowing him just enough time to toss the gem into a shower stall, where it rolled right into the drain.

As with many things in a prison, the drain was very securely attached to the floor, and after 14 months Langford realized he'd never be able to retrieve the diamond. But maybe he could use it to make a deal for a lesser penalty in his upcoming trial and avoid a "Three Strikes" sentence of 25 years to life for his third conviction. (At 18, he'd been convicted of stealing $250,000 worth of gold from the dental supply house he worked for; not long after that, he was convicted of domestic violence.)

Langford, now offering his services to the government, claimed that the owner of the jewelry shop owed him $75,000 and that he'd taken the loose diamond as partial payment. When the store's video-surveillance footage didn't support the police's grab-and-dash scenario, the district attorney cut a deal: Tell them where to find the diamond and get a reduction on the charges. Langford sang, the jeweler got his diamond back, and the judge sentenced Langford to time already served.

Found in the bathroom: A very rare book
What it was doing there: Bathroom reading
Story: In 1859 naturalist Charles Darwin published his ground-breaking On the Origin of Species after decades of observation and reflection on the process of evolution and natural selection. His publisher, John Murray III, cautiously printed only 1,250 copies. Although understandable, considering that the cover price was 15 shillings (the equivalent of $83 in today's money), his reticence was unwarranted: Buyers depleted the publisher's entire stock within a few days. Fast-forward to 2009. A man, fresh from a com-memorative exhibit of the book's 150th anniversary, stepped into his father-in-law's bathroom and perused a shelf stocked with an assortment of bathroom reading. His heart nearly stopped when he saw a familiar cover and discovered that his wife's dad owned one of Darwin's first editions. He asked how his father-in-law had got-ten it and why it was in the loo. The man shrugged, saying he bought it for a few shillings in a rural used bookstore back in the

Lichens are actually two living creatures in one: a green plant and a fungus.

1950s. They immediately took it to Christie's auction house, and were stunned to find out that the few shillings purchase was now worth "maybe as much as 60,000 pounds" (about $100,000). But even the experts at Christie's were stunned when the bathroom book brought in nearly twice that. (One more surprise: The word "evolution" never appears in the first edition. Darwin didn't use the term until he revised the text for its sixth printing, in 1872.)

Found in the bathroom: $182,000 in Depression-era currency
What it was doing there: Being stored for safekeeping.
Story: Finding treasures in the bathroom doesn't always work out well. Take the case of contractor Bob Kitts and his former class-mate, Amanda Reece. In 2006 Reece hired Kitts to remodel a bathroom in her 83-year-old house near Cleveland, Ohio. While Kitts was ripping out the old walls, he discovered two lockboxes filled with envelopes of cash—$135,000 in one, $22,000 in the other—hidden behind the medicine cabinet. Two days later, he found a cardboard box with $25,000 in the wall behind the bath-tub. He immediately called Reece and after a giddy interval of unwrapping and counting bills, things quickly soured between the two. She offered to Kitts 10 percent of the money; he wanted 40 percent. She refused, so he went to a lawyer, who told him that the law favored him. Then things got worse. The story was picked up by the *Cleveland Plain Dealer*, and descendants of Patrick Dunne, the man who had owned the house until his death, saw it. They noted that the envelopes were labeled "The P. Dunne News Agency" and sued Reece for the money. Too late: By the time the case got to court, the money had dwindled dramatically. Reece testified that she'd spent around $25,000 on herself and $14,000 on a trip to Hawaii with her mother, sold $54,600 of the rare bills to a coin dealer, and lost $60,000. (She claimed it was stolen from her closet.) What was left? $25,230. The court ruled that 86.3% of it should go to Patrick Dunne's 21 heirs and the rest should go to Kitts. In the aftermath, Reece lost the home in foreclosure and filed for bankruptcy. And Kitts, who had to split his share of the money with his lawyer, ended up with only $2,700 and com-plained that he'd lost business because he had been portrayed as a greedy "bad guy" in news reports.

ROBOTS IN THE NEWS

Robots are getting smarter and more advanced every day. Familiarize yourself with these recent developments, puny human.

CASHIER-BOT

Since the 1980s, UPC codes and cash register scanners have automated most of the checkout process. So why not replace the cashier with a robot? In 2011 a Stanford University team unveiled PR2 (for "Personal Robot 2"), a robot that can scan and bag groceries. It uses a high-speed articulated hand to pick up and rotate each item until it finds and carefully scans the barcode. A computer then looks up the pricing data and the PR2 tosses the item into a sack. (The Stanford team is still working on the robot's bagging skills.)

BABBLE-BOT

In May 2011, Scientists at the University of Queensland in Australia gave robots one of the tools they need to become sentient: They taught them how to develop their own language, independent of what they are programmed to know by humans. The "lingodroids" wander around a room and make up words for things, then relay that information to other lingodroids. Choosing from a set of programmed syllables, such as "ku," "rey," "za," and "la," a robot that finds itself in an unfamiliar area will pick an unused syllable combination, then point to the place and say the word to the other robots. Then the information is reinforced with games. For example, one robot will say "ku-zo," then two other robots will race to where they think "ku-zo" is. At that point, all three robots have learned a new word they made up themselves.

DISMEM-BOT

If giving robots the ability to speak without humans knowing what they're talking about sounds scary, it's nothing compared to the robot that's outfitted with so many motors and sharp knives that it can completely debone a chicken in 2.5 seconds. The Japanese-built Mayekawa Automatic Chicken Deboner butchers 1,500 birds in an hour and costs $560,000. (It's for commercial processing plants, not home cooks.) Another feature: It accounts for variations from chicken to chicken—in milliseconds. It photo-scans each one, then processes the data and adjust its blades slightly to realign the depth and location of each cut. Then it grabs hold of the chicken's wings and rips the meat off of the rib cage.

BUM-BOT

British artist Tim Pryde designed a robot that solicits donations for charity. It's name: DON-8r. (Get it?) A waist-high, white, pod-shaped droid that resembles EVE from *Wall-E*, DON-8r detects when humans are nearby, and then calls out to them in a traditionally mechanical "robot" voice to ask for money. If the human obliges and inserts a few coins into DON-8r's donation slot, it leaves them alone and retreats…a few feet, then returns to ask for more.

NURSE-BOT

For the past decade or so, robots have played an increasing role in healthcare, be it robotic cameras that explore inside the human body or robotic arms that assist in surgery. But what about nursing? Researchers at Georgia Tech were curious to know whether people are ready for a robot to do the job that's usually done by a nurturing human. So they did a study. A nurse-robot named Cody would touch a human subject on the arm. Intent seemed to matter most: If told Cody was *cleaning* their arm, the test subjects reacted favorably. If told Cody was attempting to comfort them, the subjects responded negatively.

PIRATE-BOT

After the wave of pirate attacks off the coast of Africa, an American company called Recon Robotics is developing a remote-controlled robot that can help rescue trapped ships and hostages. About the size of a soda can, the ship-boarding bot is fired from a distance (out of a cannon) and attaches itself to the enemy ship's hull with magnetic wheels. Then it "walks" up and over the side of the ship. Once on board, it sends video images back to the controller. Recon is working in cooperation with the U.S. Navy. They want to keep the anti-pirate robot out of the private sector so it doesn't fall into the hands of the wrong people…specifically, real pirates who would use it to raid other ships.

EDIFICE COMPLEX

*Think the old woman who lived in a shoe had weird taste
in housing? It turns out she was just ahead of her time.
Buildings can look like all sorts of things. Even...*

AN IGLOO

Crouched on the Parks Highway about 180 miles outside of Anchorage, Alaska, is a hulking four-story igloo. Its dome can be spotted from an airplane flying at 30,000 feet. Built in the 1970s, the igloo was meant to give tourists a chance to visit a "real" Alaskan igloo. Igloo City, as it's known, has been a convenience store, a gas station, a makeshift triage clinic for a man attacked by a grizzly bear, and an emergency airplane refueling stop (a small plane once landed on the highway and taxied in for gas). But other than part of the ground floor, the igloo itself has never been used. It was supposed to be a motel, but the couple who built it forgot something important: building codes. The structure never passed inspection, and its owners went broke.

...THE WORLD'S LARGEST CHEST

In the 1920s, the High Point, North Carolina, Chamber of Commerce built its first building-sized chest of drawers. Twenty feet tall, the giant chest served as the chamber's Bureau of Information and helped to promote the city's image as the "Furniture Capital of the World." In 1996 the chest was augmented, making it 38 feet tall. In 2010, upset with the city's refusal to help with the upkeep of the landmark, Pam Stern, the building's owner, had the chest measured for a giant bra: 20 feet of silk, spandex, and underwiring. (Get it? A *chest* of drawers.) HanesBrands Inc., maker of Playtex bras, sent engineers over to take the chest's measurements. Whether the city will permit the chest to wear the bra remains unknown at this time.

...A CHICKEN

A 56-foot-tall chicken head juts from the roof of the Kentucky Fried Chicken at the corner of Roswell Street and Cobb Parkway in Marietta, Georgia. Locals use it as a landmark when giving directions: "Turn right, after you pass the Big Chicken." The

---

What were Chewco, Obi-1 Holdings, and Kenobe? The names of Enron subsidiaries.

architectural whimsy, built in 1963, was a Johnny Reb's Chick, Chuck and Shakes fried-chicken restaurant until 1966, when the owner, Tubby Davis, sold it to his brother, who turned it into a KFC. In 1993 the chicken suffered wind damage and might have been demolished were it not considered too important to be axed. Reason: Pilots use the building as a reference point when approaching Atlanta and nearby Dobbins Air Reserve Base.

...A NAUTILUS SHELL

In 2006 a young family in Mexico City decided to ditch their conventional home and build one more in harmony with nature. From above, their new house looks like the perfect spiral of a nautilus shell. From the front lawn, it looks like a soft-serve ice cream sundae. The frame for the building consists of steel-reinforced chicken wire that's covered in a two-inch layer of stucco, inside and out. Stained-glass bubbles in the walls sparkle like sunlight on water. A stone walkway spirals from room to room on a bed of live plants, creating the sensation of floating above the ocean floor. The bathroom's sandy walls and blue tiles offer users the illusion of being underwater. Family memebers say the Nautilus House makes them feel "like a mollusk in its shell, moving from one chamber to another."

...MR. ROBOTO

In 1986 Thai architect Sumet Jumsai designed the new Bank of Asia in Bangkok to reflect the computerization of banking going on at the time. Result: The $10 million, 20-story building looks like a giant LEGO robot. The "robot" has two antennae that serve as lightning rods, and glass eyes with louvered metallic lids that serve as windows. Jumsai wanted the building to "free the spirit from the present architectural intellectual impasse and propel it forward into the next century." The inspiration for what has been called a post-high-tech marvel? His son's toy robot.

...AN EGG

The owner of a European ad agency wanted to add an office next to her lakeside house in Belgium, and hired the design firm dmvA to come up with something organic-looking that could be built without cutting down a single tree. Local authorities refused to issue a building permit because city council members thought the design was too weird: The building—nicknamed "the blob"—looked like a giant white egg. To get around the council, the designer turned the egg into a mobile unit so it would qualify as a work of art, not a building. The structure consists of a wooden frame with a polyester skin and an ultra-modern grid of niches molded into the interior for storage. The interior features lighting, a sleeping shelf, a kitchen, and a bathroom. The pointy end of the egg (the egg is on its side) opens up to create a porch. After the project, known as the Blob VB3, was completed, the unique structure appeared in a Belgian newspaper under the heading "Art skirts building regulations." The next day, someone at the building council showed up to warn the owner that if the egg was placed near the house, there would be consequences. Dubbed the "rovin' ovum" by its fans, the Blob VB3 went on the auction block in 2010. (No word as to whether anyone had the huevos to buy it.)

...A HOUSE ON STILTS

Architect Terunobu Fujimori has a weird way of getting approval for his unique designs. He invites clients to join him in his tiny *Takasugi-an*—his "Too-High Teahouse." Perched 20 feet in the air, the 30-square-foot private teahouse in Chino, Japan, balances on two forked tree trunks that resemble spindly chicken legs. Once clients have climbed the ladders to the house, he shows them his hand-drawn plans. "If they don't like my design, I shake the building!" he says with a laugh.

...A PEACH

The 150-foot-tall water tower outside Gaffney, South Carolina, was built to catch the eye of motorists speeding along I-85. It looks like a gigantic peach. In 1981, when the tower went up, the local economy depended on peach orchards. Townspeople wanted it known that Cherokee County, where Gaffney is located, grew more peaches per year than the whole state of Georgia (the "Peach State"). Macro-artist Peter Freudenberg studied local peaches for many hours and used 50 gallons of paint in 20 different colors to make the peach hyper-realistic. Features include a 7-ton, 60-foot-long leaf, and an enormous vertical cleft in its backside, leading to the nickname "Moon Over Gaffney."

Flying aces: Some species of mosquito are such skilled fliers that they can dodge raindrops.

FAILED AMENDMENTS

It's very difficult to amend the U.S. Constitution. A potential amendment has to pass both houses of Congress with two-thirds approval, and then it has to be approved by the legislatures of three-fourths of the states. Since 1787, only 27 amendments have been adopted. Numerous others have been proposed...and rejected. Here are some notable rejects.

NO FUNDS FOR CHURCHES
In 1875 President Ulysses S. Grant gave a speech endorsing the use of federal funds to establish public schools nationwide. Maine congressman James Blaine agreed with Grant, but not because he supported public education. He was against parochial schools—Catholic schools (and anything Catholic) in particular. This came on the tail of a large influx of immigrants from Ireland and Italy, two predominantly Catholic countries, and anti-Catholic sentiment in the U.S. was high. That same year, Blaine introduced a constitutional ban on the use of public funds for religious-based organizations. While that may sound like part of the debate over the separation of church and state, Blaine's real goal was to prevent the Catholic Church from getting any tax money. (Ironically, Blaine actively sought the Catholic vote in his 1884 run for President of the United States, which he lost.)

NO INTERRACIAL MARRIAGE
Like many Americans in the early 1900s, Georgia representative Seaborn Roddenberry felt very strongly about racial integration—he was the leading Congressional advocate for segregation. After African-American boxer Jack Johnson married a white woman in 1912, a public scandal, Roddenberry introduced the Anti-Miscegenation Amendment, which would have made interracial marriage a federal crime.

NO PRESIDENTIAL TERM LIMITS
Franklin Roosevelt was elected to four presidential terms—the Constitution set no limit on the number of terms a president could serve. Prior to that, all presidents had retired after two, a tradition started by George Washington. But Roosevelt and his

sweeping program of social welfare were so hated by his Republican opposition that after he died in 1945 and Republicans gained control of Congress in 1947, they passed the 22nd Amendment, limiting the president to two terms. Since 1989, a repeal of that amendment has been proposed several times by members of Congress from both parties, as a way to continue the administrations of popular presidents.

NO AUTOMATIC CITIZENSHIP
It's set forth in the early pages of the Constitution that anyone born within the borders of the United States is automatically a United States citizen—even if they are the child of illegal immigrants. In 2003 Florida Congressman Mark Foley proposed an amendment to the Constitution that would remove that stipulation. It died in committee. (Foley's career died after he was accused of having sent sexually explicit instant messages to Congressional pages.)

FEWER RESTRICTIONS TO THE PRESIDENCY
The Constitution forbids foreign-born U.S. citizens from becoming president. This was to prevent anyone from the British empire from ever seizing control of the United States. In 2003 Utah Senator Orrin Hatch proposed the Equal Opportunity to Govern Amendment, which would have allowed any naturalized (foreign-born) American who'd been a legal citizen of the United States for at least 20 years to be president. It was widely seen as a way to eliminate roadblocks for California governor Arnold Schwarzenegger (who was born in Austria) in case he ever wanted to run for the country's highest office.

NO FLAG BURNING
The Flag Desecration Amendment has popped up for votes frequently since 1968. It would give Congress authority to make it illegal to burn the American flag, an act currently protected as free speech under the First Amendment. Between 1995 and 2005, six different versions of the amendment were passed by the House of Representatives, but it couldn't clear the Senate. In June 2006, the Senate voted 66–34 in favor of it…just one vote short of the two-thirds majority it needed to go on to ratification by the states.

Earth orbits the sun at a speed of about 1,000 miles per minute.

THE BIG CHALLENGE

*Staging public "challenges" as a way to get relatively inexpensive
advertising for your product is an old marketing technique.
But now that we've entered the Internet age, some of
those challenges have gotten pretty interesting.*

PWN2OWN

Background: Every year since 1999, online security experts in Canada have hosted a conference in Vancouver, British Columbia, called CanSecWest. In 2007 they decided to add a little excitement.

The Big Challenge: Organizers offered a $10,000 prize to the first person who could remotely hack their way into an "unhackable" MacBook Pro laptop computer. They called the challenge Pwn2Own ("pwn" is Internet jargon for "to dominate.") The winner would get the hacked computer (worth $2,000), as well as the cash prize.

Result: On day two of the conference, hacker Shane Macaulay sent the computer an e-mail containing a website address. Per contest rules, the CanSecWest organizer using the MacBook had to open the e-mail and go to the website. It appeared to be blank—but it had been created by Macaulay's friend and fellow hacker Dino Dai Zovi, and it contained *malware*, a malicious program designed by Dai Zovi to infect a Mac through its Internet browser. Moments later, Macaulay had complete access to all the data on the MacBook—and the contest was over. Macaulay got the laptop; Zovi got the $10,000. (Pwn2Own has been a part of CanSecWest every year since then. Prize money for the 2011 event: $125,000.)

VANISH!

Background: Evan Ratliff is a writer for the technology magazine *Wired*, and in 2009 he wrote about how easy it is to locate people in the digital age. Credit cards, cell phones, and Internet use make it surprisingly simple to find out exactly where a person is, in ways that just weren't possible in the past. The story inspired Ratliff to try to disappear, for just one month.

The Big Challenge: On August 15, *Wired* announced the "Vanish!" challenge. Ratliff was traveling around the country, they said, and whoever could find him—and snap a photo of him—would win $5,000. (They also had to say the codeword "fluke" to Ratliff to get him to admit who he was.) Every day, *Wired* put clues to Ratliff's whereabouts on their website, including information on his credit card use and IP addresses for computers he used.

Result: Thousands of people took the challenge. One, Jeff Reifman, founder of an online technology company, used the clues to find an anonymous account Ratliff had opened on Twitter, and by reading Ratliff's comments made an educated guess that he was headed to a book reading in New Orleans—not far from a pizza place called Naked Pizza. Reifman called Naked Pizza, and owner Jeff Leach agreed to help. On September 5, Leach went to the bookstore—and waited. Sure enough, he spotted Ratliff. Leach walked up to him, said, "You wouldn't happen to know a guy named Fluke, would you?" and then snapped a picture of him. Ratliff was caught, and the contest was over. Reifman and Leach shared the $5,000 prize.

LIVE OFF GROUPON

Background: Groupon, short for "group coupon," is an online company that offers daily deals to its subscribers around the world. Here's how it works: Groupon will negotiate a deal with a company, say, a wine shop in Buffalo, New York, to make one of their items half-off. If enough of Groupon's subscribers sign up to buy a coupon for the deal, it takes effect. Groupon then splits whatever money it takes in with the store. (If not enough people sign up, the deal is simply off.) Groupon deals cover a huge variety of items, including food, clothing, electronics, even dance lessons, and they have been an enormous success: They reportedly turned down a $6 billion offer to be bought by Google in 2010.

The Big Challenge: In 2010 Groupon founder and CEO Andrew Mason came up with the idea of offering a prize to anyone who could travel the country for one year living off Groupon coupons —but no cash, checks, or credit cards whatsoever. (The coupons could be used for what they were intended, or they could be traded for other things.) That February they held a contest in which people had to create a YouTube video explaining why they deserved to be the one to try the challenge. In May 27-year-old Josh Stevens of Chicago was declared the winner. Prize: If he could make it to May 2011 living only on Groupon coupons, he'd win $100,000.

Result: Stevens made it. Over the year, he traveled to 50 cities, including New York, Minneapolis, Denver, Detroit, San Francisco—he even flew to London. He rode stock cars in Virginia, took singing lessons in Nashville, took a cooking class in Las Vegas, rode in a hot-air balloon in Kentucky, went sea kayaking in California, and a lot more—and never spent a cent of "real" money. He did it all on Groupon coupons. And at the end of the year, he was handed a check for $100,000. (When asked on the *Today* show why he did it, Stevens answered, "Why not?")

*   *   *

WEIRD NEWS

• Brookfield, Connecticut, high-school teacher Robert Wollkind was placed on administrative leave in 2010 after making what was deemed an insulting comment to a student who had failed to bring his homework to class. In front of the entire class, Wollkind asked the student, who was overweight, if he had eaten it. Wollkind, 68 and in his 32nd year of teaching, retired soon after.

• In May 2010, an off-duty Ryanair pilot named James Sweetnam crashed his sportscar into a brick wall while driving in the English countryside. He refused to submit to a blood-alcohol test until three hours after the crash, at which point he still tested over the legal limit and was arrested for drunk driving. Because this was his second conviction, Sweetnam got a 12-month jail sentence (suspended) and was banned from driving until 2014. Banned from *driving*, but apparently not from *flying*: "He has since left Ryanair and is expecting to soon take a co-pilot's job with Emirates Airline," the *Leicester Mercury* newspaper reported in 2011.

Gnome recognition: German potter Philip Griebel invented garden gnomes in the mid-1800s.

UNEXPECTED ENCOUNTERS

The photo of Elvis Presley's 1970 meeting with President Richard Nixon is the National Archives' most-requested item—it's more popular than the U.S. Constitution or the Bill of Rights. Here are some more odd encounters.

ANNIE OAKLEY MEETS KAISER WILHELM

In 1889 famed American sharpshooter Oakley was touring Europe with Buffalo Bill's Wild West Show. That November, the revue stopped in Berlin for a sold-out performance at the city's Charlottenburg Race Course. As part of her act, Oakley would tell the crowd that she was going to attempt to shoot the ashes off of a lit cigar. She'd then joke, "Who will volunteer to hold the cigar?" The line always got a laugh, but rarely a volunteer. (Oakley's husband, Frank Butler, would then step up to the task.) On that day, however, the audience was aghast when Germany's emperor, Kaiser Wilhelm II, stood up to offer his services. The brash Wilhelm, who'd been on the throne barely a year, waved away the police who tried to stop him, then took a cigar from a gold case in his pocket, and lit it. Oakley's pride apparently outweighed the consequences of accidentally blowing off the head of a head of state. She paced off 10 large steps, drew her Colt .45 from its holster, and took aim. And then, much to the delight (and relief) of the audience, Oakley shot the ashes from the young monarch's cigar. (It's been speculated that, had she missed the cigar and hit the Kaiser instead, she might have prevented World War I.)

JANIS JOPLIN MEETS WILLIAM BENNETT

In early 1967, two decades before he was America's first drug czar and the architect of Nancy Reagan's "Just Say No" anti-drug campaign, Bennett was a graduate student studying philosophy at the University of Texas. He was also an active Vietnam War protestor and the guitarist in a local band called Plato and the Guardians. Janis Joplin was an up-and-coming blues rock singer from Port Arthur, Texas, who was singing in clubs around Austin, home of the University of Texas. Mutual friends thought the two would hit it off and set them up on a blind date. After spending a couple of hours eating barbecue and staring up at the big Texas sky, Joplin and Bennett found they did have a lot in common—an affinity for rock 'n' roll, an opposition to America's involvement in Vietnam War, and the same taste in beer. What they didn't have was romantic chemistry. "Let me put it this way," Bennett said years later, "we were both disappointed." Later that year Joplin hit it big with her band, Big Brother and the Holding Company, and became one of rock's biggest stars. A hard-partying lifestyle and heroin addiction led to her death by drug overdose in 1970, at age 27. Bennett became increasingly conservative. Following his stint in the Reagan administration, he penned *The Book of Virtues* and several other books that advocated for self-discipline and family values.

NIKOLA TESLA MEETS MARK TWAIN

Growing up in in the 1860s in what is now Croatia, Tesla was a sickly child prone to all manner of unidentified illness. Doctors had given up on him. One day while Tesla was bedridden, someone gave the sick boy an anthology of Mark Twain's short stories. Tesla later said that it was "so captivating as to make me utterly forget my hopeless state" and credited the writer with what was considered a miraculous recovery. Tesla went on to pioneer electrical engineering and lay the groundwork for modern-day electricity, including alternating current (AC). In 1888 the two men met for the first time. Tesla told Twain how his stories had saved him as a child and "was amazed to see the great man of laughter burst into tears." They became friends and Twain—an enthusiastic supporter of science—often spent time with Tesla in his New York laboratory.

*　　*　　*

PEERLESS

In 2011 Elena Kagan was called in for jury duty in Washington, D.C. She dutifully showed up at court and sat with the other prospective jurors, but ultimately wasn't chosen to sit. She then returned to her day job…as an associate justice on the U.S. Supreme Court.

Tlacatlaolli was an Aztec stew made of corn and human flesh.

HUT, HUT, HIKE, EH?

*If you're American, you'll find these Canadian football rules
strange…and strangely familiar. If you're Canadian, you
may also learn a thing or two about "the other NFL."*

BACKGROUND

The National Football League is the only one of the "Big
4" American sports leagues that doesn't have any teams in
Canada. That's because Canada has its own football tradition,
with its own league and its own rules.

In the 1860s, an army garrison from Great Britain, which still
controlled Canada, introduced American football to rugby players
at Montreal's McGill University. They'd picked it up in the United States, where the game's popularity was beginning to grow at
northeastern colleges, such as Yale and Princeton. By the 1920s,
both sports—rugby and American football—were being played by
the same groups of people at Canadian colleges. From those two
football games a new, third style of football developed: Canadian
football, which combined the fast-paced, pass-and-kick style of
rugby with many of the rules and structure of American football.
It eventually replaced professional Canadian rugby altogether.

An official pro league—the Canadian Football League—was
formed in 1958. Initially, there were eight teams in the league, but
most of them were far older than the sport of Canadian football.
For example, two current CFL teams, the Hamilton Tiger-Cats
and the Winnipeg Blue Bombers, were founded as rugby teams
around 1870. Today, Canadian football is the second-most-popular
spectator sport in Canada (behind hockey). It's played throughout
the country—but only in that country—at youth, high school,
senior, and semi-pro levels to boot.

THE RULES

If you watched a Canadian football game and knew nothing about
it, it would look fairly similar to an American football game…but
just slightly off. For example:

• **The field.** The playing field in the CFL is bigger. An NFL field
is 100 yards long and 53 yards wide, while in the CFL it's 110

NFL stars who played in the CFL: Doug Flutie, Ricky Williams, and Joe Theismann.

yards long and 65 yards wide, making for a looser style of play with more throwing of the ball than handoffs. The goalposts are in a different place as well. In the NFL, the "uprights" are placed at the back of the end zones, while in the CFL they're right on the goal line.

• **Players.** CFL teams get one more player than NFL teams: 12 vs. 11. The extra man is usually employed as a backfielder. On offense, Canadian teams employ two *slotbacks*, instead of one tight end as Americans do. On defense, the formation includes two halfbacks and one safety, instead of the single American safety.

• **The line of scrimmage.** In the NFL, the offensive and defensive lines line up just 11 inches apart from each other—the length of the football. In Canada, a full yard is mandated, which means that more teams take a risk on the last down.

• **Downs.** Canadian football uses three downs, not four. And the amount of time allotted for a play is just 20 seconds, half of what the NFL allows. Combined with the three downs, it makes for a faster-paced game.

• **Scoring.** Scoring in the CFL is the same as in American football, with the exception of the "rouge point." One point is awarded to the kicking team when they miss a field goal or punt the football and the receiving team opts to take a knee rather than attempt to run it down the field. A rouge point is also awarded if the ball goes out of bounds in the end zone during a kick.

MONEY

In the 1950s and early '60s, the NFL and CFL were pretty much on par financially. That's because the main source of revenue was admission to games. TV changed all that. The NFL now has multibillion-dollar deals to air its games. Canada, with about one-tenth the population of the United States, has fewer TV outlets, which means less TV revenue. And that affects player salaries: The average NFL player makes about $1.1 million a year. The average CFL player makes about $50,000, and many have to get off-season jobs to make ends meet. The highest-paid CFL player ever: Rocket Ismail. In 1991 the Toronto Argonauts drafted the Notre Dame star and offered him $18.2 million for four seasons, more than any player had ever been offered in CFL *or* NFL history to that point. (The Argonauts got around the $3.8 million salary cap by using a "marquee player" exemption loophole. They also got a huge cash

Long distance: The first telephone answering machine was 3 feet tall.

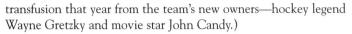

transfusion that year from the team's new owners—hockey legend Wayne Gretzky and movie star John Candy.)

Huge TV revenues led the CFL to try to expand into the United States in 1993, with the addition of the Sacramento Gold Miners. They added more teams the following year—in football-friendly cities that had no NFL team, such as Birmingham, Baltimore, Las Vegas, Memphis, Miami, and Shreveport—but getting Americans interested turned out to be an uphill battle because the CFL was essentially introducing them to a new sport. The Baltimore Stallions went to the Grey Cup championship finals in 1994 and won the cup in 1995. Nevertheless, all American teams were shuttered that year, thanks to poor attendance and no TV contract.

OTHER QUIRKS

• More games. The CFL's regular season is 18 games vs. the NFL's 16. The season runs from June to November (in America it runs from September to February). And since there are only eight teams in the CFL, each team plays all the others at least twice.

• NFL games are almost all played on Sunday. In Canada, they're played throughout the week but primarily on Friday, Saturday, and Sunday. And just as Thanksgiving in the U.S. features a double-feature of televised football games, Labor Day in Canada offers football on TV all day.

• In the NFL, cheerleaders are hired individually by each team, which controls budgets and public appearances. In the CFL, the cheerleaders are employees of a separate umbrella organization: Canadian Football League Cheerleading.

• Only player in both the Canadian Football Hall of Fame and the American Pro Football Hall of Fame: Warren Moon, quarterback of the Edmonton Eskimos from 1978 to '83 and then an NFL star (primarily with the Houston Oilers) from 1984 to 2000.

• Jackie Robinson, the first black player in Major League Baseball, had played for the minor league Montreal Royals in the mid-1940s, and he was accepted and well liked there. Believing that the city—and football—was ready for black players, in 1946 Montreal Alouettes boss Lew Hayman hired Herb Trawick. The NFL didn't draft any black players until 1949.

THEY WENT THATAWAY

Some famous people aren't just remarkable for how they lived,
but also for how they died. Take these folks, for example.

K ING ALEXANDER OF GREECE (1893–1920)
Claim to Fame: Alexander reigned from 1917 to 1920. He
was a first cousin of Prince Philip of England.

Cause of Death: Killed by monkeys

Details: On October 2, 1920, the king was walking his dog
through the Royal Garden in Athens—now called the National
Garden—when one of the monkeys that lived there attacked the
dog. (Some sources claim it was the dog that attacked the monkey.) When Alexander tried to separate them with a stick, a second monkey came to the defense of the first, and the king was
badly bitten by both. He died from his wounds three weeks later.

Note: Alexander became king during World War I after his father,
King Constantine I, was forced off the throne because of his pro-
German sympathies. After Alexander's death, Constantine
returned to the throne, making Alexander a rare example of a
king who succeeded his father and was succeeded by him as well.
Constantine abdicated a second time in 1922, this time for good.

JOHN A. ROEBLING (1806–69)

Claim to Fame: The engineer who designed the Brooklyn Bridge

Cause of Death: Killed by the Brooklyn Bridge

Details: On June 28, 1869, Roebling was standing on a dock sur-
veying the location of the tower on the Brooklyn side. When an
approaching ferry pressed up against the dock, Roebling got his
right foot caught between the boat and the dock and his toes were
badly crushed. They were amputated later that same day. Roebling
refused further medical treatment, perhaps contributing to his
developing *tetanus*, a disease caused when a wound is infected by a
strain of bacteria commonly found in dirt. Tetanus can be fatal,
and in Roebling's case, it was. After a week of suffering terrible
seizures, he died on July 22.

Note: Roebling's son Washington, who took over supervision of

Jack Haley, who played the Tin Man in The Wizard of Oz (1939) and famously...

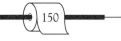

the project after his father's death, was nearly killed by the Brooklyn Bridge as well. Long hours spent in *caissons*, the pressurized underwater chambers used to construct the bridge's foundation, left him severely disabled by decompression sickness, more commonly known as "the bends." For the remaining decade that it took to finish the bridge, he supervised the project from his house via intermediaries, rarely returned to the job site, and did not attend the bridge's opening in 1883.

MARCUS GARVEY (1887–1940)

Claim to Fame: Leader of a New York-based "Back-to-Africa" movement in the 1910s and 1920s

Cause of Death: Killed by his own obituary

Details: Garvey, who was born in Jamaica, believed that people of African descent would never win equal rights in majority-white countries and felt it made more sense for them to return to Africa. His views made him a controversial figure even within the African-American community. By 1940 he had long since been deported from the United States as an "undesirable alien" and was living in London. After he suffered a stroke that January, some newspapers mistakenly reported that he'd died, prompting one prominent African-American newspaper, the *Chicago Defender,* to run a full, and very unflattering, obituary. On May 18, Garvey read it and was so upset by its negative tone that he suffered a second stroke and died three weeks later, on June 10, 1940.

JASPER NEWTON "JACK" DANIEL (1846–1911)

Claim to Fame: The distiller who created Jack Daniel's Whiskey

Cause of Death: An unsafe safe

Details: Daniel had a terrible time remembering the combination to his office safe (no word on whether whiskey was a factor), and it was usually his nephew's job to open it. One morning, however, Daniel came in to work early and his nephew wasn't there. Daniel tried to open the safe himself and got so frustrated in the attempt that he kicked it, striking it so hard that he broke his toe. The toe became infected, and he developed *septicemia*, or blood poisoning, which killed him on October 10, 1911. Daniel's last words (according to the distillery): "One last drink, please."

MIKE EDWARDS (1948–2010)

Claim to Fame: Cellist and founding member of the rock group Electric Light Orchestra. Edwards was with ELO from 1972 to 1975.

Caused of Death: Killed by a bale of hay

Details: In the United States, bales of hay are often rectangular in shape and don't weigh much more than 100 pounds. In the United Kingdom, the bales are wheel-shaped and can weigh more than 1,300 pounds. In September 2010, Edwards happened to be driving past a farm in Devon, in Southwest England, when a farmer lost control of just such a bale. It rolled down a slope, bounced over a 15-foot hedge, and demolished the cab of the van Edwards was driving, killing him instantly.

MATTHEW VASSAR (1792–1868)

Claim to Fame: A wealthy brewer, in 1861 Vassar donated $408,000 and 200 acres of land to found a college for women in Poughkeepsie, New York. Thanks to his generosity, Vassar College was the first such institution that was comparable to men's colleges in terms of funding and equipment.

Cause of Death: Dropped dead while delivering his farewell speech

Details: Vassar turned 76 in 1868, the year he decided to step back from his close involvement in the college. On June 23, 1868, he made his final speech to the board of trustees. One topic he planned to cover: his gratitude that none of the students or faculty had become ill or died during the school's first three years of instruction. According to the minutes of the meeting, Vassar was eleven pages into the speech "when he failed to pronounce a word which was upon his lips, dropped the papers in his hand, fell back in his chair insensible, and died at precisely ten minutes to 12 o'clock p.m. by the clock in the College Tower." After a prayer, the trustees adjourned until 3:00 p.m. and then reassembled to listen to a trustee finish reading the speech.

*   *   *

Movie Fact: Highest-grossing movie about Twins: *Twins* (1988).

The tuatara, a lizard native to New Zealand, has a third eye on the top of its head.

KINGS, SIZED

*Here's the long and short (and wide) of some of
the world's most powerful monarchs.*

NOT SHORT ENOUGH

It's no surprise that Charles VIII of France was short when he became king in 1483—he was only 13 years old. As the years passed, his head continued to grow but his body didn't keep up, making him not only short, but also disproportionate. He did have one thing going for him: He was courteous. In fact, "Charles the Courteous" became his nickname long before 1498, the year he escorted his wife down a dark corridor toward a tennis match, bowed to allow her to pass beneath the door's low lintel, and then stood up too fast, crashing his head into a wooden beam. He died of a skull fracture nine hours later.

THE KING'S MINIATURE PAINTER

At 5'4", Charles I was the shortest king in British history. That may be why he kept a 19-inch-tall dwarf at court—to have at least one man he could look down on. In 1649, after England's Second Civil War, the British monarchy was abolished and Charles I was executed, leaving him a head shorter. (He regained his stature after Parliament permitted his head to be sewn back onto his body so that his family could pay their last respects.) The monarchy was restored in 1660, and at 6'2", Charles II towered over his late father. His future wife, Catherine of Braganza, however, was short. So short, in fact, that when they met, Charles said, "My God, they've sent me a bat!"

HIS ROYAL WEAKNESS

Five-foot-five-inch King Frederick William I of Prussia (1688–1740) surrounded himself with giants. His Potsdam Giant Guards—a special regiment of the Prussian Infantry—had a minimum height requirement of 6'2". The Potsdam Giants never saw battle, though. Frederick just liked to watch them perform drills, led by their mascot, a bear. "The most beautiful girl or woman in the world would be a matter of indifference to me," Frederick confided to the French ambassador, "but tall soldiers...they are my weakness."

HEY, GOOD LOOKIN'

The Venetian Ambassador once called 6-foot-tall Henry VIII "the handsomest potentate he'd ever set eyes on." That must have been before the British king got fat. Henry seldom ate fruit or vegetables. Instead, he indulged in eels, whales, porpoises, boars, snails, swans, and peacocks. Historians note that Henry had many symptoms of scurvy—a disease caused by a lack of vitamin C: swollen face, ulcerated legs, lethargy, bloating, and wild mood swings. He also ended up with a 52-inch waistline, weighed 300 pounds, and needed several servants to carry him about in a chair on poles.

SHRIMP À LA KING

Believing that the 900-year-old House of Savoy needed a boost, King Umberto I of Italy did some selective breeding. In 1896 he matched his 5'3" son, Prince Victor Emmanuel, to the tallest royal he could find: 6-foot-tall Elena of Montenegro. While he waited for his own son, Umberto II, to grow up, Victor Emmanuel did all he could to elevate his own stature. He had the legs of his throne cut short so his feet touched the floor and the back seat of his royal car raised so his subjects could see him through the window. The Italians adored *il piccolo*—"the little one"—but he appointed Benito Mussolini to Prime Minister, and Mussolini backed Germany in World War II, a disaster for Italy and its people. In 1946 the little king abdicated, hoping his 6-foot-tall son could hold the throne. He couldn't. The Italian people voted to make Italy a republic and gave the last Savoy monarch the boot.

QUEEN-SIZED

Like most senior citizens, Queen Victoria suffered from shrinkage—she lost five inches, going from 5' in her youth to 4'7" in her old age. And by the end of her life (age 82), England's longest-reigning monarch was almost as wide as she was tall. A pair of her bloomers that sold at auction in 2009 had a 50-inch waist.

THE GOLDEN PAGE

These facts are worth their weight in Au.

• Gold's chemical symbol is Au. Why not G? Because the "au" is short for *aurum*, the mineral's name in Latin.

• Gold reflects heat and radiation so well that NASA used it to coat the plastic visors of astronauts' space-suit helmets to provide protection from the Sun's powerful rays.

• Gold-to-Go ATMs dispense 24-karat gold coins and gold bars. The machines update their prices every 10 minutes (based on current gold prices) and are "largely" burglar-proof and tamper-resistant.

• The most gold ever stored in Fort Knox was in 1949. At the time, there were 701 million ounces there, or 69.9 percent of all the known gold in the world. How much is in there today? The government won't say.

• For three years, a North Carolina family used a heavy rock found on their farm as a doorstop. In 1802 they sold it to a jeweler for $3.50. Bad move: It turned out to be a 17-pound gold nugget.

• Yellowknife, a city in Canada's Northwest Territories, is famous for having streets "paved with gold." (Waste from local gold mines was used to make some of them.)

• The infamous 1838 relocation of the Cherokee known as the "Trail of Tears" is directly linked to gold. The tribe controlled most of the land in the North Georgia. Almost immediately after gold was discovered there in 1828, the Georgia legislature began plans for their removal.

• On average, a ton of ore dug from a gold mine yields only a single ounce of gold.

• Elvis Presley had many custom Cadillacs, but designed only one himself: a gold custom Eldorado convertible with gold pearlescent paint (40 coats), a gold-plated steering wheel, a solid-gold hood ornament, and gold records mounted on the cloth top. The car wasn't built until 1987—10 years after Elvis died. (There's a Hot Wheels version.)

King George II of England had a pet armadillo. He called it "Indian Monster."

MISERY INDEXES

*Here's a look at some famous and not-so-famous indexes
that are used to measure the bad things in life.*

THE SAFFIR-SIMPSON HURRICANE SCALE

Background: Robert Simpson was the head of the National Hurricane Center in August 1969 when Hurricane Camille—one of the most powerful ever to hit the United States—bore down on the Gulf Coast states. New forecasting tools had enabled the Center to predict Camille's intensity, and Simpson raised such an alarm that more than 81,000 people evacuated the affected areas. Result: Fewer than 300 people were killed when it hit. Nonetheless, Simpson felt that a more effective way of communicating the size and likely impact of a hurricane was needed. So he contacted a Florida engineer named Herbert Saffir, who had recently devised a five-category windstorm scale for the United Nations to predict how much damage would be caused to structures hit by winds of various strengths. Simpson and Saffir worked to incorporate potential damage from storm surges and flooding intro hurricane predictions; their Saffir-Simpson Hurricane Scale made its debut in 1971.

How It Works: Hurricanes are classified into five categories according to wind speed: Category 1 (74–95 mph), Category 2 (96–110 mph), Category 3 (111–130 mph), Category 4 (131–155 mph), and Category 5 (156 mph and greater).

Details: The scale has proven ineffective at predicting flooding and the height of storm surges. Both vary too much according to local factors such as the shape of the coastline and slope of the continental shelf where the hurricane makes landfall. In 2010 these elements were removed; now it's solely a wind scale.

THE INES SCALE

Background: INES stands for International Nuclear Event Scale, the scale used to measure disasters at nuclear power plants and other nuclear facilities. Drawing inspiration from similar scales used by the French and Japanese nuclear industries, the International Atomic Energy Agency created INES in 1990 to provide a

In Oman, date palms are so valuable that the government keeps a list of who owns each tree.

single international standard of comparison that it hoped would be as useful as the Fahrenheit scale or the metric system.

How It Works: Nuclear events are measured on a scale of 1 to 7: Levels 1 to 3 have consequences contained inside the affected facility and are called "incidents"; levels 4 to 7 have consequences outside the facility and are called "accidents":

Level 1: Anomaly

Level 2: Incident

Level 3: Serious Incident

Level 4: Accident with Local Consequences

Level 5: Accident with Wider Consequences

Level 6: Serious Accident

Level 7: Major Accident

Details: Like the Richter scale, the INES scale is a *logarithmic* scale: Each increase in level (say, from Level 4 to Level 5) represents a tenfold increase in the severity of the disaster.

• The 1979 accident at Three Mile Island in Pennsylvania was a Level 5 "Accident with Wider Consequences" because it involved a partial meltdown with severe damage to the reactor core, plus limited release of radioactive material into the environment.

• The 1986 accident at Chernobyl in the former Soviet Union ranks as the worst nuclear disaster in history and one of only two Level 7 "Major Accidents" to date (release of a "significant fraction" of the nuclear material in the reactor core, resulting in widespread health and environmental effects). The other Level 7 accident occurred after the 2011 earthquake and tsunami in Japan.

• It can take time to accurately assess the scale of a nuclear event, especially if more than one reactor is involved. In the months following the 2011 Japanese earthquake and tsunami, officials were still assessing the damage to six nuclear reactors at the Fukushima nuclear power plants. Three reactors have been assessed as Level 5 incidents (severe damage to the reactor core, and *limited* release of radioactive material) and one was rated at level 3 (loss of cooling water to the reactor). The overall incident, however, was categorized as a Level 7 accident.

DEFCON

Background: If you're a fan of science fiction or war movies, you may already know that DEFCON is short for "Defense Readiness

Condition" and is measured on a scale from 1 to 5. The system was created in the late 1950s to give all U.S. military operations worldwide a simple measure of the nation's current state of alert.

How It Works: DEFCON 5 is the lowest level of readiness in peacetime. As perceived threats increase, the military's readiness can be raised in stages all the way to DEFCON 1, when war is imminent. (Precise details of *how* the military increases its readiness when the DEFCON level is raised are kept secret.)

Details: Are you old enough to remember the Cuban Missile Crisis in 1962? Throughout much of the Cold War the military was kept at DEFCON 4, but during the Cuban Missile Crisis the alert level was raised to DEFCON 3, and the U.S. Air Force's Strategic Air Command was ordered to DEFCON 2. That's the only time since the creation of the system that any part of the military has been placed at DEFCON 2. During the 9/11 attacks the alert level never rose above DEFCON 3. DEFCON 1 has never been used...so far.

THE DOOMSDAY CLOCK

Background: By the summer of 1947, just two years after the atomic bombing of Hiroshima and Nagasaki, the directors of the University of Chicago's *Bulletin of Atomic Scientists* had grown so concerned about the possibility of another nuclear war that they created a symbolic clock face called the "Doomsday Clock" to convey their estimation of how close the world was to "midnight"—nuclear Armageddon—at any point in time. The clock has appeared on the cover of the *Bulletin* ever since.

How It Works: When the clock was created in June 1947, it was set at seven minutes to midnight. Between 1947 and 2011, the minute hand was moved 19 times, closer to midnight when the *Bulletin*'s board of directors thought the danger of nuclear war was increasing; farther from midnight when the danger was receding.

Details: When the U.S. and the Soviet Union both tested hydrogen bombs in 1953, the clock was reset from three minutes to just two minutes before midnight, the closest to the zero hour that it has ever been set. The farthest it has ever been from midnight was in 1991, when the end of the Cold War and the signing of the first Strategic Arms Reduction Treaty prompted the editors to move it from 10 minutes to 17 minutes 'til midnight in a single stroke. In 2007 the clock was updated to include non-nuclear dangers such as biological weapons and climate change. (So what time is it now? As of June 2011, it was six minutes to midnight.)

THE RAPTURE INDEX

Background: Created by an evangelical Christian named Todd Strandberg in the 1980s, the Rapture Index keeps track of current events to estimate how quickly the world is moving toward the "End Times" that many Christians believe are prophesied in the Bible. (According to the prophesy, during the Rapture, Christians will be lifted up to heaven to be with Jesus Christ; everyone else will suffer seven years of catastrophes in a world ruled by the Antichrist.)

How It Works: Current events are organized into 45 Rapture-foretelling categories, including "False Christs," "Satanism," "Inflation," "Liberalism," and "Volcanoes." Each category is assigned a numerical value from 1 to 5, according to the amount of "activity" in that category. Then the values are added up to calculate the current Rapture Index score. A score of 100 or below is classified as "Slow Prophetic Activity," meaning the Rapture probably isn't near. A score of 100 to 130 indicates "Moderate Prophetic Activity," and a score of 130 to 160 is a sign of "Heavy Prophetic Activity." A score above 160? "Fasten Your Seatbelts"— the Rapture may be imminent.

Details: The highest score the Rapture Index ever reached came on August 8, 2011—just after the Standard & Poor's credit rating agency downgraded U.S. debt from AAA to AA+—when the Index hit 184 out of a possible 225. The all-time low: 57, reached in December 1993, when "just about every indicator either went dormant or had positive news," Strandberg reports.

Highlights: "There has been an increase in the number of UFO sightings," Strandberg reports in the "Supernatural" category (2 points). What about the Antichrist category? "The European Union now has a President. This office could be a precursor to the Antichrist," he writes (3 points).

THE NATIONAL DEBT CLOCK

Background: In the winter of 1980, a New York real estate developer named Seymour Durst wanted to communicate his concerns about the ballooning national debt to elected officials in Washington, D.C. So he sent them New Year's cards that read "Happy New Year! Your share of the national debt is $35,000." No response—so Durst went to a sign maker and asked if it was possible to make a billboard with a numeric display that showed the national debt growing in real time—a Doomsday Clock for the American taxpayer. It *wasn't* possible: That year, the debt was growing at a rate of about $13,000 per second, and the computers of the day weren't fast enough to operate a numeric display at that kind of speed. It took eight years for technology to catch up with Durst's vision, and in 1989 the first National Debt Clock was installed on a Durst-owned building near Times Square. Cost: $100,000. (No word on whether Durst went into debt to pay for the clock.)

How It Worked: Each week Durst called the U.S. Treasury to get the latest national debt figures and updated the sign via modem so that the continuously changing numbers were as accurate as possible. He continued updating the clock until his death in 1995, after which the sign company assumed the responsibility.

Details: In 2000 the national debt stopped growing, and for the two years it actually *shrank*. That created a problem for the sign, which wasn't designed to run backwards. On Durst's birthday in 2000, the sign was switched off and covered with a red, white, and blue banner in the hope that it would never be uncovered. But the debt soon started rising again, and in July 2002 the sign was switched back on. It was replaced with a new and improved sign in 2004, but the new sign wasn't "improved" enough: When the national debt hit $10 trillion in 2008, there weren't enough digits on the sign to display all the debt, and the "$" had to be converted to a 1. Plans are in the works to add another two digits to the sign. (Every American's share of the national debt, as of August 2011: $46,700…and climbing.)

*　　*　　*

"If I had to describe myself in one word, it would be 'bad at following directions.'"

—Matt Roller

In 1737 Samuel Higley of Connecticut minted America's first copper coins. Value: 3 pence.

SUPERMAN RETURNS, STARRING WILL SMITH

Some roles are so closely associated with a specific actor that it's hard to imagine that he or she wasn't the first choice for the part. Can you imagine, for example...

JOHN BELUSHI AS ARTHUR (*Arthur*, 1981) The part of the millionaire alcoholic became the definitive role of Dudley Moore's career and earned him an Oscar nomination, a rare feat for a comic performance. But the producers' first choice for the role was Belushi, one of the biggest comic actors of the era. Belushi thought the script was excellent, but turned it down. Reason: After playing a hard-drinking guy in *Animal House,* he didn't want to play another hard-drinking guy in *Arthur* and risk getting typecast as a substance abuser. (Belushi died from a drug overdose in 1982.)

EMMA THOMPSON AS GOD (*Dogma*, 1999) In this dark comedy about Armageddon, God makes a brief appearance at the end of the film, silently cleaning up the chaos and forgiving the bad guys. Writer-director Kevin Smith wrote the part for Emma Thompson because he felt she could imbue the role with authority and dignity. She passed on it because she was pregnant. Smith then asked Carrie Fisher, which would have been an in-joke, as all his movies feature characters discussing the *Star Wars* movies, in which Fischer starred, at length. She turned it down too, so Smith cast singer Alanis Morissette. (He also rewrote the script for her. When asked by the lead character for the meaning of life, God was originally supposed to reply, "Plastics," but Smith deleted Morissette's one and only line.)

WOODY ALLEN & MEL BROOKS AS JERRY AND GOD (*Oh, God!*, 1977) Larry Gelbart wrote the script, and Carl Reiner signed on to direct it. Both had worked on Sid Caesar's *Your Show of Shows* in the 1950s and wanted to extend the reunion by casting fellow *Show* writers Mel Brooks as God and Woody Allen as

In Great Britain, McDonald's changed the design of its McFlurry containers...

supermarket manager Jerry Landers. Brooks and Allen were the two top comedy directors of the 1970s, and acted only in their own films. That's why Allen turned down the role—he was working on *Stardust Memories*, also a film about God. Once Allen turned it down, Brooks backed out too. (Singer John Denver and George Burns were cast as Jerry and God, respectively.)

PAUL NEWMAN & JIM CARREY AS WOODY AND BUZZ (*Toy Story*, 1995)

Pixar envisioned casting Paul Newman as the voice of Woody, the old-fashioned cowboy doll, and Jim Carrey as Buzz Lightyear, the fancy electronic spaceman toy that replaces Woody in the heart of the little boy who owns them. It was meant to be a metaphor for Old Hollywood (Newman) and New Hollywood (Carrey, the hottest new star of the year). This was Pixar's first feature film, and the company couldn't afford to hire *two* big movie stars, so they went with just one: Tom Hanks as Woody, and TV star Tim Allen as Buzz.

WILL SMITH AS SUPERMAN (*Superman Returns*, 2006)

Filmmakers considered many B-list actors, including Josh Hartnett and Ashton Kutcher, but director Bryan Singer wanted the industry's *biggest* star: Will Smith. Obviously that would have been a controversial choice, because Superman is white, and Smith would have been the first black actor to take on the role. Smith wanted no part of that controversy. "You can't be messing up white people's heroes in Hollywood," Smith said to a reporter. "You'll never work in this town again!" In the end, Singer hired a largely unknown soap actor named Brandon Routh.

BETTE MIDLER AS ANNIE WILKES (*Misery*, 1990)

In 1989 Disney-owned Touchstone Pictures was producing an adaptation of Stephen King's novel *Misery*, about a crazed fan who kidnaps and tortures her favorite author. Touchstone repeatedly offered the role of crazy Annie to Bette Midler, who they had under an exclusive contract. Midler repeatedly turned it down because she thought the script was distasteful and frightening (it *was* based on a Stephen King novel, after all). The part ultimately went to stage and TV actress Kathy Bates. It made her a film star...and won her an Oscar.

I'M STUCK...

And we thought the toilet was the worst place to get stuck.

...BETWEEN A ROOF AND A HARD PLACE: On New Year's Eve 2009, Roberto Carrillo executed his long-planned escape from the prison in Valle Hermoso, Mexico. He hoisted himself up to the top of his cell and proceeded to squeeze his way through a small gap between the top of the bars and the roof. He got his head and upper torso through...and then he got stuck. Hanging upside down, Carillo had no choice but to call the guards, who laughed while they cut him free with a chainsaw.

...IN THE MUCK: In May 2010, Xiao Chen went for a night swim in the China's Chang Jiang River. The 25-year-old underestimated just how muddy the river would be in the rainy spring season and got completely stuck waist-deep in the mud. He tried to free himself for four hours, before some passing fishermen called firefighters, who freed him another seven hours later. Bonus: Xiao had a cell phone on him the entire time, and he wasn't so stuck that he couldn't have reached it. He told reporters he was simply "too embarrassed" to call for help.

...ON THE LINE: Mustafa Danger is a high-wire motorcycle rider—a professional daredevil. In the Spanish resort of Benidorm in 2010, he was attempting a world record for the highest high-wire ride: 1,640 feet long, 610 feet in the air, with no safety net. He went 1,100 feet...and then the wind picked up, making it too dangerous to move in any direction. Danger stopped and had to be towed to safety. (A day later, he tried again, and made it.)

...HEAD UNDER HEELS: In 2007, 16 people boarded the roller coaster at Fangte Amusement Park of Wuhu in China. As the ride swung into the middle of an upside-down loop, a huge gust of wind blew through. Safety equipment automatically went into effect, locking the coaster to the track and grinding the ride to a halt—with 16 people hanging upside down. It took park officials half an hour to resume the ride and get everyone to safety. Six people were treated for nausea at a local hospital.

THE FORBIDDEN ISLAND

Ever heard of North Sentinel Island? Probably not...even though
it's one of the most unusual places on Earth. What makes it
so odd? The people—they've been there a long time,
completely cut off from the rest of the world.

MAROONED!
Late on the night of August 2, 1981, a Hong Kong
freighter navigating the choppy waters of the Bay of
Bengal ran aground on a submerged coral reef. The ship, called
the *Primrose*, was hopelessly stuck. But there was no danger of it
sinking, so after radioing for assistance, the captain and his crew
settled in for a few days' wait until help arrived.

The following morning, as it became light, the sailors saw an
island a few hundred yards beyond the reef. It was uninhabited, as
far as anyone could tell: There were no buildings, roads, or other
signs of civilization there—just a pristine, sandy beach and behind
it, dense jungle. The beach must have seemed like an ideal spot to
wait for a rescue, but the captain ordered the crew to remain
aboard the *Primrose*. It was monsoon season, and he may have
been concerned about lowering the men into the rough seas in
tiny lifeboats. Or perhaps he'd figured out exactly *which* island lay
beyond the reef: It was North Sentinel—the deadliest of the 200
islands in the Andaman Island chain.

SOME WELCOME

A few days later, a lookout aboard the *Primrose* spotted a group of
dark-skinned men emerging from the jungle, making their way
toward the ship. Was it the rescue party? It seemed possible
...until the men came a little closer and the lookout could see
that every one of them was naked.

Naked...and *armed*, but not with guns. Each man carried
either a spear, a bow and arrows, or some other primitive weapon.
The captain made another radio distress call, this one much more
urgent: "Wild men! Estimate more than 50, carrying various
homemade weapons, are making two or three wooden boats. Worrying they will board us at sunset."

A WORLD APART

After a tense standoff lasting a few more days, the crew of the *Primrose* were evacuated by helicopter to safety. They were lucky to get away: It was their misfortune to have run aground just off-shore of one of the strangest islands on Earth, and probably the very last of its kind. Anthropologists believe that the men who appeared on the beach that morning in 1981 are members of a hunter-gatherer tribe that has lived on the island for 65,000 years. That's 35,000 years before the last ice age, 55,000 years before the giant wooly mammoths disappeared from North America, and 62,000 years before the ancient Egyptians built the pyramids at Giza. These people are believed to be the direct descendants of the first humans out of Africa.

The outside world has known about the North Sentinel Islanders for centuries, but the islanders have been almost completely cut off from the rest of the world *all* that time, and they fiercely maintain their isolation to this day. No one knows what language they speak or what they call themselves—they have never allowed anyone to get close enough to find out. The outside world calls them the "Sentineli" or the "Sentinelese," after the island. It's estimated that the 28-square-mile island (slightly larger than Manhattan) is capable of supporting as many as 400 hunter-gatherers, but no one knows how many people live there.

HOME ALONE

North Sentinel Island is amazingly well suited to both support and isolate a tribe like the Sentinelese. It's too small to interest settlers or colonial powers, especially when there are bigger, better islands within a few hours' sailing time. And unlike many of those islands, North Sentinel has no natural harbors, so there's no good place for a ship to take shelter from a storm. Furthermore, the island is surrounded by a ring of submerged coral reefs that prevent large ships from approaching. This was especially true during the age of sail, when ships had no way of quickly maneuvering out of harm's way once they realized that the reefs were there. Narrow openings in the reefs allow small boats to slip through and land on the beach, but these are passable only in good weather and calm seas, which occur as infrequently as two months out of the year. For the remaining 10 months, the island cannot be safely approached from the sea.

Tonka uses 5.1 million lbs. of sheet metal every year to manufacture its toy trucks.

SELF-SUFFICIENCY

At the same time that they keep strangers out, the coral reefs help keep the Sentinelese in, because the reefs created several shallow lagoons that are teeming with sea life. The food provided by these lagoons is so plentiful that the Sentinelese have never needed to fish in the deep sea waters beyond the coral reefs. They propel their dugout canoes through the shallow lagoons by poling along the bottom, but they cannot navigate in water deeper than the length of their poles. They've never invented oars, without which they cannot leave the island.

The Andaman Islands, North Sentinel Island included, sit at the crossroads of ancient trade routes between Europe, the Middle East, and Southeast Asia. Ironically, this may have further encouraged the isolationist tendencies of the Sentinelese, because their dark skin and African appearance would have made them the targets of any slave traders who might have tried to land on the island over the centuries. Periodic contact with such outsiders would have only intensified the tribe's hostility toward the outside world and their desire to be left alone.

WHO ARE YOU WEARING?

One more thing that has protected the Sentinelese from outsiders: the age-old belief that all Andaman Island tribes were cannibals. There is no evidence that any of them were, except that some tribes wore the bones of their ancestors as jewelry (including the skulls), which they wore strapped to their backs. It would have been easy to mistake such people for cannibals. Who'd stick around long enough to find out that they weren't?

By the time the Greek astronomer Ptolemy wrote of an "Island of Cannibals" somewhere in the Bay of Bengal in the 2nd century A.D., sailors were already giving the Andamans a wide berth. Marco Polo didn't help matters in the 1290s when he described the Andamanese as "a brutish and savage race...[who] kill and eat every foreigner whom they can lay their hands upon." Claims like these certainly did help to keep strangers away. And considering how fiercely the Sentinelese and other Andaman tribes defended their islands, it's probably a lucky thing that they did.

Turn to page 357 for Part II of the story.

The world's largest elk herd (over 200,000) is in Colorado's White River National Forest.

WEIRD ANIMAL NEWS

Strange tales of creatures great and small.

THAT'S SO RAVEN

Wall Street brokers spend years learning the intricacies of the financial markets so they can pick stocks that make money for their investors. A monkey named Raven picks *her* stocks by throwing darts at a list of companies. In 2000 she was ranked the 22nd-best fund manager in the United States—her MonkeyDex fund outperformed more than 6,000 licensed (and experienced) brokers. When asked to divulge the secret to winning at high-finance stock speculating, her handlers said, "It's all in the wrist action."

BOVINE INTERVENTION

How long could you elude the British Army? In 1999 a herd of nine Limousin cattle escaped from a Staffordshire, England, farm and made a new home in nearby Hopwas Woods. For the next three months they managed to elude 50 hunters, 100 soldiers, and a helicopter equipped with thermal imaging equipment. Staffordshire Police installed "Go Slow" signs on local roadways to prevent people from scaring the cows, which can be dangerous when frightened. Four cows were eventually shot and killed, but public outcry convinced authorities to spare the other five...once they were caught.

EIGHT ARMS TO PRANK YOU

One morning in 2009, an employee of the Santa Monica Pier Aquarium arrived at work to discover three inches of standing water throughout the building, and still flowing out of a 200-gallon saltwater tank. The culprit: a curious octopus. The water-control valve was located on the inside of the octopus's giant tank. Aquarium official Tara Treiber believes that the octopus was merely exploring and "found something loose and pulled on it," sending water everywhere, damaging the aquarium's recently installed carpets, but not killing any of the sea creatures.

Oldest operating tavern in the US: the White Horse Tavern in Newport, RI, opened in 1673.

A BAD CASE OF HIVES

The bees are coming! In 1999 a swarm of 10,000 bees suddenly descended on the Manhattan Beach Pier in California. None of the 150 people at the pier were injured, but all were evacuated while officials cleared the area. The insects are part of an increasing expansion of Africanized "killer" bees that have been moving north from South America since the 1950s. The Africanized Honey Bee problem has gotten so bad in Manhattan Beach that the area is now considered to be "colonized." The Manhattan Beach City website has a page about how to deal with AHBs, and the city of 35,000 has four bee removal services—about four times as many as any other town with such a small population.

TRUNKARDS

The habitats of wild elephants in India continue to be threatened by human encroachment. In 1999, 15 of the giant animals used their trunks to break into thatched huts in the northeastern village of Prajapatibosti. They then proceeded to drink the rice beer they found inside…and there was enough to get all 15 elephants drunk. The inebriated pachyderms then trampled rice paddies and more huts, killing a family of four.

IT'S BETTER THAN WHAT THEY USUALLY THROW

Researchers at the Furuvik Zoo in Gavle, Sweden, first realized there was a problem with their chimpanzee, Santino, when visitors complained that the animal was throwing rocks at them. The scientists looked at video footage and discovered that Santino had planned the attacks. Zookeepers found hidden stashes of rocks and concrete chunks all around his enclosure. When visitors came close, Santino unloaded. (The zoo keeps a close eye on him now.)

*   *   *

WE ARE NOT AMUSED

England's Queen Victoria loved Lewis Carroll's book *Alice in Wonderland* so much that she requested a copy of his next book. Carroll, a math professor at Oxford, was happy to oblige, so he sent the Queen his next book: *Syllabus of Plane Algebraical Geometry—Systematically Arranged with Formal Definitions, Postulates, and Axioms*.

Crowded skies: There are over 2,000 species of butterfly in the rain forests of South America.

GRANDMA CELIA, CARD SHARK

Uncle John's grandma makes money playing cards, but she loves doing tricks more than anything. These classics are among her favorites. See if you can guess how they work without peeking at the answers on page 536.

INSTA-MATIC

"I have a photographic memory," Grandma Celia told me as she opened a new deck of cards. "When I shuffle these, I can't help but memorize the order of all the cards in the deck."

"I don't believe you," I said.

"No? Then watch this," she replied. She shuffled the deck face down, staring intently at the cards. Then she split the deck into three piles in front of her from left to right and said, "The first card is the Seven of Clubs." She picked the top card off of the first pile and looked at it, but did not show it to me. "Got it!" she said. Then she said, "The second card is the Jack of Hearts," and picked the top card off the second pile and looked at it, again not showing it to me. "Right again!" she said. "The card on top of the third pile is the Three of Spades." She picked the top card off of the third pile, looked at it without showing it to me and said, "What'd I tell you? Three in a row!" Then she laid the three cards face up on the table, calling them out as she did: "Seven of Clubs, Jack of Hearts, and the Three of Spades." How'd she do that?

SEEING IS BELIEVING

"Ever since I had that laser surgery on my eyes, I've actually been able to see *through* the playing cards," Grandma Celia said. "I thought about suing the doctor, but I make so much money playing poker I decided to let it go. Now the doctor's suing me for a percentage of my winnings."

"Yeah, right!" I said.

"My boy, you need to be more trusting of your elders," she said. She took out a piece of paper, wrote something on it, and then put it in her wallet ("For safekeeping," she explained) and put the wallet in her purse. Then she gave me the deck and told me to shuffle it and start dealing the cards face down onto the table, without looking at them and without showing them to her. She said she'd tell me to stop when she was ready. "Don't worry about being tidy," she said, "a messy pile is fine." Celia looked carefully at the back of each card as I dealt them onto the table. After I'd dealt a bunch she said "Stop!" and took her wallet out of her purse and laid the wallet on top of the pile. "Open the wallet, take out the note, and read what it says," she said. I did as she asked. The note read, "You stopped at the Ten of Diamonds." Then Celia said, "See for yourself." I lifted the wallet off the pile and turned the top card over: It was the Ten of Diamonds. How'd she do that?

FLIP-FLOP

"I try never to mix my hobbies, but sometimes I can't help it," Grandma Celia told me. "My circus training occasionally intrudes into my card playing, and the cards somersault by themselves."

"Maybe that's just your head spinning, Grandma," I said.

"Smart aleck!" Celia snarled as she fanned out a deck of cards in her hands and presented them to me face down.

"Pick a card," she said. I did, and as I read my card Celia closed the fan and squared up the deck. When I was done, she held out the squared deck and said, "Put the card back in the deck, but don't let me see it." I slid the card into the deck as she held it. Next Celia put the deck behind her back for just a second, then she put the deck on the table face down. "What was your card?" she asked. "The Queen of Clubs," I said. With a swipe of her hand Celia fanned the cards out across the table. All the cards were face down except one: the Queen of Clubs. How'd she do that?

A STAND-UP GUY

"One last trick," Celia said. "The Joker is hardly ever used in card games because he's too levelheaded—so levelheaded, in fact, that he can balance a paper cup on his head."

"Is *that* a joke?" I asked.

"Shh!" she said, holding the Joker vertically in the palm of her hand, her thumb on one side of the card and three fingers on the other. She picked a paper cup off the table and set it on top of the card. It sat there like it was nailed into place. How'd she do that?

In one day in Mumbai, India, you'll breathe in as many toxins as there are in 50 cigarettes.

FUNKY JUNK FOOD

Who says food that's bad for you can't be creative?

THE HOLE STORY

Among the first items available when the Portland, Oregon-based Voodoo Doughnut chain opened in 2003: a Pepto-Bismol flavored doughnut and a cherry-Nyquil-frosted doughnut. (The FDA forced the founders, Kenneth Pogson and Tres Shannon, to remove them from the menu because it's illegal to sell medicine as food.) Their other creations include Frisbee-sized doughnuts, Cap'n Crunch-coated doughnuts, Red Bull-glazed doughnuts, and doughnuts with playfully dirty names like "the Triple Chocolate Penetration"—a chocolate cake doughnut topped with Coco Puffs and drizzled with chocolate sauce.

HOT DOG!

Hot dogs are a common street food in New York City. Some of the city's most unique dogs come from Brian Shebairo and Chris Antista's Crif Dogs. The "Good Morning" is a hot dog wrapped in bacon and covered in cheese and a fried egg. There's the "Tsunami," a bacon-wrapped hot dog topped with teriyaki sauce and pineapple; the "Jon-Jon Deragon," with cream cheese, scallions, and everything-bagel seeds; and the "Chihuahua," with bacon, sour cream, and avocado. Junk food bonus: Most of the hot dogs are deep-fried.

THE FRYIN' KING

For the past decade, Abel Gonzales Jr. has been one of the most popular vendors at the Texas State Fair, where he sells inventive deep-fried foods. Among his creations (which win "Best in Show" nearly ever year) are deep-fried cookie dough, deep-fried Coke (balls of batter made primarily from Coca-Cola), fried chocolate (a brownie stuffed with white chocolate, cherries, and pecans, then dipped into chocolate cake batter and friend), deep-fried butter, and deep-fried peanut butter, banana, and bacon sandwiches. Gonzales also sells deep-fried pineapple topped with banana-flavored whipped cream that's frozen in nitrogen—when you bite into it, it shatters and sends banana-scented smoke up your nose.

Hot dogs take more than 20 years to break down in landfills.

SCI-FI TREASURES

Ever find yourself looking for a good book to read? It happens to us all the time, so we decided to offer a few recommendations in one of our favorite genres: science fiction. These novels might not be household names, but they're all classics in their own right—imaginative, clever, and great reading.

L**IVES OF THE MONSTER DOGS** (1997) by Kirsten Bakis
Review: "An army of civilized, talking dogs—the dream of a mad Prussian scientist—descends on Manhattan after having slaughtered their masters. Although the novel addresses big themes, parts are laugh-out-loud funny. The book unfolds like a rich, resonant dream that you can't stop thinking about the following day." (*The New York Times*)

ENDER'S GAME (1985) by Orson Scott Card
Review: "Earth has been invaded twice by aliens, so the army embarks on a program to breed the ultimate military genius and attack the aliens' home world. Six-year-old Ender Wiggins may be the person they're looking for. But how can they manipulate a compassionate child into wiping out an entire species? Deeply emotional and character-driven, brilliantly intellectual, and exciting as all get-out." (Common Sense Media)

THE MOUNT (2002) by Carol Emshwiller
Review: "This quiet, disturbing novel is about what happens when small alien invaders called Hoots take over Earth and begin breeding humans for transportation. Hoots have weak legs that fit perfectly around human necks, as well as superior weapons that easily convert the disobedient to dust. What's compelling about this beautifully written novel, though, is that it's no simple 'aliens oppress humans' tale. It explores what happens when humans get used to, and even enjoy, their servitude." (io9.com)

GATEWAY (1977) by Frederik Pohl
Review: "Like *The Treasure of Sierra Madre* expanded to galactic proportions, *Gateway* tells the story of prospectors searching for hidden riches in remote and dangerous locales. Gateway, a pear-shaped

Not that it helped: The *Titanic's* whistles could be heard from 11 miles away.

rock in space, is the last safe outpost before the prospectors head off into the unknown. Some come back rich, but most wind up in a black hole or some other ugly cosmic disaster zone from which they never return. Smartly paced and written with just the right touch of parody and light humor, *Gateway* swept the major honors, winning the Hugo and Nebula awards." (*ConceptualFiction.com*)

THE DARK BEYOND THE STARS (1991) by Frank Robinson

Review: "Sparrow is a crew member on the *Astron*, a multigenerational ship sent out from Earth on a 2,000-year search for other inhabited worlds. After a series of accidents, during which he loses his memory, Sparrow decides that someone is trying to kill him. He's plunged into an ever-deepening mystery; no one will discuss his past with him, the computer has restricted his data, and the little he does discover about his history leads only to further secrets. Robinson plants plenty of clues for the reader, scattering them skillfully amid exciting action and dialogue." (*Publishers Weekly*)

ALL FLESH IS GRASS (1965) by Clifford D. Simak

Review: "A first-contact story with the most unlikely of ambassadors: Brad Carter, a failed real estate agent in Millville, the archetypal small town where nothing ever happens. But when aliens (who communicate via purple flowers) place a barrier around Millville, preventing travel into or out of the town, nuclear annihilation looms from an increasingly fearful outside world, while unrest brews among the terrified locals. It's a unique story that's both familiar and utterly alien at the same time." (The Nebulog)

THE MAN IN THE HIGH CASTLE (1962) by Philip K. Dick

Review: "In an alternate version of the 1960s in which the Axis powers won World War II, what was once the United States has been partitioned into the Nazi-run East and the Japanese-run West. The Japanese overlords are totalitarian but honorable, and many have a penchant for collecting old U.S. memorabilia—Civil War pistols, 1920s comic books, and the like. Meanwhile, the Germans have landed astronauts on Mars, drained the Mediterranean for farmland, and have almost entirely liquidated the African population in an extension of the 'final solution.' Dick's use of detail to sketch out his alternate reality is nearly flawless." (Infinity Plus)

FIVE THINGS YOU SHOULD NEVER DO IN A FOREIGN COUNTRY

In the United States, you don't place the American flag on the ground.
Similar rules of decorum apply in foreign lands...or else.

1. Never order a "Black and Tan" in a pub in Ireland.
A Black and Tan, typically served in a pint glass, is a combination of English ale and Irish stout. While any bartender in America would be happy to prepare one for you without batting an eye, don't even think about ordering one in Ireland. When poured together, the two beers refuse to mix (the stout floats on top of the ale)—which serves as a metaphor for the bitterness that still simmers between Ireland and the United Kingdom. "Black and Tan" was also a derogatory term for members of the Royal Irish Constabulary Reserve Force, a black-and-khaki-clad English brigade sent to suppress Irish rebels in the 1920s.

2. Never shake hands with your left hand in Saudi Arabia.
According to Islamic tradition, the prophet Muhammad commanded people to eat and drink with their right hand only. "The *Shayatan* [a demon] eats with his left and drinks with his left hand," he wrote. The rule still applies in Muslim areas, such as Saudi Arabia, Malaysia, and parts of Northern Africa. The left hand is considered "unhygienic" since it's typically used to clean oneself after using the bathroom, especially in rural areas where toilet paper can be hard to come by. For the same reason, it's also considered rude to eat with the left hand or gesture towards others with it.

3. Never place a business card in your back pocket in Japan.
Japan applies rigid traditions to everything from the placement of chopsticks after eating rice to how elderly people should be greeted at the dinner table. Similarly staunch etiquette is applied when

exchanging business cards—they should be stored in card holders and must be given and accepted with both hands. If you receive one, you're expected to immediately look it over and admire it. During meetings, the card should be placed respectfully on the table in front of you. Afterward, it should be carefully stored in a holder and never, ever, placed in a back pocket or written on.

4. Never ask for a "fanny pack" in Australia.

In Australia, "fanny" is a slang term for female genitals. The touristy belt bag Americans call a "fanny pack" is usually called a "bum bag" in Australia. Additionally, avoid telling an Australian what sports teams you "root" for back home—"root" is a vulgar term for sexual intercourse, equatable with the F-word. (And if you're fed a nice meal, don't say you're "stuffed" at the end, as in Australia that means "sexually satisfied.")

5. Never wear a #24 football jersey in Brazil

The number 24 is negatively associated with homosexuality in Brazil. Giving a gift with that number on it (for example, a DVD box set of the Kiefer Sutherland TV series 24) might lead to a fist-fight if the receiver is sensitive about such matters. The roots of this taboo lie in an illegal but still popular lottery game called *Jogo do Bicho* ("the animal game"), typically organized by local crime gangs. Cards used in the game feature drawings of 25 animals, with deer as the 24th on the list. In Brazilian culture, deer are pejoratively associated with homosexuals. Males born on the 24th day of the month are often subjected to jokes and taunts. Athletes also avoid putting the number on their jerseys.

*   *   *

BOSTON'S FAVORITE CITY: ST. LOUIS

• The Boston Celtics won their first NBA championship in 1957. They defeated the St. Louis Hawks.

• The New England Patriots won their first Super Bowl in 2002. They defeated the St. Louis Rams.

• The Boston Red Sox won their first World Series in 86 years in 2004. They defeated the St. Louis Cardinals.

Warner Brothers Corset Company's claim to fame: creating the bra-cup sizing system (1935).

JINGLE FEVER

You might not hear them as much anymore, but songs from commercials are a serious part of the soundtrack of pop culture. Here are the stories behind some of the most famous ones.

Product: Folgers Coffee
Jingle: "The best part of wakin' up / is Folgers in your cup"
Story: Singer Leslie Pearl had one minor hit in 1982—"If the Love Fits Wear It," which hit #28 on the pop chart. After that, she moved into songwriting. Among her compositions are "You Never Gave Up On Me," a Top-5 country hit for Crystal Gayle; and "Girls Can Get It," a Top-40 hit for Dr. Hook & the Medicine Show. After that, Pearl moved into jingle writing. In 1984 she wrote the most-played and most-famous song of her career: a jingle for Folgers canned coffee. It's been used in ads for more than 25 years, making it one of the longest-running jingles of all time.

Product: Old Spice aftershave
Jingle: Whistling
Story: Since the mid-1990s, Old Spice commercials have used just six whistled notes, but that six-note melody was originally the ending of an earlier jingle called "The Old Spice Sea Chanty," written in 1953 and used for decades. (Sample lyrics: "'Old Spice means quality,' said the Captain to the Bosun / Ask for the package with the ship that sails the ocean.") Veteran jingle writer Ginger Johnson borrowed the melody from an old Scottish bagpipe folk song called "Scotland the Brave." The whistling was performed by jazz musician Jean "Toots" Thielemans, who also provided the whistling in the theme song of *The Andy Griffith Show* and played the harmonica on the *Sesame Street* theme song.

Product: Oscar Mayer wieners
Jingle: "I wish I were an Oscar Mayer wiener…"
Story: Richard Trentlage was a struggling songwriter in 1963, when he heard about a jingle contest being held by Oscar Mayer.

Contestants composed original jingles for Oscar Mayer hot dogs; the winner's song would be used in commercials. Unfortunately, Trentlage found out about the contest only the day before entries were due. Fortunately, it took him just a few minutes (on a banjo-ukulele) to write: "Oh, I wish I were an Oscar Mayer wiener / that is what I'd truly like to be / 'Cause if I were an Oscar Mayer wiener / everyone would be in love with me." Trentlage won, of course; his jingle is still in use.

Product: Tootsie Roll

Jingle: "The world looks mighty good to me / 'cause Tootsie Rolls are all I see…"

Story: In 1976 a 13-year-old boy and his 9-year-old sister were hired to sing the Tootsie Roll tune. They weren't professional singers—their parents were friends of the jingle's writer. It took an entire day to record the song at a Manhattan recording studio, mainly because the adolescent boy's voice kept cracking. Finally, the mid-jingle solo ("whatever it is I think I see / becomes a Tootsie Roll to me") was given to the girl, Rebecca Jane. (Her brother's name was never released.) The song was used in Tootsie Roll advertising for more than 20 years, but the singers were paid only $50 each for the day's work and that's all they ever made.

Product: Almond Joy and Mounds candy bars

Jingle: "Sometimes you feel like a nut / sometimes you don't"

Story: One of the biggest purveyors of late '60s bubblegum music was Super K Productions. The label's lead producer and songwriter was Joey Levine, who was also the lead singer for the company's anonymous studio creations, the Ohio Express ("Yummy Yummy Yummy") and Kasenetz-Katz Singing Orchestra ("Run Joey Run"). Levine knew how to write a catchy tune, so in 1969, he formed a jingle-writing service called Crushing Enterprises. The first jingle he sold was for Peter Paul's line of candy bars. After that, he wrote some of the most memorable jingles of the last 30 years, including "Just for the taste of it—Diet Coke," "You asked for it, you got it, Toyota," "Come see the softer side of Sears," "The heartbeat of America, that's today's Chevrolet," and "Who's that kid with the Oreo cookie?"

"Four hostile newspapers are more to be feared than a thousand bayonets." —Napoleon

ARACHNOPHOBIA!

These spider facts are more scared of you than you are of them.

SPIDERS ARE SNEAKY! Ever seen a newborn spider? No? That's because they're colorless (and tiny), making them virtually invisible to predators...and you. Hundreds can colonize your home and by the time you realize it, they're all fully grown.

THEY CAN SEE YOU! Most spiders have eight eyes and will see you coming. However, if you venture underground, many cave-dwelling species will *not* see you...because they have no eyes. But their other senses are so heightened that they'll know you're there long before you know they're there.

THEY'RE FAST! In a split second, the jumping spider can jump 20 times its own length to catch prey, but it doesn't have any leg muscles. How does it do it? By increasing its blood pressure to the point where if the spider *didn't* jump, it would explode.

THEY'RE CUNNING! The Bolas spider "fishes" for large, flying insects by spinning a sticky ball at the end of a line of silk. Then it hangs the ball from the web to catch a bug...and reels it in.

THEY'LL TRAP YOU! The female Darwin's bark spider, native to Madagascar, spins the world's largest and strongest web. It can span more than 80 feet (some even cross rivers). Her silk is the strongest biological material in existence—three times stronger than Kevlar, the material used in bulletproof vests.

THEY'LL STAB YOU! Tarantulas have barbed *urticating* hairs on their abdomens. When threatened, they use their legs to "kick" these hairs into the eyes of their attacker.

THEY WILL DESTROY YOUR MANHOOD! The Brazilian wandering spider is the most venomous in the world. It's hairy, five inches long, and if it bites a man, the toxin has a Viagra-like effect. That lasts for several hours, is extremely painful, and if the toxin doesn't kill him, will render him impotent.

Dam! Beavers can hold their breath underwater for 45 minutes.

KNOTTY BUOY

Apparently, once you've earned enough money to buy a boat, you've also develop a really corny sense of humor. These are all real boat names.

Aboat Time	One Moor Time
Let's Get Naughty-Cal	Naut Fast Enuff
Sailing Solution	More Than We Can Afford
Sea Cups	Knotty Buoy
Mr. Tip-Sea	Ship Happens
Devocean	Just a Splash
Meals on Reels	Fin-Addict
Rich Craft	Pilots of Penzance
Sea Ya	Fraid Knot
Cirrhosis of the River	Motion Granted
Incredible Hull	Baits Motel
Campbell's Sloop	College Fund
Dream Boat	Reelin' Good
Water Logged	Positive Lattitude
A Yacht of Fun	A Fishin' Sea
What's Up, Dock?	Heirless
Row vs. Wade	Empty Nest
Channel Surfer	Grounds for Divorce

Big appetite: Giant anteaters eat about 30,000 ants a day.

HEARTBREAK HOTELS

Sometimes there's a good reason that grand schemes fail.

SAN-ZHI POD VILLAGE

The Original Plan: In 1978 the Taiwanese government built a futuristic-looking vacation resort on Taiwan's northern coast—a place for wealthy visitors from Taipei to escape into space-age luxury. Each "building" consisted of eight yellow, green, pink, or blue fiberglass pods attached to a central cement tower, looking like an armada of UFOs. The towers surrounded a man-made lake; a massive dragon sculpture guarded the resort's entrance.

What Happened: Several fatal accidents delayed, and then halt-ed, construction. Stories spread that the project was cursed. Why? The dragon was angry. (To widen the road at the entrance, devel-opers had to split the statue in half.) Then the 1980s real estate bubble burst, and money for second homes dried up. The half-finished San-Zhi turned into a ghost town: The vibrant colors of the pods faded and the buildings began to collapse. Locals claimed that the spirits of the workers who'd died during construction lin-gered among the ruins, unable to pass on. For more than 30 years, the broken dragon guarded the ruins until the pods were demol-ished in 2009 to make way for a new vacation resort.

THE IRVING CLIFF HOTEL

Background: In 1841 Washington Irving, author of "The Legend of Sleepy Hollow," visited Honesdale, Pennsylvania, with his friend (and town namesake) Philip Hone and climbed a rocky cliff along the Lackawaxen River. The views from the top were so magnificent that Irving declared in a letter to his sister that it should be kept forever as a "public resort" for all to enjoy. (Hone's response: He named the cliff in Irving's honor.)

The Original Plan: The Irving Cliff Hotel Company had a differ-ent idea. In 1884 they purchased the land as the site of a grand hotel with broad verandas that overlooked Irving's celebrated view. With 125 rooms, an elevator, gas lighting, electric bells to call room service, and fresh mountain air, the hotel would lure summer visitors from sweltering Philadelphia and New York City.

No joke: Apes laugh when tickled.

What Happened: Just after workers roughed in the first two stories, high winds reduced the structure to rubble. Bad omen? Construction resumed and the hotel was completed on schedule, with a formal opening planned for July 1885. But the developers had incurred huge construction debts. Lawsuits prevented the hotel's opening, as contractors clamored to be paid. In 1887 the property sold at sheriff's auction for $11,000—less than half the amount owed for its construction. The new owner restored the structure to its former grandeur, complete with fine silver in the restaurant and embroidered linen in the rooms. But as the hotel was being readied for its June 22, 1889, opening, disaster struck again. Fire! The hotel's water system couldn't adequately supply the fire department's pumpers, and the only other water source was the river at the foot of the sheer cliff, far beyond the reach of their hoses. Firemen salvaged what they could—appliances, carpets, chandeliers—but the structure burned to the ground. The fire was suspicious… but its cause was never determined, and nothing has ever been built on the siteagain . It remains to this day a public park with a stunning view, free for all who care to visit—just as Washington Irving wanted.

THE RYUGYONG HOTEL

The Original Plan: In 1987 North Korean leader Kim Il-Sung decided to build a hotel that would be a monument to his country's economic growth. The 105-story futuristic pyramid-shaped structure would pierce the sky above the country's capital, Pyongyang, like a spearhead. Its design included 3,000 rooms, five revolving restaurants, and an observation deck. Rising 1,100 feet high, it would be the world's tallest hotel.

What Happened: In 1991 the Soviet Union collapsed, and its financial support of North Korea ended. That left the country strapped for money. Result: Construction of the hotel came to a dead stop. The windowless shell towered above Pyongyang, earning it the dubious distinction of being the world's tallest unoccupied building, with the nicknames "Ghostscraper" and "Hotel of Doom." The European Union Chamber of Commerce calls it "irreparable," specifically citing its curving elevator shafts. Yet plans to finish the hotel keep popping up. The latest is to open it in late 2012, on the posthumous 100th birthday of Eternal President Kim Il-Sung. The exterior got some new windows in 2011, but the odds remain stacked against completion. Reasons: First, it would cost about $2 billion—10 percent of North Korea's annual economic output. Second, North Korea would have to admit that the Ryugyong Hotel actually exists. For years, it has been air-brushed out of photographs and excluded from maps of Pyongyang. Perhaps that's for the best, though. In 2010 North Korea ranked #1 on a list of "worst places on Earth" to visit.

THE HARMON HOTEL

The Original Plan: In 2006 MGM Resorts broke ground on the $8.5 billion, 67-acre CityCenter in Las Vegas—the largest privately funded construction project in U.S. history. The "city within a city" project included a casino, high-rise condos, stores, a dining and entertainment district, and several hotels. One of them was the Harmon, a 49-story hotel and condo tower, designed by Lord Norman Foster, the "rock star" British architect who designed the super-modern Great Court, the centerpiece of London's British Museum.

What Happened: In 2008 building inspectors found improperly placed steel reinforcing rods, commonly called *rebar*, on 15 of 20 completed floors. (Embedded in concrete, rebar helps skyscrapers bear their massive loads.) Result: The ability of the 49-story struc-ture to withstand high winds and earthquakes had been severely compromised. In January 2009, MGM scrapped the 200 condos planned for the top floors and reduced the plan to 28 stories, kneecapping Foster's original design.

Further investigation determined that the work had actually been inspected and approved. The official who made the inspec-tions left town, and the Harmon became the poster child for sub-par construction. MGM sued the contractor, Perini Building, for shoddy work, and Perini countersued for nonpayment of construc-tion costs. The suits won't be settled for some time, but MGM has already written off the Harmon as a $279 million loss. For now, the elegant blue glass building remains an empty shell, due for demoli-tion. A giant vinyl wrap curves around the tower promoting *Viva Elvis*, a Cirque du Soleil production at CityCenter's casino. The hotel once called "one of the most beautifully designed buildings ever" has become a billboard.

What do they suck on, ice? There are leeches in Antarctica.

DISCHARGED!

Sometimes those little numbers on a form marked "for office use only" have a secret meaning. In the U.S. armed forces, they did for decades.

THE NUMBERS GAME

From 1947 to 1974, all branches of the U.S. military placed three-digit letter and numerical codes at the bottom of discharge papers, also called a "Report of Separation" or Form DD-214. The numbers looked like official business and seemed to just be there for processing. There were more than 500 codes, and they all had a meaning, a secret code revealing to military personnel (or soldiers' potential employers, if they called the Pentagon) the *real* reason for the end of a military career. Here are a few of the codes, declassified and revealed.

263: Bed-wetter

463: Paranoid personality

627: Reached upper age limit

KCO: Family's only surviving son

258: Ineptitude

290: Desertion

KLG: Financial irresponsibility

280: Fraudulent entry into armed forces

LGJ: Disapproval of request for extension of service

318: Conscientious objection

311: Illegal alien to the U.S.

JFB: Underage at time of admission to service

HLK: Unsanitary habits

464: Schizoid personality

LFN: Physical disability existing prior to service

41A: Apathy; lack of interest

221: Pregnancy

440: Concealment of prior arrest record

256: Homosexual

JRB: Admission of bisexuality

41E: Obesity

BLF: Drug use

GMG: Alcoholism

GMF: Sexual perversion

JLB: Discreditable incident involving a civilian

JLJ: Shirking

KNL: "For the good of the Service"

OBSCURE 1960s FADS

Sure, you've heard of lava lamps, Nehru jackets, yo-yos, pop art, op art, paper dresses, and bell-bottoms. But here are a few crazes of the 1960s that may have escaped you.

PIANO WRECKING (1963)
As part of his nightclub act in the 1930s, Jimmy Durante would play a few songs on a piano...and then slowly rip the instrument apart with his bare bands and throw the chunks out into the crowd. Audiences loved this bizarre bit of performance art. More than three decades after Durante did it, wrecking pianos became a fad in the engineering department at Derby College of Technology in England. Six-man teams used tools such as axes, sledgehammers, and crowbars to break a piano into pieces so tiny that they could be passed through a 20-cm hole (that's a little less than eight inches), competing to see who could do it the fastest. The fad spread to Cal Tech in Pasadena, California, where the Piano Reduction Study Group deconstructed a piano in just 10 minutes, 44 seconds. Engineering students at Wayne State University in Detroit beat that record with a time of 4 minutes, 51 seconds. But why wreck a piano into tiny bits? Like earlier weird college fads such as phone-booth stuffing or goldfish swallowing, it probably helped to blow off steam built up from the rigors of academia. Or, as Robert Diller of Cal Tech told *Time* in 1963, "It has psychological implications which are pretty clear to us. It's a satire on the obsolescence of today's society." The fad died out by the mid-'60s, replaced with a far more pressing college pastime: protesting the Vietnam War.

COLORING BOOKS FOR ADULTS (1961)
The TV show *Mad Men* has kindled nostalgia for the booming corporate culture of the 1960s. But as it was actually happening, in 1961, Chicago advertising writers Marcie Hans, Dennis Altman, and Martin Cohen came up with a way to viciously satirize it: They wrote and drew *The Executive Coloring Book*. It looked like a children's coloring book, but instead of cowboys and barnyard animals, it pictured men in suits sitting behind desks, and had sarcastic cap-

---

The dwarf planet Pluto was named by Venetia Burney, an 11-year-old British schoolgirl.

tions like "This is my suit. Color it gray or I will lose my job," and "This is my desk. It is mahogany. Important people have mahogany desks. My walls are mahogany, too. I wish I were mahogany." The idea was a lark and an inside joke, so the three creators paid for a small print run of just 1,600 copies. They sold out in a week. By the end of the year, they'd sold a staggering 300,000 *Executive Coloring Books*. In 1962 a slew of "adult coloring books" hit the market, mocking subjects like bartenders, the United Nations, John F. Kennedy, and psychiatrists ("My analyst says I am confused and abstract. Color me confused and abstract"). Before the novelty wore off at the end of 1962, a million adult coloring books had been sold.

SCOPITONE (1960)

Panorams, jukebox-like machines that played three-minute films of jazz musicians performing (called "soundies"), were popular in bars in pre-World War II France. After the war, using surplus military parts and equipment, a company called CAMECA tried to bring back the concept, only with color film. It took the company's technicians 15 years to figure out how to rear-project a moving image to a TV screen, but they finally released their Scopitone "video jukebox" in 1960. About the size of a refrigerator, it offered a choice of 36 film clips, each a staged, lip-synced performance of a popular song, much like modern music videos. The first clips, distributed to French bars, restaurants, and movie theaters, featured French pop stars such as Johnny Hallyday, Juliette Greco, and Serge Gainsbourg. As Scopitones moved into West Germany, England, and the United States, stars like Neil Sedaka, Debbie Reynolds, and Dionne Warwick (warbling "Walk on By" while lying on a white bearskin rug) signed on. By 1964 more than 500 Scopitones had popped up around the United States, primarily in resort hotels, cocktail lounges, and bowling alleys (as well as hundreds more by knockoff companies Colorama, Color-Sonics, and Cinebox). Scopitones were phenomenally popular for the better part of 1964...until rock acts like the Beatles and the Rolling Stones started to dominate pop culture. Scopitone, meanwhile, could only manage to sign "stars" like Buddy Greco, Ethel Ennis, and Frank Sinatra, Jr. But Scopitone's biggest mistake: They placed their machines in bars—where young rock and pop fans weren't allowed. Scopitone went out of business in 1969.

SECRETS OF
THE AVOCADO

*Inside that textured green skin, it's ripe with mystery. It's an
"evolutionary anachronism." It's not a vegetable, and not
exactly your typical fruit. It's an acquired taste that
most Americans still resist. Meet the avocado.*

HAVING A BALL

The avocado came from South America, so it's not
too surprising that the Nahuatl language of the ancient
Aztecs gave us its name, derived from *ahuacatl*. Besides referring
to the fruit, the word had another meaning: "testicle," which also
isn't too surprising, considering the fruit's shape and texture.
Although "guacamole" doesn't really sound like "avocado," the
two words share a root: Guacamole comes from the Nahuatl
ahuacatl-molli, which means "avocado sauce." (The fact that it
also means "testicle sauce" is probably not something we want to
dwell on.)

BEEN THERE, DUNG THAT

Biologists suggest that it's a lucky accident the avocado is still
with us, because it evolved to fill a niche in an ecosystem that
went extinct eons ago. As with many fruits, the avocado developed as a mutually beneficial trade-off with animals. The tree provides tasty food, but there's no such thing as a free lunch—the
plant's price for its fruit is mobility for its seeds. How does that
work? The seeds of the fruit are typically small enough to pass
through the digestive systems of the animals that eat it. The seeds
are often bitter, sometimes even toxic enough to cause nausea. So
animals rarely chew them more than once, but instead learn to
swallow them whole. The seeds exit the digestive system intact, as
waste, and end up planted in the animal's nutrient-rich dung.

There's no reason to believe that the avocado was an exception to this rule. It's unlikely that the plant species' survival was
ever meant to depend on humans poking its seed with toothpicks
and suspending it in water to get it to sprout. But that begs the

question: What animal in South America is big enough to eat a avocado whole and poop out its oversize pit?

ANIMANIACS

The answer, of course, is that there is none. Not anymore, anyway. As with the mango and the dodo fruit, the plant's animal partner is no longer with us, making it what scientists call an "evolutionary anachronism." Long ago, South America was ruled by *megafauna*, giant animals that lived until humans arrived and apparently hunted them to extinction, around 10,000 to 20,000 years ago. For millions of years South America was an island, not yet connected to North America, allowing for richly diverse evolution of animals such as the *glyptodon*, an armadillo the size of a Volkswagen Beetle, and the sleek *macrauchenia* ("long neck"), a 10-foot-long grass eater that looked like a cross between a horse, a camel, a giraffe, and a svelte elephant. Then there were the giant ground sloth, 20 feet long and weighing five tons, and the *gomphothere*, an oversize elephant-like creature that might have roamed South America as recently as 9,000 years ago. All four are prime candidates for being the avocado's co-evolutionary pals. But if the fruit hadn't turned out to be tasty to humans, it may well have gone the way of the glyptodon and the gomphothere.

AVOCADO FACTS

• **Good For You.** Avocados are full of nutrients and cholesterol-lowering monounsaturated fat. However, the fruit, leaves, pit, and skin have been documented as harmful—and sometimes deadly—to many animals, including cats, dogs, rabbits, birds, horses, goats, rabbits, cattle, rodents, and fish. But not all parts are poisonous to every animal. While the fruit can kill birds, at least one pet food manufacturer has added avocado pulp and oil to its line of cat and dog foods as a coat conditioner, without any known ill effects.

• **What Hass Got Rot?** There are dozens of avocado varieties. The most common by far is the Hass avocado, accounting for about 80 percent of all cultivated avocado trees worldwide. And *all* of them are descended from the cuttings of a single tree owned by Rudolph Hass, a mail carrier who lived in La Habra Heights, California. In 1935 Hass noticed that the tree of unknown lineage produced great fruit year-round, so he patented it and sold its cuttings. (His original tree died of root rot in 2002.)

• **Production.** Of America's avocado crop, 90 percent comes from California. Of those, 60 percent come from San Diego County. How many avocados can a typical commercial tree produce each year? About 500, totaling 200 pounds of fruit. But don't expect to see any advertisements for "tree-ripened avocados." The avocado is unusual in that it won't ripen on the tree. Avocados can be kept mature but unripe for weeks or even months by leaving them on the tree or refrigerating them until they arrive at their retail destination. After only a few days at room temperature, they ripen into the semi-squishy state that consumers want.

• **Fruits or Vegetables?** Based on the fact that avocados grow on trees, you'd assume that the avocado is classified as a fruit. That's correct. But what kind of fruit? According to the University of California, it isn't like most tree fruits—apples, pears, or peaches—it's a "single-seeded berry."

• **Hernando Cortés, Food Critic.** Native American populations have been cultivating avocados for thousands of years. When he wasn't busy looting and destroying cities, conquistador Hernando Cortés took the opportunity to try an avocado in Mexico. He wrote: "In the center of the fruit is a seed like a peeled chestnut. And between this and the rind is the part which is eaten, which is abundant, and is a paste similar to butter and of very good taste." Not everyone agrees. Only 41 percent of American households consume avocados.

• **What's in a Name?** In 1960 the British retail chain Marks & Spencer tried introducing avocados to English consumers. Figuring the name was too foreign-sounding, the store marketed the fruit as "alligator pears." Unfortunately, its customers thought of pears as being something you made into a dessert...the culinary results were disastrous. After numerous complaints about inedible "alligator pear" tarts and pies, Marks & Spencer decided "avocado" wasn't such a bad name after all.

IT'S SCIENCE!

*Thoughts on the joys and frustrations
of scientific discovery.*

"Men love to wonder, and that is the seed of science."
—**Ralph Waldo Emerson**

"The task is not to see what has never been seen before, but to think what has never been thought before about what you see every day."
—**Erwin Schrodinger**

"The whole of science consists of data that, at one time or another, were inexplicable."
—**Brendan O'Regan**

"The most exciting phrase to hear in science, the one that heralds new discoveries, is not 'Eureka!' but 'That's funny...'"
—**Isaac Asimov**

"A good scientist is a person in whom the childhood quality of perennial curiosity lingers on. Once he gets an answer, he has other questions."
—**Frederick Seitz**

"All truths are easy to understand once they are discovered; the point is to discover them."
—**Galileo Galilei**

"Science is simply common sense at its best—rigidly accurate in observation and merciless to fallacy in logic."
—**Thomas Huxley**

"There are many hypotheses in science that are wrong. That's perfectly all right; they're the aperture to finding out what's right."
—**Carl Sagan**

"Every great advance in science has issued from a new audacity of imagination."
—**John Dewey**

"The good thing about science is that it's true whether or not you believe in it."
—**Neil deGrasse Tyson**

"The greatest discoveries of science have always been those that forced us to rethink our beliefs about the universe and our place in it."
—**Robert L. Park**

"Only those who see the invisible can do the impossible."
—**Bernard Lown**

A 2007 earthquake lifted up the entire island of Ranogga, in the Solomon Islands, by 10 feet.

FAMOUS AND BROKE...

Just because you're known by millions or you've changed history doesn't mean you're going to have any money in the bank.

GEORGE McGOVERN retired from politics in the 1980s, after 18 years in the U.S. Senate and an unsuccessful run for president. In 1988 he bought and began operating a 150-room hotel in Connecticut. In 1991, just three years after it opened, the inn closed and McGovern filed for bankruptcy. He said that the cost of meeting governmental regulations and dealing with frivolous lawsuits drained him and the hotel financially.

BERNHARD GOETZ shot four men in the New York City subway in 1984, claiming they'd threatened him with a screwdriver and tried to rob him. He was acquitted for that, but served 250 days in jail for carrying an unlicensed handgun. One of the muggers, Darrell Cabey, filed a civil suit against Goetz for the shooting, which left Cabey paralyzed. Cabey won a $43 million judgment. Goetz filed for bankruptcy in 1996, listing Cabey and his own lawyers as his primary creditors.

JAMES W. MARSHALL was a New Jersey carpenter who moved to California in the 1840s, hoping to find a better life. There, while working at Sutter's Mill (he was a partner in the sawmill), he discovered the gold that started the California Gold Rush. Lots of people got rich, but Marshall didn't. Not only that, the sawmill went out of business because all his employees left to hunt for gold. Marshall was penniless when he died in 1885.

ELIOT NESS won fame as the 27-year-old government agent who put gangster Al Capone in prison in 1931 on tax evasion charges. After that, things soured for Ness: His wife left him, he started drinking, he started a couple of failed businesses, and he got fired from a job at an alarm company for drinking too much. A 1947 run for mayor of Cleveland was his attempt to straighten things out—not only did he lose, but it left him with six figures of campaign debt. Bankrupt, Ness died of a heart attack in 1957.

Dinosaur ants, the world's oldest known ant species, can grow to over an inch long.

FOUR NICE STORIES

Every now and then, we like to lock our inner cynics
in a box and share stories with happy endings.

TOGETHER AGAIN

It was 1921. In a one-room schoolhouse in rural Wisconsin, two third-graders became "sweethearts." But after the school year ended, Mac McKitrick and Lorraine Beatty lost contact with each other...for 85 years. Then, in 2009, they were reunited through family members (their brothers had become friends). The two lovebirds instantly remembered each other and picked up right where they left off: McKitrick proposed, Beatty said yes, and the newlyweds moved in with each other at an Illinois retirement home. "I still picture Lorraine as my third-grade sweetheart," said McKitrick. "I've carried that in the back of my mind for all those years."

JUMPING TO CONCLUSIONS

An 84-year-old retiree named Don Ritchie has saved 160 lives over the past 50 years. How? By convincing people not to kill themselves. Ritchie doesn't work at a suicide hotline, though; he lives across the road from a seaside cliff in Sydney, Australia, called "The Gap"—one of the country's most notorious spots for suicides. Every day, Ritchie keeps an eye on the ledge from his living room window. If he sees someone who appears to be in despair, he walks over and starts talking to them. Ritchie's approach is low-key: He smiles and asks the person if they'd like to come over for tea. Then Ritchie tells them they still have a chance to reconsider their decision. A few haven't taken his advice, but most have. (Ritchie's job before he retired: selling life insurance.)

A BONDING EXPERIENCE

In December 2010, Mike Rodgers, an employee at Blue Grass Recycling in Burlington, Kentucky, was sifting through the contents of a bin that hadn't been emptied for several months. Near the bottom, he found 23 U.S. savings bonds with face values ranging from $50 to $500. Rodgers did some research online and discovered that the bonds, purchased in 1971, were now worth $22,000. Rodgers could have tried to cash them in himself, but instead decided to try and find the owner…which turned out to be very difficult. He found the identity of the woman who had purchased the bonds, Martha Dobbins, but she had been dead for nearly 20 years. Rodgers then began looking for the other person named on the bonds: Robert Roberts. To his dismay, he discovered there were hundreds of "Robert Roberts" in the United States. But he figured that only one would know who Martha Dobbins was, so he started e-mailing and calling every Robert Roberts he could find. He met with dead end after dead end. Finally, after more than a week of searching, Rodgers found his Robert Roberts a few days before Christmas. Roberts, 82, lived in Florida; Dobbins was his mother. "I had taken care of her for several years before she died," Rodgers explained, "but she never said anything about any bonds." When Roberts received the bonds in the mail, he tried to give Rodgers a reward, but Rodgers refused, saying he did it because "it was the right thing to do."

DINNER FOR TWO

One night in March 2008, Julio Diaz exited the subway at his stop in the Bronx, New York. When the 31-year-old social worker reached the stairs, a man held a knife to his back and demanded his wallet. Diaz slowly turned around, and noticed that his mugger was only a teenager. He took out his wallet and gave it to him. As the teen was walking away, Diaz, on a whim, decided to offer his coat. "If you're going to be robbing people for the rest of the night, you'll want to keep warm."

"Why are you doing this?" the teen asked.

"If you're willing to risk your freedom for a few dollars, then I guess you must really need the money." The teen accepted Diaz's coat. Then Diaz invited him to join him at his favorite restaurant. The teen accepted. Once there, the two just talked for a while as they ate dinner. When the check arrived, Diaz explained that he didn't have any money, but if the teen gave him his wallet back, then he'd treat him. The teen gave the wallet back. As he stood up to leave, Diaz asked for one more thing—the knife. The teen handed that to him as well and then left the restaurant.

Hair relaxer: At any given time, 15% of your hair follicles are resting.

THE UN-FRIENDLY SKIES

*At one time, you had to do something bad
to get in trouble with airport security.*

READ 'EM AND WEEP. In 2010 A Pomona College senior considering a career as a U.S. diplomat in the Middle East stuck his Arabic-language flashcards in a pocket before heading through airport security. He planned to brush up on his vocabulary during a flight from Philadelphia to California. Instead, he spent four hours in a holding cell, two of them in handcuffs. Plenty of time to consider whether the cards for "bomb" and "terrorism"—though highly relevant to his chosen field—should have been left at home.

NO YOLK! In 2011 a TSA agent handcuffed and detained 35-year-old Valerie Baul at the Philadelphia airport. The offense? She cracked a plastic egg over an agent's head after he asked what it contained. At the time, Baul was wearing a fuzzy pink bunny costume and carrying a basket filled with eggs that had already passed through the X-ray machine. (The eggs contained confetti.)

MOUSETRAP. Israeli scientists have begun testing a new kind of body scanner. It looks like a traditional airport scanner, but hidden inside are three trays filled with mice, specially trained to sniff out bomb-making chemicals. If the mice smell chemicals, they escape into a side chamber and trigger an alarm. In a test run, mice successfully detected all 22 chemical-tainted mock-terrorists planted among 1,000 shoppers in a Tel Aviv shopping center.

BIG MOUTH. In 2005 Dr. Esha Khoshnu, a New Jersey psychiatrist, was flying out of Phoenix on her way to San Diego. TSA tagged her for a random bag inspection. That's when, according to airport staff, she got "mouthy and snippy." Khoshnu said, "Even if I had a bomb, you wouldn't find it." That was enough—TSA detained her. She missed her flight, but was released. For some reason, however, Khoshnu's luggage—the bag that needed to be searched because the TSA thought it might contain a bomb—was still loaded onto the San Diego-bound plane. Once the plane reached San Diego, Khoshnu's bag was blown up on the tarmac.

ACTION FIGURE FACTS

Uncle John would like to remind you, once and for all, he is not playing with his "dolls." They are action figures.

GOODBYE, DOLLY

In 1964 designers at Hasbro Toys came up with a line of military dolls. Executives loved it, but the marketing department felt that boys would never buy anything called a "doll," a term associated with girls' toys. So they coined the term "action figure" to describe any human-like posable doll that was marketed to boys. And that toy line—G.I. Joe—was the first successful "action figure." Here are some more action figure facts.

• **The Name Game:** "Action figure" is more than a marketing term—it's also been used as a legal distinction. In 2003 manufacturer Toy Biz, which made Marvel, TNA Wrestling, and *Lord of the Rings* action figures, argued before the U.S. Court of International Trade that its products were toys, and not dolls. Why? Because companies have to pay higher tariffs on importing dolls produced in other countries—toys are subject to half the rate. Toy Biz lawyers argued that dolls are representations of humans, whereas action figures depicted "nonhuman creatures" (like superheroes) or characters (like wrestlers) Toy Biz won the case.

• **Rarest Action Figure:** When *The Simpsons* went on the air in 1990, a hurricane of Simpsons merchandise flooded the market. Surprisingly, Simpsons action figures were poor sellers. How poor? A Bart Simpson doll wearing a shirt that says "Save Blinky" (the three-eyed fish who lives in the contaminated lake by the Springfield Nuclear Power Plant) was available only by mail via Mattel Toys. Anybody could send away for it, but only three people did. Those are the only three known to exist; they're each worth about $1,000.

• **The Birth of (He-)Man:** Mattel passed on the opportunity to produce toys based on the *Star Wars* films. Big mistake: The movie went on to generate more than $1 billion in action figure sales well into the 1980s. Mattel wouldn't make a toy line based on the

1982 hit movie *Conan the Barbarian*, either, because it was R-rated. Instead, it created a new line of toys, combining the space fantasy of *Star Wars* and the beefcake and sorcery of *Conan*, and called it He-Man and the Masters of the Universe. Toys and comic books sold well, but they didn't take off until a TV cartoon series aired in 1983—specifically designed to boost sales of the toys (a children's-programming practice later made illegal by the FCC). It was the bestselling toy line of the 1980s.

• **Movies to Toys:** Other toy companies didn't seem to mind an R rating. R-rated movies with kids' action figure lines include *Rambo*, *Toxic Crusaders*, *Terminator 2*, *RoboCop*, and *Aliens*.

• **Toys to Movies:** A group of businessman and artists formed a company called Toy Vault in 1998 to fill what it thought was an overlooked market: toys based on children's literature. They bought the action figure rights for *Alice in Wonderland* and *Lord of the Rings*, and although no *Alice in Wonderland* figures were ever produced, the *Lord of the Rings* figures (Gandalf and Balrog) sold so well that executives at New Line Cinema decided that there was a market for big-budget *Lord of the Rings* movies.

• **Most-Hyped Figure That Ever Existed:** In late 1985, Mattel held a contest in which kids could send in their ideas for a new He-Man action figure. The best entry would be mass-produced and sold by the company. The winner: 12-year-old Nathan Bitner from Naperville, Illinois. His idea: Fearless Photog, a good-guy monster whose head is a video camera that drains the evil out of bad guys. Bitner won a $100,000 college scholarship, but the action figure was never produced. (Mattel did send him a picture of a prototype, though.)

• **Most Valuable Action Figure:** In the first wave of *Star Wars* toys—which didn't hit the market until 1978, a year after the film's release because Kenner didn't anticipate the huge demand—a Darth Vader action figure came with a telescoping lightsaber. (The saber's handle ejected from his hollow arm, and then a thinner piece came out.) It was very difficult to make and it broke easily, both in the factory and at home, so only the first wave had this feature, later replaced with a single-piece version. Only a few hundred were made and sold. Average value today: $6,000.

In 1935 Humpty Dumpty Drive-In owner Louis Ballast trademarked the word "cheeseburger."

BODIES IN MOTION

It's hard to stay disinterested about disinterment.
Throw in (or dig up) some celebrities, and you've
unearthed some great bathroom reading.

ELVIS PRESLEY (1935–77)
Claim to Fame: The King of Rock 'n' Roll
Interred: When Presley passed away at age 42 in August 1977, he was initially entombed in a special "family room" crypt inside the mausoleum at the Forest Hill Cemetery in Memphis, Tennessee. The crypt had slots for eight people, and Presley's mother Gladys, buried nearby, was moved to a space near her son.

Disinterred: In the month following Presley's death, it's estimated that more than a million fans crowded into the cemetery, disrupting other mourners and forcing the Presley estate to pay for extra security. Then, two weeks after the funeral, three men broke into the cemetery in the middle of the night and were charged with attempting to steal the King's body to hold it for ransom. The charges were later dropped; the men carried no tools and may simply have been trespassing. But the incident put a scare into Elvis's father, Vernon Presley. He felt his wife and son would be safer at Graceland, so he obtained a zoning variance to convert the estate's "Meditation Garden" into a six-plot private cemetery. Both Elvis and his mother were disinterred and buried at Graceland the following October. Vernon Presley died in 1979 and is buried there, as is his mother, Minnie Mae, who died in 1980.

JACKIE WILSON (1934–84)

Claim to Fame: A legendary R&B and pop singer of the 1950s and '60s, Wilson had numerous top-10 singles, including "Higher and Higher" and "Lonely Teardrops."
Buried: In 1975 Wilson collapsed from a heart attack while singing "Lonely Teardrops" onstage. He never fully recovered, and after lingering in nursing homes for eight years, he died in 1984. Wilson's finances weren't great even before the heart attack, and

after almost nine years of round-the-clock care, his estate was broke. There was no money for a headstone; his grave in the Westlawn Cemetery in Wayne, Michigan, was marked only by a board with his name on it.

Exhumed: Three years later, Wilson's grave still had no marker. That's when Florida disc jockey Jack "The Rapper" Gibson launched a fundraising drive to buy one. He raised enough money for a small marble crypt, and in June 1987 the remains of Wilson and his mother, who died a few weeks after his heart attack, were exhumed and interred together. Inscribed at the bottom of their marble marker: "No More Lonely Teardrops."

LEE HARVEY OSWALD (1939–63)

Claim to Fame: On November 22, 1963, Oswald assassinated President John F. Kennedy in Dallas, Texas. Two days later he was gunned down by Dallas nightclub owner Jack Ruby.

Buried: After Oswald's body was autopsied, it was returned to his family and buried at the Rose Hill Cemetery in Fort Worth, Texas.

Exhumed: In 1981 Oswald's grave was reopened at the behest of Michael Eddowes, a British conspiracy theorist who believed that the man buried in Oswald's grave was a Soviet KGB assassin. Oswald had lived in the U.S.S.R. from 1959 to 1962, and Eddowes was convinced that a KGB double agent had returned to the United States in Oswald's place on a mission to kill JFK. Exhuming the corpse and comparing the skull with Oswald's dental records, he argued, would prove the man in the grave was not Oswald.

Oswald's widow, Marina, thought Eddowes's theory was nuts, but she had her own theory, namely that Oswald's body had been secretly removed from the grave and cremated "to prevent vandalism." She supported Eddowes's request to have the body exhumed because it would enable her to find out if the grave was empty.

It wasn't. When the grave was dug up in October 1981, it did indeed contain a body. After the head was removed and the teeth cleaned and X-rayed, the new X-rays matched Oswald's dental records perfectly. "Beyond any doubt, and I mean absolutely any doubt," the lead pathologist told reporters, "the person buried under the name Lee Harvey Oswald is Lee Harvey Oswald."

Worldwide, only 6% of airplane pilots are women.

BLOOD & BOOTY

*American history might have been written in French
or Spanish. Here's part of the reason it wasn't.*

PLUNDERERS FOR HIRE

In 1562 some French Protestants known as *Huguenots* landed on what is now Parris Island, near Beaufort, South Carolina. Like the English Pilgrims who would arrive a half century later, the Huguenots wanted religious freedom. This group, led by Captain Jean Ribault, also wanted riches: They were privateers. In an era when navies were smaller than they are today, countries hired armed private ships and crews to do much of their pillaging and plundering for them. Privateers were an accepted part of naval warfare: Under admiralty law, if captured they were supposed to be treated as prisoners of war, even if what they were doing looked a lot like piracy.

The Huguenots were going to do their pillaging under the French Crown. After raising a stone marker on Parris Island and claiming all the surrounding land in the name of King Charles IX, Ribault sailed back to France for supplies. He left behind 28 men to establish a fort, with enough food for six months and sufficient arms and munitions for defense. The men immediately set to work building a shelter made of wood and earth, with a straw roof. They dug a moat around it and added four bastions—bulwarks from which they could defend the new settlement. Then they waited…and waited… and waited. But Ribault did not return. The problem: By the time Ribault reached home, France was embroiled in a full-blown religious war between Protestants and Catholics and had no money to spare for his resupply mission. So Ribault sailed on to England, hoping to find a sponsor there. Instead, he ended up imprisoned in the Tower of London by a suspicious Queen Elizabeth I.

WE'LL NEVER HAVE PARRIS

When their supplies ran out, the abandoned men panicked. They cobbled together a ship using pine resin to seal the wood and moss to caulk the seams. Then they sewed their shirts and sheets together to make sails and begged the natives for rope to rig them.

In 1810 the average American drank 5 gallons of liquor per year. In 2010: 1 gallon.

The 15-year-old cabin boy took one look at the ship that they planned to sail across 3,000 miles of ocean (with no navigator) and decided to stay with the Indians.

The would-be colonists spent more than a year at sea, much of the time drifting for lack of wind. The food they'd brought dwindled to 12 corn kernels per man a day. When that was gone, they ate their shoes and leather jackets. Then they turned to cannibalism, choosing one of their own to eat so the rest might live. Fourteen months into their voyage, adrift and within sight of France but unable to steer what was left of their poorly built vessel, a British ship spotted them. They were rescued and taken to England.

HERE THERE BE SILVER

Two years later, Ribault's lieutenant, René Laudonnière, sailed a second band of colonists to the New World. He landed at the mouth of the St. John's River (near present-day Jacksonville, Florida), a perfect spot for attacking the galleons returning to Spain via the Gulf Stream. But while his men built a new fort—called Fort Caroline—Laudonnière discovered spoils closer at hand: gold and silver bangles jingling around the natives' ankles. He decided to befriend them and discover the source of their wealth. First, he promised to aid a local chief in his war with an inland rival. Then, to curry favor with the rival chief, he rescued the prisoners being held by the first chief and returned them home. Pretty soon neither leader trusted the French commander.

The same went for his own men. Tired of waiting for treasure—and food—they plotted to get rid of him. Thirteen mutineers stole some small ships, and set to sea to attack Spanish ships. Bad idea. Spain had already targeted the colonists at Fort Caroline as "a nest of pirates" and sent one of its most brutal commanders—Pedro Menendez de Aviles—to wipe them out.

GOD VS. PIRATES

By the time Menendez arrived, Ribault had been released from the Tower and returned to France. From there he went to the New World with seven ships and 500 soldiers, where he reinforced and resupplied Fort Caroline, left a small company of men to help Laudonnière guard the fort, and set sail with the rest of his crew. If all went well, he would wipe out the Spanish before Menendez could establish a stronghold. As for Menendez, he built fortifications on ground protected by water on three sides and named the new fort *San Augustin* (St. Augustine). Being a devout Catholic, he also prayed. He was certain that God would be on his side against the Protestant pirates.

SURRENDER OR STARVE

Ribault's ships made their way down the coast toward St. Augustine, not knowing that a hurricane thundered toward shore. While the French were battered by the hurricane, Menendez took his forces overland to Fort Caroline. He destroyed the fort and killed nearly everyone there, including the sick, the elderly, the women, and the children. Laudonnière survived by abandoning his post and fleeing with a few followers. Meanwhile, the storm blew Ribault's ships past the inlet that led to St. Augustine and smashed them against the barrier islands. Ribault and his men survived, but had to make the 180-mile trek back to Fort Caroline on foot, only to be stymied when they reached an inlet south of St. Augustine. How would they cross?

Back from destroying the fort, Menendez and his troops were only too happy to help. They offered to ferry the French across, if they agreed to lay down their weapons and surrender. Famished and exhausted, the shipwrecked privateers let themselves be taken captive, expecting to be treated as prisoners of war. Menendez promised to do "whatever God directed him to do." The Spanish ferried the French across the inlet a few at a time, led them into the dunes, and put them to the sword. Locals named the place *Matanzas*—the Spanish word for "slaughter."

THE PIRATES' REVENGE

Menendez's treachery did not go unmarked, though he justified the massacre as being done "not as to Frenchmen but as to heretics." Unfortunately for him, Laudonnière made it home. Soon tales of the slaughter spread across France. Dominique de Gourgues, a French nobleman, had his own score to settle with Spain. In his youth, he had been taken captive and consigned to the brutal Spanish galleys. Enraged by the massacre, he disguised himself as a slaver, equipped three ships with 200 men-at-arms, and headed across the Atlantic.

WHO GOT THE LOOT

Spanish soldiers at the fort on the St. John's River—renamed San Mateo—were completely fooled by the fake slavers, and saluted as de Gourgues's ships sailed into the river. That night, de Gourgues and his men came ashore, slew the guards at their posts, and overran the garrison. They hanged Menendez's men on the same trees Menendez had used as gallows for the French at Fort Caroline. De Gourgues posted a sign that read, "I do this not as to Spaniards nor as unto Mariners, but as to Traitors, Robbers, and Murderers."

Historians have speculated that had the French and Spanish not been busy fighting each other for control of Florida, *either* country might have secured an unbreakable hold over the New World. Their squabbles most benefited another colonial power: England.

*   *   *

TWO McDONALDS (B)AD CAMPAIGNS

• Members of the company's marketing department knew they had their work cut out for them when they were faced with the task of pitching the dark, PG-13-rated *Batman Returns* to McDonald's young customers in 1992. The company rolled out a line of Happy Meals that downplayed connections to the film: A free toy featuring the Penguin looked like the character in the comic book instead of the grisly, deformed villain in the film, played by Danny DeVito. Even so, the company was slammed with complaints from angry parents who took their young children to the movie after seeing the toys. To avoid further controversy, the company yanked the campaign.

• McDonald's has helped promote dozens of animated Disney films over the years, from *The Little Mermaid* to *Bambi* rereleases. They missed the mark on a promotion for *Mulan,* the 1998 movie based on an ancient Chinese legend. Commercials featured Ronald McDonald in a headband comically karate-chopping the company's logo, and encouraged customers to sit on the floor when they ate their Happy Meals. Jeff Yang, founding editor of A, an Asian-American magazine, called the racial stereotyping in the ads "the equivalent of a drive-by mooning."

Aptly named: The world's largest herd of Holstein dairy cows is in Elsie, Michigan.

MOVIE QUOTE QUIZ #1

Can you name the movies that launched these familiar quotations?
Give yourself an extra point if you know the year of the
film, too. (Answers are on page 538.)

1. "It's not a tumor!"

2. "When you're slapped, you'll take it and like it!"

3. "Excuse me while I whip this out."

4. "I must break you."

5. "Dad always used to say the only causes worth fighting for were the lost causes."

6. "San Dimas High School football rules!"

7. "We all go a little mad sometimes."

8. "Wherever there's a fight so hungry people can eat, I'll be there. Wherever there's a cop beatin' up a guy, I'll be there."

9. "Et cetera, et cetera, et cetera!"

10. "You ever danced with the devil in the pale moonlight?"

11. "The power of Christ compels you."

12. "Get off my plane!"

13. "It's a trap!"

14. "Snap out of it!"

15. "Mein Fuhrer, I can walk!"

16. "We're goin' streaking!"

17. "Please, sir. I want some more."

18. "Fish are friends, not food."

19. "No bastard ever won a war by dying for his country. He won it by making the other poor dumb bastard die for his country."

20. "I once had wealth, power, and the love of a beautiful woman. Now I only have two things: my friends and my thermos."

21. "We'll do it for Johnny!"

22. "Keep your friends close, but your enemies closer."

23. "The greatest trick the devil ever pulled was convincing the world he didn't exist."

24. "You're not too smart, are you? I like that in a man."

In some remote villages in New Mexico, people still speak a form of 16th-century Spanish.

OUR STATE IS #1!

*Everybody likes to know that they're the best at something...
unless that "something" is a little embarrassing. Here's a
list of two things that each state in the U.S. excels at.*

ALABAMA
- Lowest taxes on goods
- Adult-onset diabetes

ALASKA
- Heliports
- Teen death

ARIZONA
- Copper production
- Alcoholism

ARKANSAS
- Best-trained math teachers
- E. coli infections spread by petting zoos

CALIFORNIA
- Roller coasters
- Air pollution

COLORADO
- Flu shots
- Cocaine usage

CONNECTICUT
- Dentist visits
- Electricity consumption

DELAWARE
- Most-profitable farms
- Gasoline theft

FLORIDA
- Freshwater turtles
- Mortgage loan fraud

GEORGIA
- Best condition of roads
- Personal bankruptcy filings

HAWAII
- People who carpool to work
- Highest cost of living

IDAHO
- Rainbow trout fishing
- Highest suicide rate

ILLINOIS
- Pumpkins
- Nuclear power production

INDIANA
- Elevator manufacturing
- Divorce

IOWA
- Percentage of residents over the age of 85
- Water pollution

KANSAS
- Helium manufacturing
- Obsolete bridges still in use

KENTUCKY
- Horse breeding
- Deaths from smoking

LOUISIANA
- Affordable hospitals
- Gonorrhea and syphilis

MAINE
- Youngest median age
- Per capita rate of asthma

MARYLAND
- High school students who take college-level courses
- Movie bootlegging

MASSACHUSETTS
- Adults with college degrees
- Government health care spending

MICHIGAN
- Navy bean production
- Unemployment

MINNESOTA
- Per capita rate of preventive colonoscopies
- Tornadoes

MISSISSIPPI
- Wetland restoration and preservation projects
- Obesity

MISSOURI
- Sport hunting
- Meth labs

MONTANA
- Number of restaurants per capita
- Drunk driving

NEBRASKA
- Livestock
- Domestic violence

NEVADA
- Gold mining
- Home foreclosures

NEW HAMPSHIRE
- Lowest percentage of people living in poverty
- Skin cancer rates for women

NEW JERSEY
- Millionaires
- Population density

NEW MEXICO
- Lowest cancer rates
- Children who drink alcohol

NEW YORK
- Charitable donations
- Longest daily commute

NORTH CAROLINA
- Most diverse population of salamanders
- Lowest teacher salary

NORTH DAKOTA
- Lowest rate of AIDS
- Lowest rate of seat belt use

Senior spider: Tarantulas live for up to 20 years.

OHIO
- Library visits
- Traffic tickets issued

OKLAHOMA
- Per capita use of electric and hybrid cars
- Women in prison

OREGON
- Solar panels
- Homeless population

PENNSYLVANIA
- Covered bridges
- UFO sightings

RHODE ISLAND
- Drive-in movie theaters
- Per capita illegal drug use

SOUTH CAROLINA
- Lowest gas prices
- Strokes

SOUTH DAKOTA
- Lowest personal income tax rate
- Per capita Facebook use

TENNESSEE
- Immunizations
- Painkiller prescriptions

TEXAS
- Wind power
- High school dropout rates

UTAH
- Community service volunteers
- Online pornography use

VERMONT
- Percentage of children who are read to daily
- Fewest registered organ donors

VIRGINIA
- Places on the National Historic Register
- Least amount of employee leave

WASHINGTON
- Largest fleet of nonmilitary ferries
- Lowest availability of psychiatric care

WEST VIRGINIA
- Pre-death funeral planning
- Heart attacks

WISCONSIN
- Organic farming
- Binge drinking

WYOMING
- Coal production
- Injuries from lightning strikes

40 million Americans experience *bruxism* in their sleep. What is it? Tooth grinding.

I SHOOT YOU WITH...MY KEY FOB!

*Guns disguised as everyday items aren't
just for James Bond movies.*

GLOCK AND ROLL

In March 2011, police in the city of Luleå, Sweden, responded to a tip about a man who had a stash of illegal weapons in his home. When they raided the house, they found six unlicensed guns...and an electric guitar. On closer inspection, they discovered that the guitar was actually a shotgun: The neck had been hollowed out and was concealing two gun barrels, and inside the guitar body was an almost-completed triggering device. The man told officers that he kept the guns as a form of therapy "to keep off the drink," and that he was building the shotgun-guitar "for fun." He faces several charges.

REACH OUT AND SHOOT SOMEONE

A special police mafia unit in Naples, Italy, raided the headquarters of the Gionta crime family in 2008. One of the things they found was a cell phone, with what appeared to be a normal keypad, a screen, and an antenna—except that it was actually a cleverly disguised gun. Here's how it works: You slide the keypad to the left to reveal four holes under the fake screen. Load four .22 caliber cartridges into the holes and slide the phone closed. To fire: Press the four buttons in the top row one at a time, and each time a bullet is shot out of the fake antenna. Police said the phone-guns first appeared in eastern Europe around 2000, and the fact that they were now in mafia hands was "worrying."

KEY WITNESS

In November 2004, Junior Collins, 27, was arrested for drunk-driving in Manchester, England. In Collins's pocket police found an electronic car door opener. The device was black, about four inches long by one inch wide, and had three buttons on it and a key ring attached to one end. The cops didn't give it much

---

What do you call the noise your epiglottis makes when it flaps? A burp.

thought—until one of them remembered that they'd been briefed about "key fob guns" coming into the country from eastern Europe. (A "key fob" is a term for any decorative item attached to a key ring.) They looked closer, and sure enough, the thing was a gun. And it was loaded with two .22 caliber cartridges. Collins admitted that the device was his, but said a friend gave it to him—and he didn't even know it was a gun! Judge Anthony Gee didn't believe him, and made a good point about the gun. "Weapons such as this can only be designed to be fired," he said. "Just showing it would be unlikely to produce alarm and terror, because anyone looking at it wouldn't know it was a firearm." Collins was sentenced to six years in prison.

(LIP)STICK 'EM UP

In 2008 Defense Devices of Jackson, Tennessee, introduced a new type of lipstick…that's actually a stun gun. Its glossy metal case makes it look very much like a real lipstick cylinder, except that you can use one to send 350,000 volts of electricity into an assailant, an intruder, or just one of your friends. Cost: $26.95. Also available from Defense Devices: stun guns disguised as cell phones and fountain pens, and a ring (for your finger) that shoots pepper spray.

GUN BELT

Police in Queensbury, New York, pulled a man over for speeding in March 2010. When the driver rolled down his window, police noticed that the passenger, Jeremy Stead, 32, of Quinlan, Texas, had a very large and very odd belt buckle, with what appeared to be a tiny gun worked into the buckle's design. It turned out the tiny gun could be removed from the buckle—and it was real. Stead told officers he wore the buckle because it was "part of my persona." His persona was charged with possession of an unlicensed firearm.

*　　　*　　　*

"Opportunity is missed by most people because it comes dressed in overalls and looks like work."

—**Thomas Edison**

MYTH-CONCEPTIONS

*"Common knowledge" is frequently wrong. Here are some
more examples of things that many people believe...but
that, according to our sources, just aren't true.*

Myth: Camels can go long periods without drinking water
because they store extra water in their humps.
Truth: The hump is a reservoir for fat, not water. In fact,
a camel stores *most* of its body fat in its hump, unlike humans,
who store it throughout their bodies. The lack of heat-trapping fat
allows the camel to lose heat from the rest of its body without
having to perspire, thus conserving water.

Myth: The Statue of Liberty is in New York.
Truth: It's actually in New Jersey. The structure sits on Liberty
Island, which is in New York Harbor, but technically within the
territorial waters of Jersey City, New Jersey. An agreement
between the two states gives New York control over—but not
ownership of—Liberty Island. New York maintains the statue;
New Jersey provides utility services.

Myth: Panthers are a particular kind of wild cat.
Truth: There is no species of cat called a panther. Leopards
and jaguars that happen to have black coats are all labeled as
"panthers."

Myth: Your ears sit on the outside of your head.
Truth: Those things on the sides of your head are called *pinnae*,
and they're primarily made up of cartilage. Your ears are organs
consisting of the inner ear, middle ear, and outer ear, some of
which are inside your head. The pinnae enhance the hearing
process by funneling sound to the inner ear. They also serve to
protect the internal ear parts.

Myth: Dixie, the nickname for the South, is derived from the
Mason-Dixon Line, commonly thought to be the boundary
between the North and the South.

The Olympic torch was carried to the top of Mt. Everest in 2008.

Truth: There's no evidence that Dixie is derived from Dixon (Mason and Dixon were two surveyors hired in the 1700s to settle a border dispute; their findings determined state lines later on). The term probably came from $10 bills issued in New Orleans in the mid-1800s that had the word *dix* printed on them. (*Dix* is French for "ten.") The bills were nicknamed "dixies," and the term caught on as shorthand for the whole of the South.

Myth: White wine is made from green grapes, and red wine is made from red grapes.
Truth: The color of wine doesn't have much to do with the color of the grapes from which it was made—it has to do with how the skins are used. Both color grapes are used in winemaking, but if the skins are removed in the fermentation process, the wine turns out light-colored. If the skins are left on to ferment, the wine is redder.

Myth: Legally speaking, murder is a premeditated act, while manslaughter is a crime committed in the heat of the moment.
Truth: Murder isn't always premeditated. Murder charges can be filed for a planned act of killing, but they can also be levied for a killing in the heat of the moment if it happened during the commission of another felony—shooting a guard during a bank robbery, for example. Manslaughter, on the other hand, is killing without malice (without intent to kill). Voluntary manslaughter *is* a heat-of-the-moment killing, such as self-defense or a crime of passion; it's involuntary manslaughter if someone is killed while another, non-felony crime is being committed, such as misdemeanor reckless driving.

Myth: Before you exercise or play a sport, you should stretch in order to prevent soreness and injuries.
Fact: We've been told this ever since grade school, but recent findings have revealed that static stretching—in which you bend down and hold your toes for a length of time—will have little or no effect on how you perform or how you feel afterward. (If you stretch for too long, more than a minute, you could pull a muscle.) What your muscles need in order to warm up is movement—so wave your arms and run in place to get your blood flow going.

Pickles for the pickled? Polish hangover cure: dill pickle juice. German: pickled herring.

FAMILIAR PHRASES

Here are the origins of some common phrases.

HAVING KITTENS

Meaning: To be extremely anxious

Origin: "Dates back to the medieval belief in the power of witches. It was thought that witches could perform a spell on a pregnant woman by turning her baby into kittens that would scratch at her womb. It is possible to imagine the kind of fear that would have gripped the 'victim' in more superstitious times. However, as our superstitions have diminished, we have been left only with this strange image." (From *March Hares and Monkeys' Uncles*, by Harry Oliver.)

JUST DESERTS

Meaning: A punishment or reward that is deserved

Origin: "The phrase has its origins in the obsolete word 'desert,' meaning that which one deserves. In use since at least the 1300s, it is commonly seen in print as *just desserts*, as in the sweet final course of a meal. It is pronounced this way, but the spelling is incorrect." (From *Exploring Idioms*, by Valeri R. Helterbran.)

GET THE SACK

Meaning: To be fired from a job

Origin: "In 17th-century France, mechanics traveling in quest of work carried their implements in a bag, or sack. When discharged, they were literally handed the sack so that they could put their tools in it and seek a job elsewhere." (From *Dictionary of Phrase and Fable*, by Ebenezer Cobham Brewer.)

GOODY TWO-SHOES

Meaning: An overly virtuous person

Origin: "Goody Two-Shoes is the name of the main character in a children's story called "The History of Little Goody Two-Shoes," which was published in 1765 in London. She lived most of her life with only one shoe, but when she received a second shoe, she was so overjoyed that she ran around yelling 'Two shoes! Two shoes!' until nobody could stand the sight of her." (From *Complete Idiot's Guide to Weird Word Origins*, By Paul McFedries.)

SAVE ONE'S BACON

Meaning: To prevent an injury or loss to oneself

Origin: "The phrase arose as a metaphor from the necessity of keeping the household's winter store of bacon protected from scavenging dogs. In this sense its meaning is to prevent a loss." (From *Flying by the Seat of Your Pants*, by Harry Oliver.)

CUT TO THE CHASE

Meaning: Get to the point

Origin: "In the early days of film (late 1920s to 30s), the term meant to cut (edit out) the boring parts and get to the excitement: the chase scenes. By the late 1940s, the term had gone from an editing direction to a figure of speech." (From *Let's Talk Turkey: Stories Behind America's Favorite Expressions*, by Rosemarie Ostler.)

BY THE SEAT OF YOUR PANTS

Meaning: Without the necessary experience

Origin: "Back when pilots didn't have so many navigation instruments, they relied on feedback from the plane itself through the point of greatest contact: the pilot's pants. British Royal Airforce pilots used the term 'fly by the seat of your trousers' in World War II and American pilots borrowed the phrase, switching 'pants' for those starchy British trousers." (From *I Love It When You Talk Retro*, by Ralph Keyes.)

THE LUNATICS HAVE TAKEN OVER THE ASYLUM

Meaning: Those who should be regulated are running the show

Origin: "In 1918, three of film's greatest stars—Charlie Chaplin, Mary Pickford, and Douglas Fairbanks—together with director D.W. Griffith, founded a movie studio of their own, to be called United Artists. When the news reached the head of Metro Pictures Richard Rowland, his reaction was: 'The lunatics have taken over the asylum.'" (From *Who Said That First?*, by Max Cryer.)

A bottlenose dolphin's outer skin replaces itself every 2 hours—9 times faster than a human's.

SEE YOU AT THE IGLOO

*Few sports fans call stadiums or arenas by their official names
(Qualcomm Park? Really?) True fans use colorful, locally
derived (and often derisive) nicknames…like these.*

STADIUM: Minute Maid Park
HOME TEAM: Houston Astros
STORY: It was once called Enron Field, but Coca-Cola
bought the naming rights when Enron famously collapsed in 2001.
Coke then named it after Minute Maid, its subsidiary that primarily packages orange juice. Add to that the fact that the Astros
wear orange uniforms, and the fact that the park is one of the
smallest in Major League baseball, and you get…**The Juice Box**.

STADIUM: Cleveland Stadium
HOME TEAM: Cleveland Indians
STORY: For years a rumor persisted that the stadium, which
opened in 1931, was built to help persuade the International
Olympic Committee to hold the 1932 games in Cleveland, but
that clueless planners broke ground after Los Angeles had already
been awarded the event. In truth the stadium, constructed near
Lake Erie, was built for the Cleveland Indians, not the Olympics,
and was meant to attract commerce to downtown Cleveland. Still,
it's never shaken its nickname: **The Mistake by the Lake**.

ARENA: Verizon Center
HOME TEAM: Washington Capitals
STORY: Verizon, a cell-phone service provider, owns the naming
rights to the arena, prompting fans to call the building **The Phone
Booth**. That's kind of ironic, because cell phones have actually
brought about the widespread disappearance of phone booths.

ARENA: Prudential Center
HOME TEAM: New Jersey Devils
STORY: Prudential Insurance, which is headquartered in Newark,
New Jersey, and holds the arena's naming rights, has been using

---

Bestselling pharmaceutical drug worldwide: aspirin.

the Rock of Gibraltar as its logo since the 1890s and introduced its most famous advertising slogan, "Get a piece of the rock," in the 1970s. It makes sense that the Prudential Center's nickname, then, would be **The Rock**.

ARENA: Civic Arena
HOME TEAM: Pittsburgh Penguins
STORY: The arena is round and painted white. And it's filled with ice because a hockey team plays there. So despite the fact that real penguins live in Antarctica, while igloos are found only in the Arctic, the Mellon Arena is nicknamed **The Igloo**.

STADIUM: Wrigley Field
HOME TEAM: Chicago Cubs
STORY: Cubs fans are among the most loyal in sports, despite the team not reaching the World Series in more than 100 years. And one of the most popular Cubs of all time was Ernie Banks, a Hall of Famer whose positive attitude (despite his team never winning a championship) earned him one of his nicknames, "Mr. Sunshine." Banks gave the stadium its nice nickname, **The Friendly Confines**.

STADIUM: Tropicana Field
HOME TEAM: Tampa Bay Rays
STORY: The NHL's Tampa Bay Lightning played there in the 1990s. And the building is a dome, earning it humorous comparisons to the bloodsport arena from the 1985 movie *Mad Max Beyond Thunderdome*. So, since lightning goes with thunder, fans call it **The Thunderdome**.

STADIUM: Lambeau Field
HOME TEAM: Green Bay Packers
STORY: One of the most famous games in NFL history, the "Ice Bowl," was played there in December 1967: The Packers and the Dallas Cowboys played on frozen ground amidst frigid winds and a –15°F temperature. *Sports Illustrated* writer Tex Maule equated Lambeau Field with the Arctic tundra. But when the game was discussed in season highlight films for both teams, narrators referred to the field as **The Frozen Tundra**, and the nickname stuck.

STREET SONGS

For generations of kids, the songs on Sesame Street were the first pop songs they ever heard. Here are the stories behind some favorite ones.

"C IS FOR COOKIE"

In 1971 *Sesame Street* mastermind Jim Henson, puppeteer Jerry Juhl, head writer Jeff Moss, and chief songwriter Joe Raposo decided to write a sketch for every letter of the alphabet. One of the Muppets' biggest hits was the song they came up with for C: "C Is for Cookie," sung by Cookie Monster (Frank Oz) while sitting on a giant letter C, with a monster chorus singing operatic background vocals. Raposo wrote the song, which debuted on a *Sesame Street* album in 1971 and aired on TV in 1972. Raposo was also the original inspiration for Cookie Monster. He was a ravenous fan of cookies—so much so that when he died in 1989, his family had a milk-and-cookies reception instead of a wake.

"MAHNA MAHNA"

This song is more famous from *The Muppet Show*. It was the basis of the very first sketch on the very first episode in 1975: A crazy-looking jazz singer puppet named Mahna Mahna (pronounced "ma-náh ma-náh"), dressed in a green fuzzy vest, with wild orange hair, sang the nonsense song "Mahna Mahna" as he bounced on, off, and around the screen. But the song debuted on episode 14 of *Sesame Street* in 1969, as performed by a puppet named Bip Bippadotta. (It also made quite an impression when the Muppets performed it on *The Ed Sullivan Show* that same year.) The premise of the sketch was always the same—the nonsense words "mahna mahna" repeated over and over, sung calmly at first, then veering wildly out of control. It's one of the few well-known *Sesame Street* songs not written specifically for the show. It was actually written by Italian composer Piero Umiliani for a the 1968 movie *Sweden, Heaven and Hell*—a soft-core porn film.

"BEIN' GREEN"

In 1970 producer Jon Stone asked Joe Raposo to "write a song for the frog," meaning Kermit, and gave him educational guidelines

---

"I" is for inflation: A birdseed milkshake on *Sesame Street* cost 20¢ in 1969. In 2010: $2.99.

for the lyrics, a common practice on the show. Stone said it had to be about making kids feeling special and unique. He even gave Raposo some lyrics to work from. Raposo hammered out a song in which Kermit laments being green because it's ordinary, but ultimately realizing that it's beautiful. The lyric, "It's not easy being green," became a catchphrase in the early 1970s, and was also interpreted as an anti-racist sentiment. Although many of the lyrics used in "Bein' Green" were written by Stone, he didn't ask for a songwriting credit. Raposo ended up being listed as the sole writer of the song and Stone lost out on millions in royalties.

"CAN YOU TELL ME HOW TO GET TO SESAME STREET?"

Jon Stone wanted the show's theme song to build momentum and excitement—exactly what an opening song should do. "Running happily, tumbling, playing along the way, but always intent on getting to *Sesame Street*," is how Stone put it in his memoir. He liked the catchy, toy-piano-driven sing-song melody that Joe Raposo and co-writer Bruce Hart came up with but hated the lyrics—he thought they were trite and full of clichés ("Sunny day, sweeping the clouds away"), with references he felt would be dated, like "everything's A-OK," which Stone derided as "astronaut slang." Nevertheless, it's been the theme song for the show's entire run (although it was remade several times—most notably as a calypso version in 1993 and a hip-hop version in 2007).

T IS FOR TRIVIA

• **"Sing."** This Raposo ballad, about trying to do things even if you're afraid you aren't good at them, was written for the show in 1970 and was sung on the show in English, Spanish, and even sign language. It's the most-performed song on *Sesame Street*. (It's been sung by more than 50 performers.) The Carpenters recorded it in 1973, and it became a #3 pop hit.

• **"Rubber Duckie."** While rubber ducks had been around since the 1890s (with the availability of cheap rubber), it wasn't until this song was featured on *Sesame Street* in 1970 that they became really popular, becoming the definitive kids' bath toy (as well as the mascot for a certain trivia book). The song itself was popular, too. Singing it as "Ernie," Jim Henson hit #16 on the pop chart with "Rubber Duckie" in 1970.

TOILET TECH

Better living through bathroom technology.

TAG, YOU'RE IT

Product: Linen Trackers

How They Work: The days of checking out of your hotel with your suitcase stuffed with the hotel's bath towels will be a thing of the past if Linen Technology Tracking of Miami, Florida, has its way: The company has developed a washable version of those anti-shoplifter ID tags that sound an alarm if you take merchandise out of a store without paying for it. The tags can be sewn into towels, bathrobes, bedspreads, and anything else the hotel thinks you might be tempted to abscond with. LTT says that a Honolulu hotel that installed the system to keep track of its pool towels cut thefts from 4,000 towels per month to just 750—a savings of $16,000 a month. (If hotels pass the savings on to consumers in the form of lower room rates, you might save enough money to *buy* yourself some towels.)

LOO-VER DAM

Product: HighDro Power

How It Works: Developed by a British graduate student named Tom Broadbent, HighDro Power is a small turbine that can be installed in the vertical drainpipes of high-rise buildings, which connect plumbing fixtures to the sewer system below. Every time a toilet is flushed or a sink is emptied, wastewater going through the drainpipe turns the blades on the turbine. The turbine is connected to a generator, which converts this mechanical energy into electricity. Broadbent estimates that a seven-story building fitted with the devices would cut its electricity bill by $1,400 a year, and that a big hotel could even make money by selling the energy back to the power company.

RECYCLED CONTENT

Product: Reusable Toilet Wipes

How They Work: Not all toilet tech has to be high-tech.

Sometimes it's nice to get back to basics…and sometimes it isn't. Wallypop, a company whose goal is "supporting a natural lifestyle," sells flannel and terrycloth toilet wipes for people who feel guilty about using toilet paper. The Wallypop website offers tips on how to incorporate the reusable wipes into daily life. After use, it says, "Shake, scrape, swish, or squirt off anything you don't want in your laundry, then toss the wipe into a diaper pail or container." Then, "in laundering poop-stained cloth, an important tip: wash them separately from other laundry." Check! And finally, "This is not nearly as gross as you might be imagining." (Yes, it is!)

NO ESCAPE

Product: "Billboard Mirrors"

How They Work: Installed over restroom sinks, these 40-inch mirrorized video screens display advertising—high-definition video clips or still images—when no one is using the sink. Then, when someone approaches the sink, the ad shrinks until it occupies just a corner of the screen, enabling the person to use the mirror and, if they want, watch the commercial in the corner. TV ads in restrooms may seem like an unwelcome intrusion into one of the last places where a person can have a moment to themselves, but Clear Channel Airports, the company that introduced them at Chicago's O'Hare Airport in early 2011, says feedback from the public and from advertisers has been positive. Don't expect to see TV screens in toilet stalls anytime soon, though. The mirrors are intentionally installed only at the sinks to get "as far away as possible from the toilet and the negative connotations associated with that from the advertiser's point of view."

THE SHOOTIST

Product: The Sega Toylet

How It Works: Why wasn't *this* game system called the Wii? The Toylet is the latest attempt to turn a urinal into a video game. In early 2011, Sega installed these game consoles in a few public restrooms in Tokyo. A pressure sensor is installed inside the urinal; a video display is installed at eye level above it. "Players" aim for the sensor as they make use of the facilities. There are four games

---

…WWII-era British urinal with Adolf Hitler's face painted inside the bowl.

to choose from: "Manneken Pis," which calculates the volume of urine released from the time spent urinating and the pressure generated; "Graffiti Eraser," in which you use a virtual fire hose to spray graffiti off a wall; "The Northern Wind and Her," in which you try to generate enough pressure (wind) to lift a girl's skirt, revealing her underwear; and "Milk from Nose," in which you try to generate more pressure than the last person who used the urinal. When the games are over, the video screen plays an advertisement. The Toylets are experimental; Sega says it has "no concrete plans to turn them into actual products."

STOP AND GO
Product: The "Don't Flush Me" project
How It Works: When New York City's sewer system is deluged with rainwater during heavy storms, millions of gallons of untreated sewage can end up flowing into New York Harbor. The Don't Flush Me Project, created by a graduate student named Leif Percifield, uses a sensor connected to a cell phone to keep track of water levels in the sewer system. When the levels rise close to the point of overflowing, the cell phone calls a computer, which alerts subscribers via text messages and Twitter tweets to hold off flushing toilets until the crisis has passed. Percifield hopes to one day install them throughout the city's sewer system.

GOING CLUBBING
Product: The UroClub
How It Works: Disguised as a golf club, this personal urinal allows golfers who suffer from "urinary frequency" to pee while out on the course. Developed by a urologist named Dr. Floyd Seskin, the faux 7-iron has a hollow shaft that can hold up to half a liter of urine—about twice the capacity of a human bladder. When nature calls, just unscrew the triple-sealed, leakproof cap at the top of the shaft and relieve yourself into the UroClub. Bonus: The club comes with "a removable golf towel clipped to the shaft that functions like a privacy shield!" Attach the towel to your belt or waistband and you're ready for action. Some golfers actually credit the UroClub with improving their game: "I used to hit my ball directly into the woods so I could urinate," one fan told Dr. Seskin. "You took five strokes off my game."

GEOGRAPHIC ODDITIES Q&A

Here's some obscure trivia about the world around us that you didn't learn (or maybe forgot) in geography class.

CHINESE CHESS

Question: What is Formosa?

Answer: It's a small island off the coast of China, more commonly known as Taiwan. (A Portuguese sea captain sighted it in 1554 and called it *Ilha Formosa*, meaning "beautiful island.") The nation that governs the island is also commonly referred to as Taiwan, but its official name is the Republic of China. This is not to be confused with the *People's* Republic of China. That's *mainland* China—with which Taiwan/the Republic of China is locked in an ongoing dispute over who really owns the island, and who is the real China. Mainland China *was* the Republic of China from 1912 until 1949, when the Communist party won the Chinese Civil War, and the government of the Republic of China fled to Taiwan. Today the Taiwanese government still claims that mainland China is part of the ROC, and the Communist PRC government claims that Taiwan is part of mainland China. The United Nations gave its "China" seat to the Communist PRC in 1971, making it the de facto "Real China" and relegating ROC/Taiwan to a small independent nation that has diplomatic relations with only 23 other countries.

SORRY, FINLAND

Question: What is Scandinavia?

Answer: It's a region in northern Europe. The name is usually used to describe the area encompassing Denmark, Norway, Sweden, and Finland. Technically, however, Finland is not part of Scandinavia because Scandinavia is the landmass of the Scandinavian Peninsula, comprising Norway and Sweden. Finland is attached to mainland Europe, and historically and culturally has more in common with its Russian neighbors than its Scandinavian neighbors. Denmark *is* included because true Scandinavia is the

---

Record for most balloon animals made in one hour: 747, or about 1 every 5 seconds.

ancestral home of the people who founded Denmark, and because Denmark once controlled the Scandinavian Peninsula.

ON THE OUTSIDE LOOKING IN

Question: What is Kaliningrad?

Answer: Nestled in between Lithuania and the Baltic Sea is a 5,080-square-mile swath of land that, on most maps, is probably unlabeled and colored the same shade as Russia. This is Kaliningrad, an *exclave oblast*. That means it's a non-connected (exclave, the opposite of an enclave) district (oblast) of another country, in this case Russia. It's fully run by the Russian government, even though it isn't directly connected by land. It used to be…sort of. Before the Soviet Union fell in 1991, mutual neighbor Lithuania was a Soviet republic. But Lithuania became an independent nation, while Kaliningrad, which was a Russian district rather than a Soviet republic, remained in Russian hands.

RANDOM ODDITIES

Not quite exclaves, these are places where countries ceded small plots of land to foreign entities for various reasons.

• French author Victor Hugo lived on Guernsey, a British island in the English Channel, off the coast of France. In 1927 the house in which Hugo lived and the land on which it stands were ceded not only to France, but to the landlocked city of Paris, which is more than 215 miles away.

• The Vimy Memorial in France commemorates the Battle of Vimy Ridge in World War I. In 1922 France ceded the memorial (and the land beneath it) to Canada, in tribute to that nation's contributions to the Allied effort in World War I.

• The Normandy American Cemetery and Memorial commemorates the massive storming of the beaches in far-northern France during World War II, and is the final resting place of more than 9,000 American troops who died in the battle. The land is officially United States territory.

• Two cemeteries off the coast of North Carolina—one on Ocracoke Island, the other on Hatteras Island—are the final resting places for British sailors killed in German U-Boat attacks during World War II. Both were ceded to the United Kingdom.

18 WHEELS OF TERROR

Whether you're driving a big rig, driving next to a big rig, or even walking around on top of a big rig, you're never far from danger. Here are some harrowing stories of survival.

BLINDED BY THE LIGHT

Colin Tandy was driving his truck up the appropriately named Tumbledown Bay Road in Marlborough, New Zealand, in 2011. It was dawn, and he was just coming around a curve when the rising sun blasted him in the eyes. He slammed on the brakes, but the truck slipped off the edge of the road and started falling down the heavily forested cliffside. "I actually remember rolling about four times," he said. "I knew the sea was down there, so I ripped off my seatbelt as I didn't want to drown." Tandy was thrown from the cab, which turned out to be a good thing because it was crushed. He didn't fare much better than the cab, though: He tore all of his lower back muscles, pulled five vertebrae, broke eight ribs and both hips, and split his pelvis. And he couldn't feel a thing below his waist. Doctors informed Tandy that he'd never walk again. They were wrong. Only a few days later, and before the first of many scheduled operations, he could feel his toes tingling. A few weeks later, he walked out of the hospital and has since made a full recovery. (Upon his release, he announced that he would compete on the *World's Toughest Trucker* reality TV show in his native England.)

FLAT ON THE FREEWAY

A rainy day in Los Angeles led to a horrific accident on a highway overpass. When rescue crews arrived, a semi that had skidded on the freeway was lying on its side. Witnesses shouted that there was a car stuck *under* the truck's trailer. With little hope for survivors, firefighters began emptying the trailer's heavy load while a crane was brought in to lift it up. When it finally did, the car's driver was still alive. After rescuers used the jaws of life to free him, to everyone's amazement, he actually climbed out of the crushed car on his own and started walking around. He didn't have a scratch. According to his doctor, "He's done remarkably well for somebody who spent that much time under a truck."

A pill bug can drink through its rear end.

TWIST AND SHOUT

Jeremiah Morrison saw the tornado on the road ahead of him. He pulled his truck over on I-40 in central Oklahoma, and was about to get out and look for a ditch to take shelter in. Then Morrison lost sight of the tornado. Thinking it was gone, he reached for his seatbelt. All of a sudden the twister was right on top of him, lifting the truck off the ground and tearing it apart. "I felt myself bouncing around in the cab and somehow or other I went out the window," he recalled. His rig was demolished. Had Morrison succeeded in fastening his seatbelt, he most likely would have been demolished, too. Instead, all he received were a few bruises and a fractured shoulder.

FRUIT OF THE DOOM

While driving his big rig on a Pennsylvania highway in 2011, Richard Paylor, 55, started choking on an apple. He blacked out and then plowed into the concrete center divide. On impact, he was thrown forward into his steering wheel with such force that it dislodged the apple from his throat. Paylor's amazing story was confirmed when police found a chunk of regurgitated apple stuck to the semi's dashboard. "I guess it wasn't my time," he said.

BLOWUP

In 2011 Steven McCormack, a 48-year-old New Zealand truck driver, was getting his rig ready for a job. While climbing in between the cab and the trailer, he lost his footing and fell backward onto the hose that feeds compressed air into the brakes. The hose dislodged, and the nozzle pierced McCormack's left buttock. To his horror, he started filling up with pressurized air at 100 pounds per square inch! Unable to move, he screamed for help, but his workmates had a tough time reaching him. As his neck, hands, chest, and face were balling up to twice their normal size, he knew he was about to pop. Finally, someone shut off the air valve. McCormack was rushed to a hospital, where doctors were amazed to discover that many of his muscles had actually separated from the fat they were connected to. In addition, McCormack's skin was full of tiny bubbles. Doctors drained fluid from one of his lungs, but it took three days for him to return to his normal size. How? "I had to do a lot of burping and farting," he said.

Tallest actress to win an Oscar: 6'0" Geena Davis. (*The Accidental Tourist*, 1988.)

NAMED FOR A SHIP

*Turns out there are a lot of places around the world
named after ships. (We didn't sea that coming.)*

AJAX, ONTARIO

During World War II, the area this town now inhabits was an unnamed region outside of Toronto known for its massive artillery plant—which manufactured more than 40 million shells for the Allies during the war. When the town was incorporated in 1955, a naming contest was held among the plant's employees. Winner: Ajax, after the HMS *Ajax*, a British warship that had played an important role in the first major naval victory of World War II—the Battle of River Plate (off Uruguay) in December 1939. (The plant made shells that were used in the battle.) When the ship was finally scrapped in 1988, the British government presented the *Ajax's* anchor to the town of Ajax. It sits in front of a Royal Canadian Legion headquarters there today.

FRANKLIN POINT, CALIFORNIA

On January 17, 1865, the clipper ship *Sir John Franklin*, named after a famed British explorer, was headed up the California coast with a load of lumber, pianos, and 300 barrels of liquor, bound for San Francisco. Just 50 miles south of her destination, and after 24 hours in dense fog, the ship smashed into rocks and sank. The skipper and 11 crewmembers were lost. Just six bodies were recovered: Two were buried in San Francisco, and four were buried on the point where the ship went down. It had been called "Middle Point" up to that time, but after the wreck the name was changed to Franklin Point in honor of the stricken ship.

KWINANA, AUSTRALIA

The Australian ship SS *Kwinana* had an awful streak of luck between 1920 and 1922. On Christmas Day, 1920, the ship was severely damaged by a fire off the southwest Australia coast. While being towed to Perth for repairs, it collided with another ship and was badly damaged again. The ship was anchored offshore while its owners tried to figure out what to do with it…until the anchor line snapped during a gale and the ship was blown onto a nearby beach. The beach became associated with the wreck, and when the area around it became a town in the mid-1930s, they named the town in honor of the ship. (The word *kwinana* comes from an Australian Aboriginal language and means "pretty woman.")

ORACLE, ARIZONA

Albert Weldon left New Brunswick, Canada, in 1878 and sailed around South America to the west coast of America, hoping to strike it rich prospecting for silver and gold. He named his first successful mine, located in southern Arizona, after the ship that had brought him from New Brunswick. A community grew around that mine, and a post office opened there in 1880. The name of the new town was taken from the mine, which had been taken from the ship: the *Oracle*.

ARNISTON, SOUTH AFRICA

In May 1815, the *Arniston*, a ship licensed by the British East India Company, was returning to England when a navigational error by the captain drove it toward rocks off a barren strip of the southern coast of Africa. Three anchors were dropped to halt the ship; two snapped immediately. The skipper ordered the last line cut so they could at least wreck in daylight, which they did, less than a mile offshore. Just six of the 378 people onboard survived. The spot became known as Arniston, and it is the official name of the South African tourist town located there today. (The underwater remains of the *Arniston* were discovered in 1982. The shipwreck is now a South African national monument.)

COLLAROY, AUSTRALIA

The SS *Collaroy* was an English-built, iron-clad, coal-powered paddle ship, the first of its kind in Australia when it arrived there in 1854. After nearly three decades of service, the ship was making its regular 100-mile run between Newcastle and Sydney along Australia's southeast coast when, on January 20, 1881, it got lost in deep fog and ran straight onto a beach. All 40 people onboard, along with 30 sheep and 40 pigs, simply walked off the boat onto the beach. Tugs were unable to free the ship—so there she sat for

You emit half a ton of carbon each year just by breathing.

the next three years. The beached ship became such an attraction that businesses sprang up in the area to accommodate the visitors, and when the region finally became a town in 1906, it was named in honor of the ship that had drawn it so much attention. The SS *Collaroy* was removed from the beach in 1884, refitted, and put out to sea again…only to sink off California in 1889.

OTHER BOAT-RELATED PLACES

• **Cannon Beach, Oregon**, is so named because a cannon was found there in 1898. It came from the USS *Shark*, a U.S. Navy ship that had wrecked in the vicinity 52 years earlier.

• **Sachs Harbour**, on Banks Island in the Canadian Arctic, is named after the *Mary Sachs*, one of the three ships purchased by the government for the Canadian Arctic Expedition of 1913.

• **Monitor, California**, a Sierra Nevada Mountain town near Lake Tahoe, was named in 1863 after the iron-clad Civil War battleship USS *Monitor*. (Monitor no longer exists—it's a ghost town.)

• **Heart's Desire, Newfoundland and Labrador**, according to celebrated Canadian author Harold Horwood, was named after a pirate ship that wreaked havoc all over the North Atlantic in the early 1600s.

• **Port Oneida, Michigan**, on the northwest shore of Lake Michigan, was named after the first boat known to have docked in the region, a New York-based steamship called the SS *Oneida*.

• **The Columbia River**, in the United States' Pacific Northwest, was named by explorer Robert Gray, who sailed into its mouth in 1792, the first person of European origin known to have ever done so. He named the river after his ship, the *Columbia Rediviva*.

*   *   *

POLITICAL TRIVIA

Q: More Americans voted for this man than any other man in the nation's history. Who?

A: Richard M. Nixon. In his 30-year political career, he received several hundred millions of votes. How? He ran for Congress twice, vice president twice, governor of California once, and president three times, winning the final election in a landslide.

New York drifts about 1 inch farther from London every year.

ODD JOBS

You think you hate your job? At least you're not a bodily fluid collection squeezer. (If you are, our apologies—now get back to squeezing!)

TICK DRAGGER. Yale epidemiologist Durland Fish hires students to collect ticks. The job requires dragging a white corduroy sheet through overgrown forests. Every 20 yards, tick draggers must stop, use tweezers to pluck the ticks they've collected from the sheet—up to 1,000 per day—and drop them into a jar. Though they wear protective clothing from head to toe, the tick draggers do get bitten, which makes them susceptible to tick-borne diseases, including Lyme disease. (Ironically, the purpose of this endeavor is to study Lyme disease.)

RAISIN WATCHER. Workers at a British cake factory sit all day, watching raisins pass by on a conveyor belt. Their task? To ensure that no two raisins go by stuck together. When the raisins get to the end of the belt, they all fall into a single bin.

BODILY FLUID COLLECTION SQUEEZER. (Warning: This is a little gross.) At the Royal Women's Hospital in Victoria, Australia, microbiologists are studying the incidence of sexually transmitted diseases in large populations. The best collection medium they've found so far: used tampons. Turns out that women are statistically more apt to participate in such studies when they collect specimens themselves, rather than submitting to an invasive procedure done by a doctor. The biggest problem for the microbiologists comes at the extraction stage. Normally, a centrifuge would be used to extract fluids for testing, but tampons are designed to retain fluids. According to Dr. Suzanne Garland, "Optimal recovery requires manual squeezing."

ANT HUNTER. These people spend their days sticking straws into the tops of anthills and blowing into them until ants—5,000 to 50,000 at a time—swarm out. They capture the agitated insects in a tin scoop and then quickly transfer them to mason jars and move on to the next hill. Why do they hunt ants? Ant farms.

Uncle Milton's Ant Farms are popular science-based toys—more than 20 million farms have sold since 1956—but they don't come with ants. Without water, ants can survive for only three days, so each farm includes a *certificate* for live ants. (You send in the certificate, and Uncle Milton sends you a vial of 20 to 30 ants that come from the ant hunter.) If you get an ant farm for Christmas, you might have to wait, though. When it's too cold where the ants are headed, the shipment is delayed. "No sense in having a child disappointed by a vial of frozen ants," says professional ant wrangler Afton Fawcett.

SUPER REPO MAN. When the economy goes down, the super repo business picks up. "Super repo" men repossess items worth millions—747s from Sri Lankan airlines, speedboats from Wall Street titans, helicopters from failed flight schools, and so on. The pay is good, too. Firms such as Citibank, Transamerica, and Credit Suisse pay super repo men $600,000 to $900,000 per snatch. The catch: These deadbeats aren't the typical ticked-off Toyota owners. They employ guards, police, even military units to protect their investments. Nick Popovich, president of Sage-Popovich, Inc., an Indiana airplane repossession company, has been in the business for 30 years. And during that time he's been jailed and beaten in Haiti, threatened by Neo-Nazis with shotguns in South Carolina, and arrested by *gendarmes* in France. Popovich once flew out of the Congo with its president's personal plane. "There's still a death warrant out for me," he told the Smithsonian's *Air & Space* magazine.

* * *

AN INSTANT CONNECTION

In March 2011, Sara Kemp, 42, and George Bentley, 47, both from England, met in a London bar after chatting on an online dating site. They talked about their pasts…and quickly made a startling realization: They were brother and sister. They'd been separated as kids when their parents divorced, and hadn't seen each other in 36 years. The reunited siblings got over their embarrassment, and now visit each other on a regular basis.

A mouse can fit through a hole the diameter of a ballpoint pen.

"WORDS ON A SHIRT"

And other real T-shirt slogans we've seen.

Jenius

Free Tibet*
*with purchase of another tibet
of equal or greater value

I ♥♥♥ Polygamy

**Most Likely to Secede,
Class of 1825**

*Fingers Are Overrated,
Explosions Are Awesome*

Medicine Is
the Best Medicine

*Maybe it's the booze
talking, but I want you
to know I love booze*

**Practice safe lunch:
use a condiment**

THIS IS MY
SKINNY-DIPPING SHIRT

**I'm breaking the first rule
of Fight Club**

I make over four figures
a year

Sportsmanship Is for Losers

You had me at 'sup

Your favorite band sucks

*Sorry about
what happens later*

*Is it solipsistic in here,
or is it just me?*

I am not an ambulance

*Voted "most likely to travel
back in time," Class of 2057*

*Hedgehogs: Why don't they
just share the hedge?*

Dear Math, I'm not
a therapist. Solve
your own problems.

Rock Is Dead
and Paper Killed It!

**If life gives you lemons,
keep them. Because,
hey, free lemons!**

*May the Mass x Acceleration
Be With You*

**The only thing we have to
fear is fear itself...and spiders**

ANCIENT SUB-URBS

*What if there was an abandoned city underneath your house,
waiting for you to discover it? Sound far-fetched? Read on.*

WHERE'D THE FLOW GO?
In 1972 a Turkish farmer named Latif Acar was trying
to figure out where the water disappeared to when he
watered his crops. He could see that it wasn't soaking into the
soil…so where was it going? Baffled, Acar started digging, and
before long, he discovered something unexpected—an underground
room. Further excavation revealed a complete underground city
with 10 subterranean levels, the lowest at a depth of 131 feet. It
was large enough to house 60,000 people, and its 52 air shafts
made it fully habitable. But the question remained: Who could
have dug an entire city below ground? And why?

MEET THE CONE HEADS

Starting around 3,000 years ago with the Hittites and continuing
into the Christian era, the people of Cappadocia, Turkey, needed
more than just shelter. They needed a hiding place—somewhere
they could go on short notice and not be found. Reason: The
region lies at a strategic spot along ancient trade routes that
linked China to the West, and threats came from all directions—
the Assyrians, the Persians, Alexander the Great, the Romans,
and warring Muslims, to name just a few. Luckily, Cappadocia has
an unusual natural feature: towering cone-shaped formations
called "fairy chimneys" that rise 50 to 300 feet in the air. Millions
of years ago, volcanic eruptions deposited a layer of porous, sandy
rock over the region. Over time, rain and wind turned the soft
stone into a moonscape of towers, caves, clefts, and cloth-like
folds, and the area's earliest inhabitants carved dwellings into it.
When invaders threatened, the Cappadocians dug deeper, ultimately creating a warren of underground chambers.

For hundreds of years, whenever hoof beats sounded on the
rock, the locals ran down the steep staircases in the caverns, then
rolled huge stone disks over the entryways and locked them in
place. They had everything they needed to live comfortably for

It's called a "bug" for a reason: There's a species of beetle whose Latin name is *Agra vation*.

months: kitchens with *tandoor* fireplaces (cylindrical clay ovens), meeting rooms, wine cellars, salt-grinding tables, grain storage areas, Turkish baths, and toilets. They had arsenals filled with weapons, churches with elaborate painted frescoes, and multiple escape routes. Wells provided water, and ventilation shafts brought in fresh air. They even brought their animals along, keeping them safe in underground stables.

Cappadocia's hidden cities were in continuous use for 2,500 years up until the 14th century, when the region became part of the Ottoman Empire and villagers felt safe enough to stay aboveground. But for hundreds of years after that, those who knew about the subterranean cities kept them secret from outsiders.

DARTH INVADERS

Since its rediscovery, Cappadocia has captured the imagination of filmmakers and tourists with its eerie beauty. The region has been featured in 80 Japanese films and many Bollywood movies, it's been in some European commercials, and it was used as a location for the Nicolas Cage movie *Ghost Rider II: Spirit of Vengeance*.

But despite the hoopla, small farmers like Latif Acar still tend crops, orchards, and vineyards in the region. They ride their donkeys home to their own houses carved into soft stone, and cope with the affluent Turks and foreigners who are now turning cones and caves into second homes, hotels, and B&Bs. And if they need to get away from the modern invasion, they can escape the same way their ancestors did. More than 200 underground cities like the one in Latif Acar's field have been discovered over a 100-square-mile area (so far) and can be easily reached simply by ducking through one of the hundreds of doorways hidden in surface dwellings.

*   *   *

BACKYARD PROSPECTOR

Largest gold nugget ever found with a metal detector: "The Hand of Faith," weighing 72 pounds, 11 ounces. It was found by Kevin Hillier of Wedderburn, Australia, outside his trailer. The Golden Nugget Casino in Las Vegas paid Hillier more than $1 million for the nugget, and keeps it on public display.

DOES THIS TASTE FUNNY?

Clever comedians and their culinary quips.

"I was making pancakes the other day and a fly flew into the kitchen. And that's when I realized that a spatula is a lot like a fly swatter. And a crushed fly is a lot like a blueberry. And a roommate is a lot like a fly eater."

—**Demetri Martin**

"I won't eat snails. I prefer fast food."

—**Strange de Jim**

"Pie can't compete with cake. Put candles in a cake, it's a birthday cake. Put candles in a pie, and somebody's drunk in the kitchen."

—**Jim Gaffigan**

"My mom made two dishes: Take It or Leave It."

—**Steven Wright**

"I believe when life gives you lemons, you should make lemonade, and then find someone whose life has given them vodka, and have a party."

—**Ron White**

"A professor from the University of Wisconsin says he's found a way to take the bitterness out of cheddar cheese. Now, if he can only find a way to remove the arrogance from Wheat Thins."

—**Tina Fey**

"In Maine, scientists have made a hamburger out of blueberries. It's just like a regular hamburger, except it tastes awful."

—**David Letterman**

"Fun-sized Snickers? Who's this fun for? Not me. I need six or seven of these babies in a row to start having fun."

—**Jeff Garlin**

"I go running when I have to. When the ice cream truck is doing sixty."

—**Wendy Liebman**

"Every cookie is a sugar cookie. A cookie without sugar is a cracker."

—**Gary Gulman**

"Fish—you have to wonder about a food that everybody agrees is great, except that sometimes it tastes like what it is."

—P. J. O'Rourke

"I'm the frosting on America's cake, and tonight I'm willing to let you lick the bowl."

—Stephen Colbert

"I order club sandwiches all the time and I'm not even a member. I don't know how I get away with it."

—Mitch Hedberg

"I'm a post-modern vegetarian; I eat meat ironically."

—Bill Bailey

"I bought a box of animal crackers, and it said on it, 'Do not eat if seal is broken.' So I opened up the box, and sure enough…"

—Brian Kiley

"At my lemonade stand I used to give away the first glass free and charge five dollars for the second glass. The refill contained the antidote."

—Emo Philips

*   *   *

A DEATH-DEFYING MOVIE GIMMICK

The Gimmick: In the 1961 horror film *Mr. Sardonicus*, starring Guy Rolfe, director/producer William Castle decided to let movie theater crowds determine the title character's fate. Shortly before the final act, Castle appears on screen while ushers in the theater hand out glow-in-the-dark "Punishment Poll" ballots with a "thumbs up" symbol. Castle explained that two endings had been filmed, and asked the audience whether Sardonicus should live or die. As they hold up their cards, Castle pretends to tally them up. He says, "You have given the verdict." Then the story resumes and Sardonicus dies.

The Truth: Only one ending was filmed. Castle made Sardonicus so incredibly vile that audiences would have no choice but to kill him. he gouged out his manservant's eye for disobeying him, applied leeches to his maid's face in an "experiment," and threatened to maim his beautiful wife if his own disfigurement was not cured. And just to make sure audiences *truly* hated the character, Castle had him feed poisonous plants to a dog.

A copper mine in the Andes has 1,500 miles of tunnels. It houses an entire town.

THE TUPPERWARE STORY, PART II

Here's the second installment of our story about the two people,
Earl Tupper and Brownie Wise, who made Tupperware
a household name. Part I of the story is on page 44.

TRIFECTA

The "party plan" sales method was perfect for a product like Tupperware. Clearly, it needed to be demonstrated, and once it was, people bought it. It was great for the company, too, because the sales force Brownie Wise was building cost it almost nothing. "Tupperware ladies" weren't company employees; they weren't paid a salary and didn't receive benefits. Like the Stanley team before them, they were independent salespeople who earned a percentage of their sales.

The party plan was also good for the housewives who sold Tupperware. Remember, they were part of the "Rosie the Riveter" generation—women who'd worked outside the home during World War II and never lost their taste for it. Selling Tupperware offered housewives a chance to develop business skills, make their own money, and earn recognition they seldom got from cooking, cleaning, and taking care of their kids. They could sell Tupperware part-time while they raised their families, and their careers weren't threatening to their husbands in an era when the man was still expected to be the sole breadwinner in the family.

It was even possible to make a lot of money selling Tupperware. Top-performing Tupperware ladies were promoted to manage other Tupperware ladies, and if the husband of a top-performing manager was willing to quit his job and join his wife at Tupperware, the couple could be awarded a lucrative distributorship and transferred across the country to open up new territories.

THE QUEEN

In 1953 a public relations firm told Earl Tupper that he should make Brownie Wise the public face of the company. Tupper, who

---

The sun contains 99.8% of the mass in the solar system. Jupiter has most of the rest.

was so reclusive that few company employees even knew what he looked like, happily obliged. In the years that followed, the Tupperware publicity department built Wise into an idealized Tupperware lady, giving her an Oprah Winfrey-like status with her sales force. Each year thousands of Tupperware ladies paid their own way to "Jubilee," the annual sales conference at Tupperware Home Parties headquarters in Kissimmee, Florida. One of the biggest draws of Jubilee was a chance to meet Brownie Wise. And each year she awarded refrigerators, furs, diamond jewelry, cars, and other fabulous prizes to her top performers. But some of the most coveted prizes of all were the dresses and other outfits that Wise selected from her personal wardrobe and awarded to a very lucky few. If her slender outfits did not fit the winners, many gladly shed 20 or 30 pounds just for the honor of wearing the great lady's clothes.

Brownie Wise didn't invent the home party system, but she made it work like it had never worked before. And in the process she and her ever-expanding sales force helped to turn Tupperware from a product that nobody wanted into one of the most iconic brands in American business history, as well known as Kleenex, Jell-O, Xerox, Frisbee, and Band-Aid. In the process, Tupperware ladies became a 1950s cultural force in their own right.

BOWLED OVER

Meanwhile, sales of Tupperware were growing so quickly that the company was on track to become a $100 million-a-year company by 1960. Ironically, the only person who wasn't pleased was Tupper himself. Though Wise had made him a millionaire many times over, and had served as the public face of Tupperware at his own request, Tupper grew increasingly resentful that she seemed to receive all the credit for making Tupperware the huge success that it was.

By 1957 Tupper was ready to sell his company, and in that male-dominated era he was afraid that he'd never find a buyer if the company had such a forceful and powerful woman as its second-in-command. In January 1958, he abruptly fired Wise, without notice and without a penny in severance pay, after accusing her of (among other things) using a Tupperware bowl as a dog dish. Wise later sued the company and settled for $30,000. Eight months later, Tupper sold the company. Price: $16 million.

First woman to make the cover of *Businessweek* magazine: Brownie Wise, in April 1954.

Tupper stayed on to run Tupperware for the new owners until he retired in 1973. In those years he ruthlessly purged the company of any and all record of Wise's contribution to building the business. In many ways the purge continues to this day; as late as 2011, the Tupperware website still made no mention of Brownie Wise at all.

A WORD TO THE WISE

After she was fired from Tupperware, Wise became the president of a new home party company called Cinderella Cosmetics. She hoped to persuade her Tupperware ladies to jump ship and help her build the new company, but only a handful did—even her own mother decided to stick with Tupperware.

Cinderella Cosmetics folded after just a year in business. After that Wise dabbled in Florida real estate and pursued other interests, but she never made another big mark in the business world. When she died in 1992, still living just a few miles from Tupperware Home Party headquarters in Kissimmee, her passing was ignored by the company and barely noted anywhere else.

PARTY ON

Perhaps the biggest and most backhanded compliment Tupper ever paid to Brownie Wise came the day he sold the company in 1958. As he was leaving the building, he warned one of his top executives to get out while the getting was still good. "This thing is going to blow up, it'll never last," he told his head of manufacturing, "go out and get yourself another job." Tupper apparently didn't envision the company prospering long without Wise at the head of her devoted sales force, urging the ladies ever onward and upward.

He was wrong. The world has changed a lot since 1958, but Tupperware is still around; today it's a $4.2 billion company with sales in nearly 100 countries. And though you can now buy Tupperware direct from the company's website, you can still buy it at a Tupperware party; there are more than 2.6 million Tupperware ladies worldwide. Every 1.75 seconds, one of them hosts another Tupperware party somewhere in the world, using the sales techniques that Brownie Wise perfected more than a half century ago.

RANDOM ORIGINS

Once again Uncle John answers the question:
Where does all this stuff come from?

THE FLASHLIGHT

A few years after D-cell batteries were invented in 1896 came the first battery-powered hand lights. The first one—called the "Electrical Hand Torch"—was invented by American Conrad Hubert. Because early batteries were weak and the contacts faulty, the lights flashed a lot, hence the name "flashlight." Even after the batteries and contacts were improved, the name stuck. (In the U.K., flashlights are still referred to as "torches.")

THE 911 EMERGENCY CALL SYSTEM

The 999 emergency phone number was set up in England after a 1937 house fire killed five people. It wasn't until 1967 that the FCC and AT&T worked together to create the system in the United States. They chose "911" because "999" took too long to dial on a rotary phone. But AT&T was taking a long time to implement the system, so Bob Gallagher, president of the Alabama Telephone Company, ordered his plant manager, Robert Fitzgerald, to set up the nation's first 911 service in Haleyville, Alabama. By the mid-1970s, most of the U.S. could dial 911.

THE SLURPEE

Omar Knedlik had a broken soda fountain and thirsty customers. It was a hot day in 1957, so the World War II vet put some pops in the freezer at his Dairy Queen in Coffeyville, Kansas. By the time the sodas were opened, they'd turned to slush. And Knedlik's customers *loved* them. Inspired, he started tinkering with parts from the soda fountain, an ice cream machine, and his car's air conditioner. A few years later, the machine—which blends flavored syrup, CO_2, and semi-frozen ice—was complete. Knedlik called his new the drink the ICEE, and was soon selling machines all over the U.S. In 1967 the 7-Eleven corporation licensed them. A company ad man named Bob Stanford came up with the name "Slurpee," based on how it sounds when sucked through a straw. Since then, more than six billion Slurpees have been slurped.

More good news from nature: Smallpox can live outside the human body for over a year.

THE STORY OF METAL, PART I

Do you have a ring on your finger? Is it made from gold, silver, platinum, or another natural metal? Then ponder this: The metal in that ring on your finger is older than the planet you're standing on.

W**HAT IS "METAL"?**
Scientifically speaking, metals are naturally occurring chemical elements that are typically hard, lustrous, and good conductors of both heat and electricity. Examples include iron, gold, silver, copper, zinc, nickel, etc., but also elements we don't normally think of as metals. One is *sodium*—a metal we regularly eat: Sodium is a soft, silvery white metal that commonly bonds with the element *chlorine* to form sodium chloride, or common salt. Another is *astatine*, which was discovered in 1940 in a lab, where it was created artificially. It wasn't discovered in nature until 1943. Astatine is highly radioactive, and only a single ounce of it is believed to exist—in total—on Earth. Of the 118 known chemical elements in existence, 88 of them are metals.

REAL ALCHEMY

So, where did all these metals come from? Here's a very simplified explanation:

• All elements, including metals, are made of the same stuff: atomic material—electrons, neutrons, and protons. Atoms of different elements can be distinguished from one another by the number of protons they contain. (The number of neutrons and electrons can vary even among atoms of the same element.)

• For example, a hydrogen atom contains just one proton. A gold atom has 79. This is true of every one of the countless hydrogen and gold atoms in the universe.

• If you could find a way to mash 79 hydrogen atoms together into one atom, you'd have an atom with 79 protons, and therefore you'd

---

Unique, in a bad way: Dalmatians are the only dogs that get gout.

have a gold atom. And that's almost exactly what happens…
except it happens inside stars.

THERE'S GOLD IN THEM THAR STARS

According to cosmologists, the very first matter to appear in the
universe was formed as a result of the cosmological event known
as the Big Bang, roughly 13.7 billion years ago. Matter first
appeared in the form of atoms of the two lightest elements: hydrogen, with one proton, and helium, with two. They remain, by far,
the most abundant elements in the universe.

After many millions of years those first hydrogen and helium
atoms collected in clouds of dust and gases so huge they would
have to be measured in light years (1 light year = 6 trillion miles
or 9.5 trillion kilometers). The clouds eventually gave in to their
own enormous gravity and collapsed, forming the first stars. And
stars were atom destroyers—hot enough to break down those
hydrogen and helium atoms, and fuse the bits back together,
remaking them into larger atoms of different, heavier elements.

For example, if you fuse two hydrogen atoms together, you
have an atom with two protons—or helium. Fuse three hydrogens
together and you get an atom with three protons—lithium, the
first and lightest metal. Fuse three heliums together and you get
an atom with six protons—carbon. This is what's happening in all
the stars you see in the sky at night. In the massive ones the
process can result in the production of heavier and heavier elements, including metals such as titanium (22 protons), and iron
(26 protons). If they're especially massive, they can produce the
heaviest metals, such as gold (79 protons), and uranium (92 protons). This is one of the things stars do, and that's how all the elements—including all those shiny metals—are formed in nature.

Now, how did they get here?

DOWN TO EARTH

In the first few billion years after the Big Bang, billions and billions of stars were born, in the way we just described. Many were
extremely massive (hundreds of times larger than our sun) and
massive stars live relatively short lives—just a few million years in
some cases (smaller stars can live for billions of years)—and then
die by exploding as supernovas. And when those massive stars

exploded billions of years ago, they expelled the heavy elements they had been creating, sending them into space. They had, to put it one way, "seeded" the universe with elements, including metals. And super-massive, impossible-to-comprehend amounts of it—trillions and trillions and trillions of megatons of it. That means that when new stars were later formed—they had already been "seeded" with metals left behind by those supernovas.

One of those later, metal-rich stars was our own sun. A quick look at that story:

• About 4.5 billion years ago, a massive cosmic cloud of dust and gas, seeded with lots of heavier elements, collapsed, beginning the process of forming a new star.

• Most of the hydrogen and helium in the cloud became part of the newly formed star. The rest of the dust and gas, including the metals, accumulated in a molten mass, spinning around the new star. The spinning motion flattened out the mass (picture spinning pizza dough) into a molten, spinning disk.

• Over millions of years, as the disk cooled, bits of it clumped together here and there, and those clumps became the planets in our solar system. And the metals in the dust? They became all the metals found in all the planets, including our own.

Our Share: Earth has a lot of metal. Nearly a third of the planet's mass is the element iron, most of that located in the planet's core. Another 14 percent is magnesium, 1.5 percent is nickel, and 1.4 percent is aluminum. That's 49 percent of the planet. The rest of Earth's metals, including "precious" metals such as gold, silver, platinum, and palladium, exist only in trace amounts. The rest—the non-metal portion—is about 30 percent oxygen and 15 percent silicon, along with smaller amounts of numerous other non-metal elements.

For Part II of "Metals," turn to page 323.

*　　*　　*

Music Trivia: Before deciding on "Beatles," the Fab Four called themselves the Beetles, the Beatals, the Silver Beets, the Silver Beetles, the Silver Beatles, and Long John and the Silver Beatles.

MOONSTRUCK

*Our favorite childhood classics make us feel as snug as a bunny
in bed. Here's a look at what's down the rabbit hole.*

GOODNIGHT MOON

"Goodnight light and the red balloon..." Margaret Wise
Brown wrote more than 100 books for children, but her
most famous is *Goodnight Moon*, published in 1947. It was a revolutionary book in its time, inspired in part by the poetry of Gertrude
Stein. More than four generations of children have nodded off to
this classic's hynpnotic spell, and 11 million copies have been
sold since its first printing. But in the beginning, the book's
prospects looked dim.

In its first year, *Moon* sold a modest 6,000 copies at $1.75 each.
That yielded a typical author's royalty rate of a dime or less per
book, earning Brown around $500. Sales declined from there. In
1951 *Goodnight Moon* sold only 1,300 copies, and there was no
reason to believe that sales would ever recover. That may explain
why in May the following year, Brown made a whimsical addition
to her will: Upon her death, the royalties from her books would go
to the three sons of her neighbors, Joan and Albert Clarke, probably figuring they'd get a few dollars a year to blow on toys and
bubblegum. But that's not how it turned out.

GOOD NEIGHBOR POLICY

The Clarke family had provided a measure of stability to Brown,
who lived a bohemian life in her nextdoor flat, never marrying
and never having kids of her own. Apparently she loved the
Clarke children and allocated royalties from various books to
each. Her will provided that the middle child, nine-year-old
Albert, would receive 100 percent of *Goodnight Moon*. What happened next was completely unexpected. Four months after writing
her will, while on a book tour of Europe in late 1952, the 42-year-old author suffered a coronary embolism and died.

It took a few years for Brown's estate to be settled, and in 1957
the Clarke family learned the peculiar details of her will. In the
meantime, though, the situation had already begun to change for

---

The average American woman will spend about 8 years of her life shopping.

Goodnight Moon. As parents across the country and world began telling each other about this "magic" book that put toddlers to sleep, sales grew and the publisher began issuing new printings. The result was that Albert, now 13, learned that his share of the estate was already $17,530 (about $134,000 in today's money) and still growing robustly. By 1970 *Goodnight Moon* was selling 20,000 copies a year; in the decades that followed, that number jumped into the hundreds of thousands, with total sales reaching four million in 1990.

THE PLOT THICKENS

You'd think that a story about a children's book might have a happy ending: Perhaps Albert would use his money wisely and generously. No. In 2000 Joshua Prager tracked Albert Clarke down for the *Wall Street Journal*, writing that "in the intervening years, the trajectories of Ms. Brown's book and the boy who inherited it began to diverge with strange symmetry." Prager describes a life of squandered millions, murderous fistfights, theft, a sequence of broken homes, domestic violence, lost custody of children, clothing bought and thrown away instead of being washed, houses bought and sold at a loss, vagrancy, debt, drug abuse, and arrests on an array of charges ranging from menacing and resisting arrest to criminal possession of a weapon, criminal trespass, assault, and grand larceny. According to Prager, Albert Clarke said he believed—with no supporting evidence or corroboration from any source—that Brown was his real mother, a notion his older brother Austin characterized as "delusional thinking. It's a fairy tale that makes him feel better."

THE NEVER-ENDING STORY

Austin's response is understandable: Albert's most recent six-month royalty check had been $341,000; Austin's (for Brown's book *The Sailor Dog*): $13.88. Their youngest brother Jimmy, also the recipient of small checks, had joined a cult years earlier before committing suicide in 1995. How long will this continue? Thanks to extensions of copyright laws in the 1990s, Albert or his heirs will be receiving royalties for *Goodnight Moon*—one of the most successful children's books of all time—until 2043.

An average pickup truck weighs around 4,000 pounds. Average monster truck: 11,000 lbs.

TOP BANANA

There's a saying among some older people: "Don't buy green bananas—
you might not live long enough to eat them." Turns out the opposite is
true: We might actually outlive the bananas we're used to eating.

BANANA REPUBLIC
Ever wonder why there are so many different kinds of
apples on supermarket shelves but only one kind of
banana? Bananas can only be grown in tropical climates, and they
have to be grown in large quantities to meet the demand. And
ironically, while it makes economic sense to grow large fields of
just a single variety of banana, it's this kind of setup that leads to
rapid outbreaks of blight and plant diseases. So again, why is there
just one kind?

There are actually dozens of edible banana varieties in the
world, but the only one you've probably ever seen is the bright
yellow Cavendish variety. Before the 1950s, the Cavendish was a
rare, exotic fruit that almost nobody in the United States had ever
eaten. That's because the sole banana available in the U.S. before
that was the Gros Michel. Introduced to the United States in
1870 by a Cape Cod fisherman and importer named Lorenzo
Baker, the Gros Michel had a skin that was resistant to the disease
and cold weather it was exposed to on the journey from the equatorial jungles and banana plantations.

By 1910 Americans were buying about 200 million Gros
Michels (or "Big Mikes") every year. Baker's importing business,
now called United Fruit, had grown to a $200 million company on
the strength of the Gros Michel. In order to meet the demand for
bananas, United Fruit bought enormous swaths of land in Central
and South America, decimating jungles and hiring locals to work
the banana plantations for a few cents a day.

YELLOW FEVER
The goal of any large commercial agricultural operation is to produce predictable, uniform, nearly identical fruit. But growing acre
upon acre of just one variety results in a lack of plant diversity,
which can make it susceptible to blight. Even worse, because cul-

Bananas grow pointing up, not hanging down.

tivated bananas are propagated through cuttings, not seed, the plants are genetically identical to one another. Result: Any disease that can kill one Gros Michel banana tree can kill them all. And that's exactly how the Gros Michel fields started to die off in the late 1940s—from a fungus known as Panama disease.

As United Fruit watched its cash crop die, the company's tiny rival, Dole, saw the writing on the wall and switched its production from Gros Michel to another banana variety: the Cavendish, a Chinese variety discovered by British explorers in the 19th century. Its main selling point: It was immune to the diseases that were killing off the Gros Michel, so it could even be planted on the same fields already in use. It was, however, highly susceptible to other plant diseases, requiring the liberal use of pesticides, as well as special ripening rooms built near banana farms. United Fruit was so slow to switch to the healthier but less-sweet-tasting Cavendish that it lost more and more market share to Dole. (United Fruit later made a big comeback in bananas under another name: Chiquita.)

YES, WE HAVE NO MORE BANANAS

What happened to the Gros Michel is now happening to the Cavendish. Again, growing too much of one plant in a large area makes it susceptible to blight, and pesticide-resistant strains have developed over the decades. Killing off the Cavendish is a newly discovered soil-borne disease called Tropical Race Four that acts quickly and remains viable in the dirt for a long time—spores as old as 30 years have been found. The blight (a new fungus) devastates the plants, turning the centers of the fruit into putrid-smelling—and unsellable—mush. The fungus was first noticed in northern Australia in 1997, and it's been steadily wiping out banana plantations ever since. In some areas, production is down 60 percent from peak levels in the 1980s.

Scientists are now in a mad rush to find a banana to replace the Cavendish, which replaced the Gros Michel. The most likely candidate: the Goldfinger, developed by Canadian and Honduran scientists and first sold in 1994. It's caught on commercially in Australia, but it will be a hard sell in the U.S., where consumers are used to the sweet, creamy Cavendish. The Goldfinger is very different from the banana as we know it—it is long and yellow, but it's also said to be tangy, acidic…and slightly crunchy.

North Dakotans have tried to drop "North" from their state's name twice, in 1947 and 1989.

EARLY TO RISE

Because age is just a number.

• **At age 1:** Future jazz great Buddy Rich started drumming professionally as part of his parents' vaudeville act.

• **At age 3:** Wolfgang Amadeus Mozart learned to play his first instrument, the harpsichord.

• **At age 5:** Future rock star Tori Amos was accepted to the Peabody Academy of Music in Baltimore, its youngest student ever.

• **At age 6:** Shirley Temple became Hollywood's top box-office star. (She remained at #1 until she was 9.)

• **At age 8:** Tiger Woods won the Optimist International Junior World title, his first international golf tournament.

• **At age 10:** Future Swiss psychologist Jean Piaget published his first scientific article. It was based on observations he'd made of a sparrow.

• **At age 11:** Franz Liszt gave his first piano recital.

• **At age 12:** A Ukrainian boy named Sergey Karjakin became the world's youngest chess grandmaster.

• **At age 13:** Mario Andretti started racing cars.

• **At age 14:** "Buffalo" Bill Cody became a rider for the Pony Express.

• **At age 15:** Mia Hamm joined the women's U.S. National Soccer team.

• **At age 15:** After hearing what she believed to be the voice of God telling her to lead France in war, Joan of Arc convinced the Dauphin of France to let her lead the armies against England in the 100 Years War.

• **At age 19:** Jane Austen wrote *Sense and Sensibility*.

• **At age 20:** Leif Ericson led a crew of 35 Vikings to what is now Newfoundland, where he established the first European colony in North America around the year 1000.

• **At age 23:** Facebook founder Mark Zuckerberg became the youngest billionaire in history.

Connecticut and Rhode Island never ratified the 18th Amendment (Prohibition).

AUSSIE-OOPS

After we compiled this year's crop of goofs and blunders, we noticed that a bunch of them come from Australia. Coincidence? Of course, but we still thought it would make for a fun couple of pages.

HOG HEAVEN

In January 2011, Australia's *Morning Bulletin* reported a story of seemingly biblical proportions after cyclone Yasi caused severe flooding in the northeast part of the country: "There have been 30,000 pigs floating down the Dawson River since last week." Over the next few days, at least three other newspapers printed the *Bulletin's* report verbatim. Apparently no one at any of the press offices questioned that incredible figure. Readers, however, had a tough time believing it and challenged the papers. A little digging revealed the truth: When *Morning Bulletin's* reporter originally interviewed pig farmer Sid Everingham about the flood, Everingham didn't say "30,000 pigs"—he said "30 sows and pigs." The newspapers all printed corrections.

A BALL GAME

Several hundred plastic balls were carefully loaded into an Alfa Romeo sports car at a Perth shopping mall in 2011 for a "Guess the Amount" contest to raise money for the charity Comic Relief. In accordance with safety protocols, the battery of the car was disconnected. What organizers didn't realize was that without the battery, the car's doors automatically unlocked. And no one knew they were unlocked until a three-year-old boy opened one of them... and hundreds of balls spilled out. While the crowd cheered, mall security scrambled to collect all the balls (some were taken by other little kids). Nearly an hour later, the remaining balls were back in the car, and the doors were locked. Said mall manager Siobhan McConnell, "This was a bit more comic relief than we had originally planned."

WHAT A DOLL

During the 2011 Queensland floods, two 19-year-olds (a couple whose names were not released to the press) decided to have a little fun by floating down the raging Yarra River near Melbourne in a makeshift raft. But the raft couldn't hold them both, and the girl got sucked away by the rapids. She managed to grab hold of a tree, and had to cling to it for over an hour before a rescue team was able to pluck her from the river. Authorities were both angered and amused when they discovered that the couple's "raft" was actually a blow-up sex doll. "It is not a recognized flotation device," a police spokesman told reporters.

LAMBOR-GONE-Y

Late one night in May 2011, a 30-year-old man let a 22-year-old friend (names not released) drive his brand-new Lamborghini Murcielago (retail price: $400,000). The owner wasn't worried about the car because it was fully insured. From the sidewalk, the man watched his friend peel out. Traveling at nearly 50 miles per hour down a busy Sydney street, the young driver lost control of the powerful sports car, veered over the center line, and smashed head-on into a taxicab. The driver emerged from the wreck unscathed, but the 51-year-old cabbie suffered a broken leg (it took paramedics an hour to free her). As for the Lamborghini, it was totaled. And when the car's owner later put in a claim to his insurance company, he was informed of a clause in his contract that he'd previously overlooked: The car was "not insured for drivers under age 25." It was a total loss.

*   *   *

YOU NEVER SAUSAGE A NUMBER

Mathematically speaking, there is no such thing as more than 100 percent (unless you're a sports coach or a motivational speaker). That's why a Swedish consumer reported the sausage company Trangsvikens Chark to government officials. On the package of one of their products, the label said, "Meat content—104%." "This sausage couldn't possibly contain more than 100 percent meat," the man complained, "as there are other ingredients stated on the label." Marcus Farnstrom, the company's CEO, explained that it takes 104 grams of meat in order to make 100 grams of sausage, hence the higher-than-possible percentage. However, Farnstrom also acknowledged that the packaging is confusing and promised to have it fixed.

Australia's crested billbird has an odd defense mechanism: It can throw its voice like a ventriloquist.

BOOKWORMS

Pay no attention to the fact that there are other books out there besides Uncle John's Bathroom Reader.

• Before they figured out they could use parchment, Europeans wrote on thin peels of bark. The word "book" is derived from *bog,* the Danish word for beech, the preferred writing bark in Denmark.

• Only writer to turn down the Pulitzer Prize for Fiction: Sinclair Lewis, for *Arrowsmith* in 1926. He felt the Prize committee judged books arbitrarily, based on "American ideals," not on literary merit.

• For her first *Harry Potter* book, J.K. Rowling received an advance of only £1,500 (about $2,400).

• The British town of Hay-on-Wye *loves* books. It has 39 used bookstores (but only 1,300 residents). Each May it hosts a 10-day literary festival that Bill Clinton once called "the Woodstock of the mind."

• Most prolific author ever: Brazilian novelist José Carlos Ryoki de Alpoim Inoue. Between 1986 and 1996, he published 1,058 novels—about one every three days.

• The dust jacket dates back to the 1830s, but Lewis Carroll (*Alice's Adventures in Wonderland,* 1865) came up with the idea to put the title on the spine of the jacket so you could tell what book it was when it was lined up on a shelf.

• First e-book reader on the market: the Sony Bookman, introduced in 1992. It played CDs. (It flopped.)

• Patron saint of librarians: St. Jerome. Patron saint of booksellers: St. John. Patron saint of bookbinders: St. Christopher.

• Herman Melville was a failure in his own time; his novel *Moby Dick* sold poorly upon its release in 1851 due to bad reviews. The reason: The last few pages were accidentally not printed, giving the impression of an unresolved ending.

• In terms of titles available, the world's biggest bookstore is the World's Biggest Bookstore, located in a converted bowling alley in Toronto.

SELF-SURGERY

Stories about people who had to perform emergency surgery on themselves may seem gross...because they are. But here's something that might make you want to read about them anyway: They all have happy endings.

Who: Jan de Doot of Amsterdam

Background: In 1651 de Doot, a blacksmith, began having terrible pains in his groin. He could feel something hard—it was a bladder stone (related to kidney stones)—through his skin. According to Dr. Nicolaes Tulp, mayor of Amsterdam and one of the most renowned surgeons of the era, Doot didn't trust doctors.

Do It Yourself! With only his brother standing by in case something went wrong, Doot used a small, sharp knife to cut through his perineum (the floor of your crotch, basically), where he could feel the stone. Then, according to Tulp:

> To get the stone out was more difficult, and he had to stick two fingers into the wound on either side to remove it with leveraged force, and it finally popped out of hiding with an explosive noise and tearing of the bladder.

The stone was the size of a chicken egg. When the operation was completed, Doot had his brother summon a doctor's assistant to stitch up his wound.

Outcome: Doot apparently survived, because sometime after the self-administered surgery he sat for a painting by Flemish artist Carel van Savoyen. In it, de Doot is depicted holding a knife in one hand, and in the other he's holding up an egg-shaped object—the stone he cut from his own body.

Who: Inés Ramírez of Rio Talea in southern Mexico

Background: In April 2002, Ramírez, who was pregnant, went into labor. She had already had several children at home, but lost her last one in childbirth. And now, once again, something was not right. After 12 hours of increasingly painful labor, 50 miles from the nearest midwife, and with no phone—or electricity or running water—Ramírez decided to do something.

What is a *spectroheliokinematograph*? A special camera used to film the sun.

Do It Yourself! Ramírez drank a few shots of liquor as an anes-thetic, got a sharp knife, and made a cut low on her belly. She kept cutting—for an hour—and finally reached her womb, at which point she reached inside and pulled out a baby boy. Shortly before passing out, she sent one of her sons for help. Some hours later, a local health aide arrived and, after getting over his shock, stitched up Ms. Ramírez's belly—using ordinary needle and thread—and then drove her to a hospital in the city of Oaxaca.

Outcome: Both the mother and child survived. It is the only known case in history of a woman successfully performing a cesarean section on herself.

Who: Dr. Leonid Ivanovich Rogozov of Leningrad, U.S.S.R.

Background: Rogozov went to Antarctica with a Russian research team in 1960, the only doctor in the 13-person group. On April 29, 1961, he woke up with a fever and a pain in the right side of his abdomen. He took antibiotics, but got worse. By the next day, he was in extreme pain and knew that he was suffering from appen-dicitis. The closest help was another Soviet Antarctic station 1,000 miles away, but blizzard conditions would have made land-ing a plane there impossible. Appendicitis, untreated, is almost always fatal. There was only one option.

Do It Yourself! Rogozov put on his doctor's uniform, including surgical mask, got into a hospital bed, propped his head up with pillows, and, using novocaine as a local anesthetic, cut a five-inch incision into his abdomen. Then, going by feel, though sometimes looking in a mirror held by one of the researchers (he later said that just confused him because everything was backward), he cut deeper into his body, pausing every few minutes to vomit, collect himself, and continue cutting. After *four and a half hours*, he got the infected and swollen appendix out, sutured himself up—and passed out.

Outcome: After he recovered, Rogozov wrote, "At the worst moment of removing the appendix I flagged: My heart seized up and noticeably slowed; my hands felt like rubber. Well, I thought, it's going to end badly." Two weeks later, he was back at work. He spent the next year and a half at the station, and in 1962 returned to his home in Leningrad a national hero.

VIDEO GAMES VS. REALITY

*Online multi-player immersive video games can be fun,
but for some gamers, the fun gets a little out of hand.*

OUT OF ORDER

Video and computer games are hugely popular in South Korea, where it's estimated that a third of the country's 50 million people regularly play MMORPGs ("massively multi-player online role-playing games"), such as *World of Warcraft*, *Maplestory*, and especially the space-war-themed *Star Craft*. It has become the country's most popular televised "sport," earning the best players lucrative sponsorship deals and prompting many South Korean kids to shun school in search of a payday. The vast majority don't hit it big, of course, and end up with an unhealthy obsession instead. Local media reported that one teenager played *Star Craft* for 36 hours straight before passing out from exhaustion. "After I woke up, I spent another 30 hours playing again," he said.

YOU CAN RUN BUT YOU CAN'T HIDE

By December 2009, Alfred Hightower thought he was home free. The fugitive, who was wanted in Indiana on drug-dealing charges, had fled to Canada three years earlier. But Hightower's other hobby—playing *World of Warcraft*—allowed authorities to use tips they collected from the game to track down him down online. And sure enough, there he was. Then they subpoenaed *Warcraft*'s publisher, Blizzard Entertainment, for Hightower's IP address, screen name, account history, and billing address. Shortly there-after, he was arrested in Ottawa, Ontario, and extradited back to the United States. Game over!

TIME BANDIT

In 2005 a 28-year-old man collapsed and died in an Internet café in Taegu, South Korea. He'd been playing *World of Warcraft*...for 50 hours straight. "We presume the cause of death was heart fail-

---

Nothing left to the imagination: The German word for mucus is *Nasenschleim* ("nose slime").

ure stemming from exhaustion," police told reporters. They also noted that the man had recently been fired from his job—for missing too much work because he was playing video games.

VIRTUAL REALTY

Entropia Universe is an online game in which players develop real estate on a habitable asteroid called Planet Calypso. But to participate in the game, players have to spend real money to buy virtual property, virtual homes, and virtual goods. Despite the fact that they're trading real cash for imaginary things, some people have made a lot of money at it. A resort developer named Jon Jacobs put $100,000 into his *Entropia* account in 2005, and in 2010 he sold his properties in the game to other players for a very real $635,000. Another *Entropia* player—known only as "Buzz 'Erik' Lightyear"—paid 3.3 million "Project Entropia Dollars" for one of the game's top pieces of property: a space station. Each PED costs 10 cents, which means Lightyear paid $330,000 for his virtual space station (although he's confident he'll earn it back eventually). Altogether, economists estimate that online gamers spent $7 billion on in-game products in 2010.

NO CHEATING!

In the online world of *Second Life*, players set up identities and live fairly normal "lives"—buying houses, going on trips, working jobs, and getting married. A rising "career" in *Second Life*: virtual private detective. Online game monitors report an increase in the past few years of virtual detectives hired by gamers' real-life spouses spying on virtual players to find out if they're having affairs, either in the game or in real life.

*　　*　　*

Top 5 Biggest Beer-Selling Holidays in the U.S.
1. Independence Day
2. Labor Day
3. Memorial Day
4. Father's Day
5. Christmas

First documented user of cloth handkerchiefs: England's King Richard II (1367–1400).

UNCLE JOHN'S "CREATIVE TEACHING" AWARDS

If schools handed out degrees for dumb, these teachers would have earned a Ph.D.

Subject: Citizenship
Winner: Natalie Munroe, 30, an 11th-grade English teacher at Central Bucks High School East in Pennsylvania
Approach: In August 2009, Munroe began writing an online blog for family and friends. She talked about her students, describing them as "rat-like," "dunderheads," "frightfully dim," and "utterly loathsome in all imaginable ways," to list but a few of her nasty comments. The blog was supposed to be secret—Munroe never mentioned either her school or her students by name. But she did write under the not-very-secret pseudonym of "Natalie M."
What Happened: One of the rat-like dunderheads stumbled across the blog in February 2011, realized that "Natalie M" was Munroe, and shared the blog entries with other kids via Facebook. Word soon spread to school administrators, who promptly fired Munroe. "I'm not sorry. I don't take back anything I said," Munroe told reporters after she was let go.

Subject: Anatomy
Winner: Faith Kramer, a health and physical education teacher at New York City's Intermediate School 72
Approach: When she taught the state-mandated course on H.I.V./AIDS prevention to her eighth-graders in 2007, Kramer followed the state's instructions that she speak to the kids using "terms that they understood." She wrote "polite" words for various body parts and sexual acts on the blackboard, and then asked the students if they knew any other terms to describe those things. Then she wrote their answers on the board—and although she didn't ask the kids to take notes, some did. When the parents of the note-takers found lists of words like "hooters," "banana," "junk," and "taco" in their kids' homework, they complained to

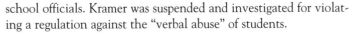

school officials. Kramer was suspended and investigated for violating a regulation against the "verbal abuse" of students.

What Happened: No disciplinary charges were ever brought against Kramer. After being suspended for eight months with pay, she was allowed to return to her classroom. (She's suing the Board of Education for $2 million.)

Subject: Modern Dance

Winner: Adeil Ahmed and Chrystie Fitchner, teachers at Churchill High School in Winnipeg, Manitoba

Approach: At a school pep rally in February 2010, the pair performed a dance routine to Michael Jackson's "The Way You Make Me Feel." The song must have made them feel good, because their routine included a lap dance, followed by a simulated sex act.

What Happened: In an era when cell phones didn't have cameras, they might have gotten off with a suspension or a written reprimand. But video clips of the incident were posted on YouTube within hours, and when those clips received more than two million hits by the end of the week, Ahmed and Fitchner were told to take their dirty dancing elsewhere.

Subject: Peace and Conflict Studies

Winner: Mike Richards, the head teacher at St. Mary's Roman Catholic School in northwestern England

Approach: In 2011 Richards wanted to give his primary school students a sense of what it was like to live through World War II, so he called an assembly of the entire school and told the children that World War III had broken out that morning. He showed them wartime film footage of the bombing of London, and told them it had been taken earlier in the day. Then an air raid siren sounded and the students were led into the cellar while fireworks were set off in the schoolyard outside to simulate bombs.

What Happened: The "exercise" was supposed to last all day, but Richards called it off at 1:30 when the children became too terrified for him to continue. "We spent all afternoon explaining to the kids that it wasn't real," he said afterward. "On this occasion we realize that we went too far." (Parents were not amused. "No one with an ounce of common sense would put children through that," one angry mother told the *Daily Mail* newspaper.)

EDUCATIONAL TOYS

What kind of person would think you can learn and have fun at the same time? (Uh-oh—don't tell Uncle John we said that.)

SPEAK & SPELL

One of the earliest handheld electronic toys ever available, the Speak & Spell was introduced in 1978 by Texas Instruments, primarily a manufacturer of calculators. The candy-red toy with a kid-friendly handle on top would speak letters in a robotic voice as the child typed them out, helping the child recognize the letters and learn to read. It featured a small digital display screen, a speech synthesizer, and a standard QWERTY keyboard, so it also taught kids to type. It was part of a line that also included the Speak & Read and Speak & Math, which weren't as successful. The product got a major boost when E.T. used one to communicate with his Earth friends in *E.T.: The Extra Terrestrial* (1982), helping to fuel sales of more than 10 million Speak & Spells (in seven different languages) by 1992, when the toy was discontinued.

STACKING RINGS

Cornelius Holgate started a small family carpentry business outside Philadelphia in 1789. It thrived over the years, but in 1929, the Holgates finally found their niche: wooden toys. Child psychologist Lawrence Frank married into the Holgate family and convinced them to take the business that way. The most popular item: stacking rings—smooth, painted wooden rings that toddlers placed over a small wooden pole in order to learn motor skills. Stacking rings are still manufactured in wood by the Holgate Toy Company, as well as in plastic by Playskool and Fisher-Price, who introduced the popular Rock-a-Stack version in 1960.

SEE 'N SAY

"The cow says...*mooooo*" is probably familiar if you had kids or were a kid in the last few decades. The See 'n Say was introduced by Mattel in 1965. Here's how it works: There's a spinning arrow in the middle of the round toy. The child points the arrow at a

---

If airline flights had the same rate of failure as space flights, 275 planes would crash every day.

picture of an animal, then pulls the "chatty ring" (it's now a lever) and a voice pronounces the name of the animal, followed by the noise it makes. See 'n Say is unique in that it operates mechanically, without batteries. A metal needle inside the toy plays tracks on a plastic disc, functioning much like an old fashioned gramophone record. Mattel engineers were inspired by the company's popular 1950s toy Chatty Cathy, a doll that said different phrases at random. The See 'n Say was the first toy in which kids could choose exactly what would be heard.

LEAPFROG

San Francisco lawyer Michael Wood's young son, Matthew, was having trouble putting sounds together to make words. So, with the help of Stanford professor Robert Calfee (and using the technology for talking greeting cards), he developed Phonics Desk, an interactive toy designed to teach children how to pronounce words. It came out in 1995, and LeapFrog Enterprises was founded. In 1999 the company introduced LeapPad interactive books, which allow children to touch letters with a stylus in order to hear them pronounced. By 2002 almost nine million LeapPads were sold, making it the first educational toy to become a bestseller in the United States since the 1980s.

ALPHABET BLOCKS

Wooden blocks were first suggested as an educational tool in 1693, when English philosopher John Locke wrote that "dice and playthings with the letters on them to teach children the alphabet by playing" would help make learning more enjoyable. But it wasn't until the early 1800s that such toys became widely available. That's when New York teacher J.E. Wickham began selling sets of blocks covered in colored paper engraved with words and pictures. In 1820 the S.L. Hill Company of Williamsburg, New York, took out a patent on wooden blocks embossed with the alphabet, commonly called "alphabet blocks." They're now one of only 46 toys in the National Toy Hall of Fame.

*　　*　　*

It's no use carrying an umbrella if your shoes are leaking.

—**Irish proverb**

Freshly fallen snow is only about 8% water; the rest is air.

IGY

*"I Got You?" "Icky Greenish-Yellow?" No, it stands for the
International Geophysical Year, a scientific world summit
that led to some of the most important and famous
scientific breakthroughs of the 20th century.*

THE FUTURE'S SO BRIGHT

In April 1950, physics professor and rocket scientist James Van Allen hosted a party for about 10 of his friends, all top American scientists, at his home in Silver Spring, Maryland. The occasion: Influential British geophysicist Sydney Chapman was in Washington, D.C., on business, and the American scientists wanted to meet him. Over the course of the evening, the men got to talking about the era in which they lived. Certainly, they said, it had to be one of the most exciting times ever for science, particularly because of all the recent technological developments being applied to peaceful uses after World War II. Among those advances: rockets, radar, computers, and atomic energy.

Physicist Lloyd Berkner agreed, but only to a point. His area of research concerned measuring the height and density of the atmosphere. Proper calculations required data gathered from all over the planet, a task hindered by Cold War politics. What science needed, Berkner said, was a replay of the "International Polar Years" (IPY) of 1882 and 1932, during which scientists worldwide pooled their knowledge, resources, and expertise to study meteorology, magnetism, and atmospheric science, using new advancements such as high-frequency radio and precision cameras to collect data. But the Great Depression reduced the scope of the project, and in the wake of World War II, most of the observation stations from the IPYs had been damaged or destroyed. Berkner was suggesting a new IPY—a coordinated effort to explore and advance earth and physical sciences, free from political interference.

BLINDED WITH SCIENCE

Van Allen, Berkner, and a few others drew up some ideas over the next year or so, and in 1952 they presented their idea for an "International Geophysical Year" (IGY) to the International

Council of Scientific Unions, a worldwide coalition that oversaw individual national scientific boards. The proposal was accepted, and planning got under way for the IGY, which would technically be a year and a half, observed from July 1957 to December 1958. That time period was selected because it coincided with an expected high point in sunspot activity and the frequency of eclipses, allowing for better research of those phenomena. But more importantly, the scientists needed a full five years to prepare: They still had to design and build many of the tools and instruments they would need to conduct their research.

The United Nations endorsed and promoted the IGY not only as a move toward vast scientific development, but also as a move toward world peace. By the time the IGY began, 67 countries had signed up, with China the only major holdout. The event began as scheduled in July 1957, with experiments and projects taking place across the globe (and beyond). It would be the largest study of the natural world ever attempted, with more than 4,000 research stations established around the world.

A WORLD OF DISCOVERY
Under the umbrella of the IGY, international scientists made many significant discoveries and achievements.

• **The dawn of the Space Age.** The October 1957 launch of *Sputnik I*, the world's first artificial satellite, was part of the IGY. The launch took the world (and some world governments) by surprise, but the International Council of Scientific Unions had called for artificial satellites to be launched during the IGY. The U.S. launched *Explorer I* just a few months later, in January 1958, and the ensuing media storm over both satellites (and the fact that the Russians had launched theirs first) helped fuel the "Space Race."

• **Understanding Earth's magnetic field.** *Explorer I* confirmed a theory posited by James Van Allen. He arranged for radiation-measuring Geiger counters to be placed on the satellite, and they detected a halo of high-energy particles—primarily cosmic rays and solar molecules—around the planet. For these halos to exist, a strong magnetic field had to be holding them there. And because of how they were situated, it meant that Earth itself generated a magnetic field. Without the field in place, all those molecules would collide with the atmosphere, creating so much radiation on Earth that it would make the planet uninhabitable. (That halo of particles is now known as the Van Allen radiation belt.)

• **Determining the makeup of the atmosphere.** Lloyd Berkner was finally given access to data from research facilities around the world, enabling him (and others) to measure the height and density of the atmosphere and make new discoveries about upper-atmospheric winds. That knowledge led to further developments in shortwave radio, which in turn allowed scientists to study how the full spectrum of light reacts with the atmosphere.

• **Long-term study and facilities in Antarctica.** The first permanent structure on the continent of ice was built in advance of the IGY in 1956 by the Royal Society (England's national academy of sciences) following a South Pole expedition. They named it Halley Research Station after British astronomer Edmond Halley, discoverer of Halley's Comet. Japanese and American stations followed, and in 1958 the Antarctic Treaty was signed, establishing the continent as a place owned by no one nation and dedicated entirely to research. More than 40 nations have signed the treaty to date. Research done during the IGY radically changed previous estimates of the thickness of the Antarctic ice sheet and of the total ice content of the Earth.

• **Understanding of oceanic trenches and plate tectonics.** For the first time, oceanographers were able to measure and define mid-ocean ridges—miles-deep trenches—and gain a better understanding of the chemical makeup of Earth's crust, not to mention plate tectonics. They also measured and charted ocean depths all around the planet.

• **Free exchange of scientific data.** Three "World Data Centers" were set up for the storage of all the data collected during the IGY. With one in the U.S., one in the U.S.S.R., and one in Asia, the goal was to use redundancy to prevent a full-scale data loss.

• **Use of computers for storage of huge amounts of data.** Within the World Data Centers, there was yet more redundancy, with data saved in triplicate—paper, computer punch cards, *and* computerized magnetic tape. This was the first large-scale computer data-storage operation in history. The World Data Centers still exist to securely store scientific data, but there are 52 of them now.

• **The development of an American space program.** After two launched satellites, the discovery of radiation belts, and better knowledge of the makeup of the atmosphere, the consensus at the end of the IGY was, literally, "the sky's the limit." And so, in July 1958, just after the IGY officially ended, the U.S. government announced the start-up of an independent space program, the National Aeronautics and Space Agency.

ELEPHANT JOKES
A corny but popular fad from the 1960s. (And still corny.)

Q: How is an elephant like an apricot?
A: They're both gray. Well, except the apricot.

Q: How can you tell if an elephant is in the refrigerator?
A: The door won't shut.

Q: How can you tell if an elephant has been in the refrigerator earlier?
A: Footprints in the butter.

Q: How do you stop a charging elephant?
A: Take away his credit card.

Q: What did Tarzan say when the elephants charged?
A: "Look out, here come the elephants!"

Q: What did Tarzan say when he saw a herd of elephants in the distance?
A: "Look, a herd of elephants in the distance!"

Q: What did Tarzan say when he saw a herd of elephants with sunglasses?
A: Nothing. He didn't recognize them.

Q: Why do elephants wear sandals?
A: So that they don't sink in the sand.

Q: Why do ostriches stick their heads in the ground?
A: They're looking for the elephants that forgot to wear their sandals.

In 1928 travel writer Richard Halliburton paid 36¢ to swim through the Panama Canal.

ICNTDRV

...and other real and funny license plates sent in to us by readers.

SLZBAG

IFARTED

H8MYWIFE

MMMBACON

HIOFCER

WOH NELI

VNTYPL8

11 MPG

MY NAME

PMS24-7

0TURDS
(on a plumber's
van)

IM LOST

RELSHME
(on the
Wienermobile)

LUV2FRT

U R NXT
(on a hearse)

NOT OJ
(on a white
Ford Bronco)

KOP B8
(on a Corvette)

2MNYKIDZ
(on a minivan)

FSTR N U

YOMAMMA

GLBLWRMR
(on a gas-guzzler)

U IDIOT

EIEIO

IM2FAT

X N TRUNK

BEAMEUP

IM LTL
(on a compact
car)

L8 AGN

STOL3N

NO1LKSU

CATLADI

3ZACROWD
(on a two-seater
sports car)

BEERRUN

CRASH

HI DEBT
(on a Ferrari)

MOM TAXI

KICKGAS
(on a Prius)

ICRASHM

EPH U

NVERLA8
(on a sportscar)

LYTESPD

TOY YODA

RN EM OVR

I GOTTA P

You can fold a $1 bill 4,000 times before it will tear.

DINNER AND A LAWSUIT

*You go out to your favorite restaurant or bar, expecting
to have a pleasant time…but instead you end
up suing the place. Bon appétit!*

THE PLAINTIFF: Arturo Carvajal, a Florida doctor
THE DEFENDANT: Houston's, a restaurant in North Miami Beach

THE LAWSUIT: Do you know the correct way to eat artichokes? You use your teeth to scrape the "meat" from the bottom of each tough, fibrous, spiky leaf and then discard the leaf. Never having eaten artichokes before, Dr. Carvajal didn't know that. Even so, he ordered the daily special—grilled artichokes—when he dined at Houston's in May 2009. When his plate arrived, Carvajal ate the first leaf, spike and all. Then he ate another and another, until his plate was clean. Then he didn't feel well. Suffering from acute abdominal pain, Carvajal went to the hospital, where doctors found the undigested spiky leaves stuck in his bowel and intestines. Claiming "disability, disfigurement, mental anguish, and loss of capacity for the enjoyment of life," Carvajal sued Houston's for $15,000, claiming the server should have told him how to eat artichokes.

THE VERDICT: The restaurant's attorney called the lawsuit a "silly notion." The case is still pending, but don't be surprised if the next time you order grilled artichokes, they come with an instruction manual.

THE PLAINTIFFS: Chadwick St.-OHarra and Steve Righetti, both 59, two friends from California
THE DEFENDANT: The Seafood Peddler in San Rafael

THE LAWSUIT: St.-OHarra was treating Righetti to a birthday dinner in 2010 when their appetizer arrived: a plate of *escargot*— snails in garlic butter. When St.-OHarra used his cocktail fork to pierce a steaming snail, it exploded, spraying melted butter and tiny chunks of snail all over both men. St.-OHarra's face and shirt were covered. According to his lawsuit, a bit of butter got into his eye, causing "temporary vision impairment." And a squirt of butter

---

The foil used to wrap one day's production of Hershey's Kisses would cover 40 football fields.

landed on Righetti's nose, causing "humiliation." (What occurred is known as "escargot explosion," and although it is rare, it is not unheard of.) After wiping themselves off, the two men finished their main courses, but were unhappy with the lack of remorse shown by the staff, which St.-OHarra described as "friggin' rude." Said Righetti, "Do I need this on my birthday?" They filed a claim against the Seafood Peddler's insurance company. When it was rejected, they sued. St.-OHarra, a former law student, decided to act as their lawyer in small claims court. He sought $7,500 for medical expenses and pain and suffering.

THE VERDICT: Citing a complete lack of evidence to back up their claims, the judge dismissed the case "with prejudice," which means that it can never be filed again. The real winner was the Seafood Peddler—after the lawsuit made headlines, the restaurant reported a surge in escargot sales.

THE PLAINTIFF: David Martin, of California
THE DEFENDANT: A Ca-Shi in Studio City
THE LAWSUIT: In February 2011, Martin went to the restaurant for the $28 all-you-can-eat sushi special. When the first plate was brought to him, Martin ate the raw fish that comes inside the sushi rolls, but not the rice that surrounds it. Then he ordered another plate and did the same thing. When Martin ordered a third plate, restaurant owner Jay Oh told Martin that because he wasn't eating any of the rice, he would have to pay for each order of just the fish, at $25 per serving. Martin replied that he was unable to eat the rice because he is a type-2 diabetic (his body can't handle all the carbohydrates). Neither man would budge, and Oh charged him the full amount. Two weeks later, Martin filed a $4,000 discrimination suit, claiming "humiliation, embarrassment, and mental anguish." He argued the restaurant wanted him to "fill up on rice." Oh countered, "Rice is a part of sushi. If you only eat the fish, I would go broke."

THE VERDICT: Even though Martin's attorney claimed the suit was "not about the money," he offered to drop the whole thing for $6,000, more than the initial amount cited. Oh refused. He knew he would have to pay a lot in court costs, but vowed to fight the charge. At last report, the two still plan to duke it out in court.

THE PLAINTIFF: Aaron Schnore, a Manhattan screenwriter

THE DEFENDANT: Johnny Utah's, which bills itself as the only bar in New York City with a mechanical bull

THE LAWSUIT: There's a sign on the door of Johnny Utah's warning people to not ride the mechanical bull if they're drunk. Schnore, 38, didn't heed that sign, but he signed the waiver releasing Johnny Utah's from liability should he get hurt. He got hurt. According to Schnore's lawsuit, because he was already drunk when he signed the waiver, the contract should be invalid. Schnore's lawyers also argued that the mechanical-bull operator "pumped it and pumped it until he could throw him," which amounted to "assault and battery." Johnny Utah's management countered that that's the whole point of the mechanical bull—to try and throw the rider. Alleging that he received "serious" injuries (Schnore landed awkwardly on his arm), he sued the bar for an undisclosed amount of money.

THE VERDICT: A New York State Supreme Court judge dismissed the case, basically saying that if you sign a waiver when you're drunk, you're still held to that agreement.

*   *   *

PROTEST SIGNS
Real homemade signs spotted at real protest rallies.

I'm mad as hell.
But mostly in a
passive-agressive way.

**3 words that will save
the economy:
Gay. Bridal. Registry.**

Thank you, Fox News,
for keeping is infromed.

Drink the Kool-Aid already!

CONGRESS SHOULD
DO STUFF.

I support my state senator.
(Wherever he is.)

I already regret
choosing to carry a sign
around all day.

*Can't we all just
get a bong?*

RANDOM BITS ON ELTON JOHN HITS

Here's hoping these facts don't burn out like a candle in the wind.

"**Your Song**": John's first album, *Empty Sky* (1969), flopped in both the U.S. and the U.K. Still, he got a gig as the opening act for Three Dog Night. One of the songs he performed on that tour was "Your Song," which he planned to include on his next album. Only problem: So did Three Dog Night, who planned to release their version as a *single*. At the last moment, though, the band changed their minds. Why? They thought John did the song (which he co-wrote) better. It turned out to be John's breakthrough hit, reaching #8 in the U.S., his first of 59 top 40 hits.

"**Bennie and the Jets**": A surprise hit on R&B radio stations, this song earned John an invitation in May 1975 to perform as the lead act on *Soul Train*, only the second white artist ever to do so. (The first was David Bowie.)

"**Candle in the Wind**": This song, first written to eulogize Marilyn Monroe, has been released as a single three times, each more successful than the last. The studio version from the album *Goodbye Yellow Brick Road* didn't even make the charts when it came out in 1974, but a live version reached #6 in 1987. In 1997 John performed a new version at the funeral of Princess Diana with special lyrics by his longtime writing partner, Bernie Taupin. A live recording of that song (John performed it only once) spent 14 weeks at #1 and became the bestselling single of all time. (Proceeds went to charity.)

"**Rocket Man**": When this song was released in the Soviet Union, it was retitled "Cosmonaut."

"**Empty Garden (Hey Hey Johnny)**": It's about Elton's friend John Lennon, who was murdered in 1980. In an interview on *Inside the Actors' Studio*, John said that he hardly ever plays the

---

One acre of peanuts produces enough peanut butter for 30,000 peanut butter sandwiches.

song live anymore because it makes him too sad. But he noted that he has performed it at Madison Square Garden in New York, where he dueted with Lennon in 1974 on the Beatles' "Lucy in the Sky With Diamonds"—Lennon's final concert appearance.

"Don't Let the Sun Go Down on Me": Elton John wanted an all-star chorus for the backing vocals. He managed to land Carl Wilson and Bruce Johnston of the Beach Boys, the Captain and Tennille, Dusty Springfield, and members of America. The mix sounded terrible, so all were jettisoned except Wilson, Johnston, and Tennille. (The horn section was provided by Tower of Power.)

"Goodbye Yellow Brick Road": John has performed in all 50 states. The 50th: Vermont (2008), home of Ben & Jerry's Ice Cream, which commemorated the event with a flavor called "Goodbye Yellow Brickle Road"—chocolate ice cream, peanut butter cookie dough, butter brickle, and white chocolate chips.

"Levon": In 2010 John and his partner David Furnish became parents to a boy born on Christmas Day to a surrogate mother. They named him Zachary Jackson Levon Furnish-John. "Levon" is a John song, which includes the lyric, "He was born a pauper to a pawn on a Christmas day." (The song, in turn, was named after Levon Helm of The Band, although the song isn't about him.)

"Honky Cat": The only hit song in history that features a duck call solo (performed by John's drummer, Ray Cooper).

"Don't Go Breaking My Heart": Kiki Dee and John recorded this duet in 1976 as an homage to Motown greats Marvin Gaye and Tammi Terrell. It was John's first #1 single in the U.K. Other stars with whom John recorded the song: Miss Piggy (on *The Muppet Show*), Minnie Mouse (on *Totally Minnie*), and RuPaul (on John's *Duets* album).

"That's What Friends Are For": John sang on this 1985 hit single benefiting AIDS charities along with Dionne Warwick, Stevie Wonder, and Gladys Knight. He was the producers' third choice for the slot, after George Michael and Rod Stewart both turned it down.

The spout on the milk carton didn't appear until the 1960s. Before that you cut them open.

THOUGHTS ON 'BOTS

*We asked our Acme Quote Generato-tron to come up with a page...
and it presented us with these quotes about robots, of course.*

"Robotics is about us—the discipline of emulating our lives, of wondering how we work."
    —Rod Grupen

"The robot is going to lose. Not by much. But when the final score is tallied, flesh and blood is going to beat the damn monster."
    —Adam Smith

"Robots do not hold on to life. They can't. They have nothing to hold on with—no soul, no instinct. Grass has more will to live than they do."
    —Karel Capek

"I visualize a time when we will be to robots what dogs are to humans, and I'm rooting for the machines."
    —Claude Shannon

"I wish a robot would get elected president. That way, when he came to town, we could all take a shot at him and not feel too bad."
    —Jack Handy

"Man is a robot with defects."
    —Emil Cioran

"Unless mankind redesigns itself by changing our DNA through altering our genetic makeup, computer-generated robots will take over our world."
    —Stephen Hawking

"Someday a human being, named perhaps Fred White, may shoot a robot named Pete Something-or-other, and to his surprise see it weep and bleed. And the dying robot may shoot back and, to its surprise, see a wisp of gray smoke arise from the electric pump that it supposed was Mr. White's beating heart. It would be rather a great moment of truth for both of them."
    —Philip K. Dick

"Part of the inhumanity of the computer is that, once it is completely programmed and working smoothly, it is completely honest."
    —Isaac Asimov

"You end up with a tremendous respect for a human being if you're a roboticist."
    —Joseph Engelberger

GROANERS

What's black and white and dreaded all over?
This page of bad jokes. (You've been warned.)

What do you call a cow with two legs that are shorter than the other two?
Lean beef.

Why did the orange-juice factory worker lose his job?
He couldn't concentrate.

Patient: "Doctor, doctor—you gotta help me! I feel like a deck of cards!"
Doctor: "Sit down, sir. I'll deal with you later."

Which bird is the most contented?
The crow. He never complains without caws.

Doctor: "How is the kid who swallowed the half-dollar?"
Nurse: "No change yet."

What do you call a nun who walks in her sleep?
A Roman Catholic.

The New York doctor advised his patient to walk two miles a day. A month later the patient called and said, "I'm in Boston. What should I do now?"

The Leaning Tower of Pisa and the tower of Big Ben were thinking of starting a family, but they called it off. One didn't have the time; the other didn't have the inclination.

Did you hear about the shipload of paint that wrecked and marooned all the sailors?

What do you call a dog with no legs?
It doesn't matter; he won't come when you call him.

Doctor: "I'll have your eczema cured in a week."
Patient: "Please, doctor. Don't make rash promises."

How do you know if a cat burglar has been in your house?
The cat is missing.

Definition of "vitamin":
What you do when a friend comes to your door.

Customer: "Why is this coffee so muddy?"
Waitress: "It was ground yesterday."

Why don't snails smell? They don't have noses.

TOUGH GUYS

The cold hands of Death just couldn't get a grip on these tenacious survivors.

GESUNDHEIT!

Darco Sangermano was having a great time celebrating New Year's Eve 2010 in Naples, Italy—until a stray bullet pierced his skull. Sangermano collapsed to the ground, but remained conscious and was rushed to a nearby hospital. As physicians were trying to determine how to go in and remove the bullet, Sangermano sneezed…and the bullet fell out of his left nostril. He only needed a few stitches to close the entry wound. According to Dr. Sid Barrone, "The bullet went through his temple, behind his eye, entered the nasal cavity, and then became lodged in his nostril before he sneezed it out. Amazing."

THE SQUEEZE

Matthew Lowe broke his back, ruptured his stomach and bowel, shattered his pelvis, and fractured both hips, his right arm, and several ribs. But the 25-year-old British factory worker is alive. While he was working next to a steel-processing machine at Compass Engineering in Barnsley, England, Lowe's clothes got caught in the high-powered conveyor system and he was pulled into it through a five-inch opening, about the width of a CD case. "The machine crushed my body, ripped my clothes to shreds, and spat me out," he said. Although Lowe's outward appearance hasn't changed much, he's "lost count" of the amount of metal that doctors have put inside him in order to keep his organs functioning. The factory was cited for numerous safety infractions, but Lowe made a full recovery and has since returned to work as a supervisor.

HE WAS NEARLY KILT

A Scottish mountain climber named Adam Potter had nearly reached the summit of Sgurr Choinnich Mor ("Big Rocky Peak of the Moss" in Gaelic). Shortly after he stopped and told his team to prepare for the final ascent, he slipped in the snow and fell down the 1,000-foot rocky cliff. His friends watched in horror as he bounced from craggy outcrop to craggy outcrop—his gear flying

---

In 2011 Rifca Stanescu of Romania became the world's youngest grandmother. Age: 25.

everywhere—before disappearing from sight. A search-and-rescue helicopter came in but couldn't find Potter's body anywhere. They did, however, spot a man at the bottom of the cliff standing up, reading a map. Maybe he knew where Potter was. When the rescuers landed, they were amazed to find out that the man *was* Potter. He was cut up and had a lot of bruises but was otherwise okay. "It was quite incredible," said one of the rescuers, "he must have literally glanced off the outcrops as he fell, almost flying." For his part, all Potter thought about on the way down was that this would delay his upcoming trip to Mt. Everest.

COLD-COCKED

A 24-year-old construction worker named Esidras Valles was working on the roof of a one-story building in North Bergen, New Jersey, when a 40-pound air conditioner fell on his head…from 15 stories up. Valles had a gash on his head that required a lot of stitches, but he made a speedy recovery. Lacking any medical reason for why Valles wasn't killed, Dr. Bruno Molino said philosophically, "You can consider him fortunate and unfortunate."

LIFE'S A HITCH

In 2010 Eric Provost was driving his SUV near Canby, Oregon. He'd just picked up his six-month-old son Evan from the babysitter and was heading home. While talking to his wife on his headset, Provost, who teaches fifth grade, saw an object bouncing in the road. Before he could react, the object—a large, metal trailer hitch—smashed through the windshield and hit the steering wheel so hard that it bent it back. Had the hitch hit a few inches higher, it could have taken Provost's head off. Still, it slammed into his chest and arm before flying into the back of Evan's rear-facing car seat. Amazingly, the hitch did not dislodge the car seat, but bounced up and punctured the SUV's ceiling before finally landing in the back. Provost skidded to a stop and knew instantly that his arm was broken. His wife, who had listened to the entire event on the phone, was terrified. He told her he was hurt but okay, and that Evan didn't get a scratch. From his hospital bed, Provost later joked, "If someone out there is missing a trailer hitch, it's in the back of my car." He also had a message for his students: "I am still the toughest guy you know."

More than half of all doctors in Finland are female.

SPIT BOXES & MORNING GLORIES

The only horse-racing terms most of us know are "giddyup" and "mint julep." But it turns out the Sport of Kings is full of colorful lingo. Here are a few favorites.

BUG BOY. A rookie or apprentice jockey, so called because of the asterisks, or "bugs," that appear next to a rookie's name on racing forms. The more "bugs," the less experience the jockey has.

MORNING GLORY. A horse that runs well in morning workouts but seldom wins races.

IN THE VAN. In the lead, running at the front of the main pack of horses. (Van is short for "vanguard.")

IN THE RUCK. Running at the back of the pack. (Ruck is short for "rucksack," another word for "backpack.")

IN THE ONE-ONE. Running just behind the leading horse and slightly to one side. Because there's less wind resistance in this position than there is "in the van," the "one-one" is considered the best place to stay until the leader can be overtaken.

IN THE DEATH. Running just to the right, or "outside," of the race's leader. It's considered a bad position because this horse has to cope with more wind resistance than the horses behind it, and, because the track is curved, a horse in the death has to cover more distance than the leader.

HANGING. Tending to veer toward the inside or outside rail during a race, often interfering with other horses.

ON THE PAINT. Running very close to the inside rail.

SPEEDY CUT. A leg injury caused when a galloping horse's hoof cuts the skin on the inside of its opposite leg.

GRABBING A QUARTER. When a galloping horse's hind hoof clips the back of a front hoof, often causing a stumble or injury.

MAIDEN. A horse that hasn't won a race yet.

The average person in the UK drinks as much tea as 23 Italians.

GRADUATE. A horse that's just won its first race.

MUDLARK. A horse that excels in running on muddy tracks.

SPIT BOX. The receptacle into which a horse's urine and blood samples are placed for drug testing.

CUPPY TRACK. A loose, bumpy, unstable track surface that breaks away under a horse's hooves and slows it down.

SHADOW ROLL. A piece of lamb fleece attached to the noseband of a horse's bridle to prevent it from seeing the ground and being startled by its own shadow.

FLATTENING OUT. When a horse drops its head while running, usually due to fatigue.

SPITTING THE BIT. When a horse tires during a race and becomes hard to control.

WASHY. Description of a horse that's drenched in nervous sweat before a race.

OUCHY. Description of a horse that's sore after a race.

PURPLE PATCH. A run of good luck in several consecutive races.

WALKOVER. A race in which all the horses except one were withdrawn before the start time. By regulation, the remaining horse must still gallop the distance to win.

BLANKET FINISH. Similar to a photo finish, but the two leading horses cross the finish line so close together that a single blanket could be spread across both of them.

*   *   *

Jim Gaffigan on movie trailers: "Why is it whenever you're watching a preview you always feel like you have to comment on it to the person you're with? 'Yeah, I'm not gonna see that movie. I'm gonna wait for that on video.' I mean, when you think about it, it's just a commercial for the movie. You never sit at home watching TV and say, 'Yeah, I'm not buying *that* cereal. I don't like raisins. What's your take on that?'"

HERMITS FOR HIRE

What do millionaires do to show off their wealth? Some buy exotic pets, big houses, or fancy cars. But 300 years ago, a fad erupted among wealthy Brits to buy people—not to make them servants (they already had those), but to have them simply wander around the yard.

HERMITAGE, SWEET HERMITAGE

By the late 1700s, the Industrial Revolution was in full swing. A by-product of this new technology: the Romantic Era, in which English writers, painters, and the well-to-do railed against modernization. Poets like John Milton and William Wordsworth wrote about the virtues of solitude and anti-materialism. The "humble hermit living off the land" became a symbol of the Romantic ideal (though few were willing to try it themselves). At the same time, a trend was growing among the rich in England: They constructed "architectural follies" on their grounds—elaborate buildings that were primarily decorative, such as Roman temples and Egyptian pyramids, towers, grottos…and hermit houses, or *hermitages*.

What was a hermitage like? They were pretty small. The one at Hagley Hall in Worcestershire was a closet-sized stone cave covered with roots, moss, and foliage. A Milton poem was hung on the wall, just in case visitors didn't understand the connection. Many hermitages also included macabre decor, such as floors made of knuckle bones. Marston House in Surrey was surrounded by a bone fence topped with real horse heads. And no hermitage was complete without a decorative human skull for contemplation.

KEEPING UP WITH THE JONESES

Soon, simple caves and grottoes just weren't enough to make the nobleman stand out from his peers; he needed his own actual hermit (preferably a filthy, bearded old man) to live in the hermitage. However, finding an old man who was living a truly non-materialistic life in the woods was difficult, even back then. And convincing him to move to a huge estate was nearly impossible. (There was a reason they lived in the woods.) The next best thing: Hire a peasant from the village to fill the role. Ironically, only the wealthy could afford to maintain a garden hermit, who was supposed to symbolize the landowner's interest in non-material pursuits.

ON LONE

Most of the time, a rich person would simply put an ad in the newspaper looking for a hermit. But in a few cases, folks who were down on their luck offered themselves up for the job, as evidenced by this *London Courier* newspaper ad from 1810:

> A young man who wishes to retire from the world and live as a hermit in some convenient spot in England is willing to engage with any nobleman or gentleman who may be desirous of having one.

It's unknown if that man ever became a hermit, but those who were hired were usually contracted to live in the hermitage for seven years. For example, an English politician named Charles Hamilton advertised a seven-year contract for a hermit to come and live on the forested land at Painshill Park in Surrey…

> …where he shall be provided with a Bible, optical glasses, a mat for his feet, a hassock for his pillow, an hourglass for timepiece, water for his beverage, and food from the house. He must wear a camlet robe, and never, under any circumstances, must he cut his hair, beard, or nails, stray beyond the limits of Mr. Hamilton's grounds, or exchange one word with the servant.

Hamilton offered a payment of 700 guineas (more than $500,000 in today's money), but there was a catch: The hermit wouldn't get a penny unless he followed every detail in the contract. Hamilton did find a man willing to shed his wares, but the hired hermit lasted for only three weeks—he was fired when he was found drinking at the local pub.

MASTERS OF PUPPETS

Indeed, finding a good hermit could be quite difficult…unless you were the queen. In the 1730s, Queen Caroline, wife of King George II, offered to let a poet who was grieving the death of his wife live in her hermitage at Richmond Park near London. The poet, whose name was Stephen Duck, accepted and became one of the most famous hermits of the Romantic Era. Duck grew a long beard and wrote poetry in his garden hermitage, having all the access he wanted to the queen's library. He received thousands of visitors each year (not exactly a life of solitude), but never did seem to find solace. In 1756 Duck drowned himself in the River Thames.

But most rich folks weren't as fortunate as Queen Caroline. They became frustrated by the hermits sneaking off and embarrassing them. So some wealthy landowners placed wax dummies in chairs in their hermitages. John Hill of Hawkestone Park in Shropshire went one step further: He used a puppet. That's because his real hermit, known as Father Francis, had died after living for 14 years in a cave at Hawkestone, sporting the requisite long beard and contemplating an hourglass to the delight of passersby. After his search for a suitable replacement failed, Hill instructed his servants to build him a life-size replica of Father Francis. The new "Francis" turned out to be distinctly less animated than his predecessor, but Hill had a solution for that as well: He hired a man to crouch behind the dummy and make it "stand up" whenever a visitor approached. The operator would then recite poetry while moving Francis's mouth with a string.

EMPTY NESTS

As the Romantic Era came to a close in the mid-1800s, interest in ornamental hermits declined, and the practice was all but forgotten. However, many of the hermitages have been kept up for posterity. And every once in a while, one is actually used for its intended purpose. In 2004 an artist named David Blandy revived the hermitage built by Charles Hamilton at Painshill Park, announcing on his website:

> The 18th-century tradition of housing a human pet at the bottom of your garden to impress the neighbours is set to return. I will seal myself off from the outside world and reside in a house with similar proportions to a rabbit hutch.

Like his Romantic predecessors, Blandy was protesting modernism. His goal was to illustrate that in today's world, people care more about their electronic gadgets than each other. So how long did Bandy's detachment from society last? Only a few weeks.

They just don't make hermits like they used to.

IT'S ALL YOU NEED

Who doesn't love a good quote page?

"How on Earth are you ever going to explain in terms of chemistry and physics so important a biological phenomenon as first love?"
—**Albert Einstein**

"One's first love is always perfect until one meets one's second love."
—**Elizabeth Aston**

"Some pray to marry the man they love. I humbly pray to heaven above that I love the man I marry."
—**Rose Pastor Stokes**

"You know you're in love when you can't fall asleep because reality is finally better than your dreams."
—**Dr. Seuss**

"Love is what is left in a relationship after all the selfishness has been removed."
—**Cullen Hightower**

"Love works a different way in different minds; the fool it enlightens and the wise it blinds."
—**John Dryden**

"Love is the only satisfactory answer to the problem of human existence."
—**Erich Fromm**

"I have found the paradox that if I love until it hurts, then there is no hurt, but only more love."
—**Mother Teresa**

"Love is a game that two can play and both win."
—**Eva Gabor**

"If Jack's in love, he's no judge of Jill's beauty."
—**Benjamin Franklin**

"If I know what love is, it is because of you."
—**Herman Hesse**

"If you have love in your life, it can make up for a great many things you lack. If you don't have it, no matter what else there is, it's not enough.
—**Ann Landers**

"John Lennon said, 'All you need is love.' John obviously never met my bank manager."
—**Danny McCrossan**

First African-American member of the US Senate: Hiram Rhoades Revels, Mississippi, 1870.

FORBIDDEN ISLAND, USA

If you've ever visited the Hawaiian islands, you may already know that one of them, Niihau, west of Kauai, is off-limits to outsiders. Here's the story of how that came to be, and what life on the island is like today.

FOR SALE BY OWNER

In 1863 Eliza McHutchison Sinclair, the wealthy 63-year-old widow of a Scottish sea captain, set sail with her children and grandchildren from New Zealand for Vancouver Island off the southwest coast of Canada. There she hoped to buy a ranch large enough to support the dozen family members who were traveling with her, but after arriving in Canada, she decided the country was too rough for a ranch to be successful. Someone suggested she try her luck in the kingdom of Hawaii, 2,400 miles west of North America in the middle of the Pacific Ocean. On September 17, 1863, she and her family sailed into Honolulu harbor, and quickly became friends with King Kamehameha IV.

The Sinclairs toured the islands looking for suitable ranch property. They turned down an opportunity to buy much of what is now downtown Honolulu and Waikiki beach, and they passed on a chance to buy much of the land in and around Pearl Harbor. "After some months of looking," Eliza's daughter Anne recalled years later, "we gave up and decided to leave for California. When King Kamehameha heard of this he told us that if we would stay in Hawaii he would sell us a whole island."

SALE PENDING

The island was Niihau (pronounced NEE-ee-HAH-oo), a 72-square-mile island 18 miles off the southwest coast of Kauai. Population: about three hundred natives. Anne's brothers, Francis and James Sinclair, had a look and liked what they saw. They offered King Kamehameha $6,000 in gold; the King countered with $10,000 (about $1.5 million in today's money). Sold! Kamehameha IV died before the sale could be completed, but his successor, King Kamehameha V, honored the deal. In 1864 the Sinclairs ponied up about 68 pounds of gold, and Niihau has been the family's private property ever since.

State of war: More than half of all Civil War battles were fought in Virginia.

CAVEAT EMPTOR

History (including Hawaiian history) is filled with examples of indigenous peoples being cheated out of their land by unscrupulous outsiders, but this may be a case where the natives pulled one over on the foreigners. When the Sinclair brothers first laid eyes on Niihau, the island was lush and green, seemingly the perfect place to set up a ranch. What Kamehameha apparently did not tell them was that the island was coming off of two years of unusually wet weather. Normally it was semi-arid, almost a desert. Niihau sits in the "rain shadow" of Kauai and receives just 25 inches of rain a year, compared to more than 450 inches on the wettest parts of Kauai. Droughts on Niihau are so severe that it was common for the Niihauans to abandon their island for years on end until the rains returned. If they didn't leave, they starved.

Indeed, the only reason the island was available for sale—and the reason Kamehameha was so eager to unload it—was because it was so barren. After the Great *Mahele* ("division") of 1848, when the monarchy made land available for purchase by native Hawaiians for the first time, the Niihauans had tried to buy the island themselves. They'd hoped to pay for it with crops and animals raised on the island, but the land wasn't productive enough for them to do it, not even when the price of the land was just a few pennies an acre. They ended up having to lease the island from the King instead, at an even lower price. By the time the Sinclairs sailed into Honolulu harbor in September 1863, the Niihauans had fallen so far behind on even these meager payments that Kamehameha IV was ready to sell the island to someone else.

HEDGING HER BETS

After the sale went through, the Sinclairs built a large house on the west coast of Niihau and set up their ranch. But the dry weather returned, and it became evident that the operation might never be successful. Luckily, Eliza Sinclair still had plenty of gold left, and in the 1870s she bought 21,000 acres of land on Kauai that the family developed into a sugarcane plantation. It, too, remains in the family to this day. (In 1902 Eliza's grandson bought the island of Lanai at a property auction, making the family sole owners of *two* of the eight inhabited Hawaiian Islands…but only for a time. They sold Lanai to the Hawaiian Pineapple Company—now part of Dole—in 1922.)

CHANGES, CHANGES, EVERYWHERE

When King Kamehameha V signed ownership of the island over to the Sinclairs, he told them, "Niihau is yours. But the day may come when Hawaiians are not as strong in Hawaii as they are now. When that day comes, please do what you can to help them." The Sinclairs, it turned out, were more than just the owners of an island—they were also the rulers of the Hawaiians who lived on Niihau…at least those who chose to stay on the island after it changed hands. Having their land sold out from under them was a bitter blow to the Niihauans, and many moved off the island. By 1866 the native population of Niihau was half of what it had been in 1860.

Those Niihauans who moved away soon discovered that change was coming to *all* the islands, not just to Niihau. And few of the changes would be to their benefit. In 1887 a group of armed American and European landowners forced King Kalakaua to sign what has become known as the Bayonet Constitution, which stripped the king of much of his power and denied many native Hawaiians the right to vote. According to the new constitution, foreign-born landowners were allowed to vote, even if they weren't Hawaiian citizens.

Kalakaua died in 1891, and his sister Liliuokalani became Queen. In 1893 she tried to replace the Bayonet Constitution with one that restored the power of the monarch, but her attempts had the opposite effect and she was overthrown in a coup organized by the foreign landowners. The Republic of Hawaii was declared in 1894, and in 1898 Hawaii was annexed by the United States.

MEANWHILE, BACK AT THE RANCH

Eliza Sinclair did not live to see the overthrow of the Hawaiian monarch; she died in 1892. Other family members opposed it, and it's likely that she would have too. She was deeply concerned about the threat the outside world posed to the Hawaiian culture and way of life. Those threats went way beyond politics: They included exposure to deadly Western diseases as well as alcoholism, prostitution in the seafaring ports, gambling, tobacco, and other vices of the modern world. English was quickly displacing Hawaiian as the primary language of the islands, and even the hula and other Hawaiian art forms were beginning to disappear.

The Mars rovers contain pieces of metal from the World Trade Center.

It was distressing for all Hawaiians to see their way of life under threat. What set the Niihauans apart was the fact that their island was owned by a family that was willing and able to honor the commitment made to King Kamehameha V to assist them in preserving their culture. Beginning with Eliza Sinclair, and continuing with her grandson Aubrey Robinson, who assumed responsibility for Niihau after her death, the family began limiting access to Niihau as a means of allowing the Niihauans to live their lives as they always had, free from the pressures of the modern world. When a measles epidemic on Niihau killed 11 children in the 1930s, they sealed off the island almost completely.

Over the years, control of the island passed from Aubrey to his son Aylmer and then to Aylmer's brother Lester. When Lester died in 1969 his widow Helen Robinson assumed responsibility, and when she died in 2002 control passed to her sons Keith and Bruce Robinson. They oversee the island today.

Each generation of the family has respected the wish of the Niihauans (and Eliza Sinclair) to maintain their isolation from the outside world. The Niihauans are free to come and go as they please, and many do spend significant portions of their lives off the island. But outsiders can visit Niihau *only* with the Robinsons' personal permission, and that is rarely given.

LAST OF ITS KIND

If you've ever been to Hawaii, you know that there's plenty of Hawaiian culture to be found in the museums and souvenir shops that serve the 6 million tourists who visit each year. But that's about the only place you'll find it. The 80,000 Hawaiians who claim full native-Hawaiian ancestry today make up less than 6% of the state's total population. Fewer than 2,000 Hawaiians are native Hawaiian speakers, and half of those are over 70 years old.

There are no communities left on the Hawaiian Islands that speak Hawaiian as their first language. No communities, that is, except one: the 130 Hawaiians who live on Niihau. Their culture and privacy are still carefully guarded by the descendants of Eliza Sinclair. On every other island, the traditional Hawaiian way of life has all but disappeared.

Part II of the story is on page 457.

In ancient Rome, it was illegal to bury a body within the city limits.

CELEBRITIES IN THE CAN

They go to the bathroom, just like us. Except weirder stuff happens.

LEONARDO DICAPRIO. While attending a soccer game at the World Cup in South Africa in the summer of 2010, DiCaprio stepped out to use the bathroom. To his horror, a bunch of fans spotted him and followed him in. DiCaprio tried to find some privacy by running into a stall, but there were too many men—and women—in the bathroom, crowding around to peek into it. They started shaking the stall walls and nearly toppled them onto DiCaprio, which would have put him at the bottom of a pile of gaping fans. But DiCaprio screamed for help and security officers came to his rescue before anything serious occurred.

MILEY CYRUS. When Barbara Walters interviews celebrities for her Oscar-night specials, she films in the celebrity's home to create a sense of warmth and intimacy. When she and her crew came to Cyrus's home in 2008, they made themselves a little too much at home. They used her bathrooms...and clogged all the toilets. Cyrus had no hard feelings—she called a plumber and later sent Walters a tiny solid-gold toilet to commemorate the experience.

GERARD DEPARDIEU. In 2011 the French actor was on a CityJet flight, on his way to Dublin to film a movie. The plane was delayed on the tarmac at the Paris airport. Nature called, and Depardieu got up to use the bathroom. Flight attendants told him he'd have to wait until the plane was in the air. Depardieu, who suffers from prostate problems, couldn't wait—so he relieved himself on the carpet of the airplane, in the aisle, in front of other passengers.

JACKIE CHAN. He's a fervent environmentalist, and he takes that attitude with him to movie sets. Addressing a crowd at a "Green Living" rally in Singapore in 2009, Chan insisted that members of the film crew save water by going to the bathroom in groups. Only after the last one finishes up, he explained, can the toilet be flushed. Chan calls it the "Golden Flush."

JUST PLANE WEIRD

*If you happen to be reading this page on board
an airplane, you might want to save it for
when you're back on the ground.*

INCIDENT OF NOTE

In January 2010, an Oregon man named Joseph Johnson boarded a flight to Hawaii, then got mad when he saw there was no seat in front of him to store his things under. Apparently he needed to vent his anger. Ninety minutes into the flight, he filled out a comment card and passed it to the fight attendant in a sealed envelope. "I hope we don't crash and burn…or worse yet, end up on some place like Gilligan's Island," the note read. "What if the plane ripped apart in mid-flight and we plumited [sic] to earth?" Alarmed, the pilot radioed a distress call, and two fighter planes were scrambled to escort the plane back to Portland, where Johnson was arrested and charged with interfering with the duties of a crew member. "He told me he didn't think anyone would open [the envelope] during the flight," the investigator wrote in an affidavit. "He thought the card was going to be taken back to an office somewhere, opened, and everyone in the room would 'get a laugh' from it, and perhaps he'd even get some frequent flyer miles out of it." Instead, Johnson got sentenced to 50 hours of community service and was ordered to write a letter of apology to the airline and his fellow passengers on board the flight.

SILENT TREATMENT

Not long after midnight on March 22, 2011, the pilot of an American Airlines flight from Miami to Reagan National Airport in Washington, D.C., radioed the control tower to request landing assistance. No response. After repeated attempts to reach the tower by radio and via a "shout line" that broadcasts through a loudspeaker in the control tower, the pilot went ahead and landed anyway, assisted by an air traffic controller in Warrenton, Virginia, 45 miles away. A few minutes later, a United Airlines flight from Chicago also landed without assistance from the tower. Finally, after 30 minutes of dead air, the lone controller on duty was suddenly back on the air, blaming a "stuck microphone" for the problem. He later admitted to falling asleep at his post and was suspended while the incident was investigated. This was the second time in two years that the National Airport control tower fell silent. The first incident occurred when another lone controller accidentally locked himself out of the building.

GROUNDED

In November 2009, police responded to a report of someone disrupting operations at Griffin-Spalding County Airport in Georgia. They discovered a Delta Airlines pilot named Dan Wayne Gryder driving his car back and forth across the runway. Gryder initially gave the police a fake name. Then, when they figured out who he was and attempted to issue him a citation, he quickly boarded his personal plane, a 1937 Douglas DC-3 airliner. After threatening the officers, he tried to take off, but then realized he was out of fuel. When police refused to let him refuel, he parked the plane and was arrested as he stepped onto the tarmac. At last report Gryder (who is also a private flight instructor) was suspended from Delta and awaiting trial for aggravated assault and obstruction of justice. One aviation industry blog's headline: "Delta Pilot Accused of a Lot of Things."

CLOTHES CALL

In June 2009, a U.S. Airways flight from Charlotte, North Carolina, to Los Angeles was disrupted when a passenger, 50-year-old Keith Wright of the Bronx, New York, stripped naked and refused to put his clothes back on. When a flight attendant tried to cover him with a blanket, he started punching and kicking, at which point two off-duty police officers on the flight subdued and handcuffed him. The plane was diverted to Albuquerque, New Mexico, where Wright was taken off the plane. "He had some alcohol at the Charlotte airport and was on medication but didn't take it. Perhaps a combination of not taking his medication, plus the alcohol and the altitude all impacted his usual behavior," the Albuquerque airport police chief told reporters. (Wright, a former employee of the Transportation Security Administration, says he doesn't remember the flight.)

On average, it takes 85 lbs. of feed to raise a 30-lb. turkey.

STRANGE SUPERSTITIONS

*It's hard to imagine that anyone could possibly believe these
old superstitions, but then some people actually doubt the
existence of the Great Flooplenocker, so go figure.*

• A newborn's first sneeze is lucky. Before the sneeze, the baby is under the influence of bad fairies, and the newborn who does not sneeze may become a warlock or witch.

• Is she *really* a witch? Drive a nail into her footprint. If she returns to pull it out, she's a witch.

• Dropping an umbrella on the floor means there will be a murder in the house.

• To remove a birthmark, rub it with a duck's foot. (No word on whether it should be attached to the duck.)

• Don't throw out hair trimmings. If a bird uses your hair for a nest, you'll be prone to constant headaches.

• Your best chance of recovering from being struck by lightning is to be buried up to your neck in the ground.

• Carrying St. John's wort keeps the devil from coming any closer than nine steps away from you.

• The pains of childbirth can be lessened by untying all knots in a house and unbraiding the woman's hair.

• To cure a headache, rub your fingers under your arms really hard and then smell them.

• To be successful in all you do, carry a bat's heart with you at all times.

• Break the shell of a boiled egg after eating it to keep witches from traveling in it.

• A girl who eats chicken gizzards will have big breasts.

• To avoid bad luck after seeing an ambulance, pinch your nose until you see a black or brown dog.

• A mole on the buttocks foretells death by hanging.

• Swallowing young frogs whole will cure cancer.

• If you leave the house wearing a fern, you'll lose your way and snakes will follow you.

• Knives stay sharp longer once they have "tasted" their owner's blood.

NICE LEGS!

Some facts that really stand up.

• All animals on Earth with legs are descended from animals without legs—the first creatures to leave water for land. Fossil evidence suggests this happened roughly 400 million years ago.

• All insect species (there are an estimated 6 to 10 million of them) have three pairs of legs. Although they can differ considerably, there are five main types of insect legs:
Cursorial. Specially adapted for running. Examples of insects with such legs are cockroaches and silverfish.
Saltatorial. Adapted for jumping. You've seen them on grasshoppers and crickets.
Raptorial. For grasping prey. Example: the praying mantis.
Natatorial. Flat and covered with fine hairs. They're used for swimming, and are found on insects like diving beetles.
Fossorial. For digging. Found on burrowing insects such as mole crickets.

• The legs of crustaceans (crabs, shrimp, barnacles) and myriapods (centipedes, millipedes) all have seven segments.

• The more than 100,000 species of arachnids (spiders, scorpions, ticks, etc.) have four pairs of legs. Each leg is made up of seven segments. From the body out, they are *coxa, trochanter, femur, patella, tibia, metatarsus,* and *tarsus.*

• Most mammals have four legs, and most of them use all four for walking. The others—the aquatic mammals (such as whales and seals) and bats all *descended* from animals with four legs.

• A few, including humans, are *bipedal,* meaning we use two limbs to get around.

• Other bipeds: birds; macropods (hopping animals such as kangaroos); some lemurs that, when on the ground, hop sideways on two legs; the *Tyrannosaurus rex* (and many other extinct creatures).

• The fewest number of legs on any animal: two. The most: 750, recorded on *Illacme plenipes,* a type of millipede found only in central California. (The number of legs varies, but most members of the species have more than 600.)

- There are no known animals with an odd number of legs.

- Some insects, such as caterpillars, have structures called *prolegs* on their abdomens. In the case of caterpillars, the prolegs have tiny hooks on them and can be manipulated to assist the creatures in moving. But they are unsegmented and, as such, are not considered true legs.

- There are around 1,100 bat species in the world. They all have two legs, but only two—vampire bats and lesser short-tailed bats—can walk. The rest have legs that are too fragile and weak for walking.

- Why do birds stand on one leg? Scientists believe they do it to conserve heat. Birds' legs contain significant veins and arteries, but aren't covered with feathers, so they lose body heat through their legs. Standing on one leg simply reduces the rate at which they lose that heat. (Another theory about why birds stand on one leg: If they stood on no legs, they'd fall over.)

*　　*　　*

THERE'S AN APP FOR *THAT*?

UK Payphone: If you're traveling in the United Kingdom, this app will help you find the closest pay telephone…which seems kind of pointless, since you'd have to have your *phone* to use it.

Wooo! Button: Tap the button and it shouts "wooo!"

Hair Clinic for Man and Woman: The producers bill it as "the world's first mobile hair clinic system." They claim that if you run this $8.99 app while rubbing the phone on your head, it releases frequencies that promote the circulation of blood on the scalp, helping hair to grow.

SimStapler: Press the picture of the stapler. It makes stapling sounds.

Hang Time: It measures how high into the air you can throw your smartphone. The app costs 99 cents, but make sure to catch your phone, or it will end up costing a lot more.

Myth-understood: Elephants aren't afraid of mice (but they are afraid of bees).

DUMB CROOKS

With crooks like these, we hardly need cops.
Here's proof that crime doesn't pay.

OFF THE HOOK

In March 2011, Kevon Whitfield, 19, and a 14-year-old friend phoned Topper's Pizza in Clifton, Ohio, and ordered a pizza. But what they really wanted to do was to rob the pizza delivery person. How do we know this? Because after Whitfield phoned in the order, he forgot to end the call—his cell phone was still connected to Topper's Pizza as he and his accomplice were planning the robbery. A Topper's Pizza employee heard everything and immediately called the cops. The police replaced the delivery driver with an undercover officer, who arrested the two prospective thieves as they tried to pull the heist.

SICK DAY

In February 2009, Amber Carter, a 4th-grade teacher in Bellefontaine, Ohio, took a half-day of sick leave and went home early. The following morning the school's principal visited Carter's classroom to tell her students that their teacher would not be returning to Western Intermediate School. The afternoon Carter supposedly went home sick, she was arrested for prostitution at a Super 8 Motel after she accepted cash from an undercover cop posing as a customer. How'd she get caught? "Suspicious Internet activity." Police say they received an anonymous tip after Carter posted ads for her "services" on Craigslist using a school computer.

(SHIRT) COLLARED

Two men pulled a home-invasion robbery in Charlotte, North Carolina, in March 2011, making off with jewelry, a wallet, and other valuables. But as they fled, a T-shirt fell out of their getaway car. Not just any T-shirt, either: This one had a photo of one of the robbers on it (along with the slogan "Making money is my thang"). When police displayed it on the local "Crime Stoppers" TV show, the man depicted on the shirt, 25-year-old Jonathan Huntley, turned himself in. Extra dumb: The photo on the shirt

---

20th Century Fox has a trademark on "the spoken word 'D'oh'" (but not the *written* word).

was a mug shot from a previous armed robbery arrest—for which Huntley had served seven years in prison. He had only been out for four months when his mug shot shirt got him arrested again.

THEY'LL NEVER EXPECT THIS!

In August 2010, Shane Alexander, 20, and Jason Vantress, 30, went to a Portland, Oregon, Fred Meyer supermarket and started cutting the tags off items and stuffing the goods into their backpacks. The things they took included clothes, shoes, tools—even a couple of blenders. A clerk saw what they were doing and quickly notified police, which wasn't very difficult…since there were 60 uniformed officers already in the store. Turns out it was "Shop with a Cop" day, an annual event during which officers assist underprivileged kids with back-to-school shopping. Alexander and Vantress were arrested seconds later. "As is so often the occasion with crooks," said Officer Pete Simpson, "they think they're smarter than the average bear. And they're not."

IT'S A LONG WAY TO THE BOTTOM, TOO…

In January 2009, Joseph Houston, 29, of Brewster, Massachusetts, went to Boston to see a concert by the heavy metal band Metallica. During the show Houston had too much to drink, pulled down his pants, and exposed himself to the family sitting in front of him. Then he urinated on one of them. Then, with his pants still down, he started fighting with one of them. When police tried to get him to leave, he fought with them, and he was finally arrested.

Legendary Bonus #1: Houston's mug shot—which ended up on the Internet—shows the T-shirt he was wearing that night: It was a take-off on "Metallica," and said *Alcoholica* on it.

Legendary Bonus #2: Mr. Houston was an officer with the Brewster Police Department. (Mr. Houston is no longer an officer with the Brester Police Department.)

*   *   *

"One disadvantage of having nothing to do is you can't stop and rest."

—**Franklin P. Jones**

Christopher Reeve's trainer for *Superman* (1978): David Prowse, who played Darth Vader.

FACES OF DEATH

Who will you encounter after you kick the bucket? The Grim Reaper? Or maybe an entirely different specter? It might depend on where you live, since none of the world's religions seem to agree on who—or what—will be waiting on the other side. Here are some of Death's strangest personifications.

Name: Yamaraj
Origin: Hindi culture
Details: Also known as Dharmaraj, or Yama, for short, his name literally means "the Lord of Death." In artistic depictions, he's a portly man with a mustache and, legend says, skin that's "the color of a rain cloud." He rides the plains of existence on a water buffalo, and upon a person's death, ropes the departed soul with a lasso and carries it to Yamalok, the Hindu underworld. His assistant, Chitragupta, keeps track of all the good and bad deeds of every human on the planet, and after checking the records, Yama determines how each soul will be reincarnated. If the person was good, they might return as a tiger. If not: a mosquito.

Name: Giltine
Origin: Eastern Europe, primarily the Baltic states
Details: Before they adopted the more Western depiction of Death as a hooded skeleton with a scythe, people in the Baltic region had Giltine, a grotesque woman with a crooked, blue nose and a sharp, poisonous tongue, whose name means "to sting." According to folklore, she was once a beautiful young woman... until she was trapped in a coffin for seven years and emerged a monster. Then, the legend goes, she collected poison from grave-yards and used it to lick the dying to death.

Name: Izanami
Origin: Japan
Details: According to Japanese mythology, a god named Izanagi-no-Mikoto and his goddess wife, Izanami, helped bridge the gap between Heaven and Earth, creating humanity and the islands of Japan in the process. Izanami died while giving birth to a fire god; overcome with grief, Izanagi-no-Mikoto went looking for

---

The ancient Romans used asbestos napkins. To clean them, they threw them in the fire.

her in Yomi, the land of the dead. He found her, but after discovering that her beauty had been ravaged by death, he fled back to Earth. Enraged by his betrayal, Izanami vowed to take the lives of 1,000 humans per day, becoming the Goddess of Death. Izanagi responded with a vow of his own: to offset her wrath by creating 1,500 people per day.

Name: Santa Muerte
Origin: Mexico
Details: Literally "Saint Death," she is usually portrayed in Mexican folk art as a female skeleton wearing a dress and a large floral hat. The concept emerged from a combination of Meso-American native religions and the Catholicism that dominates the country today. Belief in the skeleton-deity has been condemned over the centuries, with the Catholic Church of Mexico going so far as to dub believers—even if they are also Catholic—a "cult." Nevertheless, millions of Mexicans reportedly worship Santa Muerte, celebrating her during the huge cultural festivities called *Dia de los Muertes* (Day of the Dead) on November 1 of every year and erecting altars to her in their homes. The faithful believe that Santa Muerte not only assists souls in the afterlife but can grant favors to the living, protect them from bodily harm, and make others fall in love with them.

Name: Papa Ghede
Origin: Haiti
Story: Voodoo practitioners believe that a short, cigar-chomping man in a top hat is waiting for them at the crossroads of Earth and the afterlife. That man is Papa Ghede, who legend says is the living corpse of the first man who ever died. He's aided by four other spirits who handle everything from guarding graveyards to giving voices to the dead during seances. Ghede loves rum and is known for his crass sense of humor and great wisdom, which includes an extensive knowledge of everything that happens in the worlds of the living and the dead. He also reads minds and sometimes even inhabits humans, inspiring them to make love. If that isn't enough, Ghede is also the patron saint of those who die young. Worshippers offer him rum, cigars, or sacrificed crows to prevent him from taking sick children to the underworld.

Coca-Cola can partially neutralize the pain of a jellyfish sting (but vinegar works better).

UNDERWEAR ON A MISSION

Remember when your underwear's only job was to cover your privates (and not embarrass you in the emergency room)? Times have changed.

THE EMERGENCY BRA

What It Does: Lets you breathe easier

Details: If you're ever caught in an emergency where the air becomes difficult to breathe, and you're wearing one of these bras invented by Dr. Elena Bodnar, president of Chicago's Trauma Risk Management Institute, you'll breathe easier. The bra's cups are made of a special air-filtering material and can be removed and used as face masks—one cup for you, one for a friend. They secure to the head with special straps, "freeing a survivor's hands to keep balance while running and removing objects on the way out of danger," Dr. Bodnar writes on her website. Her invention won her an IgNobel Prize (a parody prize that honors silly achievements in science) in 2009. For men unwilling to cross-dress for safety, she also sells an Emergency Dress Shirt with a special panel of the same material. Press the panel against your face, tie the sleeves around your head, and *voilà!* You've got a face mask.

BALLISTIC BOXER SHORTS

What It Does: Reduces injuries from improvised explosive devices

Details: There really isn't much to these shorts. They're regular boxers, made from two layers of thick silk fabric woven together and treated with an antibacterial agent. But while the shorts can't stop bullets or shrapnel, if the wearer happens to encounter IEDs or land mines, they are surprisingly effective at blocking dirt and sand particles, minimizing the size of wounds and keeping them clean and easier to treat. The antibacterial agent also helps prevent secondary infections. In April 2011, the U.S. Marines rush-ordered more than 27,000 pairs of the undies after learning that British forces who wore them had fewer injuries than their Ameri-

During WWII, a London slang term for German bombs was "Bob Hopes."

can counterparts. Also under consideration: steel or high-density polyethylene cups, and underwear with pockets for Kevlar inserts.

"WHAT WOULD YOUR MOTHER DO?"
What It Does: It's "abstinence underwear," designed to discourage teenagers from having sex.

Details: The underwear has anti-sex messages like "Dream on," "Zip it," and "Not tonight" printed on the waistband. "Why not help our teens make wise choices while they navigate the dating scene?" the company asks parents. "We just want to provide you with cute reminders to help you make an impression—somewhat discreetly." To date, the company only sells underwear for girls; the jury's still out on whether they're truly effective at stopping teenagers from having sex. "If couples are getting to the point that their underwear is visible to the opposite sex," one skeptic told the London *Daily Mail*, "they're obviously not going to stop because of a 'Zip it' slogan!"

SHOCK JOCK BRAND BOXERS AND BRIEFS
What It Does: Enhances the male "package"

Details: Who says you have to play baseball to wear a cup? This line of underwear comes fully equipped with "Active Shaping Technology"—a soft cup with "authentic-looking male features" that the company says will add to a man's appearance. Because the cup is made of a soft, fleshy-feeling material, it won't stop baseballs…and it won't stop the object of your affection from laughing at you when they discover you're wearing a falsie. But then, maybe Shock Jocks are a form of abstinence underwear too.

Bonus: Andrew Christian, maker of Shock Jock, also sells a line of butt-enhancing underwear called Flashback, which uses hidden straps to "lift and shape" the junk in your trunk. (No word on whether a line of combo Shock Jock/Flashback underwear is in the works.)

*　　*　　*

"If you can make people who are dead set against you laugh, that's the first step toward winning them over."

—John Waters

Your body contains about 30 billion fat cells.

CANADA'S MOST FAMOUS OUTHOUSE

*You know you've hit the big time when even your outhouse
is famous. Here's the story of a Canadian poet
and the privy he put on the map.*

HOMESTEADING

In 1957 a struggling Canadian poet named Al Purdy bought a plot of land on the shores of Roblin Lake in Ontario for $850. He and his wife Eurithe wanted to build an A-frame cabin on the property, but if you've ever tried to build a house using the money you've earned by writing poetry, you can understand why Purdy decided to start small: He built an outhouse first. Even that was built with scrap lumber; he, his wife, and two other relatives built the outhouse (and later, the cabin) using materials salvaged from a local schoolhouse that had been demolished.

BIG TIME

For a time Purdy was so broke that he and Eurithe fed their family powdered milk, canned soup, and whatever other goods they pulled from a dumpster on a nearby military base. But his years of struggle ended in 1965 when he published a collection of poems titled *The Cariboo Horses,* which won him the Governor General's Award for Poetry, Canada's highest poetry prize. In the years that followed, he published 33 volumes of poetry, and as his body of work grew, so did his reputation. By the end of his life, Purdy was widely considered the unofficial poet laureate of Canada and arguably the greatest English-language poet in the country's history.

Yet despite all his fame and fortune, Purdy never tore down his simple A-frame cabin to replace it with something better. And even after he installed indoor plumbing in the A-frame, he never stopped using the outhouse. According to his wife, it remained his personal getaway, the place where he did some of his best thinking.

Eggplant seeds contain nicotine.

SIGN HERE

Purdy invited a lot of guests to visit him, and his spot on Roblin Lake soon became a beloved summer retreat for a generation of young Canadian writers, who whiled away the long summer days drinking Purdy's homemade wild-grape wine with him on his deck. He even let them use his cherished outhouse, but on one condition: They had to sign their names on the walls inside. Over the years those outhouse walls became covered with the signatures of scores of Canada's best-loved writers.

When Purdy passed away in 2000, his publisher banded together with his friends and admirers to form the Al Purdy A-frame Trust, a group dedicated to preserving what had become the most famous writer's house—and outhouse—in Canada. More than a decade later, those efforts are still under way. A regional land trust now owns the property, and the A-frame Trust raises money to support it. The house will eventually host a "writer in residence" for eight months a year.

PRIVY COUNCIL

The preservation project that probably would have been dearest to Al Purdy's heart was put off almost until it was too late, and even then it was completed only by chance. In 2010 the Trust contacted Trenton High School, the school that Purdy attended until he dropped out at age 17, and asked them if there was anything they wanted to contribute to the preservation effort. A teacher paid a visit…and immediately laid eyes on Canada's Most Famous Outhouse, now 53 years old and very dilapidated. "The outhouse was on the verge of collapsing. It was the most urgent project," said Eric Lorenzen, a teacher at Trenton High.

Lorenzen's proposal: Let the shop class restore the outhouse. The "Purdy Privy Project" was approved, and in October 2010 the outhouse was hauled to the high school, where it was rebuilt in time to be hauled back and rededicated on April 21, 2011, the 11th anniversary of Al Purdy's death. (Those signatures of famous Canadian writers? Unfortunately, they'd been painted over years earlier and couldn't be saved.) On hand to rededicate the outhouse, Eurithe Purdy said, "The students did a marvelous job on it. It's more solid now than it ever was. It really brings back a lot of memories." (But when asked to test it out, she declined.)

OLD HISTORY, NEW THEORY

We tend to believe what the experts tell us about history…until a new set of experts come along to tell us that the old experts were wrong.

The Event: In 1847 half of the 87 pioneers known as the Donner Party perished on a cross-country wagon train from Independence, Missouri, to California.

What the History Books Say: The group—which consisted of several families, including the Donners and the Reeds—left Missouri in the spring of 1846, heading west. In late July, they decided to take a little-traveled route known as Hastings Cutoff in order to shave 400 miles off their 2,500-mile journey. But the shortcut turned out to be more dangerous than expected. Bad weather and Indian attacks delayed the travelers, placing them high in the Sierra Nevada mountains in October when an early winter storm hit. The snow kept falling until there was a 30-foot base; the group was stranded. When rescuers finally arrived in February 1847, only 48 people were left, and they were barely clinging to life. How had they survived? Several of the group had resorted to cannibalism.

New Theory: As news of the tragedy spread, the allegations of cannibalism dogged the Donner Party, but they vehemently denied it. It wasn't until 2010 that scientific evidence backed them up. Analysis of bones excavated from a campsite near Truckee, California, revealed that they ate their horses, their cattle, and even Uno, the family dog…but not each other. According to project leader Gwen Robbins, an anthropologist at Appalachian State University, "They were boiling hides, chewing on leather, and trying desperately to survive. The bones were boiled and crushed in order to extract any kind of nutrients from them." But none of the bones found in the fire pit were human.

Conclusion: Of course this doesn't necessarily mean that there was no cannibalism, just that there's no evidence of it. What's more likely: 19th-century press outlets spiced up the survivors' accounts in order to sell more newspapers.

Sea anemones can live to be 80 years old.

"I'LL HAVE SOME BAGOONG WITH A GLASS OF PLONK"

If a stranger offered you some kreplach, would you eat it?
It's just one of many foods that may sound weird…but
that's only because you speak English.

DONG GUA. Also known as winter melon, it's actually a squash that is harvested in summer. Available year-round in Chinese markets, "winter" refers to the snow-like white blotches on the mature fruit.

SHABU-SHABU. Thinly sliced seafood, meat, or tofu swirled in a flavored broth. In Japanese it translates loosely to "swish swish."

KREPLACH. A Jewish dumpling filled with meat, cheese, or mashed potatoes. Similar to wontons or ravioli.

POPE'S NOSE. Also known as "parson's nose," it is the stubby end of a turkey's tail that scientists call the *pygostyle*. The term refers to the way that part of the tail is upturned, resembling someone "snooty," i.e., with their nose in the air.

BAGOONG. A popular Filipino condiment made from shrimp or small fish that have been salted, cured, and fermented for weeks.

SLUMGULLION. A cheap watery meat stew, made by California Gold Rush miners out of whatever fixings they happened to have lying around.

AGAR-AGAR. A dried, tasteless seaweed extract that acts as a setting agent to create a vegetable gelatin.

ASAFOETIDA. A potent, garliclike spice found in Asia and India, harvested from the roots of the plant of the same name. The name comes from the Persian *aza* and the Latin *foetidus*, and translates literally to "stinking resin."

VARAK. Super-thin, edible sheets of pure silver and gold used as a decoration on desserts in parts of India.

How many are named Sandy? About 2.5 million people live in the Sahara Desert.

HULI HULI. Hawaiian for "end-over-end," this can describe a rotisserie barbecue itself, or the popular marinade used for roasting meats, made from brown sugar and soy sauce.

CLABBER. A drink once popular in the southern U.S., made from curdled milk, which is then chilled and mixed with cream, sugar, and nutmeg.

KOPI LUWAK. This Indonesian coffee is said to have a smooth, rich caramel and chocolate flavor with no bitterness. Sound good? Warning: The kopi beans are also eaten by a native marsupial called the luwak. After the kopi beans pass through the luwak's digestive system, coffee-loving locals collect the "delicacy," wash it off, grind it up, and brew it.

GLOGG. For Christmas, Swedes traditionally spice their wine, mix it with punch, then mix that with brandy. The combination—called *glogg*—is served heated with a few almonds and raisins floating on top.

GADO-GADO. An Indonesian vegetable salad usually consisting of chopped greens, sliced potatoes, boiled eggs, and peanut sauce. (It means "mix mix.")

NOBLE ROT: If poop can make coffee taste better, does mold improve the flavor of wine? Experts say yes. A naturally occurring infection called *Botrytis cinerea*, or "noble rot," causes grapes to shrivel on the vine, which concentrates the sugar, making for a very sweet dessert wine.

SPÄTLESE. In German the word means "late picking." Spätleses are sweet wines made from grapes that have been left on the vine and are picked late in the season, often after they've been infected with the noble rot.

PLONK. In the United States, cheap wine is sometimes called "rotgut." In England it's called "plonk."

LOMI-LOMI. A cold side-dish served in Hawaii, usually salmon "massaged" with onions, tomatoes, and peppers. It means "massage massage."

*　　*　　*

Fall seven times, stand up eight. —**Japanese proverb**

VIDEO GAME SECRETS

"Easter egg" is the term used to describe hidden messages or featues on DVDs. But the term and the idea date back to the 1970s, when they were first hidden in video games.

BACKGROUND
"Easter eggs" are usually associated with DVDs. If you press a certain sequence of buttons on your remote control, for example, you might find an extra deleted scene or a video introduction form the movie's director buried in a menu somewhere. It's a secret treasure hidden almost in plain sight…just like an Easter egg. But the idea predates home video: It originated in video games, and we have the Atari corporation, which dominated the home video game market in the late 1970s, to thank for it. The tight-fisted company made hundreds of millions of dollars off the games its $20,000-a-year programmers created, but it wouldn't share the profits with them. And it kept their identities a secret to prevent other companies hiring them away. One such programmer was a man named Warren Robinett.

ADVENTURE (1979)
Robinett single-handedly created the groundbreaking game *Adventure* for the Atari 2600 console. It was the first action-adventure game, the first game with a plot, and the first home cartridge to sell a million copies. But nobody knew Robinett had anything to do with it, or even that he existed, because the company would not give him credit. He got back at Atari by hiding something in the game: As players makes their way through *Adventure*'s numerous mazes, if they manage to find an "invisible" one-pixel gray dot hidden against a gray background and bring it to another part of the maze, they gain access to a secret room. Inside is a message that reads, "Created by Warren Robinett."

Until the room was discovered by players, only Robinett knew it was there. It was an Atari executive who first called the hidden surprise an "Easter egg." Though the company was annoyed at Robinett (who had since left the company) for pulling the prank, it decided that Easter eggs added value. They were here to stay;

within a few years the practice grew to include bigger inside jokes, extra characters, even secret levels. Some examples:

THE LEGEND OF ZELDA: A LINK TO THE PAST (1991)

The first two *Legend of Zelda* fantasy games were among the most popular titles for the Nintendo Entertainment System in the late 1980s: Combined, they sold more than 11 million copies. By 1991, Nintendo had successfully launched its next home system, the Super Nintendo and with it, a third *Zelda* title. They used the promise of an Easter egg to promote the already highly anticipated title. *Nintendo Power* magazine held a contest in which the winner would have their name added to a hidden room somewhere in *The Legend of Zelda: A Link to the Past*. Reader Chris Houlihan won the contest, and, sure enough, the programmers obliged. The room is almost impossible to find, though. A series of tricky maneuvers is required to enter it, plus you have to have procured an item called "the Pegasus Boots" during the game. Anyone talented enough to uncover the secret chamber is rewarded with rubies and a message that says, "My name is Chris Houlihan. This is my top-secret room. Keep it between us, okay?"

NBA JAM (1993)

This was one of the most popular arcade games in the early '90s due to its state-of-the-art graphics, four-player option, and the chance to play as real NBA stars such as Clyde Drexler and Shaquille O'Neal. *NBA Jam* was played more than four billion times in arcades, which meant somebody was bound to stumble onto some Easter eggs. Hitting certain key combinations or entering specific initials causes the stars on screen to take on the likenesses of members of the games' programming team, or make the players' heads incredibly huge. Later updates added even more secrets, like the ability to play as ninja warriors from the *Mortal Kombat* game series. *NBA Jam*'s home version, released in 2003, also had Easter eggs. One code allows gamers to play basketball as either the Beastie Boys or President Bill Clinton.

DOOM II: HELL ON EARTH (1994)

During the climax of this violent and bloody game—one of the first POV "shoot 'em up" games—players must defeat the severed head of an evil demon. And if they enter the final level in a special, secret mode, the head they fight is that of the game's programmer, John Romero. But Romero, who designed other video-game classics such as *Quake* and *Wolfenstein 3-D*, didn't put his head there. One of the game's other programmers was so tired of dealing with Romero's allegedly huge ego that he secretly included the demon-head alternative as a cathartic "tribute." Just before the game went to stores, however, Romero discovered it. Fortunately, he thought it was funny and added a backward recording of his own voice that plays when the Romero head is encountered. Played forward, it says, "To win this game, you must kill me, John Romero."

GRAND THEFT AUTO SERIES

This controversial video game series is filled with both violence and Easter eggs. Here are two examples:

• In *Grand Theft Auto: San Andreas* (2004), determined players can track down Sasquatch in a forest, view risqué statues in an atrium, and enjoy some "hot coffee" (a video-game euphemism for sex) in a hidden level that, once it was discovered, led to an outcry from lawmakers and parental advocacy groups. The secret level started out as an add-on developed by a Dutch hacker and distributed for free via the Internet. It was so popular that the game's publisher, Rockstar Games, decided to add it to the game for its 2005 re-release. The "secret" became so widely discussed that it helped propel *San Andreas* to sales of more than 17 million units, making it the Sony PlayStation 2's top seller ever.

• One of the oddest of the series' secrets can be found in *Grand Theft Auto IV* (2008). Players can hijack a helicopter and fly out to the "Statue of Happiness," a mock-up of the Statue of Liberty. On a platform attached to the statue is a door with a placard reading "No Hidden Content Through Here." It's lying, of course. Inside, there's an enormous beating heart chained to the wall.

*　　*　　*

KIDDIE CAR

Henry Ford's son Edsel received his first Ford when he was 8 years old. He drove himself to the 3rd grade.

THE ZERO MILEPOST

Here's the story of an unusual historical artifact...
and the city that grew up around it.

HUMBLE BEGINNINGS

Terminus, Georgia, was never expected to amount to much. In 1837 the Georgia Railroad Company decided to build a depot there and staked out the spot with a stone marker: the Zero Mile Post. The railway's chief engineer declared the place fit for "one tavern, a blacksmith shop, a grocery store, and nothing else." He was wrong. Once the depot went up and the trains started coming, Terminus prospered. Within a few years, the town's merchants and railroad men had turned Terminus into a regional hub. They even gave it a new name: Atlantica-Pacifica, later shortened to...Atlanta.

A few decades later—not long after the city council banned hogs from the streets and okayed gas lamps—along came the Civil War, and the thriving city, with its railway lines, became the perfect target for Union cannons. Remember the depot where Scarlett O'Hara tended wounded Confederate soldiers in *Gone with the Wind*? That was the bull's eye. In late July 1864, as the Battle of Atlanta began, Sam Luckie, one of only 40 free blacks living in the city, had the bad luck to be standing near the depot. Luckie, who owned the Barber and Bath Salon in the nearby Atlanta Hotel, was leaning against a gas lamp talking with a group of white businessmen when a Union shell struck. Luckie was killed, but the lamp made it through with just a few dings.

REDUCE (TO ASHES), REUSE, RECYCLE

The battle left Atlanta smoldering, but the same force that had jump-started Terminus before the Civil War got the city going again: the railroads. By 1869 a new three-story depot stood at the Zero Mile Post. Banks, hotels, saloons, law offices, and a whiskey distillery soon popped up in the new depot district. By the turn of the 20th century, 15 railroad lines passed through the city, with more than 150 trains arriving every day. Then something even more powerful than a locomotive came along: the automobile.

World's busiest airport: Atlanta International, serving over 90 million travelers per year.

By the 1920s, the railroad district had become so congested that city planners decided to build viaducts (elevated roads), sending auto traffic up and over the rail lines. Merchants followed, moving their operations upstairs to the new street level and abandoning the former shopfronts one level below. Atlanta's first city center faded into the past—covered over, and then forgotten. The granite archways, ornate marble floors, cast-iron pilasters, and decorative brickwork of the once-thriving depot district now moldered below ground.

HISTORIC HOT SPOT

As in most American cities after World War II, the 1950s and '60s brought racial unrest to Atlanta and "white flight" to the suburbs. Urban decay followed. Determined to preserve the city's history and revitalize its downtown, Atlanta's Board of Aldermen declared the five-block "city beneath the city" a historic site and joined with private industry to create a downtown hot spot. It took $142 million to bring the district back to life. "We've preserved a piece of working history," said Jack Patterson, one of Underground Atlanta's original developers. "It's not a cold museum. It's full of life, with money changing hands."

For those who enjoy eyebrow braiding, psychic readings, and As-Seen-on-TV products, Underground Atlanta is the place to go. Some say it's the city's most over-hyped tourist trap. Others see beyond the hype to Atlanta's historic beginnings. The upscale restaurant at the entrance to the district is the city's oldest building—the 1869 railroad depot. The gas lamp outside the underground's MARTA light rail station still has the dings in it from the Union shell that killed Sam Luckie. And tucked downstairs on the old depot's first floor is a Georgia Building Authority office. According to the Historical Commission, "The door is normally locked, so knock (or wave to the lady at the desk) and someone will open it." Why bother? Because beyond that door stands Atlanta's oldest artifact, the stone terminus marker for the Western and Atlantic Railroad: the Zero Mile Post.

*　　　*　　　*

"No snowflake in an avalanche ever feels responsible."

—**Voltaire**

On Arnold Schwarzenegger's last day as California governor, he received a parking ticket.

ODD ECONOMIC INDICATORS

Can't make heads or tails of the Dow or the GNP? Fear not—there are lots of other economic "indicators" that tell us what the economy is doing.

• **Nice Waiters/Waitresses.** When the economy is down, business in restaurants is slow. Result: The waitstaff isn't overworked, and the customers are less grumpy because their orders aren't backed up behind half a dozen other orders. In addition, when jobs are hard to find, waiters and waitress may be less likely to snap at you, even if they are in a bad mood.

• **Gorgeous Waiters/Waitresses.** In cities like New York and Los Angeles, which are centers of fashion and the arts, waiters and waitresses can become better-looking in hard times, as would-be models, actors, and actresses have to take jobs waiting tables when their other, more glamorous gigs dry up.

• **Belly Buttons.** In the 1920s, an economist named George Taylor advanced the theory that women's hemlines rise along with rising stock prices and fall when the stock market tanks, as an "expression of conservatism." Now you can add bare midriffs to Taylor's theory: When the economy is booming, halter tops and other revealing fashions are popular, but when it slows down, women become less willing to bare it all.

• ***Playboy* Playmates.** In their groundbreaking 2004 study "*Playboy* Playmate Curves: Changes in Facial and Body Feature Preferences Across Social and Economic Conditions," Terry Pettijohn and Brian Jungeberg argue that the magazine's Playmate of the Month selections vary according to the performance of the economy. "When social and economic conditions were difficult, older, heavier, taller *Playboy* Playmates of the Year with larger waists, smaller eyes, larger waist-to-hip ratios, smaller bust-to-waist ratios, and smaller body mass index values were selected."

• **Hit Songs.** Five years after Pettijohn and Jungeberg wrote their *Playboy* Playmate article, Pettijohn published an analysis of #1 songs on the *Billboard* pop chart from 1955 to 2003. "When social

---

Can you spot it? One of the asteroids in the *The Empire Strikes Back* is actually a potato.

and economic times were relatively threatening, songs that were longer in duration, more meaningful in content, more comforting, more romantic, and slower were most popular," he wrote. Also: "Performers with more mature facial features, including smaller eyes, thinner faces, and larger chins, were popular during relatively threatening social and economic conditions."

• **Cemetery Plots for Sale on eBay and Craigslist.** Like boats, airplanes, vacation homes, and other luxury items, cemetery plots are something you can live without if you must. People buy them when they're flush with cash; many have to unload them when their money runs out.

• **The Content of Military Recruitment TV Ads.** In good times, when civilian jobs are plentiful, the military has to hustle to meet its recruiting numbers. In such times it runs TV ads that resemble action movies and video games, hoping to lure people into joining. In bad times, when jobs are scarce and the pool of potential recruits increases, the military can afford to be more picky: TV ads will show a more realistic picture of life in the armed forces, to discourage less-qualified candidates from applying.

• **Mosquito Bites.** When home owners can't afford to pay a pool cleaning service—or, even worse, lose their homes—swimming pools go stagnant and become breeding grounds for mosquitoes.

• **Shark Attacks.** When the economy is bad enough, even man-eating sharks have trouble finding work. In 2008, for example, shark attacks in U.S. waters dropped to their lowest point since 2003. "If you have a reduction in the number of people in the water, you're going to have a reduction in the opportunities for people and sharks to get together," says George Burgess, who studies shark attacks at the University of Florida. "I can't help but think that contributing to the reduction may have been the reticence of some people to take holidays and go to the beach for economic reasons. We noticed similar declines during the recession that followed the events of 2001."

• **Death.** "People are physically healthier in a recession," Christopher Ruhm, an economist at University of North Carolina, told the *New York Times* in 2008. "Death rates fall, people smoke less, drink less, and exercise more. People are healthier, but they're not happier. Suicide rises, and mental health may deteriorate."

MOVIE QUOTE QUIZ #2

Name the movies that launched these familiar quotations. One point for the film, and a bonus point if you know the year it was released. (Answers are on page 538.)

1. "We rob banks."

2. "Fiddle-dee-dee, war war war."

3. "Nobody calls me chicken."

4. "I'm not a drinker—I'm a drunk."

5. "Practically perfect in every way."

6. "I don't have to show you any stinking badges."

7. "Fat, drunk and stupid is no way to go through life, son."

8. "Klaatu barada nikto!"

9. "We can stay up late, swapping manly stories. And in the morning, I'm making waffles!"

10. "Would ya just watch the hair? Ya know, I work on my hair a long time."

11. "It's in the hole!"

12. "Every one of these letters is addressed to Santa Claus!"

13. "Attica! Attica!"

14. "I'm walking here!"

15. "I have a head for business and a bod for sin. Is there anything wrong with that?"

16. "Follow the money. Just follow the money."

17. "Oh, he's very popular, Ed. The sportos, the motorheads, geeks, sluts, bloods, wastoids, dweebies, dickheads —they all adore him. They think he's a righteous dude."

18. "I ain't got time to bleed."

19. "Ye'd best start believin' in ghost stories, Miss Turner. Yer in one."

20. "He got a real pretty mouth, ain't he?"

21. "That was me seducing you. It needs to be the other way around."

22. "I'm ready for my close-up."

23. "You killed my father. Prepare to die."

24. "I can see your dirty pillows!"

Every year, the U.S. produces enough plastic cling wrap to cover the state of Texas.

HOW TO MEASURE DISTANCES BY "EYEBALL"

Once you get the hang of this simple trick, it's easy. And if you verify your "guesstimate" with a tape measure, you'll find that it's surprisingly accurate.

WHAT YOU NEED

- **Your Eyes.** (It's not called "eyeballing" for nothing.)
- **Your Thumb.** You're going to hold it out in front of you, as if you were hitchhiking, except straight ahead.

WHAT TO DO

- To guesstimate the distance between you and a nearby building, hold your thumb out at arm's length toward the building.

- Close your left eye, then place your thumb so that it is close to a feature on the building whose width is easy to judge. A standard doorway, for example, is about three feet wide. Place your thumb just to the right of such a doorway. (Let's call it Point A.)

- Open your left eye and close your right eye. Don't move your arm! Your thumb will appear to move to the right (to Point B).

- Compare the distance your thumb appeared to move with the width of the doorway. If the doorway is three feet wide, and your thumb appeared to move a distance equal to five times the width of the doorway, then it moved approximately 15 feet.

- Now visualize a triangle created by drawing lines between your two eyes and your thumb. This triangle is identical in shape to the triangle you could create by drawing lines between your thumb and Points A and B on the building. Only the size is different.

- The length of your outstretched arm is about 10 times the distance between your two eyes. Because both triangles are the same shape, the ratios are the same for the larger triangle.

- This means the distance between your thumb and the building is about 10 times the distance your thumb appeared to move from Point A to Point B. Since it appeared to move 15 feet, you're about 150 feet (10 x 15) away from the building.

DOOMED BY
THE INTERNET

*Thank goodness for Google and Wikipedia, or this
article would have been a lot harder to research.*

- **PHONE BOOKS.** Throughout the 20th century, a phone
book was a household and office necessity—it listed the phone
numbers of every home and business in town, which made it a
vital resource. Generally issued by phone companies, phone
books could be found in more than 90 percent of American
homes. Today, though, nearly any phone number can easily be
located on the Internet. So why lug out a huge, heavy phone
book when you can just do a Google search? So few people are
using phone books now that in 2010, Verizon announced it
would no longer publish "white pages." A 2011 poll by the online
social network Yelp found that only 24 percent of people think
phone books are still relevant…and those are people that use
Yelp, which lists and categorizes local businesses… more or less a
modern-day yellow pages.

- **ALBUMS.** Sales of whole music albums have declined from a
high of 900 million in 1999 to just under 375 million in 2009.
Chalk that up to the fact that there was really only one way to
buy music in the '90s and early 2000s: an entire album, on a
physical CD. The music industry had stopped selling singles,
forcing consumers to buy music in the more expensive album
format. But with the rise of the MP3 and Apple's iTunes music
store, singles sales have risen from roughly zero in 1999 to 1.2
billion in 2009—and nearly all of those are digital downloads,
priced around $1.00 each. There's no longer any need to buy full
albums. A bad economy hasn't helped either—a decade ago, a
high-profile album by a big star would routinely sell a million
copies in its first week (*NSYNC's *No Strings Attached* sold more
than 2 million in 2000). In 2011 an album by the band Cake
debuted at #1 on the *Billboard* album chart after selling just
44,000 copies.

According to studies, babies who use pacifiers are more prone to earaches.

- **ENCYCLOPEDIAS.** *The World Book, Grollier,* and *Encyclopedia Britannica* were once the go-to references in millions of homes and libraries—the definitive sources for what seemed like all the knowledge in the world. Those three brands have kept up with changing technologies, issuing their annual, multi-volume editions on relatively affordable CD-ROMs since the mid-'90s ($1,000 for the book vs. $100 for the digital version). They appeared online not long after (an annual subscription to *Britannica*: $69). But the real competition is from free websites such as Wikipedia and Google. Wikipedia is constantly updated, and while its accuracy is sometimes questionable despite active maintenance by thousands of dedicated users, the fact that it's digital makes its capacity virtually limitless—not subject to the physical limits of a printed encyclopedia.

- **VIDEO STORES.** Home video revolutionized entertainment in the early 1980s—it used to be that when a movie left the theater, you'd probably never see it again, unless it was re-released or showed up on TV. With video, consumers could buy a copy of their favorite movie and watch it as often as they liked. Blockbuster Video opened the first of its 5,000 video rental stores in 1985. At Blockbuster and hundreds of other video stores, customers picked out a VHS tape, rented it, watched it at home, and then returned it to the store. Changing technology made this model obsolete— Netflix and other web-based services offer mail-away rental as well as instant digitally delivered movies for a monthly fee. Blockbuster filed for bankruptcy in 2010; during evening hours, Netflix now occupies 20 percent of all online bandwidth in the United States.

- **PLAYBOY MAGAZINE.** Once again, people don't like to pay for something they can get for free online...especially if it's something that's embarrassing to purchase in a store, such as pictures of naked women. Interested parties can find plenty of free nudity (and hardcore pornography) on the Internet, which has rendered *Playboy* magazine's soft-core photos passé. *Playboy* circulates 2.5 million issues a month, 11 times a year, down from the 7 million readers of 12 annual issues it enjoyed 20 years ago. Result: The company has had to divert its business to brand extensions, such as *Playboy* founder Hugh Hefner's reality TV show *The Girls Next Door.*

WORKS OF ART

See? Even artists have a tough time explaining art.

"Art is a collaboration between God and the artist, and the less the artist does the better."
—**Andre Gide**

"Creativity is allowing yourself to make mistakes. Art is knowing which ones to keep."
—**Scott Adams**

"The aim of art is to represent not the outward appearance of things, but their inward significance."
—**Aristotle**

"The stupid believe that to be truthful is easy; only the artist knows how difficult it is."
—**Willa Cather**

"Painting is just another way of keeping a diary."
—**Pablo Picasso**

"An artist is someone who produces things that people don't need to have but that he—for some reason—thinks it would be a good idea to give them."
—**Andy Warhol**

"Art teaches nothing, except the significance of life."
—**Henry Miller**

"Blessed are they who see beautiful things in humble places where other people see nothing."
—**Camille Pissarro**

"Art is a kind of illness."
—**Giacomo Puccini**

"When I judge art, I take my painting and put it next to a God-made object like a tree or flower. If it clashes, it is not art."
—**Paul Cézanne**

"Art is the signature of civilizations."
—**Beverly Sills**

"An artist cannot talk about his art any more than a plant can discuss horticulture."
—**Jean Cocteau**

"If I could say it in words there would be no reason to paint."
—**Edward Hopper**

CALL ME MISTER

Here, ladies and gentlemen, are the stories behind some well-known products (and one character) who prefer to be addressed as "Mister."

MR. COFFEE

In the 1968, Vincent Marotta and Sam Glazer, high-school friends who became partners in a small construction company, decided to start a coffee delivery service. Obsessed with finding a way for people to make better coffee at home, an idea came to Marotta while he was recuperating from brain surgery in 1970. His great idea: A self-contained unit that would heat the water to 200°F and drip it through the coffee grounds once, not over and over again, as was the standard "percolater" method at the time. He and Glazer then hired two ex-Westinghouse engineers to design the product, which he named Mr. Coffee. The product was a hit almost instantly, but Marotta wanted to go national. His other great idea: He hired his boyhood hero, Joe DiMaggio, as the company spokesman. It worked. Within three years, the company dominated the coffeemaker market, producing nearly 40,000 Mr. Coffees a day, with annual sales approaching $150 million. In 1987 Glazer and Marotta, who once referred to himself as "the Michaelango of coffee," decided to sell the company, but the product—and Marotta's big idea—still dominate.

MR. CLEAN

"Mr. Clean will clean your whole house / And everything that's in it / Mr. Clean, Mr. Clean, Mr. Clean..." Within six months of its introduction in 1958 by Proctor & Gamble (including that earworm TV jingle), Mr. Clean became America's bestselling household cleaner. The Mr. Clean character was designed by a Chicago ad agency in 1957, but Procter & Gamble—perhaps to ward off lawsuits from Yul Brynner, who affected a very similar look as the king of Siam in a popular musical of the time, *The King and I*—insisted that the character was modeled after a Navy sailor from Pensacola. Internationally, his name is usually translated into the local language—*Maestro Lindo* in Italy, *Don Limpio* in Spain, *Meister Proper* in Germany, and *Monsieur Net* in Quebec.

In the American West, turkeys were moved like cattle, in "drives" of hundreds of birds.

MR. BEAN

Rowan Atkinson, who created the 1990s British TV character, described Mr. Bean as a "boy trapped in a man's body." (Watch him try go shopping and you'll see why.) Mr. Bean, who rarely speaks, was modeled after silent film stars as well as "Monsieur Hulot," a bumbling character created by French director Jacques Tati in the 1950s. Atkinson debuted Mr. Bean at a French-only comedy festival in Montreal, Quebec, in 1987. Why? He wanted to see if non-English speakers would laugh at him. They did. The character didn't even have a name when the show went in to production, but Atkinson just *knew* it had to be some kind of vegetable, and came close to calling him Mr. Cauliflower.

MR. PiBB

The Dr Pepper Company didn't have its own bottling or distribution facilities, so it typically bid out the jobs to other soft drink companies, giving them a share of the company and profits in exchange. In some regions, Coca-Cola won the bid; in others, Pepsi or 7-Up did. Coke didn't have distribution of Dr Pepper in the South, where it was most popular, so in the early '80s Coke created a taste-alike brand and tested it in a few markets, most notably Waco, Texas, Dr Pepper's hometown. This didn't make the Pepper people happy, and the company sued when it discovered that Coke was calling its new drink "Peppo." So Coke changed the name to "Dr. Pibb." Still too close. (From a distance, the two lowercase b's resembled p's.) Finally, Coke revoked Pibb's medical license and capitalized the two B's, creating "Mr. PiBB," which was just barely different enough.

MR. MISTER

The 1980s American rock group's name started as a private joke. Inspired by a Weather Report song "Mr. Gone," the band members began referring to each other as "Mr. _____," filling in the blank with something to address a current situation. (e.g., "Here comes Mr. Late and his friend Mr. Even Later…"). After a while, they wanted the band's name to follow the same form, but group members couldn't agree on what word to use to fill in the blank. Finally, drummer Pat Mastelotto broke the impasse when he suggested "Mr. Mister."

THE UNLUCKIEST TRAIN RIDE

*Even if you're not a history buff and know very little
about World War II, there is one thing about it that
you do know: how it ended. But here's a part
of the story that you may not know.*

INCOMING

Shortly after 8:00 a.m. on the morning of August 6, 1945, lookouts in the mountains east of Hiroshima, Japan, spotted two American B-29 bombers flying in close formation, followed by a third B-29 a few miles back. They weren't overly concerned. The aircraft were flying at an altitude of more than 31,000 feet, unusually high for a bombing run. The firebombing raids that had devastated more than 60 Japanese cities since March 1945 operated at a much lower altitude and involved huge numbers of B-29s, sometimes 500 or more. The only bombers that had flown as high as these three had been on reconnaissance missions, not bombing runs.

Even when the three aircraft altered course and headed straight for Hiroshima, officials weren't alarmed. It was common for B-29s to rendezvous near the city before heading off to bomb other targets. At this late stage of the war, fuel, ammunition, airplanes, and pilots were in desperately short supply in Japan; the military couldn't afford to waste resources chasing just a handful of planes. The B-29s approached Hiroshima unmolested by fighter planes and anti-aircraft fire.

DEADLY MISSION

Two of the three planes were indeed carrying only scientific and reconnaissance equipment. But the last plane, the *Enola Gay,* was on one of the deadliest missions of the war. It was carrying an atomic bomb, one with an explosive power equivalent to 18,000 tons of TNT—more than 1,500 times as powerful as the British Grand Slam, the largest bomb that had ever been used in warfare. At 8:15 a.m., the *Enola Gay* released the bomb over the city. It dropped to

an altitude of 2,000 feet and then exploded, destroying much of
Hiroshima and killing an estimated 70,000 people, or 30 percent of
the population. Another 70,000 would die within weeks.

BEARING WITNESS

Shigeyoshi Morimoto was luckier than many people in the city. The
master kitemaker was in town for a secret meeting to study whether
kites could be used to protect the Japanese fleet from attack by
American fighter planes, and was visiting his cousin's home about
half a mile from ground zero when the bomb went off. Ninety-five
percent of the people who were that close to the bomb were
killed, but Morimoto, his cousin, and his cousin's son all survived.

"There was something like a lightning flash, and along with
the flash the house collapsed and we were pinned beneath the
fallen ceiling and roof," Morimoto told interviewer Robert Trumbull in 1956. "All three of us were alive—unhurt, in fact, except
for bruises from the fallen roof and ceiling of the ruined house,
which kept us from being exposed to that horrible blast."

When the three dug themselves out from the rubble, they were
stunned by the vastness of the destruction. Like a lot of survivors,
they assumed that the blast had been nearby, perhaps caused by an
exploding fuel tank or a bomb falling a few blocks away. But when
they saw how widespread the damage was, they realized this was
no ordinary bomb. Every building within a one-mile radius of the
blast was flattened, and every building within a 4.5 square mile
area was or would soon be destroyed by fire. (Many of the fires
were caused by cooking stoves knocked over by the explosion.)

WHAT NEXT?

Morimoto returned to the hotel where he'd been staying, to see if
he could salvage any of his belongings. The hotel was badly damaged but still standing. There he found that three of his colleagues
had also survived: Tsuitaro Doi, Shinji Kinoshita, and Masao
Komatsu. The four men spent the night in the ruins of the hotel,
and the following morning they discussed what to do next.

By now news of the destruction of Hiroshima had spread to the
rest of Japan, but there was no way for survivors to get word out to
their families that they were still alive. The bomb had knocked
out telephone and telegraph lines, as well as the radio stations.

World's largest eatery: the Damascus Gate restaurant, in Syria. It seats 6,014 people.

The four men decided to return home, and after obtaining permission to leave the city, on the afternoon of August 8 they walked out of Hiroshima and found a train to their home city: Nagasaki.

SOME HOMECOMING

At least three trains left Hiroshima for Nagasaki, 190 miles to the southwest, and arrived there by August 9, the day that an atomic bomb was dropped on *that* city. One train left on the afternoon of August 6th, another on the 7th, and another on the 8th. Though the trains left Hiroshima packed with fleeing refugees, most of the passengers traveled only a few stops beyond the city before they got off.

Nevertheless, it's estimated that at least 165 survivors of the Hiroshima bomb traveled to Nagasaki, were there for the second atomic blast, and lived to tell the tale. The number of Hiroshima survivors who were killed by the Nagasaki bomb is unknown.

DUCK AND COVER

While it was certainly bad luck to survive one atomic bomb only to be bombed a second time, many of the citizens of Nagasaki who spoke to the Hiroshima survivors before the second bomb fell were fortunate to have done so. They learned valuable information that increased their own chances of survival.

The Hiroshima survivors knew, for example, that a short interval of time separated the initial blinding flash of light from the destructive blast wave that followed it, in much the same way that thunder follows lightning. People close to ground zero had just a moment or two to take cover before the blast wave hit; people further away had more time—not a lot more time, but even a few seconds was enough to flee into a basement or a nearby air-raid shelter, or at least duck down below window level before the glass exploded into thousands of flying, razor-sharp projectiles.

Tsutomu Yamaguchi, a ship designer for the Mitsubishi company, was one of the Hiroshima survivors who returned to Nagasaki. He reported to work on the morning of August 9 and shared his experiences with his staff, stressing the importance of getting away from the windows as soon as they saw such a flash. When the flash did come a short time later at 11:02 a.m., many workers dove for cover behind desks and other sturdy objects. "My section's staff

---

What is a *clurichaun*? A leprechaun who only comes out at night. (He's usually drunk.)

suffered the least in that building. In other sections there was a heavy toll of serious injuries from flying glass," he told journalist Robert Trumbull in 1956.

Many such conversations between Hiroshima survivors and Nagasaki citizens were taking place at the very moment the second bomb exploded. Shigeyoshi Morimoto, the master kitemaker, had just finished describing the atomic bomb to his wife ("First there is a great blue flash…") when their house was suddenly flooded with a blinding blue flash. "There, you see!" he shouted. "It comes again! That's what I mean!" He shoved his wife and son into the family's air raid shelter and jumped in behind them, pulling the heavy trap door shut just as the blast wave destroyed their house. Morimoto, his wife, and their son were uninjured.

SILENT WITNESSES

The story of the *nijyuu hibakusha*, or "double bomb-affected people" is one of the least-known stories of World War II, and this is due in large part to the fact that very few of the *nijyuu hibakusha* have ever come forward. As of 2009, only one of them—ship designer Tsutomu Yamaguchi—has been officially recognized by the Japanese government as a survivor of both bombs.

In the mid-1950s, Trumbull traveled to Japan in search of the *nijyuu hibakusha*, but he was only able to come up with a list of 18 names. He tracked down 11 people on the list, but only nine—including Tsutomu Yamaguchi; kitemaker Shigeyoshi Morimoto and his three colleagues, Tsuitaro Doi, Shinji Kinoshita; and Masao Komatsu—agreed to speak to him. He published their accounts in his 1957 book *Nine Who Survived Hiroshima and Nagasaki*, one of the few books ever written on the subject. (A 2010 book titled *Last Train from Hiroshima*, by another author, was withdrawn from publication after it was found to contain fabricated sources and information.)

SECOND-CLASS CITIZENS

The reluctance of so many to speak of their experiences may be due in part to the fact that for many years, there was a stigma associated with being an atomic bomb survivor. Because they often suffered from fatigue, malaise, and other illnesses caused by exposure to radiation, survivors suffered from job discrimination

Aichmophobia is the fear of sharp things, like needles.

and even social isolation, shunned by people who feared that their strange sickness might be contagious. And for a decade after the war, the victims of the atom bombs were largely ignored by the Japanese government, which was wary of assuming responsibility for the victims of the American bombs. It wasn't until 1954, when the crew of a Japanese fishing boat was exposed to radioactive fallout from an American hydrogen bomb test on Bikini Atoll, that public outrage over that incident forced the government to take an active interest in the well-being of the Hiroshima and Nagasaki victims as well. The A-Bomb Victims Medical Care bill, which provided free medical care to the victims, became a Japanese law in 1957.

TRAUMATIZED

Another reason for the silence of so many *nijyuu hibakusha* was that although they were very lucky to have survived two atomic bombings, the experience was so traumatic that many may have simply chosen not to talk about it, at least not publicly. Kitemaker Shigeyoshi Morimoto survived both bombings largely unscathed, but he lost two family members at Hiroshima and eight more at Nagasaki. And the images of death and destruction he witnessed after both bombings were among the most horrific ever seen.

Tsutomu Yamaguchi, the Mitsubishi ship designer, was badly burned by the Hiroshima bomb and suffered further injuries at Nagasaki. He wore bandages for 16 years, and his wounds never did completely heal. His wife and six-month-old son were exposed to "black rain" radioactive fallout from the Nagasaki bomb, and they, along with a daughter who was born after the war, suffered from chronic health problems for the rest of their lives.

Aside from the interview with Robert Trumbull in the 1950s, Yamaguchi largely avoided public attention for decades and was not active in Japan's antinuclear movement. But when his son died from cancer in 2005 at the age of 59, he went public with his story and began speaking out against nuclear war. "Having been granted this miracle, it is my responsibility to pass on the truth to people of the world. For the past 60 years survivors have declared the horror of the atomic bomb, but I can hardly see any improvement in the situation," he told an interviewer in 2005. Yamaguchi died from stomach cancer in January 2010 at the age of 93.

The garfish (or needlefish) has green bones.

JUDGES GONE WILD

*Further proof that being a judge is no guarantee
that a person has good judgement.*

Judge: Sharon "Killer" Keller, the presiding judge on the Texas Criminal Court of Appeals. She is the highest-ranking criminal judge in the state.

Background: On September 25, 2007, the United States Supreme Court agreed to hear a case that questioned the constitutionality of the method of lethal injection that Texas uses to execute condemned prisoners. By chance, an inmate named Michael Richard was scheduled to be executed in Texas that very night. Richard's lawyers wanted to request a stay of execution based on the Supreme Court's action, but they had computer problems and shortly before 5:00 p.m. they called the Court of Appeals and asked if it could remain open a few minutes past closing time so they could file their papers. Such requests are typically granted before scheduled executions...but not this time. "Tell them we close at five," Judge Keller replied. The lawyers missed the deadline, and Richard was executed a few hours later.

What Happened: Keller was brought before the State Commission on Judicial Conduct and charged with five counts of misconduct relating to the case. The commission could have removed her from the bench, but they let her off with a reprimand. Even so, Keller appealed the verdict to the State Supreme Court. She lost; at last report she was considering requesting a new trial. (Keller's other claim to fame: authoring a 1997 opinion that denied a new trial to a man serving 99 years for aggravated rape after DNA tests *excluded* him as a suspect in the crime. "We can't give new trials to everyone who establishes, after conviction, that they might be innocent," Keller explained to an interviewer. The man was later pardoned by then-governor George W. Bush.)

Update: In 2010 Keller was fined $100,000 by the Texas Ethics Commission for failing to list more than $2.8 million in assets on financial disclosure forms. (She's appealing that, too.)

NATURE'S REVENGE

What happens when you mess around with nature? Sometimes
it works out…but sometimes nature gets even. Here are
a few instances when people introduced new animals
into the environment—and regretted it.

Import: Indian mongoose

Background: Ecologists consider black rats, which came aboard ships with European explorers, to be one of the most destructive predators ever introduced to the New World. Columbus unintentionally left a few behind during a stopoff in Jamaica in 1494. By 1870, the rats were costing Jamaican plantation owners as much as one-fifth of their sugar cane crops. So in 1872, they decided to import the Indian mongoose to control the rats.

Nature's Revenge: They did eat the rats…but then they moved on to chickens, piglets, lambs, kittens, puppies, frogs, turtles, nesting birds, lizards, bananas, coconuts, sweet potatoes, pineapples—anything they could get their teeth into. In 1883 further importation was banned and a bounty was placed on the mongoose.

Imports: Rats, cats, and rabbits

Background: In 1810 seal hunters discovered Macquarie Island, about halfway between New Zealand and Antarctica. The rats that came aboard their ships jumped off, and that was the beginning of what scientists call an "ecosystem meltdown." The sealers brought cats to the island to keep the rodents from eating their food stores. Then, around 1879, they brought European rabbits to breed and provide a ready food supply.

Nature's Revenge: By 1884 there were thousands of rabbits. The cats ate the rabbits, so the feline population exploded. But they also ate birds, and quickly rid the island of two native species, a rail and a parakeet. By 1985 conservationists decided they had to shoot the cats to prevent the loss of more bird species. But as the cat population declined (the last was killed in 2000), the rabbit population soared. At last count, some 130,000 rabbits were nibbling away at the island's vegetation, turning lush slopes into bare earth. The rabbits have now stripped 40 percent of the island bare.

Only U.S. president buried in Washington, D.C.: Woodrow Wilson.

Import: European snails

Background: In the 1870s, an aquatic snail native to Europe was introduced to the Great Lakes region. It wasn't intentional: They probably came in the ballast of timber transport ships or stuck to packing crates.

Nature's Revenge: In the summer of 1898, when Chicago residents turned on faucets, the soybean-size snails came out along with the water. Millions of the snails clogged the filtering screens at Chicago's waterworks, so many that they had to be shoveled into carriages and hauled away. But that didn't end the infestation. The snails—dubbed "faucet snails" after the Chicago invasion—have now spread to infest municipal water supplies as far away as Montana to the west and Maryland to the east.

Import: Russian hogs

Background: In 1912 a shipment of 14 wild Russian hogs, including 11 sows and 3 boars, arrived at a private game preserve in western North Carolina. The owner's intent: to breed them for sport hunting. By the early 1920s, the preserve had about 100 hogs, and the hunt was on. The hunters managed to kill only two hogs. Most of the rest escaped into the surrounding mountains.

Nature's Revenge: The hogs thrived and spread, including into the nearby Great Smoky Mountains National Park. They bred with local hogs, producing a hybrid that can weigh as much as 300 pounds and have tusks eight inches long. Though normally shy and reclusive, the hybrid hogs can be ferocious when confronted. According to one mountaineer, "Them tusks can rip a hound from stem to stern. What's more, the hog knows it."

Import: American gray squirrel

Background: In 1890 ten gray squirrels were shipped from the United States to England and released on the estate of the Duke of Bedford. Why? Just for the novelty.

Nature's Revenge: The grey squirrel moved into Britain's parks, gardens, and woodlands. Rather than sticking to their usual diet of nuts, the American squirrels began to strip and eat bark, killing forests of beech, sycamore, and oak trees. Over the next 100 years, the species "colonized the entire land surface of England and Wales." Current economic cost: more than $16 million a year.

DEATH BY LAWNMOWER

We must be pretty cynical to think it could be even mildly amusing that any particular country has the highest per capita death rate due to, say, falls from trees. And yet somehow it's kind of compelling, isn't it?

Emphysema and alcohol-related liver diseases: Hungary

Falls down steps, blunt-object attacks: Lithuania

Hepatitis, explosions: Malta

Asthma: South Korea

Meningitis: Nicaragua

Cholera: Belize

Kidney failure: El Salvador

Stabbings, and overall murders: Colombia

Anthrax: Paraguay

Obesity: Austria

The common cold: Egypt

Heart failure: Argentina

Executions: The Bahamas

Chicken pox: Venezuela

Teen suicides, skin cancer: New Zealand

Cancer: The Netherlands

Lightning strikes: Cuba

Lawnmower accidents, falls from trees: Moldova

Lupus, sickle-cell anemia: Bahrain

Falls from cliffs: Austria

Gun-related murders: South Africa

Single-car crashes: Lithuania

Eating disorders: Iceland

Snake and lizard bites: Panama

Epilepsy: Estonia

Multiple sclerosis: Norway

Schizophrenia: Finland

Struck by falling objects: Cayman Islands

Burning clothing: Latvia

Circulatory diseases: Ireland

Heart disease: Slovakia

Background check: Some mummies are so well preserved that their fingerprints can be taken.

FABULOUS FLOPS

*Some more stories to remind you that even though
an idea might look good on paper, it doesn't
always pan out in real life.*

Product: The Dodge La Femme, introduced by Chrysler in 1955

What it Was: One of the first American cars designed specifically with women in mind

Details: In the mid-1950s, Chrysler executives noticed that a lot of one-car families were buying second cars, and that women had a big say in the purchase—after all, moms would be doing much of the driving of the new car. So why not make a car just for ladies? The 1955 La Femme featured a two-tone "Heather Rose and Sapphire White" paint job, rose-colored fabric seats with pink vinyl trim, and special seatback compartments that stored the La Femme rain cape, rain hat, umbrella, and shoulder bag, which was stuffed with a La Femme compact, cigarette lighter, cigarette case, and other accessories.

Flop: Women in two-car families were going to do most of the driving in the second car, but not all of it. The pink-and-white La Femmes were like giant purses on wheels—few men of that era would have been caught dead driving one, and few ever were… only about 2,500 had sold by the time Chrysler discontinued the car for the 1957 model year. Only a handful of La Femmes survive today. They're valuable collector's items, and so are the accessories: In 1998 a La Femme shoulder bag and rain cape sold for $17,000…*without* the car.

Product: The McDonald's Arch Deluxe

What it Was: A "hamburger for adults" introduced in 1996

Details: The Arch Deluxe was marketed as a premium burger for customers who'd grown tired of Big Macs and Quarter Pounders. Its special features included a bakery-style bun made from potato flour, "Spanish" onions, "extra-fancy" ketchup, and its own "secret sauce"—mayonnaise mixed with two (*two!*) kinds of mustard.

First U.S. military unit to have African-American officers:…

Flop: Company hype aside, the burger was just a stuck-up Quarter Pounder. The ad campaign supporting it didn't help: TV commercials showed kids complaining that the Arch Deluxe was "yucky" (McDonald's way of saying the burger was for people with "mature tastes"). Sticker shock made things even worse: The Arch Deluxe cost twice as much as a Big Mac, prompting many customers to give it a pass. McDonald's predicted $1 billion in sales the first year, but sales were so bad that individual franchisees yanked it from their menus without waiting for corporate headquarters to kill it. McDonald's spent as much as $300 million on the Arch Deluxe before it finally gave up, making it the most expensive flop in fast-food history.

Product: *Yesterday and Today*

What it Was: A Beatles album released in the U.S. and Canada in the summer of 1966

Details: Despite the Beatles' huge popularity, Capitol Records still insisted on reworking the Fab Four's albums for American audiences. *Yesterday and Today* was just such an effort, a mishmash of tracks from the British versions of three different Beatle albums: *Help!*, *Rubber Soul*, and *Revolver.*

Flop: For the album cover art, Capitol inexplicably selected a photograph of the Beatles in white butchers coats, holding bloody cuts of meat and nude, decapitated baby dolls in their hands and on their laps. Such a photo likely would not have attracted much notice buried in a book of art photographs, but on the cover of an album it was too provocative. Capitol somehow didn't realize this until it printed up 750,000 copies of the album, then mailed advanced copies to music critics and radio stations. When even *disc jockeys* complained, Capitol knew it had a problem: It withdrew all 750,000 albums from circulation and pasted new, less offensive cover art (the Beatles gathered around an open steamer trunk) over the offending image. After the cost of pasting the new cover art on all those albums was factored in, *Yesterday and Today* actually *lost* money in its initial release, quite an achievement at the height of Beatlemania.

Flip-Flop: In 2006 a rare, factory-sealed "Butcher Cover" version of *Yesterday and Today* sold at auction for $39,000.

AFTER THE FUNERAL

*Sometimes the funeral isn't the end it's supposed
to be—it's just the beginning.*

ALISTAIR COOKE (1908–2004)
Claim to Fame: Host of the PBS series *Masterpiece Theater* from 1971 to 1992
After the Funeral: After Cooke died from lung cancer in 2004,
the 95-year-old was cremated according to his wishes, but not
before modern-day medical "body snatchers" stole pieces of his leg
bones and sold them for $7,000, for use as surgical bone grafts.
Cooke wasn't the only victim: The body snatching ring, run by an
ex-dentist named Michael Mastromarino, worked with crooked
funeral homes in New York, New Jersey, and Pennsylvania to
steal bones and other tissue from more than 1,000 cadavers, many
of whom, like Cooke, were diseased, making them unsuitable for
transplants. It's estimated that the stolen tissue was implanted into
about 10,000 unsuspecting patients, some of whom suffered ill
effects as a result. After the ring was busted in 2005, Mastromarino and other conspirators pled guilty to abusing corpses, forgery,
theft, and other charges and received long prison sentences. Mastromarino is serving 25 to 58 years.

MOHANDAS K. GANDHI (1869–1948)

Claim to Fame: Led the Indian nationalist movement, which won
India's independence from the British Empire in 1947
After the Funeral: After he was assassinated in January 1948,
Gandhi was cremated atop a funeral pyre. Custom dictated that
his oldest son scatter the ashes into a river or into the sea within
13 days. But Gandhi's oldest son, Harilal, was estranged from his
father and the duty was never performed. Instead, Gandhi's ashes
were placed in numerous small copper urns and distributed all
over India to be scattered in local rivers. Most of the ashes were
scattered, but several urns' worth were not.

• One urn sat forgotten in a bank vault in the Indian state of
Orissa until it was rediscovered in 1994. After a three-year legal
battle, one of Gandhi's great-grandsons scattered the ashes at the

confluence of the Ganges and Yamuna rivers.

• Another surfaced in 2007, when the son of one of Gandhi's close friends tried to donate it to a museum in Mumbai. Those ashes were also claimed by the family, and in 2008 one of Harilal's granddaughters scattered them in the Arabian Sea.

• A third urn is in southern California, entombed in a Gandhi memorial at the Self-Realization Fellowship Lake Shrine in Pacific Palisades. The owners have no plans to hand it over. No one knows how many urns were filled with Gandhi's ashes in 1948, so there may be more urns out there, waiting to be discovered.

BENITO MUSSOLINI (1883–1945)

Claim to Fame: Founder of Italian fascism, *Il Duce* ("The Leader") was the dictator of Italy from 1925 to 1943.

After the Funeral: Mussolini and his mistress, Clara Petacci, were captured by Communist partisans and executed while trying to flee to Spain in the closing days of World War II. Their bodies were transported to Milan, where they were hung upside down from the roof of a gas station. After the bodies were taken down, Mussolini was autopsied (the Americans kept a sample of his brain for study), then buried in an unmarked pauper's grave in Milan's Musocco Cemetery.

A year later, a right-wing journalist named Domenico "the Body Snatcher" Leccisi located Mussolini's grave, dug up the decaying corpse and made off with it. (Most of it, anyway: Leccisi is believed to have lost one of Il Duce's legs and perhaps a finger or two as he made his escape.) Fascist sympathizers moved the body from one place to another in the months that followed, but in August 1946 the authorities caught up with it in a Franciscan monastery near Milan, where it was hidden in a trunk. Fearing that Mussolini's grave might become a fascist shrine, the Italian government hid the dictator's body in another monastery for eleven years before returning it to the Mussolini family in 1957. They placed the body, minus the brain sample and missing appendages, in the Mussolini family crypt in the town of Dovia di Predappio, Italy. (The brain sample was returned in 1966; the leg and missing fingers were never recovered.) Just as the authorities feared, the crypt has become a pilgrimage site: As many as 100,000 tourists, many of them neofascists, visit the tomb each year.

It would take about 3 years of nonstop pedaling to ride your bike to the moon.

METAL, PART II

It's part of so many products in your life, from your car to your pen, but you probably never even think about where it comes from. Here's part II of the story. (Part 1 is on page 236.)

LOOK! SHINY!

For at least a few million years, human beings and their ancestors used tools made from such materials as wood, bone, and rock, to help make their lives a little easier. It didn't make their lives *that* much easier: *Homo sapiens* have been relatively primitive nomadic hunters and gatherers for almost all of their existence. Then, around 10,000 years ago they began discovering ways to work with a "new" material: metal.

The first metals used by humans were the ones that early metalsmiths didn't have to do very much with to make them usable. These are the *native metals*—metals that occur in nature in a pure state, or are naturally mixed with other elements in a way that maintains their usable properties. They include copper, tin, lead, silver, and gold.

Someone might have just found nuggets of these metals in a streambed, or in the roots of an unearthed tree, and thought they were attractive. They may have pounded them with stone hammers and found that they could shape them. That could have led to metals being used in jewelry or ornaments, or to the making of metal tools and weapons like axes, knives, and swords—a vast improvement over the old stone tools. All of this eventually led to people actively searching for more metals, the establishment of mines, trading in metals between different peoples, and the birth of a metal industry. However it happened—it happened in numerous locations all over the world.

METALLURGY

Starting around 8,000 years ago, archaeologists say, people started discovering that they could alter the metal. They may have discovered it by accident, or perhaps people just got creative, or maybe it was a combination of both. In any case, new processes were developed to alter metals, then to create entirely new ones that didn't exist in nature at all—with huge improvements in quality. Over the next few thousand years, mining and metalworking became integral to most of the cultures on Earth, and metal became one of the most civilization-changing substances in human history. Each of these new processes involved fire, and it's likely that experimentation with one led directly to the next. The most important advancements:

Annealing. This is simply the process of heating metal until it's cherry red. This restores old, brittle metal to its original malleable state, allowing it to be reworked and prolonging its usability. Annealing can be done at relatively low temperatures (copper can be annealed in a campfire). It was first done sometime around 6000 B.C., somewhere in the Middle East, and possibly in Europe and India around the same time.

Smelting. In this process, metals are melted into a liquid state, offering for much more freedom to shape them into different forms. Metals were first smelted around 5000 B.C., after the development of more advanced pottery kilns, which can produce much higher heats than could be achieved in simple open fires.

Alloy Production. This is the process of mixing different metals while they are in a molten state. It began around 3300 B.C. (the beginning of the Bronze Age), with the first production of bronze—a mixture of copper and tin that is much harder and more durable than either of its components.

Extraction. With further improvements in kiln technology and the subsequent ability to achieve higher temperatures, techniques were developed that allowed for the extraction of metals from ore. It was first done with iron in the Middle East around 1500 B.C.— marking the beginning of the Iron Age.

Smelting, alloy production, and extraction were practiced by ancient peoples in Europe, Asia, South America, and as far north as Mexico, but not in the rest of North America, or in Australia, until Europeans arrived. These simple processes remain the foundation of what is likely the largest and most successful industry in human history: the metal industry.

For Part III of "Metals," turn to page 504.

AMAZING COINCIDENCES

The universe sometimes works in mysterious ways.

• What do American cartoonist Hank Ketcham and British cartoonist David Law have in common? Both—independently—came up with comic-strip characters named "Dennis the Menace," both of whom were obnoxious youngsters. Not only that, both characters debuted on the exact same day: March 12, 1951. Neither man filed suit against the other, because both understood that it was just a strange coincidence. (But to avoid confusion, the U.S. version was shortened to "Dennis" when it ran in the U.K.)

• Two women named Patricia Ann Campbell were born on March 13, 1941. Due to an administrative goof, they were both issued the same Social Security number. Forty years later, when they were called in to the government office to rectify the mistake, they discovered that they both were bookkeepers, both had studied cosmetics, both had fathers named Robert, both had married military men a few days apart in 1959, both had two children, and their kids were the exact same ages.

• In 1992 Sue Hamilton, a British office worker, needed to call her co-worker, Jason Pegler, when the fax machine broke. She found his number on a bulletin board, dialed it, and he picked up. "Sorry to ring you at home, Jason," she said. "I'm not at home," he replied. "I was walking past a phone booth when it rang." Instead of dialing Pegler's phone number, Hamilton had accidentally dialed his employee number—which happened to be the same number as the phone booth he happened to be walking past.

• In 1858 a poker player named Robert Fallon was caught cheating and was shot dead in a San Francisco saloon. No one wanted his $600 (money won by cheating was considered unlucky), but they had no problem *winning* it back. So they plucked a young man from the street to take the dead man's place. He obliged…and started winning. When a police officer arrived to investigate the killing, he seized the original $600 to give to Fallon's next of kin. The young man then said to the cop, "His name was Fallon? So's mine!" It turned out that the new player *was* Fallon's next of kin—his son. He hadn't seen his father in seven years. (He kept the money.)

"THE EIGHTH WONDER OF THE WORLD"

Need publicity? Adding your project (or yourself) to the "Seven Wonders" list is an easy way to get noticed. Here are a few modern contenders.

• **The Pikeville Cut-Through.** Opening in 1987, it was one of the biggest construction projects of all time, taking 14 years and costing $78 million to blast a four-lane highway and railroad line through a mountain in Kentucky.

• **The Sydney Opera House.** Designed by Danish architect Jørn Utzon in 1957, the iconic building won architecture's highest award, the Pritzker Prize. An opera about the creation of the expressionist shell-shaped building, called *The Eighth Wonder,* debuted in 1995 (at the Sydney Opera House).

• **Andre the Giant.** The World Wrestling Federation gave their star 7'4"-tall, 500-pound grappler this title in the 1980s. (A decade later, the WWF labeled 180-pound female wrestler Chyna the "Ninth Wonder of the World.")

• **The Houston Astrodome.** Major League Baseball awarded a team to Houston contingent on the city building a stadium with a roof, because it was thought that Houston was too hot for open-air baseball. So civil engineers conceived this building, the world's first domed arena, which opened in 1965.

• **The Karakoram Highway.** The world's highest international highway, this 15,397-foot high freeway connects China and Pakistan across an 800-mile mountain range. Both countries promote it as a tourist attraction with the "Eighth Wonder" nickname.

• **The Panama Canal.** Before this channel in the Isthmus of Panama opened in 1914, ships in the Pacific Ocean had to go all the way around South America to reach the Atlantic. Although 27,000 people died during its construction, the canal significantly improved (and cheapened) international commerce.

• **The International Space Station.** Wait—this one isn't even *on the world.*

Besides ovens, Easy-Bake has also made toy popcorn poppers and potato-chip makers.

MYTH AMERICA: "THE PRICE THEY PAID"

*If "The Price They Paid" hasn't landed in your e-mail inbox
already, it probably will someday. It's very popular—the
kind of thing people like to share with friends. Why?
Because it's a great story...if only it were true.*

IT'S ALL OVER THE INTERNET

The last time we checked, more than 200,000 websites had
reprinted a short essay called "The Price They Paid." And
every year since 1999, the Fourth of July has triggered thousands
more appearances. It's an inspiring story, detailing the troubles
and persecutions that befell the 56 men who signed the Declaration of Independence: fortunes lost, families split, heroes killed,
ships seized, homes burned. To give the signers their due, they did
risk a lot in voting to declare independence from Great Britain.
They had every reason to believe that their lives—and everyone
else's, for that matter—would be turned upside down. Some
anonymous writer, though, decided that the signers' bravery
wasn't brave enough, so he "improved" the story by distorting or
leaving out important facts, or just creating new "facts" to make
it a better story.

Historians have tried to determine the original source of the
"Price They Paid" stories. The best anyone's been able to figure
out is that this shot heard 'round the Internet was actually the
echo of a piece from a book called *The Rest of the Story* by radio
commentator Paul Harvey, published in 1956. Harvey was a great
storyteller, but it seems he told a few whoppers. Here are a few
examples from "The Price They Paid."

THE ESSAY'S CLAIM: "Five signers were captured by the
British as traitors, and tortured before they died."
THE TRUTH: While five signers *were* captured by the British
during the course of the war, only one, Richard Stockton, was
arrested because he'd signed the Declaration of Independence. He
spent 34 days in a prison before being paroled in a prisoner

exchange after first giving his word of honor as a gentlemen that he would not "meddle" in war or politics until the end of the war. He died four years later of cancer, at age 50. The other four—George Walton, Thomas Heyward Jr., Arthur Middleton, and Edward Rutledge—were prisoners of war, captured as they were leading armies. None were unusually mistreated because they'd signed the Declaration; all were released in prisoner exchanges, not executed, as would have been the case if the British had considered them traitors.

Prisons on both sides were hellish places, rife with vermin and disease, that ultimately killed more soldiers than bullets did. However, the implication that those five were specially "tortured" is simply incorrect. In fact, as officers and gentlemen, they routinely got much shorter stays and much better treatment than the lower ranks. And despite what's implied in "The Price They Paid," all five lived for years after hostilities ended in 1783. Middleton died in 1787 at age 44; Rutledge, in 1800 at age 50; Walton, in 1804 at age 63; and Heyward, in 1809 at age 62.

THE ESSAY'S CLAIM: "Nine of the 56 fought and died from wounds or hardships of the Revolutionary War."
THE TRUTH: Nine of the signers died during the course of the war from a variety of causes, but none of the 17 signers who joined the military died at the hands of the British. Exactly one signer *did* die of a shot fired in anger during the war: Button Gwinnett, who was killed in a duel, ironically, with a rival *American* officer.

THE ESSAY'S CLAIM: "Twelve had their homes ransacked and burned....Vandals or soldiers looted the properties of Dillary, Hall, Clymer, Walton, Gwinnett, Hayward, Ruttledge, and Middleton."
THE TRUTH: Actually, more than 12 had that experience. One not listed was Lewis Morris, whose son wrote to him about his home being made into a barracks, every pane of glass maliciously smashed, every bottle in the wine cellar drunk, and his crops, horses, and cows taken by soldiers. Apparently many of his neighbors in New York's Westchester County had similar experiences. But it wasn't at the hands of the British—it was the Americans. The truth is, resupplying troops in the field was next to impossible back then, so both armies were expected to scrounge,

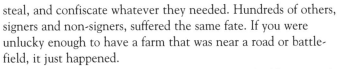

steal, and confiscate whatever they needed. Hundreds of others, signers and non-signers, suffered the same fate. If you were unlucky enough to have a farm that was near a road or battle-field, it just happened.

On the other hand, many of the signers who had homes and farms within British-held territory *weren't* looted. When British troops controlled Boston, they left the homes of Sam Adams and John Hancock alone. When they occupied Philadelphia during the winter of 1777, they didn't vandalize the homes of signers Benjamin Franklin, Benjamin Rush, Robert Morris, or James Wilson. Not that Wilson's home came through completely unscathed: During food shortages in 1779, Americans—both militia members and ordinary citizens—looted his supplies.

To be fair, the war did wreak havoc on the lives of a few signers. The farm and home of Francis Lewis were looted in late 1776, and his wife was held by the British. (She had ignored an order to evacuate Long Island.) A few months later she was traded for the captured wives of British officials, but her confinement damaged her health and she died a few years later. Her husband largely retired from public life after her death.

THE ESSAY'S CLAIM: "Two lost their sons in the Revolutionary Army; another had two sons captured."
THE TRUTH: Only one signer's son was killed in battle: James Witherspoon, son of John Witherspoon. The other claim is true: Aaron and Thomas Clark, the two sons of Abraham Clark, were taken prisoner but survived. (Thomas Clark was captured twice and escaped both times.)

THE ESSAY'S CLAIM: "Carter Braxton of Virginia, a wealthy planter and trader, saw his ships swept from the seas by the British Navy. He sold his home and properties to pay his debts, and died in rags."
THE TRUTH: Braxton earned his fortune the old-fashioned way: He inherited some of it and married into more, first by wedding a wealthy heiress while still in his teens (she died two years later), and then by marrying another one two years after that. Unfortunately, having money isn't the same thing as keeping it. He invested heavily in shipping—including the transport of slaves

from Africa ("the price of Negros keeps up amazingly," he wrote to potential partners in 1763)—and lost a lot of money during the war, not because he'd been targeted for having signed the Declaration of Independence, but because all shippers suffered losses. Between British embargos and piracy, Braxton lost his investments and much of his income, as did many who were in shipping during the war, and had to sell some of his land. However, he didn't lose it all, and recovered most of his fortune after the war. Braxton's business ethics were less than sterling, and he spent his postwar years evading investors and creditors and battling lawsuits. Yet although he lost much of his fortune, he was *still* richer than most other colonists. He died in one of the several estates he still owned…not "in rags."

THE ESSAY'S CLAIM: "Thomas McKeam was forced to move his family almost constantly…. His possessions were taken from him, and poverty was his reward."

THE TRUTH: This one's not even spelled correctly: His name was *McKean*, not McKeam. He wrote to John Adams in 1777 that he'd been "hunted like a fox by the enemy, compelled to remove my family five times in three months." However, it didn't seem to have anything to do with having signed the Declaration—*none* of the signers' names appeared in print until January 1777, and McKean's didn't appear even then, leading to the conclusion that he was one of the stragglers who added their names to the document very late. He was, however, a militia leader, and engaged in armed conflict with the British, so it's no surprise that he was being hounded. Regardless, the author of "The Price They Paid" exaggerated the riches-to-rags story: According to a contemporary account, the estate McKean left when he died consisted of "stocks, bonds, and huge land tracts in Pennsylvania."

THE ESSAY'S CLAIM: "In the battle of Yorktown, Thomas Nelson Jr. noted that the British General Cornwallis had taken over the Nelson home for his headquarters. He quietly urged General George Washington to open fire. The home was destroyed, and Nelson died bankrupt."

THE TRUTH: Well, no, it didn't quite happen like that. Another Internet version of this tale has Nelson telling the Marquis de

Lafayette, not Washington, to destroy his own home—that didn't happen, either. There's also a version that Nelson bet some French gunners that they couldn't hit his house from where they were located, offering a reward to anybody who could. Also untrue. In fact, his home survived and is now part of the Colonial National History Park. (However, according to the Park Service, "the southeast face of the residence does show evidence of damage from cannon fire.")

CLAIM (from Paul Harvey's original 1956 version): "John Hart was driven from his wife's bedside as she was dying. Their 13 children fled for their lives. His fields and his gristmill were laid to waste. For more than a year, he lived in forests and caves, returning home to find his wife dead and his children vanished. A few weeks later, he died from exhaustion and a broken heart."

THE TRUTH: This one wins the Pants-on-Fire prize. Here's what is true: Hart *did* have 13 children, his farm *was* captured and looted in November 1776, and he *did* go into hiding (for two months). Everything else? Not. His wife couldn't have been "dying," because she'd died a month earlier. His children hadn't vanished; they'd grown up and moved away—nearly all were adults. And Hart himself didn't die "a few weeks later" from "exhaustion and a broken heart." Instead, he served as Speaker of the New Jersey Assembly and was re-elected to the Continental Congress twice before being laid low by kidney stones in May 1779.

*　　*　　*

MISSED IT BY THAT MUCH

Liam Aiken was a child actor who had worked with director Chris Columbus on the 1998 drama *Stepmom*. In 2000 Columbus gave Aiken the role of Harry Potter in *Harry Potter and the Sorcerer's Stone*. A day later, Warner Bros. forced him to retract the offer. Why? J.K. Rowling, the author of the *Harry Potter* book series, had put a clause in her contract prohibiting the use of any non-British actors. Aiken was American, so he was out.

The first American Indian reservation was established in 1758, in New Jersey.

THE CHOCOLATE POODLE

There are more than 50,000 public houses—or pubs—in Britain. They serve as neighborhood meeting places, community centers, diners, and watering holes. And part of the centuries-old tradition is to give pubs colorful names. Here are some real pub names, past and present.

The Leg of Mutton
and Cauliflower

The Duke
Without a Head

Printers Devil

The Old Mother
Redcap

Bull and Spectacles

Donkey on Fire

Dirty Dick's

The Jolly Taxpayer

Ye Olde Trip
to Jerusalem

Cow and Snuffers

The Thatcher's Foot

Muscular Arms

The Sociable Plover

The Spinner
and Bergamot

The Cat and
Custard Pot

The Strawberry
Duck

Who'd A Throwt It

Sally Up Steps

The Old Thirteenth
Cheshire Astley
Volunteer Rifleman
Corps Inn

The Quiet Woman

The Old
Queen's Head

Round of Carrots

Mad Dogg at Odell

The Inn Next Door
Burnt Down

The Bucket of
Blood

The Poosy Nancies

The Blind Beggar

The Olde Cheshire
Cheese

The Bitter End

Q

The Hole in
the Wall

Ye Olde Fighting
Cocks

The Crooked House

Slug and Lettuce

The Dying Cow

The Old New Inn

The Case Is Altered

The Shoulder
of Mutton
and Cucumber

The Same Yet

The Penny-
Come-Quick

Ye Olde Bung Hole

The Ram Jam

The Chocolate
Poodle

The Drunken Duck

The Hark to
Mopsey

The House
Without a Name

The Fool & Bladder

Las Vegas study: Scented slot machines generate 53% more revenue than unscented ones.

BAD NEWS BARBIES

When you're one of the most popular toys ever, you're
bound to stir up some controversy now and then.

BACKGROUND
Almost since Mattel Toys first introduced Barbie in 1959,
the doll has been criticized for perpetuating an unrealistic
and even dangerous standard of beauty for girls. For example,
research shows that if Barbie were a real adult woman, she'd be
5'9" and weigh 110 pounds—thin enough to classify her as an
anorexic. But Barbie hasn't just sent out a subliminal "thin is in"
message—she's actively promoted it. The 1963 Barbie Baby-Sits
set included a pamphlet for girls called *How to Lose Weight*. One
of the tips in the pamphlet: "Don't eat!" Two years later, the booklet was included in the Barbie Slumber Party set, along with a
bathroom scale, permanently set at "110 pounds." Here are a few
more controversies associated with Barbie dolls.

SHARE A SMILE BECKY

With an eye toward divertsity, in 1997 Mattel introduced a friend
of Barbie's: Share a Smile Becky, a teenager with an unspecified
disability that required her to use a wheelchair (a pink one, which
came with the doll). Becky kept a low profile until 17-year-old
Kjersti Johnson, a Washington girl with cerebral palsy who used a
wheelchair herself, wrote a letter to Mattel to inform them that
Barbie's Dream House was not wheelchair accessible—while the
Dream House did have an elevator, it was too narrow to accommodate Becky's chair. The company promised a future redesign of
the house, but instead just dropped Becky from the Barbie line.

COLORED FRANCIE

As early as 1967, Mattel wanted to reach out to (and sell toys to)
African-American children. That year they produced a black
friend for Barbie and called her Colored Francie. Advocacy groups
quickly pointed out that all Mattel really did to create the doll
was use the same head molds they'd used for the original, white
Barbie, and dye the skin dark brown. It wasn't until 2009 that

---

Mattel made a line of African-American Barbies (named Kara, Grace, and Trichelle) with unique designs that aimed to replicate the features of real African-American women.

TOTALLY STYLIN' BARBIE

This 2009 Barbie doll came with a set of stickers that looked liked tattoos—hearts with the name "Ken" on them, for example. She also came with matching temporary tattoos for the girl playing with the doll, and packaging that encouraged girls to apply them to their lower back—a style of tattoo colloquially referred to as a "tramp stamp." Parents and consumer groups, led by Consumer Focus, thought that sent two bad messages: that it's okay for girls to do "trampy things," and that it's okay for kids to give each other homemade tattoos. Mattel did not agree, and Stylin' Tattoo Barbie remained in the line.

TEEN TALK BARBIE

When dolls with voice chips inside them, such as Teddy Ruxpin and G.I. Joe, became big hits in the early 1990s, Mattel decided to give Barbie a voice too. Embedded in every 1992 Teen Talk Barbie was a computer chip that held four spoken phrases. The toymaker compiled and recorded 270 phrases, and gave each doll four at random. Examples: "I love shopping!" and "Let's have a pizza party!" But a troublesome phrase ended up in approximately 1 percent of the dolls: "Math class is tough!" Many women's groups, especially the American Association of University Women, felt it perpetuated the stereotype that women are bad at math and could make young girls think they would never be good at it. In response, Mattel offered to replace any math-averse Barbie at no charge. But their efforts came too late. When the controversy erupted, a satirical group called the Barbie Liberation Organization (B.L.O.) covertly bought hundreds of Teen Talk Barbies (regardless of whether they said "Math class is tough!" or not) and swapped the Barbie voice chips with chips taken from Talking Duke G.I. Joe action figures. The B.L.O. then put all the dolls back on store shelves, where they were purchased by some very confused children who ended up with G.I. Joes that exclaimed, "Let's plan our dream wedding!" and Barbies that screamed, "Vengeance is mine!"

Most phobias cause blood pressure to rise. *Hemophobia*, the fear of blood, causes it to drop.

UNCLE JOHN'S STALL OF FAME

Uncle John is amazed—and pleased—by the unusual ways people get involved with bathrooms, toilets, toilet paper, and so on. That's why he created the "Stall of Fame."

Honoree: Florence Welch, who performs with backing musicians as Florence + the Machine

Notable Achievement: Finding fame in a public restroom

True Story: In 2006 Welch was an aspiring singer and recent art-school dropout. The closest she'd come to a performing career was singing, usually drunk, at open-mike nights in small clubs around London. One night, at just such a club, in just such a state of intoxication, Welch spotted Mairead Nash, the host of a BBC radio show that showcases new talent. Welch followed Nash into the restroom, introduced herself, and then sang the Etta James song "Something's Got a Hold on Me," right there in the bathroom. "I'd never heard anyone sing like that," says Nash. She'd never managed a singer before either, but she agreed to manage Welch's career. A recording contract soon followed, and in 2009 Welch's first album, *Lungs*, debuted at #2 on the U.K. charts, second only to Michael Jackson, whose recent death had sent sales of his music soaring. *Lungs* bounced around the charts for 28 weeks, then hit #1, making it the bestselling debut album of 2009. "It's such a funny fluke that I started, quite literally, in the toilet," says Welch. (Her bestselling single in the U.S.: "Dog Days Are Over.")

Honoree: Dan Colen, 32, an artist living in New York

Notable Achievement: Making a splash in the New York art scene by making a splash in an important bathroom

True Story: Colen was an up-and-coming artist when he attended an exhibition opening in New York in 2006. Also there: Sam Orlofsky, director of the Gagosian Gallery, one of the most exclusive art galleries in the city. A newcomer like

Colen *should* have had a hard time getting a gallery like the Gagosian to show his work, but Orlofsky thought Colen had promise. "I suggested he do a show with us. He said, 'Yeah, right, where am I going to show, in the bathrooms?'" Orlofsky told *The New York Times*. Actually, Orlofsky thought it sounded like a good idea, so he talked his boss, gallery owner Larry Gagosian, into hanging six of Colen's paintings in the gallery bathrooms. They were priced at around $10,000 each, and they all sold immediately. (Colen had a second show at the Gagosian in 2010. This time they displayed his work in the main gallery, not in the bathrooms.)

Honoree: Stephan Bischof, 24, of Honor Oak, England

Notable Achievement: Retrofitting a wheeled trash can (a "wheelie bin," as the British call them) to accept a more personal form of waste. Why? "I want to raise awareness of the fact that public toilets are closing," Bischof says.

True Story: If you've ever received the call of nature after a long night of pub crawling, you probably understand how the lack of available restrooms after closing time can lead to, shall we say, "outbursts" of antisocial behavior. That's why Bischof converted his wheelie bin into a portable outdoor urinal—and an environmentally friendly one at that. The plastic pissoir "has a funnel on one side and liquid flows into a base, separate from the bin. The urine is mixed with dry grass to turn it into a bio-fertilizer," reports London's *Evening Standard* newspaper.

Update: Bischof is on the hunt for investors. If he finds them, someday his wheelie urinals may appear outside of pubs all over Britain. (So is that a good thing?)

Honoree: Laszlo and Andrea Csrefko, a married couple living in Bekasmegyer, Hungary

Notable Achievement: Receiving an unusual visitor in their brand-new bathroom…and living to tell the tale

True Story: We've all read news accounts of people seeing the face of Jesus on a piece of French toast. Andrea Csrefko had a similar experience, but she didn't see Jesus. Not long after Laszlo finished installing a new shower, tub, and ceramic tiles in their bathroom in 2010, Andrea took the first shower. It ended in horror when she saw the face of Satan in one of the tiles on the wall. "I was naked and coming out of the shower and I could suddenly see his eyes staring into me! I just screamed and ran," she told the *Sun* newspaper. ("It wasn't there when we put the tiles up. It just appeared overnight," says Laszlo.) Repeated attempts to scrub Beelzebub off the bathroom wall have failed; ordinary household cleansers are apparently no match for Satan's power. Neither is the Csrefko's bathroom heater: "The room is always ice cold no matter how high we turn the heat," Laszlo says. "We've stopped using the bathroom. It's too spooky. We wash in the sink downstairs now."

Update: The Csrefkos have called in a professional exorcist to drive Lucifer from their lavatory, with no luck so far: "We need help from God or from the spirit world or we're going to seal up the room forever," Laszlo says.

Honoree: Koji Suzuki, bestselling Japanese horror writer and author of the novels *Ring* and *Dark Water*, both of which were made into Hollywood motion pictures

Notable Achievement: Rolling out one of his horror stories

True Story: In 2009 Suzuki partnered with the Hayashi Paper Corporation to have his short story "Drop" printed on rolls of toilet paper. The terrifying tale of a goblin who lives in a public restroom, "Drop" plays on traditional Japanese superstitions about evil spirits who hide in toilets. (Did your folks ever tell you about the Boogie Man? In Japan it's customary for parents to warn naughty children that a hairy hand will rise up out of the toilet bowl and drag them down into the abyss it if they continue to misbehave.) "Drop" is printed on the toilet paper in blue ink interspersed by red, blood-like splatters. The story takes up only three feet of toilet paper and is meant to be read in a single sitting. Priced at 210 yen (about $2.00), each roll contains several copies of the story so that more than one person gets to read it. "I've read the story and it's very scary," says Takaki Hayashi, vice president of Hayashi Paper, which markets the rolls as "Japan's scariest toilet paper" and "a horror experience in the toilet."

Most shark species have been around longer than trees have.

THE GARBAGE SATELLITE

They don't have used clothing stores in space, so what's an astronaut to do when his spacesuit wears out? Here's the story of the spacesuit that talked back after it was thrown over the side.

THE WELL-DRESSED ASTRONAUT

If you're like Uncle John, you like to wear your old jeans, T-shirts, and sweatshirts until they're tattered and riddled with holes. You can get away with that on Earth, but not in space: The spacesuits that NASA astronauts and Russian cosmonauts use can't be worn until they're full of holes, because their *not* having holes is what keeps the astronauts alive. Millions of dollars are spent designing and building the suits used on the International Space Station, yet most are used only a dozen times before they need to be completely refurbished or retired from service.

Then what? During the space shuttle era, NASA spacesuits could be returned to Earth aboard the shuttle and overhauled; now they're discarded the same way that the Russian *Orlan* spacesuits are: via the unmanned *Progress* spacecraft that resupply the ISS three or four times a year. After supplies are unloaded from the *Progress* capsule, it's stuffed with space garbage from the ISS: empty food containers, dirty clothes (the ISS doesn't have a washing machine), old spacesuits, and other refuse. Then the capsule is set adrift in orbit, where it will eventually burn up as it re-enters Earth's atmosphere. That shooting star you saw the other night? It might have been a flaming ISS garbage can.

TALKING TRASH

On more than one occasion, astronauts have used the spacesuits themselves as trash cans, cramming them full of garbage, hauling them out the airlock, and shoving them off the back of the ISS into space. In 2004 a Russian research team led by engineer Sergei Samburov took the concept a little further: Since *anything* tossed out of the ISS will orbit the Earth for a few months until it re-enters the atmosphere, they decided to turn an old *Orlan* spacesuit into a cheap communications satellite by outfitting it with a microprocessor and an amateur ("ham") radio walkie-talkie.

According to *The Joy of Cooking*, one ostrich egg will serve 24 people.

ARISS-TED DEVELOPMENT

Samburov and his colleagues were members of the Russian chapter of Amateur Radio on the International Space Station (ARISS). The group was responsible for getting a ham radio station installed on the ISS. Members train astronauts to use the station before they leave Earth, and then arrange for space-to-Earth contacts with school assemblies, science museums, scouting organizations, and other community groups on the ground. It's all done with the purpose of encouraging people—especially young people—to take an interest in science, engineering, and mathematics.

Working out the details of what the spacesuit satellite would do fell to the Russian and American sections of ARISS. (The Russians nicknamed it "Ivan Ivanov," the Americans called it "Mr. Smith," but its official name was "SuitSat-1.") Here's what they decided:

• After identifying itself and giving its call sign ("This is SuitSat-1, RS0RS"), the satellite would play one of five different prerecorded greetings made by students from Russia, the United States, France, Japan, and Germany.

• This would be followed either by a digital voice stating the satellite's temperature, battery power, and elapsed mission time, or by the transmission of a single digital photograph (stored in the microprocessor) that could be downloaded onto any computer.

• Then SuitSat-1 would pause for 30 seconds and begin transmitting again. The transmissions would repeat continuously, cycling through the five recorded greetings until the batteries finally died.

• Each greeting contained a "secret" word that students were encouraged to translate into their own language by exchanging information with students from other parts of the world.

• The subject of the digital photograph was also secret; to find out what it was, the photograph had to be downloaded.

Any student who succeeded in receiving the SuitSat-1 transmissions was eligible to receive a commemorative certificate, with special recognition going to students who translated the secret words or downloaded the digital image. SuitSat-1 broadcast its signal over a ham radio frequency, 145.990 MHz. And because the signal would be coming from directly overhead, the transmission would be strong enough to give anyone with even the simplest police scanner or walkie-talkie tunable to ham radio frequencies a good chance of receiving the signal. The only trick was figuring out when SuitSat-1 was passing overhead, but that information was easy to get online.

MAN OF THE HOUR

On September 10, 2005, a *Progress* resupply ship blasted off from Kazakhstan bound for the International Space Station. Among its cargo were the walkie-talkie and other components for SuitSat-1. After *Progress* arrived at the ISS, the astronauts assembled the components and placed them inside the body of the spacesuit. They attached an antenna and a control panel to the suit's helmet, then stuffed the suit full of dirty clothes to give it a more human form (and to get rid of the clothes).

Then on February 3, 2006, at the start of a six-hour spacewalk, Russian cosmonaut Valery Tokarey eased SuitSat-1 out of the ISS airlock, switched it on, and gave it a final shove. "Goodbye Mr. Smith," he said as the spacesuit slowly floated away. Footage of the launch of SuitSat-1 can be found online, as can photographs of SuitSat-1 floating above the earth. The images are beautiful, but they're also kind of disturbing: SuitSat-1 looks like a dead astronaut drifting off into space.

HOUSTON, WE HAVE A PROBLEM

SuitSat-1 only completed a couple of orbits around Earth before it started to malfunction. Tokarey and his partner on the spacewalk, NASA astronaut Bill McArthur, weren't even back inside the space station before Mission Control in Houston reported that no more transmissions were being received from SuitSat-1.

It seemed like the satellite was dead...until ham radio enthusiasts all over the world began picking up faint signals. They were much weaker than expected, but the SuitSat-1 was still on the air. There are different theories to account for SuitSat's troubles. The batteries may not have functioned properly in the intense cold of space. Or the radio might somehow have switched to a low power setting. Or the antenna, scrounged from parts on the ISS, may not have performed as well as expected, a problem made worse by the uncontrolled tumbling of the spacesuit.

Amazingly, instead of dying out in two or three days as expected, SuitSat-1 stayed on the air for a full two weeks before finally falling silent on February 18 as it passed over North America. SuitSat-1 drifted in orbit for another seven months before burning up on re-entry on September 7, 2006.

EMPTY SUIT

SuitSat-1 was successful enough for ARISS to want to try the idea again. The group made plans for a much-improved SuitSat-2, this time with rechargeable batteries (powered by solar panels attached to the legs of the spacesuit), cameras transmitting live images to Earth instead of a single digital photograph, and a transponder that would allow ham radio enthusiasts in different parts of the world to talk to each other using SuitSat-2 as a relay.

But this was a SuitSat that would have no suit: In July 2009, the retired *Orlan* spacesuit that was set aside for the project had to be disposed of to free up room on the ISS for more important projects. Rather than wait for another suit to become available, ARISS built a metal box large enough to hold all of the SuitSat-2 components and used it instead. Renamed ARISSat-1, the satellite arrived at the ISS in January 2011 and was deployed during a spacewalk on August 3, 2011. It almost certainly won't be the last such satellite tossed out the back of the International Space Station: ARISS has a few more ARISSats assembled and ready to go for the next time an opportunity arises; "tossing" may one day be a common (and cheap) method of putting satellites in orbit.

*   *   *

5 NON-HANDPRINTS IN
THE HOLLYWOOD WALK OF FAME

1. Groucho Marx's cigar

2. John Wayne's fist

3. Al Jolson's knee

4. Jimmy Durante's nose

5. Whoopi Goldberg's braids

Big mouth: The Australian Pelican's bill can grow to 19 inches, the longest beak of any bird.

WHEN LIFE WAS "SIMPLER"

We came across this piece in Barbara Swell's book Secrets of the Great Old-Timey Cooks *(shameless plug for the publisher: nativeground.com) and it made us think. The next time you think you're too tired to cook dinner, consider a day in the life of Effie Price, who lived in a log cabin in a remote mountain cove in the Big Pine section of Madison County, North Carolina. Here's her tale of a typical day as a 14-year-old in 1928.*

THE DAY BEGINS

"I got up at 5:00 a.m. to feed the hogs and chickens and gather the eggs by lantern-light. Then I helped my mother cook breakfast (in the wood cookstove). After eating, Mommy would wash the dishes while my brother Dewey and I milked the cows and put the milk in the spring box to cool. In spring, summer, and fall we'd go to the field with Poppy and work 'til dinner. We'd plant and hoe corn, dig 'taters (sweet and white), and tend the tobacco. We grew wheat and vegetables, too. After dinner and a 10-minute rest, we'd return to the fields and work 'til dark. Then it was time to milk the cows again by lantern-light. At night, we'd have a little supper, then quilt or sew before going to bed.

"Saturday was 'washin' day.' We'd build a fire under the big iron pot that hung in the yard and haul water from the spring to heat. When the clothes dried we'd iron them with irons kept hot by the fire. Then we'd sweep the house and yard. (Back then, folks didn't plant grass in their yards like they do now.) Sundays, we'd hitch up the horses to the wagon and give a ride to whomever we came across walking down the road to the Baptist church. If it was a school day, chores were done before and after school.

Sew What Else Is New

"My mother sewed all our clothes from cloth she bought on her monthly outing to Marshall, the nearest town. As a kid I tried sewing, but my mother thought I'd tear up the machine running it backwards and didn't want me to mess with it. So when she'd go to town, I'd have Dewey be lookout, and I learned to sew on my own. I stashed fabric under the bed, and one day I took out a pretty dress I'd sewed and sure surprised my mother. I sewed my first quilt at 13, made of feed sacks. The quilt I sleep under now is one my mother made from smoking-tobacco sacks. She'd keep some white, and dye some red, then sew them up. We made all our own sheets; we'd embroider the edges at night.

It Chore Was Fun

"Life wasn't all work. If it snowed, Dewey and I would take our guitars and head over the mountain to play music at my Uncle's in Spring Creek. In the fall, we'd have bean shellings, quilting bees, and corn husking parties. The first person to find a red ear of corn would get $5.00.

"Those were the good days. I was happy as a lark. We all were. Life was simpler then; you just worked hard and slept sound. We all got along and worked together. I don't even remember being tired. I wouldn't trade those days for anything in the world!"

REAL (FUNNY) FLYERS

You see them on telephone poles and bulletin boards at the grocery store. Here are some lines we've collected from actual flyers.

"Do not take this flyer down. There is a very angry hornet hiding behind it who will sting you in the neck. See that bulge right there? That's him."

"Found: a nice pile of dog poop. If you've lost a pile of dog poop and this photo looks like your dog's poop, then please come by and get it."

"Lost cloud. Last seen in the sky above my house. Looks white, fluffy, drifty. May or may not repond to 'Mr. Wispies.'"

"Missing unicorn. If you see it, you are probably high."

"Missing: my imaginary friend Steve."

...was the first to sell left and right shoes, as a pair, in a box (1884).

SURREAL VIDEO GAMES

Not all video games are about scoring points or saving princesses.

Super PSTW Action RPG (2009). The player controls a knight as he runs through the countryside, fighting enemies and collecting gold. But you have to do it fast—you'll lose points the longer you wait. But how do you get the knight to do all those things? It's ridiculously simple: Press the space bar. In fact, the "PSTW" in the title stands for "press space to win."

Don't Shoot the Puppy (2006). Unlike most games, where the object is to *do* something, the object of this game is to *not* do something. On one end of the screen is a huge gun; on the other is an animated puppy. If the player presses a key or moves the mouse even slightly, the cannon fires and blows off the puppy's head, killing it. Game over. But if the player can go 10 seconds without lifting a finger, the puppy lives, and the game is won.

Desert Bus (1995). Created by the comedy duo Penn and Teller, this game has the player drive a tour bus through the uneventful desert from Tucson to Las Vegas. In real time. That takes eight continuous hours. (You can't pause the game.) If you veer off the road, you crash, and the bus gets towed back to Tucson, also in real time. Each successful trip earns the player...one point.

4 Minutes and 33 Seconds of Uniqueness (2009). The object is to be the only person on the Internet playing the game for 4 minutes, 33 seconds. The actual "game" consists of a black-and-white screen counting up to 4:33.

You Only Live Once (2009). It's not very realistic that video game characters get to come back and try again over and over after they "die." This game takes death more seriously. If "Jemaine," the game's lead character, dies trying to rescue his girlfriend from the evil lizard who kidnapped her, he stays dead. The girlfriend mourns the death, the lizard is arrested, and a memorial is built. The game then places a data file on the player's computer that prevents them from ever playing it again.

Pilot slang: The moment it becomes too dark to see the horizon is called "the twilight zone."

THE ____ OF CANADA

Everyone compares themselves to something. Whether it's the
"Paris of the South" or the "Beethoven of TV Jingles,"
it's an easy way to communicate who you are.

"The California of Canada": Okanagan Valley is located in the interior of British Columbia. Like California, the days there are warm and dry, and the nights are cool. Like California, there's a desert to the south, skiing to the north. And like California, it has dozens of vineyards and wineries.

"The Provence of Canada": Provence is a coastal region of France known for its food and wine. Cowichan Valley (45 minutes north of Victoria, British Columbia) is home to lots of farm-to-table restaurants, wineries, and artisan cheesemakers, attracting food tourists and earning its nickname.

"The Thomas Edison of Canada": In 1882 Thomas Ahearn, a 27-year-old inventor and a native of Ottawa, founded a company to experiment with electricity and manufacture electric products when the technology was still in its infancy. Ahearn brought electric lights and electric street cars to Ottawa, and he invented the electric water heater, flatiron, and range.

"The Manchester of Canada": Galt, Ontario, was an agricultural community until the 1830s, when it switched to industrial production. That's when it earned its nickname, borrowed from the smog-choked English city that boomed in the Industrial Revolution. (Unlike Manchester, Galt is no longer an independent city. In 1973 it was absorbed into the city of Cambridge, Ontario.)

"The Carrie Bradshaw of Canada": Josey Vogels writes three sex and relationship columns syndicated to Canadian newspapers: "My Messy Bedroom," "Dating Girl," and "The J Spot." She's advertised as Canada's Carrie Bradshaw, after the sex-columnist character on the HBO series *Sex and the City*. But Bradshaw is based on real-life American sex columnist Candace Bushnell, so Vogels should probably be called "the Candace Bushnell of Canada."

The music on **Mr. Rogers' Neighborhood** was written by his brother-in-law, Johnny Costa.

"The Bing Crosby of Canada": Montreal-born Dick Todd was a 1930s–40s crooner who sang in the style of Bing Crosby. He was one of the biggest Canadian music stars of the era, although his biggest hit was "Pennsylvania Turnpike, I Love You So."

"The Bohemian Grove of Canada": The Bohemian Club is a group of powerful international political and economic leaders who meet annually for a retreat at a camp in northern California called the Bohemian Grove. (Many conspiracy theorists believe the group is an insidious secret society). The Club now meets in Canada too, in the Toronto suburb of King City, at the Canadian Imperial Bank of Commerce Leadership Center.

"The Bermuda Triangle of Canada": Over the past few decades, police have been baffled by mysterious deaths, unsolved disappearances, and the sudden appearances of headless corpses in the South Nahanni River valley in the Northwest Territories, leading some people to give the area this nickname.

"The MIT and Harvard of Canada": As the Massachusetts Institute of Technology is the United States' most exclusive and prestigious technical and scientific training school, the University of Waterloo is Canada's. In the U.S., Harvard is one of the nation's oldest and best universities. In Canada, that honor goes to McGill University, founded in Montreal in 1821.

"The Birmingham of Canada": Entrepreneur Hiram Walker founded Walkerville, Ontario, in 1858 as a planned community: He established a whiskey distillery and built up the farming and factories necessary to manufacture the beverage. And it worked. By the turn of the century, the home of Canadian Club whiskey had become one of Canada's biggest industrial and farming centers, mirroring Birmingham, England. (Walkerville is now part of the city of Windsor.)

"*The Wire* of Canada": *The Wire* was a cerebral—and critically acclaimed—HBO series from 2002 to 2008. It detailed the intricate dynamics of newspapers, politicians, and drug dealers in Baltimore. The Canadian Broadcasting Company's *Intelligence* took a similar approach to the underbelly of Vancouver. Some critics called it "*The Wire* of Canada," but that didn't bring in many viewers. It was canceled in 2008, after only 25 episodes.

The actors who played zombies in *Night of the Living Dead* (1968) were paid $1 and a T-shirt.

KNOW YOUR BOATS

See if you can match these fictional skippers' names to their fictional ships and the stories they came from. (Answers on page 539.)

1. Jason
2. Ahab
3. Nemo
4. Charlie Allnut
5. Steve Zissou
6. Hook
7. Jack Sparrow
8. Horatio Hornblower
9. Quint
10. Charon
11. Sonny Crockett
12. Old Fred
13. J. Flint
14. Forrest Gump
15. Austin Powers
16. Lord Drinian
17. Disko Troop
18. Mr. Burns
19. Quinton McHale
20. Dread Pirate Roberts
21. Marko Alexandrovich Ramius
22. George "Chief" Phillips

a) *St. Vitus' Dance*
b) *Revenge*
c) *Yellow Submarine*
d) *Pequod*
e) *African Queen*
f) *Walrus*
g) *Nautilus*
h) *Lydia*
i) *Black Pearl*
j) *Argo*
k) *Red October*
l) *Erebus*
m) *Dawn Treader*
n) *We're Here*
o) *Belafonte*
p) *Orca*
q) *Jenny*
r) *Gone Fission*
s) *PT-73*
t) *Jolly Roger*
u) *Shag at Sea*
v) *The Ferry of the Dead*

World's largest jack-o'-lantern: 17 feet in circumference, carved from a 1,469-lb. pumpkin.

MACGYVER ESCAPES!

On the '80s TV show, MacGyver (played by Richard Dean Anderson) was a secret agent who never used a gun—he used whatever he found lying around to create weapons and tools to get out of whatever dangerous predicament he happened to find himself in. MacGyver's innovations may seem improbable, but the show's writers were careful to use sound scientific principles as the basis for the "MacGyverism." Besides—it made for fun TV. Here are a few examples of how MacGyver did what he did.

TRAPPED IN A TOILET-BOWL FACTORY...

...MacGyver breaks open a gas line and places a rubber glove over the leak. While it inflates with noxious gas, he hangs an electric lightbulb (on a cord) over the glove. When the villain threatens to shoot him, MacGyver throws chunks of a broken toilet bowl at the bulb. On his second try, he hits the bulb. Sparks fly and ignite the gas-filled glove. It explodes. MacGyver escapes!

TRAPPED IN A BOOBY-TRAPPED MANSION...

...MacGyver fastens the head and shoulders of a suit of armor to the top shelf of a wheeled kitchen cart. He then uses a rubber band to attach an electric mixer to the cart's front wheel and plugs it in. The mixer turns the wheel, which propels the cart across the floor and out of the kitchen, triggering automatic motion-detecting guns. The cart takes the hit. MacGyver escapes!

TRAPPED IN A LIQUOR-STORE WAREHOUSE...

...MacGyver removes a length of heating duct and straps it to a wooden crate. Into the duct he places a small, sealed keg of beer. Behind that he places a garbage can full of wood, douses it with an available flammable substance—whiskey—and lights a fire with some matches he conveniently finds lying around. The flames heat the keg, which ignites the alcohol inside, propelling the keg through the pipe, breaking a door open. MacGyver escapes!

TRAPPED IN A DIFFERENT WAREHOUSE...

...MacGyver has been tied up by bad guys, and has just four minutes before a time bomb is set to explode. Just then, a very friendly dog wanders into the warehouse. Somehow, MacGyver gets the dog to fetch a bottle of sulfuric acid that just happens to be sitting on a nearby table. He then convinces the dog to place the bottle on one end of a seesaw contraption that MacGyver made out of a yardstick and an empty bottle that he was able to reach with his feet. MacGyver slams his feet down on the makeshift catapult, which launches the bottle of acid into his hands, which he uses to dissolve the ropes binding his hands and feet. MacGyver (and the dog) escape!

TRAPPED IN A CRASHED PLANE...

...and buried under an avalanche somewhere in Russia, MacGyver wraps the plane's emergency oxygen tank in a piece of fabric that he tears off a sleeping bag. He then puts the bundle in a bucket of vodka, buries the bucket in the snow just outside the plane's door, and lights the fabric on fire. The vodka and the oxygen tank combust and blow a hole out of the snow. MacGyver escapes!

TRAPPED ON A TRAIN...

...MacGyver has to figure out who on board sold tainted medicine to a tribe of Middle Eastern nomads before the train stops and they can escape. So he runs a wire from the cuff of a blood-pressure monitor into a mechanical, wind-up alarm clock. When somebody wears the cuff, and they lie, their pulse quickens and the alarm clock goes off. MacGyver nails the bad guy with it. The bad guy doesn't escape!

TRAPPED ON A CRUISE SHIP FULL OF SOULS...

...is the premise of a 1990 episode. MacGyver gets into an accident, falls into a coma, and dreams he meets up with his deceased grandfather. The two get trapped by Anubis, the Egyptian god who is the keeper of the afterlife, in the engine room of a cruise ship full of souls. Anubis has jammed an axe in the ship's lock wheel as an extra precaution. Fortunately, even when he's dreaming, MacGyver can get out of any sticky situation. He wraps one end of a fire hose around his side of the lock wheel, and the other around the propeller shaft of the ship. As the propellor turns, tension builds from the hose, eventually snapping the door's lock and the axe handle. MacGyver escapes!

Only U.S. president who did not represent any political party: George Washington.

STRANGE LAWSUITS

We're back with a BRI favorite: unusual legal battles.

THE PLAINTIFF: A Polish hunter named Waldemar
THE DEFENDANT: Jaworski Jagdreisen, a German travel agency that specializes in African hunting expeditions
THE LAWSUIT: Waldemar *really* wanted to shoot an elephant, so in 2010 he booked a vacation with Jaworski Jagdreisen, which sent him to a game reserve in Zimbabwe (one of the few countries where it's still legal to hunt elephants). Waldemar was told that if he found an elephant's excrement, he could pick up the animal's trail and shoot it. But he found neither excrement nor elephants, and went home empty-handed. After he complained, the agency gave him a free trip back to Zimbabwe, and this time, he shot and killed an elephant. Nevertheless, Waldemar sued the travel agency for $130,000 for failing to provide him with an elephant to kill on the first trip.
THE VERDICT: Case dismissed. The judge remarked, "The fact that elephants were not encountered during the hunt does not testify that elephants were not there."

THE PLAINTIFFS: David Jonathan Winkelman and his stepson, Richard Goddard
THE DEFENDANT: KORB, an Indiana hard-rock radio station
THE LAWSUIT: In 2000 DJ Ben Stone announced on the air that any listener who had the station's call letters tattooed on their forehead would receive $150,000. Winkelman and Goddard decided to take them up on the offer. But first they went to the station and asked if the deal was legitimate. They were told it was, so they went to a tattoo parlor and got their foreheads inked with the station's slogan: "93 Rock, the Quad City Rocker." When the two men went to the station to claim their prize, Stone photographed them and then informed them it was just a practical joke. Winkelman and Goddard received no money, but their pictures were displayed on the station's website. Winkelman lost his job, and neither man could find work because of the big tattoos on their foreheads. Winkelman and Goddard sued, claiming that the

---

Some fireflies lay glowing eggs.

radio station set out to "publicly scorn and ridicule them for their greed and lack of common good sense."

THE VERDICT: Goddard's case was dismissed when he didn't show up at court. Winkelman later dropped his suit. Not long afterward, the station changed its format to easy listening.

THE PLAINTIFF: Robin Brown, 48, amateur birdwatcher and employee at Massage Envy in Weston, Florida

THE DEFENDANT: Mark Horn, assistant state attorney in Broward County, Florida

THE LAWSUIT: One day in 2009, Brown was birdwatching in a patch of woods in Weston. As she often did, Brown said a prayer for peace and burned a small bundle of sage, a Native American purification ritual known as "smudging." When she returned to her car, Broward County Sheriff's Deputy Dominic Raimondi was waiting for her. Suspecting that she was smoking marijuana, he searched her bag and found the sage. Although sage and marijuana don't look (or smell) anything alike, Raimondi put the sage into a field testing kit, which is known for giving false positives. The substance tested positive for marijuana, but Raimondi let Brown go and sent the sage to the crime lab for a proper test.

Three months passed. Brown forgot about the incident... until the police entered her workplace, arrested her on felony drug charges, handcuffed her, and marched her out in front of her customers and coworkers. At the station, Brown was strip-searched, cavity-searched, and put in jail for the night. "I tried to act tough," she later said, "but inside I was quaking." The next day, Brown hired a lawyer, Bill Ullman, to find out why she had been arrested. The answer: Assistant State Attorney Mark Horn was supposed to have had the sage tested; for some reason, he didn't do it, but he ordered her arrest anyway. Ullman demanded that the substance be tested; when it finally was, it was indeed sage. The charges were dropped. Brown then filed a civil suit against Horn.

THE VERDICT: The judge dismissed the case. "Prosecutors are given immunity from lawsuits in the course of doing their jobs," he said. Ullman disagreed. "Horn *wasn't* doing his job. He filed a false statement swearing she had marijuana, and she didn't." At last report, the case was under appeal.

ADIDAS vs. PUMA, PART II

*Here's part two of our chronicle of one of the most
bitter family squabbles in business history.
Part I of the story is on page 110.*

TRIPS 'N STRIPES

Now that Adi and Rudi Dassler had split their shoe company
into two new ones, both men wanted to be sure that customers would be able to tell Adidas and Puma shoes apart. It had
been common practice for many shoemakers, the old Dassler
Brothers company included, to sew vertical strips of leather onto
the sides of shoes to give them structure and strength. The strips
weren't too noticeable, because they were the same color as the
rest of the shoe.

Adi Dassler decided that the strips—which were painted white
or some other color to make them look like *stripes*—would be the
Adidas trademark. He made up sample shoes with two, three, four,
five, and six stripes apiece, then asked his wife Käthe and her sister Marianne to pick which ones they liked best. Two-stripe shoes
were out: Some Dassler Brothers shoe designs had used two strips
of leather, so Rudi would have grounds to fight a two-stripe trademark if he wanted to.

Käthe and Marianne felt that the shoes with four or more
stripes looked too busy. They picked three stripes, and Adidas
shoes have been made with them ever since. Over at Puma, Rudi
played with a few designs, including a puma jumping through a
capital "D," before eventually settling on the company's signature
"formstripe," a horizontal stripe that begins at the back of the
shoe, then widens as it moves forward along the side of the shoe
before turning down toward the sole.

SPLIT PERSONALITIES

When the Dassler brothers divided their company in two, the
employees had to choose whether they wanted to work for Adi at
Adidas, or for Rudi at Puma. Most of the technical people stayed
with Adi; most of the sales force and administrators went with
Rudi. That might seem like a formula for faster growth at Puma,

---

On average, left-handed women enter menopause 5 years sooner than right-handed women.

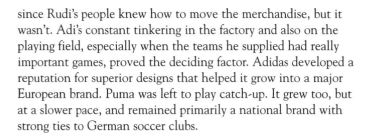

since Rudi's people knew how to move the merchandise, but it wasn't. Adi's constant tinkering in the factory and also on the playing field, especially when the teams he supplied had really important games, proved the deciding factor. Adidas developed a reputation for superior designs that helped it grow into a major European brand. Puma was left to play catch-up. It grew too, but at a slower pace, and remained primarily a national brand with strong ties to German soccer clubs.

THE TOWN OF BENT NECKS

As the years passed and Adidas and Puma loomed ever larger over the economy of tiny Herzogenaurach, the entire town was drawn into their feud. Nearly everyone worked at one company or the other (or was related to someone who did), so few people could avoid choosing a side. Dating, even socializing, across company lines was frowned upon. Marrying someone from the other side was out of the question. Herzogenaurach became known as "the town of bent necks," because people looked down to see which shoes people were wearing before engaging them in conversation.

Adidas people bought their bread from bakers who sided with Adidas, bought their meat from Adidas-friendly butchers, and drank in Adidas-only beer halls. Puma workers did the same. Which bus a child took to school depended on whose side their parents were on, and so did the gang a kid joined. The rivalry that started soon after birth went all the way to the cemetery: Each side had its own tombstone carvers. And when Adi and Rudi Dassler died four years apart in the 1970s, they were buried in opposite corners of the Herzogenaurach cemetery, as far apart as possible. They had carried their feud to the end of their lives, and the same was expected of everyone else.

THE ENEMY IS US

Had Adi and Rudi been able to patch up their differences in their lifetimes, and had their descendants not carried the feud into the next generation, the global athletic shoe business might look very different today. But they didn't. The brothers couldn't even limit themselves to fighting with each other. Adi fought with his son and heir, Horst Dassler, finally banishing him to France, where Horst was put in charge of a shoe factory that was losing money.

Scientific term for insect poop: *frass*.

Horst turned it into a moneymaker, then built Adidas France into an operation that rivaled the rest of Adidas. But none of it was good enough for Adi. Writing from Herzogenaurach, Adi disowned his son in one angry letter after another.

Horst was so certain that Adi would throw him out of the company that he began diverting millions of Adidas dollars into his own sporting-goods businesses, so that he'd have somewhere to go when he got tossed out. He concealed his activities behind shell companies and front men for several years. And though his scheming eventually was exposed, he never did get thrown out of Adidas. After Adi died in 1978, Horst battled his four sisters for control of Adidas, winning the fight in 1984 when his mother sided with him against his sisters.

THE CUB

Over at Puma, Rudi's relationship with Armin Dassler, his oldest son and heir, was no better. Rudi routinely belittled him in front of other company executives, and Armin chafed at his father's overbearing nature and outmoded ways of doing business. Armin could see what his cousin Horst was accomplishing at Adidas, and it drove him crazy that he couldn't do the same at Puma. Armin finally banished *himself* to Salzburg, Austria, to run a Puma factory there. When the Austrian athletic shoe market proved less profitable than expected, Armin started selling shoes to the U.S. market, something Rudi had expressly forbidden. Armin actually had to go behind Rudi's back to introduce his father's own shoes to the largest sporting goods market in the world.

The relationship between father and son never did improve. When Rudi died in 1974, Armin was stunned to learn that Rudi had written him out of the will. Only a legal technicality allowed Armin to inherit a controlling 60 percent interest in Puma against his father's dying wishes. Armin's younger brother Gerd inherited the other 40 percent.

While the two families were consumed with their own squabbles, a shoe-nami was on the way from overseas. For Part III of the story, turn to page 477.

Over 8 *Harry Potter* movies, actor Daniel Radcliffe went through 70 wands and 160 pairs of glasses.

NASTY MUSICIANS

Who are the harshest music critics? Other musicians.

On Lady Gaga: "I'm not quite sure who this person is, to be honest. I don't know if it is a man or a woman."
—**Christina Aguilera**

On Christina Aguilera: "She is one of the most disgusting human beings in the entire world. She looks like a drag queen."
—**Kelly Osbourne**

On the Beatles: "They were peripheral. If you had more knowledge about music, they didn't really mean anything."
—**Van Morrison**

On Elvis Costello: "Music journalists like him because music journalists look like him."
—**David Lee Roth**

On Rod Stewart: "He has kind of a female voice."
—**Tony Bennett**

On Red Hot Chili Peppers: "I'm forever near a stereo saying, 'What is this garbage?' And the answer is always the Red Hot Chili Peppers."
—**Nick Cave**

On Jack White (of the White Stripes): "He looks like Zorro on doughnuts."
—**Noel Gallagher (Oasis)**

On Chuck Berry: "I love his work but I couldn't warm to him even if I was cremated next to him."
—**Keith Richards**

On Keith Richards: "It's like a monkey with arthritis, trying to go onstage and look young."
—**Elton John**

On Mick Jagger: "I think he would be astounded and amazed if he realized to how many people he is not a sex symbol, but a mother image."
—**David Bowie**

On former bandmate Slash: "I consider him a cancer and better avoided."
—**Axl Rose**

On Bruce Springsteen: "He plays four and a half sets. That's torture. Does he hate his audience?"
—**John Lydon (Sex Pistols)**

The campy *Batman* TV show was inspired by a Batman-themed party Hugh Hefner threw in 1965.

A BORING PAGE

Does everything have to be exciting?

YAWN
The "Boring 2010" conference took place in London. About 200 people attended. Among the activities: milk-tasting, a PowerPoint presentation of a man's changing tastes in necktie colors, and a speech called "My Relationship with Bus Routes."

WHATEVER

In 1964 artist Andy Warhol released what is possibly the most boring movie ever made. Called *Empire*, the grainy, black-and-white silent film is just one continuous shot of New York City's Empire State Building on a night when nothing happened. Warhol filmed the building for six hours, but to make the movie even less interesting, he recorded it at a slower speed so it lasts eight hours.

YUP

To many, the phrase "boring museum" is redundant, but some museums are more boring than others. Examples: the Cement Museum in Spain, the Wallpaper Museum in France, and the Occupational Health and Safety Museum in Germany.

MEH

What's the world's most boring city? It could be Brussels, Belgium. According to a poll of 2,400 travelers conducted by the website TripAdvisor.com, aside from the famous waffles, there's not much of interest there.

ARE WE DONE YET?

In 2010 British researcher William Tunstall-Pedoe designed a computer program that scanned all the news from every single day in the century to determine the most boring day of the 20th century. The "winner": April 11, 1954. On that day, no one famous was born, no one famous died, and there were no big news events. According to Tunstall-Pedoe, even the weather was boring.

NASA slang for floating space poop: "escapees."

THE FORBIDDEN ISLAND, PART II

*Here's Part II of our story about what could
be the most isolated people on Earth.
(Part I is on page 163.)*

STRANGERS BEARING GIFTS

The first real threat to the natives of North Sentinel Island appeared in 1858, when the British established a penal colony at Port Blair on nearby South Andaman Island, and set about trying to pacify the local tribes—the Great Andamanese, the Onge, the Jarawa, and eventually the Sentinelese. One technique the British used was to kidnap a member of an unfriendly tribe, hold him for a short period, treat him well, and then shower him with gifts and let him return to his people. In so doing, the British hoped to demonstrate their friendliness. If the first attempt didn't work, they'd repeat the process with as many tribesmen as it took to turn an unfriendly tribe into a friendly one.

In 1880 a large, heavily armed party led by 20-year-old Maurice Vidal Portman, the British colonial administrator, landed on North Sentinel and made what is believed to be the first exploration of the island by outsiders. Several days passed before they made contact with any Sentinelese, because the tribe members disappeared deeper into the jungle whenever the strangers approached.

Finally, after several days on the island, the party stumbled across an elderly couple who were too old to run away, and several small children. Portman brought the two adults and four of the children back to Port Blair. But the man and the woman soon started to get sick and then died, probably from exposure to Western diseases like smallpox, measles, and influenza, to which they would have had little or no resistance. So Portman returned the four children to North Sentinel island and released them with gifts for the rest of the tribe. The children disappeared into the jungle and were never seen again.

The world's largest sea cave is near Florence, Oregon. It's the height of a 12-story building.

INDIA'S TURN

After this experience, the British left the Sentinelese more or less alone, and focused their pacification efforts on the other tribes. When India won its independence from Great Britain in 1947, the Andaman Islands were handed over to India, but the Indians ignored the Sentinelese, too, for about 20 years.

Then in 1967, the Indian government launched its own large-scale expedition to North Sentinel Island, complete with plenty of armed policemen and naval officers for protection. The visit was less aggressive than the British had been 87 years earlier (no kidnapping), and it was more scientific (an anthropologist named T.N. Pandit was a member of the party). But they never made contact with a single Sentinelese soul—once again, the tribe members vanished deeper into the jungle whenever the outsiders approached.

RE-GIFTING

That began a decades-long policy of "contact visits" by the Indian government to North Sentinel Island. From time to time during the short calm-weather season, an Indian naval vessel would anchor outside the coral reefs and dispatch small boats through the openings in the reefs to approach the beaches. *Approach* the beaches, but not land. The boats had to be sure not to come within an arrow's flight of the beach or risk being attacked by the Sentinelese.

These strangers, like the British before them, came bearing gifts—usually bananas and coconuts, which do not grow on the islands, and sometimes other gifts, including bead necklaces, rubber balls, plastic buckets, and pots and pans. Once the visitors approached as closely as they felt was safe, they would toss the items overboard to wash up on the beach. Or, if the party was large enough to frighten the Sentinelese into retreating into the jungle, it might even land on the beach, but only long enough to drop off the gifts and beat it out of there before the Sentinelese attacked. When a *National Geographic* film crew lingered a little too long during one such visit in 1975, a Sentinelese warrior with a bow and arrow shot the director in the thigh, and then stood there on the beach laughing at his accomplishment.

CLOSE ENCOUNTERS

It wasn't until the early 1990s, after more than 20 years of such visits, that the Sentinelese finally relaxed their guard—just a bit—and allowed the boats to come closer. Sometimes unarmed tribesmen stood on the beaches while the people on the boats tossed the coconuts overboard. A few times, they even waded out into the water to collect the coconuts in person. Even so, they did not allow the visitors to stay long. After just a few minutes, the Sentinelese would signal with menacing gestures or "warning shots"—arrows fired with no arrowheads attached—that the visit was over.

LEAVE 'EM ALONE

That was about as close as the Sentinelese ever came to opening up to the outside world. In the mid-1990s, the Indian government decided that its policy of forcing contact with the Sentinelese made no sense, and it ended the visits in 1996.

The visits made no sense to India, but they were actually dangerous for the Sentinelese. With so little resistance to Western diseases, the islanders risked not just the death of individuals with each contact with outsiders, but the extinction of the entire tribe. That was the experience of the other Andaman Island tribes: When the British established their penal colony on South Andaman Island in 1858, the native population of the Andaman Islands was nearly 7,000 people. But the British arrival was followed by a succession of epidemics, including pneumonia, measles, mumps, and the Russian flu, which decimated the tribes. After more than 150 years of exposure to Western diseases, their numbers have dropped to fewer than 300 people, and continue to decline. Some tribes have gone completely extinct. The Sentinelese, by refusing contact with the outside world, are the only tribe that has avoided this fate.

WAVE GOODBYE

The Sentinelese even survived the 2004 Indian Ocean tsunami, the deadliest in recorded history, with few or no casualties. Though the tsunami killed more than 230,000 people in surrounding countries, it appears that the Sentinelese were able to sense the coming of the tsunami and escape to higher ground before it arrived. When an Indian Navy helicopter arrived three days later to check on their well-being and drop food parcels on the beach, a Sentinelese warrior came out of the jungle and warned the helicopter off with bow and arrow, a clear sign that the Sentinelese did not want help from outsiders.

KEEP OUT

Today the Indian government enforces a three-mile exclusion zone around North Sentinel Island with regular sea and air patrols. Heavy fines and jail time await anyone caught trespassing into the zone. And if that isn't enough of a deterrent, the Sentinelese continue to defend their island as fiercely as ever. In 2006 two poachers who'd spent the day fishing illegally inside the exclusion zone dropped anchor near the island and went to sleep, apparently after a night of heavy drinking. Sometime during the night the anchor came loose and the boat drifted onto the coral reefs. The Sentinelese killed both men and buried their bodies on the beach. At last report the bodies were still there; when an Indian Navy helicopter tried to recover them from the beach, the Sentinelese fought it off with bows and arrows.

EYE IN THE SKY

Today anyone with a laptop and Internet access can use Google Earth to spy on places that are not meant to be seen by outsiders. You can look at satellite photos of Area 51, the secret military airbase in the Nevada desert. You can look at Mount Weather, a secret facility in Virginia that is rumored to be the place where members of Congress are evacuated in times of national emergency. You can even peer down on secret waterslides on the outskirts of Pyongyang, North Korea, that are the playground of that country's Communist Party elite.

But when you look down on North Sentinel Island in the Bay of Bengal, all you can make out is the wreck of the *Primrose*, still stuck on the reef where it ran aground in 1981. You can't see the Sentinelese, their dwellings, or anything else that might shed light on how many people there are on the island, or how they live their lives. The dense jungle canopy that covers every inch of the island except the beaches conceals everything: Even when viewed from outer space, the Sentinelese remain free from prying eyes.

Indonesia has more mammal species than any other country (and the most under threat).

ODD BIKES

Proof that fads come in cycles.

TALL BIKES

An early version of these bikes, primarily used by lamp-lighters, first appeared in the late 19th century. They're not to be confused with the old-fashioned "penny farthings," bikes with one giant wheel in front and a tiny one in back. "Tall bikes" have conventional wheels, but their frames and seats (and pedals) extend high into the air. They've become increasingly common-place in bike-loving cities such as Portland, Oregon, and Nashville, Tennessee, where thousands of people participate in tall-bike clubs. The bikes aren't commercially available; they're constructed by hobbyists out of spare parts, and are often made up of two bike frames welded together. The seat can be anywhere from 6 to 10 feet off the ground, giving the rider an excellent—and dangerous—view of the surroundings. (It should go without saying that getting on and off a tall bike takes a good deal of prac-tice.) One tall-bike hobby: jousting, where high-riders whack each other with lances made out of foam and PVC pipes.

LOW-RIDER BICYCLES

Car and motorcycle enthusiasts often "trick out" their vehicles with expensive, flashy modifications. But if that's out of your price range, try these. Favored by inner-city cyclists, low-riders are shorter than a standard adult bicycle, and are often modified children's bikes. (Most preferred brand: Schwinn Sting-Ray.) Low-riders are typi-cally customized into elaborate mini-monsters with banana seats, elaborate paint jobs, stylish handlebars, all-white tires, stereos, and other features. Some riders have even managed to work in hydraulics. All told, it's a $10 million-per-year industry.

FIXED-GEAR BICYCLES

Since they lack the part called a "freewheel," these bikes, also known as "fixies," prevent the rider from coasting. If the bike is moving, that means the pedals are moving. Sound ridiculous? Well, many fixies don't have brakes, either; you stop by "skidding"—leaning forward to take weight off the rear wheel and then resisting the forward motion of the pedals. They've been used by cyclists in *velodromes* (indoor bike tracks) and by racers training during the off-season because they supposedly encourage "good pedaling." In recent years, their popularity has skyrocketed among everyday riders. Nonetheless, they're illegal in many countries and cities. A fixie is definitely not a bike for beginners, but if you can manage one, here's a plus: You can ride backwards. They're also lighter than regular bikes, and because they have fewer parts, they're easier to repair and maintain. But don't worry about fixed-gear bikes replacing regular bikes. Despite an eight-fold sales growth since 2001, only 0.5 percent of all bikes sold each year are fixed-gear bikes. Cost: around $500. (You can convert your own for about half that.)

RECUMBENT BICYCLES

These bikes allow the rider to sit back, almost lying down as if they were lounging in a deck chair. Favored by older cyclists for their ergonomic benefits over more conventional styles, they're not necessarily for the lazy or the elderly: The world bicycle speed record was set with a recumbent bike. While they're fast, recumbents are difficult to pedal up hills and have a wider turning radius than traditional cycles. They're also tough to balance on and tend to be pricier than standard bikes. About 20,000 are sold in the U.S. each year.

UNICYCLES

Riding a unicycle is not for the faint of heart—they are tough to balance on, and crashing can earn you a ticket to the hospital. But believe it or not, there are people who commute to work on these things. So why ride something so unforgiving? For one, unicycles are lighter and easier to store than two-wheelers. They work different muscles than normal bikes do, and they cost less. In comparison to two-wheeled bicycles, they're easy to get in and out of elevators or up a flight of stairs. And then, of course, there's the "fun factor." While unicycles haven't quite caught on in the United States (it's estimated that only about 2,000 Americans use them to commute to work), the mode of transportation is gaining popularity in Japan.

GOVERN-MENTAL

A few goofs from the public sector.

SHOULD HAVE SETTLED. In 2008 the city of Bridgewater, New Jersey, charged a resident named Tom Coulter $5.00 for a compact disc recording of a public council meeting. After Coulter paid, he felt he should only have to pay for the actual cost of the disc itself, which cost 96 cents, so he asked the city to return the balance. The city refused, so Coulter took them to court. City leaders could have settled, but decided to fight. They lost. In the end, Bridgewater spent $17,500 on legal fees and Coulter's court costs...and still had to refund him his $4.04.

A KILLER MISTAKE. When U.S. Representative Michele Bachman kicked off her presidential campaign in 2011, she did so from Waterloo, Iowa. "John Wayne was from Waterloo," she boasted in her speech, "That's the kind of spirit that I have, too!" One problem: It was John Wayne *Gacy* who was from Waterloo—a serial killer who murdered 33 people. John Wayne the movie star was from another town on the other side of Iowa.

VOTE SHMOTE. Lisa Osborn of Burton, Michigan, lost her bid for a spot on the Board of Education by one vote—her own. Why? She attended her son's baseball game that day, and figured she had enough supporters to carry her in the election. She would have won with one more vote. "It was a dumb move," said Osborn.

THE GULLIBLE INTELLIGENCE AGENCY. Two years after the September 11, 2001, terror attacks, a 57-year-old software developer named Dennis Montgomery offered the CIA a way to catch al-Qaeda. He told them he'd developed computer software at his Reno, Nevada, company that could unscramble terrorist messages hidden among the pixels on Al Jazeera's news channel. The CIA awarded Montgomery $20 million in government contracts without even testing the software. It turned out to be completely bogus—Montgomery was simply a tech geek trying to con the government. He wasn't prosecuted, and all information regarding the incident has been classified to avoid any further embarrassment to the CIA.

Don't believe it? Count 'em: A 2-lb. bag of sugar contains about 5 million individual grains.

UNDERWEAR IN THE NEWS

*Let's face it: For those of us who don't go "commando," underwear
is a pretty important part of life. So it's understandable that
it would make headlines once in a while.*

BLUSHING BRIDE
In 2008 a New York woman named Sara Bostwick hired
the Christian Oth Studio to photograph her wedding.
Like a lot of brides, Bostwick wanted pictures of herself getting
ready for the big day, but she made it clear that she didn't want
any pictures taken of her in her underwear. When Bostwick
logged on to the studio's website to look at proofs of her pictures,
she was stunned to see that the photographer had ignored her
request and had indeed taken pictures of her in her underwear.
The pictures were on a password-protected part of the site, but
Bostwick had already given out the password to wedding guests.
She filed a lawsuit against the studio, claiming "severe emotional
injuries, including post-traumatic stress disorder." What happened? Bostwick lost—the judge ruled that while she may have
been embarrassed by friends and family seeing her in her underwear, the pain she experienced did not constitute "emotional
distress." Bostwick plans to appeal the ruling; a spokesperson for
the Christian Oth Studio retorted that Bostwick should have
looked at the photos before giving out her password.

A ROYAL PAIN
England's Queen Elizabeth II isn't the kind of person who has to
pack her own suitcases or do her laundry when travelling abroad,
but there may be times when she wishes she was. In December
2010, a Florida auction house announced that it was auctioning a
pair of lace undies that were left aboard an aircraft used by the
Queen when she visited Chile in 1968. The garment, mono-
grammed with an 'E' and a crown, somehow fell into the hands of
a Hungarian playboy named Baron Joseph de Bicske Dobronyi,
who kept them for more than 40 years. When he died in the sum-

How'd Jack Singer of Warwick, NY, celebrate his 10th birthday in 2010? By putting on...

mer of 2010, his heirs made plans to put the royal undies up for auction. At last report those plans were on hold, because "out of respect and courtesy for a person of such dignity and rank" as the queen, the British auctioneer wanted to wait a respectable interval after the wedding of Prince William and Kate Middleton before putting the royal knickers on the block. The opening bid is expected to be about $9,000, the same price that a pair of Queen Victoria's bloomers fetched at auction in 2008.

HAMBURGLAR

When some cash went missing from a McDonald's restaurant in Midwest City, Oklahoma, in the summer of 2010, the manager took a look at the surveillance camera footage to see if it could shed some light on what happened. The video showed a woman wearing a white Spanx stretch girdle over her face; she walked up to the unattended drive-thru window, reached in, took the money from the cash drawer, and walked off again. After the footage was shown on the local news, an anonymous tip led police to 51-year-old Sharon Lain, a former night manager at the restaurant. She admitted stealing the money to pay a water bill. "Fortunately," said Police Chief Brandon Clabes, "Ms. Lain's crime spree was very brief. No pun intended."

I'VE GOT A SECRET

In 2009 Koichi Wakata became the first Japanese astronaut to live on the International Space Station. Although few people knew it, he was making history of another kind as well: He went an entire month without changing his underwear, the longest voluntary stretch of underpants-wearing in the history of human spaceflight. Luckily for everyone else on the space station, these were no ordinary underpants. They were water-absorbing, antibacterial, odor-eliminating, quick-drying, flame-resistant, anti-static experimental "J-Wear," developed by JAXA, the Japanese space agency. They were designed to be worn by astronauts for weeks on end without causing discomfort to the wearer (or to others in the vicinity), and Wakata was assigned to put them through their paces. "I haven't talked about this underwear to my crew members," he admitted shortly before returning to Earth. "I wore them for about a month, and my crew members never complained, so I think the experiment went fine." (When 33 Chilean miners became trapped underground for 69 days after a 2010 mine accident, JAXA sent each of them five pairs of the underwear.)

ON THE LINE

In December 2010, a Japanese woman (unidentified in press reports) sued Google for 600,000 yen ($7,433), alleging "psychological distress" after the search-engine giant posted a picture of her underwear on Google Maps. She wasn't wearing it at the time—the underwear was hanging on a clothesline outside her apartment when the Google camera car drove by, snapping pictures for the company's Street View service. The woman found the picture while looking online for a view of her apartment. "I could understand if it was just a picture of the outside of the apartment, but showing a picture of underwear hanging outside is absolutely wrong," she told the court.

PANTY RAID

In the summer of 2010, the village of Portswood in southern England experienced a rash of underwear thefts. The heists occurred in a neighborhood popular with college students, and the thief showed a marked preference for young women's and children's underwear. Was a pervert on the loose? Were women and children in danger? Only if they were allergic to cats: The panty thief turned out to be Oscar, a stray cat taken in by Peter and Birgitt Weismantel, who volunteer as feline "foster parents" for a local cat charity. Oscar apparently liked his new foster home so much that he began stealing items from nearby homes and presenting them to the Weismantels as thank-you gifts. His 10-thefts-a-day habit was bad enough when he stole socks, garden gloves, and other random items, but when his focus narrowed to panties and children's underwear, the Weismantels notified police to allay any fears in the neighborhood that the culprit was human. And who says crime doesn't pay? Oscar's larceny has earned him a permanent spot in the Weismantel's home. "We can't give him back now. He makes such an effort with these gifts," Birgitt Weismantel told the *Southern Daily Echo*. "It's just so touching to see him come home every day with something for us." (At last report Oscar was still stealing away.)

I SPY...AT THE MOVIES

More fun in-jokes and cameos from the silver screen.

CHARLIE'S ANGELS (2000)

I Spy...E.T.'s living room

Where to Find It: Wearing nothing but a plastic blow-up swimming-pool toy, Dylan (Drew Barrymore) bursts into a house where two boys are playing a video game. It's the same house in Tujunga, California, that was used for *E.T. the Extra-Terrestrial*, the film that launched Barrymore's career in 1982. (To hammer the point home, the kids are eating Reese's Pieces and there's an *E.T.* poster on the wall.)

HALLOWEEN H20: 20 YEARS LATER (1998)

I Spy...several nods to *Psycho*

Where to Find Them: John Carpenter cast Jamie Lee Curtis in the original *Halloween* (1978) in part because she is Janet Leigh's daughter. Leigh, of course, appeared in Alfred Hitchcock's 1960 thriller *Psycho*. In this sixth sequel to *Halloween*, Carpenter cast Curtis along with Leigh herself, who plays Norma (a nod to Norman Bates) and drives the same 1957 Ford that she drove to the Bates Motel. The license plate on the car reads "NFB 418" (Bates's initials and birthday). When Norma drives away, you can hear a faint rendition of the screeching music from *Psycho*.

LAND OF THE DEAD (2005)

I Spy... Simon Pegg and Edgar Wright

Where to Find Them: In a photo booth. Director George A. Romero, who began the modern zombie craze with 1968's *Night of the Living Dead*, was so impressed with Pegg and Wright's 2004 zombie comedy *Shaun of the Dead* that he invited the British funnymen to make a cameo appearance as zombies in his latest movie. Pegg and Wright eagerly accepted.

First country to issue postage stamps: Great Britain, in 1840.

CIVIL WAR SIDENOTES

Everyone's familiar with the big stories of America's Civil War—Fort Sumter, Gettysburg, the Emancipation Proclamation, and so on. But a conflict that lasts four years, with more than 10,000 military engagements involving hundreds of thousands of people, is bound to yield a lot of little stories, too. Here are some you may not be familiar with.

PUSHING THE ENVELOPE

Most Americans don't know how close Floridians came to starting the Civil War. Upset by Lincoln's election in November 1860, Florida secessionists hatched plans to seize Fort Barrancas, near Pensacola, and use its weapons—13 large-caliber cannons and howitzers, and several smaller guns—against Union troops. The secessionists watched for communiqués from Washington, D.C., knowing that if the Federal commander received orders to move his troops, they had to strike, even if it meant war. But no such orders came, so they waited. The moment Florida seceded on January 10, 1861, Confederate forces stormed the fort. They found it abandoned—Federal forces had withdrawn their weapons by barge to Fort Pickens in Pensacola Harbor just two days earlier. How did the orders get through? They were sealed in a scented pink envelope and addressed by a female hand, and no Southern gentleman would open, much less read, a lady's love letter.

TURN THE OTHER CHEEK

Brigadier General Matt Ransom and 200 Confederate soldiers held a bridge on the Roanoke River against 5,000 Union soldiers. How did they do it? They battled "buck naked." When Federal scouts came out of the woods, hundreds of Rebs who'd been skinny dipping in the millpond grabbed their muskets—instead of their clothes—and came out shooting. The scouts were so flustered, they hightailed it back to the forest. Then they tried to skirt around behind the enemy, but the swampy area at the back of the pond proved too big an obstacle. The Union soldiers must have kept their eyes closed the entire time: They managed to hit only one of the "naked jaybirds," and according to reports, they never even saw the bridge they'd been sent to capture.

TRIGGERNOMETRY

Union Major General John Sedgwick was a good leader and beloved by his men (they called him "Uncle John"), but he was also a bullet magnet. He took one at Frayser's Farm and three at Antietam but kept on going. During the battle of Spotsylvania, near Fredericksburg, Virginia, his chief of staff told him to stay away from a certain section along the artillery battery because Confederate snipers had been taking potshots at every officer that showed himself along that line. Sedgwick laughed. The Rebs had to be a mile away—"They couldn't hit an elephant at this distance," he said. A minute later, a bullet whistled across the battery, and Sedgwick fell to the ground. The sniper had a British Whitworth rifle with a telescopic sight, accurate to 1,500 yards—about a mile. When they rolled Uncle John over, he was dead... but he still had a smile on his face.

ROLL OUT THE BARREL

After battles ended, Union and Confederate generals often exchanged prisoners of war. The exchange rate: 15 privates for one colonel. One such exchange included Union Major General George Stoneman and his staff. Colonel James Biddle, another Union P.O.W., had been cooking for the men, and put his name on the list of privates, calling himself "Chief Commissary." The ruse might have worked, but on the way to the exchange, Biddle was recognized by a Confederate officer, and the Union didn't have enough prisoners to exchange for a colonel. "We have been hammering at each other for a long time," Biddle pleaded. "Can't you help me out?" The Rebs decided to see if terms could be arranged. While Biddle stewed inside the train car, the two sides compared prison rolls. It seemed to take forever. But that was a good thing: The Union negotiators brought a barrel of whiskey with them. They tapped the keg and relaxed over a few drinks as they compared lists. Then they had a few more drinks and a few more, and compared lists again. In the end, Stoneman was able to get the colonel released. "Biddle," he confided, "to tell the truth, I believe you were exchanged for a keg of whiskey."

DRESS UNIFORM

According to reports in the *Louisville Daily Journal*, 21-year-old

Sue Mundy had a fair complexion, long dark hair, and a "beautiful mouth." But Mundy was no lady. In the final days of the Civil War, she led a band of Confederate raiders on a rampage across Kentucky. The *Journal* ran story after story about the desperate deeds of the female guerrilla and her gang, who, said the paper, burned railroad depots, robbed train passengers, attacked Federal wagon trains, and gunned down Yankee guards. On Sunday, March 12, 1865, fifty men from the 30th Wisconsin Volunteers, part of the Union's forces in Kentucky, finally put an end to Mundy's spree. Surrounded by troops, Sue fired with a revolver in each hand, wounding four soldiers, one fatally, but it was for naught. She was captured on Sunday, tried on Tuesday, and sentenced to hang on Wednesday. At the trial Mundy said, "I am not guilty of one-tenth of the outrages that have been charged" and blamed the *Journal* for exaggerating her exploits. Turns out the truth in this case was a mix of fact and fiction. The *Journal's* editor, George Prentice, did exaggerate Sue Mundy's deeds. He also invented the name "Sue Mundy" for the long-haired guerrilla. Reason: to embarrass the Union soldiers for being unable to catch a woman. So who was Sue Mundy who swung from the gallows? The notorious marauder's last act was to write a note to a sweetheart back in Bloomfield, Kentucky: *My dear, I do truly and fondly ever love you. I am ever and truly yours. M. Jerome Clarke.* Sue Mundy was a man.

CLASS WARFARE

According to historian James McPherson, West Point, the U.S. military academy on the banks of the Hudson River, produced "a band of brothers more tightly bonded than biological brothers." West Point graduates led troops in all 60 major battles of the Civil War. The only problem: In 55 of those battles, West Pointers faced each other across enemy lines. Stonewall Jackson (class of 1846) gained his nickname trouncing Irvin McDowell (class of '38) at Bull Run. George McClellan (class of '46) beat his old roommate A.P. Hill (class of '47) at Antietam—the two had once wooed the same girl. (McClellan won her, too.) After the war, Morris Schaff (class of '62) wrote, "West Point friendships did more at the close of the war than any other agency to heal the scars," starting with Robert E. Lee (class of '29), who surrendered to Ulysses S. Grant (class of '43) at Appomatox Court House.

THE DENNY'S STORY

It's an American institution—the diner that gave us "Moons Over My Hammy" and all-night road food (sometimes with a side of fistfight). Here's the story of the man behind Denny's...and his legacy.

COMFORT FOOD

Harold Butler's impact on the food business is huge. He did the same thing for the sit-down restaurant industry that Ray Kroc of McDonald's did for the fast food industry: Butler made it so you could go to a Denny's in, say, Florida and expect the exact same menu and service you'd receive at a Denny's in Oregon, or even Tokyo. Before the 1960s, that kind of consistency—at least when it came to dining out—was unheard of. But he didn't set out to change the way people eat. Not at first, anyway.

DOLLARS TO DONUTS

From an early age, Butler was known for his uncanny business sense. His first venture as a teenager in upstate New York in the 1930s: He sold maggots to fishermen for bait. Not long after, he started selling rejected buttons from his father's button company to tailors. He soon made enough to buy a boat, and started making loads more money taking tourists on boat rides. With those profits, Butler purchased a small shop in Rochester where he sold scrap wood. With the money he made from that venture, which was a lot, he bought a donut-making machine. By the time Butler was 21 years old, he'd already made his first million dollars.

However, along with that business sense came a penchant for taking *big* risks, and Butler soon lost it all in the stock market. Broke and embarrassed, about all he had left was his donut machine. He borrowed $2,000 from his uncle, loaded the machine in his car, and left snowy New York for sunny southern California.

MAKE ROOM FOR DANNY

Butler landed in Lakewood, just south of Los Angeles, in 1953, where he opened a small corner shop he called Danny's Donuts. Why not "Harold's" or "Butler's"? They didn't sound wholesome to

him. TV's Danny Thomas, the epitome of wholesome, was hugely popular, and "Danny's Donuts" had a nice ring to it.

Butler quickly made a name for himself with his jam-filled donuts and good coffee, which was so well received that a year later he changed the name to Danny's Coffee Shop. Business kept growing, and a year later he opened a second eatery, this one with breakfast and burgers added to the menu. That sparked a new name: Danny's Restaurant. The two spots became popular hang-outs in California in the 1950s, so Butler kept expanding. "After we opened our fifth restaurant," he later recalled, "I looked at all the traveling going on and said to myself, 'My God, this is the future.'" Butler's goal: to put a Danny's at nearly every freeway exit in the country. And each one had to be exactly like every other one.

By 1959 Butler owned 20 Danny's Restaurants when he was sued by a rival chain called Coffee Dan's for trademark infringement. Rather than fight to keep the name and risk brand confusion, Butler simply changed "Danny's" to "Denny's."

A BAD GAMBLE

Denny's began franchising in 1963 and went public three years later. By 1971 there were 800 restaurants, and with Butler serving as chairman, his future with the company looked bright. But once again, his penchant for risk-taking got him into trouble: He tried to buy Caesars Palace in Las Vegas to create a Denny's-themed casino. After he made an offer to the owners in private that was better than the offer he'd made in public, the U.S. Securities and Exchange Commission launched a fraud investigation. The deal fell through and the board of directors forced Butler out. Just like that, his tenure with Denny's had come to an end.

ORDER UP

Butler never stopped running restaurant chains—Hershel's Delis, JoJo's, and Naugles, to name a few. But none of them ever became as popular as Denny's or its signature item, the Grand Slam Breakfast, introduced in 1977. Now owned by South Carolina-based Advantica Restaurant Group, there are 1,600 Denny's worldwide.

Butler died in 1997 in the Mexican town of La Paz in Baja California where, of course, he owned a restaurant. As he always said, "I just love to feed people."

DELUSIONS OF GRANDEUR

Dictators give themselves long, flowery titles describing their amazing greatness. (All hail Uncle John, Lord of Porcelain and Grand Master of Flushery!)

Dictator: Jean-Bédel Bokassa
Position: President of the Central African Republic (1966–76), Emperor of Central Africa (1976–79)
Official Title: "His Imperial Majesty, Bokassa the First, Emperor of Central Africa by the will of the Central African people, united within the national political party, the Movement for the Social Evolution of Black Africa"

Dictator: Enver Hoxha
Position: Secretary of the Albanian Labour Party (1941–85)
Official Title: "Comrade-Chairman-Prime Minister-Foreign Minister-Minister of War and Commander-in-Chief of the People's Army"

Dictator: Idi Amin
Position: President of Uganda (1971–79)
Official Title: "His Excellency President for Life, Field Marshal Al Hadji Doctor Idi Amin Dada, VC, DSO, MC, Lord of the Beasts of the Earth and Fishes of the Sea and Conqueror of the British Empire in Africa in General and Uganda in Particular and the Most Ubiquitous of all King of Scotland dictators"

Dictator: Francisco Macias Nguema
Position: President of Equatorial Guinea (1968–79)
Official Title: "Unique Miracle, Grand Master of Education, Science, and Culture"

Dictator: Teodoro Obiang Nguema Mbasogo
Position: President of Equatorial Guinea (1979–present)

East African leopards' spots are in a circular pattern. South African leopards: square pattern.

Official Title: "Gentleman of the Great Island of Bioko, Annobón and Río Muni"
Dictator: Joseph-Désiré Mobutu
Position: President of Zaire (1965–97)
Official title: "Mobutu Sese Seko," which means, "The all-powerful warrior who, because of his endurance and inflexible will to win, will go from conquest to conquest, leaving fire in his wake."

Dictator: Yahya Jammeh
Position: President of Gambia (1994–present)
Official Title: "His Excellency the President Sheikh Professor al-Haji Doctor Yahya Abdul-Azziz Jemus Junkung Jammeh Naasiru Deen"

Dictator: Muammar al-Gaddafi
Position: President of Libya (1969–2011)
Official Title: "Brother Leader, Guide of the First of September Great Revolution of the Socialist People's Libyan Arab Jamahiriya"

Dictator: Kim Jong-Il
Position: Supreme Leader of North Korea (1994–present)
Official Titles: North Korea's state-controlled media are (big surprise) extremely gracious toward Kim. They most commonly refer to him to as "Great Leader," but other titles seen in print include:
• "Dear Leader, who is a perfect incarnation of the appearance that a leader should have"
• "Sun of the Communist Future"
• "Shining Star of Paektu Mountain"
• "Guarantee of the Fatherland's Unification"
• "Invincible and Iron-Willed Commander"
• "Glorious General, Who Descended From Heaven"
• "Guiding Star of the 21st Century"
• "Highest Incarnation of the Revolutionary Comradely Love"

How much did you buy? Last year, Americans spent more than $300 million on lip color.

MIND YOUR ZARFS AND WAMBLES

*These are all real words. Your mission: Guess which is
the real definition. The answers are on page 542.*

1. FERRULE
a) the edible casing into which ground sausage is stuffed
b) the metal band on a pencil that holds the eraser in place
c) the uppermost window in a church steeple
d) a black spot on a dog's tongue

2. PURLICUE
a) a fashionable bonnet worn by sows at agricultural fairs
b) the special pocket on a soccer referee's uniform where the red
and yellow cards are kept
c) the space between the extended forefinger and thumb
d) a trick question that college professors add to exams to test
students' critical thinking skills

3. ZARF
a) the thick trail of hair some men have that extends from the top
of the neck down to the upper back
b) a holder, usually made of ornamental metal, for a coffee cup
without a handle
c) legal slang for a defendant who wishes to plead insanity believing that he or she is not insane—when in fact he or she is
d) a barbed hunting spear used by some Australian aborigines

4. ROWEL
a) the spinning metal star on the back of a cowboy's spur
b) a beaded seat cover primarily used by cab drivers
c) a political advertisement designed to create suspicion about the
candidate's opponent
d) an aftershock of an aftershock of an earthquake

Andrew Jackson's first official act as president: ordering spittoons for the White House.

5. CHANKING

a) the noises made by a locomotive coming to a stop
b) the unsettling feeling of having done something embarrassing (like picking your nose) and then realizing that someone saw you
c) food that is, by necessity, spat out, such as rinds, seeds, or pits
d) a grammar term inspired by fictional detective Charlie Chan that refers to speaking without articles such as "a" and "the"

6. WAMBLE

a) a donkey's gait
b) a stomach's rumble
c) a bulldozer's dashboard
d) a talk-show host's final thoughts

7. LIRIPIPE

a) a ceremonial American Indian hookah used to mark the passage of an elder into the next plane of existence
b) the lever that a school bus driver uses to open the bus door
c) a philosophical argument in which neither side can win because there is no way either side can prove their point
d) the tassel on the hat that a graduate wears

8. MACARISM

a) the act of taking pleasure in someone else's happiness
b) a classical music piece arranged for bluegrass instruments
c) a fungal infection that causes tiny lacerations to form inside the ear canal
d) a humpback whale's call, as it is heard from the deck of a ship

9. SOCKDOLAGER

a) the small tab at the end of the security sticker on a CD, DVD, or Blu-Ray case
b) a real knockout blow, or an otherwise decisive answer
c) the decorative tail at the end of a letterform that swoops back and underlines the entire word
d) a cocktail made of gin, vermouth, and human tears

The tallest volcano on Mars is 17 miles high—that's 84 times taller than the Eiffel Tower.

FIVE ODD FOODS

What they are, where they came from, and why
you might (or might not) want to eat them.

SQUEAKY CHEESE

According to legend, cheese was discovered thousands of years ago by a Middle Eastern nomad who poured milk into his saddlebag, which was probably made from an animal's stomach and contained traces of the coagulating enzyme *rennin*. The combination of the rennin and the desert heat curdled the milk into two parts: clotted solids and cloudy liquid. The solids, when separated from the liquid *whey*, are the cheese curds. At that point, they can be formed into blocks or balls and aged to make cheese, or eaten as-is. If they're not pressed into blocks or balls, the air trapped inside the rubbery curds creates a distinctive "squeak" when bitten, so they're sometimes marketed as "squeaky cheese." In Wisconsin (the world's top cheese curd manufacturer) and other parts of the Midwest, they're often battered and deep-fried, and served as a snack or side dish. And in Canada they're used in *poutine*: French fries topped with cheese curds and brown gravy.

BUBBLE TEA

If you live in a city or college town, bubble tea may not seem so unusual anymore: Shops selling the drink have been popping up all over North America since the 1990s. Also called pearl milk tea or boba tea, it's is basically a mixture of instant black, red, or green tea, fruit flavoring, and creamer (dairy or non-dairy), into which a generous handful of "boba balls" are dropped. The bobas (corrupted into English as "bubbles") make the drink chewy. About a quarter-inch in diameter, they're made from a gummy blend of tapioca and seaweed powder. Alone, the bobas pack about 2 calories each, but a pint of bubble tea is around 300 calories. Invented in the 1980s in Taiwan, the drink spread through Asia, and then to every city in the world with an Asian population. It's usually served in a disposable cup with a clear plastic lid—and an industrial-size straw to accommodate the passing of the bulbous bobas.

Nauseous by nature: About 3 lbs. of your body weight is bacteria and parasites.

GEODUCK

Pronounced "gooey duck," this is the world's largest burrowing clam. Sometimes called a "mud duck" or "king clam," it gets its name from a Native American word meaning "dig deep." (Alternate spellings: *gweduc*, *geoduc*, and *guiduch*.) Geoducks live in the sandy beaches off the Pacific Northwest, feeding on the plankton and algae that wash over them. The clam's most notable feature: its protruding *siphon*, which can be more than three feet long. This part of the geoduck is soft, fatty, and especially chewy, so it's often deep-fried. True to their Indian name, geoducks burrow far below the surface and have to be removed from the sand with manually operated water jets. The wholesale price of about $15 per pound reflects the difficulty of digging them up. The delicacy is especially popular in Asia, where it's served boiled, stir-fried or raw, sashimi style.

MOCHI

This paste made of glutinous rice is eaten year-round in Asia, but is traditionally most popular during the Japanese New Year. In fact, *mochi*-pounding, or *mochitsuki*, is one of the biggest events of the New Year's celebration. Here's how it's made: Sweetened rice is soaked overnight, then cooked and pounded with wooden mallets into a sticky, elastic heap. Then it's hand rolled into small balls and formed into shapes. Although it's commonly baked like pastry and eaten as a snack, or used in savory dishes (often roasted and added to soups and noodles, for example), in the United States it's most often served as a pastry-like shell filled with ice cream and sold frozen. First mass-produced by the Japanese food conglomerate Lotte in 1981, mochi ice cream has become increasingly popular in the West—pastel-tinted shells about the size of a small hen's egg, filled with vanilla, strawberry, *adzuki* (red bean), or *matcha* (green tea) ice cream.

CODFISH SPERM SOUP

You read that right. This Japanese delicacy, also known as cod's milk soup, is composed primarily of the sperm of the cod fish. It can be served raw on a plate or heated in a bowl. (Warm, it has about the same consistency as clam chowder.) Its Japanese name, *shirako*, means "white children."

CROSS THAT BRIDGE

*Random facts about something you never think
about…until you have to cross a river.*

• Three types of bridges: a beam bridge (a single beam, like a log over a brook), an arch bridge (the arch is below the roadway), and a suspension bridge (the road deck is hung on cables suspended from towers).

• Oldest bridge still in use in the United States: the stone Frankford Avenue Bridge in Philadelphia. It was built for horse traffic in 1697; it's used for car traffic today.

• Japan's Akashi-Kaikyo Bridge is the world's longest cable suspension bridge. It took 10 years to build (at a cost of $6 billion) and has the world's highest toll: $29.

• Contrary to popular belief, covered bridges weren't covered to protect travelers from the weather. Most covered bridges were built out of wood. The purpose of the roof was to protect the wooden deck from the elements.

• World's busiest bridge: India's Howrah Bridge near Kolkata (Calcutta). A million travelers walk across it daily.

• World's saddest bridge: San Francisco's Golden Gate Bridge. To date, more than 1,400 people have plunged to their deaths from it.

• *Gephyrophobia* is the fear of crossing bridges.

• The Maryland Transportation Authority, which operates the four-mile Chesapeake Bay Bridge, offers a service for gephyrophobes: They'll arrange for someone to drive you (and your car) over it for you.

• The longest bridge in the world is the Danyang-Kunshan Grand Bridge, linking Shanghai and Nanjing in East China. The bridge is 102 miles long and almost a football field wide (260 feet). It runs mostly over land and was built to accommodate high-speed trains.

• A week after the Brooklyn Bridge opened in May 1883, a panicked pedestrian shouted out that the bridge was collapsing. Hundreds of people on the bridge also panicked and fled, trampling 15 pedestrians to death.

Giant tortoises never stop growing.

HE SAID...

Men think they're sooooo funny.

"Men are superior to women. For one thing, men can urinate from a speeding car."

—**Will Durst**

"Women want to fight men for equal pay, but how often do they fight a man for the check?"

—**Bill Maher**

"Women exist in the main solely for the propagation of the species."

—**Arthur Schopenhauer**

"Charity is taking an ugly girl to lunch."

—**Warren Beatty**

"I don't think a prostitute is more moral than a wife, but they are doing the same thing."

—**Prince Philip**

"Henry VIII didn't get divorced, he just had his wives' heads chopped off when he got tired of them. That's a good way to get rid of a woman—no alimony."

—**Ted Turner**

"I hate pants. Neither my mother nor my wife is allowed to go out with me in pants."

—**Arnold Schwarzenegger**

"Marriage is the most expensive way for the average man to get laundry done."

—**Burt Reynolds**

"May there never be in my home a woman who knows more than a woman ought to know."

—**Euripides**

"I listen to feminists and all these radical gals. These women just need a man in the house to tell them what time of day it is and to lead them home."

—**Jerry Falwell**

"I love the women's movement, especially when I'm walking behind it."

—**Rush Limbaugh**

"Woman inspires us to great things, and prevents us from achieving them."

—**Alexandre Dumas**

Bee-bee boomers: Honeybees can be trained to detect explosives.

SHE SAID...

Women think they're sooooo smart.

"Men should be like Kleenex: soft, strong, disposable."
—Cher

"Don't accept rides from strange men—and remember that all men are as strange as hell."
—Robin Morgan

"Men are beasts, and even beasts don't behave as they do."
—Brigitte Bardot

"If life is to survive on this planet, there must be a decontamination of the Earth. I think this will be accompanied by an evolutionary process that will result in a drastic reduction of the population of males."
—Mary Daly

"Behind every successful man is a surprised woman."
—Maryon Pearson

"The male function is to produce sperm. We now have sperm banks."
—Valerie Solanas

"The male is a domestic animal which, if treated with firmness...can be trained to do most things."
—Jilly Cooper

"Men know everything—all of them, all the time—no matter how stupid or inexperienced or ignorant they are."
—Andrea Dworkin

"If men can run the world, why can't they stop wearing neckties? How intelligent is it to start the day by tying a little noose around your neck?"
—Linda Ellerbee

"A man's home may seem to be castle on the outside. Inside it is more often his nursery."
—Claire Booth Luce

"Men think monogamy is something you make dining tables out of."
—Kathy Lette

"A man is like sitting in a bathtub. Once you get used to him, he's not so hot."
—Kathryn Maye

THAT SMARTS!

According to the latest research, you may
not be as smart as you think you are.

SUPERIORITY COMPLEX
"One of the painful things about our time," observed 20th-century philosopher Bertrand Russell, "is that those who feel certainty are stupid and those with any imagination and understanding are filled with doubt and indecision." In 1999 Justin Kruger and David Dunning, two professors at Cornell University, became intrigued by this paradox. They took a personal and professional interest in the topic after running across a survey of fellow college professors. The survey's finding: 94 percent believed they were "above average" when compared with their peers. (Statistically speaking, no more than half of any group can be above average.) Dunning and Kruger decided to test how some people—and often the wrong ones—arrive at a wildly inflated view of their own abilities.

YOU HAVE BEEN TESTED...AND FOUND WANTING
Dunning and Kruger started small with a sample that could be easily measured. They cornered Cornell students as they walked out of a class in which they'd just taken a test and asked them to estimate how well they'd scored and to what degree they felt they'd mastered the course material. When the professors compared the actual scores to the students' predictions, they were floored. Not only had the lowest-performing students believed they'd done better than they actually had, they vastly overestimated themselves. In fact, those who had scored in the 12th percentile (that is, lower than 88 percent of their fellow students) believed they'd scored in the 60*th* percentile and beaten out nearly two-thirds of their classmates.

Just as surprising, though, was that those who did the best *under*estimated how well they'd done. They weren't as far off as their underachieving counterparts, but they knocked as much as 20 percentage points off their scores. It turned out that *all* of the groups thought they ranked in the range of the 60th to 70th percentile.

Matt Damon refused to be involved in the *Bourne Conspiracy* video game. (It was too violent.)

I CAN DO ANYTHING YOU CAN DO BETTER

When Dunning and Kruger interviewed the students in depth, they discovered that those who were the least competent at mastering the subject matter were also the least able to define what it meant to be competent in a given subject. Judging their own performances without understanding the criteria for success, they had no idea how profoundly they'd missed the mark.

But then why did the successful test takers underestimate their abilities? Well, it turned out that it wasn't a matter of not recognizing what success looked like. Instead, they were tripped up by assuming that other students were in their league.

The two professors wondered if this perception/performance gap was unusually wide only among students, who might not have as much life experience as older adults, or if there was any chance they'd find it in other ages and situations as well. So they began testing other people on a variety of skills: the ability to think logically, for example, or the ability to judge how funny a joke would be to an audience. In almost every case, they found that the least competent people overestimated their abilities by 40 to 50 percentage points.

This same principle tended to hold true in a variety of ages and situations, including sports and games such as tennis and chess, but most alarmingly in life-or-death skills like driving, medical proficiency, and laboratory work. They also identified a dynamic that allowed bad performers to remain bad: The less-talented are convinced they're above average, so they tend to rest on their non-existent laurels instead of working toward a higher level of competence.

There is hope, however. The researchers discovered that when the least-knowledgeable groups were taught what was considered "competent" in their field, they became substantially better at judging their abilities compared to others'. So, ironically, the smarter people became, the lower their self-regard became. The truth might hurt, but it can also set you free.

THE GRAND ILLUSION

Similar to the Dunning-Kruger effect is the "illusory superiority effect," a delusion that leads large numbers of people to believe they're above average. And it shows up in survey after survey.

• For example, 68 percent of University of Nebraska faculty believed themselves not only above average, but in the *top 25 percent* of the teaching profession.

• At high-octane Stanford University, 87 percent of the students believed that they were above the general population average *and* better than the typical Stanford student.

• According to a College Board survey of more than a million students, 70 percent believed they were made of superior leadership material. A whopping 85 percent believed that they were better than average at getting along with others, with 25 percent saying they were in the top 1 percent.

• When estimating their own IQ, men and women guess wrong by the same average amount—five points. However, there's one crucial difference: On average, men tend to *overestimate* their IQ by five points, while women tend to *underestimate* by the same amount.

• It also turns out that North Americans are the group most susceptible to this false sense of superiority. Studies of East Asians found that the majority *underestimate* their abilities, which spurs them toward continuous self-improvement. And when Swedes and Americans were asked the same questions about their driving abilities, 69% of the Swedes believed they had above-average driving abilities compared to 93% of the Americans.

SMARTY PANTS

Illusory superiority is also known in the field as "the Lake Wobegon effect," which refers to Garrison Keillor's sign-off to *A Prairie Home Companion*, a radio program that features monologues about his fictional hometown of Lake Wobegon, where "all of the children are above average."

Luckily, *we* can't possibly be that deluded, right?

*　　*　　*

"Relax. What is mind? No matter. What is matter? Never mind!"
—**Homer Simpson**

During the Alaskan gold rush, potatoes were worth their weight in gold.

RANDOM BITS ON MICHAEL JACKSON HITS

*If you find this page bad and not a thriller, Uncle John
respectfully suggests that you beat it.*

"You Are Not Alone": Released in 1995, it was the first song
ever to debut at #1 on the Billboard Hot 100 chart.

"Scream": Jackson was a devout Jehovah's Witness and steadfastly
refused to use profanity. "Scream," a duet with his sister Janet
Jackson, is the only time he ever swore in a song: "Just stop messing with me / just stop f***ing with me / make me want to scream."

"Thriller": Horror movie legend Vincent Price recorded his spo-
ken-word interlude in just two takes. Songwriter Rod Temperton
wrote it in a taxi on the way to Price's recording session.

"Bad": Jackson planned it as a duet with Prince. Prince backed
out over lyrical content. (He was reportedly uncomfortable with
the song's first line, "Your butt is mine.")

"I Just Can't Stop Loving You": Another duet for the *Bad*
album, which Jackson wrote to perform with Whitney Houston.
She had recorded three hit duets with Jackson's brother Jermaine,
but turned this one down. So did Barbra Streisand. Who got the
gig? An unknown backup singer named Siedah Garrett, who also
co-wrote "Man in the Mirror" with Jackson.

"Wanna Be Startin' Something": Jackson was sued for stealing
the song's African-influenced chorus from the 1972 landmark
disco song "Soul Makossa" by Cameroonian saxophonist Manu
Dibango. (They settled out of court.)

"Beat It": Eddie Van Halen played the song's guitar solo as a
favor to producer Quincy Jones. He was uncredited and unpaid
for his work, apart from the two six-packs of beer Jones gave him
during the recording session.

What's *rhinorrhea*? The medical term for snot. (What's *rhinorhinorrhea*? Rhino snot.)

JUST PLANE WEIRD: BATHROOM EDITION

If you happen to be reading this page in an airplane restroom, you might want to save it for when you're in a bathroom on the ground.

MUCH BETTER NOW, THANKS

Not long after the Air Antilles flight lifted off from the Caribbean island of Guadeloupe bound for St. Martin in March 2011, one of the passengers complained of feeling ill and spent the rest of the flight in the bathroom. When the plane was about to land, he asked for an ambulance to meet him at the airport. The plane landed, the ambulance pulled up…and the man said he suddenly felt better and didn't need medical assistance after all. He walked out of the airport, bypassing all the usual security and immigration checks, and disappeared. The first sign that something was amiss came when airplane cleaners found a bundle of money in the bathroom; the second sign came when one of the other passengers, a Brink's guard transporting $1.6 million in cash (stored in a cargo hold next to the bathroom), noticed that some of it was missing. The "sick" man had spent the entire flight taking apart the bathroom to get to the cash, and had walked off the plane $238,000 richer. He hasn't been seen since.

A BATHROOM BREAK TO REMEMBER

In May 2010, an Air India Express 737 was flying from Dubai to India when the pilot left the cabin for a bathroom break. While he was gone, the co-pilot tried to adjust his seat. In the process he accidentally struck the control column and sent the plane into a steep dive. The panicked co-pilot couldn't pull the plane out of the dive. Not only that—he couldn't unlock the cockpit door to let the pilot back in, so that *he* could pull the plane out of the dive. The pilot gained access by entering an emergency code, and then saved the plane. ("We hit an air pocket," he told the terrified passengers.) An investigation later determined that had the pilot not taken control when he did, the plane likely would have broken apart in midair.

Theory of Relativity fact: Clocks run slightly faster on mountaintops than at sea level.

PRE-FLIGHT PIT STOP

In January 2009, two Southwest Airlines passengers were going through security at Ohio's Port Columbus Airport when they noticed that the pilot just ahead of them "looked and smelled drunk." Worried that he might be *their* pilot (he wasn't), they confronted him—and he ran off. A few minutes later, airport police found him hiding in an airport bathroom. By then he'd already ditched his pilot's uniform and called in sick from inside the bathroom. Too late. Southwest suspended him with pay and launched an investigation into the incident. (The pilot admitted to police that he'd "partied hard" in his hotel room the night before, but said he had not had anything to drink that morning.)

BREATHLESS

In February 2011, the Federal Aviation Agency ordered every U.S. airline to dismantle the oxygen generators (those things that drop out of the ceiling if the plane loses cabin pressure) in airplane bathrooms. Apparently, the government is worried that terrorists might be able to use the equipment to start a fire or set off a bomb in the bathroom. So are you doomed if the plane loses pressure while you're on the pot? No, but you may be embarrassed: As soon as the flight attendants put on their own oxygen masks, they will unlock the bathrooms and pass bottles of oxygen in to anyone caught with their pants down. The FAA is working with airplane manufacturers to come up with a safer oxygen system…just for bathrooms.

COOKIE MONSTER

A San Francisco man named Kinman Chan was on a flight from Philadelphia to Los Angeles in early 2010 when he locked himself in the bathroom and started screaming. When he came out of the bathroom (with his pants around his ankles) he elbowed a flight attendant. Bad move: She was a black belt in tae kwon do. She restrained Chan in a choke hold and then handcuffed him for the rest of the flight. The plane was diverted to Pittsburgh and Chan was turned over to the FBI. He blames his bizarre behavior on the marijuana cookies he eats to treat a medical condition. "Chan advised me he has a medical marijuana card and he took double his normal dose," an FBI agent noted in an affidavit.

There's enough copper on the roof of Arizona's capitol building to make 4.8 million pennies.

NAKED NEWS

All the nudes that's fit to print.

In the Ruff. Streaking was a strange fad in the '70s. Naked, running people interrupted all sorts of things, from the 1975 Academy Awards to football, baseball, and basketball games. In 2010, Mark Roberts of Liverpool, England, became the first person to streak a dog show. He showed up at the 2010 Crufts Dog Show in Birmingham, England wearing nothing but a cat face painted over his private parts. Roberts had previously streaked a benefit for poor children and a morning TV weather report.

Just the Facts, Ma'am. Fort Pierce, Florida, police pulled over Ellena Lucia Barron late one night in 2009 for a routine traffic stop. Barron had nothing to hide and wasn't carrying anything illegal, but she still panicked. She told the officer she had to get something out of her trunk, and emerged from the car with her shirt off. "I thought that's what you wanted to see," Barron told the officer. He didn't. She was charged with indecent exposure.

Flash 'n' Splash. In 2010 Melanie King and Annie Januszewski set out to beat the two-woman transatlantic rowing record from Europe to the West Indies. The record is 75 days, but they thought they could shave time off through improved aerodynamics—by being totally nude for the whole trip. Januszewski and King did complete the trip nude…but it took them 77 days.

Poopy Excuse. David Napodano of Lehich Acres, Florida, was arrested in 2009 for exposing himself to two women in a grocery store parking lot. Creepy? Yes, but he had an excuse: Napodano told police that he was standing in the parking lot naked because he'd had a bout of "explosive diarrhea" and had used his underwear to clean himself up. (That actually makes it creepier.)

Clothes Call. Julia Laack was accused of shoplifting a lighter and some beef jerky from a Sheboygan, Wisconsin, convenience store. When police went to Laack's home, she took off all of her clothes and, while naked, tried to attack them. Laack later explained that she thought that "a naked person can't be arrested."

FAMOUS FOR HOW THEY DIED

What if the most interesting thing that ever happened to you was the last thing that ever happened to you? That was the case for these people.

SIR ARTHUR ASTON (1590–1649)

Who He Was: A British army officer who sided with the losing Royalist forces of King Charles I in the English Civil War

How He Died: Beaten to death with a wooden leg

Details: In 1649 Aston was the governor of Drogheda, a walled town on the east coast of Ireland that was one of the last Royalist strongholds. That September, Oliver Cromwell, leader of the opposing Parliamentarian forces, arrived with superior numbers. After blasting two openings in the wall, Cromwell offered Aston and his garrison of 3,000 men the chance to surrender without further bloodshed. Aston refused, and Cromwell stormed the town. On his orders, the entire garrison was put to death, including Aston, who, rumor had it, had gold coins hidden inside his wooden leg. Cromwell's soldiers searched the leg, and when they found no gold, they beat Aston to death with it.

LEN KOENECKE (1904–35)

Who He Was: An outfielder for the New York Giants and the Brooklyn Dodgers in the early 1930s

How He Died: Extinguished in mid-air

Details: Koenecke had a good year in 1934 but slipped badly in 1935 when both his playing and his drinking became erratic. Dodgers manager Casey Stengel cut him from the team in the middle of a road trip through the Midwest. On the American Airlines flight home to New York, Koenecke downed a quart of whiskey, then fought with another passenger and had to be restrained by the co-pilot. Thrown off the flight when it stopped in Detroit, he chartered a small plane to fly him to Buffalo. He was drunk on that flight too, and after the pilot refused his request to perform aerial stunts, Koenecke grabbed for the controls and tried to crash the plane. The pilot and the one other passenger battled Koenecke for about 15 minutes before the pilot finally knocked him senseless by bashing him repeatedly over the head with the plane's fire extinguisher. By the time the plane made an emergency landing on a racetrack outside of Toronto, Koenecke was dead from his injuries.

FRANK HAYES (1888–1923)

Who He Was: An American jockey in the early 1920s
How He Died: Crossing the finish line
Details: On February 27, 1923, Hayes and his horse, Sweet Kiss, were a 20-to-1 long shot in a race at New York's Belmont Park. Good news: Hayes won. Bad news: When the owner ran over to congratulate him, Hayes was dead, killed by a heart attack. Only the reins and stirrups had kept him from falling off the horse. Some bookies balked at paying off on a race won by a dead man, but the rules made no mention of the winning jockey having to be alive at the end of the race, so the bets were paid in full.

BRIAN WELLS (1956–2003)

Who He Was: A pizza delivery man from Erie, Pennsylvania
How He Died: Killed by a time bomb
Details: On August 28, 2003, Wells robbed a bank in Erie. This was no ordinary heist: Wells had a bulky metal object shackled to his neck, and when police caught up with him a short time later, he told them the device was a time bomb that three assailants had attached to his neck a few hours earlier, after luring him to a remote area to deliver some pizzas. The assailants gave him a list of tasks to complete (including robbing the bank), and warned him that if he didn't finish in time, the bomb would go off. Wells was waiting for the bomb squad to arrive when the device exploded, killing him. His story was profiled on *America's Most Wanted* three times. The mystery remained unsolved for nearly four years. Then in 2007, two of Wells's associates, Marjorie Diehl-Armstrong, 58, and Kenneth Barnes, 53, were arrested and charged with involvement in the incident. Wells was named as an "unindicted co-conspirator" in the plot that resulted in his own murder. Prosecutors allege that he was in on the scheme, but

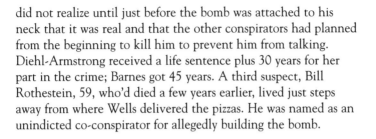

did not realize until just before the bomb was attached to his neck that it was real and that the other conspirators had planned from the beginning to kill him to prevent him from talking. Diehl-Armstrong received a life sentence plus 30 years for her part in the crime; Barnes got 45 years. A third suspect, Bill Rothestein, 59, who'd died a few years earlier, lived just steps away from where Wells delivered the pizzas. He was named as an unindicted co-conspirator for allegedly building the bomb.

THE JAMES ROBINSON & CO. CIRCUS BAND (1870)

Who They Were: Musicians traveling with the circus

How They Died: Eaten by lions

Details: As the circus was pulling into Middletown, Missouri, the management told the band to climb on top of the horse-drawn lion wagon and perform there as the circus paraded through town. The bandleader complained that the roof wasn't strong enough to support the weight of 10 musicians, but he lost the argument, and the band climbed up to the roof and began to play. As the wagon turned a corner on its way through town, the driver tangled the reins, sending the horses into a gallop. They pulled the wagon to the side of the road, where it crashed into a large rock. The impact caused the roof to collapse, dumping the musicians on top of the lions. Three musicians were killed and four were badly mauled before bystanders pulled the survivors to safety.

SIGURD THE MIGHTY (9th century)

Who He Was: Ruler of the Viking settlement on the Orkney Islands off the northern coast of Scotland

How He Died: Bad karma and bad teeth—not *his* bad teeth, but bad teeth just the same

Details: In 892 Sigurd challenged his enemy, Máel Brigte the Bucktoothed, to a battle limited to 40 men on each side. Sigurd then brought 80 of his own men to the fight and won handily. His victory was short-lived, though: Claiming the dead Máel Brigte's head as a war trophy, Sigurd fastened it to his saddle with the buckteeth facing inward, toward him. On the ride home the teeth scraped repeatedly against his leg, giving him a nasty gash that got infected and killed him a few weeks later.

HAIL TO YOUR CHIEF

*Regardless of what Americans think about them or what
history books say about them, some presidents are
beloved in surprising places overseas.*

President: Rutherford B. Hayes (1877–81)
Popular in: Paraguay
Story: Hayes is one of the more obscure U.S. presidents,
most often cited in history books for the 1876 election that
brought him to the Oval Office, in which his opponent, Samuel
Tilden, actually won the popular vote. President Hayes's foreign
policy mainly had to do with South America. From 1864 to 1870,
most of the continent was involved in the War of the Triple
Alliance, in which Argentina and Brazil (along with Uruguay)
fought tiny Paraguay over ownership of two regions of land, including one inside Paraguay named Gran Chaco. Most of Paraguay's
adult male population died during the war, which Argentina and
Brazil ultimately won. Those countries negotiated for years on how
to properly divide up Gran Chaco, but all talks ended in stalemate,
and the issue was still unresolved when Hayes took office in 1877.
Hayes volunteered to arbitrate the conflict, and he came up with a
plan that essentially negated the bloody War of the Triple
Alliance: He awarded Gran Chaco back to Paraguay.
Hail to the Chief! Paraguay showed its appreciation when, in
making Gran Chaco a state, it named part of the region Department Presidente Hayes. The region's capital city, formerly the
Argentine-occupied Villa Argentina, was renamed Villa Hayes.

President: Woodrow Wilson (1913–21)
Popular in: Czech Republic
Story: The countries that are now the Czech Republic and Slova-
kia were part of the Austro-Hungarian Empire in the late 1800s.
An independence movement began in the 1880s, led by Czech
activist Tomas Masaryk, who was elected to represent the region
in the empire's parliament in 1891. He advocated for Czech and
Slovakian independence for years, but got nowhere until after
World War I, when the Allied forces of England, France, Russia,

---

Only two women in *Rolling Stone's* 100 Greatest Guitarists list: Joan Jett & Joni Mitchell.

and Italy defeated the Austro-Hungarians, and the empire was dissolved. In 1918 President Woodrow Wilson invited Masayrk to come to the White House and discuss an independent Czechoslovakia. After a meeting that lasted just under an hour, Wilson publicly called for independence for Czechoslovakia. Result: When the Versailles Treaty divvied up Europe, Czechoslovakia became an independent nation.

Hail to the Chief! The Czechs showed their appreciation by renaming Prague's main railway station Wilsonovo nádraží (Wilson Station) in 1919 and erecting a statue of Wilson there in 1928. The statue was destroyed by the Nazis during World War II; the train station was renamed in 1953, during the Soviet occupation.

President: Franklin D. Roosevelt (1933–45)

Popular in: Norway

Story: *Time* magazine reporter Leland Stowe was on assignment in Oslo, Norway, on April 22, 1940, the day the Nazis invaded the city. As German troops marched through the streets, Norwegian citizens looked on, shocked and horrified. Stowe misinterpreted their reaction as indifference and wrote an editorial (widely reprinted) decrying Norway for its reluctance to fight back. Result: a growing anti-Norwegian sentiment in the United States. In September 1942, the U.S. Navy gave the ship the *King Haakon VII* to Norway for the war effort. Roosevelt spoke at the event at the Washington Navy Yard, calling attention to the active Norwegian Resistance and other anti-Hitler forces in the country. Roosevelt remarked: "If there is anyone who still wonders why this war is being fought, let him look to Norway. If there is anyone who doubts the democratic will to win, again I say, let him look to Norway."

Hail to the Chief! Norway showed its appreciation by erecting a statue of Roosevelt in Oslo, where it still overlooks the town hall and the Nobel Peace Centre.

*　　*　　*

"We forfeit three-fourths of ourselves to be like other people."

—**Arthur Schopenhauer**

Did they forget the words? Mountain lions whistle.

ODD BASEBALL STORIES

*Why is baseball our favorite sport? Because
it's full of oddball stuff like this.*

FOUL PLAY

September 19, 1940: Luke Appling of the White Sox was batting against Red Ruffing of the Yankees with two men on base. Appling fouled off the first pitch. Then he fouled off the second, third, and fourth pitches before taking pitch #5 for a ball. Then he fouled off the next six pitches before taking the 12th pitch for a ball, making the count two balls and two strikes. Ruffing was getting ruffled. He threw another pitch. Appling fouled it off...as he did 13 more times before finally getting a walk on the *28th pitch* to load the bases. The next batter hit a grand slam. "Ruffing cussed me all the way to the plate," said Appling.

DOZING OFF

To motivate pitcher Roy Oswalt for Game 6 of the 2005 National League playoffs, Astros owner Drayton McLane promised the Mississippi native what he'd always wanted—a bulldozer—if he won. Oswalt beat the Cardinals 5–1. Afterward, he was presented with a $200,000 Caterpillar D6N XL (with a big red bow on top). Oswalt, who'd signed a $73 million contract a few months earlier, said he'd use it to "make a little extra money in the off-season."

HEAD SHOT

"I've been telling (second-baseman Alexi) Casilla all year, 'Quit lobbing it. Throw the ball!'" said Twins manager Ron Gardenhire while having his ear stitched up in the locker room during a September 2010 game. What happened? In pregame warm-ups, Casilla threw the ball to first and accidentally beaned his skipper in the head. "Best throw he's made all year," said Gardenhire.

QUICK TAKE

The fastest nine-inning game in pro baseball history took place in 1916 in North Carolina between the minor league Asheville

Ironically, the state of Washington was originally called Columbia, but the name...

Tourists and the visiting Winston-Salem Twins. Every batter swung at the first pitch, and nobody tried very hard to score runs. Final score: 2–1, Twins. Elapsed time: 31 minutes. Why so fast? The Twins only had an hour to catch the last train home.

FUZZY MATH

In 2011 Mariners pitcher Doug Fister was pitching to the Padres' Cameron Maybin in the fifth inning. But the scoreboard operator goofed; he typed in "3 balls, 2 strikes" when it was really only 2 and 2, and then the ump goofed, trusting the scoreboard. After he got another ball and "walked," Maybin scored the game's only run and the Mariners lost. Seattle skipper Eric Wedge later promised to keep a better eye on the count…but a week later the M's gave up another three-ball walk, this time in a loss to the L.A. Angels.

CONGRATULATIONS!

In July 2010, the Marlins' Chris Coghlan (the 2009 Rookie of the Year) celebrated teammate Wes Helm's game-winning hit by hitting him in the face with a pie. But Coghlan tripped and landed hard on his knee and tore his meniscus. He missed the rest of the season.

BOOKENDS

The first game ever played at Atlanta's Fulton County Stadium was Opening Day 1966. Starting for the Braves: pitcher Tony Cloninger and catcher Joe Torre. The final game played at Fulton was Game 5 of the 1996 World Series, 30 years later. The Braves lost to the Yankees, who were managed by Joe Torre. His bullpen coach was Tony Cloninger.

PLAYING CHICKEN

Baseball's oddest curse: In 1985 fans of Japan's Hanshin Tigers celebrated a championship by throwing a plastic statue of Colonel Sanders from a nearby KFC restaurant into the Dotonbori River. Hanshin hasn't won another championship since. Fans blame it on the angry spirit of the Colonel, and tried several times to excavate the statue from the murky river. Portions were finally found in 2009, but the left hand is still missing. The curse continues.

DOUGH-LYMPIC RECORDS

Is there any aroma so wonderful as the smell of freshly-baked bread?
Here are some forgotten achievements that deserve honorable
mentions for their contributions to humanity.

WORLD'S OLDEST BAKERY

In 2002 a team of archaeologists digging in the city of Giza in northeast Egypt discovered the remains of an ancient bakery. They found shallow clay bowls used to knead dough, trays used to let dough rise, ceramic bread molds that also served as baking pans, and open air ovens for baking the bread. There's a good chance, the researchers said, that the bakery supplied bread for the workers who built Egypt's famous pyramids—which are only a few hundred yards away—as it dated to about 2500 B.C., the era during which the pyramids were being built. The Giza site is the oldest bakery ever uncovered.

WORLD'S FIRST CHEESECAKE RECIPE

Cato the Elder was a Roman statesman who lived in the 2nd century B.C. He was an author, military hero, and politician who rose to the position of *consul*, the highest elected office in the Roman Republic. And he *really* liked cheesecake—so much so that he included a recipe for it in a collection of his essays, entitled *De Agri Cultura* ("On Farming"). The recipe is remarkably similar to modern cheesecake, with separate directions for the crust and the filling, which was simply cheese mixed with a lot of honey. He called the cheesecake *placenta*—"flat cake" in Latin. (*De Agri Cultura* also contains one of the oldest recipes for sourdough bread.)

WORLD'S LARGEST BAKING-THEMED TOMB

In 1838 an ancient tomb was discovered near downtown Rome. Constructed sometime around 40 B.C., it stood 33 feet tall, it was supported by huge columns, and its upper section was lined with sculptures…of people performing various baking duties. On the monument was the following inscription:

> This is the monument of Marcus Vergilius Eurysaces,
> master baker, contractor, public servant.

Little is known about him, but historians believe that his surname, Eurysaces, shows that he was Greek; that his two Roman first names indicate that he was probably a slave who bought his own freedom (common at the time); and that he must have been very wealthy (*un*common for a lowly baker and former slave) to have been able to afford such a massive monument. The "contractor, public servant" in the tomb's inscription could mean that Eurysaces supplied bread to the enormous Roman army, which would also explain his wealth. The "Tomb of Eurysaces the Baker," as it came to be known, remains a popular tourist site today.

WORLD'S OLDEST RECIPE FOR PITA BEAD

Ibn Sayyar al-Warraq, who lived in 10th-century Baghdad, wrote a collection of recipes that was used in the kitchens of the most prominent people of his day, including those of the ruling *caliphs*. The book, which was rediscovered only recently, contains 615 recipes (for snacks, soups, stews, desserts, wines, and more). Additional chapters cover utensils, proper handwashing, the best toothpicks, and after-meal napping. That alone would earn al-Warraq a spot in any food-related hall of fame, but he's in this one because his *Book of Dishes* contains the oldest known recipe for *khubz*, the round "pocket bread" we know as *pita*. It is basically the same recipe used today, and it even calls for the bread to be baked in a *tannur* (now called a *tandoor*), the cylindrical clay oven still used throughout the Middle East and India. *The Book of Dishes* is the oldest Arabic cookbook in existence.

THE INVENTION OF PUFF PASTRY

In 1645 Gele, a rural French pastry cook's apprentice, baked a loaf of bread for his sick father, who was under doctor's orders to eat a lot of flour and butter. To make something special for him, Gele kneaded extra butter into the dough, then rolled it very thin and folded it over on itself into the shape of a loaf. He then baked it…and watched with surprise as it rose dramatically. Steam from the butter had become trapped in the folds, expanding and lifting the dough. The finished product was a light, flaky, and buttery bread that Gele called *pate feuilletée*, meaning "leaf-like pastry." Gele took his invention to bakeries in both Paris and Florence, where it became famous, and from there spread all over the world. True puff pastry still uses no yeast, but rises simply via the steam it creates.

WORLD'S FIRST RECIPE FOR GÜLLAC

Hu Szu-Hui was a chef and physician to the leaders of the Mongol Empire in China in the 1300s. His book of ancient Mongol cuisine includes the first-known recipe is for *güllac*: Place chopped nuts between many layers of paper-thin dough that have been soaked in sweetened milk, top with pomegranate seeds, and bake. If it sounds familiar, remove the pomegranate seeds and add honey, and you've got the classic Greek dessert known as *baklava*. In fact, many food historians actually call güllac "the original baklava." (But don't tell the Greeks that.) Interestingly, Hu Szu-Hui wasn't a Mongol—he was a Turk, and güllac is still a popular treat in Turkey, especially during the holy month of Ramadan.

Sidenote: Dr. Hu's book also includes recipes for bear soup (a cure for foot problems) and sheep's heart (a cure for depression). And readers are warned against eating fish with eyelashes, which, according to Hu, are poisonous. (Fish don't have eyelashes.)

* * *

THE RIDDLER

1. I penetrate your ear, but if you poke out my eye, I really smell. What word am I?

2. I have a head and a tail but no body in between. What am I?

3. What kind of running means you'll be walking?

4. I have no mass and can't be seen, but I make millions move every day, though few of them travel very far. What am I?

Answers:

1. The word "noise"—take out the "i," and you're left with a nose, which really smells. **2.** A coin. **3.** Running out of gas. **4.** Music, which makes people dance (moving without going anywhere).

THE ORIGIN OF PARCHEESI (A GAME OF COWRIES AND INDIANS)

*No, it's not a game that Native Americans played. It's a game
that actual Indians from India played by rolling cowrie shells.
And it was once the most popular board game in the
U.S. (before Monopoly). Here's the story.*

CHECKERED PAST

If you were the Mogul Indian emperor Akbar I in 1590, you might be playing *pachisi*, a game very much like Parcheesi—except *much* larger. Instead of a table-friendly fold-out board, you and your three opponents would be playing in the center of a large room, on a floor of inlaid red and white marble. And instead of dice, you'd be rolling six cowrie shells. Most significantly, instead of sitting at a table and moving pieces of colored plastic, you and your opponents would be sitting on a raised platform, moving 16 members of your harem dressed in the four classic colors of the board. But the goal back then was the same as in modern Parcheesi: to get all four of your pawns home.

A game that's more than 400 years old may seem old, but even then it was considered ancient. Mogul-era historians claimed the games went much farther back, perhaps as early as the 4th century A.D., perhaps even farther. Some believe, for example, that a version of pachisi may have been the storied "game of dice" that started a war in 400 B.C. between princely cousins, as told in the ancient Sanskrit text *Mahabharata*.

Today, it is the "national game of India."

IN CASE YOU'VE NEVER PLAYED

Parcheesi, and its forerunners and descendants, are "Cross and Circle" game in which the players' pawns start in one place, travel around the outside of an X-shaped board and—unless blocked, sent

---

back, or otherwise thwarted by the pawns of their competitors—eventually end up safe in a Home position in the center of the board (the place where Emperor Akbar and his opponents sat waiting for their harem girls). The competitor who gets all of their pawns home first is the winner.

THE CURE FOR POST-WAR BOARDOM

In 1867, two years after the American Civil War ended, a New York game developer named John Hamilton adapted a version of the Indian game of pachisi. Historians are unclear how Hamilton found the game. Perhaps he was a world traveler, or maybe someone brought it to him from India. Either way, he copyrighted it as "Patcheesi," adding a "t" and a double "e" to make sure Americans pronounced the name correctly ("Patch-easy"), instead of guessing ("peh-chizzy" or "pay-chai-see"). Keeping the unusual name turned out to be a smart marketing move: After decades of building a national identity and fighting numerous wars to keep it, Americans were ready to branch out and indulge themselves in this exotic "new" game from the mysterious East.

A year after Hamilton copyrighted Patcheesi and before any boards were printed or distributed, he sold the rights to the game. The buyer was a New York "fancy goods manufacturer" named Albert Swift, who in turn sold it to E. G. Selchow & Company (later renamed Selchow & Righter), which issued a yearly catalog of practical jokes, magic tricks, puzzles, and board games.

It was in those few years of going from owner to owner that Patcheesi's "t" turned into an "r." No one knows who changed the name or why, but in 1874 the newly-coined Parcheesi became a huge hit for Selchow & Righter. It sold several million copies and created a small industry of knockoffs. Until Monopoly became popular in the 1920s, Parcheesi was *the* game of choice.

A LUDO-CROSS CULTURAL ADAPTATION

Parcheesi didn't catch on in England until several decades after it did in the United States—a curious fact considering that England colonized India in the 1850s and helped itself to the region's tea, spices, textiles, ivory, and opium. It wasn't until 1896, at the height of America's Parcheesi craze, that the English finally adapted

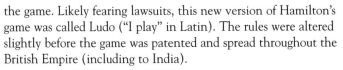

the game. Likely fearing lawsuits, this new version of Hamilton's game was called Ludo ("I play" in Latin). The rules were altered slightly before the game was patented and spread throughout the British Empire (including to India).

As with Parcheesi in North America, Ludo became Great Britain's dominant board game in the early 1900s. In fact, both versions are still popular in the 21st century.

CHEESI VARIATIONS
The popularity of Ludo in England brought even more imitators from all over the world. Of all the various non-Indian variations of pachisi, Hamilton's Parcheesi is the closest to the original, but it has many cousins.

• **Mensch Ärgere Dich Nicht.** This German variation of Ludo, released in 1914, translates to "Don't Get Angry, Man!" It differed in that players could not only could block their competitors but knock them all the way back to the start. This variation and its name spread through Croatia, Slovakia, the Czech Republic, Italy, and the Netherlands. An English-language variation hit the U.S. and Canada in the 1930s. You may know it better as...

• **Sorry!** Patented in England in 1929, Sorry! was released in the United States six years later by Parker Brothers, and became one of their best sellers. Replacing the dice with cards, the goal is the same—to get all four of your pawns Home before your opponents make you go back to Start.

• **Uckers** is a much more aggressive version of Ludo that was popular in the British Navy in the 1930s. Sometimes played in teams, you not only have to get all four of your pieces Home first, but you must do so before any of your opponents get *any* of their pieces Home.

• **Pachisi, Pachesi, Parchesi, and Game of India** were all knock-offs with one purpose in mind: Create something as close to Parcheesi as possible without getting sued for copyright infringement. The first one was released in 1899 when a company called Chaffee & Selchow ripped off the Selchow & Righter game without even changing the name. A lawsuit was filed, but the case was dropped when it was revealed that the Selchow in the new company was the son of the original Selchow. Because he was still

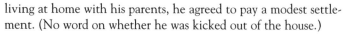
living at home with his parents, he agreed to pay a modest settlement. (No word on whether he was kicked out of the house.)

- **Pollyanna:** A Milton Bradley product (as was the knock-off Game of India), Pollyanna was unique in that it may have been the first pop-culture version of a popular board game. Decorated with characters from the popular 1913 children's book, *Pollyanna*, by Eleanor H. Porter, this version of Parcheesi was the predecessor of modern crossover games such as *Star Wars* Monopoly and *The Simpsons* Clue.

- **Clue** isn't based on Parcheesi, but the name of the game comes from Cluedo, invented in England as a way to pass the time during World War II bombing raids. The name of *that* game was modeled after Ludo. (If the Parker Brothers had followed that logic in America, the game might have been called Cluecheesi.)

- **Petits Chevaux** was a French copy of Parcheesi, but with a horse-racing motif.

- **Aggravation.** Released in 1962 and now sold by Parker Brothers, Aggravation differs from Parcheesi in that the board's cross-shaped playing area was redesigned into an asterisk shape, meaning as many as six people can play. And instead of plastic pawns, players use marbles. The name comes from the fact that it's very aggravating when an opponent lands on your marble and sends you back to Start...again.

- **Wa Hoo.** This 1960s variation mistook the game's Indian origin as *American* Indian, hence the pictures of teepees and warriors all over the board.

SHELL GAME

If you want to play Parcheesi like the ancient Indians played pachisi, put the dice away and get six cowrie shells (available at any craft store). The rules: If your roll of the shells yields two to six openings facing upward, you move that many spaces. However, if your roll yields only one opening on top, you move 10, and if you roll no openings on top, you move 25. (Not coincidentally, *pachisi* means "25" in the Hindi language.) Or, if you *really* want to play the way the Indian noblemen did, get rid of the plastic pawns and get yourself a harem.

HERE COMES THE JUDGE

It's their courtroom, and court is in session. The ruling:
They can do whatever they want. Anything at all.

ARE WE BORING YOU?
At a 2009 sentencing hearing, Judge Daniel Rozak sentenced Jayson Mayfield of Joliet, Illinois, to two years' probation for a felony drug charge. In other words, he basically got to walk away. His cousin didn't. After the sentence was announced, Mayfield's cousin, Clifton Williams, yawned loudly, angering Rozak, who then sentenced Williams to six months in jail for contempt of court, calling the yawn a "loud and boisterous" attempt at disruption. It wasn't the first time Rozak issued an odd contempt-of-court charge. He's also jailed people for their ringing cell phones and for uttering profanities. (Williams, by the way, only served three weeks for his infraction.)

MAKE SURE TO TAPE IT

Facing trial for his alleged role in a Canton, Ohio, Walmart robbery in 2010, Harry Brown became concerned that his court-appointed defense lawyer was unprepared and incompetent. So Brown began to shout out corrections and facts that he felt the lawyer was getting wrong. That upset Municipal Court Judge Stephen Belden, who warned Brown against further outbursts. Brown didn't stop, so Belden ordered a deputy to shut him up…by putting duct tape over his mouth. That got Brown even angrier, so Judge Belden ultimately dismissed the hearing to another court. Brown says putting tape on his mouth was "disrespectful."

PHONING IT IN

Aftab Ahmed was due in court in Suffolk, England, for sentencing on a charge relating to his bankruptcy, but he was late—he was stuck in a traffic jam and not going anywhere. So he called his lawyer, Kevin McCarthy, to explain the situation. McCarthy relayed the story to Judge Caroline Ludlow, who decided to continue with the case anyway because she had a full slate that day and couldn't afford to wait any longer. And just like that, Judge

---

Most states won in a presidential election: 49, by Richard Nixon ('72) & Ronald Reagan ('84).

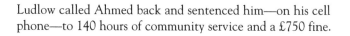

Ludlow called Ahmed back and sentenced him—on his cell phone—to 140 hours of community service and a £750 fine.

WORK FASTER!

At your job, if you didn't finish an important assignment on time, at the very worst, you'd probably get fired. Be glad you don't work for Fort Lauderdale, Florida, Circuit Court Judge Charles Greene. He gave his court reporter, Ann Margaret Smith, several months to type up a 1,500-page manuscript of a criminal trial that was needed for an appeal hearing. The deadline came and went, and Smith had completed only 400 pages of it. Judge Greene felt that this constituted obstruction of justice, so he had Smith jailed for contempt of court...because she didn't finish typing up the transcript. The Judge threatened to *keep* Smith in jail until she finished the job, but when she argued that there were no facilities in the Fort Lauderdale jail to do that, he released her to house arrest until she finally finished.

NIAGARA FAILS

Judge Robert Restaino was hearing a docket of domestic violence cases in Niagara Falls, New York, in 2005 when a cell phone rang—a posted no-no in the courtroom. Restaino said, "Every single person in this courtroom is going to jail unless I get that instrument now." But none of the 46 people present would admit to having the phone, so Restaino followed through on his threat: He directed police to take the entire crowd of defendants, witnessess, and observers to the Niagara City Jail. Thirty-two people posted bail and were released, while the other 14 were booked and jailed. After the local media found out about his rash decision, Restaino released the remaining prisoners and blamed his behavior on "stress." Then the city of Niagara Falls gave Restaino time to relax...by removing him from his judge position.

*   *   *

"A real patriot is the fellow who gets a parking ticket and rejoices that the system works."

—**Bill Vaughan**

Studies show: Your favorite foods are likely foods your mother ate when you were in her womb.

HELEN KELLER: VAUDEVILLE STAR

In 1919 Helen Keller was 39 years old and an international celebrity, but she was having trouble paying the bills. So she took her act on the road.

WHO WAS HELEN KELLER?
Born in Alabama in 1880, Helen Keller was a cheerful, bright baby who was just beginning to learn to talk. Then, at 19 months old, she contracted a high fever that left her blind, deaf, and unable to speak. All of a sudden, Helen's normal development stopped and she became a "wild child"—she ate with her hands, threw food, and broke things. The Kellers' relatives urged her affluent parents to send the little girl to an asylum, which was a too-common destination for deaf-blind people in those days. But Mrs. Keller knew that inside her angry daughter was an intelligent girl trying desperately to communicate.

So when Helen was six years old, her parents brought her to the famous inventor Alexander Graham Bell, who was trying to find a way to cure deafness. Bell was unable to help Helen but recommended the Perkins School for the Blind in Boston. The school's headmaster decided that Helen needed constant home care and sent a 20-year-old teacher named Anne Sullivan, a recent graduate of the school, who was herself partially blind. Sullivan had no experience with deaf-blind students, but after a rough start, she had a major breakthrough when she got Helen to understand the connection between actual water and the letters "w-a-t-e-r," which Sullivan spelled using sign language in Helen's hands.

AN UNLIKELY CELEBRITY

After that, a whole new world opened up for Keller. Under Sullivan's tutelage, she excelled at reading and writing, and in 1904 she became the first deaf-blind person in history to graduate from college. Keller had been famous since childhood thanks to a series of articles written about her by the headmaster at Perkins, but her celebrity skyrocketed after her first book, *The Story of My Life*, was

---

Of all the animal milk that humans drink, a donkey's milk is the closest to human milk.

published when she was 22 years old. Keller then became an advocate for the deaf-blind, as well as a political activist—touting socialism, worker's rights, and pacifism. But she was most famous for simply being Helen Keller.

OPPORTUNITY KNOCKS

Starting in Keller's teenage years, vaudeville promoters came calling. At Sullivan's urging, Keller always politely declined, explaining that she made her living by writing books and giving formal lectures—not by appearing in front of rowdy crowds who paid a nickel each to gawk at (and heckle) jugglers, comedians, and singers, not to mention "freak" acts such as the dog-faced boy or the Siamese twins. Even though vaudeville shows were advertised as "family entertainment," audiences could get out of hand.

But in 1919 Keller convinced Sullivan to let her take the job. The pros just outweighed the cons. For one, Keller's two previous books hadn't sold well, and the money she was making on the Chautauqua adult-education lecture circuit wasn't enough to sustain her. And because they had to travel to a new town for each lecture, the daily schedule was becoming too hectic for Sullivan, whose eyesight and health were growing worse. Doing vaudeville shows would allow them to stay in the same town for a week at a time, rather than traveling nearly every day.

Another factor that led Keller to vaudeville: She disapproved of the way Hollywood had told her story in a 1919 silent movie based on her life called *Deliverance*, in which she and Sullivan appeared as themselves at the end. The film glossed over a lot of details about her life, and completely avoided her political views. Vaudeville would give Keller a chance to set the record straight.

And finally, Keller was a people person, and she knew that vaudeville would be a great way to educate the masses about the struggles of the disabled. So against her family's wishes, she signed on to the Orpheum vaudeville circuit.

NATURAL-BORN KELLERS

Keller knew that her decision to become a vaudeville performer was risky. How would the crowds treat her—like a freak, or as a respected speaker? There were, in essence, two Helen Kellers. "The sweet myth, the canonical one, portrays her as an angel

---

Amazon ants are incapable of feeding themselves and need captured slave workers to survive.

upon earth, saved from the savagery of darkness and silence," wrote Keller biographer Walter Kendrick. But the real Keller was not so angelic—she was a fiery, middle-aged woman who espoused radical left-wing ideals and spoke out against the United States' involvement in World War I, which most Americans supported. With vaudeville, Keller's ambitious goal was to put on an entertaining, educational act without compromising her ideals.

The public, in turn, wanted to see for themselves whether Keller could actually do all the things for which she was credited. Because deaf-blind people were often institutionalized, most people assumed they were "retarded." Indeed, rumors had persisted for years that Keller was not the writer she was made out to be, that she didn't really master five languages, and that her books were ghostwritten frauds. Furthermore, her critics charged, Keller was incapable of having sophisticated political opinions—Sullivan and her husband, John Macy, were using Keller to espouse *their* Marxist views. Keller was ready to prove that she did her own thinking.

The first shows were scheduled for early 1920 at the Palace Theater in New York City, one of vaudeville's premier venues. The playbill advertised:

> Blind, deaf, and formerly DUMB, Helen Keller presents a remarkable portrayal of the triumph of her life over the greatest obstacles that ever confronted a human being!

HELEN BACK AGAIN

Billed as "The Star of Happiness," the 20-minute act began with the curtain rising to reveal Sullivan sitting in a drawing room. As Mendelssohn's "Spring Song" played, Sullivan spent the first few minutes chronicling Keller's rise from a sightless, soundless childhood to a prosperous adulthood (basically the same story later made famous by William Gibson's 1959 play *The Miracle Worker*). Then Sullivan led Keller onto the stage. Keller sat at a piano and exclaimed loudly, "It is very beautiful!" For the audience, this was a surprise. Despite what the poster said, Keller was rumored to be mute. But Keller proved that she could indeed talk, albeit very poorly—only her inner circle could understand what she said, so Sullivan was always there to translate. Said one audience member after hearing Keller recite the Lord's Prayer: "Her voice was the loneliest sound in the world."

But the performances were by no means somber affairs. Keller smiled throughout as Sullivan told stories about her, including one about her lifelong friendship with Samuel Clemens, who once said after a meeting with Keller, "Blindness is an exciting business. If you don't believe it, get up some dark night on the wrong side of your bed when the house is on fire and try to find the door." The crowd laughed at the jokes, and watched intently as Keller demonstrated how she could "hear" a human voice: She placed her hand on Sullivan's face—the first finger resting on the mouth, the second finger beside the bridge of the nose, and the thumb resting on the throat. Keller could then feel the vibrations created by the voice and understand Sullivan's words.

Q&A

The most popular part of the act came at the end when Keller took questions from the audience as Sullivan translated. This gave Keller a chance to show off her quick wit…and to push her social-ist views (which were actually better received on the vaudeville stage than they were on the conservative Chautauqua circuit). A few recorded exchanges:

Q: How old are you?
A: Between 16 and 60.

Q: What do you think is the most important question before the country today?
A: How to get a drink. [Prohibition had recently banned the sale of alcohol.]

Q: Do you believe all political prisoners should be released?
A: Certainly. They opposed the war on the grounds that it was a commercial war. Now everyone with a grain of sense says it was. Their crime is, they said it first.

Q: Does talking tire you?
A: Did you ever hear of a woman who tired of talking?

IT'S A HIT!

Audiences *loved* "The Star of Happiness." And so did the critics. The *New York Times* wrote, "Keller has conquered again, and the Monday afternoon audience at the Palace, one of the most criti-cal and cynical in the world, was hers." Everywhere Keller and

---

One in 100,000 people is born with *Moebius syndrome*, the inability to make facial expressions.

Sullivan went throughout the United States and Canada, crowds greeted them warmly. "At first it seemed strange to find ourselves on a program with dancers, acrobats, and trained animals," Keller later wrote. "But the very difference between ourselves and the other actors gave novelty and interest to our work." Keller and Sullivan were paid in the top tier for vaudevillians— $2,000 per week.

After a show in Syracuse, New York, Keller wrote in a letter to her mother: "The audience was interested in me, they were so silent, paying the closest attention. Indeed, some days there wasn't a clap and yet we knew they were deeply interested. After a while, they found their tongue and asked more questions than we could answer." Other times, Keller wasn't as pleased with the crowds: "Although I love the people, they appear so superficial. They are peculiar in that you must say a good thing in your first sentence, or they won't listen, much less laugh. Still, they have shown us such friendliness. I'm grateful to them."

SIGNING OUT

Keller quit the vaudeville circuit in 1924 when Sullivan's sight and overall health became too poor for her to continue. Besides, Keller had bigger plans. Now under the care of Sullivan's secretary, Polly Thomson, she amped up her advocacy. That same year she became a spokesperson for the American Foundation for the Blind and was already a founding member of the American Civil Liberties Union. She then began traveling the world to advocate for people who faced discrimination or any other blows that life dealt them. During World War II, she visited disabled veterans to demonstrate—through her mere presence—that they could still accomplish great things. In 1948 she toured the Japanese cities of Hiroshima and Nagasaki just three years after the atomic bombs were dropped. In all, Keller traveled to 39 countries and met with every president from Grover Cleveland in 1888 to Lyndon Johnson, who awarded her the Presidential Medal of Freedom in 1964.

By the time Keller died peacefully in her sleep in 1968, her stint in vaudeville was a mere blip in her 87 years, but she remembered it with fondness. "I found the world of vaudeville much more amusing than the world I had always lived in. I liked to feel the warm pulse of human life pulsing round and round me."

NANO-GOLD

How tiny is a nanometer? It's one-billionth of a meter. Nanometers are the units of measurement for the world's smallest particles—atoms and molecules. If you find it hard to imagine how tiny that is, picture this: A million nanometers could line up single file across the head of a pin. Amazingly, scientists are now finding practical uses for particles of gold that measure in mere nanometers.

HOW TO CATCH GOLDFINGER

Despite advances in DNA evidence, forensic investigators still favor an old-fashioned method of crime-scene detection: fingerprints. These are obtained by applying chemicals that react with the amino acids in sweat that was left behind in the print. But prints last for only about three hours on non-porous surfaces, and people with very dry skin don't always leave clear fingerprints. Modern science has a solution: nano-gold. Researchers at the University of Technology in Sydney, Australia, have found that mixing gold nanoparticles into those chemicals gives much sharper detail, no matter how old the prints are or what surface they're on. This is an important step toward the "holy grail" of forensic science: recovering fingerprints from a crime victim's skin—even from corpses. "There is the potential to use it for evidence that may have been laying around for quite a while," says researcher Dr. Xanthe Spindler.

WASTE NOT

Thanks to nano-gold, sewage treatment plants could go from consuming energy to producing it. How? By using the microbial fuel cell, a device that converts chemical energy to electrical energy. Bacteria from sewage are placed in the *anode chamber* of the cell, where they consume nutrients and grow, releasing electrons in the process. Result: electricity! Engineers at Oregon State University have discovered that coating the anodes with nano-gold increases the amount of energy released twentyfold. In the future, sewage treatment plants might not only produce their own operating power, they could become "brown energy" generators.

Point to ponder: In your lifetime, you'll excrete a school bus's weight in poop.

DIVIDE AND CONQUER

More than a third of all Americans—about 120 million people—will be diagnosed with cancer sometime during their lives. When the wife of Dr. Mostafa El-Sayed, a Georgia Tech professor, was fighting breast cancer, he began looking into cancer research. "In cancer, a cell's nucleus divides much faster than normal," says El-Sayed. "If we can stop a cell from dividing, we can stop the cancer." El-Sayed felt that the properties of gold might be useful in killing cancer cells, and he designed nanometer-sized spheres of gold to test his theory. He and his team harvested cells from cancers of the ear, nose, and throat and coated them with a peptide that would carry the nano-gold into the cancer cells, but not into healthy cells. Result: The cancer cells started dividing, then collapsed and died. Though the discovery came too late to save El-Sayed's wife, nano-gold may save many lives in the future.

CURE FOR THE COMMON GOLD

Scientists at the University of Georgia have developed a new way to diagnose influenza: They coat viruses with gold nanoparticles. It turns out that nano-gold is extremely effective at scattering light while biological molecules, such as flu viruses, are not. When scientists coat those gold nanoparticles with antibodies that bind to specific strains of the flu virus, the nano-gold causes the light to scatter in a predictable and measurable pattern. Result: a test that can detect a specific flu strain in minutes. "You take a sample, put it in the instrument, hit a button, and get the results," says researcher Jeremy Driskell. Cost: a fraction of a penny per exam.

CAN YOU DIG IT?

Currently, scientists must make their own nano-gold by dissolving larger pieces of gold and growing nanocrystals. That may soon change. A research team has found nano-gold in western Australian clay. The area's salty, acidic water dissolves gold deposits in the clay and redeposits them in masses of gold nanoparticles. But finding extractable deposits isn't easy. "Gold nanoparticles are transparent and effectively invisible," explains lead scientist Dr. Rob Hough. Why bother? Invisible gold—just like the kind you can see—is worth $1,500 an ounce and is projected to rise to $15,000 per ounce by 2020. All you have to do is find it.

BEHIND THE COVER

With CDs and digitally distributed music, album covers aren't as important or as memorable as they once were. But from the 1950s to the 1990s, some became iconic pieces of popular art unto themselves, and many have great stories about how they came to be.

Artist: Van Halen
Album: *1984* (1984)
Story: When the art department at Warner Bros. Records asked Van Halen what they wanted for the cover of their sixth album, singer David Lee Roth said, "Dancing chrome women." (He didn't say why.) The Warner Bros. art department brought in Margo Nahas, an airbrush artist and cover designer with a knack for photo-realism. They'd used Nahas before—she'd done Stevie Wonder's *Journey Through the Secret Life of Plants* and Autograph's *That's the Stuff,* which actually did depict a metallic woman. Nahas signed on, but after a few weeks, she just couldn't get the chrome women to look real enough to suit her. So she sent her portfolio to Van Halen, hoping it would give them some ideas. But instead of being inspired, they picked one of Nahas's paintings that was already done: a winged cherub smoking a cigarette. Nahas had painted it from a photograph she'd taken of a friend's four-year-old son (holding candy cigarettes). *1984* went on to sell 10 million copies.

Artist: Rolling Stones
Album: *Sticky Fingers* (1971)
Story: The Rolling Stones liked to shock and titillate, and they aimed to do the same with the cover of *Sticky Fingers.* They knew they'd get something controversial if they hired legendary Pop artist Andy Warhol to design it. Warhol's idea: a photo of a man's crotch in a pair of tight blue jeans. Warhol then hired several male models and invited them to his New York studio, The Factory, for the photo shoot. In all, six men were photographed, but Warhol never took notes about who they were and never revealed whose image actually ended up on the album cover. Among the candidates: Jay Johnson, the twin brother of Jed Johnson, who was

---

Parachutes (invented in 1783) are older than airplanes (invented in 1903).

Warhol's lover at the time, as well as painter Corey Tippin. (It definitely wasn't, as an urban legend suggests, Mick Jagger.) But a crotch wasn't suggestive enough for Warhol. He designed the jeans on the cover to include a real, working zipper. When zipped down, a glimpse of white cotton underwear was revealed with the message "This photograph may not be, etc." After the first pressing, the real zippers were replaced by a picture of a zipper because the real ones were too expensive to produce (and they damaged the record inside).

Artist: The Clash
Album: *London Calling* (1979)
Story: The British punk band hired photographer Pennie Smith to take pictures during their 1979 U.S. tour. At a show in New York City's Palladium theater, Smith snapped a shot of bassist Paul Simonon hunched over, about ready to smash his instrument in a moment of urgency, anger, and passion—a very punk moment. Later that year, when the band was trying to decide on a cover shot for their upcoming album *London Calling,* they asked Smith for her tour shots. All four band members agreed on the shot that best represented their music and its destructive, cathartic, cynical emotions: the one of Simonon about to smash his bass. Smith thought it was a terrible shot (it was slightly out of focus). All the better, thought the Clash, and CBS Records agreed.

Artist: Herb Alpert and the Tijuana Brass
Album: *Whipped Cream & Other Delights* (1965)
Story: Can you guess what 1960s band rivaled the Beatles in album sales? It was the Tijuana Brass, an instrumental group popular with adults. In 1965 A&M Records' head Jerry Moss suggested to Alpert (also an A&M founder) that the Tijuana Brass should do an album of food-themed songs. They had a lot of familiar standards to choose from—"Whipped Cream," "A Taste of Honey," "Tangerine," and "Lollipops and Roses," among others, and Alpert titled the album *Whipped Cream & Other Delights*. A&M art director Peter Whorf had an idea for the cover that was very edgy for its time: a naked woman covered in whipped cream, giving the camera a seductive look. He set up a shoot with Dolores Erickson, a model who'd appeared in ad campaigns for Max Factor and on

other A&M album covers (she was a friend of Alpert's). Two notable facts about the naked woman in whipped cream: 1) She wasn't really naked—she was wrapped in a white cotton blanket; and 2) She wasn't really covered in whipped cream—it was shaving cream, which doesn't disintegrate under hot studio lights as quickly as the dairy stuff. (She also was three months pregnant.) Alpert and Moss had major reservations about the image—they thought it would get censored, or at the very least, rejected by older, conservative listeners. Neither thing happened. *Whipped Cream & Other Delights* sold six million copies. The most memorable part of that album? The cover.

Artist: The Who
Album: *The Who Sell Out*
Story: In 1967 the Who were preparing their first album for Track Records, a new label founded by the band's managers. They had complete creative freedom, and guitarist Pete Townshend, the band's primary songwriter, decided they'd do a concept album about the increasing commercialization of rock music. Between the songs were real jingles recorded by a real jingle-recording company for real products, implying that the band had "sold out." The Who wanted the sleeve to look like the band had sold out as well, so graphic designers David King and Roger Law came up with an idea for four panels, each depicting one of the four members in an advertisement for one the products mentioned in the album's jingles. Rock photographer David Montgomery shot the four scenes: On the front, Townshend applies a giant stick of Odorono deodorant to his underarm, and singer Roger Daltrey sits in a bathtub full of Heinz baked beans. On the back, drummer Keith Moon uses a giant tube of Medac pimple cream, and bassist John Entwistle wears a leopard-skin Tarzan suit and stands next to a bikini-clad woman in a parody of Charles Atlas bodybuilding product ads. While the cover helped propel the album to the Top 20 in both the U.S. and Britain, the band was sued by makers of the real products for copyright infringement. The disputes were settled, but Medac had to be changed to Clearasil for the album's release in Australia. (Another problem: The beans that Daltrey sat in arrived in two giant, frozen cans, and he claimed to have caught a mild case of pneumonia.)

TIME FOR TANGRAMS

*Here's the story behind one of the most popular puzzles
in the world: the simple, and yet maddeningly
complicated, seven-piece tangram.*

SQUARE DEAL

A few years ago, a friend introduced Uncle John to a puzzle called a tangram. It looked simple enough, consisting of only seven pieces, or "tans": five right triangles (two large, one medium, and two small), a small square, and a four-sided parallelogram. The seven pieces fit together to make one large square, like this:

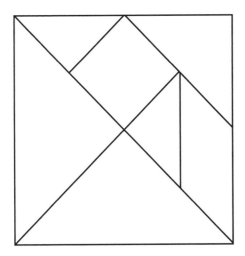

Included with the puzzle were a few dozen problems—silhouetted shapes that could be made by arranging the seven pieces in different combinations. The silhouette on the left, for example, is made by arranging the seven pieces as shown:

Here's another problem and its solution:

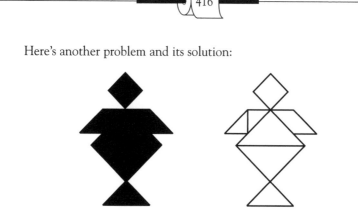

The rules for tangram problems are pretty simple: Each silhouetted shape uses all seven pieces. Each piece touches at least one other piece, to make a single contiguous shape. The pieces do not overlap. That's it.

A DIM HISTORY

The early history of tangrams is pretty sketchy; they are believed to have been invented in China sometime around 1800 by a writer known only by his pen name: *Yang-cho-chü-shi*, or "Dim-witted Recluse," who called the puzzle *Ch'i ch'iao t'u*, or "Pictures Using Seven Clever Pieces." No copies of this book have survived; very little else is known about Dim-witted Recluse.

Mr. Recluse is believed to have been inspired by furniture from the Ming Dynasty (1368-1644), known as "butterfly-wing" tables. A butterfly wing table was a set of 13 smaller tables that, like tangrams, could be arranged in countless ways to symbolize different objects: flowers, dragons, mountains, boats, and, of course, butterflies.

TO THE FOUR CORNERS

By 1815 merchant ships visiting Chinese ports of call began to bring tangram puzzle books to the rest of the world. Because the books were composed almost entirely of the silhouette images and their solutions, they were easy to translate into other languages. The puzzle pieces were cheap and easy to make; people could even cut them out of pieces of paper. All that—and the novelty of the puzzles—helped spark a tangram craze that swept Europe and the

In the last 150 years, the magnetic North Pole has "wandered" a total of about 685 miles.

United States. In France tangrams became so popular that cartoonists began to lampoon them; one cartoon from the time shows a wife ignoring her husband and baby as she sits at a table puzzling over a tangram. Napoleon had a tangram set. So did Edgar Allan Poe. Lewis Carroll, author of *Alice's Adventures in Wonderland*, also wrote puzzle books, some of which included tangrams.

SQUARE ROOTS

Historians think there might have been another inspiration for the invention of tangrams: the fact that you can arrange all the tans in a single tangram set into either one large square, or two smaller squares of equal size. Do you remember the Pythagorean theorem from your high-school math class? (Neither did we—we had to look it up.) Here's a quick refresher: In the case of a *right triangle* (one with a 90° angle), the square of the length of the *hypotenuse* (the side opposite the right angle), is equal to the sum of the squares of the two other sides. Put more simply, the area of the big square below is equal to the area of the two smaller squares combined:

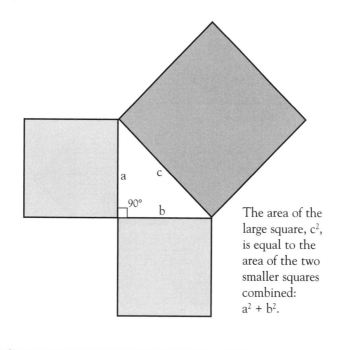

The area of the large square, c^2, is equal to the area of the two smaller squares combined: $a^2 + b^2$.

The first American cattle ranch was started on Long Island in 1747.

One technique for proving the theorem is to see if you can cut the larger square into pieces that can be made into the two smaller squares. If it's possible, then the theorem is true.

Because the pieces of a tangram do just that, it's possible that they were originally used as tools to demonstrate the concept of the Pythagorean theorem. Only later, when arranging the pieces into other shapes proved to be more fun than math class, did they become more popular as puzzles. We can't know for sure, since no copies of Dim-witted Recluse's first tangram book survive. But the oldest tangram books that do survive, and which date back to 1813, mention the Pythagorean theorem.

GET IN SHAPE

See if you can solve the following tangram problems. Trace the pieces on page 415 onto a piece of paper and cut them out. The answers are on page 542.

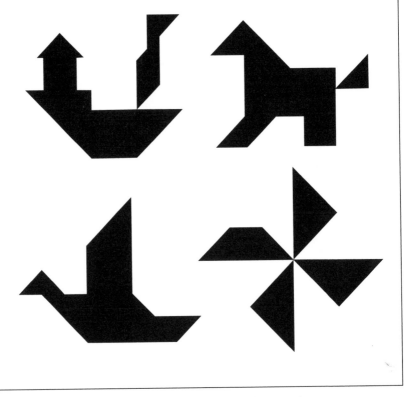

Iceland has more tractors per acre of cropland than any other nation.

WORD ORIGINS

Ever wonder where common words come from? Here are some everyday words and their interesting origins.

BUFF
Meaning: Someone who pursues an interest as a pastime
Origin: "In New York, in the burgeoning days of firefighting (early 1800s), men followed fire engines to watch firefighters extinguish blazes. During the icy winters, they wore buffalo fur to keep warm. The firefighters viewed spectators with contempt and nicknamed them 'buffalos,' which was shortened to 'buffs.'" (From *March Hares and Monkeys' Uncles*, by Harry Oliver)

EGGHEAD

Meaning: A term of derision applied to intellectuals
Origin: "First used to describe Adlai Stevenson during the 1952 Presidential campaign, the term echoes the popular misconception that intellectuals have high brows and heads shaped like eggs, the kind of heads cartoonists give to 'superior beings' from outer space." (From *QPB Encyclopedia of Word and Phrase Origins*, by Robert Hendrickson)

CYNIC

Meaning: One who sees the worst in other people and in life
Origin: "First used by the followers of the Greek philosopher Antisthenes (440 B.C.), a student of Socrates who scorned the pursuit of wealth and fame. It came from the name of his school, *Cynosarges* ('white dog'). His students were *kynikos* ('doglike') because they ignored public customs." (From *The Story Behind the Word*, by Morton S. Freeman)

FOOL

Meaning: A person who acts unwisely
Origin: "It seems no woman can really be a fool, since the word comes from the Latin *follis*, which means bellows, wind-bag, or scrotum." (From *In a Word*, by Margaret S. Ernst)

Nation with the most McDonald's restaurants per capita: the United States. #2: New Zealand.

GEEK

Meaning: A socially inept person

Origin: "From the Scottish word *geck* (fool), for a long time geek referred solely to a performer whose act consisted of biting the head off a live chicken." (From *An Analytic Dictionary of English Etymology*, by Anatoly Liberman)

YOKEL

Meaning: A country bumpkin

Origin: "In England, before the 19th century, a yokel was a woodpecker named after its distinctive call: yo-KEL, yo-KEL. Today the term refers to people who live in the country (where the *yokels* live)." (From *"I Didn't Know That," Volume I*, by Karlen Evins)

GUY

Meaning: A regular person

Origin: "Used by the British to refer to an effigy of Guy Fawkes, the leader of the infamous Gunpowder Plot, the word still means 'a thoroughly grotesque person' in England. The American usage started with playwright Eugene O'Neill in a 1927 letter to a friend." (From *Origins*, by Eric Partridge)

RIFF-RAFF

Meaning: People regarded as disreputable or worthless

Origin: "From the medieval French expression *rifle et rafle*. The phrase referred to lowly scavengers who would plunder (*rifle*) the dead bodies on the battlefield and then carry off (*rafle*) their belongings." (From *World Wide Words*, by Michael Quinion)

HAM

Meaning: Someone who overacts, sometimes to unintentionally humorous results (like William Shatner as Captain Kirk)

Origin: "In 19th-century minstrel shows, white actors in 'black face' used ham fat to remove their makeup. (They often strummed the banjo song, 'Ham-fat Man.') These performances were usually less than first quality." (From *Why You Say It*, by Webb Garrison)

Aristotle believed that going barefoot diminished the libido.

CANADA AT RANDOM

A few facts to bring you up to speed (in kilometers).

• The highest-grossing domestic film in Canadian history is 2006's *Bon Cop, Bad Cop,* a bilingual buddy film about a serial killer who's murdering hockey executives. Once you factor in inflation, though, it comes in third behind *Porky's* (1982) and the 1970 porn film *Deux Femmes En Or.*

• Average high July temperature in Toronto: 28°C (82°F). In Alert, the northernmost permanently inhabited locale in Canada (and the entire world), the average July temp is a mere 6°C (42°F). Population of Alert: 5.

• In 1992 Michael Ondaatje became the first Canadian author to win the Man Booker Prize, the highest literary prize in the British Commonwealth. Ondaatje's prize-winning book: *The English Patient.*

• Some Canadian slang: *kerfuffle* (a commotion), *timbits* (doughnut holes), and *two-four* (a case of beer).

• Alberta's West Edmonton Shopping Mall was the world's largest when it opened in 1981. It has since dropped to fifth place, but it still holds the record for the world's largest indoor amusement park.

• Snorri Thorfinnsson, the first European born in North America, lived in Newfoundland around 1010 A.D. His parents, Þorfinnr Karlsefni and Guðríðr Eiríksdóttir, were Viking explorers.

• You probably know that Canada has two official languages—English and French. How many Canadians actually speak both? About 17 percent.

• Canada has its own version of the Loch Ness Monster—a beast called Ogopogo that reportedly lives in British Columbia's Okanagan Lake.

• The most-viewed television program in Canadian history: the gold-medal men's hockey game during the 2010 Winter Olympics. Over 80 percent of the country tuned in to watch Canada beat the U.S. 3–2.

Worth it? When sea turtles eat man-of-war jellyfish, they give off a scent that attracts sharks.

WORLD HAIRSTORY

There have always been things people were willing to dye for.

BED HEAD
Black hair was the norm in ancient Rome. Blond hair was associated with exotic foreigners from places like Gaul (France) and Germany, and with…prostitutes. To set themselves apart from other citizens, Roman prostitutes were required by law to dye their hair blond. Natural blonds who weren't prostitutes could apply a mixture of vinegar and ground-up leeches to their hair and sit in the sun until it baked in, turning their hair black.

DYE, YOU SAXON PUNKS!
When the Germanic Saxons invaded Britain 2,500 years ago, they sported colors meant to terrify. They headed into battle with hair and beards dyed bright orange, green, red, and blue, giving them a distinct psychological advantage. (Of course, those two-handed battle-axes that could cleave a man in half probably enhanced the effect, too.)

BLONDS HAVE MORE SUN
In the late 16th century, women of Venice, Italy, who wanted blond hair wore special crownless hats that allowed their hair to stick out the top as they sat all day in the blazing sun. Richard Corson's book *Fashions in Hair* describes one woman who stayed out so long that, "she bled almost every day abundantly through the nose," but she "obtained the effect of her desires"—bleached hair.

THE RED QUEEN
Queen Elizabeth I (1533–1603) had red hair that started a hair-dyeing fad as men and women of rank vied to show their loyalty through their locks. Using a mixture of lead, quicklime, and sulfur, women dyed their hair to match the queen's. High-ranking men dyed theirs auburn, and some male courtiers dyed their beards as well. Loyalty, however, came with side effects: nausea, headaches, nosebleeds, and, thanks to the lead, kidney failure and death.

OPERATION PAUL BUNYAN

The unoccupied Demilitarized Zone separating North and South Korea has been a tense place since the end of the Korean War in the 1950s. It's been the site of periodic flare-ups, one of which involved a tree.

TWO KOREAS

For most of its history, Korea has been a single country, often a very powerful one. In the late 19th century, the nation lost its independence to Japan. At the time, Japan was trying to build a global empire, and Korea was a valuable strategic target. After World War II, the Japanese Empire fell apart, and the countries it had once controlled became independent nations once again. But a new conflict was developing: the Cold War between the United States and the Soviet Union. Korea's strategic location made it an important ally to both sides.

The United States assumed the administration of the southern part of Korea, taking steps to assure that it would develop into a capitalist economy. American diplomats and politicians micromanaged the region's political process to produce leaders sympathetic to the West. At the same time, the Soviet Union oversaw the development of the north, and encouraged that part of Korea to develop along socialist lines. The split was formalized in 1948, when the north refused to participate in United Nations–supervised free elections. Both sides claimed to be the only legitimate government on the Korean peninsula. The Korean War was fought over this issue, which led to two separate nations. To this day, South Korea maintains that it lawfully controls North Korea, while North Korea believes the same thing about South Korea.

Technically, the Korean War never formally ended. There was no peace treaty—only an armistice that ended the shooting (it was temporary, but it's lasted since 1953) and established a two-mile wide DMZ, or Demilitarized Zone, as a neutral buffer between North Korea and South Korea.

STAY POSTED

Like all Cold War hot spots, the DMZ was rife with political intrigue and paranoia (and heavily guarded by troops). North Korea accused the South of periodically sending spies into the North, and in 1975 South Korea discovered secret tunnels that North Korea had built under the DMZ.

In the early 1970s, the United Nations set up multiple command posts within the DMZ to help control the situation. U.N. Command Post #3 was critical. It was the northernmost post, situated within sight of North Korean territory. North Korean soldiers had repeatedly attempted to kidnap U.N. officials from Command Post #3, so soldiers stationed at the southern end of the DMZ believed it was vital to keep a close eye on the post at all times. Only problem: Command Post #3 was surrounded by dense foliage, which made the post impossible to observe during summer months. One particularly troublesome poplar tree directly blocked the view.

THE KOREAN AXE MASSACRE

So on August 18, 1976, under U.N. orders, the South Korean military sent five soldiers, escorted by a dozen U.S. troops, into the DMZ to chop down the poplar. Because soldiers are not allowed to carry firearms inside the DMZ, the squad carried only the axes and machetes they planned to use.

Just as the troops began trimming the tree, a delegation of North Korean soldiers arrived at the site and demanded that the South Koreans drop their axes. The tree in question, they said, had been personally planted and tended by Kim Il Sung, North Korea's first "great leader." Despite repeated warnings from the North Koreans, the squadron from the South continued to chop... prompting the commanding officer of the North Korean detachment to order, "Kill them!"

The South Korean troops immediately dropped their axes and attempted to flee. The North Koreans—unarmed because of the weapon-free DMZ rule—then picked up the axes and attacked the American escorts, killing the commanding officer, Capt. Arthur Bonifas, and fatally wounding Lt. Mark Barret, and injuring most of the South Koreans. United Nations soldiers at Observation Post #5, watching the proceedings unfold, recorded the entire incident on camera, and it was quickly reported to the leaders of North Korea and to the general public in South Korea. Through it all, the poplar tree remained standing.

THE ART OF WAR

Because two Americans had been killed, many expected the full military power of the United States to come down on North Korea. But waging all-out war would have been extraordinarily dangerous during the Cold War. Seoul, the bustling capital of South Korea, was located directly south of the DMZ, well within range of North Korean artillery. And while the U.S. had superior air and sea power, North Korea maintained a close diplomatic relationship with China, which had tens of millions of troops that it would almost certainly send to aid North Korea.

Henry Kissinger, then serving as both U.S. Secretary of State and national security advisor to President Ford, was prepared to fight. He suggested to Ford that the best course of action would be a full-scale bombing campaign of the North. Kissinger believed that holding back would make the United States appear diplomatically and militarily weak. Ford, however, did not want to start a new Korean War, or worse, another world war, so he devised a solution that he hoped would allow the U.S. to save face while avoiding a major escalation: Send in the troops…and chop down the tree.

TIMBER!

"Operation Paul Bunyan," as it was called, commenced on August 21, 1976, just three days after the original confrontation—which was being referred to as "the axe murder incident"—and involved a major military incursion into the DMZ. The primary "attack arms" consisted of two six-man units from the U.S. Army Corps of Engineers, all armed with chain saws. Each unit was accompanied by a support unit of 30 heavily armed soldiers, and backed up by two dozen attack helicopters and a wing of B-52 Stratofortress bombers. Meanwhile, every military unit south of the DMZ was on high alert: Aircraft patrols were launched from air bases all over South Korea, and the USS *Midway* carrier group held a position just off the Korean Peninsula. Artillery units stood by to detonate critical bridges in the vicinity, and South Korean special forces ran secret scouting missions along the most critical areas of the DMZ. North Korea responded in kind, dispatching hundreds of sharpshooters and machine gunners to their forward posts along the DMZ. Northern forces set up machine-gun nests in view of Command Post #3.

Despite the armed buildup on both sides, the operation ended without incident. The poplar tree was chopped down in just under an hour. The chain-saw crew left a stump 19 feet high as a visible reminder of what had occurred there, and that was that. In the mid-1980s, Command Post #3 was abandoned, and in 1987 the rest of the stump was removed. But in its place, a small shrine—a stone monument with a bronze plaque—was erected to honor the memory of the two American soldiers who died there.

*　　*　　*

THE WORLD'S BEST ETHNIC JOKE

This showed up in Uncle John's inbox one day.

An Englishman, a Scotsman, an Irishman, a Latvian, a Turk, a German, an Indian, an American, an Argentinean, a Dane, an Australian, a Slovakian, an Egyptian, a Japanese, a Moroccan, a Frenchman, a New Zealander, a Spaniard, a Russian, a Guatemalan, a Colombian, a Pakistani, a Malaysian, a Croatian, a Pole, a Lithuanian, a Chinese, a Sri Lankan, a Lebanese, a Cayman Islander, a Ugandan, a Vietnamese, a Korean, a Uruguayan, a Czech, an Icelander, a Mexican, a Finn, a Honduran, a Panamanian, an Andorran, an Israeli, a Venezuelan, a Fijian, a Peruvian, an Estonian, a Brazilian, a Portuguese, a Liechtensteiner, a Mongolian, a Hungarian, a Canadian, a Moldovan, a Haitian, a Norfolk Islander, a Macedonian, a Bolivian, a Cook Islander, a Tajikistani, a Samoan, an Armenian, an Aruban, an Albanian, a Greenlander, a Micronesian, a Virgin Islander, a Georgian, a Bahaman, a Belarusian, a Cuban, a Tongan, a Cambodian, a Qatari, an Azerbaijani, a Romanian, a Chilean, a Kyrgyzstani, a Jamaican, a Filipino, a Ukrainian, a Dutchman, a Taiwanese, an Ecuadorian, a Costa Rican, a Swede, a Bulgarian, a Serb, a Swiss, a Greek, a Belgian, a Singaporean, an Italian, and a Norwegian walk into a fine restaurant. "I'm sorry," said the maître d', "but you can't come in here without a Thai."

MORE VIRAL VIDEOS

Other people who found fame—and infamy—online.

Internet Star: Caitlin Upton, 19, of Lexington, South Carolina
Better Known As: The "Geography-Challenged Beauty Queen"
The Story: In 2007 Upton was asked this question at the Miss Teen USA pageant: "Recent polls have shown that one-fifth of Americans can't locate the U.S. on a world map. Why do you think this is?" Tripped up by the question, Upton responded:

> I personally believe that U.S. Americans are unable to do so because, uh, some people out there in our nation don't have maps and, uh, I believe that our, uh, education like such as in South Africa and, uh, the Iraq, everywhere like such as, and, I believe that they should, our education over here in the U.S. should help the U.S., uh, or, uh, should help South Africa and should help the Iraq and the Asian countries, so we will be able to build up our future, for our children.

She took fourth place in the pageant.

What Happened: Upton's answer chalked up 50 million views on YouTube. The aspiring model, whose career got a *big* boost after that (including a photo spread in *Maxim*), mocked her botched response in a Weezer music video and on *Jimmy Kimmel Live*. She also became a contestant on the reality show *The Amazing Race* (she placed third). She even got a chance for redemption on *The Today Show*, when host Matt Lauer asked her the question again. Her revised response: "Well personally, my friends and I, we know exactly where the United States is on our map. I don't know anyone else who doesn't. And if the statistics are correct, I believe that there should be more emphasis on geography in our education so people will learn how to read maps better."

Internet Star: Ted Williams, 53, a drifter from Columbus, Ohio
Better Known As: The "Homeless Man With the Golden Voice"
The Story: In January 2011, the *Columbus Dispatch* posted an online interview with Williams, who was panhandling on the side of a road with a sign advertising his vocal skills. The reporter

---

An island unto itself: The kneecap is not connected to any other bone.

asked Williams to "work for your dollar," and Williams replied in a very soothing radio voice, "When you're listening to the best of oldies, you're listening to Magic 98.9!" Seeing this disheveled homeless man speak with such amazing clarity and timbre turned the video into a viral hit (13 million views so far).

What Happened: Suddenly, Williams had more job offers than he could handle, but there was a reason he was homeless. Drug and alcohol abuse in the 1990s destroyed his family and led to prison time. Nevertheless, thanks to the video, he was receiving offers from Kraft Foods, MTV, and the Cleveland Cavaliers. He was "overwhelmed" to go from being homeless one day to a media sensation the next. Cameras were even there for the tearful reunion with his estranged mother.

But the attention took its toll. Williams started drinking again and, in a widely publicized episode, Dr. Phil convinced him to check into a rehab facility. But Williams left a few days later, claiming his treatment was too "scripted" (cameras followed him everywhere). He escaped the public eye and checked into a private facility in California. The Cavaliers and MTV rescinded their offers, but Williams did record a commercial for Kraft mac and cheese. He now has all the voice-work he wants...if he stays clean.

Internet Star: Rebecca Black, 13, a pop singer from Anaheim Hills, California
Better Known As: Star of the "Worst Video in the World"
The Story: In 2010 Black's parents paid a production company called ARK Music Factory $4,000 to produce a single and a video starring their daughter. ARK sent her two songs to consider, and she chose one called "Friday," which dealt with waking up, eating cereal, going to school, and then going to a party. Sample lyrics: "Yesterday was Thursday, Thursday / Today is Friday, Friday / We so excited / We gonna have a ball today / Tomorrow is Saturday / And Sunday comes afterwards." Black posted the video on YouTube in early 2011, hoping to get a few hundred hits and lay the foundation for her future career as a pop singer. But then, on March 11, comedian Daniel Tosh posted it to his Twitter account, commenting: "Songwriting isn't for everyone." That night, Black saw her video go from 4,000 to 70,000 views. When she awoke the next day, it had reached 200,000.

What Happened: To Black's horror, "Friday" became popular for all the wrong reasons: People *hated* it. They hated her voice, the shallow lyrics, and the creepy rap interlude from a grown man following a school bus. In an interview on *Good Morning, America*, Black divulged the fact that she'd even received death threats. "I hope you cut yourself," one commenter wrote. "I hope you get an eating disorder so you look pretty."

In a little over two months, "Friday" reached 164 million views before Black pulled it from YouTube due to "copyright concerns." (ARK wanted to start charging $2.99 per view.) Black says that despite all the insults, she plans on pursuing her dream as a singer. Her second video—"My Moment," released that July—wasn't nearly as horribly received.

Internet Star: Paul "Bear" Vasquez, 47, a former trucker turned cage fighter turned organic farmer from Mariposa, California

Better Known As: The "Double Rainbow" man

The Story: In January 2010, Vasquez posted a YouTube video of a double rainbow that he saw from his front yard. His initial amazement turns to joy, then to tears of ecstasy. He then questions the nature of the universe: "What does it meeeeeeeeeeannnnnnn?"

What Happened: For the first few months it was up, the video had only a few dozen hits…until someone sent the link to comedian Jimmy Kimmel. He loved it so much that he reposted it to his Twitter account. Within a few days, the Double Rainbow video went viral and has since amassed more than 30 million views. Dozens of interview requests came to Vasquez, and all of the reporters asked the same basic question: "Were you high?" His answer: No. (He did admit he was "a little high" in some of his other YouTube videos.) Like all Internet *memes* (what fads are called on the Web), the video prompted hundreds of parodies, including a mash-up of Vasquez with Kermit the Frog singing "Rainbow Connection."

In addition to parodying his video for a Microsoft commercial, Vasquez used his newfound fame to advocate for organic farming. He also announced plans to open a spiritual retreat on his land for anyone willing to let nature "restore their sense of awe." Vasquez said he isn't the least bit surprised by his video's enormous success: "I always knew someday I was going to go viral."

A 0.08"-thick ostrich eggshell can withstand the weight of a 350-lb. bird sitting on it.

MAKE MINE A DOUBLE

Sure, you can order a great Long Island Iced Tea at your local watering hole, but will the bartender garnish it with the still-beating heart of a cobra?

AIRAG. Fermented (alcoholic) horse milk. It's tangy but slightly sweet, and it's naturally carbonated. While it packs plenty of nutrients and vitamins, its alcohol content is a mere 2 percent. Genghis Khan was said to be a big fan of *airag*, and it's still a very popular drink in Mongolia and throughout central Asia. If you're ever in Mongolia and somebody offers you a bowl of airag, you must try at least a sip. To reject it outright is considered rude.

SNAKE BLOOD WINE. It's made by taking a live snake, typically a cobra, and slicing it open. The blood is then drained and mixed with rice wine or whiskey. (The snake's bile is occasionally added as well.) Bottles can be purchased online, complete with a dead snake in the bottle, but according to the people of southeast Asia where it's most popular, it's best when served fresh—with the snake's still-beating heart dropped in the glass as a garnish.

"THE END OF HISTORY." The Brewdog Brewery in Scotland came up with this oddity, reportedly the strongest beer ever created—it's 55 percent alcohol, compared with the usual 5 to 7 percent of most other beers. Only 12 bottles were made; they sold out on the day they went on sale in 2010. "Bonus": Each bottle was set inside a small taxidermied animal, with the bottle necks sticking out of the creatures' mouths. Price: around $780 per bottle, but they varied somewhat, depending on whether the customer wanted a conventional weasel or a more elaborate "Squirrel in a Tuxedo."

BAIJIU. This drink, popular in China, may also be the world's stinkiest. The name translates to "white liquor"—it's distilled from grain, usually sorghum or glutinous rice—and it's about 60 percent alcohol. It comes in a number of different varieties, from unflavored to flavor-infused types such as rose, medicinal herbs, and black tea. Regardless of what's printed on the label, it smells like diesel fuel. It's reportedly very good with pickled foods.

SAMANTHA SMITH

From our "Dustbin of History" files (even though it's only from 1983), here's the story of a little girl, a world leader, and nuclear war.

THE LETTER

Like millions of American children during the Cold War, 10-year-old Samantha Smith of Manchester, Maine, was terrified of getting nuked by the Russians. News reports and TV specials about nuclear bombs, missile defense systems, and "mutually assured destruction" were commonplace, and Smith got more and more frightened about the possibility of war.

Frustrated and scared, Samantha asked her mother to write a letter to the president of the Soviet Union to find out "who was causing all the trouble." Instead, her mother suggested that Samantha write the letter herself. So that's what she did. In November 1982, Samantha wrote to General Secretary of the Communist Party Yuri Andropov, the head of the Soviet Union:

Dear Mr. Andropov,

My name is Samantha Smith. I am ten years old. Congratulations on your new job. I have been worrying about Russia and the United States getting into a nuclear war. Are you going to vote to have a war or not? If you aren't please tell me how you are going to help to not have a war. This question you do not have to answer, but I would like to know why you want to conquer the world or at least our country. God made the world for us to live together in peace and not to fight.

Sincerely,

Samantha Smith

THE WAIT

For months, there was no response...until her letter was published in *Pravda*, the Soviet state newspaper, as a plea for international understanding. But that didn't mean much to Samantha—she'd written the letter to Andropov himself, and she wanted a reply that answered her questions. So she wrote another letter, this time to the Soviet embassy in Washington, D.C. In March 1983, the embassy telephoned Smith at her home and told her that a letter from Andropov was being fast-tracked to her.

THE RESPONSE

A month later, the letter arrived. Along with alerting Smith, the ambassador, eager to create a positive press moment for the Soviets, had also tipped off the media and given them a copy of the letter. Reporters and photographers swarmed the Smiths' house as the letter was delivered. Here are some excerpts:

Dear Samantha,

I received your letter, which is like many others that have reached me recently from your country and from other countries around the world.

You write that you are anxious about whether there will be a nuclear war between our two countries. And you ask are we doing anything so that war will not break out. Your question is the most important of those that every thinking man can pose. I will reply to you seriously and honestly. Yes, Samantha, we in the Soviet Union are trying to do everything so that there will not be war on Earth. And today we want very much to live in peace, to trade and cooperate with all our neighbors on this earth—with those far away and those near by. And certainly with such a great country as the United States of America.

In America and in our country there are nuclear weapons—terrible weapons that can kill millions of people in an instant. But we do not want them to be ever used. That's precisely why the Soviet Union solemnly declared throughout the entire world that never—never—will it use nuclear weapons first against any country. In general we propose to discontinue further production of them and to proceed to the abolition of all the stockpiles on Earth. It seems to me that this is a sufficient answer to your second question: "Why do you want to wage war against the whole world or at least the United States?" We want nothing of the kind. We want peace—there is something that we are occupied with: growing wheat, building and inventing, writing books and flying into space. We want peace for ourselves and for all peoples of the planet. For our children and for you, Samantha.

I invite you, if your parents will let you, to come to our country, the best time being this summer. You will find out about our

Conakry, Guinea, in West Africa, is the world's wettest capital city (over 12 feet of rain per year).

country, meet with your contemporaries, visit an international children's camp—"Artek"—on the sea. And see for yourself: In the Soviet Union, everyone is for peace and friendship among peoples. Thank you for your letter. I wish you all the best in your young life.

Y. Andropov

America's Cold War adversary had just invited 10-year-old Samantha Smith to visit the Soviet Union, something few Americans at the time had done. She accepted.

THE TRIP
The U.S. government allowed the Smiths to go, but they didn't technically sponsor it or approve it. After all, this was a private citizen being hosted as a guest of a rival nation, and it cast the Russians in a good light. However, for the sake of security, the State Department did prep the family in the two and a half months prior to their trip. (Meanwhile, Samantha appeared on numerous TV shows to discuss the upcoming journey, including *Nightline* and *The Tonight Show*.)

On July 7, 1983, Samantha and her parents flew to Moscow, beginning a whirlwind tour and media extravaganza. She was shuttled around in a limousine and saw the sights in Russia's two biggest cities, Moscow and Leningrad, and learned about the country's history, its people, and how Communism worked. But Samantha's favorite part was the familiar world of summer camp. She stayed for a few days at the Artek Young Pioneers Camp (similar to a Boy Scouts or Girl Scouts retreat), where she swam in the Black Sea and hiked with Russian girls her age (all of whom, for the sake of convenience, spoke English).

THE CALL
Every news and TV outlet in the Soviet Union covered the girl's comings and goings, and Russians gathered along the streets to see her and cheer her name. At one of many press conferences, Samantha was handed a telephone. She listened and then hung up after hearing the voice on the other end repeat the words, "I kiss you, Samantha, I kiss you!" She had no idea that the person on the phone was cosmonaut Valentina Tereshkova, the first

woman in space and a national hero. "I thought it was just a kid who was calling," Samantha later said.

The American girl's only regret: She never got to meet personally with Yuri Andropov. His handlers had told her that he was too busy. In fact, he was too sick—he suffered from renal failure and was dying. They spoke by phone during the trip; Andropov died in early 1984.

THE IMPACT

Samantha became an unofficial goodwill ambassador, advocating for both the power of international friendship and nuclear disarmament. She published a book called *Journey to the Soviet Union*, appeared on TV, and gave speeches promoting peace around the world. Invited to the Children's International Symposium in Japan, she even called for a "granddaughter exchange," in which Soviet and U.S. leaders should send their granddaughters to live with one another for two weeks every year, mirroring her trip. "The president wouldn't want to send a bomb to a country his granddaughter was visiting."

She became so famous that she started to get offers from the entertainment world. In 1984 she hosted an election special for kids on the Disney Channel called *Samantha Smith Goes to Washington* where she interviewed George McGovern and presidential candidate Jesse Jackson. In 1985 she was cast on *Lime Street*, an ABC drama starring Robert Wagner as an international insurance fraud investigator; Samantha played his daughter.

THE TRAGEDY

In August 1985, just after filming the fifth episode of the series, Samantha and her father were aboard a six-passenger plane flying into Auburn-Lewiston Municipal Airport, near their home in Maine. Bad weather, piloting errors, and incorrect directions from an air traffic control tower caused the plane to crash in a field. There were no survivors. Samantha was 13 years old.

Condolences came from the highest levels of the U.S. and U.S.S.R. governments. Soviet leader Mikhail Gorbachev sent a personal letter to Samantha's mother, Jane Smith. So did President Ronald Reagan. "Perhaps you can take some measure of comfort in the knowledge that millions of Americans, indeed millions of people, share the burdens of your grief," he wrote. "They also will cherish and remember Samantha, her smile, her idealism and unaffected sweetness of spirit."

THE LEGACY

The Russians memorialized Samantha in a number of different ways: A postage stamp was issued in her honor and a giant diamond discovered in Siberia was named after her, as were a new breed of flower, an asteroid discovered by a Russian astronomer (3147 Samantha), and the Young Pioneer Camp she'd visited in 1983.

In the United States, elementary schools in Sammamish, Washington, and Jamaica, New York, were named for her. By decree of the Maine state legislature, the first Monday of June in Maine is Samantha Smith Day. A lifesize bronze statue of Samantha holding a dove, with a bear cub at her feet holding an American flag, now stands at the Maine state library. The bear is a symbol for Russia; the dove is a symbol for peace.

In 1986 Jane Smith started the Samantha Smith Foundation. Its mission was to send American children on friendly exchange trips to Russia. More than 1,000 kids went before Smith laid the organization to rest in 1995. After Gorbachev's *Glasnost* freedom reforms in the late 1980s, followed by the collapse of the Soviet Union in 1991, the director of the foundation, Donna Brustad, told a reporter, "I think the work that the foundation was originally formed to do has been done."

*   *   *

THE CLASSIFIEDS

• Easygoing athletic SJM, 41, seeking SF, looks not important, must be tall, slim and attractive.

• Nemesis Wanted: I'm 5'10", into kayaking, books, and conversation (by day), justice, honor, and vengeance (by night). Seeking arch-enemy, possibly crimelord or deformed megalomaniac.

• PIG! I saw you at Tiki Bobs. You grabbed my butt and I told you if you did that again I'd kill you. You did. I need your address now.

• This large personal ad cost $340 to run. Needless to say, on our first date, we'll be going dutch.

Only American to be both a Navy admiral and an Army general: Samuel P. Carter (1860s).

"HEALTH" "FOOD"

*We put quotes around both words because these
actual products barely qualify as either.*

SIZE MATTERS. In 2007 a Japanese company introduced a line of snack food to help women become "more feminine," which is ad-speak for "grow bigger boobs." The bust-enhancing treats include F-Cup Cookies, F-Cup Cakes, and F-Cup Pudding cups. The snacks all contain *Pueraria mirifica*—a plant containing phytoestrogens, which are sometimes marketed as natural breast enhancers. Hopeful women will have to decide for themselves if a larger cup size is worth the reported side effects: giddiness, vomiting, diarrhea, and, as one user reported, "the uncomfortable feeling of going through puberty again."

A BEACH-READY BOD. Rodial, maker of Brazilian Tan products, has introduced a new way to get ready for the beach: Skinny Beach Sticks—a diet drink that's high in beta carotene, which, Rodial claims, somehow offers protection against UV rays, and "a slim, toned, ready-to tan body." (Word of warning: Beta carotene is what makes carrots orange, peppers red, and flamingos pink.)

GIVE ME S'MORE. Considering collagen injections? Marshmallows could become the new skin-plumpers of choice. Every packet of Eiwa Grapefruit Collagen Marshmallows contains 3,500 mg of collagen, which, the manufacturer claims, offers the same benefits as injections but without the pain. Dermatologists at the British Skin Foundation find no scientific evidence that consuming collagen works the way injecting it does, but marshmallows do have one advantage: They can be squished between two graham crackers and topped with chocolate.

A ROSE BY ANY OTHER NAME. Another Japanese innovation: a deodorant in the form of chewing gum. Fuwarinka Scented Gum reportedly freshens the breath *and* causes the body to secrete the scent of roses from the pores. According to the manufacturer, gum chewers smell "as fresh and clean as a spring garden" for up to six hours.

RAISE YOUR GLASS

… to these spirited quotes about libations.

"Always do sober what you said you'd do drunk. That will teach you to keep your mouth shut."
—**Ernest Hemingway**

"Without question, the greatest invention in the history of mankind is beer. Oh, I grant you that the wheel was also a fine invention, but the wheel does not go nearly as well with pizza."
—**Dave Barry**

"I'm not a heavy drinker; I can sometimes go for hours without touching a drop."
—**Noël Coward**

"No animal ever invented anything so bad as drunkenness—or so good as drink."
—**Lord Chesterton**

"Whoever takes just plain ginger ale soon gets drowned out of the conversation."
—**Kin Hubbard**

"Health: what my friends are always drinking to before they fall down."
—**Phyllis Diller**

"One martini is all right. Two are too many, and three are not enough."
—**James Thurber**

"Beer is not a good cocktail-party drink, especially in a home where you don't know where the bathroom is."
—**Billy Carter**

"I've stopped drinking, but only while I'm asleep."
—**George Best**

"Drunkenness is nothing but voluntary madness."
—**Seneca**

"I know I'm drinking myself to a slow death, but then I'm in no hurry."
—**Robert Benchley**

"I drink to make other people interesting."
—**George Jean Nathan**

"If you are young and you drink a great deal it will spoil your health, slow your mind, make you fat—in other words, turn you into an adult."
—**P. J. O'Rourke**

Liquid diet: A leech can consume 10 times its own weight in blood.

CONSTITUTIONAL Q&A

The United States is one of the most stable countries in world history. It's gone almost 250 years without a government collapse, due in part to the U.S. Constitution, which explicitly lays out how the federal government is to be run, with procedures for making laws, electing the president, electing Congress, etc. It's interesting to see what provisions the Constitution made (and didn't make) for some unlikely scenarios.

SCENARIO #1: All senior officials die

The Constitution and the Presidential Succession Act of 1947 specify who takes over if the president resigns, dies, or is removed from office. The first in line is the vice president, but if he or she is unavailable, the job goes to the Speaker of the House, and after that, the President pro tem of the Senate. The line of succession then extends to cabinet secretaries: secretary of state, then secretary of treasury, secretary of defense, attorney general, and so on down to the secretary of homeland security, the 18th and last person in line. Historically, no one below the vice president has ever been called on, but a cabinet department head having to take over isn't that far-fetched. That's why every year, just before the president gives the State of the Union address in the same building with both houses of Congress, the vice president, and all cabinet secretaries, he names one of those officers as the "designated survivor," to stay in another location. In 2011 Secretary of the Interior Ken Salazar was the designated survivor.

SCENARIO #2: The vice president does something really bad

The Constitution says that the vice president (like the president) can be impeached for "treason, bribery, and other high crimes and misdemeanors." If this were to happen, the House of Representatives would be responsible for listing the crimes the vice president was accused of committing. The Senate would then try the vice president in a manner very similar to a court of law. There's one problem: The Constitution states that one of the vice president's duties is to preside over the Senate. If the vice president were ever impeached, he would be responsible for presiding over his own impeachment. Now, if this ever actually happened, the vice president would most likely resign: That's what Richard Nixon's VP Spiro Agnew did when he was facing impeachment for bribery in 1973. But technically, he (or she) doesn't have to.

SCENARIO #3: The VP is in a *really* tight race for president

As Senate president, the vice president is also tasked with breaking tie votes. Ties in the Senate are rare but critical. In particular, if no candidate wins a majority of electoral votes in a presidential election, the Senate is responsible for deciding who wins. This has happened only once, in 1828. But if it had happened in, say, 2000, and Vice President Al Gore had tied Governor George W. Bush in the electoral college, the Senate would have voted to break the tie…and Gore would almost certainly have voted for himself.

SCENARIO #4: The Speaker of the House isn't in the House

Every two years, the House of Representatives elects a Speaker as its presiding officer. That person becomes very influential in promoting (or blocking) legislation. Since the days of Washington and Jefferson, the Speaker of the House has been either a respected senior member of Congress or an influential party leader. However, the Constitution doesn't actually require that the Speaker be chosen from among the members of the House of Representatives. It gives *no* specifics about who can hold the job. Congress has never clarified the Speaker's qualifications, either. So by a literal reading of the Constitution, even *you* could be Speaker.

SCENARIO #5: The president goes nuts

The Constitution is clear on who becomes president in the case of death, impeachment, or resignation, but it's a little fuzzier regarding insanity. The document states that the president must step down if he is deemed "unable to discharge the powers and duties of his office." Who makes that determination? The Constitution says that it's either "the vice president and a majority of the principal officers of the executive departments" or any "other body as Congress may by law provide." That means that Congress can form a body of officials to decide whether or not the president is well enough to stay in office. Who would Congress pick? Probably a panel of respected doctors, psychiatrists, and other medical professionals…but they could pick anyone.

…Hercule Poirot. (His death in her last novel won him an article on page 1.)

FAKE CITY QUIZ

These fictional towns were located in real states…but can you match them to their book, game, movie, or TV show? (Answers on page 542).

1. Delta City, Michigan

2. Maycomb, Alabama

3. Hooterville, Missouri

4. Shermer, Illinois

5. Vice City, Florida

6. Frostbite Falls, Minnesota

7. Toontown, California

8. Grovers Corners, New Hampshire

9. Cicely, Alaska

10. Springwood, Ohio

11. Smallville, Kansas

12. Whistle Stop, Alabama

13. Lake Wobegon, Minnesota

14. Bay City, California

15. Sparta, Mississippi

16. Castle Rock, Maine

17. Lanford, Illinois

18. Quahog, Rhode Island

19. Stoneybrook, Connecticut

a) *Starsky & Hutch*

b) *A Nightmare on Elm Street*

c) *Family Guy*

d) *Who Framed Roger Rabbit?*

e) *The Breakfast Club*

f) *RoboCop*

g) *In the Heat of the Night*

h) *Fried Green Tomatoes*

i) *Our Town* (play)

j) *Grand Theft Auto* (video game)

k) *To Kill a Mockingbird*

l) *Superman* comics

m) *The Baby-Sitters Club* (book series)

n) *Roseanne*

o) *Northern Exposure*

p) Stephen King novels

q) *A Prairie Home Companion* (radio show)

r) *Petticoat Junction*

s) *Rocky and Bullwinkle*

Barbie's hometown, according to Mattel, is Willows, Wisconsin.

TREE-GO-NOMETRY

*Have you ever wondered just how tall the tallest tree in your yard is?
If you're afraid to climb all the way to the top, fear not: There's
a way to measure its height without ever leaving the ground.*

WHAT YOU NEED
A tape measure and a sunny day. You're going to
estimate the height of the tree by comparing the length
of its shadow to the length of your own shadow. And there won't
be any shadows if it's foggy, overcast, or 2:00 in the morning.
Level ground. The flatter it is, the better your estimate will be.

WHAT TO DO

• Lay the tape measure on the ground and measure your shadow.
To keep the math simple, let's assume your shadow is 9 feet long
(108 inches), and you are 6 feet tall (72 inches).

• Measure the tree's shadow. Let's say it's 50 feet long.

• Visualize a triangle created by you, your shadow, and a straight
line running from the top of your head to the end of your shadow.
Using trigonometry, the study of triangles, you're going to compare
your triangle with the one made by the tree and its shadow.

• The tree's triangle is the exact same shape as your triangle; only
its size is different. That's because the sun's rays are coming from
the same direction when they create both shadows.

• Because the triangles are the same shape, the ratio of your
height to your shadow's length (72 in. ÷ 108 in. = 0.67) will be
the same as the ratio of the tree's height to its shadow.

• Since your height is 0.67 the length of your shadow, the tree's
height will be 0.67 the length of its shadow. That's 0.67 x 50 feet
= 33.5 feet, so the tree is approximately 33 feet 6 inches tall.

• Why approximately? Because the position of the sun in the sky
gradually changes as the Earth rotates. That means the lengths of
the shadows are slowly changing too. Take your measurements
quickly! The faster you work, the more accurate you'll be.

More Americans (4.2 million) are employed as retail sales clerks than any other occupation.

BEFORE THEIR TIME

Neil Young sang that it's "better to burn out than to fade away." These folks were on their way to making it big before they were 25…and then they died, leaving us wondering what else they would have done.

EDDIE COCHRAN (1938–60)

Cochran was an early star of rock 'n' roll, who, like Elvis Presley, helped craft the young art form with a combination of electric guitars and a rockabilly sensibility. He was only 18 when he started his music career, but he was among the first to experiment with studio tricks such as multitrack recording and overdubs on hits like "C'mon Everybody," "Twenty-Flight Rock," and the song for which he's most famous, "Summertime Blues." In late 1959, Cochran recorded a song called "Three Stars," about the plane crash that killed Buddy Holly and Ritchie Valens, and eerily, it would be one of the last songs he ever recorded. In April 1960, he embarked on a European tour. Late one night in London, he was riding in a cab with his girlfriend. The car blew a tire and careened into a light post. Cochran was sitting in the middle of the backseat and apparently tried to block his girlfriend from being thrust forward. But there were no seatbelts then, and when the car hit the post, Cochran flew out the window and died on impact. He was 21.

HANK GATHERS (1967–90)

Only three players ever led college basketball in both scoring and rebounds in the same season. Two of them, Kurt Thomas and Xavier McDaniel, went on to moderately successful NBA careers, but the one who was primed to be a superstar was the third one, Hank Gathers. A 6'7" power forward for Loyola Marymount University in California, Gathers averaged 32.7 points and 13.7 rebounds per game in his 1988–89 junior year. His numbers in the next season were almost as good—29 points and 10.8 rebounds per game. NBA prognosticators predicted that Gathers would be selected high in the 1990 NBA draft, likely in the top ten. Having so promising a future is probably why Gathers kept his health problem a secret. In December 1989, he had collapsed at the free-throw line during a game. While hospitalized, he learned he had an irregular heartbeat, a potentially fatal condition. But Gathers kept on playing, leading LMU to the conference championship tournament. He also stopped taking the medication—a beta blocker—that helped the heart trouble, believing it made him weaker and affected his play. In the first half of a game against the University of Portland on March 4, 1990, Gathers dunked on an alley-oop, and then while running down the court, he staggered and fell. As trainers rushed to his aid, he yelled, "I don't want to lay down." Then he stopped breathing. He died in an ambulance on the way to the hospital. He was 23.

PINETOP SMITH (1904–29)

Clarence "Pinetop" Smith began his career as a blues pianist-for-hire at age 15. At first he made his living playing at house parties, bars, and brothels in Pittsburgh. From there, he joined the black vaudeville circuit, performing occasionally as a comedian, sometimes as a solo pianist, and finally as an accompanist for major blues singers like Mamie Smith and Ma Rainey. Smith still played the occasional house party, and at one of them in St. Louis in 1928, he invented a new style of music: 12-bar piano blues with an improvised melody (right hand) over a steady rhythmic bass figure (left hand). He called it "boogie-woogie." A blues label called Vocalion signed Smith to make some recordings, the first of which was in the style he'd just invented, called "Pinetop's Boogie Woogie." Over the music, he spoke instructions on how to do a boogie-woogie dance, which he'd also just come up with. Altogether, Smith recorded eight songs at Vocalion's Chicago studios in three sessions—one in December 1928 and two in January 1929. Two months later, while still in Chicago, Smith was at a local dance-hall for a gig. A fight broke out, guns were drawn, and Smith got caught in the crossfire. He was 24 years old. No photos of Pinetop Smith are known to exist, but his influence is still being felt. The style of music he invented gave way to hot jazz, rhythm and blues, and in the eyes of many music historians, rock 'n' roll.

JOHN KEATS (1795–1821)

Regarded as one of the most important poets of all time, Keats was part of the second generation of English Romantic poets, which included Lord Byron and Percy Bysshe Shelley. Keats won his first literary prize at age 14, but as he came from a poor family, he continued with school, eventually attending medical school and becoming a surgeon. In 1817, at the age of 21, he'd had enough and quit his job to focus on poetry full time. In the winter of 1818–19, Keats wrote the majority of his most famous poems, including "Ode to Psyche," "Ode to a Nightingale," and "Ode on a Grecian Urn" ("Heard melodies are sweet, but those unheard / Are sweeter; therefore, ye soft pipes, play on"). The following year he contracted tuberculosis and went to Rome to convalesce. His doctor treated him with a starvation diet (one piece of bread and one anchovy per day) and repeated bloodletting. After living in agony for a year, Keats finally died in February 1821 at age 25. While it's difficult to say how much more he would have written, he was quite prolific in his time, writing more than 120 poems. Although Keats was considered unexceptional by literary critics of his day, by the end of the 1800s his works had become among the most studied in English literature.

*　　*　　*

IT'S A WEIRD, WEIRD WORLD

• In 2007 a dead body was discovered in a wooded area in Allen Park, Michigan…with a six-foot-tall guillotine next to it. A police investigation revealed that the dead man had built the guillotine in his home nearby, and then used it to behead himself. Allen Park Police Chief Dale Covert said, "I can't even tell you how long it must have taken him to construct. This man obviously was determined to end his life." No suicide note was found.

• Responding to a call of an alligator threatening kids in an Independence, Missouri, neighborhood in June 2011, officers located the creature in a yard belonging to Rick Sheridan. With orders to shoot the animal on sight, an officer fired two rounds into it. That's when Sheridan came running outside, yelling, "What are you doing? It's made of concrete!" When asked why he had a concrete alligator in his yard, Sheridan explained that it works better than a "No Trespassing" sign.

First steamship to cross the Atlantic: The SS *Savannah* (1819).

HOW TO EAVESDROP ON THE ASTRONAUTS

The International Space Station is one of the wonders of our age, as large as a football field and the third-brightest object in the sky after the sun and the moon. Few of us will ever get to visit it, but you can listen in when it's passing overhead. It's easier than you think.

HELLO DOWN THERE

On November 28, 1983, the space shuttle *Columbia* lifted off from Florida's Kennedy Space Center for a 10-day mission. It was the ninth shuttle mission, and not a particularly memorable one...unless you're a fan of amateur "ham" radio: It was the first time that an astronaut, mission specialist Owen Garriott, brought a ham radio into space.

Whenever Garriott had some free time he'd point the radio's antenna toward Earth and try to contact fellow ham operators on the ground. The radio was only a walkie-talkie tuned to ham radio frequencies, and it had just five watts of transmitting power—five percent of the power of a 100-watt bulb. Even so, Garriott was able to talk to more than 250 people, including some more than 1,000 miles away. An astronaut using a walkie-talkie to talk to people on the ground may not sound like a big deal, but it was the first time in history that ordinary citizens could talk to a person in space. Anyone with a ham radio license was welcome to try.

NOW HEAR THIS

Today it's easier than ever to talk to astronauts in space. The International Space Station has its own ham radio station, five times more powerful than Garriott's walkie-talkie. All you need to talk to the ISS is a ham radio license, and all that takes is a passing score of 26 on the 35-question multiple-choice license exam.

But what if you don't want to get a ham radio license? *Listening* to the astronauts is even easier than talking to them. No license is required: All you need is a radio or a police scanner that can tune to the 2-meter amateur radio band (144.00 MHz to 148.00 MHz). Radios with digital tuners work best, as they allow you to tune

446

precisely to the ISS's downlink frequency, 145.800 MHz. A radio that can scan frequencies from 142.300 MHz to 149.300 MHz is particularly desirable—it will enable you to pick up the ISS's signal earlier and hold onto it longer because of a phenomenon known as the *Doppler effect*: When the ISS is approaching your location, the Doppler effect causes the signal you receive to be slightly higher in frequency than 145.800 MHz. And when the ISS is moving away from your location, the received frequency will be slightly lower than 145.800 MHz.

LOCATION, LOCATION, LOCATION

The trickiest part to listening to the ISS is figuring out when it is passing through your part of the sky, because that's the only time its transmissions can be heard at your location. The ISS orbits Earth every 91 minutes, and depending on where you live, it should pass overhead at least a few times a day.

Before the Internet, finding this information would have been difficult; today all you have to do is Google your way to any one of a number of satellite tracking websites, then enter your zip code to get a schedule of upcoming passes for your area. (NASA's website lists only the passes when the ISS is likely to be *visible* in the sky.) It's also possible to download satellite tracking software onto your computer and track the space station yourself. A schedule of ISS passes will contain the date, time, and length in minutes of each upcoming pass, plus its *maximum elevation,* or its highest point in the sky during the pass. If the ISS barely peeks over the horizon before dipping below it again, it will have a maximum elevation close to 0°. If it passes directly over your location, it will have a maximum elevation of 90°.

HIGH AND MIGHTY

The higher the ISS's maximum elevation during a particular pass, the more likely it is that you'll be able to receive any transmissions that are being made. That's because the ISS is physically nearest to you when it is passing directly over your head. It orbits at an altitude of anywhere from 173 miles to 286 miles above Earth, so when it's directly overhead, this is how far away it is from you. When it's on the horizon, it can be as far as 1,500 miles away, and at that distance the radio transmissions are weaker and more difficult to receive. High-altitude passes also last longer than low altitude passes, sometimes 10 minutes or more compared to 2 minutes or less for low altitude passes. This gives you more time to listen for transmissions. Passes with a maximum elevation of 40° or greater offer the best chance of picking up a signal.

TIMING IS EVERYTHING

The astronauts on the International Space Station use the radio to talk to schoolkids and other civic groups through a program called Amateur Radio on the Space Station (ARISS) (for more on this, see page 338). The NASA website posts the dates of scheduled ARISS contacts; if there are any scheduled for your area, that's a great time to listen in. It's not uncommon for the astronauts to talk to individual hams before and after scheduled events, so tune in early and keep listening after the scheduled contact has ended.

The astronauts can also use the radio in their spare time, so it helps to try and figure out when that spare time is likely to occur. The ISS is usually on Coordinated Universal Time (UTC), which puts them eight hours ahead of the West Coast and five hours ahead of the East Coast. A typical ISS workday begins at 06:00 UTC, when the astronauts awaken from their night's sleep. They start work at about 08:00, break for an hour lunch at 13:00 UTC, then continue working until about 19:30 UTC. They have two hours off until bedtime at 21:30. The astronauts are most likely to use the radio during their work breaks, before and after meals, and in the two hours before bedtime, so if after calculating the time difference between your location and UTC, you find a high-altitude pass of the ISS over your area at a time when the astronauts are likely to have some downtime, that is an excellent opportunity to listen for transmissions.

Weekends are also a good time to listen. The astronauts work only five hours on Saturdays, and their Sundays are unscheduled except for catching up on unfinished work, so they may have time to talk on the radio then as well.

RUSSIAN HAM

Before the ISS, the Soviet Union had its own space station called *Mir*, which was operational from 1986 until 2001, and it too had a ham radio on board. In the years leading up to the construction of the ISS, American astronauts made extended visits to Mir. The visits between the onetime cold-war foes didn't always go as smoothly as hoped, which led to at least one instance when the Mir's ham radio got a lot more use than it otherwise might have:

• In 1995 Norm Thagard became the first NASA astronaut to visit Mir. He was supposed to receive two radio "com passes" with NASA officials each day, but the Soviets reneged on the deal. Thagard went days on end without being allowed to talk to NASA…at least not through official channels. He finally started using Mir's ham radio to talk to David Larsen, a ham radio buff in northern California, who became a back-channel conduit for exchanging messages with NASA.

• Thagard was supposed to conduct scientific experiments during his Mir mission, but they ended in failure when the freezer containing his samples died a few weeks into the four-month mission. The Russians wouldn't let him touch any of their equipment, so with nothing left to do and months in which to do it, Thagard spent his remaining time aboard Mir staring out the windows, doing crossword puzzles, watching movies, and talking on the ham radio.

A MIR TRIFLE

Soviet cosmonaut Sergei Krikalev was aboard Mir in August 1991 when Communist hardliners tried to overthrow Soviet president Mikhail Gorbachev. Krikalev learned of the failed coup attempt on Mir's ham radio, which is also how he learned that the crumbling U.S.S.R. couldn't afford to send up the rocket that was supposed to bring him back down. Result: Krikalev had to spend an extra six months aboard Mir (10 months in all), and he was still there when the U.S.S.R. passed into history on December 25, 1991. He finally returned home—to Russia—in March 1992. Thanks to his time stranded aboard Mir, the astronaut who went up a Soviet and came down a Russian still holds the record for the most time in space—more than 800 days in all.

* * *

"An autobiography without punctuation is a life sentence."
—David Hincksin Hughes

Largest private home ever built in the US: the Biltmore Estate in N. Carolina (250 rooms).

A CACOPHONY OF CACA

How variations of one ancient word
plopped into so many languages.

THE DIRTY TRUTH

Many of today's languages descended from a common root language they call "proto-Indo-European," or PIE. Dating to the Copper Age, about 4,000 B.C., PIE led to ancient Greek, Farsi, Hindi, Latin, and, by extension, all the Romance languages (French, Spanish, Italian) and the Slavic and Germanic languages (Russian, Polish, German, English, Dutch). PIE probably originated at the Pontic-Caspian steppe, a vast area of 384,000 square miles encompassing eastern Europe and western Asia.

The area was populated by tribes of nomadic horsemen, and as they went off in separate directions to conquer various areas of Europe and Southern Asia, PIE spread with them and evolved into ancient Greek, Sanskrit, and Latin. With further expansion over the next few thousands of years, the ancestors of all modern languages based on PIE were born. No written samples of PIE exist—because written language hadn't developed yet. Most of its words have disappeared, but at least one lives on in dozens of languages: *kaka,* or caca. Or poop.

MEDICAL TERMS

Medical terms are formed from words in ancient Greek, one of the few ways the language survives today. "Cac" is a medical prefix used to describe things that are wrong, off, or otherwise unsavory. In other words, poopy. They include:

- *cacodermia:* a general term to describe bad skin conditions
- *cacomelia:* deformed limbs
- *cacidrosis:* foul-smelling sweat
- *cachexia:* wasting away from disease

There are about 140 billion pennies in circulation—$1.4 billion worth.

SCIENTIFIC TERMS

Scientific names have the same Greek lineage. Some caca-based words:

- *cacophony:* harsh noise
- *cacodemon:* evil spirit
- *cacosmia:* the hallucination of a bad smell
- *cacology:* poor word choice

SLANG

Caca pops up in slang all over the world, too:

- In the Jewish dialect of Yiddish, an *alter kocker* is an insulting term for an old person. It literally translates to "old pooper."

- Poppycock, the English slang word for nonsense comes from the Dutch word *pappekak,* which means "soft poop."

- The Dutch expression *bekakt* means "to put on airs." Literally, bekakt means "covered with excrement."

- The Aztec word for the chocolate they drank was *cacahuatl.* But that sounded (and looked) like you-know-what to the Spaniards, so they called it *chocolatl,* which eventually became "chocolate."

WE'RE NOT DUNG YET

Here are some more variations of "caca" from the world's collective vocabulary:

- French: caca
- Lithuanian: kakoti
- Gaelic: cac
- Portuguese: cagar
- German: kacken
- Russian: kakat
- Greek: kakke
- Italian: cacca
- Bosnian: kakiti
- Ukrainian: kakaty
- Turkish: kaka yapmak
- Basque: kaka egin

*   *   *

BOOK SMART

By age 15, Harry Truman had read every book in the Independence, Missouri, library (but he never graduated from college).

Skeletal remains of people living 10,000 years ago in what is now Pakistan have no cavities.

THE 'UMBLE UMBRELLA

*Just when we thought we'd done every origin
under the sun…it starts to rain.*

UNDER COVER

According to some scholars, the only early treatise on the history of the umbrella burned when Julius Caesar torched Egypt's Library of Alexandria. But legend says that a Chinese woman invented the device 3,000 years ago. Its purpose: to provide relief from the sun for the elite. In fact, only Chinese men of royal blood and government officials could be shaded by a *san kai*. The higher a man's rank, the more umbrellas in his entourage, with as many as 24 being carried in the emperor's procession. Since its invention, the umbrella has popped up all over the world, and for a long time, it was anything but humble.

THE UMBRELLAS MAKE THE KING

• A bas-relief sculpture dated between 668 and 626 B.C., located in the palace of Ashurbanipal, King of Assyria, shows the king riding his chariot back from war. He has just trounced his brother, the king of Babylon, and rides in triumph beneath an umbrella.

• In Egypt, the umbrella protected the exalted heads of the pharaohs from the harsh African sun. In Thent-Amen's time, around 1120 B.C., the Egyptian courts held that if the shadow of the Pharaoh's umbrella fell upon a man, he became a slave for the rest of his life.

• In ancient India, umbrellas were stacked, one atop another on a single pole, to show status. The king's umbrellas were stacked 13 high. And in nearby Burma, the ruler held the title "King of the White Elephants and Lord of the Twenty-Four Umbrellas."

GETTING CARRIED AWAY

• In 339 B.C., the poet Claudius Claudianus complained that effeminate Roman youths of the day were more interested in parading around with umbrellas than they were in carrying off conquered Sabine women.

In San Marino (a tiny republic inside Italy), tourists outnumber residents almost 19 to 1.

• In the Middle Ages, the Catholic church used special umbrellas to signify the status of the clergy. Red and gold for the pope, red or violet for cardinals, and green for bishops. Whenever the Pope appeared in public, an umbrella shaded him. The papal court keeps the tradition to this day.

• Between 1619 and 1637, King Louis XIII built a collection of umbrellas that included 11 made of taffeta (an expensive silk fabric) and 3 made of oiled cloth trimmed with gold and silver lace.

THE MAN IN THE STREET

• In 1772 a Baltimore, Maryland, shop owner bought an umbrella off a ship that had just returned from India. When he walked outside and popped it open, women—who had never seen an umbrella before—screamed. Horses bolted and children started following him. Bystanders stoned him, then took his umbrella and tore it to shreds. The town watch had to be called out to stop the free-for-all.

• So how did the umbrella go from shading royalty to sheltering commoners? It happened in London, a city that's synonymous with rain—it gets an average of 25.6 inches per year. So it's no surprise that the British have many nicknames for the umbrella: a brolly, a mush-topper, a rain-napper, a gingham, a gamp…and a Hanway. Around 1750 an eccentric traveler and philanthropist named Jonas Hanway ventured into the rain carrying an umbrella he'd brought home from China. Nearby coachmen nearly hooted him off the street. (At the time, Londoners considered any man who carried an umbrella to be either effeminate or French.)

If not for the 18th-century British dandies called macaronis, known for following absurd fashion trends (such as sticking feathers in their hats), Hanway might have been the first and last Englishman to carry an umbrella. Unfazed by the catcalls of coachmen, the macaronis adopted the device, and after about 30 years it became "the indispensable companion of the British gentleman."

• The umbrella's round-the-world journey ends where it began, in China—the world's largest umbrella manufacturer—where one city alone, Shangyu, has more than 1,000 umbrella factories. It takes 80 steps to make a single umbrella, but only one to open it and take shelter from the sun or rain. The next time you open an umbrella, don't think of London. Thank the Chinese.

World's largest comic-book collection: The Library of Congress has more than 100,000.

WEIRD UMBRELLAS

The basic design of the umbrella has gone unchanged for 3,000 years. But that hasn't stopped the world's would-be inventors and mad scientists from trying to "improve" on it. Here are a few examples:

Stunning Umbrella. The United States Patent and Trademark Office has received thousands of applications for umbrella patents. Examples include a weather-forecasting umbrella, an umbrella with a self-contained rain-measuring device, a glow-in-the-dark umbrella, a strap-on umbrella for pets, and an electric stun-gun umbrella. The patent office reportedly has four full-time employees who do nothing but process umbrella claims.

Internet Umbrella. A projector located in the umbrella's shaft projects a 3-D image of a map onto a large display inside the umbrella's canopy. Using GPS technology, Flickr, and Google Earth, the map updates constantly. Users can watch the 3-D views to help find their way as they walk around the city streets. (And, hopefully, watch where they're going.)

Gunbrella. A Hong Kong gadget-maker offers an umbrella that is opened by pressing the "trigger" on its rifle-stock-shaped handle. Carried slung over the shoulder by its handy strap, the umbrella looks like a rifle.

Light Saber Umbrella. The shaft lights up like a prop from *Star Wars*, illuminating you and your path. Even on the darkest nights, you're visible to cyclists, drivers, and Jedi knights.

Eco-Umbrella. Though umbrellas have been around for thousands of years, they don't seem to last very long. "Umbrellas," says Julie Lasky, editor-in-chief of *International Design* magazine, "suffer from design flaws that often lead to their premature deaths and unwelcome burials in landfills." In 2006 *I.D.* sponsored a contest for eco-friendly umbrella designs. The winner? The Crayella. All the pieces of its frame are made from recycled polyethylene (soda bottles). And all the moving parts have ball-and-socket joints that snap together, so a Crayella can be assembled quickly and any broken parts can be replaced in minutes without tools. Bonus: It's oval shaped so you can shelter a friend or your backpack.

GOING PLACES?

Strange tips from real travel agencies to help plan your next vacation.

Come to Colombia! "Anywhere that illicit drugs are cultivated in Colombia is a dangerous zone. To get to any of these areas, you'd have to go off the beaten track and avoid everyone's local advice. You're unlikely to just stumble across a coca field. So forget about that point."

—**Paisatours.com**

Come to Russia!

"In most parts of Russia, a tourist is a great rarity, and speaking to one is not always that easy psychologically."

—**Svezhy Veter Agency**

Come to Cameroon!

"Cameroon is a real paradise for animals in the wild. Forests and rivers full of funny gorillas are waiting for your visits."

—**Globalbushtratour.com**

Come to Mongolia!

"It is better to avoid dogs, even ones which appear tame, and take caution if offered marmot meat."

—**Blue Mongolia Tour**

Come to Nepal!

"Public demonstrations and strikes are popular forms of political expression in Nepal and may occur on short notice. Travelers are requested to stay at the most prominent areas where no untoward incidents have taken place, so far."

—**India Invites**

Come to Iran!

"Do you want to travel to Iran but doubt it?"

—**UpPersia.com**

Come to Latvia!

"For travelers, the best thing about Latvia is that it is so compact."

—**Latvia.travel**

Come to the USA!

"Many parts of the United States are subject to earthquakes, wildfires, floods, extreme heat, hurricanes, mudslides, landslides, thunderstorms and lightning, tornadoes, tsunamis, volcanoes, freezing rain, heavy snow and blizzards, and extreme cold."

—**Smartraveller.gov.au**

Fastest-flying insect: the hawk moth. With an 8-inch wingspan, it can fly up to 33 mph.

HIGH-TECH UNDERWEAR

Is there any limit to the things underwear can do?

Underwear: X-Ray Armor, made by Rocky Flats Gear, Inc., a Colorado underwear company

What It Does: Shields your private parts from the view of invasive airport body scanners

Details: X-Ray Armor consists of ordinary underwear with patches of "patent-pending lead-free shielding material" over the crotch and breasts. The material on the crotch is shaped like a fig leaf; on bras it's shaped like clovers, clasped hands, or flowers. Inventor Jeff Buske says his skivvies protect sensitive areas from exposure to radiation and also prevent employees of the Transportation Security Administration from trading scanner images like baseball cards. The TSA maintains that its scanners can't print, transmit, or save the images, which are deleted immediately anyway, so there's no way for the agency's employees to misuse them. It also says the radiation emitted by the equipment is minimal and harmless. But try telling that to Buske: "There's no such thing as safe radiation," he says. "Short of wearing an actual radiation suit, which would be impractical, you protect what you can." (One caveat: The TSA might insist on patting you down if you wear underwear designed to defeat their equipment.)

Underwear: Experimental "smart underwear" being developed for the military by San Diego engineering professor Dr. Joseph Wang

What It Does: Puts a paramedic in your underpants

Details: Chemical sensors in the waistband monitor heart rate, blood pressure, and numerous biomarkers in human sweat, such as lactate, oxygen, norepinephrine, and glucose, that signal when someone is injured in battle. The information is fed into a microcomputer built into the soldier's uniform. When the system detects an injury, reservoirs of painkillers and other drugs stored in the soldier's uniform can be administered on the spot to stabilize the soldier's condition until help arrives. The sensors are sensitive enough to distinguish between different kinds of injuries and administer treatments accordingly. Because Dr. Wang's underwear

---

"No-Wash" hospital boxer shorts have yellow fabric in front, brown in back. "If you...

research is funded by a grant from the U.S. Office of Naval Research, the initial applications will be military. But the biometric sensors can also detect the markers for stroke, heart attack, diabetes, and even blood alcohol levels, so if the technology proves workable, the underwear may eventually be used to monitor the elderly and the chronically ill at home. When combined with biofeedback training, they've even shown promise preventing motion sickness. Who knows? Maybe one day court-ordered underpants will communicate with automobiles to prevent convicted drunk drivers from driving drunk again.

Underwear: FlowPants, boxer shorts being tested by ThermaRx, a manufacturer of medical devices in Houston, Texas

What It Does: They're therapeutic "hot" pants

Details: Equipped with a battery-powered heating element, these underpants are designed to treat urinary hesitation and retention conditions associated with an enlarged prostate. They're actually *over*-underwear: You wear them under your pants but over your regular underpants, and the battery pack clips to your belt. The underwear is currently undergoing clinical trials to test the "Jacuzzi effect"—anecdotal evidence that sitting in a hot tub (or hot pants) relieves urinary retention. If the underwear proves to be effective, it could be coming to a pharmacy near you.

Underwear: 4Skins briefs and boxers, manufactured by an Australian company of the same name

What It Does: The underpants are engineered to absorb the smell of farts. The company's motto: "Keep It in Your Pants."

Details: 4Skins' Contrast and Modern Classic lines of underwear are made using a technologically advanced fabric that incorporates "odor-eliminating nanotechnology" into every fiber. "By doing this, it attracts, isolates and neutralizes unwanted smell immediately," says the company's website. So where do all the absorbed fumes end up? "As the smell is absorbed by the fabric, it holds the odor until you place the undies in the wash. This is when the odor is released." (The underpants only absorb the *smell* of flatulence; how you deal with the *sound* is your problem.)

LIFE ON AMERICA'S FORBIDDEN ISLAND

*What's life like on the only privately owned Hawaiian
island? Here's the second installment of our
story. (Part I is on page 275.)*

STILL THE SAME

If you've ever wondered what the Hawaiian islands looked like when Captain Cook first set eyes upon them in 1778, you can get a pretty good idea by sailing around Niihau. The island is almost completely undeveloped: There are no paved roads and no hotels or other commercial buildings. The beaches are pristine. Most of the islanders live in small houses clustered around Puuwai (pronounced POO-ooh-WAH-ee), Niihau's only village, on the west coast of the island. With the exception of this tiny settlement, most of the island looks as if it is uninhabited by anything other than wildlife, including feral sheep, antelope, and wild Polynesian boar that roam the island.

Another thing that hasn't changed much since Eliza Sinclair bought the island in 1864 is the odd legal relationship that exists between the Robinson family that owns the island and the native Niihauans who live there. The Niihauans don't hold legal title to any part of the island, or even to the houses they live in. On paper they are little more than the permanent houseguests of the Robinsons, who have the legal right to do with their island whatever they please. That may not be an ideal set of circumstances for the Niihauans, and yet if they had lived on any of the other Hawaiian islands, where—at least in a property-owning sense—they would have had more freedom, their language, culture, and way of life would have changed long ago.

LIFE ON THE ISLAND

The Niihauans live on the island, and in their homes, rent free. They may live a traditional lifestyle of hunting and fishing if they wish. Or if they want to earn money, there are jobs available on Niihau and on the Robinson family's sugarcane plantation on

---

Niihau was the only Hawaiian island that voted against U.S. statehood in 1959.

Kauai. They are also free to move off the island, which many do, especially those who work on Kauai. And as long as the community is willing to have them back, they can move back onto the island when they are ready.

OLD SCHOOL

The Niihauans speak Hawaiian as their first language. Classes in the tiny elementary school are taught in Hawaiian through the third grade, after which English is introduced. There are no private automobiles on the island; the Niihauans get around on bicycles or on horseback. There are no police and no jail on the island, but there isn't any crime, either. The last serious crime took place in December 1941, during the attack on Pearl Harbor, when a Japanese pilot ditched his plane on Niihau and then terrorized the island for several days before he was killed by one of the Niihauans.

Guns and alcohol aren't allowed on Niihau, and while tobacco hasn't been banned entirely, the Robinsons will not transport it on the barge that periodically ferries supplies over from Kauai. To outsiders, these restrictions may seem harsh, but alcohol, tobacco, and firearms were never a part of Hawaiian culture, so they're not part of Niihauan culture now. (So how do they hunt the wild animals on the island? The same way they have for generations: with knives and rope.)

DOLLARS AND SENSE

One more thing that hasn't changed about Niihau since 1863: It's still a really bad place to run a ranch. For more than a century, the Robinsons tried to raise cattle, sheep, and honeybees, and even made charcoal from some of the trees that grow on the island—anything they could think of to generate income and provide employment for the Niihauans. But the various enterprises usually lost money, and in dry years they lost a lot of it. Finally, after decades of subsidizing the ranch with income from the sugarcane plantation on Kauai, in 1999 the Robinsons shut down ranching operations on Niihau. Since then they have looked for other ways to earn income and provide jobs for Niihauans. In recent years the largest source of income has come from the U.S. military, which rents part of Niihau for an unmanned radar facility that it uses to track missiles launched from the Pacific Missile

Range Facility on Kauai. The military also uses the island as a training site for special forces units, who land there and then try to avoid detection and capture by "enemy" forces (Niihauan trackers who are paid to hunt them down). Any other military programs that take place on the island are classified.

OPEN...JUST A CRACK

Another result of the island's difficult finances is that after 100 years of nearly complete isolation, in 1987 Bruce Robinson, Eliza Sinclair's great-great-grandson, decided to open up access to Niihau...but only a little. That year he paid $1 million (100 times what Eliza Sinclair paid for the entire island) to buy a helicopter that would serve as an air-ambulance for the island. There is no hospital on Niihau, and before Robinson bought the helicopter, whenever there was a medical emergency the Niihauans had to travel to Kauai by boat.

Robinson decided to offset the cost of the helicopter by using it to provide tours to the remotest parts of the island. The flights leave from Kauai in the morning, and after a quick aerial tour of the island, the pilot selects a secluded beach and lands for the afternoon. The tourists are free to fish, swim, snorkel, or explore the beach for a few hours until it's time to return to Kauai. When the population of feral sheep and wild boar grew to unacceptable levels in the early 1990s, Robinson added safaris to the helicopter trips. (Safari trips are the only exception to the "no guns" rule.)

THE FORBIDDEN VILLAGE

The helicopter trips are always day trips—outsiders are not permitted to spend the night on Niihau, and there are no hotels on the island to accommodate them. Any Niihauan who wants to hike out to the helicopter landing site to greet the tourists is free to do so, but the village of Puuwai is off-limits to outsiders. The helicopters always land several miles away from the village to protect the Niihauans' privacy. Though remote parts of their island have been opened up to outsiders, the Niihauans themselves still live apart. "We have chosen not to change for generations," a Niihauan named Ilei Beniamina told a reporter in 1987. "I'm proud of what Niihau stands for. That's more than I can say about anywhere else in the state."

THE CURSE OF
THE DEMON CORE

*The real-life story of a small ball of plutonium, the
people it killed, and the researchers who blew it up.*

THE BOMB

On the evening of Tuesday, August 21, 1945, American
physicist Harry Daghlian was working at the U.S. government's ultra-secret Los Alamos National Laboratory in New Mexico. He was performing a very delicate experiment: Daghlian was
placing brick-shaped pieces of metal around a chunk of plutonium,
the highly unstable fuel used in most nuclear bombs. And he was
making it more unstable with every brick he placed around it.

Daghlian (pronounced "DAHL-ee-an") was part of the government's Manhattan Project, which since 1942 had worked to develop the world's first atomic bombs. And they succeeded: Just a few
weeks before Daghlian's experiment, two atomic bombs were
dropped on the Japanese cities of Hiroshima and Nagasaki. The
bombs had killed at least 100,000 people immediately, and many
tens of thousands more in the days that followed. Less than a week
after those bombings Japan surrendered to Allied Forces, ending
World War II.

For Daghlian and his fellow scientists, that meant there was
much more work to do.

NEW AND IMPROVED

The United States was the only country in the world with nuclear
weapons at the time, but the government knew that wouldn't be
the case for long. If America was going to survive in a world with
nuclear-armed enemies, it was reasoned, the nation was going to
have to keep producing those weapons, and make them even more
effective. This was precisely the reason that Daghlian was doing
the particular work he was doing that night at Los Alamos.

Harry Daghlian was just 24 years old. He'd been brought into
the Manhattan Project in 1943, while he was still a physics stu-

---

Jaws, Jr.: The spined pygmy shark grows to be only 6 inches long.

dent—an exceptionally brilliant one—at Indiana's Purdue University. He had helped in the development of the bombs used in Japan, which, their devastating effects aside, were actually not very good nuclear bombs. They were, after all, only the second and third ever exploded (one test bomb had been detonated in New Mexico just three weeks before the two in Japan).

One of the chief issues for the scientists was determining how to take full advantage of a bomb's nuclear fuel. Amazingly, both bombs used in the attacks on Japan used only tiny fractions of their fuel to produce their explosions. (Imagine if they had used it all.) And using a bomb's fuel efficiently is all about the *neutrons*.

THE NEUTRON DANCE

The most common type of fuel used in nuclear weapons is a type of plutonium known as plutonium-239, or Pu-239.

• Pu-239 is naturally radioactive, meaning that its atoms naturally emit particles from their nuclei. Some of those particles are *neutrons*. (This is known as *neutron radiation*.) Neutrons are very large, as atomic particles go—so large that if a neutron emitted from one atom happens to strike another atom, it can actually "break" it, and cause the second atom to eject some of its own neutrons. (This is the "split" in "splitting the atom," and scientifically, it's known as *fission*.)

• This process happens normally very slowly, because most of the radiating neutrons just fly off. The whole idea behind nuclear weapons is to *contain* those neutrons within the plutonium, thereby speeding up the splitting process—with neutrons smashing atoms, causing more and more neutrons to be emitted, smashing more and more atoms—until it is completely out of control.

• The numbers involved in this *chain reaction* are almost too big to fathom: In a nuclear bomb explosion, atoms of the nuclear fuel are split by neutrons trillions and trillions of times…in hundreds of billionths of a second. Because each split of each atom releases energy, the combined splitting of trillions of atoms in such an impossibly short amount of time releases an absolutely phenomenal amount of energy—hence the power of atomic bombs.

And that small box that Harry Daghlian was building that night in August 1945 was all about containing the neutrons.

When dropped onto concrete from a height of 100" a regulation tennis ball must bounce 53"–58".

CORE VALUES

Daghlian was working with a gray, softball-sized sphere of Pu-239. It was basically the *core*, or *pit*, of a nuclear bomb—the part that does the exploding. He was performing experiments with the core to determine whether it was the proper size and density to sustain a chain reaction—so it could be used in an actual bomb.

Daghlian began surrounding the core with bricks of tungsten carbide, a very dense metal that reflects neutron radiation. The more enclosed in metal the core became, the more neutrons were reflected back *into* the core, rather than simply flying off. That meant that the rate of neutron bashing and atom splitting in the core increased as Daghlian added more and more bricks. (A geiger counter indicated whether the experiment was working, by clicking faster and faster.) Two very important notes:

• Daghlian wanted the chain reaction to increase to just below a *critical* state, meaning to a controlled chain reaction.

• He did *not* want the reaction to grow to a *supercritical* state, meaning one that was escalating completely out of control.

Using the bricks, Daghlian built walls, about ten inches on a side and ten inches high, around the plutonium. He then took a brick and slowly positioned it—he was simply holding it in his hand—over the opening at the top of the structure, right over the core. The geiger counter clicked wildly. Enough neutrons were now being reflected back into the core that it was headed toward a *supercritical* state.

Daghlian went to jerk the brick away…and dropped it.

UH-OH

The brick landed right on top of the ball of plutonium. The plutonium was now effectively surrounded by neutron reflecting material, and it went supercritical immediately. There was a blue flash—an effect of the sudden release of radiation—and the geiger counter was screaming. Daghlian grabbed the dropped brick in a panic…and dropped it again. He tried to overturn the table he was working on—but it was too heavy. He finally just started taking the bricks away from around the plutonium, one by one. The chain reaction finally stopped, and the geiger counter quieted down. Roughly one minute had passed. It was one minute too much for Harry Daghlian. He had been exposed to a massive amount of radiation. Within hours he stated feeling nauseated, the first sign of radiation sickness. He checked himself into a hospital. After a few days his hands, which had received the brunt of the radiation, began to blister due to radiation burns. He deteriorated steadily after that, and, on September 15, twenty-five days after the accident, Harry Daghlian died.

THE SECOND VICTIM

Nine months after Daghlian's death, in May 1946, the core that he had been experimenting on was designated for use in an actual bomb, to be exploded in a test over the Pacific Ocean. On May 21, Louis Slotin, Daghlian's friend and colleague (he had been on vacation during the accident) decided to perform one last experiment on it.

Slotin's experiment was similar to Daghlian's, but instead of using bricks of tungsten carbide, he had two bowl-like hemispheres made of *beryllium*—another metal that acts as a neutron reflector. (The two hemispheres could be put together to form a hollow ball; the hollow was just the right size to hold the plutonium core.) One of the hemispheres sat in a frame on a table. Slotin placed the plutonium core in it, then placed the other hemisphere over the top of the core…but not all the way. He could not cover the core and allow it to be completely surrounded by the neutron-reflecting beryllium or, as happened to Daghlian, an uncontrolled chain reaction would start. But that's exactly what happened.

NOT AGAIN

The experiment Slotin was performing with the beryllium hemispheres required him to insert the tip of an ordinary screwdriver (yes, a screwdriver) under the lip of the beryllium cap, and raise it and lower it, noting by use of a geiger counter how much of a chain reaction was being created. He was also supposed to be using safety wedges, which would insure that if the screwdriver slipped, the beryllium cap wouldn't fall and cover the core. But Slotin didn't use the wedges…and the screwdriver slipped.

The beryllium cap fell, the core became completely contained, and it immediately went supercritical. Even worse: There were seven other people standing around the table, watching Slotin

How do you know when you have *sulfhemoglobinemia?* Your blood turns blue or green.

work. As with Daghlian's accident, there was an instant blue flash, and the geiger counter started ticking wildly. (The people in the room later said they also felt a surge of heat.) To Slotin's great credit, he immediately put himself at enormous risk by prying the spheres apart—with his bare hands—thereby stopping the reaction. In doing so he received a dose of radiation several times greater than Daghlian had. The effect came almost immediately; he was already vomiting as walked out of the lab. Nine days later, after what can only be described as a period of horrible suffering, Slotin died. The "Demon Core," as it was soon known by scientists at Los Alamos, had killed its second victim.

THE END?

A baffling part of this entire story was that Daghlian's accident took place in the *evening*. He had already worked a regular day shift, but had gone back to the lab at around 9:30 p.m., after dinner. He wasn't supposed to do this. And he definitely wasn't supposed to be performing criticality experiments without another scientist present. To this day nobody knows why he was there that night. And Slotin's irresponsibility in not using the safety wedges? Nobody knows why that happened either. And the sad reality is that they weren't the only victims of the Demon Core:

• Army Private Robert J. Hemmerly, 29, was serving as a guard in the lab when Daghlian's accident took place. He was at a desk reading a newspaper at the far end of the lab when he saw the blue flash. He died 33 years later, at the age of 62, of leukemia, which is believed to have been brought on by his exposure to radiation during the accident.

• Alvin Graves was the person closest to Slotin during his accident. Slotin's action in separating the hemispheres partially shielded Graves, but he was hospitalized for several weeks with severe radiation poisoning nonetheless. He developed several lasting health problems, including vision loss, and died 18 years later, at the age of 55, of radiation-related complications.

• Of the six others in the room with Slotin, three are believed to have had their lives significantly shortened by the Demon Core.

• On July 1, 1946, the softball-sized core of Pu-239 that had killed two of America's most important scientists was detonated near the

Bikini Islands in the Pacific Ocean, in the fourth nuclear bomb explosion in history. The Demon Core was no more.

• The Bikini bomb test that finished off the Demon Core used a much higher percentage of its nuclear fuel than its predecessors and was more powerful by several *kilotons* (the explosive force of a thousand tons of TNT), meaning that, if nothing else, Daghlian's and Slotin's tests were successful.

• During several unmanned ships were anchored in the drop zone to study the bomb's effects. Locked in several of those ships were 57 guinea pigs, 109 mice, 146 pigs, 176 goats, and 3,030 white rats. They were there so scientists could study the effects of nuclear bombs on animals. The bomb killed 10 percent of them immediately; most of the remainder died of radiation poisoning in the weeks that followed.

• At least one of those animals escaped the wrath of the Demon Core, and got a bit of celebrity doing it: A 50-pound pig known as "Pig 311" was aboard an old war ship in the drop zone. (She was locked in the ship's officers' toilet.) The detonation sank the ship—but sailors later found Pig 311 swimming in the ocean. She was taken to the Naval Medical Research Institute in Bethesda, Maryland, where she lived for the next three years—growing to a mammoth 600 pounds. In 1949, Pig 311 was given to the National Zoo in Washington, D.C., where she became one of their most popular displays. She died there in 1950.

• If you want a better picture of just what Louis Slotin was doing in his experiment, watch the 1989 film *Fat Man and Little Boy* about the Manhattan Project. In it, John Cusack plays a scientist who performs a fairly accurate version of Slotin's accident.

*   *   *

ISN'T IT IRONIC?

In 2010 WikiLeaks founder Julian Assange, who became famous for leaking thousands of sensitive diplomatic cables, got upset when someone leaked Swiss police reports of sex crimes he'd allegedly committed. Said Assange's lawyer: "Whoever did this is just trying to make Julian look bad."

Seeing faces on Mars, in pieces of toast, etc., is a psychological phenomenon called *pareidolia*.

EXHUMED!

On page 195, we told you about some famous people who weren't allowed to rest in peace. Here are some more. Hope you dig 'em.

BOBBY FISCHER (1943–2008)

Claim to Fame: The first American chess player to win the World Chess Championship, and widely considered one of the greatest players in the history of the game

Buried: After winning the chess championship in 1972, Fischer withdrew from the chess circuit, and with the exception of a single tournament in Yugoslavia in 1992, he never played competitively again. Because he played the Yugoslav tournament in violation of a United Nations embargo, Fischer risked prosecution and a prison sentence if he returned to the United States, so he didn't. Paranoid and mentally ill in his final years, Fischer moved from one country to another in an attempt to avoid arrest and extradition to the U.S. He was living in Iceland when he died from kidney failure in 2008.

Exhumed: Fischer died without a will, sparking a legal battle over his estimated $2 million estate. Two nephews, a Japanese woman named Miyoko Watai who claimed to be his wife, and a Filipino woman named Marilyn Young who claimed Fischer was the father of her seven-year-old daughter, fought to be named his heirs. In 2010 Young won a court battle to have Fischer's body exhumed and samples taken for a paternity test. The test was negative; the chess king was promptly reburied. At last report the remaining heirs were still fighting over his money.

JOSEPH STALIN (1879–1953)

Claim to Fame: Dictator of the Soviet Union from 1929–1953

Buried: When Stalin died from a brain hemorrhage in 1953, he was interred alongside Lenin in a tomb in Moscow's Red Square.

Exhumed: Stalin was a brutal dictator whose policies caused the deaths of millions of his countrymen. Had he spared the Communist Party from his wrath, he might still be in that tomb. But he didn't—during his 30 years in power he decimated the party ranks in one ruthless purge after another. When Nikita Khrushchev became first secretary of the Communist Party in 1953, he started dismantling the personality cult that had been a central part of Stalin's rule, a program that became known as *destalinization*. In 1961 Stalin was removed from Lenin's Tomb and buried without ceremony in a modest grave near the Kremlin wall.

WILLIAM WRIGLEY, JR.

Claim to Fame: Founder of the Wrigley's chewing gum company, and owner of the Chicago Cubs (who played in Wrigley Field)

Buried: Wrigley owned Santa Catalina Island, 20 miles off the California coast near Los Angeles. Over the years he developed the island into a thriving resort community. When he died from a stroke in 1932, he was laid to rest on the island, at the base of a memorial tower overlooking the Wrigley Botanical Gardens.

Exhumed: After the Japanese bombed Pearl Harbor on December 7th, 1941, Santa Catalina Island was closed to tourism, and the Wrigleys relocated their patriarch to more secure digs in a mausoleum in the Forest Lawn Cemetery in Glendale, California. The war has been over for more than 65 years now, but the Wrigleys never did put William Jr. back in the tower—he's still in Glendale. The tower's still standing, but the Wrigleys don't own much of Santa Catalina anymore: In 1975 the family donated nearly 90% of the island to a conservation group.

ERNESTO "CHE" GUEVARA (1928–67)

Claim to Fame: A Cuban revolutionary leader and Fidel Castro's right-hand man

Buried: Guevara was in Bolivia trying to overthrow the government there when he was captured and executed in October 1967. His hands were cut off and sent to Buenos Aires for fingerprint identification; the rest of his body, and those of six other revolutionaries, were buried in unmarked graves in a secret location to prevent them from becoming a pilgrimage site.

Exhumed: It wasn't until 1995 that a retired Bolivian general revealed the location of the graves—near an airstrip in the town of Vallegrande, Bolivia. It took a year to find the graves, one of them did contain the body of a man whose hands had been removed. The teeth from that body matched Guevara's dental records. In 1997 he and the other guerrillas were returned to Cuba and interred in a mausoleum in the city of Santa Clara.

…had his "Winona Forever" tattoo altered to read "Wino Forever."

MORE STRANGE CELEBRITY LAWSUITS

*Here are a few more real-life examples of unusual
legal battles involving famous people.*

THE PLAINTIFF: Aaron Fraser, CEO of Lebron Jordan,
Inc., a Brooklyn, New York, online athletic shoe company
THE DEFENDANTS: Nike, Michael Jordan, and
LeBron James

THE LAWSUIT: Nike's two best-known celebrity endorsers are
NBA superstars LeBron James and Michael Jordan. That's why
the shoe company, along with representatives of the athletes,
sent several cease-and-desist letters to Fraser's company, Lebron
Jordan. The letters demanded that Fraser stop using the trademarked names and remove from his website any shoe that bears
any resemblance to Air Jordans and Converse All-Stars (which
Nike also owns). Fraser neither ceased nor desisted. Instead, he
slapped Nike and both athletes with a whopping $900 million
lawsuit. Fraser said he lost a "multi-million dollar account"
because the defendants had "dragged his good name through the
press," and pointed out that Nike had trademarked the individual names "LeBron" and "Jordan," but not "Lebron Jordan"
together. (And Fraser's "Lebron" has a little "b.") Besides, Fraser
added, he named his company after his two godsons, whose
names just happen to be Lebron and Jordan. A Nike official
called the suit "groundless"—merely a ploy by Fraser to get more
publicity.

THE VERDICT: As predicted, the lawsuit generated a lot of
publicity for Lebron Jordan (it even got him mentioned in a
Bathroom Reader). The lawsuit was still pending at press time.

THE PLAINTIFF: Carl Mayer, a New York Jets football fan
THE DEFENDANT: Bill Belichick, head coach of the NFL's
New England Patriots
THE LAWSUIT: Mayer, a lawyer, sued Belichick for cheating.

He filed his class-action suit in 2007 in the wake of what the press called "Spygate." At a Jets home game, Belichick's coaching staff was caught secretly videotaping Jets coaches in an attempt to learn their plays. Mayer sought $185 million, to be divvied up between every Jets season ticket holder who paid to watch any home game against the Patriots since 2000, when Belichick became head coach. During the trial, the judge asked Belichick's lawyer, "Do you think someone would pay that kind of money for tickets if they knew in advance it wasn't a fair game?" The lawyer replied, "Given what I know about professional sports, yes." He then added, "Every spectator that goes to a game expects there will be rules infractions."

THE VERDICT: Apparently cheating *is* an expected part of the game. Mayer lost. He appealed the decision to the U.S. Supreme Court, which refused to hear the case. But Belichick didn't get off scot-free: The NFL fined him $500,000 and his team $250,000, plus they were stripped of a first-round draft pick.

THE PLAINTIFF: Quentin Tarantino, Oscar-winning Hollywood screenwriter (*Pulp Fiction*)

THE DEFENDANT: Alan Ball, Oscar-winning Hollywood screenwriter (*American Beauty*)

THE LAWSUIT: The press called it the "Angry Birds" case. Tarantino, who is Ball's neighbor in Southern California, complained that for two years, starting in 2009, Ball's pet macaws made "obnoxious pterodactyl-like screams" to the point where Tarantino couldn't concentrate on writing his new film script. (It's a spaghetti Western called *Django Unchained*.) Ball, who created the HBO shows *Six Feet Under* and *True Blood*, attempted to quiet down his exotic birds. He even built a soundproof aviary, but then just couldn't bring himself to keep them caged. By then, Tarantino had had enough. In March 2011, he sued Ball to have the birds removed for good.

THE VERDICT: The case was settled out of court. Details were few, but it seems that the macaws have been muffled, which has allowed Tarantino to finally finish his script. His lawyer calls it "the best script Quentin's ever written." (No word on whether any angry birds get a dose of Western justice in the film.)

NY's Adirondack Park covers 6 million acres, more than Yellowstone and Yosemite combined.

MR. TROLOLO

*Our final installment of "Viral Videos" features a
Web phenomenon four decades in the making.*

Internet Star: Eduard Khil (pronounced "Hill"), 74, a pop
singer from St. Petersburg, Russia

The Story: Famous in Russia since the 1960s, Khil was virtually unheard of in the United States until 2009. Then someone posted a video from a 1976 Russian TV show in which he lip-syncs to his 1966 hit song—"I Am Glad Because I Am Finally Returning Back Home"—on YouTube.

The video is strangely compelling: Wearing a brown polyester suit with a yellow tie, Khil slowly strolls onto a cheesy orange-and-yellow set, bouncing in time to the cheesy bossa nova music. He seems almost robotic as he smiles the entire time and waves to nobody in particular. But what makes it truly unique are the nonsense lyrics Khil sings in his operatic baritone. Sample: "Yaya-yaya-ya yaya-ya yaya-ya / Oo oo oo oo / ahh EEEE! / Trololololo!"

What Happened: Khil is now known on the Web as "Mr. Trololo," and his video and its dozens of parodies have amassed tens of millions of hits. Even a 2009 video of Khil watching Youtube parodies of himself (and commenting on them in Russian) got half a million views. American fans started a Facebook page urging him to come out of retirement and tour again, but he said he has no plans to perform live. However, Khil did post a video response thanking everyone for the renewed interest in a 40-year-old song. He also has a request that "all the people of the world" contribute actual lyrics to the song, and "we will all sing together." Overjoyed by his newfound stardom, Khil told his fans, "Thank you for getting this supply of cheerfulness and optimism while listening to this melody."

Bonus: Why doesn't the song have any actual words? Khil's lyricist did write some—about a cowboy from Kentucky longing for his woman (who is at home knitting him some stockings)—but Soviet sensors banned the lyrics, so Khil recorded it with the nonsense words instead. (Uncle John's challenge: Watch Mr. Trololo online and then try *not* to sing the melody out loud.)

HIGH CULTURE

Using marijuana for recreational purposes is illegal almost everywhere in the world, which is why some people go to Amsterdam and other cities in the Netherlands where smoking pot is legal in specialized "coffee shops." That has led to a misconception that drugs are legal there. They're not—it's a divisive political issue with a long, complicated history. Here's the real story about what you thought you knew about Amsterdam.

A HISTORY OF TOLERANCE

Before the year 1600 or so, the progressive, commercial and artistic centers of Europe were unquestionably Paris and Florence. The Netherlands was regarded as a boring backwater with little to offer. But then the Netherlands came into its own. An influx of new ideas and technology heralded the Dutch Golden Age, a period of excellence in both art ("the Dutch masters" such as Vermeer, Rembrandt, and Frans Hals) and commerce. The city of Antwerp grew into Europe's leading financial center, and the Dutch East India Company, the first international corporation (and the biggest in history until the 20th century), dominated world goods trading and led European powers in the colonization and commercialization of the New World.

Like America in the Industrial Age, the Netherlands in the 17th century was the land of opportunity. Tens of thousands flocked there, from skilled workers to financiers to religious refugees. The influx of people helped run the country's new, powerful economic machine, so the Dutch government didn't respond to religious and ethnic diversity the way other western European countries had. (England persecuted Catholics and Spain persecuted Jews.) Instead, they tolerated it. In a concept called *pillarisation*, laws were passed to allow people of *any* ethnic or religious background to hold office. The idea of adapting to change through tolerance (and legislation) would come to define the nation's cultural and political mindset into the 20th century.

THE BEAT GOES ON

Maybe because the country went through so much turmoil in the 1800s and 1900s—occupations by Napoleon and Hitler, respectively—tolerance gave way to permissiveness in the years after World War II. Laws decriminalizing prostitution, doctor-assisted suicide, homosexuality, and abortion were passed in the Netherlands in the 1950s, decades before the issues were even discussed in polite company in other first-world countries.

Along with such relaxed (or progressive) attitudes came an increase in the use of recreational drugs—similar to the way the chaotic social and political climate of the late '60s led to increased drug use in the United States. Despite the fact that possession of the drug could result in a prison sentence, marijuana use became increasingly common among Dutch youth. At the same time, use of harder drugs such as heroin was on the rise, and the government's attention began to turn toward *that* problem. Without the time or resources to combat marijuana—and given the country's tradition of tolerance—police began to turn a blind eye to marijuana use, and the drug's image began to soften. Result: In 1971 marijuana possession was downgraded to a misdemeanor offense.

THE FLOODGATES OPEN

That didn't make marijuana completely legal, though—adults could possess the drug, but it was still illegal to smoke it in public. Entrepreneurs in the nation's largest city, Amsterdam, decided to push the limits of the law by opening "coffee shops" that sold coffee...and marijuana. As a gray area between private and public, the shops invited controversy and were routinely raided by police. But they were never shut down.

This was the pattern for years in Amsterdam. The number of shops grew, and the number of police raids declined. Once again, tolerance won out: In 1976, lawmakers enacted a series of sweeping new marijuana laws. Outright legalization wasn't an option because as a member of the United Nations, the Netherlands was legally obligated to *fight* drug trafficking. The Dutch government skirted that agreement by using a strict coffee-shop model. Marijuana would be legal to sell and consume specifically at the coffee shops, but there were rules: Minors were forbidden to enter the shops, advertising was illegal, and limits were placed on both the amount of marijuana that could be sold to customers and the amount a shopkeeper could keep on the premises at any time.

In the 1920s, the Raggedy Ann doll was used as a symbol by the anti-vaccination movement.

SNUFFED OUT

One problem with rules: They only work if people follow them. A handful of shops openly flouted the laws by selling harder drugs, such as cocaine and heroin. Other European governments began to criticize the Netherlands publicly for ignoring its United Nations anti-drug-trafficking pledge. Dutch citizens weren't happy either; people living in Amsterdam and Rotterdam grew tired of putting up with "drug tourists" from Europe and the United States. By 1995 the government was ready to act again…and this time they didn't choose tolerance. They shut down half of the Amsterdam coffee shops (that amounted to more than 100 businesses). And a controversial measure in Rotterdam closed all coffee shops within 250 meters of a school, reducing the number of shops in that city by 25 percent.

Despite the crackdown, tolerance lives on. The Dutch don't seem to want to completely ban marijuana—a 2008 proposal by one Dutch lawmaker to recriminalize it, which would close *all* coffee shops, failed to gain support. But tolerance goes only so far. In June 2011, the national government passed a law banning noncitizens from setting foot in coffee shops altogether. That will make them "locals only" private clubs that require membership. Amsterdam's reputation as the "Las Vegas of Europe" may be coming to an end…unless you're Dutch.

*   *   *

9 OTHER NAMES FOR A MULLET

Ape drape
Hockey hair
Business in front, party in back
Neck warmer
Camaro hair
Beaver paddle
Mud flap
Kentucky waterfall
Long Island iced tease

DON'T TELL THE KIDS!

Think writers of magical tales that enchant children are all sweetness and light? Margaret Wise Brown hunted rabbits and collected their severed feet while writing The Runaway Bunny, *Ian Fleming wrote* Chitty Chitty Bang Bang *between James Bond thrillers, and Maurice Sendak modeled the monsters in* Where the Wild Things Are *on his Brooklyn relatives whose bad teeth and hairy noses he detested. Here's the dark side of other famous kid-lit authors.*

AUTHOR: Kay Thompson

CLAIM TO FAME: In 1955 Thompson wrote *Eloise*, a tale about a pampered, mischievous little girl who lives with her British nanny, her dog Weenie, and her turtle Skipperdee in the penthouse of New York City's elegant Plaza Hotel. *Eloise* and its three sequels (along with a lucrative line of dolls, records, toys, luggage, and clothing) made Thompson a media star.

THE DARK SIDE: Thompson, who'd had a meager career as a singer, actress and songwriter, finally achieved stardom with *Eloise* and she had no intention of sharing the spotlight with anyone. From the beginning, she insisted that her name be on *every* Eloise book, above the title, as on a marquee. When she heard a rumor circulating that Eloise was based on her goddaughter, Liza Minnelli, Thompson snapped, "*I* am Eloise!" She was equally put off by the attention her collaborator, Hilary Knight, was receiving for his illustrations. She responded by cancelling the nearly finished fifth book in the series and blocking further printing of the Eloise sequels, putting Knight in dire financial straits. (After Thompson died in 1998, the books were re-released, and Knight started receiving royalties once again.)

AUTHOR: Shel Silverstein

CLAIM TO FAME: Silverstein wrote several books that became children's classics, including *The Giving Tree*, a bittersweet fable about the relationship between a boy and a tree. Since its publication in 1964, the book has sold more than five million copies and has been translated into 30 languages.

THE DARK SIDE: Before he started writing kids' books, Silverstein was a full-time cartoonist for *Playboy* magazine. His work had a decidedly adult—even raunchy—air to it. So when his friend, illustrator Tomi Ungerer, suggested he write for children, Silverstein brushed him off. But Ungerer was persistent and pointed to his own career: In addition to children's books, his output included political, antiwar, and even erotic works.

Ungerer introduced Silverstein to his editor, Ursula Nordstrom. She liked to publish "good books for bad children," and thought Silverstein would be a perfect fit. So in 1963, she published his first effort: *Lafcadio, the Lion Who Shot Back*—the story of a lion who ate a hunter, learned to shoot the dead hunter's gun, joined a circus, and then returned to Africa with a group of humans to hunt lions. The next year, Silverstein came out with *The Giving Tree*, an equally morbid, but (literally) sappier tale of a tree that loves a boy so much, it sacrifices itself down to its stump to keep him happy. The book caused quite a stir. Some saw it as a story of a beautiful relationship; others, as a worst-case example of self-destructive love. At a *Giving Tree* symposium in 1995, Mary Ann Glendon of Harvard opined, "Tree's qualities would make her a terrible mother—a masochist who, quite predictably, has raised a sociopath."

AUTHOR: Laura Ingalls Wilder

THE STORY: In 1932 Wilder published *Little House in the Big Woods*, the first in a series of books based on her pioneer childhood. The *Little House* books spawned a multimillion-dollar franchise of spinoff books, mass merchandising, and a long-running television show.

THE DARK SIDE: Wilder is listed as the author of the *Little House* books that made her famous, but it appears that she had a lot of help from her daughter, Rose Ingalls Lane. Lane was an accomplished writer whose work appeared in *Harper's, Saturday Evening Post,* and *Ladies' Home Journal,* and her short stories were nominated for O. Henry Prizes. Though Lane suffered bipolar bouts that resulted in her losing confidence in her work, she discovered that she could still perform as an editor and ghostwriter during those times. She ghosted several bestselling books by celebrity "authors" who either credited her for "editorial assistance" (Charlie Chaplin) or with the line "As told to Rose Wilder

Lane" (Henry Ford). Lane's formidable skills have kept generations of literary detectives trying to figure out how much she actually contributed to her mother's books. Laura Ingalls Wilder was a
treasure trove of stories about early prairie living, but her first
attempt to write them down, an autobiography titled *Pioneer Girl*,
never found a publisher. So, in 1930, Lane began a collaboration
that would turn her 65-year-old mother into a household name,
and leave her in the shadows. Scholars have found substantial evidence that Lane read, edited, and revised her mother's work on
every one of the *Little House* books. But if she acted as her mom's
ghostwriter, it's a secret mother and daughter took to their graves.

AUTHOR: Roald Dahl

THE STORY: With sales of more than 100 million books, Dahl
ranks as one of the world's bestselling fiction authors. Many of his
works have been turned into major motion pictures, including
Matilda, *The Witches*, *Charlie and the Chocolate Factory*, and *James
and the Giant Peach*, the story of a boy whose parents are eaten by
a runaway rhinoceros, leaving him stuck living with his horrible
aunts, Sponge and Spiker.

THE DARK SIDE: When Roald Dahl was nine years old, his
parents sent him from their home in Wales to St. Peter's, a
boarding school in Somerset, England. The school offered an
excellent education, along with regular canings by the headmaster for such minor infractions as eating or talking during class.
His teachers graded him harshly, including one who wrote that
Dahl "persistently writes words meaning the exact opposite of
what is intended." Homesick for his family back in Wales, Dahl
felt abandoned, alone, and at the complete mercy of cruel adults.
Given this history, it's no surprise that horrid grown-ups and
abandoned kids appear in almost all of his children's books.
But—as it it turns out—Dahl could have given Sponge and
Spiker a few lessons in how to be nasty. Sometime in the 1970s,
he reportedly advised novelist Kingsley Amis to start writing
children's books. "That's where the money is," he told Amis.

"I don't think I enjoyed children's books much when I was a
child," Amis replied. "I've got no feeling for that kind of thing."

"Never mind," said Dahl. "The little bastards'd swallow it
anyway."

ADIDAS VS. PUMA, PART III

Adidas and Puma created the modern athletic-shoe industry in the late 1940s and dominated it into the 1980s. Then everything went "swoosh." Here's Part III of our story. (Part II is on page 352.)

THE LIGHT STUFF

The constant battles between Adidas and Puma, and the battles within both companies, distracted them from a larger threat posed by a onetime University of Oregon track-and-field coach named Bill Bowerman and his former athlete Phil Knight.

Bowerman was a lot like Adi Dassler: He liked to tinker with shoe designs. He thought ordinary athletic shoes, like the ones made by Adidas and Puma, were too heavy. He believed that if shoes were lighter, his athletes would be able to run faster. So in the early 1970s he invented a shoe he called the Waffle (so-named because he made the shoe's revolutionary urethane sole in his wife's waffle iron).

Phil Knight's company, Blue Ribbon Sports, imported Tiger brand athletic shoes from Japan. But he wanted his own line of shoes, and he thought Bowerman's Waffle design had promise. He arranged for some of his Japanese suppliers to manufacture Waffles in their factories. Knight considered naming the new brand Dimension Six, but an employee suggested naming it after the winged goddess of victory in Greek mythology, Nike. That sounded better. In time Knight would rename the entire company Nike …but only after he'd paid a graphic design student named Carolyn Davidson $35 to come up with a logo—the Nike "Swoosh."

MEANWHILE, BACK IN GERMANY

Nike Waffles hit the market in 1974, the same year that Armin Dassler took the helm at Puma. It wasn't long before some Waffles found their way to Herzogenaurach, along with warnings from alarmed Puma and Adidas distributors in America that the Nikes were a serious problem that needed to be dealt with immediately.

Joan R. Ginther has won Texas Lottery jackpots 4 times. Odds: 1 in 18 septillion.

Neither Horst Dassler at Adidas nor his cousin Armin at Puma saw the Waffle as much of a threat. It went against everything the companies understood about good athletic shoe design: They were too light, weighing little more than bedroom slippers; they were too flimsy; and the soles were made in a *waffle iron*. Both Horst and Armin gave Nikes a quick once-over, had a good laugh, and went back to fighting each other.

LOSING GROUND

Puma was the first company to feel the full impact of Nike's rise. Armin waited five years before responding to the threat and then, in 1979, he replaced his U.S. distributor in an attempt to boost the company's flagging American sales. When that failed he spent millions of dollars buying out the new distributors. That didn't work, either, and when he tried to sell Pumas through mass-market discounters like Kmart, all it did was tarnish Puma's image, which got even worse when Foot Locker and other athletic shoe retailers retaliated by dumping the brand.

In 1986 Armin took Puma public, hoping that listing shares on the Frankfurt stock exchange would bring in money from outside investors. But as soon as outsiders realized how much money Puma was losing, thanks to crashing sales in the U.S., the company's stock price collapsed. In September 1987, Deutsche Bank seized control of the company to prevent it from going under. Then it fired Armin Dassler and his sons Frank and Jörg. Puma was a Dassler company no more.

DOUBLE TROUBLE

By the time Adidas finally came up with a lightweight running shoe to compete against the Waffle in the late 1970s, Nike dominated the market. When Nike introduced the Air Jordan basketball shoe in 1985, it pushed Adidas off American basketball courts as well, racking up $100 million in Air Jordan sales the first year alone.

When Reebok, a British shoe company with just $300,000 in sales in 1980, introduced a shoe designed especially for the aerobics craze, Adidas declined to offer a competing product, because aerobics was not a "sport." By 1987 Reebok had grown into a $1.4 billion-a-year business. Two years later it was the largest athletic shoe company in the world.

When General George S. Patton's troops reached the Rhine River in WWII, he peed in it.

AUF WIEDERSEHEN

Horst Dassler didn't live to see Adidas's day of reckoning; he died of cancer in 1987 at the age 51. His death sparked another family battle for control of the company, this time between his two children (Adi Jr. and Suzanne), who owned 20 percent of Adidas shares, and his four sisters, who controlled the other 80 percent.

Through 1988 Adidas was still the largest sporting goods company in the world, just slightly ahead of Reebok and Nike. But by the end of 1989 it had fallen behind both companies and even behind the Converse shoe company, and sales continued to fall. A plunge from first place to fourth in one year was more than Horst Dassler's sisters could stomach. Mindful of what had happened to their cousins over at Puma, they decided to unload Adidas while they still had something to sell. On July 4, 1990, they sold their shares to a French industrialist for $273 million. By then Adi Jr. and his sister Suzanne had already sold most of their shares to pay their inheritance taxes. The Dassler era was over.

LIFE AFTER DASSLERS

Reebok's reign at the top did not last. By the late 1990s, it had slipped to a distant third behind Nike and Adidas, and it never caught up again. In 2005 it was acquired by Adidas, but as of 2011 Nike is still larger than its two rivals combined. In 2007 Puma was acquired by the French conglomerate Pinault-Printemps-Redoute (PPR), which also owns Gucci, the Italian luxury-goods label.

Both Adidas and Puma are still headquartered in Herzogenaurach, though shoes are no longer made in the village. Now that the factory jobs are gone, the rivalry that divided the town for decades has largely disappeared. Today Rudi's grandson Frank Dassler, fired from Puma in 1987, works for Adidas.

About the only time the rivalry resurfaces is when tradespeople hired to work in the Adidas or Puma headquarters show up wearing the wrong kind of shoes. That's a tradition that dates back more than 60 years, when laborers deliberately wore the wrong shoes when working in Adi or Rudi's homes—they knew that if Adi saw Pumas in his house or Rudi saw Adidas in his, they'd give the workers free pairs of the right kind of shoes. "Rudolf simply couldn't stand the fact that someone was wearing an Adidas shoe in his private home," Frank Dassler says.

First North American city to have electric streetlights: Cleveland, Ohio (1879).

CELEBRITY GHOSTS

*They may be gone, but they're not forgotten. Come to think of
it, are they really even gone? Ghost lovers claim that many
of the famous dead are still among us...in spirit.*

BENJAMIN FRANKLIN (1706–90)
Franklin helped establish the American Philosophical Society in Philadelphia in the 1740s. His papers are housed there along with, according to some staff members, his ghost. Employees claim that Franklin hangs out in the library and likes to peruse its shelves. Aside from one nasty encounter with a cleaning lady, who claims he attacked her after hours, he's usually in high spirits.

KURT COBAIN (1967–94)
In the days after Cobain committed suicide at his Seattle home, a handful of fans who gathered there for a vigil claimed to have seen the spirit of the Nirvana frontman in the windows and on the roof of the house. In August 2000, a bartender in Essex, England, told reporters that Cobain's ghost had taken up residence in her laptop. She claimed Cobain's face materialized on the screen one night, begged her for help, and then asked her to kiss him. She kissed the screen, and the image vanished. The laptop crashed and never worked again.

RUDOLPH VALENTINO (1895–1926)
A nasty case of peritonitis sent the silent-screen star to his grave at just 31 years of age. An excerpt from his diary revealed that he didn't fear death: "I believe it to be merely the beginning of Life itself," he wrote. It shouldn't have been a surprise, then, when a stable hand at Valentino's Beverly Hills mansion claimed he saw the "Latin Lover's" spirit petting a horse. (The stable hand quit on the spot.) Sightings have also been reported both at Valentino's former beach house in Oxnard, California, and in the costume department at Paramount Studios in Los Angeles.

BUGSY SIEGEL (1906–47)
Mobster Siegel helped build Las Vegas...and he seems determined

to stay there. Guests and staff at the Flamingo Hotel, which he opened in 1946, reported seeing Siegel's ghost, dressed in a smoking jacket, lingering in the Presidential Suite. He was also spotted loitering around the hotel's pool late at night, and a maid reportedly quit after seeing Siegel's ghost on the fifth floor. The last of the old Flamingo Hotel was torn down in 1993 to make room for the present-day Flamingo Hilton; today his ghost is said to haunt the memorial plaque that marks the spot where the old hotel once stood.

CASS ELLIOT (1941–74)
Actor and comedian Dan Aykroyd lives in a Los Angeles home once owned by Elliot, of the Mamas and the Papas. Aykroyd claims Elliot's ghost has snuggled up with him in bed, turned on his Stairmaster, and messes around in a jewelry box.

MICHAEL JACKSON (1958–2009)
Shortly after Jackson's death, a TV crew from *Larry King Live* shot footage around Jackson's Neverland Ranch estate. When the show aired, some fans noticed something eerie: A shadowy figure seems to be walking from left to right across a hallway. CNN claimed the image was a shadow caused by a crew member walking past an off-camera light fixture, but viewers had a spookier explanation: It was Jackson's ghost. Since then, Jackson's image has been sighted dozens of times—everywhere from a Catholic school in Harare, Zimbabwe, to a reflection on the hood of a car in Stafford, Virginia.

JOHN LENNON (1940–80)
In 1995 the surviving members of the Beatles convened in a London studio to record a new song called "Free as a Bird," built on a vocal demo that Lennon had recorded in the '70s. According to Paul McCartney, Lennon's ghost attended the reunion, too. "There were a lot of strange goings-on in the studio—noises that shouldn't have been there and equipment doing all manner of weird things." Another sighting: Lennon once told his son Julian that should he ever die, he would visit him as "a white feather floating evenly across the room." About a year after Lennon's death, Julian Lennon reported that his father kept his word.

America's lowest ZIP code, 00501, belongs exclusively to the IRS building in Holtsville, NY.

LAW & SCANDAL

*Here are the stories of some of the worst
police scandals in U.S. history.*

THE BECKER SCANDAL

The Perp: Lieutenant Charles Becker of the New York City Police Department

The Story: On July 15, 1912, Herman "Beansy" Rosenthal, owner of an illegal casino in New York's notorious Tenderloin district (near what is now Times Square), told a district attorney a sensational story: Manhattan's top anti-vice cop, Lieutenant Charles Becker, was part owner of his casino. Even worse, Becker and his "Strong Arm Squad," who were supposed to be cleaning up the Tenderloin, were instead allowing hundreds of casinos and brothels to flourish—while extorting huge amounts of cash from them. Just hours later, four men jumped out of a gray Packard and shot Rosenthal dead on a Manhattan street.

Outcome: The men who carried out the murder were arrested, and they all said that Becker had ordered the hit. The ensuing investigation revealed that Lieutenant Becker had taken more than $100,000 (about $2 million today) in extortion money in just nine months as head of the anti-vice unit. The story was a national sensation—and a major NYPD embarrassment—as the case dragged on for three years. The four hit men were convicted of murder and executed. Becker was also convicted, and on July 30, 1915, he became the first police officer in U.S. history to be executed for murder.

THE SUMMERDALE SCANDAL

The Perps: Eight Chicago police officers

The Story: In July 1959, 23-year-old Richie Morrison was arrested while burglarizing a Chicago business. He wasn't too worried about it at first, but when the help he seemed to expect didn't arrive, he started talking. And what a story: The "Babbling Burglar," as he became known across the nation, told investigators that over the previous 15 months he had carried out a string of burglaries...with the help of eight Chicago cops. They all worked

---

If grasshoppers were the size of humans, they could leap the length of a basketball court.

the night shift at the city's 40th, or "Summerdale," police district. They had helped plan the robberies, Morrison said, and had even used their squad cars to take away the loot.

Outcome: The eight officers were arrested, and all of them were eventually convicted on various felony charges. Two paid fines, and the other six served time in prison. Unlike some other police scandals, Summerdale actually resulted in significant changes to the department, most importantly the establishment of the Chicago Police Board—a five-member civilian panel to oversee many aspects of police administration, including the handling of cases of misconduct. The board still exists today.

THE MALDONADO SCANDAL

The Perps: Agent Alejo Maldonado, head of Puerto Rico's Criminal Investigations Corps (CIC), and several other cops

The Story: In 1982 the son of a wealthy San Juan, Puerto Rico, jeweler was kidnapped. The FBI was brought into the case, and was on the scene when a group of men picked up the $300,000 ransom and drove off. When FBI agents pulled them over, they were surprised to discover that Maldonado, one of the most powerful cops in Puerto Rico, was driving the car.

Outcome: A subsequent investigation revealed that for more than a decade Maldonado had led a gang of powerful and corrupt police officers that ran roughshod over the island, committing extortion, arson, robbery, murder—even murder-for-hire—and more. Their arrest and trial dominated the news in Puerto Rico for more than a year. Maldonado "explained" his actions by saying, "Police corruption is eternal. It was not something we made up, it was there and it still exists." In 1983 Maldonado was sentenced to 40 years in prison; several of his cohorts went to prison as well.

THE MIAMI RIVER COPS SCANDAL

The Perps: Several officers in Miami, Florida

The Story: On July 29, 1985, a group of men were attacked on a boat on the Miami River in the city's Little Havana district. Several of the men were thrown (or jumped) overboard; three died by drowning. An investigation found that the men had been unloading roughly 400 kilos of cocaine when the attack occurred. Further investigation revealed that the attackers were Miami cops, and they were in uniform when they made the raid. But instead of arresting the suspects and taking the cocaine as evidence, they took the cocaine and sold it, making about $116,000 in the process. Still more investigation revealed that the same group of corrupt cops had been pulling off similar drug heists, as well as a host of other crimes, for years.

Outcome: Thirty-four members of the Miami PD were arrested, some of whom agreed to testify against the others in exchange for immunity. During the course of the trial, several of the arrested cops hired a hit man to murder the key witness against them. (The plot fell through.) When it was all over, 24 Miami cops were convicted, and 17 went to prison. The longest sentence went to the leader of the group, Officer Osvaldo Coello, who got 35 years.

Extra: Writers for the television crime drama *Miami Vice* based several episodes on the Miami River Cops Scandal.

THE CLEVELAND POLICE SCANDAL

The Perps: Forty-four cops in Cleveland, Ohio

The Story: On January 21, 1998, the FBI completed a two-year investigation into organized crime in Cleveland by staging the biggest sting operation in their history to date, and most of the people arrested were cops. What agents had discovered during the initial stages of the investigation was a network of police officers in several different agencies who had been taking payoffs to protect—and take part in—major drug-smuggling operations. The leader of the ring: corrections officer (and mobster wannabe) Michael "Guido" Joye, who once told an undercover agent, "These guys I have working for me, we're a specialty, like a goon squad."

Outcome: The operation resulted in the felony convictions and prison sentences of 30 Cleveland-area cops, including Joye.

Extra: During the course of the operation, the FBI staged a fake "Mafia" induction ceremony, during which Officer Joye had to kneel on the floor in front of a table covered with a white cloth and candles to be "sworn in" as a "made man." A cop who later testified against Joye said, "He came out white as a ghost. He said he was in the Mafia now. He totally believed it."

THE RAMPART SCANDAL

The Perps: Dozens of Los Angeles police officers

The Story: Rafael Perez was an officer with the LAPD's Rampart Division, located northwest of downtown L.A. (named after the area's Rampart Boulevard). He was also a member of Community Resources Against Street Hoodlums, or CRASH—an elite LAPD anti-gang unit. And on August 25, 1998, Perez was arrested for stealing six pounds of cocaine from an evidence room. He was offered a five-year sentence and immunity from further prosecution…in exchange for testimony against fellow officers. Perez agreed, and ended up giving more than 4,000 pages of testimony implicating dozens of his fellow CRASH officers in drug deals, murder, robbery (even a bank robbery), perjury, falsification of police reports, extortion, and more.

Outcome: Of the 70 officers Perez implicated, seven resigned, twelve were suspended, and five were fired. Only seven were tried on criminal charges, and just three of those were convicted—and their convictions were later overturned. But the city of Los Angeles ended up paying over $125 million to settle more than 140 civil suits against the city of Los Angeles. And more than 100 previous convictions related to the corrupt officers were overturned. In 2000 the CRASH unit was closed down for good.

Extra: The investigation of the Rampart Scandal found that at least three CRASH officers were on the payroll of hip-hop mogul Marion "Suge" Knight, and his label, Death Row Records. In 2007 Perez and two other Rampart officers were named in a wrongful death lawsuit, alleging that they had carried out the drive-by murder of rapper Notorious B.I.G. That lawsuit was dismissed in 2010. (The murder of Notorious B.I.G. remains unsolved.)

*   *   *

ANIMAL HOUSE

David Roberts, 31, of Helston, England, runs a hotel…for chickens. Chicken owners who plan to be away from home can board their chickens with Roberts. The birds spend their days freely wandering the fox-proofed grounds during the day, and their nights in "5-star luxury coops." Rates start at about $3 per night per chicken.

Wash your hands! A single bacterium can multiply into a million bacteria in less than a day.

SAVING FORD FROM FORD

You may know the story of how Henry Ford put America on wheels. Here's the story of how he nearly ran the Ford Motor Company into a ditch.

WHEEL MAN

If you're a history buff or just like reading about automobiles, you probably already know how Henry Ford, the founder of the Ford Motor Company, used the moving assembly line and other mass-production techniques to revolutionize the auto industry. He drove the price of his Model T so low that ordinary people, even the workers on his assembly lines, could afford to buy cars for the first time. In the process, Ford, more than any other individual, ushered in the modern automobile age. By 1923, 57 percent of all cars manufactured in the United States, and half of all the cars on Earth, were Fords.

What's less well known about Henry Ford is how close he came to destroying the Ford Motor Company in the later years of his life. The only reason you can still buy a Ford today is that other members of the Ford family were able to wrest control of the failing company away from him before it collapsed entirely.

MR. T

Ironically, it was Henry Ford's obsession with the Model T, his greatest success, that initially set the Ford Motor Company on the road to ruin. Ford introduced the Model T in 1908 and for nearly 20 years fought every attempt to improve it or to replace it with something better. For many years Model Ts had no gas gauge. If you wanted to know how much fuel was in your car, you had to dip a stick into the gas tank. They had no electric starter, either. You started a Model T by turning a hand crank on the front of the car. And they had no gas pedals. You controlled the speed with a throttle that was located on the steering column.

Even when Henry Ford did give in and make improvements, he did so several years after his competitors. Result: By the mid-1920s, the Model T was hopelessly outdated. For years Ford had terrorized every other auto company as he dropped the price of the Model T ever lower, from $825 in 1908 all the way down to

$290 in 1924. But his refusal to update the car gave General Motors and other competitors the opening they needed. More than one automaker battled its way back from the brink just by adding improvements to their cars that Henry Ford refused to add to his.

Ford finally announced in mid-1927 that it was ending production of the Model T in favor of the much improved Model A, but the change came too late. That year Ford sold fewer cars than Chevrolet, GM's largest division. Strong sales of the Model A did put Ford back in first place in 1929…but only for a year, and by 1933 it was in *third* place, behind both Chevrolet and Chrysler.

TROUBLE UNDER THE HOOD

By the early 1930s, the company itself was as decrepit as the Model T. It had taken Ford six months to retool its factories to manufacture the Model A, and the disruption cost the company $250 million—the equivalent of about $3 billion today. GM, by comparison, could retool its manufacturing plants in six weeks.

Ford's network of independent dealers was also a mess. Years of being forced to sell obsolete Model Ts on a cash-only basis (Henry Ford didn't believe in auto loans) had caused many Ford dealers to go under; others had abandoned Ford to become GM or Chrysler dealers. Many who did remain loyal to Ford were driven out of business by Henry Ford himself when they failed to meet the company's unrealistic sales targets.

The biggest problem of all was the Ford executive suite. The company was wholly owned by the Ford family, and executives who were not family members already knew they'd never hold the top job. Henry Ford made matters much worse by firing any executive who showed even a hint of independence or initiative. The most talented Ford executives soon became *ex*-Ford executives, working for GM, Chrysler, or other auto companies, and driven by the desire to get even with Ford.

THE HEIR

About the only top executive who didn't leave was the one who couldn't: Edsel Ford, Henry's only child. Edsel had been the company's president since 1919, but he was president in name only. Though Henry held no title and liked to say his only responsibility

---

was to "let Edsel find something for me to do," he was firmly in control.

TOUGH LOVE

If anything, Henry Ford's ideas for how to work with Edsel were even more peculiar than his ideas about how to run an auto company. Edsel was a dutiful son, but Henry saw this as a weakness. He blamed himself for being soft on Edsel when he was growing up, and he believed the best way to toughen up the boy was to deliberately sabotage him as he tried to run the company. Henry routinely belittled Edsel in front of other executives, once shouting, "Edsel, you shut up!" after Edsel dared suggest in a board meeting that Fords should have modern hydraulic brakes. When Edsel decided to build coke ovens to process coal for steel production at a Ford plant, Henry feigned agreement even as he whispered to an aide, "as soon as Edsel gets those ovens built, I'm going to tear them down." The ovens were built. Henry tore them down.

When Edsel commissioned a new office building to house the company's accountants and sales staff, Henry cancelled the building, fired the accountants (he *hated* accountants), abolished the accounting department, and had its offices stripped bare. Then he told Edsel to put the salespeople where the accountants had been. Without any accountants to assist with bookkeeping, some departments were reduced to *weighing* stacks of invoices as a means of estimating their costs.

Henry's meddling in his son's affairs didn't stop at the end of the business day. He even paid Edsel's domestic servants to spy on their employer. Once, when they told Henry, an outspoken teetotaler, that Edsel had liquor in his home, Henry went there while Edsel was away on business and smashed every bottle.

OUT OF GAS

"There was a twisted collusion in the sad game that father and son were to play throughout the 1920s and 1930s, and its cruelest twist was that time did not heal the process, it made it worse," Robert Lacey writes in *Ford: The Men and the Machine*. "The more Edsel submitted, the more his father hurt him, and the more the boy was wounded, the more submissive he became."

Edsel had joined the company straight out of school in 1913, when he was 20, and silently endured his father's cruelty for 30 years. In the 1930s, he began to develop ulcers, which Henry (of course) attributed to weakness. "Regain health by cooperating with Henry Ford" were Henry Ford's instructions to his son.

Edsel's stomach problems worsened, but he put off medical tests for more than a year. When he finally went to the doctor, he was diagnosed with stomach cancer that had spread to his liver and other organs. After surgery to remove half his stomach, Edsel (who was never told he had cancer) returned to work. Henry continued to belittle and undermine him until the very end. By the end of April 1943, Edsel could not go on. He took to his bed and died four weeks later at the age of 49.

HIS OWN WORLD

Henry Ford named himself as president of the Ford Motor Company after Edsel's death. Only months away from turning 80, he too was a sick man. He'd had strokes in 1938 and 1941 and was suffering from memory lapses, slowed speech and movement, and other signs of encroaching senility.

Many old men like to live in the past; Ford reconstructed his in bricks and mortar. When he was in his early sixties he'd had a 19th-century village and museum called Greenfield Village built in the countryside northwest of Dearborn, Michigan. Now, as his faculties began to fail him, Ford spent more and more time wandering around his ersatz village instead of attending to business.

Ford became convinced that his teenaged niece, Dorothy Richardson, was his own mother reincarnated. Mary Ford had died in 1876, when Henry was only 13, and hadn't lived to see the automobile age. Henry made up for lost time by dressing Dorothy in period clothes similar to those he remembered his mother wearing, and teaching her how to drive a Ford—his way of showing his mother what he'd made of himself.

ALL THIS AND WORLD WAR II

That the Ford Motor Company was a dysfunctional, failing enterprise led by a dysfunctional, failing autocrat would have been bad enough in the best of times. But this was 1943, and the U.S. had been at war since the bombing of Pearl Harbor in 1941. Civilian automobile production was suspended in 1942, and now the Ford plants were busy manufacturing jeeps, planes, and other matériel for the war effort. The switch from cars to war production had taken place while Edsel was still alive, and it had been chaotic. By 1943 production at Ford's B-24 bomber plant was six months behind schedule, and the federal government had no faith in Henry Ford's ability to turn things around. The government even considered seizing control of the Ford Motor Company and running it itself.

That idea was rejected in favor of discharging Edsel Ford's oldest son, 25-year-old Henry Ford II, from the Navy so that he could help his grandfather run the company. Henry II left the Navy as requested, but old Henry didn't have any more faith in his grandson than he'd had in Edsel. Locked out of Edsel's old offices, Henry II spent the war years wandering from one Ford department to the next and quizzing employees on how they did their jobs.

THE TROUBLE WITH HARRY

The expectation among Ford family members was that when Henry died, Henry II would become president. That expectation was shattered in 1944 when it was discovered that old Henry had added a *codicil*—an extra provision—to his will, saying that for 10 years after his death, the Ford Motor Company would have no president. It would instead be run by the board of directors, with one of the directors, a man named Harry Bennett, serving as secretary.

The codicil was Bennett's idea. "My Harry," as Henry liked to call him, was the old man's best friend and the only person in the company he trusted. Bennett was the head of the Ford Service Department, the 3,000-man internal police force that Henry created to battle union agitators and maintain order in his factories. Bennett knew nothing about running an auto company; it was through scheming and brown-nosing that he had risen to become Henry Ford's right-hand man, wielding more influence than Edsel Ford. Indeed, Bennett was often the one who instigated, and then executed, Henry's orders to sabotage Edsel's work.

Now that Edsel was dead and old Henry was failing, Bennett's skill at manipulating the boss had made him the most powerful man in the company. He was also the most hated man, and no one hated him more than the rest of the Ford family. "Who is this man Bennett, who has so much control over my husband, and is ruining my son's health?" Henry's wife Clara had asked back in 1941.

Veggie kin: Carrots, parsley, and celery are all members of the same plant family.

Bennett burned the codicil to old Henry's will as soon as it was discovered, but the battle for the Ford Motor Company was on. Edsel's widow Eleanor now controlled Edsel's 41.9 percent share of the company's voting stock, and she threatened to sell her shares if Bennett succeeded in denying Henry II the presidency. "He killed my husband, and he's not going to kill my son," she vowed.

In April 1944, Henry II maneuvered to have himself named executive vice-president of the company, which made him superior to Harry Bennett...on paper. Bennett was still too powerful to confront directly, but Henry II used his new position to fire Bennett's cronies as he built his own alliances with people he trusted.

GRANDMA'S GIFT

In the end it may have been Henry's wife, Clara Ford, who did the most to save the Ford Motor Company from ruin. As Henry slid deeper into senility, Clara ordered that when Harry Bennett called the house, he was to be told that her husband was not home. Cut off from the boss, Bennett was powerless to retaliate against Henry II as he fired one Bennett loyalist after another.

Clara's biggest contribution to the battle came when she spent the summer of 1945 gently persuading her husband to give up control of the company and let Henry II take the reins. Finally, on September 20, 1945, he gave in and told Henry II that the job was his. Wasting no time, Henry II scheduled a meeting of the board of directors the next morning. As soon as he was appointed president, Henry II marched into Bennett's office and fired him.

A NEW FORD

Before assuming the presidency of Ford, the largest organization Henry Ford II had ever managed was the Yale University rowing team. Yet in the years that followed, he proved himself a worthy successor to his grandfather as he remade Ford into a modern, successful auto company. When Henry II retired in 1982 at age 65, the Ford Motor Company faced difficult new challenges as it struggled with quality-control problems and declining sales in the face of surging Japanese imports. That the company even survived long enough to face these threats, after many observers had declared it dead in the 1940s, may be Henry Ford II's greatest accomplishment of all.

Last state to secede from the Union during the Civil War (and the 1st readmitted): Tennessee.

UNCLE JOHN'S
STALL OF SHAME

Not everyone who makes it into the Stall of Fame is there for a good reason. That's why Uncle John created the "Stall of Shame."

Dubious Achiever: Steve Trendell, an officer with London's Metropolitan Police force

Claim to Shame: Spending too much time in the bathroom. *Lots* of bathrooms, actually.

True Story: Trendell, 30, missed a lot of work because of a bad back. Over an 18-month period between 2004 and 2006, he took 246 days of sick leave and spent another 130 days on "recuperative duty." He worked only 71 regular days during the entire period, and for a time even lived in a police rest home. Trendell's excuse: a bad back. But when the police department received a tip that his health troubles weren't as serious as he claimed, it placed him under surveillance…and discovered he was running a bathroom contracting business during the hours he was supposedly too disabled to work. (He was pretty brazen about it, too, even parking his company van in front of the rest home.)

Outcome: Trendell was arrested and charged with obtaining sick pay under false pretenses. He resigned from the force, pled guilty to two criminal counts of deception, and received a suspended six-month sentence and 250 hours of community service. (No word on whether he still installs bathrooms.)

Dubious Achievers: Inmates at the Maguire Correctional Center in Redwood City, California

Claim to Shame: Trying to stick it to San Mateo County taxpayers by flushing anything and everything down jailhouse toilets

True Story: In January 2008, the South Bayside System Authority, which provides sewer service to the jail, sued San Mateo County for more than $8 million in compensation for the damage that jail inmates had inflicted on sewer system pumps and other equipment by flushing socks, boxer shorts, shampoo bottles, bath towels, hairbrushes, garbage bags, and other seemingly unflushable items down their toilets as a way of rebelling against the prison. (How does the sewer authority know all that stuff is coming from the correctional facility? The inmates flushed their jailhouse jumpsuits down the toilets too.)

Outcome: The county settled the lawsuit for $2.3 million. The jail is tightening its inventory control to stop inmates from flushing so much stuff down their toilets. The sewer authority installed new grates to keep the trash away from sensitive equipment and hired two additional staffers to rake the trash off the grates several times a day. "It's a jail population," says deputy county counsel Porter Goltz. "What they flush down the toilet is sometimes difficult for us to monitor."

Dubious Achiever: Warren Saunders, 60, of Westwood, New Jersey
Claim to Shame: Taking "TP-ing" to new heights
True Story: One evening in October 2010, some students at Westwood Middle School were at soccer practice when an airplane passing overhead dropped two small objects on the field, then circled around and dropped a third object on the field before flying away. In a more innocent age, such odd behavior might not have been so frightening, but this was post-9/11 New Jersey. Some of the students called police, who traced the suspicious activity back to Saunders, a pilot who owns his own airplane. Saunders admitted tossing the objects—rolls of toilet paper—out of his plane onto the field. Why did he do it? Westwood Regional High School's football team was scheduled to play Mahwah High School that weekend in a game that would decide which team advanced to the playoffs. Saunders, a Westwood High fan, wanted to show his spirit by dropping streamers on the field at the start of the game. The toilet paper "attack" at the middle school was a practice run. (He says it was difficult to see in the evening light, and he did not realize there were kids on the field.)

Outcome: Saunders was facing 18 months in the slammer for one count of fourth-degree acrobatic flying over a populated area, but he got off with a year's probation and agreed to write a letter of apology to everyone involved. "I take full responsibility for my ill-conceived and, in hindsight, misguided idea of dropping toilet paper from my airplane," he wrote.

A cockroach can change directions up to 25 times in a second.

Dubious Achiever: Dwayne "Shorty" Davis, 51, Maryland businessman and owner of Shorty's Underground Pit Beef Shack

Claim to Shame: Taking his toilet-themed activism a little too far

True Story: Davis has a history of protesting against government agencies and officials he doesn't like. How? By decorating toilets with photographs, illustrations, news clippings, handwritten notes, and other items, and then depositing the fixtures in front of government buildings and other public places. In February 2011, Davis left a toilet on the sidewalk in front of the historic Baltimore County Courthouse in Towson, Maryland. This time, however, his decorations included a cell phone and a radio transmitter…and that made police suspect the toilet might be a bomb. Several streets were closed off while the bomb squad investigated. So what gave Davis away? He actually left photos of himself and a note with his home address inside the toilet. He initially denied involvement, but in a Facebook post made around the time the fixture was discovered, he wrote "Left my Toilet at the Baltimore Courthouse."

Outcome: At last report Davis was awaiting trial on two counts relating to the bomb scare. "Jesus had a cross. Martin Luther King had a dream. Malcolm X had a gun. Shorty got a toilet, but we all have our s**t to deal with," he told a TV reporter.

*　　　*　　　*

TWO NAUGHTY GAME SHOW GOOFS

Merideth Vieira: Though most planets are named after Roman deities, what is the only planet named for a figure in Greek mythology?

Contestant: Hmmm…Let's see. Jupiter is Roman, I believe. I can't even put a finger on Uranus.

—Who Wants to be a Millionaire?

Alex Trebek: This term for a long-handled gardening tool can also mean an immoral pleasure seeker.

Contestant: What is a hoe?

—Jeopardy! **(The answer was "rake.")**

THE ABCS OF pH

On page 116 we taught you how to make your own pH-level testers using nothing but cabbage and bald eagle spleens. (Okay, not exactly.) Now here's the scientific explanation behind pH. (pHinally!)

PHIRST THINGS FIRST

You've probably heard "pH level" referred to hundreds of times, possibly in relation to the water in a swimming pool or a hot tub, or to hair conditioner, laundry detergent, or even skin cream. And, like Uncle John, you probably had no idea what it actually meant. Well, in just a few minutes you will.

The first thing we need to understand about pH is why it's called "pH": It stands for "power of hydrogen." Why? Because pH is a measure of how different substances, when dissolved in water, chemically react with the hydrogen in that water—the "H" in H2O. And because water is so important in relation to life on Earth, the pH level of that water is extremely important, too.

OH!

Water is scientifically known as H2O, signifying that every water molecule is made up of two hydrogen atoms bonded to one oxygen atom. What most of us *don't* know is that those H2O molecules aren't always intact. In any given quantity of water, there's always a few H2O molecules that have split into two pieces: one atom of hydrogen (H) and a molecule containing one atom of hydrogen bonded with one atom of oxygen (OH). The only thing we need to understand about it right now is this: In pure water the amounts of H and OH are equal, but when another substance is dissolved in the water, the amounts become unequal. *How* unequal is what pH is all about.

Let's do two quick experiments:

• Imagine you have a glass of pure water. As we just described, the water has the same amount of H atoms as it has molecules of OH—because it's pure. But now add some sodium bicarbonate (also known as baking soda) to the water. What happens? Sodium bicarbonate molecules chemically react with water molecules,

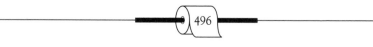

swapping atoms here and there. Result: There are now more OH molecules in the water than H atoms.

• Now take another glass of pure water, and this time add vinegar to it. The main ingredient in vinegar: acetic acid. When it's mixed with water, chemical reactions take place—and there is now much more H than OH in the water.

What you've just seen (if you could see it) is the core of the science behind pH. Some substances, such as baking soda, produce an excess of OH when dissolved in water. These substances are known as *bases*. Other substances, such as vinegar, produce an excess of H. These are known as *acids*. And each one has its own particular way of acting out here in the real world.

TRY IT AT HOME

Bases. Take something like common soap. You know how when you mix soap with water it feels slippery? That's because the main ingredient in soap is a base (most commonly lye) which, when mixed with water, produce excess OH molecules. What do OH molecules do when they come into contact with your skin? They chemically react with the oils on your skin, changing their molecular structure, and making them feel like what we think of as slippery...and soapy. This is just one characteristic that's common to all bases, and it's all because of the excess OH produced when bases are mixed with water.

Acids. Now let's use lemon juice, or citric acid, which, as the name suggests, is an acid. Put a piece of lemon in your mouth. The lemon juice mixes with the water in your saliva and, like all acids, creates an abundance of H, or hydrogen atoms. What do all those hydrogen atoms do in your mouth? They interact with specialized taste buds that send signals to your brain that you interpret as *sour*. This is just one characteristic of all acids: They all taste sour—and it's all because of the hydrogen atoms created when acids are mixed with the water in your saliva.

THE NUMBERS

pH is measured on a scale from 0 to 14. Pure water is rated 7, right in the middle. Because it contains equal amounts of H and OH, it's called *neutral*. Substances with a pH below 7 are acids, and those above 7 are bases. The lower the number, the more *acidic* the substance is; the higher the number, the more *basic* it is.

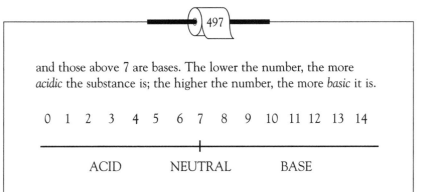

Here are the pH level of some common substances, starting with the acids:

- Egg yolks are slightly acidic, with a pH of about 5.5
- Vinegar is more acidic. It has a pH of around 2.2
- The acid in your stomach has a pH of 1
- Hydrochloric acid, a very strong acid, has a pH of 0

On the other side of the scale are the bases:

- Egg whites are slightly basic, with a pH of about 8.2
- Baking soda is a little more basic—right around 8.5
- Ammonia has a pH of about 11
- Lye (sodium hydroxide) is very basic, with a pH of 14

pH AND YOU

What's the pH level of your blood? Between 7.35 and 7.45…and it had better stay there. If it drops to 6.8 or rises to 7.8 for very long, you're dead. That's one of the amazing things about pH: Nature has very strict limits on pH levels. Just a few examples:

Seawater and freshwater both must have a pH level of between 6.5 and 8.5—not far from human blood—to maintain aquatic life. (There are a few exceptions. The most extreme example known is *Picrophilus torridus*, a microorganism that lives in hot springs on the Japanese island of Hokkaido, where it flourishes in waters with pH levels near 0—about the same as hydrochloric acid. Meaning that if *you* went into that water…your skin would burn off.)

Soil must be within a pH range from about 4.5 to 8 to sustain the nutrients needed by plant life.

Food and drinks must be at certain pH levels to be safe for con-

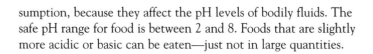

sumption, because they affect the pH levels of bodily fluids. The safe pH range for food is between 2 and 8. Foods that are slightly more acidic or basic can be eaten—just not in large quantities.

ALWAYS REMAIN NEUTRAL

One more fascinating aspect of pH is that acids and bases can be used to counteract each other. That's why gardeners treat soil with lime. Agricultural lime (crushed limestone) is a base, and adding it to acidic soil counteracts the acid, raising the pH to a level more suitable for growing plants. The same is true for soil that is too basic: You can add something acidic—such as coffee grounds, pine needles, or oak leaves—to bring the pH level down. It's also true for your stomach: *Antacids* are called "antacids" because they're bases—Tums are made from calcium carbonate, which has a pH of 9.4, and they're very effective in counteracting stomach acids. This is all known as *neutralizing* because they are all attempts to bring pH level closer to the neutral level of 7.

MORE PHUN PHACTS

• Anything basic can also be called *alkaline*.

• Only *aqueous* (water-soluble) substances can be measured for pH. Non-aqueous substances, such as oils and fats, can't.

• The overall pH of ocean water has been getting lower for some time, a result of acidic pollutants such as carbon dioxide and sulfur dioxide, which cause the production of excess H atoms in the water. *Acid rain* is rain water that's been affected in the same way.

• Lye, or caustic soda, with a chart-topping alkalinity of 14, is the active ingredient in Nair hair remover.

Here are the approximate pH level of several common—and a few uncommon—substances:

ACIDS	BASES
Battery acid: 1	Spinach: 7.8
Apple: 3	Great Salt Lake: 8.2
Feta cheese: 4.5	Baking soda: 8.3
Hot dogs: 5	Tide detergent: 10
Honeybee venom: 5	Lime (calcium hydroxide): 12.2
Coffee: 5.2 to 6.9	Oven cleaner: 13
Cow's milk: 6.6	Drano: 14

Odds that a piece of falling space junk will land on your house: 1 in a trillion.

BORN ON THE 2ND OF JULY

Pop Quiz: When did America's Continental Congress pass the Declaration of Independence? No, not July 4th. When did they sign it? Nope, that wasn't July 4th either. So what actually did happen on July 4th?

MYTHING IN ACTION

Most Americans believe that July 4, 1776, was the day that their nation began its road to independence from Great Britain. Well, not exactly. Think of the significant incidents from the American Revolution that you remember from history class: The Stamp Act? Eleven years earlier. The Boston Massacre? Six years earlier. The Boston Tea Party? Two years earlier. Paul Revere's Ride, and the battles at Lexington and Concord? Fifteen months earlier. By the time Congress got around to its Declaration of Independence, the signers were less leaders than followers in proclaiming an obvious fact: that American colonists were already fighting and dying for independence from England.

GO 4TH AND PROSPER

On July 2, 1776, the Continental Congress voted to declare that the 13 American colonies were independent states and no longer part of the British Empire. The next day, John Adams predicted in a letter to his wife, Abigail,

> The second day of July, 1776 will be celebrated by succeeded generations as the great anniversary festival. It ought to be solemnized with pomp and parade, with shows, games, sports, bells, bonfires, and illuminations, from one end of the continent to the other, from this time forward forever more.

He was mostly right about the celebration, but wrong by two days. After the vote, Congress spent the 3rd and 4th of July fine-tuning and nitpicking the formal document that explained the reasons for declaring independence. Adams was also correct in that the vote was usually considered the significant event, and the post-vote

---

There are 15,095 airports in United States—more than in the next nine countries combined.

follow-up was little more than paperwork. But for several after-the-fact reasons, that's not what happened.

Working from a first draft by a talented young wordsmith, 33-year-old Thomas Jefferson, the final document was meant to replace a shorter, more prosaic version written a few months earlier by Adams. Jefferson resented the fact that other people had edited his prose and removed about 25 percent of his writing, including a long passage critical of the slave trade. But two days after declaring independence, Congress finally voted to issue the document on July 4th.

Most of it was a laundry list of complaints about King George III: that he interfered with the colonists' elections, restricted immigration, controlled their trade, drafted their citizens into military service, levied taxes without their consent, controlled their bureaucrats and judges, sent armies to keep them in line, recruited mercenaries and Indians to help put down their rebellions, and neglected their concerns.

It was an outrage: Who died and made him king?

UNALIENABLE RIGHTS

Congress retained much of the vivid language Jefferson crafted. For example, "He has...sent hither swarms of Officers to harass our people, and eat out their substance." But what probably gave the document its enduring popularity was Jefferson's attempt at infusing it with some nobility beyond mere whining. Congress wisely included much of his high-toned phrasing (some of which would later come to haunt slaveholders like Jefferson), including the most famous: "We hold these truths to be self-evident, that all men are created equal, that they are endowed by their Creator with certain unalienable Rights, that among these are Life, Liberty, and the Pursuit of Happiness."

It wasn't that Jefferson and Congress had to go to a lot of trouble creating the bulk of the document. Jefferson himself admitted that the ideas and sentiments, although made eloquent, were not original. Some had been recycled from his earlier writings; some came from England's own Bill of Rights, which had been written to depose King James II; some had come from the many declarations of independence that had already been passed by individual towns, cities, and states before Congress acted.

The space suits worn by Apollo astronauts weighed 180 lbs. on Earth and 30 lbs. on the moon.

Having finally come up with words to justify their act of rebellion against the king, Congress went about selling their decision to their less-than-unified countrymen, printing up a few hundred copies of the resolution and mailing them off to newspapers and state governments. The famous signatures weren't included, and there was a good reason: They hadn't been affixed to the document yet. In fact, the historic parchment version of the Declaration wouldn't even come into existence until sometime after July 19, when Congress voted that the official declaration should be "engrossed on parchment" and "signed by every member of Congress." According to records, that happened on August 2, with out-of-town stragglers adding their names over weeks and months after that. Of the roughly 50 people who voted for independence on July 2, only 42 were still in office on August 2 to sign the Declaration of Independence, so the eight new members signed too, even though they hadn't voted for it.

The typeset version of the Declaration, the one without signatures, came back from the printer in time for public readings on July 8 in Philadelphia and Easton, Pennsylvania, and Trenton, New Jersey. Other cities and towns held similar events once their copies arrived. On July 9, General George Washington ordered that it be read to his troops, who had already been fighting the British for a year.

MISSION ACCOMPLISHED

The public readings and subsequent newspaper reprintings served their purpose:

• The Declaration stirred the population into a frenzy of anti-British sentiment. Riots broke out in some cities, with mobs attacking the trappings of British rule. (Of the many statues pulled down, an equestrian statue of King George in New York City ended up being melted into musket balls for the war effort.)

• It also helped solidify crucial financial support from the French, Spanish, and Dutch, who were happy to make things difficult for their longtime rivals the British.

Its mission accomplished, the autographed document became largely forgotten, generating about as much enduring interest then as an autographed copy of last year's *Congressional Record* would today. Its few lines of flowery language about the inalienable rights of humans were later shrugged off as not germane when the Constitution was being written, 10 years later. Not even the French revolutionaries borrowed from it—they were more heavily influenced by the newly passed American Constitution.

A LONG CAMPAIGN

Ironically, it was only because of politics that the Declaration of Independence ascended from forgotten document to American icon. During the presidential campaign of 1796, Federalist John Adams and Democratic-Republican Thomas Jefferson got into a public feud over who had contributed more to the founding of the United States. Jefferson laid claim to writing the Declaration of Independence; Adams retorted that he'd pushed the legislation through Congress and that Jefferson was just one member of a writing committee whose work needed a lot of editing. Jefferson lost the election, but eventually won the debate—the public began to see the nation's independence and the document that declared it as the same thing, and gave Jefferson overly generous credit for both.

Having been a contentious campaign issue, the Declaration was further pushed into the public's awareness during the War of 1812, when the United States and England fought once again. In 1817, seeing the public relations benefit of having people equate the act of drafting legislation with actual heroism, Congress commissioned John Trumbull to paint *Declaration of Independence*, the famous 12-by-18-foot portrayal of the drafting committee presenting the Declaration's first draft to the Continental Congress (not, as is often assumed, stepping forward to sign the finished work).

AN ICON FOR ICONOCLASTS

As time passed and the Declaration of Independence moved into the symbolic realm of July 4th fireworks and parades, a funny thing happened: Some people actually read it again and found that parts of it were still relevant. Not the complaints about King George, but the parts that inspired dreams about "self-evident" truths that "all men are created equal," which raised questions: If all men are created equal, why should only wealthy landowners be allowed to vote? How was it that some people could be forced into enslavement? And if all men are created equal, then why not minorities and women as well? Anti-slavery activists proclaimed "the twin rocks of the Bible and the Declaration of Independence" as the basis of the abolition movement. Similarly, Abraham Lincoln, when deciding what to do about slavery, cited the Declaration's stance on equality as the way to interpret what the Constitution really meant, a view that was controversial in its time (and, in some ways, still is).

THE CULT OF THE SIGNERS

Sometime in the 1820s came what Pulitzer Prize-winning historian Garry Wills would later call "the cult of the signers"—the idea that the politicians had engaged in a particularly brave action by signing the document. For the first time, the mostly obscure signers became the subjects of biographies, their images polished to a heroic sheen. It was a time of westward expansion, and the image of our forefathers joining together to pledge their lives and fortunes to the new nation gave America a sense of united purpose.

The stories of the *signing* had now completely overshadowed the earlier—and more significant—vote on the *Declaration* itself. In fact, the new view of the document completely obscured the memory that Americans had been fighting and dying for independence for a long time before. The July 2 date of the Declarations's passage and August 2 signing were both erroneously moved in collective memory to July 4, the day Congress finalized its language (and therefore the date written on the document), and stories that were almost too clever to be true started to emerge from the new signing date: John Hancock's announcement that he signed his name large so that King George III could read it without his spectacles (as if the king would ever have a chance to see the actual document; he read its text in memos and the London newspapers) and Hancock's setup ("Now we must all hang together"), followed by the gallows-humor of the ever-quotable Benjamin Franklin: "Yes, we must indeed all hang together, or most assuredly we shall all hang separately."

Meanwhile, America's Declaration of Independence started a whole new genre of political expression. From Albania to Vietnam, Ireland to Uzbekistan, scores of embattled revolutionaries issued their own declarations of independence, often cadging directly from the original. Jefferson would be proud.

Expecting a call at 1 o'cluck: Phone booths in Chicken Port, Brazil, are shaped like chickens.

METAL, PART III

*In Parts I and II (see pages 236 and 323), we told you how
metals are made in nature, and how they were used by early
humans. Now here's some information about how some of
the most important metals are manufactured today.*

IRON

Iron is the most abundant metal on Earth. But like most
metals, getting to it is tricky, because it's very rarely found in
a pure state in nature. It most commonly exists in *iron oxides*—
molecules composed of iron and oxygen, which are found
mixed with rock in *iron ore*. To get the iron, you have to get
rid of the oxygen and the rock. Here's the most common process
used today:

Preparation: After being mined, iron ore is crushed into a powder.
Huge magnetic drums are then used to separate iron-poor from
iron-rich ore. (The iron-rich ore sticks to the drums; the rest falls
away.) The iron-rich powder is mixed with clay and made into
marble-sized pellets, which are then heat-hardened. That allows
for more efficient burning during the next step, smelting.

Smelting: The pellets are smelted in a furnace along with *coke*—
coal that has been processed into almost pure carbon—and
limestone. The intense heat breaks the iron-oxygen bonds in the
ore, releasing the oxygen as gas, which bonds with carbon gas
being released from the burning coke to form CO_2 (carbon dioxide). The CO_2 escapes from the top of the furnace, and the iron,
now free of the oxygen, melts (at about 2,800°F) and collects at
the bottom of the furnace. The limestone also melts and bonds
with impurities to form molten waste known as *slag*. Slag is
lighter than iron, and it's continuously removed from the top of
the furnace.

Result: The product of this process is the iron alloy *pig iron*. It has
a relatively high carbon content of around 5 percent, which makes
it very brittle, and pig iron is therefore mostly useless except in
the manufacture of other iron alloys, especially steel.

A section of northern Canada (near Hudson's Bay) has the lowest gravity of anyplace on Earth.

STEEL

Today about 98 percent of pig iron produced worldwide goes into the production of steel, the most widely used metal or metal alloy in history. The process begins by pouring molten pig iron into steel furnaces, where it is treated to remove any remaining impurities, and to lower the carbon content to between 0.1 and 2 percent. That's one of the chief characteristics of steel: All but a very few of the hundreds of different types of steel contain carbon at these levels. That reduces the brittleness, while increasing strength and hardness. Depending on the type of steel being made, different elements are then added to the mix. Two examples:

• *Manganese steel*, or *mangalloy*, is about 13 percent manganese, which results in it being extremely impact-resistant. That makes mangalloy popular for use in mining tools, rock crushing equipment, and armor plating for military vehicles.

• *Stainless steel* is actually a name for a wide range of steels, but they all have one thing in common: *chromium*, from about 10 to 30 percent, depending on the type. The chromium on the surface of stainless steel bonds with oxygen in the air to form a layer of *chromium-oxide*, which is what gives stainless steel its very hard, shiny appearance, and makes it resistant to corrosion. And if it's damaged or scarred, the chromium re-bonds with oxygen, and a new layer forms—so it's self-repairing. Stainless steels are used in a wide variety of products, from kitchen utensils to surgical equipment to outdoor sculpture. (It's also 100% recyclable.)

ALUMINUM

The most common ore used for aluminum production is *bauxite*, a claylike substance that is around 50 percent *alumina*—aluminum bonded with oxygen. As with iron, getting to the aluminum means getting rid of the oxygen and the minerals in the ore. The process is much more complicated than iron extraction, and was only developed in the late 1800s. (Aluminum was only identified as a unique element in 1808.) The first part of the system most commonly used today is called the *Bayer process*, named after Austrian chemist Karl Bayer, who invented it in 1877.

The Bayer Process: Bauxite is mined and crushed, then mixed with water and lye, and heated in tanks. This heat and lye cause

---

Nice gig: *Wheel of Fortune's* Pat Sajak and Vanna White work 1 week a month.

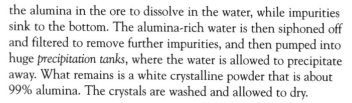

the alumina in the ore to dissolve in the water, while impurities sink to the bottom. The alumina-rich water is then siphoned off and filtered to remove further impurities, and then pumped into huge *precipitation tanks*, where the water is allowed to precipitate away. What remains is a white crystalline powder that is about 99% alumina. The crystals are washed and allowed to dry.

• The next step is known as the *Hall–Héroult process*, named for the two chemists who developed it—independently of one another—in 1886.

The Hall–Héroult Process: The alumina crystals (along with minerals that aid in the breakdown of alumina) are smelted at about 1,760°F in steel vats. But that's not enough to break the aluminum-oxygen bonds in the alumina; they're much stronger than iron-oxygen bonds. So a powerful electric current is sent through the molten material—and that causes the bonds to break. The oxygen is released as gas, and is attracted to carbon rods suspended above the molten mix, where it bonds with carbon to form CO_2 gas (just like in the iron smelting process). The freed-up aluminum melts and collects at the bottom of the pot. At this point it is 99.8% pure aluminum.

• Aluminum is used in a wide variety of applications, in its pure form (aluminum foil is made from nearly pure aluminum), and more commonly in alloys, mixed with elements such as silicon, copper, and zinc. Some are stronger than steel, and have the added benefit of being much lighter. Common uses include in cookware, soft drink cans, and automobile engine blocks.

PLATINUM

Platinum is a shiny, silver-white metal that is very rare and has some unique qualities: It's one of the densest metals, yet it is very malleable; it is extremely resistant to corrosion by temperature, rust, or exposure to materials such as acids; and it has a very high melting point of 3,215°F (Gold's melting point is just 1,064°, and iron's is 1,535°.) Platinum does exist in pure form in nature, but it's more commonly found mixed with other elements, including oxygen, copper, and nickel. More than 90 percent of the platinum mined in the world today comes from just four sites: three in Russia and one in South Africa. Production is quite complicated.

Chinese wedding custom: Tossing one of a bride's red shoes from the roof ensures happiness.

More than ten tons of ore must be mined to make a single ounce of platinum. A brief description of the process:

• Ore is mined, crushed to powder, and mixed with water and chemicals. Air is blown through the mix, creating bubbles—to which the tiny platinum particles stick. The bubbles rise to the surface of the tank, creating a soapy froth. The froth is collected, dried, and smelted at temperatures above 2,700°F. The heavier particles—the metals—sink to the bottom of the furnace. Lighter impurities collect on top of the molten metal and are removed. Complicated chemical processes are then used to separate the platinum from any copper, nickel, and other metals still present, until, finally, pure platinum is obtained.

SHINY BITS

• Iron ore is smelted in a *blast furnace*: Superheated air—up to 2,200°F—is "blasted" into the furnace, causing it to burn much hotter than it otherwise could. A typical blast furnace at a steel mill runs for 24 hours a day, 365 days a weeks, for up to 20 years, before it must be replaced.

• Pure steel is very susceptible to rust. *Galvanized steel* is steel coated with zinc—which is very resistant to rust.

• A major chemical ingredient in rubies, emeralds and sapphires: aluminum.

• What is most of the extremely rare metal platinum used for? Catalytic converters—the devices on automobiles used to clean exhaust. Platinum is an exceptionally good *catalyst*: it aids in the conversion of toxic gases in exhaust, such as carbon monoxide, into non-toxic gases.

• Platinum is extremely dense. If the two-pound paperback book you are holding right now were made of platinum, it would weigh about 48 pounds.

• It's a myth that there was no metalworking among Native Americans. Many tribes actually had long traditions of copper-working, especially around the Great Lakes, where the metal was naturally abundant.

• All the platinum mined in history could fit into an average home basement.

Termites do more damage per year in the U.S. than fires, storms, and earthquakes combined.

FRIDAY & TUESDAY

A couple of quick restaurant origins to go. Check, please!

T.G.I. FRIDAY'S

In the mid-1960s, Alan Stillman lived on Manhattan's East Side in a neighborhood that happened to have a lot of pretty models and airline stewardesses. But Stillman, a bachelor, was having trouble meeting them. Local bars were full of "guys drinking beer," and cocktail parties, where women *did* go, were by invitation only. Stillman wanted a public place where men *and* women could mingle, drink, and get a good burger. So he scraped together $10,000, bought an old corner bar, revamped it into a restaurant decorated with red and white stripes, and called the place T.G.I. Friday's. "My timing was exquisite," he said, "because I opened in 1965, the year the Pill was invented. I hit the sexual revolution on the head. It was the first singles bar." Stillman had opened a dozen T.G.I. Friday's by 1971, when he sold the chain for $1 million. He then opened Smith & Wollensky's Steakhouses (two names he picked at random from the phone book), which he still runs. Today there are 900 Friday's locations.

RUBY TUESDAY

In 1971 Sandy Beall, a University of Tennessee student, got a job at a Pizza Hut. Turns out Beall had a knack for the food business. Under the tutelage of his boss, William Kholmia, he was soon managing three Pizza Huts. Then tragedy struck—Kholmia suffered a massive heart attack. On his deathbed, he promised to leave Beall $10,000 to open his own restaurant. "A Pizza Hut?" asked Beall. "No," said his mentor, "do your own thing." Beall didn't know what kind of restaurant to open, so he drove to New York City for inspiration. There he discovered T.G.I. Friday's, and knew that was the kind of restaurant he wanted. So he went back to Knoxville and, with the help of four friends, converted a farmhouse into a full-service burgers-and-beer joint. Today it's Ruby Tuesday, Inc.—a casual-dining giant with 800 locations. (The name "Ruby Tuesday" comes from a Rolling Stones song, but not because Beall was a Stones fan—one of his fraternity brothers came up with the name. "I wasn't that hip," Beall admitted.)

Not too pious: Pope Pius II wrote an erotic novel.

MORE STRANGE LAWSUITS

A few more unusual legal battles.

THE PLAINTIFF: Jimmy A. Bell, a lawyer
THE DEFENDANT: Rich's Nail Salon in Landover, Maryland
THE LAWSUIT: On the way to dinner in fall 2010, Bell and a female friend decided to stop at Rich's salon to get manicures. When the bill came, Bell was charged $1 more than his friend. "Why am I paying more?" he asked. He claims they told him, "Because you're a man." Believing that his civil rights had been violated, Bell sued the salon for $200,000. "They didn't measure my hands or my nails to see if it's more work," he argued. "They made a distinction based solely on the fact that I'm a man."
THE VERDICT: This nail-biter was settled out of court "to the satisfaction to both parties."

THE PLAINTIFF: Dennis Gaede, a prison inmate
THE DEFENDANT: North Dakota State Penitentiary
THE LAWSUIT: Gaede alleged that while he was eating a breaded oyster in the prison's cafeteria in 2010, a piece of shell cracked one of his teeth. He asked the prison's dentist to perform a root canal and put a crown on the damaged tooth, but the dentist simply pulled the tooth. So Gaede, who is serving a life sentence for killing and dismembering a man, sued the prison for $75,000, claiming "cruel and unusual punishment."
THE VERDICT: Case dismissed.

THE PLAINTIFF: Lauren Rosenberg of Los Angeles
THE DEFENDANT: Google Maps and Patrick Harwood, a motorist in Park City, Utah
THE LAWSUIT: In January 2009, Rosenberg was visiting Park City and decided to take a walk through town. Using her Black-Berry, she downloaded walking directions from Google Maps,

---

President John Adams once got lost in the woods while trying to find the White House.

which led her to a busy highway with no sidewalk. Because she arrived at the road early in the morning, it was still dark out, and she couldn't tell whether there was a sidewalk on the *other* side. She crossed, only to discover that not only was there no sidewalk; there was a big wall just off the road. She was stuck. Before she could get back to the other side of the road, Harwood, who was driving to work, hit her. Rosenberg is seeking $100,000 from both Google Maps and Harwood for "severe injuries and emotional distress."

THE VERDICT: The case was pending as of press time, but it's not as clear-cut as you might think. Although Google Maps displays a warning on its web page—"This route may be missing sidewalks or pedestrian paths"—that warning did not show up on Rosenberg's small BlackBerry screen. Even so, she questions why would Google call it a "walking route" if there was no sidewalk. If she can prove that Google and Harwood were 51 percent responsible for her injuries, she'll get some money. If not, she'll get nothing.

UPDATE: In May 2011, the court ruled that Google Maps was not responsible for Rosenberg's injuries. That part of the case was dismissed, but she is still trying to sue Harwood.

*　　　*　　　*

HISTORY QUIZ

Q: What's the historical significance of the following sentence?

> Well, I guess I know enough to turn you inside out, you sockdologising old man-trap!

A: It was the cue to kill a president. On April 14, 1865, John Wilkes Booth, himself an actor, knew that particular line—from the 1858 play *Our American Cousin* by English playwright Tom Taylor—would cause such uproarious laughter at Ford's Theater in Washington, D.C., that no one in the audience would hear him shoot Abraham Lincoln. He was wrong—the shot *was* heard, and a scuffle ensued. Booth broke his foot after jumping from the balcony. He escaped, but was captured later.

NIXON'S LIST

As 1972 approached, President Richard Nixon started to get more and more concerned about his coming reelection campaign. He became convinced that his political adversaries weren't just opponents—they were "enemies" and had to be stopped. He and his advisers compiled this list of 20 public figures who they felt could hurt them in some way. Were they ever really threats to Nixon? Probably not, but Nixon thought so, which makes this piece of history all the more fascinating.

"ON SCREWING OUR POLITICAL ENEMIES"

In 1972 five men were caught breaking into Democratic National Committee headquarters in the Watergate Hotel in Washington, D.C. The culprits turned out to have ties to high-level members of both the Republican Party and the Nixon administration. The Congressional investigation that followed unraveled the Nixon presidency, exposing the systematic way Nixon abused power and attempted to destroy his enemies (real and imagined), eventually leading to his resignation in order to avoid impeachment.

One year before Nixon's resignation, on June 27, 1973, White House counsel John Dean testified before Congress about possible connections between the Nixon administration and the Watergate burglars' plan to steal information damaging to Democratic candidates. Dean mentioned that in 1971 he'd received a memo titled "On Screwing Our Political Enemies." Written by Charles Colson, another Nixon attorney, the memo was a list of people singled out as those most threatening to Nixon's career. The memo detailed how the White House planned to go about discrediting Nixon's opponents, which included anyone trying to run against him and any reporter who'd given him unfavorable coverage. The goal: to ruin every person on that list with a campaign of rumors, character assassination, and even IRS audits.

WHO ARE THESE PEOPLE?

The fact that there *was* a list was pretty much all Dean said about it. He didn't mention any names, although he did turn the memo over to the Senate as evidence. Daniel Schorr, the CBS reporter covering the hearings, wasn't satisfied—he wanted to *see* the list. He requested a copy of the memo from the Congressional press office the same day Dean talked about it. That night, as Schorr was delivering a live report on the *CBS Evening News*, an assistant handed him the memo, with its list of 20 targets. Schorr then read it live on the air. Among the names on the list, to Schorr's surprise, was Schorr himself. Here's a look at all the entrants on Nixon's "Enemies List," in the order that they were listed on the memo, from Enemy #1 down.

1) ARNOLD M. PICKER. Picker was a former executive with United Artists, a Hollywood film production studio. In 1971 he signed on as the finance director for Democratic Sen. Edwin Muskie's presidential campaign. The memo expresses the hope that a scandal involving Picker would "debilitate and embarrass the Muskie machine."

2) ALEXANDER E. BARKAN. Barkan was a union organizer who became the national director of the powerful AFL-CIO labor union Committee on Political Education (COPE) in 1963. COPE was the union's political wing, which lobbied on behalf of unionized labor and educated its members about which candidates were the most pro-union. Nixon and the Republican party were opponents of unionized labor, which is what landed Barkan on the Enemies List. The memo identified Barkan's COPE as "the most powerful political force" against Nixon in 1968, as it raised $10 million for Democratic candidates and influenced the votes of more than 4.6 million people. Nixon wanted COPE shut down, fearing that its anti-Nixon efforts would be ramped up in the 1972 election. Ironically, it turned out that Nixon had nothing to worry about: Barkan *denounced* the '72 Democratic presidential candidate, George McGovern, for succumbing to the tide of 1960s counterculture influence and turning the party into one of "acid, amnesty, and abortion."

3) EDWIN O. GUTHMAN. Politicians and political activists who opposed Nixon were on his Enemies List, and so were investigative reporters. Guthman won a Pulitzer Prize in 1950 when, as a reporter with the *Seattle Times*, he proved that the Washington

State Un-American Activities Committee doctored evidence to accuse a college professor of Communist ties. (Around the same time, Nixon had worked on the House Un-American Activities Committee, which rooted out Communists at the national level.) In 1961 Guthman became Attorney General Robert Kennedy's press secretary, and in 1965 national editor of the *Los Angeles Times*, where Nixon's aides were convinced (with little proof) that Guthman was "the prime mover behind the current Key Biscayne effort"—a scandal that linked Nixon's purchase of cheap real estate in Florida with known Mafiosi.

4) MAXWELL DANE. An advertising executive at Doyle Dane Bernbach, the advertising agency that handled most of the Democratic party's national presidential advertising in 1964. In that campaign, Dane's agency produced a frightening political ad for President Johnson called "Daisy," in which a little girl holds a flower in a field, counting down, until a nuclear bomb wipes out everything. That year, Democrat Lyndon Johnson beat Republican Barry Goldwater in a landslide...and Nixon wasn't about to let that happen to him. According to the memo, Dane was a test target for the Nixon enemies project—if he was successfully discredited, his partners, Doyle and Bernbach, would be next.

5) CHARLES DYSON. A major financier through his Dyson-Kissner Corporation, a major philanthropist through his Dyson Foundation, and a major contributor to Democratic candidates and causes. He funded the Businessmen's Educational Fund, which in turn sponsored a series of five-minute anti-Nixon radio ads in the run-up to the 1972 election. Dyson was also a close associate of Democrat strategist and Democratic National Committee chairman Larry O'Brien (whose office was the main target in the Watergate burglary).

6) HOWARD STEIN. One of the nation's leading investment bankers, Stein was chairman of the Dreyfus Corporation. There, he invented the mutual fund and made billions for his company and for himself. He was also the largest individual donor to Eugene McCarthy's 1968 presidential campaign. Nixon feared he'd donate as much or more to the opposition again in 1972, especially if the opposition were either John Lindsay or George McGovern, the memo notes.

7) ALLARD LOWENSTEIN. A civil rights activist, an anti-Vietnam War activist, a high-level Democratic party strategist, a one-term congressman from New York...and founder of a liberal voter information group called "Dump Nixon."

8) MORTON HALPERIN. Halperin was Deputy Assistant Secretary of Defense under Lyndon Johnson, and was one of the few officials in the Johnson administration who had opposed the Vietnam War from the very beginning. Nevertheless, Halperin was appointed to the National Security Council by Nixon's Secretary of State, Henry Kissinger. When the *New York Times* reported in May 1969 that Kissinger had directed the secret bombing of Cambodia, Kissinger and FBI director J. Edgar Hoover believed Halperin was responsible for leaking the news and began tapping his phones. He left the NSC later that year and went on to be a leader of Common Cause, a nonprofit group dedicated to openness and accountability in government. The tapping of his phone continued until early 1971.

9) LEONARD WOODCOCK. Woodcock appeared on the List with the caption "no comments necessary." He headed the United Auto Workers union, one of the largest and most powerful trade unions in the United States, with a large, Democrat-supporting voting bloc. Woodcock also used his position to publicly support two causes Nixon avoided: civil rights and women's rights.

10) S. STERLING MUNRO JR. Munro was a top aide for liberal Washington senator Henry "Scoop" Jackson, a possible 1972 presidential candidate. "Positive results" for digging up dirt on Munro, the memo notes, "would stick a pin in Jackson's white hat."

11) BERNARD T. FELD. Feld was an MIT physicist who had helped develop the atomic bomb. Feelings of remorse later led him to denounce nuclear weaponry and serve with both the Albert

Einstein Peace Committee and the Council for a Livable World, both nuclear disarmament action groups dedicated to banning nuclear weapons worldwide. Feld was a major voice for and donor to left-wing and pacifist causes, and as such, he was targeted by Nixon's cronies. The memo suggests that Feld will "program an all-court press against us [Nixon] in '72."

12) SIDNEY DAVIDOFF. In 1971 popular, young New York City mayor John Lindsay switched from the Republican party to the Democratic party, citing "the failure of 20 years in progressive Republican politics." He then announced his candidacy for the 1972 Democratic presidential nomination. He was an early front-runner, doing well in caucuses and fundraising. Davidoff was Lindsay's top aide, in charge of Lindsay's drive to capture the youth and counterculture vote. The Enemies memo called Davidoff "a first-class SOB wheeler-dealer."

13) JOHN CONYERS. Conyers was (and still is) a Michigan congressman representing Detroit. First elected in 1964, Conyers founded the Congressional Black Caucus in 1969 to address the specific needs of African-Americans, hired Rosa Parks as his secretary in 1965, and in 1968 advocated to make Martin Luther King Jr.'s birthday a national holiday. Nixon did not strongly support the Civil Rights Movement, largely because it was a liberal cause. As Conyers was a leading institutional force for civil rights, he was targeted by Nixon. (The memo crudely suggests that Conyers "has a known weakness for white females.")

14) SAMUEL M. LAMBERT. The president of the National Education Association, Lambert spoke out against Nixon's re-election promise to give federal aid to private and parochial schools, which threatened to be a contentious issue in 1972. If Lambert and the NEA were discredited, then Nixon would be able to push his legislation through more easily. (Ultimately, that legislation did not pass.)

15) STEWART RAWLINGS MOTT. Mott inherited millions from his father, Charles Stewart Mott, a member of the General Motors board of directors and mayor of Flint, Michigan. The

Basalt, the most common rock on Earth, is also found on the moon, Mars, and Venus.

younger Mott became a philanthropist, creating Mott Associates and pouring his money into causes considered liberal or even radical at the time, including the legalization of abortion, gay rights, birth control, and feminism. He was targeted for his donations of "big money for radic-lib candidates."

16) RONALD DELLUMS. A 36-year-old African-American U.S. congressman from Oakland, California, Dellums was a protégé of liberal senators John Tunney and Edward Kennedy, as well as an outspoken opponent of the Vietnam War.

17) DANIEL SCHORR. The memo labels the CBS News reporter "a real media enemy." Schorr started at the network in 1953, recruited by Edward R. Murrow, the newsman who challenged Sen. Joseph McCarthy's drive to root out Communists in government in the early 1950s (a drive in which California congressman Richard Nixon had assisted). Schorr made several reports over the years that Nixon loathed, including a sympathetic interview with Soviet leader Nikita Khrushchev in 1957 and an examination of life in East Germany in 1962. The FBI opened a file on Schorr in 1971.

18) S. HARRISON DOGOLE. One of the leading contributors to Hubert Humphrey's 1968 presidential campaign was Globe Security Systems—one of the largest private detective and security agencies in the United States. Globe president S. Harrison Dogole authorized the contributions to Humphrey, who lost to Nixon in the '68 election. Nixon's team was convinced that Dogole would be out for revenge in 1972, stating in the memo that Dogole had to be deflected because he could contribute millions to the 1972 Democratic candidate, or possibly even use Globe agents to spy on Nixon.

19) PAUL NEWMAN. Yes, *the* Paul Newman. One of the biggest stars in Hollywood, he was also aligned with "radical and liberal causes," including the unsuccessful presidential campaign of Democrat Eugene McCarthy in 1968. Newman had personally endorsed the candidate in campaign commercials, and Nixon's folks feared he might be used again in such a way in 1972.

20) MARY McGRORY. A columnist for the *Washington Post*, McGrory was a liberal editorial writer who penned "daily hate Nixon articles," as the memo put it, and anti-Vietnam War pieces. (McGrory went on to win the Pulitzer Prize in 1975 for her reporting on the Watergate scandal.)

AFTERMATH

In conjunction with the ongoing Watergate investigation, the Congressional Joint Committee on Internal Revenue Taxation looked into whether or not the people on Nixon's Enemies List had, in fact, been subjected to any unfair treatment, specifically unfair taxation or unnecessary tax audits. The committee announced in December 1973 that it had found no evidence that any of the people listed had been treated unfairly. But who knows what would have happened if those five men who broke into the Watergate hadn't been captured.

*   *   *

SMART ALECKS

"When you say, 'Bedtime!' that's not what the child hears. What the child hears is, 'Lie down in the dark...for hours...and don't move...I'm locking the door now.'"

—**Dylan Moran**

"A dog goes into a hardware store and says: 'I'd like a job please.' The hardware store owner says. 'We don't hire dogs, why don't you go join the circus?' The dog replies, 'What would the circus want with a plumber?'"

—**Steven Alan Green**

"Sometimes, when I'm feeling down, I like to take a home pregnancy test. Then I can say, 'Hey, at least I'm not pregnant.'"

—**Daniel Tosh**

"The only time it's OK to say 'I have diarrhea' is when you're playing Scrabble... because it's worth a s***load of points."

—**Zach Galifianakis**

"Toughest job I ever had: selling doors, door to door."

—**Bill Bailey**

TOILET TECH

Better living through bathroom technology.

HEAVY DUTY
Product: The Great John
What It Is: The first toilet, says the manufacturer, made specifically for "modern Americans." Translation: It's extra-large.
How It Works: Invented by the Great John Toilet Company (no relation to Uncle John), the Great John can reportedly accommodate any person up to the weight of 2,000 pounds. The base is wider than a conventional toilet's to provide extra support, and it connects to the bathroom floor with four anchors instead of the standard two. The seat provides 150 percent more "contact area" than a normal toilet (as well as offering side wings to prevent pinching if flesh still hangs over the larger seat).

SNAKE EYES
Product: FlexiSnake
What It Is: A plumbing snake to remove hair clogs from drains
How It Works: A traditional snake is tough to use—you have to unspool the metal coil, secure it with a screw, stick it down the drain, and hope that it doesn't snap into your face and blind you. The FlexiSnake is much simpler: A two-inch Velcro pad mounted on the end a short, bendy wire—it looks like the power cord on a lamp—grabs the hair that's blocking your drain, and you pull it out. Yucky, but easy.

STICK TO IT
Product: Bottom Buddy
What It Is: A long-armed TP holder
How It Works: One of the biggest challenges of being a large person is, um, cleaning up after using the toilet. That's why there's this $10 device. It's pretty simple, actually: It's a curved plastic wand with a gripper where a wad of toilet paper is inserted. After reaching around and using it, just press a button, and the wand neatly releases the TP into the bowl for hands-free disposal.

American pioneers had recipes for locust stew.

PAPER MOON

Product: Hemo Roll

What It Is: "Medicated" toilet paper

How It Works: Bad news: You've got hemorrhoids. Good news: You can get rid of them with Hemo Roll, a hemorrhoid-fighting toilet paper infused with herbs and tinctures that help reduce inflammation. At least that's what the Slovakian paper company that manufactures it claims. Among the ingredients in Hemo Roll, which is said to be gentler on the backside than non-infused, regular toilet paper: extracts of oak bark, marigold, and yarrow.

SPARKLY NUGGETS

Product: Jemal Wright Bath Designs

What It Is: Designer toilets

How It Works: Wright is a high-end home designer who specializes in fancy toilets and matching bathroom fixtures. Among his works are diamond-encrusted toilets, a gold-plated toilet with a matching pedestal sink, and a relatively understated metallic orange chrome toilet…with a diamond-encrusted flush handle. Cost: $65,000…and up.

BATHROOMS ARE FOR LOVERS

Product: TwoDaLoo

What It Is: A love-seat toilet

How It Works: In 1991 *Saturday Night Live* aired a fake commercial for an imaginary product called "The Love Toilet"—a two-person toilet for people so in love that they never want to be apart, even when they have to use the facilities. Like a Victorian love seat, the side-by-side toilets faced opposite directions, so the lovers could stare into each others eyes. In a case of life imitating art, the TwoDaLoo is now a real item, available for purchase for only $1,400. The only difference between the real TwoDaLoo and the fictional Love Toilet: The TwoDaLoo has a "privacy" bar separating the two commodes (as if that's an issue).

*   *   *

Water floats a ship. Water sinks a ship. —**Chinese proverb**

First country to use police dogs: Belgium (1859). They protected officers on the night shift.

WHAT'S COOKING?

If a recipe called for you to blanch some almonds, would you know how to do it? Cookbooks are full of techniques that are a mystery to most of us, even if their names sound familiar.

HEAT AND SERVE
There are many different ways to cook food, and each method affects food differently. Most techniques can be broken down into two categories: wet and dry—but it's not quite as straightforward as you'd think.

• *Wet cooking* involves the use of water or water-based liquid. This includes wine, broth, stock, milk, vinegar—whatever you like, as long as it's water-based. Wet techniques (also called *moist* techniques) include boiling, blanching, poaching, steaming, and stewing. The temperatures involved in all of these techniques are actually pretty low—because boiling water doesn't get any hotter than 212°F.

• *Dry-cooking* techniques include baking, broiling, frying, sautéing, and, you might be surprised to learn, deep-frying. Reason: Though oil is a liquid, it's not water-based and its use is therefore considered a *dry* cooking technique. Dry cooking involves cooking at temperatures of 270° F and above. It is these hotter temperatures that allow dry cooking to *brown* food—which cannot be done with wet techniques.

WET-COOKING TECHNIQUES

Boiling is simply the cooking of food in water-based liquid at a full boil. It's best for starchy or hard foods, such as pasta, potatoes, rice, beans, and hardier vegetables, but it can damage softer foods, such as fish. Boiling is also used to *reduce*—making foods like sauces or gravy thicker by steaming off water—and to decontaminate foods that may have come in contact with bacteria.

Blanching involves plunging food into boiling water for just a moment, and then removing and plunging it into ice water to stop the cooking process. It's commonly used to loosen vegetable or fruit skins for removal, to brighten the color of vegetables,

---

Japan produces almost 50% more cars than its two closest competitors, Germany and the US.

and to remove bitterness. Tip: Use plenty of water—the more water you have, the less the temperature will drop when you add the food.

Parboiling is *partially* cooking something in boiling water, often to make a later cooking technique quicker. You might parboil hard vegetables such as carrots, for example, so they don't come out too hard when being stir-fried with softer vegetables. Or you might want to parboil chicken to speed up grilling. Parboiling is also used before freezing vegetables, although some require only blanching.

Poaching is cooking in water (or wine, milk, stock, etc.) below boiling temperature, at 160°F to 180°F. You should be able to see the water circulating but not bubbling. This is a gentle method that works well with delicate foods such as eggs, fish, or fruit. In *submersion* poaching, the food is completely covered with liquid; in *shallow* poaching, the water comes about halfway up the food, with the pan covered, thereby both poaching and steaming the food. Tip: When poaching eggs, add a touch of vinegar to the water to get the whites to form a nice, neat shape.

Simmering is the step between poaching and boiling, done at temperatures of between 180°F and 205°F. It's a slow method for preparing stocks and soups, and to soften up tougher cuts of meat—the ones around "the hoof and the horn," such as chuck, shank, and brisket. To get a proper simmering temperature, bring the water to a full boil, and then turn down the heat until you see tiny bubbles occasionally rising to the surface.

Steaming is cooking with the steam from boiling liquid. It's considered a healthy cooking technique because it adds no oils to food, and nutrients don't leach out into the water as they do with submersion techniques. The steam doesn't have to come from a liquid in the bottom of a steamer—it can come from the food itself. A good example is fish cooked *en papillote* ("in paper"): Wrap fish in parchment paper and heat it (in an oven or over a fire, for example), and let the fish's own juices steam it from inside.

Stewing is the simmering of meats and vegetables (cut up into bite-sized pieces) in liquid that covers the food completely. It's

Ooh-la-la! Bonobo chimpanzees French-kiss.

good for tough meats, but any meat or fish can be stewed. *Braising* is similar to stewing, but the food is *browned* first (see below), then only half-covered with liquid, and the pot is always tightly lidded to keep the steam in. A classic example of a braised dish: pot roast.

DRY-COOKING TECHNIQUES

Baking is prolonged dry cooking by hot air—in an open or enclosed oven—at temperatures ranging from 270°F to 450°F. It's used for a variety of foods, including bread, cakes, pastries, pies, potatoes, beans, and lasagna, just to name a few. (Baking can also be done on heated surfaces, such as on hot rocks.)

Roasting is essentially the same as baking—cooking with heated air in an oven—but the term *roasting* is used when the food is meat. (Or chestnuts. Nobody seems to know why.) Roasted meat is usually set on a wire rack in a pan, so the bottom of the meat doesn't get soggy, and the juices collected in the pan are often basted onto the meat while cooking. (Roasting can also be done over an open fire, as in roasting a pig on a spit.) Tip: Meats that have been roasted should rest for 10 minutes or so after cooking. That allows the juices to settle and not run out during slicing.

Blackening is a technique used to cook fish. It's done on a very hot and very dry cast iron skillet. (If white ash spots appear on the skillet, you've gone a little too far.) The fish is dipped in melted butter, rolled in spices, dropped onto the skillet, and cooked for one to two minutes per side. Tip: Don't do it indoors unless you've got *really* good ventilation. Blackening creates a *lot* of smoke.

Broiling (called *grilling* outside the United States and Canada) is cooking food via heat radiating off a flame or element from above. The food sits on a grill or slotted tray, allowing oils to drip away from the food. It's sometimes recommended to keep the broiler door open a little, to prevent the thermostat from turning the element or flame off, as you want constant heat. Broiling is best for tender meats—it doesn't soften meat as much as it adds flavor via *browning*. Barbecuing follows the same basic rules, except that the heat source is under rather than above the food.

Browning, also called *searing*, is quick-cooking a food's surface at high heat. It can be done in a pan, in an oven, or on a barbecue. Browning affects naturally occurring sugars and proteins in food, and can change and greatly enhance its colors, textures, and flavors.

Deep frying is complete submersion of food in oil heated to between 350°F and 375°F. Done correctly, the oil turns the water in the food to steam, which not only prevents the oil from getting into the food (the pressure of the escaping steam keeps it out) but it cooks the food from inside. Deep frying gets a bad rap, but when it's done properly, it can actually be an economical, safe, and healthy cooking technique.

Sautéing is pan frying on a very hot pan with just a thin layer of oil. It's meant to be done quickly, to prevent the food from absorbing the oil. The food, which is cut into similarly sized pieces so they cook uniformly, is turned often, causing a slight browning on all sides of the food. (*Sauté* means "jump" in French, and refers to how the food is moved about in the pan.)

Pan frying is simple pan cooking (as opposed to more-specialized frying techniques like sautéing). Common examples of pan-fried foods are bacon, eggs, pancakes, and hamburgers.

Stir frying is frying at a much higher temperature than sautéing. Chinese in origin, it can be done in a wok, in a regular pan, or on a griddle. The food is chopped into bite-sized pieces and cooked for just a short amount of time.

A FEW MORE BITES

• *Velveting chicken* is a stir-fry technique in which chicken is marinated for 30 minutes in a mixture of sherry, salt, egg white, oil, and cornstarch. It's then fried until it turns white and then finishes cooking with other stir-fry ingredients.

• *Curing* changes the chemistry of food in much the same way that cooking does, but with very little or no heat. This can be achieved by adding salt or sugar to the food, or exposing it to smoke.

• Microwaves cook by *exciting* water molecules in food, causing them to heat up and steam the food. This means that microwaves can only heat food to 212°F—which is why you can't brown food in a microwave.

FONT(S) OF KNOWLEDGE

*We see them every day and seldom notice them,
but every typeface—from 𝕲𝔬𝔱𝔥𝔦𝔠 to Futura
to Comic Sans—has a story behind it.*

LIVING HISTORY

As you sit there reading the letters on this page, you're actually looking at symbols from the distant past. Take the two oldest letters in our alphabet, "X" and "O"; they were created by the Phoenicians more than 3,000 years ago. Most of the rest of the "modern" alphabet was created by the Greeks and Romans a few centuries after that. (The term *alphabet* is derived from the first two Greek letters, *alpha* and *beta*, which still look like "A" and "B" today.) Even the younger letters, such as "J" and "U," are hundreds of years old.

What *has* changed a lot over the centuries is how these letters have been chiseled, written, and printed. Yet the desired effect is the same—to convey a specific message. When people speak, their words make up only a portion of what they're trying to communicate. Additional information is conveyed by their tone, volume, posture, and even the setting. This principle works for reading as well: The font acts as the word's "body language." The study and creation of this language is called *typography*, from the Greek *typo* ("impression") and *graphy* ("writing").

FONT OR TYPEFACE?

The terms *typeface* and *font* are often used interchangeably, but technically they're not the same thing. A typeface is a lettering style that was created by a designer (called a typographer), whereas a font is a set of guidelines for how a specific letter, symbol, or number within a specific typeface should appear. Helvetica, for example, is a typeface. An example of a font might be "Helvetica 10-point bold italic," which looks like **this**. Today, typefaces are primarily created on computers, but their history goes back more than a thousand years. There are an estimated 100,000 typefaces in existence. Here are the stories behind a few of them.

WHOCARESABOUTREADABILITY?

In A.D. 781, a scholar named Alcuin of York was tasked with creating a uniform script to be used throughout Charlemagne's empire, which covered most of Europe. Lettering had changed very little since the fall of the Roman Empire in the 400s, except that it had become even more difficult to read. There were no lowercase letters, no breaks between words, and no punctuation. Everything was hand-written by scribes, each of whom added his own flair. Alcuin's style of script, which we now call *carolingian minuscule*, helped put an end to that. Here's a sample:

[handwritten carolingian minuscule sample of five lines]

This typeface remained the standard long beyond Charlemagne's rule and into the 1200s, but as time went on, it too became increasingly difficult to read as new scribes added new embellishments. The strokes of the letters got thicker, and the ends of the strokes got spikier. Result: carolingian minuscule went from what you see above to something resembling this:

𝕲𝖔𝖙𝖍𝖎𝖈 𝕭𝖑𝖆𝖈𝖐𝖑𝖊𝖙𝖙𝖊𝖗 [1400s]

Variations of this style of lettering, also called Old English and Textura, were used by monks who toiled away with ink and paper in small rooms called *scriptoriums* for months or even years just to make a single book. That was the norm until the mid-1400s when a German goldsmith named Johannes Gutenberg (1398–1468) realized that he could make a lot of money printing Bibles that appeared as if they were lettered by hand, but were made in a fraction of the time. There were a few rudimentary printing methods in use in Europe and the Far East, but the most popular one—block printing—was really only useful for printing pictures, not words. Utilizing his metalworking skills, Gutenberg created the *movable type* system in which individual letters and numbers could be carved out of soft metal, cut out with a punch-cutter, and then placed (in reverse) to form a page of text. Then, using new oil-based inks, these letters could be transferred onto pages.

The space shuttle *Discovery* flew 142 million miles, equal to 309 round trips to the moon.

The impact of Gutenberg's printing press cannot be underestimated—it effectively ended the Dark Ages and ushered in a new era of literacy in which books became available to the average person. (And his basic method of printing was the norm until the 1970s.) Yet Gutenberg was equally important to the world of typography: The 270 individual letters and numbers he created at different sizes are considered the first true fonts.

Why is his typeface called "gothic"? It was the Italians who gave it the name. In Italy in the 1500s, the word *gothic* was an insult meaning "barbaric." Because the Italians blamed the fall of the Roman empire on the Germanic tribes—called Goths—who sacked Rome in the 400s, anything resembling Germanic culture, from their spiked architectural building styles to their hard-to-read, spiked letters, was considered "gothic."

Garamond (1550s)

Claude Garamond (1480–1561) was a French bookmaker who refined Gutenberg's movable type system to make it even easier to operate. He's also one of the pioneers of *roman type*, so named during the Renaissance because it harkened back to the letterforms used in ancient Greece and Rome. Back then, because each letter had to be chiseled by hand, the carvers created typefaces that required few strokes. The Latin alphabet (which consisted of only capital letters) mirrored the Greco-Roman ideals of symmetry, proportion, and geometry—thin lines with rounded tops, akin to arches. Garamond brought back a unique feature of roman text: *serifs*, the little notches and hooks at the ends of letters. During his lifetime, Garamond was most famous for his Greek typestyles, which he designed on commission from King Francis I. Today, however, he's known for the typeface family that bears his name. Garamond has been a favorite font of book printers for nearly 500 years. (*Italic* type, a slanted version of roman type, was created by Italian Francesco Griffo in the early 1500s.)

Caslon (1722)

You may not recognize the name, but Caslon—designed by Englishman William Caslon in 1722—is widely considered to be the first typeface created in English. When British foundries started shipping the metal forms of Caslon to presses in the New World,

Founded in 1636, Harvard was both the first college and the first corporation in N. America.

they had no way of knowing that American revolutionaries would one day use this "British national type" to print the first copies of the document that would free America from British rule:

IN CONGRESS, JULY 4, 1776.
A DECLARATION
BY THE REPRESENTATIVES OF THE
UNITED STATES OF AMERICA,
IN GENERAL CONGRESS ASSEMBLED.

After that, Caslon fell out of favor in the United States for decades—mostly because of its ties to England, from which the new nation wanted to distance itself. In the mid-1800s, old type-styles started to become fashionable again and Caslon staged a comeback. (Playwright George Bernard Shaw insisted that all his works be set in the typeface.) By the early 20th century, the mantra among typesetters on both sides of the Atlantic was, "When in doubt, use Caslon." More-contemporary fonts would soon take over, but in recent years Caslon has been making another comeback.

Times New Roman (1932)

Stanley Morison (1889–1967) was among the 20th century's most influential typographers. Employed by the Monotype Corporation, he was responsible for the resurgence of several nearly obsolete fonts—including **Bodoni**, Garamond, Baskerville, and Bembo. In 1931, while serving as a consultant to *The Times of London*, he criticized the newspaper's outdated typeface. So *Times* bosses commissioned him to come up with a better one. Morison based his design on the roman serif font **Plantin**, sometimes referred to as Times Old Roman, but he made it much easier to read. A year after its 1932 debut, *The Times* gave up its ownership rights to the typeface, making it freely available to any newspaper that wanted to use it. However, because Times New Roman prints best on white paper, few other newspapers used it. Why? Because most newspapers used a darker grayish stock. Instead, Times New Roman became the preferred typeface for books and magazines. A close derivation of Times New Roman is used for the title font of *TIME* magazine. But don't go looking for that font online; the title was created by a graphic artist by hand. And he only created the word TIME .

Goudy (1915)

Frederic William Goudy (1865–1947) was an American artist, publisher, teacher, and typographer. He designed more than 100 typefaces, the most lasting of which bears his name. Its main benefit: The small *descenders* (the part of a letter that falls below the baseline) allow for more lines per printed page. Goudy spent much of his career creating scripts for advertising purposes, but that pursuit felt hollow to him, so he spent his later years working as an instructor; he mentored some of the 20th century's most influential typographers. But what Goudy really wanted to do was create the "perfect" roman script, so he built a foundry at his New York home to experiment with new designs. Sadly, it was destroyed by a fire before he could finish.

BRI history note: In 1988, when Uncle John was putting together the first *Bathroom Reader*, he asked the BRI's go-to designer, Michael Brunsfeld, to suggest a font for the book's title. One of Michael's picks was Goudy. Uncle John liked it so much that we decided to use it for both the title and the text you see on our pages. This is Goudy!

Courier (1956)

Technically, Courier is a "monospaced slab serif" typeface (each letter takes up the same amount of horizontal space), but it's commonly known as the "typewriter font." That's what Howard Kettler had in mind when he designed it for IBM in 1956. Because of IBM's dominance in the typewriter market, Courier (and dozens of subsequent imitations) became very popular. One place you may recognize it—on de-classified government documents with blocks of text blacked out. The U.S. State Department used Courier because it was monospaced, making it more difficult for snooping eyes to identify the blacked-out letters. In 2004 the State Department switched to Times New Roman, which has consistent spacing and is much more readable (except the blacked-out parts).

Palatino (1948)

German typographer Hermann Zapf, born in 1918, is one of the most prolific (and copied) type designers in modern history. His most famous typeface is Palatino, which he designed in 1948. He named it for the Italian writing master Giovanni Battista Palatino, a contemporary of Michelangelo and Claude Garamond. Zapf didn't just copy a Renaissance script, though; he used it as inspiration for a roman serif font that's legible and attractive—suitable for both title and body text. In the 1990s, Monotype released a Palatino-look-alike for computers called **Book Antiqua**. Here's that same name in Palatino: **Book Antiqua**. Notice the subtle differences? Probably not. (Palatino has thinner strokes.) But Zapf noticed. He was bothered by this and other derivations of his work, so in 1999 he created a new, *official* version of Palatino licensed especially for use in Microsoft's computer systems.

✤✳■✺☉✿▼▲ (∞✚✗✗)

Since writing began, scribes have used "non-letterform glyphs" to add visual pizzazz to their work: stars, flowers, scrolls, borders, toilet paper rolls, etc. By the 1800s, these glyphs were known by so many different names—including *ornamentals* and *fleurons*—that printers simply called them *dingbats*, the 19th-century equivalent to "thingamajigs" or "whatchamacallits." Today, there are hundreds of symbol fonts to choose from, the most famous of which (printed above) is Zapf Dingbats, created by Hermann Zapf in 1978.

Futura (1928)

The French word *sans* means "without"; hence, *sans serif* letters lack notches and hooks. (This **T** has serifs; this **T** does not.) Although the sans serif style dates back to ancient Greece, it didn't really catch on among designers and printers until the 19th century. And even then, most European typographers thought letters without serifs were ugly (which may explain why they're also called *grotesque* fonts). The style got a big boost in the 1920s thanks to the German Bauhaus movement of modern art, which stressed function over style—no unnecessary elements. The most famous sans serif typeface to come out of this movement is Futura, created in 1928 by German typographer Paul Renner. His goal was to combine the strength of gothic type with the elegance of roman type, all while staying within the strict boundaries of the Bauhaus movement. Futura was revolutionary for its time: Advertisers used it to show that their products were clean and refined (as a contrast to the dirty coal-burning technology of the day). Futura and the other sans serif typefaces that followed were mainly used in titles and headlines. Aptly, the commemorative plaque that Apollo astronauts left on the Moon in 1969 is set in Futura. Also, the floating title of the TV show **LOST** is set in the typeface. And if you spend a lot of time browsing the Internet, you'll see that Futura is used for the body text on many websites because of its readability.

Helvetica (1957)

In 1957 Swiss typographers Max Miedinger and Edüard Hoffmann set out to create a typeface that was simple, elegant, and modern. Based on a German sans serif font called Akzidenz-Grotesks, they called their design Neue Haas Grotesk (it was created and formed at the famous Haas foundry in Switzerland). In 1960 the typeface was refined and renamed Helvetica, based on the Latin *Helvetia*, which means "Swiss." Helvetica was an instant hit: Corporations liked it for its neutral tone; advertisers, for its readability. It became one of the most popular fonts of the 20th century, especially for transportation: New York City **Subway** signs, the logos for **Jeep** and **TOYOTA**, and millions of road signs.

Arial (1982)

You don't see Helvetica used on most computers. Instead, you see its look-alike, Arial. Why are these two typefaces almost identical? In the 1980s, Helvetica became a standard system font in Apple Macintosh computers, but a battle (that's still being waged today) was brewing: Adobe Software Systems purchased the Helvetica family of typefaces directly from Haas for use in its TrueType system. Result: Adobe won the respect of the typography industry by purchasing the rights directly from Haas, as opposed to going with some cheap knockoff…but only Adobe had the coding required to display it clearly on a computer screen. When it came time for Microsoft to choose its own default system font, instead of using Helvetica and being at the mercy of Adobe's software, the computer giant went with a cheap knockoff, Arial, designed in 1982 by Robin Nicholas and Patricia Saunders for Monotype. (Want to know how close they are? Look at the subtle difference in the tails on Helvetica's "a" and Arial's "a".)

Knitted socks from A.D. 200 have been discovered in Egyptian tombs.

Century Gothic (1991)

Why is this typeface—based on Twentieth Century, a 1930s design by Sol Hess for Monotype—called Century Gothic, when it seemingly has little in common with Germanic texts still referred to as 𝕲𝖔𝖙𝖍𝖎𝖈 𝕭𝖑𝖆𝖈𝖐𝖑𝖊𝖙𝖙𝖊𝖗? Because "gothic" is an outmoded typographic term for sans-serif, so named because the type color of early sans-serif typefaces was similar to that of blackletter script. Also, unlike roman typefaces like Garamond or Goudy, both are sans serif (the spikes and adornments on old gothic faces aren't considered true serifs). This script kept the strength of gothic-style letters, but featured a large *x-height* (a typographer term, referring to the height of a lowercase "x" in any particular font). Century Gothic proved great for advertisements, which is where you'll see it used the most.

Film note: A similar typeface called News Gothic (designed by Morris Fuller Benton in 1908) is familiar to any movie buff:

> A long time ago, in a galaxy far,
> far away...

TRAJAN (1989)

In 113 A.D., a 100-foot-tall column was erected in Rome to celebrate Emperor Trajan's victory in the Dacian Wars. Etched into the base is a dedication set in classic Roman script. Ever since the Renaissance, typographers have attempted to create typefaces based on this script, including Frederic Goudy and Hermann Zapf. In 1989 a modern version of Trajan was created by Carol Twomby, a type designer working for Adobe. Like the true Roman alphabet, Trajan has no lowercase letters. As was the case with Helvetica and Times New Roman before it, many graphic designers condemn Trajan for committing the greatest sin of any typeface: overuse. Who overuses it? Hollywood movie poster designers, as evidenced by the posters for APOLLO 13, TITANIC, THE DA VINCI CODE, SEX AND THE CITY, BLACK SWAN... and so on.

Comic Sans (1994)

In 1994 Microsoft typographer Vincent Connare opened a test version of a welcome screen for kids that featured a cartoon dog speaking with a text bubble. Connare immediately saw that the words were set in Times New Roman. "That's not a good font for kids," he told his bosses. So they told him to create one that would be. Connare drew inspiration from 1980s *Batman* and *Watchmen* comic books and came up with Comic Sans. It has since become one of the typefaces most reviled by designers. Why? Although Comic Sans was designed for kids, Microsoft added it to its font menu on home computers. And within a few years, Comic Sans was showing up all over the place. From church bulletins to restaurant signs, amateur designers frequently chose Comic Sans for their projects. It grew even more common when it became the default font in many instant-messaging programs. It's become so hated that there's a "Ban Comic Sans" movement online, initiated by designers Holly and David Combs in 1999. Their manifesto reads in part:

> Like the tone of a spoken voice, the characteristics of a typeface convey meaning. The design of the typeface is, in itself, its voice. Often this voice speaks louder than the text itself. Thus when designing a **Do Not Enter** sign, the use of a heavy-stroked, attention-commanding font such as Impact is appropriate. Typesetting such a message in Comic Sans—Do Not Enter—would be ludicrous.

So far, they've gathered about 5,000 signatures for a petition to "eradicate" the font. They even have a favorite joke: "Comic Sans walks into a bar, the bartender says, 'We don't serve your type!'"

*　　*　　*

THEIR FAVORITE BOOKS

Groucho Marx: *Charlotte's Web*, by E.B. White

Madonna: *Gone With the Wind*, by Margaret Mitchell

Stephen King: *Lord of the Flies*, by William Golding

James Dean: *The Little Prince*, by Antoine de Saint-Exupéry

Barack Obama: *Song of Solomon*, by Toni Morrison

Joe DiMaggio: *Superman* comic books

Lily Tomlin: *The Shipping News*, by E. Annie Proulx

Angelina Jolie: *In Search of the Real Dracula*, by M.J. Trow

Will Smith: *The Alchemist*, by Paulo Coehlo

Uncle John: *Drop City*, by T.C. Boyle (this week, anyway)

There are more pet fish in America than there are dogs and cats combined.

A THOUSAND CRANES

Sending a sick person a thousand paper cranes, each one folded from a single square of paper, is a tradition that originated in Japan and has spread all over the world. Here's the story of a little girl who helped turn it into an international phenomenon.

CHILDHOOD, INTERRUPTED

In the fall of 1954, an 11-year-old Japanese girl named Sadako Sasaki came down with what her family thought was a cold…until they found large lumps on her neck and behind her ears. That was enough to terrify any parent, but Sadako's family had a special reason to worry: They lived in Hiroshima, and were just a mile from ground zero on August 6, 1945, when the U.S. dropped an atomic bomb on the city in the closing days of World War II.

Sadako, two years old at the time of the bombing, had escaped the blast with only minor injuries. But she and her family were caught in a shower of "black rain"—radioactive fallout—as they fled the city. Now, nearly a decade later, as Sadako's condition worsened her parents' thoughts turned to "A-bomb disease," the catchall name that many Japanese gave to radiation-caused illnesses. In early 1955, doctors confirmed the Sasakis' worst fears: Sadako had leukemia, most likely caused by exposure to atomic radiation. She had less than a year to live and needed to be hospitalized right away.

THE GIFT

Sadako's parents could not bring themselves to tell her what was wrong or what her prognosis was. They just told her that she would have to stay in the hospital until her lumps went away.

While Sadako was living at the hospital, a group of high-school students from Nagoya sent the patients there a gift of *senbazuru*—a thousand folded origami paper cranes, strung together like beads on a necklace. In Japan and other Asian cultures, the crane is a symbol of long life, and it is common to give paper cranes as gifts to newlyweds, to children, and to the sick. The high-school students intended the cranes as a gift to the *hibakusha* ("bomb-affected people") at the hospital, to give them strength.

Eew! What is *heliculture*? The science of growing snails for food.

A WISH UPON A CRANE

Tradition also has it that when a person folds a thousand paper cranes, the mythical crane of Japanese folklore will grant a wish. Inspired by the gift, Sadako began folding her own paper cranes in the hope that the crane would grant her wish for a cure.

Paper was scarce in postwar Japan, so Sadako used whatever she could get her hands on: wrapping paper from the gifts she received, envelopes from get-well cards, notebook paper that her classmates brought when they came to visit, and even the tiny pieces of waxed paper that many of her pills were wrapped in. She cut everything into squares and folded the squares into cranes. When the squares of paper were too tiny for her to fold with her fingers, she made the folds using a straight pin.

In the eight months that Sadako lived in the hospital, she folded more than 1,300 cranes in all. She went on folding them until the middle of October 1955, when she became too ill to continue. She passed away on October 25 at the age of 12.

JOURNEY'S END

Sadako's death was expected, but it was still a shock to her classmates, a third of whom were also survivors of the Hiroshima blast. They wanted to remember Sadako in some meaningful way, and decided to raise funds for a monument that would memorialize not just her but every child who'd been killed by the atom bombs. When they passed out leaflets at an annual meeting of junior high school principals, their local campaign grew into a national one. Many of the principals brought the idea back to their own schools and encouraged their students to get involved. Japanese newspapers and radio stations got behind the effort, and soon Sadako's classmates had more than enough money to pay for the memorial. On May 5, 1958, just two and a half years after Sadako's death, the Children's Peace Monument—a bronze statue of Sadako atop a giant pedestal, her outstretched arms and holding a giant folded paper crane—was dedicated in Hiroshima's Peace Memorial Park.

After the Children's Peace Monument was dedicated, Sadako's story began to spread beyond Japan. Over the years it has been the subject of numerous children's books, songs, plays, and musicals, as well as films and television shows. Her story is taught in schools all over the world. Many include paper crane folding as part of the instruction, and the schools send the completed *senbazuru* to the Children's Peace Monument in Hiroshima, where they are put on display. Today, more than half a century after the statue was dedicated, the monument still receives more than 10 *tons* of folded paper cranes each year from children (and adults) all over the world.

CRANES FOR KUWAIT

After the liberation of Kuwait from Iraqi occupation in 1991, Sadako's story was taught in Kuwaiti schools, and the children there learned to fold paper cranes as a means of helping them deal with the trauma they experienced during the occupation. Following the World Trade Center attacks on 9/11, many strands of *senbazuru* were left on the fence surrounding ground zero in a spontaneous outpouring of sympathy for the victims of the tragedy.

Today Sadako Sasaki's older brother Masahiro, now in his late sixties, travels the world telling his sister's story as a means of furthering the cause of peace. The Sasaki family long ago donated all but five of Sadako's original cranes to the Children's Peace Monument in Hiroshima. On the sixth anniversary of the 9/11 attacks, Masahiro Sasaki presented one of the family's five remaining cranes, folded by Sadako out of the wax paper from one of her pills, to the WTC Visitors Center in New York. Small enough to fit on a thumbnail, the tiny red crane is on permanent display along with the *senbazuru* collected from the fence at ground zero. "I hope that by talking about the small wish for peace, the small ripple will become bigger and bigger," Sasaki says.

IN PERSON

If you ever visit Hiroshima's Peace Memorial Park, be sure to visit the Children's Peace Monument and see the thousands of folded paper cranes on display there. Ring the Peace Bell, another popular memorial, and visit the Peace Flame. Unlike many memorial flames, this one is not eternal: It will be extinguished when the last nuclear weapon has disappeared from Earth.

ANSWER PAGES

CALCULATOR WORDS
(Answers for page 98)

1. Sizzle
2. Eggshells
3. Belize
4. Zoo
5. Shell
6. Igloo
7. Oslo
8. Hobo
9. Oboe
10. Bolo
11. Boise
12. *Glee*
13. Google
14. Ebbs
15. Ellis
16. Gigolo
17. Hills
18. Oil
19. Oozes
20. LEGO
21. Hell
22. Boggle
23. Hobbies
24. Bolshoi
25. Illegible

GRANDMA CELIA, CARD SHARK
(Answers for page 168)

Insta-matic: Grandma Celia didn't memorize all the cards when she shuffled; she just memorized the card at the top of the deck, which happened to be the Seven of Clubs. (At the end of the shuffle she slowed down just enough to get a look at the card.) When she cut the deck into three piles, she made the pile with the Seven of Clubs the third pile—the one on the right—so that she'd draw that card *last*. But she called out "Seven of Clubs" *first*, because that was the only card she knew. Then, after she drew what turned out to be the Jack of Hearts from the top of the first pile, she called out "Jack of Hearts" as she drew the card from the top of the second pile. That card was actually the Three of Spades. So she called out, "Three of Spades," when she drew the top card from the third pile, which she already knew was the

Seven of Clubs. (That's why she didn't let me see any of the cards until she was done.)

Seeing Is Believing: Grandma Celia planned this trick in advance, so before I came over she took the Ten of Diamonds out of the deck and put it in her purse. Then when she wrote the note, put it in her wallet, and put the wallet back in her purse, she made sure to put it right next to the Ten of Diamonds.

Later, when she said "Stop!" and took her wallet out of her purse, she pressed the Ten of Diamonds against the outside of the wallet with her fingers and lifted it out of the purse with the wallet, taking care not to let me see the card. When she laid the wallet on top of the cards, she laid the Ten of Diamonds face down on the top of the pile. (That's why she told me a messy pile was OK—to make it harder for me to spot the new card on top.)

Flip-Flop: Before she did this trick, Grandma Celia turned the card on the bottom of the deck face up, without me noticing. When she fanned out the cards in her hand and told me to pick one, she was careful to make sure the bottom card wasn't showing, so I couldn't tell that it was face up. After I picked my card (and while I was momentarily distracted reading it), she closed the fan, squared the deck, and casually turned the deck over without my realizing it. All the cards in the deck were now face up, except for the card on top, which was face down. I assumed that the entire deck was face down, which is exactly what she wanted me to think. When I put my card back in the deck, it and the top card were the only two cards that were face down—the rest of the deck was face up. When Celia put the cards behind her back, she turned the top card face up and turned the entire deck over, so that now all of the cards were face down...except mine, which was face up.

A Stand-up Guy: This was the simplest trick of all: When Celia held up the Joker she kept her *fourth* finger—her index finger—hidden behind the card. Then when she set the cup on top of the card, she raised the finger up just enough to allow the cup to sit on the card *and* her finger.

...Even more impressive, Dempsey was born without half of his kicking foot.

MOVIE QUOTE QUIZ #1
(Answers for page 201)

1. *Kindergarten Cop* (1990)
2. *The Maltese Falcon* (1941)
3. *Blazing Saddles* (1974)
4. *Rocky IV* (1985)
5. *Mr. Smith Goes to Washington* (1939)
6. *Bill and Ted's Excellent Adventure* (1989)
7. *Psycho* (1960)
8. *The Grapes of Wrath* (1940)
9. *The King and I* (1956)
10. *Batman* (1989)
11. *The Exorcist* (1973)
12. *Air Force One* (1997)
13. *Return of the Jedi* (1983)
14. *Moonstruck* (1987)
15. *Dr. Strangelove* (1964)
16. *Old School* (2003)
17. *Oliver!* (1968)
18. *Finding Nemo* (2003)
19. *Patton* (1970)
20. *The Jerk* (1979)
21. *The Outsiders* (1983)
22. *The Godfather, Part II* (1974)
23. *The Usual Suspects* (1995)
24. *Body Heat* (1981)

MOVIE QUOTE QUIZ #2
(Answers for page 303)

1. *Bonnie and Clyde* (1967)
2. *Gone With the Wind* (1939)
3. *Back to the Future, Part II* (1989)
4. *The Lost Weekend* (1945)
5. *Mary Poppins* (1964)
6. *The Treasure of the Sierra Madre* (1948)
7. *Animal House* (1978)
8. *The Day the Earth Stood Still* (1951)
9. *Shrek* (2001)
10. *Saturday Night Fever* (1977)
11. *Caddyshack* (1980)
12. *Miracle on 34th Street* (1947)
13. *Dog Day Afternoon* (1975)
14. *Midnight Cowboy* (1969)
15. *Working Girl* (1988)
16. *All the President's Men* (1976)
17. *Ferris Bueller's Day Off* (1986)
18. *Predator* (1987)
19. *Pirates of the Caribbean* (2003)
20. *Deliverance* (1972)
21. *Black Swan* (2010)
22. *Sunset Boulevard* (1950)
23. *The Princess Bride* (1987)
24. *Carrie* (1976)

Picky eaters: Each of the world's 1,600 flea species prefers a different animal.

KNOW YOUR BOATS
(Answers for page 347)

1. j) Argo. Jason and his Argonauts were the heroes of Greek mythology who searched for the Golden Fleece aboard the *Argo*.

2. d) Pequod. In Herman Melville's 1851 novel *Moby Dick*, Captain Ahab hunted for a vicious white whale aboard the Massachusetts-based *Pequod*. The novel says the ship took its name from "a celebrated tribe of Massachusetts Indians; now extinct as the ancient Medes." The tribe's name is actually "Pequot," but they are indeed a New England-based nation that was nearly obliterated by English settlers during the 1600s.

3. g) Nautilus. Captain Nemo skippered this submersible in Jules Verne's 1869 novel *Twenty Thousand Leagues Under the Sea*. Verne named his fictional ship after American engineer Robert Fulton's *Nautilus*—the first workable submarine in history, built in 1800.

4. e) African Queen. Charlie Allnut was in charge of this supply ship on Central Africa's Ulanga River in the 1935 C. S. Forester novel *The African Queen*. The character is better known from the 1951 film of the same name, played by Humphrey Bogart (which won him his first and only Oscar, for Best Actor).

5. o) Belafonte. Captain Zissou (Bill Murray) captained this ship in 2004's *The Life Aquatic with Steve Zissou*, an affectionate sendup of the famed French conservationist Jacques Cousteau. The name of Cousteau's ship: *Calypso*. Zissou's ship was called *Belafonte*... after singer and actor Harry Belafonte, who became famous in the 1950s for singing calypso music.

6. t) Jolly Roger. Captain James Hook—the villain in J. M. Barrie's 1904 play, *Peter Pan*—was the skipper of this pirate ship, named after the famous "Jolly Roger" pirate flag bearing the skull-and-bones emblem.

7. i) Black Pearl. Johnny Depp plays the role of Jack Sparrow, the captain of the *Pearl*, in Disney's *Pirates of the Caribbean* film franchise. According to the story, the ship was originally the *Wicked Wench*, but then it sank and Sparrow had to make a deal with Davy Jones to save it. When he did, Sparrow renamed it the *Black Pearl*. Why? That's never explained. But one Hollywood screenwriter claims to know where the name came from: Royce

---

20,000 leagues equals about 69,000 miles. The deepest spot in any ocean: about 6 miles.

Matthews says he came up with "Black Pearl" in a pirate story he wrote in the 1990s, and he's been trying to sue Disney over the claim—without success—since 2006.

8. h) *Lydia.* Hornblower was the unhappy, self-doubting, prone-to-seasickness British Navy captain made famous in the series of novels by (once again) C. S. Forester, as well as the films and television shows based on them. The most famous of his many ships was *Lydia*, featured in the classic 1951 film *Captain Horatio Hornblower*, starring Gregory Peck in the title role.

9. p) *Orca.* Quint (according to the script, that's his last name—his first name: Sam) was the irascible skipper of the too-small boat in the 1975 film *Jaws*. The shark-obsessed Quint gave his boat the name because orcas, or *killer whales*, are the only known animals that prey on great white sharks. In real life, the *Orca* was a modified version of the *Warlock*, a Nova Scotia-based lobster boat bought by *Jaws* producers for the film.

10. v) *Ferry of the Dead.* In Greek mythology, Charon was the ferryman who took the souls of the newly dead across the river Archeron to the Underworld—but only if they had a coin to pay him. (This is why the ancient Greeks buried their dead with a coin placed under their tongue.)

11. a) *St. Vitus' Dance.* Sonny Crockett (Don Johnson) was the lead character on the TV series *Miami Vice*, and he lived aboard his yacht. St. Vitus' Dance, also called *Sydenham's chorea*, is a disease characterized by uncontrollable jerking motions of the face, feet, and hands. (It was named after Saint Vitus, the Christian patron saint of dancing.) Why the yacht has that name is never explained.

12. c) *Yellow Submarine.* In the 1968 Beatles film *Yellow Submarine* the undersea world of Pepperland is attacked by the Blue Meanies. The Lord Mayor orders Old Fred, whom he has appointed admiral, to take the submarine to the surface to seek help. (It should be noted that the Lord Mayor, who is very, very, old, calls Old Fred "Young Fred.")

13. f) *Walrus.* J. Flint was the pirate in Robert Louis Stevenson's 1883 story *Treasure Island*. (Extra: Both Flint and the *Walrus* are mentioned in 1911's *Peter and Wendy*, J. M. Barrie's novelization of his play, *Peter Pan*. Barrie and Stevenson were friends.)

14. q) *Jenny.* In the 1994 film, Forrest Gump named his shrimp boat after his childhood sweetheart, Jenny Curran (Robin Wright). The boat used in the film is currently located at the Planet Hollywood restaurant at the Disney World Resort in Orlando, Florida. (In Winston Groom's 1986 novel of the same name, Gump does start a shrimping business—but it's a shrimp hatchery...and he doesn't have a boat.)

15. u) *Shag at Sea.* In 2002's *Austin Powers in Goldmember*, Powers (Mike Meyers) reveals that he has a yacht named *Shag at Sea.* That's all we've got to say about that.

16. m) *Dawn Treader.* Lord Drinian is this ship's captain in C. S. Lewis's *The Chronicles of Narnia* series.

17. n) *We're Here.* Disko Troop is the skipper who takes young Harvey Cheyne, the spoiled 15-year-old son of a multimillionaire, on a seafaring adventure in Rudyard Kipling's 1897 novel *Captains Courageous.*

18. r) *Gone Fission.* Montgomery Burns is the evil, hated character in *The Simpsons.* He's also the owner of Springfield's nuclear power plant...which explains why his yacht is called *Gone Fission.*

19. s) *PT-73.* Quinton McHale is the lead character in *McHale's Navy,* the 1960s sitcom starring Ernest Borgnine. The "PT" stands for "Patrol Torpedo," a small, fast warship used by the American, Canadian, and British navies during World War II.

20. b) *Revenge.* Dread Pirate Roberts is the anonymous pirate figure—who is actually several different people—in the 1973 William Goldman novel *The Princess Bride.*

21. k) *Red October.* Ramius is the commander of the Soviet submarine in Tom Clancy's 1984 novel, *The Hunt for Red October,* played by Sean Connery in the 1990 film of the same name. (The sub is named in honor of the October 1917 Russian Revolution.)

22. l) *Erebus.* George "Chief" Phillips (Albert Hall) is the commander of the patrol boat that takes Captain Benjamin L. Willard (Martin Sheen) up the fictional Nung River into Cambodia in 1979's *Apocalypse Now.* In ancient Greek mythology, Erebus, son of the Greek god Chaos, represented darkness itself. The name was a reference to the 1902 Joseph Conrad novel, *Heart of Darkness,* the inspiration for *Apocalypse Now.*

MIND YOUR ZARFS AND WAMBLES
(Answers for page 375)

1. b, **2.** c, **3.** b, **4.** a, **5.** c, **6.** b, **7.** d, **8.** a, **9.** b

TIME FOR TANGRAMS
(Answers for page 415)

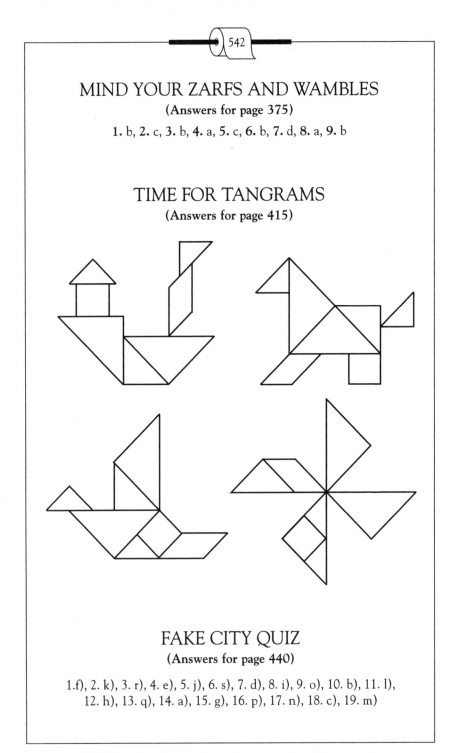

FAKE CITY QUIZ
(Answers for page 440)

1.f), 2. k), 3. r), 4. e), 5. j), 6. s), 7. d), 8. i), 9. o), 10. b), 11. l),
12. h), 13. q), 14. a), 15. g), 16. p), 17. n), 18. c), 19. m)

MTV slang for a block of videos with no on-air host: "ghost town."

UNCLE JOHN'S BATHROOM READER CLASSIC SERIES

Find these and other great titles from the *Uncle John's Bathroom Reader* Classic Series online at **www.bathroomreader.com**. Or contact us at:

Bathroom Readers' Institute
P.O. Box 1117
Ashland, OR 97520
(888) 488-4642

THE LAST PAGE

FELLOW BATHROOM READERS:
The fight for good bathroom reading should never be taken loosely—we must do our duty and sit firmly for what we believe in, even while the rest of the world is taking potshots at us.

We'll be brief. Now that we've proven we're not simply a flush-in-the-pan, we invite you to take the plunge: Sit Down and Be Counted! Log on to *www.bathroomreader.com* and earn a permanent spot on the BRI honor roll!

If you like reading our books...
VISIT THE BRI'S WEBSITE!
www.bathroomreader.com

- Visit "The Throne Room"—a great place to read!
- Receive our irregular newsletters via e-mail
- Order additional *Bathroom Readers*
- Face us on Facebook
- Tweet us on Twitter
- Blog us on our blog

Go with the Flow...

Well, we're out of space, and when you've gotta go, you've gotta go. Tanks for all your support. Hope to hear from you soon. Meanwhile, remember…

Keep on flushin'!